Object-Oriented Development in COBOL

Other McGraw-Hill Titles of Interest

DORFMAN • *C++ by Example: Object-Oriented Analysis, Design & Programming*
DORFMAN, NEUBERGER • *C++ Memory Management*
HENDERSON • *Object-Oriented Specification and Design with C++*
HOLUB • *C++: Programming with Objects in C and C++*
JOHNSON ET AL. • *Program Smarter, Not Harder: Get Mission-Critical Projects Right the First Time*
KROHA • *Objects and Databases*
MATTISON, SIPOLT • *The Object-Oriented Enterprise: Making Corporate Information Systems Work*
RANADE • *The Elements of C Programming Style*
RANADE, ZAMIR • *C++ Primer for C Programmers*
RAO • *C++ and the OOP Paradigm*
SIMS • *Business Objects: Delivering Cooperative Objects for Client/Server*
SMITH • *Concepts of Object-Oriented Programming*
SMITH • *C++ Applications Guide*
SMITH • *C++ for Scientists and Engineers*
TERRIBILE • *Practical C++*
WATSON • *C++ Power Paradigms*
WATSON • *Portable GUI Development with C++*

Object-Oriented Development in COBOL

Andrew Topper

McGraw-Hill, Inc.
New York San Francisco Washington, D.C. Auckland Bogotá
Caracas Lisbon London Madrid Mexico City Milan
Montreal New Delhi San Juan Singapore
Sydney Tokyo Toronto

Library of Congress Cataloging-in-Publication Data

Topper, Andrew.
　　Object-oriented development in COBOL / by Andrew Topper.
　　　　p.　　cm.
　　Includes index.
　　ISBN 0-07-065082-9 (p)
　　1. Object-oriented programming (Computer science).　2. COBOL
(Computer program language)　I. Title.
QA76.64.T67　1995
005.13'3—dc20　　　　　　　　　　　　　　　　　　94-32130
　　　　　　　　　　　　　　　　　　　　　　　　　　　　　CIP

Copyright © 1995 by McGraw-Hill, Inc. Printed in the United States of America. Except as permitted under the United States Copyright Act of 1976, no part of this publication may be reproduced or distributed in any form or by any means, or stored in a data base or retrieval system, without the prior written permission of the publisher.

1 2 3 4 5 6 7 8 9 0　　FGR/FGR　　9 9 8 7 6 5 4

The sponsoring editor for this book was Jennifer Holt DiGiovanna, the editors were Joanne Slike and Robert E. Ostrander. This book was set in ITC Century Light. It was composed by the author.

Printed and bound by Quebecor Printing Fairfield.

Information contained in this work has been obtained by McGraw-Hill, Inc. from sources believed to be reliable. However, neither McGraw-Hill nor its authors guarantee the accuracy or completeness of any information published herein and neither McGraw-Hill nor its authors shall be responsible for any errors, omissions, or damages arising out of use of this information. This work is published with the understanding that McGraw-Hill and its authors are supplying information but are not attempting to render engineering or other professional services. If such services are required, the assistance of an appropriate professional should be sought.

In order to receive additional information on these or any other McGraw-Hill titles, in the United States please call 1-800-822-8158. In other countries, contact your local McGraw-Hill representative.

0650829
MH94

Dedication

This book is dedicated to the most important aspect of my life, my family — Amy, Samantha, and Steven — for their unending love and support, and to my mother — Jessie Tucholski — who taught me to read, to think, to write, and to enjoy, respect, and appreciate the written word.

Contents

Preface   xiv

Chapter 1 - How Object Technology and COBOL Fit Together

1.1 Introduction	2
1.1.1 The Paradox of COBOL and Object-Oriented Development	3
1.1.2 Object-Oriented Hype	6
1.2 The Object Technology Marketplace	7
1.2.1 Current Object Technology Products	7
1.2.2 Major Object Technology Vendors	8
1.3 Factors Affecting Software Development	10
1.3.1 History of Software Development	13
1.3.2 COBOL Standards	15
1.3.3 An Objective View of Software Development	16
1.4 COBOL Extensions to Support Object-Orientation	19
1.4.1 OOCOBOL Products Available	21
1.4.2 Future OOCOBOL Products and Standards	22
1.5 Distributed Computing Standards	23
1.6 References	25

Chapter 2 - History of Object-Oriented Development

2.1 Introduction	27
2.2 Genesis of Object-Oriented Products	28
2.3 History of Object-Oriented Development	30
2.4 Emergence of OOA/D Methods	32
2.5 Current Object Technology Marketplace	34
2.6 COBOL Enters the Picture	35
2.7 Applications that can Benefit from Object Technology	36
2.7.1 Potential Benefits of Object Technology	37
2.7.2 Selecting Appropriate Object Technology	38
2.7.3 Problems with Object Technology	41
2.8 References	42

Chapter 3 - Object-Oriented Concepts and Terminology

3.1 Introduction	45
3.2 Principles of Software Engineering	47
3.2.1 Use a Formal Method	48
3.2.2 Divide and Conquer	50
3.2.3 Abstraction and Generalization	52

	3.2.4	Hierarchical Ordering and Partitioning	53
	3.2.5	Hiding Complexity	54
	3.2.6	Modularity	54
	3.2.7	Use an Incremental, Iterative Development Process	55

3.3 Terminology   56
3.4 Concepts and Principles   59
    3.4.1 What is an Object?   60
    3.4.2 Object Attributes and Properties   60
    3.4.3 Object Behavior and Operations   61
    3.4.4 Object Lifetimes and Interactions   61
    3.4.5 Object Messages   61
    3.4.6 Object Composition   62
    3.4.7 Object Types   62
    3.4.8 What is a Class?   65
    3.4.9 Class and Object Relationships   65
3.5 Example Problems   65
    3.5.1 The Library Problem   66
    3.5.2 The Automated Teller Machine Problem   67
3.6 References   74
Sidebar: What is Object-Oriented?   76

Chapter 4 - An Object-Oriented Life Cycle

4.1 Introduction   81
4.2 Traditional Software Development Life Cycles   83
    4.2.1 The Waterfall Life Cycle   83
    4.2.2 The Spiral Life Cycle   86
4.3 Life Cycle Issues in Object-Oriented Development   87
    4.3.1 Evolution in Software Development   87
    4.3.2 Prototyping   88
    4.3.3 Iteration and Incremental Development   91
    4.3.4 Conflict of Class Design vs. Application Design   92
4.4 An Object-Oriented Software Development Life Cycle   93
    4.4.1 Object-Oriented Analysis   99
    4.4.2 Object-Oriented Design   99
    4.4.3 Object-Oriented Programming   100
        4.4.3.1 Comparing Object-Oriented Programming Languages   101
        4.4.3.2 Class Libraries   105
    4.4.4 Object-Oriented Testing   106
    4.4.5 Estimating, Planning, and Managing

			Object-Oriented Development	107
	4.4.6		Object-Oriented Maintenance	108

4.5 Roles and Responsibilities of Staff 108
4.6 References 109

Chapter 5 - COBOL Considerations for Object-Oriented Development

5.1 Introduction 113
    5.1.1 History 115
    5.1.2 Existing COBOL Applications 116
5.2 COBOL as a Software Engineering Tool 118
    5.2.1 Data Types 118
    5.2.2 Data Structures 121
    5.2.3 Program Structure 122
    5.2.4 Program Calling Hierarchies 125
    5.2.5 Program Design 129
    5.2.6 Development Environments 130
5.3 Developing OOCOBOL Applications 133
    5.3.1 Analysis and Design for OOCOBOL 134
    5.3.2 CASE Tools 135
    5.3.3 Prototyping and OOCOBOL 137
    5.3.4 Other Issues for OOCOBOL Development 138
5.4 The Evolving OOCOBOL Standard 139
5.5 References 140

Chapter 6 - Object-Oriented Analysis

6.1 Introduction 141
6.2 Identifying Objects, Attributes, and Operations 143
    6.2.1 Data Modeling 144
    6.2.2 Domain Analysis 145
    6.2.3 Information Analysis of Textual
           Requirements Documents 146
6.3 Popular OOA Methods 147
    6.3.1 Shlaer/Mellor OOA 147
    6.3.2 Object-Oriented Modeling Technique (OMT) 148
    6.3.3 Object Behavior Analysis (OBA) 149
6.3 Coad/Yourdon Object-Oriented Analysis 150
    6.4.1 Introduction 151
    6.4.1 Technique 151
    6.4.2 Representations and Notations 153
6.5 Sample Problem Discussion 153

	6.5.1	Library Problem	155
	6.5.2	ATM Problem	163
6.6 Moving from OOA to OOD		174
6.7 References		176

Chapter 7 - Object-Oriented Design

7.1 Introduction		179
7.2 Using Object Models		181
7.3 Reuse of Existing Design Components		183
7.4 Reuse of Existing Programming Constructs		184
7.5 Popular OOD Methods		187
	7.5.1	Shlaer/Mellor Recursive Design	188
	7.5.2	Synthesis (Page-Jones and Weiss)	189
	7.5.3	Object-Oriented Structured Design (OOSD)	190
	7.5.4	Responsibility-Driven Design (RDD)	190
7.6 Booch Object-Oriented Design		192
	7.6.1	Introduction	192
	7.6.2	Technique	194
	7.6.3	Representations and Notations	195
7.7 Problem Discussion		196
	7.7.1	Library Problem	198
	7.7.2	ATM Problem	207
7.8 Moving from OOD to OOP		218
7.9 References		219
Sidebar: Comparing OOA/D Methods		221

Chapter 8 - Object-Oriented Programming in COBOL

8.1 Introduction		233
8.2 ANSI COBOL 97 Standard		235
	8.2.1	Defining Classes and Objects	236
	8.2.2	Referencing Objects in OOCOBOL	237
	8.2.3	Creating and Using Objects in OOCOBOL	239
8.3 Implementation Considerations		240
8.4 Reuse of Micro Focus OOCOBOL Classes		243
8.5 OOCOBOL Products Available		246
	8.5.1	Micro Focus Object COBOL Option	246
	8.5.2	Other COBOL products	246
	8.5.3	Netron/CAP	248
8.6 Sample Problem Discussion		249

	8.6.1	Library Problem	250
	8.6.2	ATM Problem	254
8.7 Testing OOCOBOL Programs		257
8.8 References		259

Chapter 9 - Building GUI Applications in Object-Oriented COBOL

9.1 Introduction	261
9.2 Popular Graphical User Interfaces	263
9.3 GUI Applications	264
9.3.1 Architecture of a GUI Application	265
9.3.2 Components of GUIs	268
9.3.3 Behavior of GUI Applications	271
9.4 Developing GUI Applications	275
9.4.1 Issues for GUI-based Development	278
9.4.2 Developing Good GUI Applications	280
9.4.3 GUI Development Tools	283
9.4.4 Class Libraries in GUI Development	285
9.5 CICS is an Event-Driven Environment	286
9.6 Client/Server Issues for GUI Development	289
9.7 OOCOBOL GUI Considerations	291
9.7.1 Library Problem	295
9.7.2 ATM Problem	297
9.6 Future User Interfaces Development	298
9.9 References	299
Sidebar: Visual Object-Oriented Programming Tools	301

Chapter 10 - Maintaining Object-Oriented COBOL Applications

10.1 Introduction	303
10.2 Maintenance Tasks	305
10.3 Types of Maintenance	307
10.3.1 Measuring Software Maintainability	308
10.3.2 Cost of Maintenance	310
10.4 Maintenance Strategies	312
10.5 OOCOBOL Maintenance	314
10.5.1 Library Problem	317
10.5.2 ATM Problem	319
10.6 General Object-Oriented Maintenance	320
10.6.1 Configuration Management Issues	321
10.6.2 Maintaining Class Libraries	322
10.7 References	323

Chapter 11 - Wrapping Existing COBOL Applications

11.1 Introduction	326
11.2 The Concept of an Object Wrapper	327
11.3 Benefits of Object Wrappers	329
11.4 Types of Object Wrappers	330
11.5 Strategies for Wrapping Objects	332
11.6 Wrapper Methods and Tools	334
11.6.1 Design Recovery and Reverse Engineering	335
11.6.2 Capturing Classes/Objects from Legacy Systems	338
11.6.3 Object-Wrapping Tools	341
11.7 Rationale for Wrapping Applications	343
11.8 Example Problem	346
11.9 Case Studies in Wrapping Applications	347
11.10 References	349

Chapter 12 - Managing Object-Oriented COBOL Development

12.1 Introduction	351
12.2 Challenges for an Object-Oriented Project	353
12.2.1 Evolution and Iteration	354
12.2.2 Prototyping	354
12.3 Managing Reuse	355
12.3.1 Introduction	356
12.3.2 A Reuse Organizational Structure	358
12.3.3 Classification Schemes	362
12.3.4 A Reusability Framework	364
12.3.5 Prohibitors to Reuse	365
12.3.6 Experiences with Reuse	365
12.4 Planning for Object-Oriented Development	368
12.5 Measuring an Object-Oriented Project	371
12.6 Configuration Management Issues	374
12.7 Quality Assurance Issues	376
12.8 References	377

Chapter 13 - Migrating to Object Technology

13.1 Introduction	383
13.2 A Strategy for Adopting Object-Oriented COBOL	385
13.2.1 Scope of Change	390
13.2.2 Software Production Framework	391
13.2.3 Software Engineering Triad	394

13.3 Software Process Modeling	395
13.3.1 Software Process Maturity Model	396
13.3.2 Models of Roles and Activities	398
13.3.3 Models of Interactions/Communication	399
13.3.4 Models of System Dynamics	399
13.3.5 Models of Continuous Quality Improvement	399
13.3.6 Goal-Oriented Models	400
13.3.7 A Common-Sense Management Model	400
13.4 Software Process Improvement	401
13.5 Training and Education	402
13.6 Technology Transition Strategies	404
13.6.1 Barb Bouldin	404
13.6.2 Roger Pressman	405
13.6.3 Watts Humphrey	406
13.6.4 The J Curve	406
13.6.5 Alternative Views on Technology Transition	408
13.7 Experiences with Object-Oriented Development	410
13.8 References	419

Chapter 14 - The Future of COBOL

14.1 COBOL 97 Standard Update	423
14.2 Emerging COBOL products	424
14.3 Distributed Object Management	425
14.4 Future Software Development	428
14.4.1 Evolution of CASE and Formal Methods	429
14.4.2 CASE as a Method Advisor	430
14.4.3 Hypertext and CASE	431
14.4.4 Reverse Engineering	432
14.4.5 Integration of Object Technology and Other Products: Object Repository	433
14.4.6 Media Use in Software Applications	434
14.5 Conclusion	435
14.6 References	436

Appendix - Example Problems	
A.1 OOA Results	439
A.2 OOD Results	452
A.3 Object-Oriented COBOL code	459
Index	483

Preface

My first experience with serious software engineering was maintaining and developing COBOL programs in a manufacturing environment. While my introduction to programming was with assembler, I was introduced to COBOL shortly afterward, and it quickly became my language of choice. Along the way, I learned how to write structured COBOL programs and incorporated those concepts into my regular development activities.

Over the years, I came to appreciate the COBOL programming language and its broad support for readability, functionality, and maintenance. Having looked at many COBOL programs that were written in an assembler like manner, with ALTER GOTOs and GOTO DEPENDING ON, I came to appreciate modular and structured programming constructs. Over the years, my appreciation for clear, concise COBOL programming increased as I matured as a software engineer.

When I heard there was going to be an object-oriented version of COBOL, I jumped at the opportunity to contribute to the success of OOCOBOL. Having learned about other OOPLs and used several — including Smalltalk, C++, and Object-Oriented Pascal — I felt a need to educate and to describe the power of the OOCOBOL language. I feel lucky to offer this book on OOCOBOL at a point in the evolution of the standard where developers still can affect the eventual language implementation. My hope is that this book, along with others to follow, will encourage discussion and comment on the benefits of object technology and the evolution of the COBOL programming language.

Goals

This book is my attempt to provide a complete resource for COBOL programmers who have little or no background in object-oriented development but want to learn and use object technology. When I decided to write this book, I defined an early outline and had in mind several important goals:

- Cover OOCOBOL completely
- Cover issues related to OOCOBOL development (i.e.,
- GUI development, OOA/D methods, etc.)
- Cover the entire OOCOBOL development life cycle
- Cover the object technology adoption process
- Cover management issues related to OOCOBOL

Along the way, I decided to include discussions on the object technology marketplace, benefits and drawbacks to using object technology, class libraries, reuse, reverse engineering and design recovery, software process models, and distributed object management. It is my hope that most every topic related to OOCOBOL is covered in this book.

Audience

This book is targeted at professional developers, managers, and COBOL programmers who are charged with evaluating and adopting object technology, as well as those who are interested in the benefits of object-oriented development and object technology. The book is structured in such a way that it can be used for a variety of purposes - from evaluating and selecting object technology to implementing reuse in an organization.

Beginning COBOL programmers also can benefit from this book, as it covers all the issues related to object-oriented development from a COBOL perspective. Seasoned COBOL programmers who want to begin experimenting with object-oriented development can use this book as a starting point. Managers of COBOL development can learn about the impact object technology has on the development process, life cycle issues, and managing reuse.

This book is also directed at graduate and undergraduate software engineering students with an eye toward COBOL and MIS development. Those colleges and universities that want to provide an object-oriented development class in COBOL can do so by acquiring the Micro Focus Object COBOL product and using the examples in this book for discussion and exercises.

Structure

The book is organized around three basic sections or views.

The first four chapters introduce the reader to object technology, the history of object technology, the concepts and terminology, and life cycle issues for using objects and messages in development.

The next five chapters (5 through 9) deal specifically with tasks in the object-oriented development process, including analysis (chapter 6), design (chapter 7), programming in OOCOBOL (chapters 5 and 8), and GUI development (chapter 9)

The final five chapters address additional technical and managerial issues in adopting object technology, including maintaining object-oriented applications (chapter 10), wrapping existing systems as objects (chapter 11), managing object-oriented development (chapter 12), migrating to object technology (chapter 13) and predictions of the future of COBOL development (chapter 14).

The book also was written with an eye towards developers who want to learn about specific aspects of object technology or OOCOBOL and can be used to supplement or in place of traditional software engineering materials. The chapters on OOA, OOD, and OOP in OOCOBOL can be used stand-alone, along with the chapters on wrapping systems and managing object-oriented development, and the example problems can be used to explain the concepts and procedures in these tasks. Together, these 14 chapters represent a complete picture of object-oriented development with COBOL.

Using the Book and the Examples

The book uses two examples, which are introduced in Chapter 3, to explain and describe each phase of the object-oriented development process, from analysis through implementation in object-oriented COBOL. Each example is represented as diagrams and specifications from OOA/D, and as excerpts of OOCOBOL code. The book also includes sidebars on standards for object terminology, comparing OOA/D methods, and visual OOPL products.

Whenever possible, the examples were developed to help clarify and explain concepts, terminology, and syntax. However, at the time that this book was completed, the ANSI COBOL standard was still under revision, and the only commercially available OOCOBOL compiler was the one sold by Micro Focus. The Micro Focus OOCOBOL product was in its initial release and did not provide complete support for the ANSI X3J4 standard. Therefore, the examples are somewhat limited in the area of OOCOBOL source code, providing only excerpts from the actual system for explanation purposes. It is my hope that when the OOCOBOL standard is sufficiently stable and the Micro Focus product is more mature these examples will be extended to include full source code and compilation support for a variety of OOCOBOL compilers.

Acknowledgments

Writing a book, while mostly a solitary endeavor, requires collaboration and benefits from comments and criticism. I would like to take this opportunity to thank the many colleagues and friends who contributed to this manuscript, for their comments, ideas, criticisms, and insight into software engineering methods. Colleagues who directly influenced the content of this book include Grady Booch, Ed Yourdon, Peter Coad, Derek Hatley, Paul Jorgensen, and Dan Ouellette.

I also would like to thank the people at Micro Focus — Dan Clark, Roly Ashley, and Mike McCandless along with the people who worked on the ANSI X3J4 committees — Joel Van Stee and Ann Wallace from IBM, Megan Adams from HP, and Don Schricker from Micro Focus. I also am indebted to Jeff Chittenden and Jim Caldarella from Citicorp, and Victor Harrison from Deere and Company for sharing their experiences with object wrappers. Finally, I thank my acquiring editor at McGraw-Hill, Jennifer Holt DiGiovanna, and Joanne Slike and John Baker for their help in editing the manuscript.

Chapter 1

How Object Technology and COBOL Fit Together

Upon reading the title of this chapter, or even this book, you may be wondering how two very different technologies, COBOL and object-oriented development, could possibly be used together in a single sentence. COBOL, the last bastion of the procedural languages of the 1960s, originally was developed to provide corporations with a language that was easier to read and maintain. Object-oriented, on the other hand, is the catchword of the day and nearly every magazine, book, or product now has this term somewhere in it.

Object technology (OT) is not a new phenomenon, and many aspects of object-orientation are incorporated into several different products. In the past few years, we have seen object-oriented programming languages (OOPLs), object-oriented database management systems (OODBMS), object-oriented environments, methods of analysis and design that are object-oriented (OOA/D methods), and even object-oriented operating systems.

As the market for object technology continues to evolve, it begins to have wider applicability to software development. While extensive experience has been gained with object-oriented development, much of it is in the area of reactive or real-time systems and very little practical development has been in the areas of commercial or management information systems (MIS). While there are many reasons for this, the most obvious is reluctance on the part of MIS organizations to throw away their existing tools and expertise in favor of newer OT.

With the creation of the X3J4.1 task group, the world of object-orientation encompassed the COBOL programming language. The task group has produced a recommended standard for COBOL that includes objects, messages, and all the other object-oriented constructs in competitive languages. Sometime in the late 1990s, an object-oriented COBOL (OOCOBOL) standard will be in place and supported across the major computer platforms.

1.1 Introduction

Given the sheer number of MIS applications, until OT is widely applied to commercial applications, the overall acceptance of OT will be minimal. For this adoption to occur, several important issues must be resolved: existing MIS development tools must be modified to support object-orientation, extensive class libraries must be developed for MIS systems, and existing systems that have been developed in COBOL must be modified to support object-oriented concepts.

Many organizations find that adopting object technology by making a transition from COBOL to Smalltalk or C++ is difficult, hazardous, expensive, and time-consuming. While some organizations have had success in making this transition, many others are hesitant and skeptical of the eventual outcome of this transition. This approach is described in Figure 1.1 and shows the hurdles or learning curves for staff in adopting object-oriented development. The left side of the diagram represents existing COBOL development staff and their expertise, while the right side represents the eventual goal of experienced object-oriented developers.

The figures shows learning curves for object-oriented development, a new programming language (C++ or Smalltalk) with its own syntax and structure, and client/server and graphical user interface (GUI) development. If you were to remove the client/server and GUI aspects, you would still be expecting your COBOL staff to move successfully through two major learning experiences.

Another approach for COBOL organizations would be to move slowly towards a COBOL language extended to support object-oriented development. To this end an X3 committee has been modifying COBOL to support object-orientation for several years. Figure 1.2 represents the migration along these lines using the same starting and ending points. If you again remove the learning curves for client/server and GUI, you are left with a single learning process for COBOL staff.

Modifications to this second approach might include acquisition of OOCOBOL class libraries, development tools, analysis and design methods, etc. and might be more extensive than illustrated, but adding a migration from COBOL to some other programming language represents a significant investment in training and lost productivity that many organizations might be hesitant to undertake. OOCOBOL allows these organizations to migrate slowly, using small increments, towards an object-oriented development

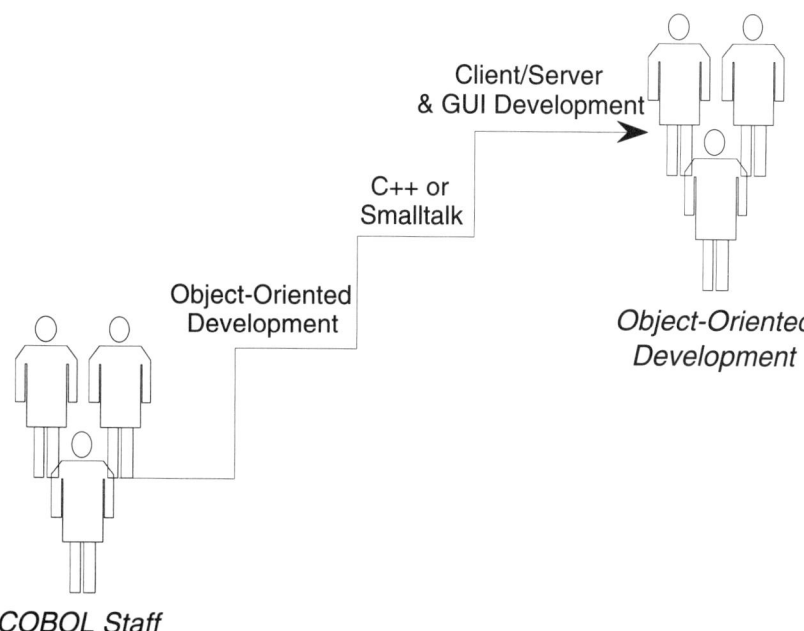

Figure 1.1 Migrating to object technology without OOCOBOL.

process and keep their COBOL expertise intact. This book describes this migration process and the available tools, methods, and issues related to adopting object technology.

1.1.1 The Paradox of COBOL and Object-Oriented Development

While at first glance, objects and COBOL might seem drastically different and paradoxical, recent product development and standards efforts have brought these two somewhat diametric items together. At a very basic level, COBOL (or for that matter any programming language) already includes support for some of the items of interest in object-oriented development. Objects can be considered as self-sustained, autonomous entities or black boxes that respond to specific requests for services. Prior to considering how COBOL and objects can be viewed together, you need to review the role of the different components of a COBOL program and the products that interact within a normal mainframe COBOL application.

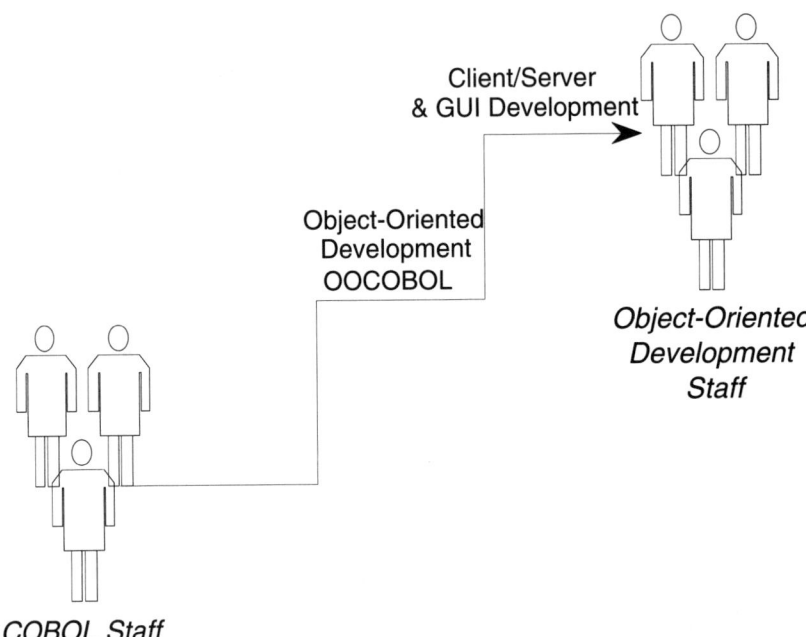

Figure 1.2
Migrating to OOCOBOL.

Any software system consists of three primary or distinct parts or portions (see Figure 1.3):

- *User Interface or Presentation* — user interaction (i.e., communication between the computer system/program and the client/user of the system)
- *Application Processing* — (control flow, logic processing, etc.) the business logic and flow of the program/system (or its behavior)
- *Data Access* — file or DBMS input and output (i.e., access to the data structures used by the program/system)

Traditional COBOL programs might include a simple user interface, perhaps a one-line command, or a complex interface, like a CICS screen with edit fields, function keys, etc. The application processing in a traditional COBOL program would be the sequence of commands in the PROCEDURE division and might include a hierarchy of control. The data access portion of a traditional COBOL program might include sequential file access, indexed file access, or even database access. Traditional COBOL programs are considered to be self-contained and often include all three of these portions.

Chapter 1 How Object Technology and COBOL Fit Together

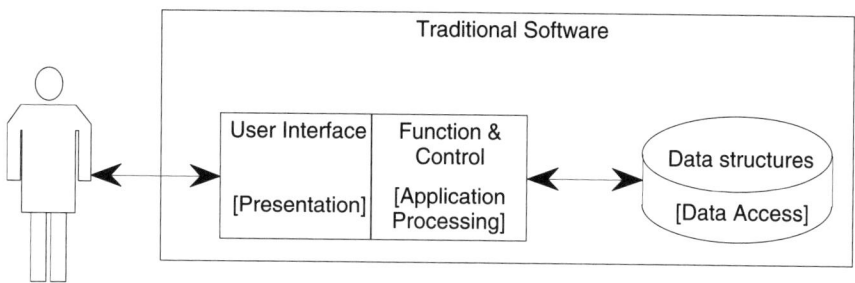

Figure 1.3
Traditional software architecture.

You could even consider a CICS COBOL program that accesses an indexed file on disk as consisting of a presentation portion that runs on a 3270 terminal and processing and data access that reside on the mainframe. You could even imagine CICS managing some of the processing for the user interface, editing the data, presenting the results, etc., and VSAM managing the data access. While both CICS and VSAM are mainframe-resident, they represent physically separate programs from the COBOL program itself. In this sense, even a traditional COBOL CICS program has portions of its processing that occur under the control of different programs.

Newer systems, especially those that use a GUI or client/server processing, might have portions of the application that reside on physically different or distinct platforms or computers. When this occurs, you will find that a COBOL program might perform only the presentation or interface and the application processing functions, with a remote database or file server performing the data access portion. Perhaps the database is available over a local or wide area network (LAN/WAN) and accessed using a standard language (SQL for example). In this case, the COBOL program contains the logic for the presentation of the information and the processing for the application, but the data access is supported via remote requests to a database or file server.

In future applications, the COBOL program might not even perform the presentation portion of an application. Consider for instance an application that includes a presentation on a PC or workstation that collects information and sends it to an application server that performs the application logic. This portion of the application might be a COBOL program running on a server that in turn requests information from another server. In this scenario, the COBOL program performs the application logic and not the presentation or the data access portion.

The movement in the software industry is towards distributed processing, and this means that future COBOL applications will be expected to support all or only part of the typical portions of a system described previously. This also leads to a set of components, or COBOL subroutines, that must have clear interfaces to allow others to use their services. The plans for the COBOL 97 standard call for support of these features, and there will be OOCOBOL compiler products available from most vendors by the year 2000. Those organizations that want to do so can move towards object-oriented development now and begin gaining experience and expertise using OOCOBOL on the PC with the Micro Focus COBOL product, then move towards full object-orientation when the mainframe-based COBOL products emerge in the years to come.

1.1.2 Object-Oriented Hype

One problem with object technology in general, as with any new technology, is the band-wagon effect it has caused in the software industry. Since the idea of object technology has grown so popular, many vendors of products, recognizing that they might be able to sell more of their products, are quickly touting them as object-oriented. There is a very dramatic effort in the industry to make everything object-oriented in an attempt to secure more sales.

Other problems with object technology parallel other technical solutions delivered over the past 30 years to the so-called software crisis. Fourth-generation programming languages (4GLs), Computer-Aided Software Engineering (CASE), expert systems, decision-support systems, object-oriented programming languages (OOPLs), and visual programming environments have all been touted as silver bullets for the software industry. Each of these technologies has been aggressively marketed and sold as the answer to any software problem and have suffered in the long run when organizations have actually applied them to real-world software projects. Object technology, like any other technical solution, can solve only specific, identified problems in software development and is not a panacea for all the problems in software engineering.

Promised benefits of object technology can be realized by organizations only after sufficient commitment, training, and application of resources. The benefits of object technology — reusable components, higher productivity, lower overall costs, easier maintenance, etc. — are achievable only when viewed in conjunction with the cultural change required to adopt any new technology. I will examine these issues in more depth in Chapter 13.

1.2 The Object Technology Marketplace

The object technology (OT) marketplace is a varied and diverse arena of different products, techniques, and environments offered by different vendors. As with the CASE marketplace, integrating all of these different products into a software development environment is difficult.

Much has been written lately about object-oriented programming languages (OOPLs), object-oriented database management systems (OODBMSs), and prototyping tools for GUIs, but very little has been published on CASE support for object-oriented analysis and design (OOA/D) techniques. Various OOA/D methods have been proposed and used by organizations over the past few years and one would expect automated support for these techniques in the CASE marketplace.

Ovum Ltd. predicts that the OT market will reach $2 billion by 1996 [OVU90]. IDC estimates that the market for OOA/D CASE tools will grow faster than traditional CASE tools until 1996 when it will reach $240 million [IDC92]. Ovum also predicts that, by 1995, there will be full support for object-oriented development in CASE tools and that sales of all aspects of the OT market will be close to $1 billion.

1.2.1 Current Object Technology Products

The current (1994) object technology marketplace is filled with many different products and players, from the major hardware and software vendors — IBM, HP, DEC, Microsoft, Borland, Computer Associates, etc. — to many smaller vendors of niche products. Figure 1.4 shows one view of the object technology market with sample product names.

One way that the object technology marketplace can be characterized is by the type of products available. The original products were OOPLs, which still represent a significant portion of the overall marketplace. These were followed by object-oriented development environments, which provided class libraries, editors, browsers, etc. for an OOPL. As organizations began using object-oriented programming (OOP), they found that they needed to describe models and system designs and so object-oriented analysis and design methods were created, which led to CASE tools to support these methods. About the same time, some database vendors found that complex data types could be supported easily in object-oriented database management systems. Soon, even the operating system marketplace was considering the possible role of objects.

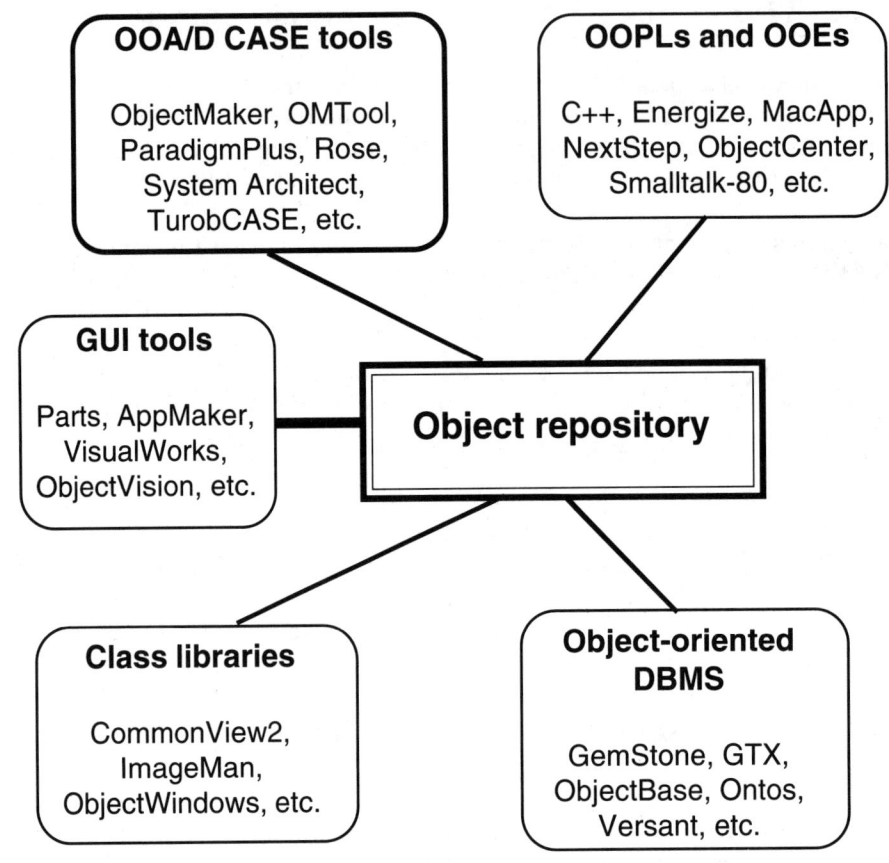

Figure 1.4 Object technology marketplace.

1.2.2 Major Object Technology Vendors

Major OOPL venders include Microsoft, IBM, HP, DEC, Borland, Sun, Centerline, and Symantic. Of these, the most popular are those targeted at the PC or workstation environments, closely followed by the Unix products. C++ has quickly become the language of choice for most object-oriented development, primarily because developers that already know C can move slowly towards C++ without loosing any facilities.

Other major OOPL vendors include Digitalk, ParcPlace, Object Technology Intl., and Easel Corp., which all support Smalltalk. Of these, Digitalk is the prominent PC-based vendor and ParcPlace is the dominant Unix vendor.

Other vendors of OOPLs include StepStone (ObjectiveC), Borland and Apple (Object Pascal), and Interactive Software Engineering (Eiffel).

The OOA/D methods are taught by a variety of vendors, and there now are CASE tools that support these methods. Major OOA/D vendors include Rational (Booch method and ROSE CASE tool), General Electric/Matin Marietta (OOMT method and CASE tool), Project Technologies (Shlaer/Mellor method), Cadre (Shlaer/Mellor and OOMT CASE), Object Technology (Coad/Yourdon method and CASE tool), Objective Systems (OOSE and Objectory CASE tool), Digitalk (Responsibility-Driven Design method), and ParcPlace (Object-Behavior Analysis method).

Other Major OOA/D CASE players include Interactive Development Environments (OOSD), Mark V Systems (CASE tool for a variety of OOA/D methods), Protosoft (CASE tool for many OOA/D methods), and Popkin Software and Systems (CASE tool for many OOA/D methods).

As objects are used more to support complex data types, the need arises to provide mechanisms to manage and access them. Persistent objects typically are stored in object-oriented database management systems (OODBMS). Major OODBMS vendors include Objectivity (Objectivity/DB), Object Design (ObjectStore), ONTOS (Ontos DB), Servio (GemStone), and Versant (Versant). Popular RDBMS vendors that now are supporting some OODBMS functions, primarily through the use of binary large objects (BLOBs), including Oracle, Ingres, Informix, Cincom Systems, and Computer Associates.

Objects also have been applied to the user interface aspect of popular operating systems. These object-oriented operating systems (OOOS) now are or soon will be available from IBM, Apple, HP, and Microsoft. IBM and Apple announced their plans to deliver Taligent, an OOOS based on the Apple Pink and Mach operating systems in 1995. Taligent will provide object system services, object frameworks, development tools, and a GUI and will require a different application development approach. HP developed and markets its own OOOS, NewWave, which sits on top of the Microsoft Windows graphical environment. Microsoft has extended their Windows GUI to support objects and actions in Chicago and the future Cairo OOOS.

As objects are used across a diverse set of operating environments, the need to manage access to them over a heterogenous network has led to the development of distributed object management systems (DOMS). Major DOMS vendors include HP, IBM, DEC, Sun, Novell, and Microsoft. As the marketplace changes, object management strategies will play a larger role in distributed computing. Several popular standards have emerged for distributed computing, including DCE, CORBA, OLE, and OpenDoc.

Another set of object technology products, visual OOPLs, have been introduced and bring the power of objects, messages, and inheritance to a visual development environment. Visual OOPL products are available from Borland, Computer Associates, Digitalk, Easel, IBM, Microsoft, and ParcPlace.

The object technology marketplace has been driven by the changing nature of software development, which has itself been required to change because of evolving hardware and software platforms and the needs of software engineering organizations.

1.3 Factors Affecting Software Development

During the past few years, some major trends have begun to dramatically change the software development industry. The following list summarizes these trends, which are discussed in the following paragraphs.

- Movement away from mainframe-centric systems towards open, distributed systems
- Movement away from "dumb" terminals towards intelligent workstations with GUIs
- Focus on reusable components
- Focus on a formal development process
- Movement towards easily extendable systems

Movement away from mainframes to distributed workstations and PCs. Organizations are moving away from centralized, mainframe-based development and deployment toward open, distributed (cooperative) processing and PC-based or workstation-based development. This trend has been called many things, including downsizing or rightsizing, but basically is a move away from proprietary, mainframe-centric systems towards open, distributed systems. Organizations find that a movement towards distributed processing and remote database access (distributed database/function) enables them to improve their overall staff productivity and to locate resources where they are most efficiently managed.

The days when everyone was developing mainframe-based systems are quickly ending, and the new viewpoint is to give everyone their own PC or workstation with their own operating system and features that typically are shared on a mainframe. This has led to a focus on distributed or cooperative processing and away from the mainframe-based file structures and databases of the late 1980s. Mainframe computers now are performing specialized application functions or acting as database servers for large networks of PCs.

Movement towards client/server applications and GUIs. Organizations also are finding that the growing acceptance of graphical environments for application deployment on a variety of platforms (PC and Unix) is pushing them away from "dumb" terminals to intelligent workstations. Using GUIs as front-ends to remote databases or distributed presentation represents a first step towards true client/server processing.

The Macintosh computer led to the acceptance of a graphical environment for computer systems and software. This was followed by the delivery of Windows from Microsoft, which did not gain widespread use until the release of version 3.0, but has enjoyed success with the current versions of Windows, 3.1, with multimedia extensions, and later with Windows NT. OS/2 version 2.0 with the Presentation Manager also has been very popular, selling over 5 million copies. Microsoft and IBM already have plans to extend their graphical environments towards OOOSs — Chicago and Cairo (Microsoft) and Taligent (IBM and Apple).

As organizations adopt client/server applications, they will move beyond distributed presentation, to distributed data access and, eventually, distributed applications or functions. Distributed data access is provided in some forms today, while the primary mechanisms for distributed function that commonly are used are remote procedure calls (RPCs). I'll discuss distributed computing in more depth in section 1.5.

Focus on reusable software components and increased software quality. As hardware becomes more and more inexpensive, software quickly is gaining the limelight in organizations as the key to improved productivity and longevity. With this focus on software comes a better understanding of the costs and benefits of software. As software costs are under more scrutiny, software development methods also are being closely scrutinized. Many organizations now are looking for less-expensive and higher-quality software than they were only a few years ago.

This has led to the belief that software development can be improved if more software can be reused over time. The focus on improving software quality has led to much speculation about component-based development where software "integrated-chips" are assembled into working applications. The benefit of using off-the-shelf components is that they already have been designed, built, and tested and therefore are more reliable than those built from scratch.

Organizations also find that, to support a variety of different physical environments — including database, networking, and presentation environments — their software should be designed to split functionality apart into distinct layers, where lower-level layers deal with specific hardware details and higher-level layers specify application functionality. This has led to a general acceptance of clearly defined interfaces that provide specific services to external components and the concept of software layers.

Focus on formal software development methods and automated tools. One area that has garnered much interest in the past few years is the use of formal software development methods and tools, including CASE, to improve the software development process. CASE has received a bad reputation in the industry, largely because of the improper expectations for these products and because of the hype associated with formal methods and tools.

Formalizing the software engineering process always has been a good idea, for technical as well as managerial reasons, and object technology offers yet another opportunity for organizations to undertake this process. Improving software quality can come only from a detailed understanding of the software process, the roles and responsibilities of staff, the products created, the techniques and tools used, and the skills of the developers. As organizations look to improve their software quality, formal development methods and tools should be considered as part of a broader strategy for defining and improving the software engineering process.

Developing systems that can be quickly and easily enhanced or changed. In the past, software was developed from the perspective of an integrated, monolithic, enterprise-wide strategy for an entire corporation. The old systems tended to be large, use shared databases, and be mainframe-centric. As a result of their size and the methods used to develop these systems — primarily ad-hoc or functional design — they were difficult to modify. These systems were complex, often not modular, and required massive amounts of documentation for maintenance.

In the future, distributed, organization-specific tactical systems will be developed instead of the large, monolithic systems of the past. These systems, which will be smaller, will communicate via clearly defined interfaces, will support specific functions or organizations, and will be easily changed. This allows organizations to build these systems and modify them quickly and easily to support the changing marketplace.

Using the principal benefits and concepts of object-orientation — modularity, encapsulation, software layers, and information hiding — these small, tactical systems will evolve to support different requirements and change functions over their useful lifetimes. In addition, structuring these systems to insulate them from low-level communication and high-level user interface issues will make them less succeptable to major redesigns when new technology is introduced.

1.3.1 History of Software Development

Early software development was primitive and relied on single processors and small amounts of memory and disk space. As computer systems evolved, the needs of software applications grew and the processing that was required became more complex. As you review the evolution of software over the past fifty years, you can characterize each 10-year period in terms of the types of input and output devices, processing, data structures, and data types used. Figure 1.6 represents these items for the past 50 years.

Initially, early software systems were developed using simple interfaces (cards), simple processing (top-down assembler), and memory-based data structures (simple structures or arrays). As software evolved, more sophisticated interfaces were developed, including the Teletype, the cathode ray tube (CRT), semi-intelligent CRTs (block-oriented devices), and eventually, PCs and workstations. As the computer interface evolved, graphical environments were developed that resembled the desktop. Graphical user interfaces (GUIs) now have become commonplace in the software industry, and many applications require these interfaces.

Likewise, as software evolved, the processing underneath the interface became more complex and the applications grew in size. Top-down processing was followed by functional or structured methods, self-sufficient modules, and control hierarchies, and this led to evolutions in procedural programming languages. Assembler led to FORTRAN, which led to COBOL, to Pascal, to C, to Ada, etc. Some in the programming community took a different approach, looking at non procedural languages, primarily to support simulations. This led to the development of object-based languages and the concept of encapsulation in program units.

Meanwhile, batch processing led to online processing, which led to storage mechanisms that supported keyed access to data. Batch programs were always sequential and had simple control structures, but online programs

Decade	Input/Output	Processing	Data Structures	Data Types
1950s	Card reader/punch	Centralized batch	Memory and tape-based sequential	Numeric and text
1960s	Stream-based (teletype and terminals)	Centralized batch with some time-sharing	Disk and tape-based sequential	Records of text or numeric
1970s	Character-base Terminals	Centralized time-sharing with TP	Disk and tape-based indexed sequential	Records of text or numeric
1980s	Page-based terminals	Centralized time-sharing with TP & DBMS	Disk-based Hierarchical, Network & Relational DBMS	Tables of records of text or numeric, some images or graphics
1990s	PCs or workstations, Pen-based, etc.	Distributed with DBMS servers	Relational and distributed DBMS	User-defined, including audio, video, graphics, images, etc.

Figure 1.5 Software characteristics over the past 50 years.

required more interaction with the user via the interface, and this led to reentrant code and recursion. Also, programs grew in size as the complexity of and the functional requirements for managing the interface grew.

Data structures became more complex, moving to stacks, queues, linked lists, sequential files on tape, then on disk, and eventually to database management systems (DBMS). Keyed access to data led to database structures (hierarchical, network, and relational), and these structures supported more complex data types. In the 1990s, non linear data structures are beginning to be used more extensively. These can take the form of digitized images, diagrams, lists of objects, audio, video, and animation. Another factor that has changed the shape of software development is the distribution of data and functionality across a network.

The software of the 1990s is characterized by powerful desktop computers (workstations and PCs) with massive memory and disk systems, graphical interfaces that support bitmapped images, some use of sound and video, and distributed data structures on a network. Downsizing has become the operative word in software development, and the mainframe now is viewed as a DBMS or application server for a network of PCs.

Client/server software, or distributed applications, has garnered much interest, and many organizations have committed to distributed functionality across their computer networks. CASE tools and object-oriented products are gaining market share, and older, procedural languages are evolving to support an object perspective.

1.3.2 COBOL Standards

COBOL has evolved along with the software development industry and has recently undergone dramatic changes to support object-oriented development. During the 1970s, COBOL was thought to be the ideal programming language with its English-like syntax and commands. While COBOL lost some of its appeal during the 1980s with the advent of 4GLs, it still has remained the dominant programming language in the industry. Prior to introducing the concepts of object-oriented COBOL, I will review the history of the COBOL language.

USAS COBOL 68 — Initial standard for COBOL. COBOL was developed by the Conference on Data Systems Languages (CODASYL) in 1959. The first standard for the COBOL programming language was issued in 1968 by the American National Standards Institute (ANSI) and CODASYL. COBOL 68 introduced the divisions in COBOL: the IDENTIFICATION, ENVIRONMENT, DATA, and PROCEDURE divisions. The 68 standard allowed for extensions to COBOL, and many compiler vendors added their own unique facilities. This led to incompatibilities between versions of COBOL 68 and hindered the overall acceptance of the standard in the industry.

ANSI COBOL 74 — First generally supported COBOL standard. In 1974, the ANSI approved a revised standard for COBOL that included better string manipulation and indexed file access. The COBOL 74 standard did not immediately achieve success in the industry because vendors didn't move quickly to support it. IBM, for example, didn't release support for COBOL 74 on the System/370 series computer until 1977.

Also, shortly after the COBOL 74 standard was released, many in the industry began to focus on structured programming concepts, but the 1974 standard did not include specific support for these programming constructs.

ANSI COBOL 85 — Structured development in COBOL. The COBOL 85 standard, which is widely used in the IBM community (COBOL II), incorporated support for structured programming. Included in the standard is support for nested programming, a CASE statement, global and local data structure, and passing parameters by content or reference. Other modifications to the language included changes to the way the PERFORM statement works and file I/O modifications.

These extensions were added by the ANSI committee to support structured programming concepts identified by Dijkstra [DIJ76], Constantine and Yourdon [YOU78], Meyers [MEY78], and others [PAR72]. These concepts included functional decomposition, modular programming, stepwise refinement, and coupling and cohesion. As the structured programming ideas were adopted, newer concepts of programming were introduced, including encapsulation, information hiding, and classification. These ideas make up the basis for the proposed COBOL 97 standard.

1.3.3 An Objective View of Software Development

One reason for using objects in the software development process is that they map very nicely to the things already in the problem domain. Other reasons for the interest in object-oriented development include the simplicity of viewing the world in terms of service requesters and providers, support for client/server development with objects, objects supporting a layered view of software, and the benefit of reusability in object technology.

Viewing the world in terms of service requesters and providers. You can view the physical world as groups of requesters and providers of services. This view is very comfortable when you begin to look at computer systems. The concept is fairly simple, and an object-oriented perspective follows this approach nicely. Objects interact by requesting and providing services to other objects. Requesters and providers must understand which type of services are available and establish a protocol (or interface) to work together in the consumer/producer relationship. Without a protocol established, services cannot be provided.

For a real-world example of providers and requesters, consider the process of acquiring telephone, electric, and cable services when you move into a new home. You, as requester, ask for services from the phone company. They, as provider, come to your home to establish the connection, and you agree to pay a monthly fee for these services.

You wouldn't have much luck asking the cable TV company for phone or electric services, and so the services available are clearly defined before the transaction can occur. Also, if you fail to pay your cable TV bill, after a prescribed period of time, you will loose these services. The relationship between you and the cable TV company requires a protocol — in this case, you pay for services and you receive them. This model of providers and requesters holds true for computer systems and especially for object-oriented systems.

Client/server development. Client/server applications have a special type of requester/provider relationship that can be exploited using object-oriented development. Under a client/server system, workstations request services, often in the form of data access or printing, from servers over a network. The workstation is the requester of services, while the server is the provider of those services.

One benefit of this view is that the requester of services, in this case the client, need not know which server will satisfy its request. In a distributed system, several competitive providers might be available and there might be reasons why one server delivers the requested service while others do not. This is especially helpful when accessing data in a distributed environment, because the client need not know where or how the server stores the data. The server might be another workstation (PC), a minicomputer, superminicomputer, or even a mainframe computer. In the event that the server is moved to some other environment or platform, the client is unaffected by this change so long as the service protocol remains consistent. I will examine other aspects of this type of relationship in other sections.

Another obvious benefit of this view is that anyone who wants to use (or reuse) the services of an object doesn't need to know who will provide the service (i.e., services are provided by black boxes that might exist anywhere in the network). This clear definition of service providers and requesters is essential as the industry moves towards distributed, heterogenous systems. Standards groups (OMG, etc.) will play a much more important role, providing definitions and specifications for common services, interfaces, and protocols across platforms in the future.

Developing software in layers. One benefit of using object technology is that it allows software to be developed in layers, with each layer interacting with other layers via a clearly defined interface. For example, consider developing a system that must use a LAN to communicate between programs. An object-oriented system can be designed and developed such that the communication or presentation portion of the system is isolated and the other potions of the application interact via this interface using a common set of services. The benefit to this approach is that if the communication or presentation portion of the application changes, perhaps because of new technology, the remaining layers of the system need not be changed if the interface stays the same. In those cases where new services are added to the communication or presentation layer, other layers might be affected but probably to a must lesser degree.

Several studies have shown that object-oriented systems tend to be more modular and thus more resilient to change than systems built using functional methods. One study [HEN93] found that object-oriented code requires fewer modules and sections to be edited, fewer lines of code to be changed, and fewer new lines of code to be added. Another study [HAY94] compared three different development approaches — functional decomposition, object-based, and object-oriented — and found that the object-oriented system had a significantly lower level of complexity in its modules and required fewer lines of code to be changed for a variety of modifications.

Software designed or organized around functions (i.e., with functional design) are composed of modules that provide simple services and are connected by usage and data transfers, whereas software designed or organized around objects are composed of modules (objects) that have many different kinds of interactions. Larry Constantine has written on this topic in [CON90].

Each approach, object-oriented and function-oriented, provide benefits and drawbacks for specific types of systems and modifications. Object-oriented software typically has fewer objects to consider so that the time to identify candidate objects for change should be smaller, but because the complexity of each object is greater than with functional modules, the time to make any change increases.

Reusing software components. Another major factor affecting the evolution of software development is the downsizing that is occurring at most organizations. Many MIS or DP groups are having to reduce staff and improve their overall software quality and productivity to stay competitive. This has led to the idea of reducing the overall costs of software development by reusing components across systems.

The concept of software reuse is not new and is covered in more detail in chapter 12, but the benefit of reuse is lower overall cost of software development. Additional benefits include reduced testing efforts, better reliability of components, and quicker/easier enhancement of existing systems.

Creating components that can be reused requires defining their inputs, outputs, and computational characteristics, as well as defining their behavior and the class or environment in which they are meaningful. Creating a library of reusable components is by far the most difficult task in achieving reuse. When class libraries are purchases, the cost of reuse becomes the cost of learning to use the classes in the library and understand how they interact.

1.4 COBOL Extensions to Support Object-Orientation

The proposed standard for COBOL in the 1990s is the ANSI COBOL 97 standard, which is expected to be released before the end of the century. This standard will incorporate objects, classes, encapsulation, and inheritance in the COBOL language. These extensions are being added to allow COBOL application development to take advantage of the benefits of object-orientation.

The basis for objects in programming stems from the development of SIMULA in the 1960s and the original OOPL, Smalltalk, developed in the 1970s and delivered in the early 1980s. Several popular OOPLs include Eiffel [MEY88], C++ [STR86], and ObjectiveC [COX91].

The object-oriented COBOL task group (OOCTG) was established in 1989 to develop a standard for COBOL that would support object-orientation. Recently, the CODASYL COBOL committee and the ANSI X3J4 committee were merged to form a single group that proposed modifications to the COBOL 85 standard. Prior to discussing the current efforts in this area, I will review the history of COBOL standards.

The OOCTG created extensions to the COBOL programming language and delivered a preliminary report in March, 1993. It is hoped that the object-oriented COBOL (OOCOBOL) standard can be approved by 1997. The current OOCTG standard contains syntax for defining classes, objects, and object interfaces.

The current OOCOBOL document recommends support for object definitions that are external to the programs that use them. The OOCTG has established objects and classes, interfaces between objects, and type checking in COBOL. Still under discussion are issues of how objects should be instantiated, if method prototypes should be supported, whether data structures should be separated from object interfaces, how objects will be bound, and how subtyping will be supported. When the OOCTG produced their report in 1993 [X3J93], most of the preliminary work was complete towards a future OOCOBOL standard.

However, how should COBOL be modified to support object-oriented constructs? Should the language support multiple inheritance or single inheritance? Should it also support persistent objects and garbage collection? Should it support type checking? Virtual methods? Should COBOL be modified to support reentrant code?

One way to consider how COBOL should be modified to support object-orientation is to review how other languages, both hybrid and true OOPLs, support object-orientation. Brad Cox identifies five characteristics of Objective-C that can be applied to all OOPLs. These include objects, messages, encapsulation, classes, and inheritance. OOCOBOL should provide support for all of these characteristics if it is to be object-oriented.

However, what level of object-orientation should be provided in the COBOL 97 standard? Peter Wegner of Brown University defines three possible levels of object-orientation:

- Object-based languages support *objects and messages*
- Class-based languages support *classes, objects, and messages*
- Object-oriented languages support *inheritance, classes, objects, and messages*

At a minimum, OOCOBOL must support the creation of objects from classes that include data structures and procedures that access those structures, methods and messages as forms of communication between programs (objects), and the associated constructs required to create working systems that interact.

For COBOL to support classes, objects, and messages, it must be modified to encapsulate data structures with the procedures that act on those structures. COBOL currently separates the procedure portion of a program from the data portion, and OOCOBOL must allow for these to be combined. The proposed standard supports encapsulation by allowing a class definition to contain multiple Identification Divisions that include both data and procedure commands [TOP93]. Subsequent COBOL programs could reference these classes and instantiate objects based on these definitions.

1.4.1 OOCOBOL Products Available

Currently, there are only two vendors that provide support for object-oriented development in COBOL: Micro Focus and Netron. Other COBOL vendors, including Computer Associates, IBM, DEC, Unisys, and HP, have plans to support the OOCOBOL standard when it is accepted.

Micro Focus COBOL already supports an object-oriented option that includes a run-time environment (RTE) and a reusable code manager. The RTE supports specialized memory management (garbage collection, etc.), macros provide for defining and creating objects, invoking objects, etc. The object-oriented option includes common data types and methods for linked lists, streams, and sets. Communication within OOCOBOL with other objects currently is limited to Smalltalk but Micro Focus plans to support communication with C++ programs in a future release.

The Micro Focus reusable code manager (RCM) supports macros and program models in COBOL that give programmers access to the run-time environment and allow them to create, initialize, and invoke objects. The RCM also can be used to maintain existing code and identify components for reuse. Screens, JCL, code, and data structures can be defined as reusable units and configuration management is supported for modification and tracking.

The Micro Focus browser allows COBOL code to be displayed, edited, compiled, debugged, and run under the RTE in a format common in other object-oriented environments. Class libraries are available from Micro Focus that support basic tasks such as managing lists, arrays, sets, and dictionaries, with support planned for the OOCTG syntax in a future release of the product.

Perhaps the most powerful aspect of the Micro Focus COBOL environment is the integrated development tools that are included. These include editors, compilers, linkers, and the Animator, which provides sophisticated debugging for new and existing COBOL programs. Together, these tools provide most of the support required in an object-oriented development environment.

Netron/CAP is a COBOL code assembly tool that supports many of the concepts of object-oriented development. Many organizations have successfully used Netron/CAP for developing COBOL systems in an object-oriented manner. Netron/CAP is based on the concept of a "frame" as the dominant component in software development and is similar to OOPLs in that these frames are combined to form working systems. More on these OOCOBOL products in chapter 8.

1.4.2 Future OOCOBOL Products and Standards

The future of OOCOBOL products looks bright. Once the OOCTG presents its report (probably by the time this book is printed) the COBOL community will begin to consider the standard and make comments on it. Hopefully, major COBOL vendors, including IBM and DEC, will provide support for the OOCOBOL standard shortly after it is accepted.

Existing COBOL development tools must be modified to support the object-oriented standard and additional products must be developed. For OOCOBOL to be effective, it must be incorporated with other, object-oriented development tools. These include browsers, editors, incremental compilers and linkers, debuggers, profilers, inspectors, debuggers, class libraries and frameworks. As I already have stated, Micro Focus has led the way with development of these tools in their existing COBOL product line and other COBOL vendors should follow this trend.

Outstanding issues that remain for OOCOBOL include technical language issues as well those of gaining acceptance from organizations that are heavily committed to COBOL applications. Technical issues include whether OOCOBOL should support multiple or single inheritance, static or dynamic binding, automatic garbage collection, how the language should support object persistence, etc.

Additional issues include how operating systems and graphical user interface APIs will be incorporated in the OOCOBOL standard, how client/server standards efforts and the Object Management Group (OMG) standard efforts will be supported by the OOCOBOL specification. Perhaps the most important issue to the success of OOCOBOL is how the language will be integrated with existing structured code and how existing systems can be made to support object-oriented concepts.

Perhaps the most pressing issue in the eventual acceptance of object-orientation is the publication and acceptance of standards within the industry for distributed object management.

1.5 Distributed Computing Standards

As I have already stated, all software systems consist of three distinct portions or functions: *human or user interface, application processing*, and *DBMS or data access*. Some applications might contain simplified user interfaces, or mix business logic with the data access, while others might have combined user interfaces and system functions. *Middleware* is a term now generally used in conjunction with client/server or distributed systems that represents the portion of an application supporting the underlying logic or business rules and any required communications with remote systems. Applications are moving towards more sophisticated middleware components as distributed or client/server systems gain prominence.

Philip Teale of IBM Canada has identified three levels of middleware: *lower*, which supports a communications model on a network protocol; *middle*, which is environment-aware and communications-model-dependent with high-level APIs; and *upper*, which isolates the application from the hardware/software environment and a communications model using a generic program model and API. Standards efforts, including the Common Object Requester Broker Access (CORBA) and Distributed Computing Environment (DCE), are attempts to define common middleware mechanisms that can be used across a variety of development environments.

Current mechanisms for middleware include remote data access, database servers, and application servers. Remote data access supports presentation and business logic on the workstation with remote requests for data from a database, typically SQL-based. Database servers provide limited presentation on the workstation with the business logic executed as stored procedures on the database server. This model of distributed computing stores the application logic in the database itself.

The third view, application servers, support presentation on the workstation, business logic on an application-specific server, and database access on a DBMS server. Remote procedure calls (RPCs), the most common mechanism for distributed computing today, facilitate DBMS and application server viewpoints in most of the major middleware available today (including OSF/CDE, Netwise, etc.). With RPCs, a server's data is accessible only through the defined set of services or an interface to the server.

Distributed object management (DOM) makes a system's resources appear as objects in a distributed system. When resources are viewed as objects, messages act as the vehicle for communication and are processed by the object management system. A DOM includes object implementations, client interfaces that allow requests to be sent and received by objects via a messaging facility, object interfaces that let distributed objects invoke the services of other objects, and a distributed set of computing resources. A common object model provides a set of abstractions understood and supported by all the DOMs.

<u>Encapsulation</u> is the grouping of object state and operations, and information hiding is supported by well-defined interfaces between objects that want to communicate. <u>Abstraction</u> is the ability to group together objects based on their common properties and behaviors. <u>Polymorphysm</u> is the ability of abstractions to overlap and intersect.

Heterogenity is supported with objects because messages are distributed to each component and are dependent only on the interfaces for each object, not on their internal structure. This provides autonomy because objects can change independently and transparently, so long as they maintain their interfaces. There are a variety of standards for distributed applications that have been proposed in the past.

The ISO Open Systems Interconnection (OSI) Reference Model identifies as key structuring concepts the use of layers of services with well-defined interfaces. The X3H7, an X3 technical committee, is charged with coordinating object-oriented development activities.

The Open Software Foundation (OSF) defined the Distributed Computing Environment (DCE) that supports encapsulation via remote procedure calls (RPCs) but does not support abstraction and polymorphism. DCE eventually will support common services, including security, file- and application-sharing over a variety of platforms. The OSF's Distributed Management Environment (DME) manages DCE for networks and systems and consists of basic management protocols, a foundation layer of object services (request brokers, etc.), a set of customizable management services, application services (installation, printing, etc.), and a Motif-based graphical user interface.

The Object Management Group (OMG) has produced the Common Object Request Broker Architecture (CORBA), which specifies a bare-bones architecture for distributed object management with five interfaces. The CORBA object model supports defining objects and their interfaces. The model is composed of objects, requests, types (classes), interfaces, and operations. Currently, the CORBA doesn't support versioning, configuration management, hot links, or transactions.

In support of dynamic client interfaces, the CORBA standard includes an interface and an implementation repository. The interface repository stores objects and IDL information at runtime and allows objects to be linked dynamically using interface primitives. The implementation repository stores the data and code required to realize an object's behavior as specified by its interface. Object adapters map the object model and implementations to the basic ORB code model.

As more vendors of computing systems hardware and software support the CORBA standard, the promise of interoperability and distributed processing over heterogenous systems will be realized. Systems built that take advantage of the CORBA standard eventually will support full distributed functionality across a wide range of operating environments. OOCOBOL must evolve to include support for the current CORBA standard as well as other OMG standards delivered in the future.

1.6 References

[ADA92]   Adams, M. and D. Lenkov, "Object-Oriented COBOL," *Object Magazine*, March/April 1992, pp. 63-68.
[CON90]   Constantine, L., "Objects, Functions, and Program Extensibility," *Computer Language*, January 1990, pp. 34-56.
[COX91]   Cox, B. and A. Novobilski, *Object-Oriented Programming: An Evolutionary Approach*, Second Edition, Addison-Wesley, 1991.
[DIJ76]   Dijkstra, E., "Structured Programming," in *Software Engineering, Concepts and Techniques*, J. Buxton et al., eds., Van Nostrand Reinhold, 1976.
[HAY94]   Haythorn, W., "What is Object-Oriented Design," *JOOP*, March-April 1994, pp. 67-78.
[HEN93]   Henry, S. and M. Humphrey, "Object-Oriented vs. Procedural Programming Languages: Effectiveness in Program Maintenance," *JOOP*, June 1993, pp. 41-49.
[IDC92]   *Object Technology: A Key Software Technology for the '90s*, International Data Corp., 1992.
[MEY88]   Meyer, B., *Object-Oriented Software Construction*, Prentice-Hall, 1988.
[OVU90]   *Technical report on Object Technology*, Ovum Ltd., 1990.

[PAR72]   Parnas, D. L., "On the Criteria to be Used in Decomposing Systems," *CACM*, vol. 15, no. 5, 1972, pp. 1053-1058.

[STE74]   Stevens, W., G. Myers, and L. Constantine, "Structured Design," *IBM Systems Journal*, vol. 13, no. 2 (1974), pp. 115-139.

[STR86]   Stroustrup, B., *The C++ Programming Language*, Addison-Wesley, 1986.

[TOP93]   Topper, A., "Object-Oriented Technology and COBOL," *Object Magazine*, March/April 1993, pp. 54-58.

[X3J93]   X3J4.1, "Object-Oriented Extensions to COBOL," Technical Report, March 1993.

[YOU78]   Yourdon, E. and L. Constantine, *Structured Design*, Prentice-Hall, 1978.

Chapter 2

History of Object-Oriented Development

Prior to looking at object-oriented development in COBOL, I will cover the evolution of the object technology marketplace in general and the emergence of the popular products and methods. As I discuss object technology in general, you can get an idea of how OOCOBOL was shaped by the marketplace. While the earliest application of objects were applied to programming languages, this was followed by the development of class libraries, analysis and design methods, databases, and finally, operating systems.

The recent alliance between IBM and Apple to form Taligent, along with the formation of the Object Management Group and the specification of the CORBA standard, have led to the widespread acceptance of object technology in the computer industry. Even Microsoft, the software industry leader, has announced its own plans for object technology in a future version of its Windows operating environment. This project, code-named Cairo, also will support some of the concepts of objects, messages, and encapsulation.

As I review the history of object technology, you should keep in mind the original concepts of object-oriented development and the factors that have affected the evolution of these products. You can gain insight into the role of objects in development by re-examining the roots of object technology and the evolutionary aspects of the technology in the marketplace.

2.1 Introduction

Object technology (OT) has its roots in the development of SIMULA in the late 1960s and the work of Alan Kay and his team at the Xerox Palo Alto Research Corp. (PARC) in the 1970s. SIMULA, which originally was developed in Norway, included most of the fundamental concepts common in all object-oriented programming languages (OOPLs) and affected the development of most of the popular object technologies that followed.

Bertrand Meyer, the architect of Eiffel, was once chairman of the Association of SIMULA Users, and Alan Kay, an originator of graphical user interfaces (GUIs) and Smalltalk, first developed his Sketchpad in the SIMULA language. Smalltalk, the original OOPL, combined the objects and classes in

SIMULA with an incremental development environment similar to that of Lisp. Bjarne Stroustrup, developer of C++ at AT&T, also originally used SIMULA, as did Jean Ichbiah, one of the designers of the Ada language.

Smalltalk 80 was the first commercial OOPL that was based on objects and classes in a GUI and led to the general acceptance of object-oriented development. Apple Computer was one of the first major users of Smalltalk and offered a version of it for the Lisa computer in 1981. Lisp was extended to support object-based concepts in 1977 by MIT, and C++ was developed by Stroustrup in 1985. Eiffel, a very powerful and elegant OOPL, was introduced by Interactive Software Engineering in 1986.

On the methods front, an object-oriented design method for Ada was described in a paper published by Grady Booch in 1982 and generalized for other OOPLs in 1991. Sally Shlaer and Steven Mellor published their own book on object-oriented analysis (OOA) in 1988. The Coad/Yourdon method was introduced in books published in 1990 and 1991, and the object-oriented modeling technique (OOMT) was defined in a book published in late 1991. Recently, much has been written on the subject or object-oriented analysis/design (OOA/D) techniques, and many CASE tools now support OOA/D methods and notations.

2.2 Genesis of Object-Oriented Products

The current crop of object-oriented development products has evolved over the past 30 years to include a wide variety of technologies and services, from analysis and design methods to database management systems and from programming languages to operating systems. All of these technologies share common properties or characteristics that make them "object-oriented." At a minimum, each of these products supports the concepts of encapsulation and information hiding, message passing, and classification by inheritance.

As previously noted, the evolution of object technology stems from the development of SIMULA, the first programming language to support objects and messages. Throughout the 1970s and into the 1980s, object-oriented programming languages were used initially for research and eventually for production systems. Two of the more popular OOPLs at the later part of the 1980s were Smalltalk and C++.

Around the mid-1980s, several key efforts were underway to begin considering designing systems using objects. Grady Booch wrote his first book on object-oriented design with Ada in 1986, and this was followed in 1988 by a book on object-oriented analysis by Shlaer and Mellor. In the early 1990s, OOA/D methods have been gaining more prominence and many techniques now are being used. CASE tools began supporting these OOA/D methods in the early 1990s and major CASE vendors, including Cadre, Intersolv, Knowledgeware, and IBM, were planning to support them in the future.

Objects began to be applied to data storage systems in the late 1980s, with efforts at the Microelectronics Computer Consortium (MCC) in Austin, Texas, as well as at IBM and HP. From these projects, and others, came persistent object management systems, precursors to the OODBMS. As the need to store and retrieve nonlinear data structures increased, including graphics, audio, and video, the need for more versatile data managers grew and the OODBMS industry was created.

Also gaining interest in the early 1990s was the concept of an object-oriented operating system. This concept would allow operating system services to be available in the form of objects and would allow users to view applications and services as integrated with the desktop environment. IBM and Apple formed an alliance in 1991 to develop a series of computers and operating environments that would be inherently object-oriented. Next, originally a developer of Unix hardware, changed their plans in 1992 and began selling only its NextStep operating environment. Microsoft announced its own plans to develop an object-oriented operating environment (code-named Cairo) in 1994.

At the same time, several important standards have been proposed in the industry for distributed computing, including the Common Object Request Broker Architecture (CORBA) from OMG, Distributed Computing Environment (DCE) from the Open Systems Foundation, and document architecture specifications from Micrsoft (OLE) and IBM, Apple, Xerox, and others (OpenDoc).

The current object technology marketplace is fractured, with few overlapping tools and methods. Some predict that the 1990s will result in a reshuffling of vendors and products and a reduction in the number of players in this industry. Others argue that the industry still is in its infancy, and thus the variety of vendors and products will continue to expand through the year 2000.

2.3 History of Object-Oriented Development

SIMULA-67 was developed at the Norwegian Computing Centre by Kristen Nygaard and Ole-Johan Dahl in 1967 [MYH68]. SIMULA was created from a variety of language constructs, and its goal was to map more directly to the objects in the problem domain so that simulation would be easier [NYG81]. Developers found that simulating things with the computer was difficult using traditional, procedural programming languages. In any procedural language, things are modeled using data fields or attributes, also called data types, but these languages (FORTRAN, COBOL, C, PASCAL, etc.) allow only for simple data types to be used — strings, integers, real numbers, etc.

The developers of SIMULA found that they needed to define their own data types, called user-defined data types, and these data types needed their own set of operations or procedures. If these types of data structures could be defined by the programmer, then they could be used in the same way that simple data types were used. To support user-defined data types, a language would have to be created that allowed for the definition of these data types within the constructs of the language.

From this viewpoint came the idea of classes (i.e., generic types of objects) and objects, which represent abstract or user-defined data types. Along with these definitions of data types and structures, the developers of SIMULA added processes or methods that could be applied against these data structures. These commonly used routines were encapsulated with the data structures themselves, and specific compiler checking was provided to ensure that only these methods could access the variables in the object to preserve information hiding and modularity.

In 1970, Alan Kay developed the Dynabook at the Xerox PARC, which included a GUI with overlapping windows, a mouse, icons, etc. In 1971, as part of the Dynabook project, a new language was created that combined the objects and classes in SIMULA with an incremental development environment of LISP. Smalltalk was the result of several language concepts being merged into a single implementation within the PARC. Along with SIMULA and LISP, Smalltalk has its roots in LOGO (some classes), CLU (abstract data types), and Director (actors and message passing). All of these languages contributed to what later became Smalltalk, which was written at the Xerox PARC by Dan Ingalls and Alan Kay in 1971.

Delivered in 1972, Smalltalk-72 became the first commercial version of Smalltalk and originally was aimed at teaching elementary school students how to program. While Smalltalk was available in the 1970s, few organizations outside research and academia used the language until the early 1980s. During the same time, MIT also developed Flavors, a set of object-oriented extensions to LISP.

The Xerox PARC licensed Smalltalk-80 to Apple, DEC, HP, and Tektronix in 1980, and two years later Apple ported it to the Lisa computer. The real interest in Smalltalk came after the publication of an issue of *Byte* magazine devoted to the language in 1981. In 1983, Object-Oriented Pascal and the Lisa Toolkit were developed by Apple, and a book on Smalltalk-80 was written by Adele Goldberg. Brad Cox developed Objective-C, and Interactive Software Engineering was founded in 1984 by Bertrand Meyer to develop object-oriented CASE tools.

In 1985, Digitalk began shipping Methods, a PC-based version of the Smalltalk language. The same year, Bjarne Stroustrup of AT&T defined C++ and Apple Computer began shipping Object Pascal and MacApp for the Macintosh computer. Bertrand Meyer developed SIMULA-85, which later became Eiffel. Meyer's goals in developing it were to support multiple inheritance, genericity, assertions, and strong typing.

In 1986, Chuck Duff of Whitewater developed Actor, Bjarne Stroustrup wrote *The C++ Programming Language*, and Grady Booch wrote "Object-Oriented Development" for the *IEEE Transactions on Software Engineering*. The first object-oriented programming, systems, languages, and applications (OOPSLA) conference was held in 1986, and Interactive Software Engineering delivered Eiffel the same year.

In 1987, Digitalk delivered Smalltalk/V for the PC and ParcPlace Systems released Smalltalk-80 for the Macintosh. In the same year, Zortech delivered a version of C++ for DOS, Windows, and OS/2. In 1988, Bertrand Meyer wrote *Object Oriented Software Construction* and the *Journal of Object-Oriented Programming* was launched. In 1989, Borland introduced Object Pascal for the PC, Apple released C++ for the Macintosh, and the Next computer was shipped. The Object Management Group (OMG) also was formed that year, and HP released NewWave, their object-oriented operating system.

In 1990, Borland introduced Turbo C++, Apple and IBM formed an alliance to develop object-oriented operating systems, and object-oriented programming (OOP) was covered in *Business Week* magazine. In 1991, the first East Coast conference on OOP was held and a Smalltalk report was published. Microsoft launched its own C++ product in 1992, and IBM signed an agreement with Versant Object Technology to incorporate object-oriented database management systems (OODBMS) into its future products. Also in 1992, the OMG released the CORBA standard for object interaction, and Object Expo and Object World were held for the first time.

In 1993, the X3J4.1 prepared a draft technical report "Object-Oriented Extensions for COBOL" and Micro Focus released the first commercial release of an Object-Oriented COBOL for DOS, Windows, and OS/2. Thus the evolution of object technology reached the COBOL community in 1993/1994 and the ANSI COBOL standard is scheduled for adoption in 1997.

2.4 Emergence of OOA/D Methods

Following the use of OOPLs, organizations began looking for methods of analysis and design to match the implementation details of objects and messages in a programming language. This closely followed the path taken by the structured development revolution of the 1970s — first focusing on programming, then on design, then on analysis. Several different methods were created and used beginning in the mid-1980s, which resulted in the publication of books and training materials that form the basic OOA/D methods now available. As these OOA/D methods gained acceptance, several Computer-Aided Software Engineering (CASE) tools emerged to support them.

One of the original object-oriented development methods was described in a technical paper in *Ada Letters* in 1982 by Grady Booch [BOO82]. This was followed in later years with a book on object-oriented design with Ada [BOO86a] and a seminal paper on object-oriented development [BOO86b] that was published in the *IEEE Transactions on Software Engineering*. Booch also wrote several books describing his method [BOO87] [BOO91], with the latest incarnation published in 1993 [BOO93]. The original Booch method was Ada-based and provided support for designing packages along with notations for showing dependencies between packages and tasks that implement objects.

The Booch method was followed by other Ada-based development techniques, including those described by Sidney Bailin, Ray Buhr, and Edward Berrard (known as the EVB method). Of these, Object-Oriented Requirements Specification (OORS) borrowed from traditional structured analysis and incorporated popular notations, including data flow diagrams, entity-relationship diagrams, and state-transition diagrams [BAI88]. Buhr described a detailed notation for design in [BUH86] that included finite state machines, Booch-like diagrams, and architectural notations. EVB Software Engineering also created and teaches an Ada-based development method described in [BAL91] based on similar Booch work.

While the Ada-based methods were evolving, others in the industry were experimenting with alternative methods of analysis and design. Data- or information-model-based methods were created and described by Shlaer/Mellor [SHL88], Coad/Yourdon [COA91], Rumbaugh *et al* [RUM91], and Martin/Odell [MAR92]. All of these methods call for the study and identification of entities in the problem domain and the description of relationships using modified entity-relationship diagrams. These methods use data models to drive the development process and fit comfortably with what many organizations already are doing with database development.

Still others in the industry were developing methods oriented towards the Smalltalk programming language developed at the Xerox PARC. Three major groups from Tektronix developed Smalltalk-based methods for analysis and design in the 1980s. The original Smalltalk-based method was based on Class-Responsibility-Collaboration (CRC) using index cards and originally was described in [BEC89]. This method evolved to become Responsibility-Driven Design (RDD) defined by Wirfs-Brock and Wilkerson and described in [WIR89] [WIR90]. Object-Behavior Analysis (OBA) is a similar method designed by Goldberg and Rubin [RUB92]. These methods differ from previous methods in their use of scenarios or object collaborations as guides to the development process.

Other methods that have been introduced recently include Objectory [JAC92], which also is based on a scenario view called *use cases* by Jacobson *et al*; Fusion, which is a combination of the best aspects of several methods used at HP [COL94]; and a method to support development with Eiffel, which was described by Nerson [NER92] and Meyer [MEY92].

CASE support for OOA/D methods has been slow in coming, but recently, several popular CASE products have been modified to support some of these methods. I discuss the issues involved in selecting and using these methods, along with issues concerning using CASE tools, in subsequent chapters.

2.5 Current Object Technology Marketplace

Some CASE tool vendors have recognized the value of object technology, in the form of OOPLs and OODBMSs, and have begun using these products themselves. Some are beginning to share their experiences with OT in papers and conference presentations. Cadre Technologies, maker of the Teamwork CASE product set, has been using object technology for the past several years. The Teamwork/Ada product is written entirely in C++, and Cadre was one of the first significant users of object-oriented design in the late 1980s.

Cadre developers have written and presented extensively on their experiences with OT and continue to expand the use of OT in their product line. Intersolv, formally Index Technology, has developed its OS/2-based tool, Excelerator for OS/2, entirely in Smalltalk. Several other tool vendors have begun providing support for OOA/D techniques or are broadening their existing support.

Research suggests that a CASE repository can substantially benefit from an underlying OODBMS with support for complex data elements, including diagrams, binary objects, object specifications, etc. For an OODBMS to be successfully used in a CASE tool, however, it must be integrated into the CASE environment and support the persistence of objects along with the management of objects and classes.

Object management becomes a critical component of any object-oriented development environment and must be included in any CASE tool used in this environment. This brings up an important question: Should a CASE repository include object management as a primary function? If so, how will this affect major repository standards already in the works (i.e., PCTE, RM/MVS, and CDD/Repository)?

Major CASE repository efforts recently have begun to consider an object-oriented perspective. Digital Equipment Corp. has included an object-oriented component in its Cohesion CASE environment, and IBM has an agreement with Atherton Technology to support object-oriented components in the AIX CASE strategy.

Other vendors have provided support for meta-methods and allow their users to tailor the tool to fit their own method or create new methods that combine aspects of different techniques. Example products include ObjectMaker from Mark V and Paradigm Plus from Protosoft, both of which also support a variety of OOA/D notations.

Further clouding the OT issue is the recent interest in client/server software, which will undoubtedly include some form of object communication in the future. Using a standard protocol or interface, objects can be distributed throughout a network and can request services from other objects using messages. The Common Object Request Broker Architecture (CORBA), as defined by the Object Management Group (OMG), is a standard for object communications. Given the members of the OMG, it is clear that future distributed (client/server) software products and architectures will be developed based on the CORBA.

2.6 COBOL Enters the Picture

COBOL 68 was the first standard COBOL produced, but it led to discrepancies among the COBOL compilers. COBOL 74, probably the most widely used COBOL standard today, brought to COBOL many modern programming language features. COBOL 85, perhaps the least-used COBOL standard (IBM's COBOL II), included support for structured programming concepts. COBOL 97, or object-oriented COBOL (OOCOBOL), will support the concepts of objects, messages, and classification.

Those who slept through the 1970s might have missed the structured revolution and still might be writing or supporting unstructured COBOL programs. The use of structured programming constructs — including single entry/exit, small independent modules, and top-down hierarchies — led to the development of the COBOL 85 standard. Structured development, including analysis, design, programming, and testing, also led to the modification of COBOL to support nested programs, calling by content, etc.

Those who remained asleep through the 1980s missed the rise and fall of the Fourth-generation languages (4GLs), along with the widespread use of the relational database (RDBMS), the graphical user interface (GUI), and the limited acceptance of Computer-Aided Software Engineering (CASE) tools. All of these efforts were not overlooked by the COBOL community, with the emergence of support for ANSI SQL, GUI development products, and links to code generators.

If any developers have been asleep through the first part of the 1990s, they might have missed the explosion in the use of personal computers (PCs), local area networks (LANs) and the movement away from mainframe-based applications to workstation or client/server applications. They also might have missed the growing interest and acceptance of object technology. For these individuals, OOCOBOL provides support for the concepts of object-oriented development and there are products available from reputable vendors that support objects and messages in COBOL.

The OOCOBOL standard, although still under revision, has been described in articles [TOP93b] and in technical papers published by the ANSI X3J4 committee [X3J93]. These papers form the basis for the features that will be in the OOCOBOL products delivered after the standard is accepted. Previous standards for COBOL (85, 74, etc.) will be compatible with the OOCOBOL standard. To support data structures and objects in older programs, the new standard will support intrinsic objects that are not encapsulated and do not support polymorphism. These intrinsic objects also can be read from and written to files, while standard objects cannot.

Under the proposed OOCOBOL standard, file access can be simplified by using the factory concept to define a class of objects that all share common access methods. With this approach, only the factory methods will be allowed to access the file.

Object-oriented COBOL will support multiple inheritance, garbage collection, and both static and dynamic binding. A new section is included in the ENVIRONMENT DIVISION, the OBJECT SECTION, which defines classes and interfaces for the program. The DATA DIVISION also has been modified to support object definitions, and the LINKAGE SECTION is used to reference data passed between objects (i.e., messages).

The PROCEDURE DIVISION can include calls to objects, creation of objects, invoking of objects, and exception handling for objects. Perhaps the most distinctive change to COBOL is the separation of objects and their methods into classes defined in physically different source files from the references to these classes in the actual program.

2.7 Applications that can Benefit from Object Technology

While many organizations are investigating object technology, there are specific types of applications that can benefit from object-oriented development and others that probably will not. Part of the process of looking at object technology should be determining if the probable benefits will exceed the expected costs. Any organization that doesn't undertake a cost/benefit analysis of object technology, or any other technology for that matter, will likely end up frustrating their staff and wasting precious resources in the process.

First and foremost, each organization should consider performing a software engineering audit or software assessment prior to evaluating object technology. Those organizations that fail to assess and evaluate their existing software engineering environments will greatly increase the likelihood of failure adopting any new technology. I will cover the issue of technology adoption in more detail in chapter 13; however, those organizations that want to assess their software development environment, the works of Roger Pressman [PRE88] and the Watts Humphrey [HUM89] can used as guidelines for this process. Beyond these basic considerations, organizations should evaluate where the potential for object technology is greatest, decide whether the technology is mature enough for their needs, and develop a plan for a transition to object-oriented development.

Prior to discussing those applications that might benefit from object technology, I will discuss the potential benefits of the technology.

- Reusability of code, designs, and models
- Increased software quality
- Increased software productivity
- Increased predictability
- Complexity controlled through classification
- Decreased maintenance

2.7.1 Potential Benefits of Object Technology

The benefit that is most often cited from object technology is increased *reusability* of code, specifications, and models, because of built-in support for inheritance, information hiding, encapsulation, and reuse through classification. Because objects can inherit properties and characteristics from parent classes, there is direct support for reuse of abstractions and mechanisms in object-oriented development. Encapsulation and information hiding also allow objects to be used without knowledge of the internal aspects or implementation details, thus facilitating reuse.

Increased *software quality* can result when tested code is used, because it has already has been unit tested and works off the shelf. This in turn can lead to an increased ability to deliver working systems in a shorter period of time. An additional benefit of object technology is the ease of enhancement/modification that objects and message provide. Encapsulation and information hiding allow objects to be modified or changed without adversely affecting any objects that interact with them. This means that systems built of autonomous objects with messages as the only form of interaction are more easily changed.

Increased *productivity* often results from reuse because new systems can be built quicker from existing objects and classes. The formula for estimating the cost of a new system using object technology is: cost of developing new + cost of using available components. While reusing existing software components does not represent a zero-dollar cost, it does tend to result in a lower overall cost of software development and delivery.

Increased *predictability* often results in systems built with object technology because of standard parts reused and standard interfaces between parts. Components that are reused have been tested and the only testing remaining is integration testing. This in turn leads to less new development and less failures in the total number of components.

Complexity is controlled in object-oriented development through classification, better requirements modeling (i.e., models map directly to the real world objects that users already are familiar with), and combining function with data. Traditional functional modeling tools (DFDs and ERDs) break apart the data and the functions and this often causes confusion and misunderstanding on the part of users, because they naturally view systems with these portions combined.

Decreased maintenance results because code is more modular, with isolated features, and the use of messages in communication leads to less impact when components are changed. Also, decreased maintenance results from less complex modules and simpler modular units (i.e., objects).

2.7.2 Selecting Appropriate Object Technology

When considering which (of if any) object technology to select and implement, there are many issues that should be taken into consideration. Applications that can benefit from the use of object technology include GUI systems, client/server systems, systems with high levels of common abstractions or mechanisms, as well as systems that tend to evolve dramatically over time.

While organizations have had success using object technology on a wide variety of applications, some general guidelines can help developers select possible projects for using these techniques. Software that executes in a graphical user interface (GUI) lends itself very nicely to object-oriented programming and thus OOA/D methods. The Apple Macintosh, Windows, OS/2 Presentation Manager, and OSF/Motif environments can provide a wealth of existing classes and objects that can be reused on new applications. Often, identifying and documenting the classification hierarchy is required before these objects can be effectively used.

Object-oriented software also fits very easily into a client/server model and can be considered as a description of the interaction between two objects: a client and a server. A client makes requests of the server to perform services, and the server provides a set of services upon request. In an object-oriented environment, both the client and the server are objects. The Object Management Group (OMG) has defined a standard communication vehicle for clients and servers called the CORBA specification. This standard defines how objects interact remotely and defines procedures for locating, invoking, and communicating between objects.

Some developers of real-time systems have claimed that the performance of object-oriented programming languages (OOPLs) is lacking, but studies suggest that a mixed OOPL and traditional programming language environment can produce adequate embedded systems [BAR91]. Much progress has been made in integrating OOPLs with traditional programming languages. As I already have shown, object-oriented software is ideal for event-driven environments and many embedded class libraries are beginning to become available. One of the examples that I design in this book, the ATM system, is an example of a reactive or real-time system, and many GUI and client/server systems exhibit event-driven behavior common in these types of systems.

Similarly, developers of MIS applications have complained about the lack of support for traditional business software under the object-oriented umbrella. While more development has occurred in C++ and Smalltalk, the OOCOBOL standard will go a long way toward removing this stumbling block. In addition, many vendors now offer object-oriented database management systems (OODBMS) that can be used in conjunction with or in place of traditional relational databases.

From a practical standpoint, most organizations will want to consider moving incrementally toward an object-oriented approach, and for this reason, those techniques that combine structured and object-oriented concepts will hold great appeal. Other considerations or suggestions for applications that might be suitable for the object-oriented techniques include client/server software, which usually is touted as part of cooperative or distributed processing environment, and vertical packaged software.

Those organizations that can identify a significant percentage of common abstractions or mechanisms should consider object-oriented development. Because one of the goals of object technology is to identify and define reusable components, it makes sense for those organizations that have common or similar systems (both functionality and data structures) to investigate object technology for the benefit of reuse across applications.

Likewise, those organizations that find the systems that they develop must be flexible and in some cases evolve dramatically over their lifetime also should look at object technology. Because object technology is based on the concept of information hiding, the modularity and extensibility of object-oriented systems is greater than traditional functional systems. Because objects hide their underlying details or implementations from outside objects, major changes to a system will have less of an impact on the system than older functional systems.

One key question to consider when evaluating object-oriented techniques is whether to adopt them and replace whatever is currently in use or adapt the existing development methods to include aspects of object-orientation. Any organization that has a significant investment in function- or data-oriented techniques should think twice before scrapping their existing approaches and beginning with object-oriented techniques.

Remembering that object technology can support all phases of the software development life cycle (SDLC), consider the following issues:

- For OOA/D support, choose a method/technique that best supports the type of software products developed (see [TOP93a] for more on this).
- For OOA/D support, look closely at automated support for the notation and method in CASE tools.
- For OOA/D support, look for available training and mentoring as described in chapter 13.
- For OOD support, look at the support for specifications targeted to OOCOBOL as some methods will be limited to specific OOPLs (e.g., Ada or Smalltalk).

- For OOCOBOL support, look at the environments supported (VSAM, IMS, etc.), multiple inheritance (from the compiler), class libraries, and development tools.
- For GUI and client/server development, look at class libraries, prototyping capabilities, support for DCE and/or CORBA, and integration with other GUI tools.
- For OODBMS, look for support for existing SQL databases and the emerging OODBMS standards in the industry.
- For object management tools and repositories, look for OODBMS support and links with CASE repositories.

2.7.3 Problems with Object Technology

While object technology represents many potential benefits to organizations, there also are drawbacks or limitations to using the technology. Some of these drawbacks result from a somewhat immature object technology marketplace, while others stem from traditional reluctance to adopt new methods or practices.

Regardless of their origin, these drawbacks should not be overlooked when evaluating object technology:

- *Bleeding-edge technology* — existing object-oriented tools and techniques might not address all of the needs of developers and might have serious limitations.
- *Incomplete OOCOBOL compiler support* across platforms.
- *Lack of measurements* related to objects and question of support for multiple inheritance in all OOCOBOL compilers.
- *Debugging* OOCOBOL systems is difficult because control flow shifts from object to object (i.e., the flow of control is harder to follow because of message propagation).
- Object-oriented designs can result in *more structurally complex modules* than traditional structured designs.
- *The ripple effect* — any change or problem that occurs in a parent object will have to be evaluated for all child objects.
- *Skepticism* can arise when the models are introduced and it isn't intuitively obvious that the method will work.
- Existing class libraries must be created expanded to cover more specialized objects *before the promise of reuse can be fully realized*.

2.8 References

[BAI88]   Bailin, S., *Remarks on Object-Oriented Requirements Specification,* Computer Technology Associates, 1988.

[BAL91]   Balfour, B., *The Evolution of an Object Oriented Development Method,* EVB Software Engineering, 1991.

[BAR91]   Barry, B. M., "Real-Time Object-Oriented Programming Systems," *American Programmer,* vol. 4, no. 10, 1991.

[BEC89]   Beck, K. and W. Cunningham, "A Laboratory for Teaching Object-Oriented Thinking," Proceedings of the OOPSL'89 Conference, *SIGPLAN Notices,* vol. 24, no. 10, October 1989, pp. 1-6.

[BOO82]   Booch, G., "Object-Oriented Design," *Ada Letters,* vol. 1, no. 3, March/April 1982.

[BOO86a] Booch, G., *Software Engineering with Ada,* Benjamin/Cummings, 1986.

[BOO86b] Booch, G., "Object-Oriented Development," *IEEE Trans. Soft. Eng.,* vol. SE-12, no. 2, February 1986, pp. 211-221.

[BOO87]   Booch, G., *Software Components with Ada: Structures, Tools, and Subsystems,* Benjamin/Cummings, 1987.

[BOO91]   Booch, G., *Object-Oriented Design with Applications,* Benjamin/Cummings, 1991.

[BOO93]   Booch, G., *Object-Oriented Design with Applications,* second edition, Benjamin/Cummings, 1993.

[BUH86]   Buhr, R. J. A., *Systems Design with Ada,* Prentice-Hall, 1986.

[COA91]   Coad, P. and E. Yourdon, *Object-Oriented Analysis,* Prentice-Hall, 1991.

[COL94]   Coleman, D., P. Arnold, S. Bodoff, C. Dollin, H. Gilchrist, F. Hayes, and P. Jeremaes, *Object-Oriented Development: The Fusion Method,* Prentice-Hall, 1994.

[HUM89]   Humphrey, W., *Managing the Software Process,* Addison-Wesley, 1989.

[JAC92]   Jacobson, I., M. Christerson, P. Jonsson, and G. Overgaard, *Object-Oriented Software Engineering,* Addison-Wesley, 1992.

[MAR92]   Martin, J. and J. Odell, *Object-Oriented Analysis and Design,* Prentice-Hall, 1992.

[MEY92]   Meyer, B., "Applying Design by Contract," *IEEE Computer,* October 1992, pp. 40-52.

[MYH68]   Myhrhaug, B., K. Nygaard, and O-J. Dahl, *Common Base Language,* Norwegian Computing Center, 1968.
[NER92]   Nerson, J., "Applying Object-Oriented Analysis and Design," *CACM,* vol. 35, no. 9, pp. 63-74.
[NYG81]   Nygaard, K. and O-J. Dahl, "The Development of the SIMULA Languages," *History of Programming Languages,* Academic press, 1981.
[PRE88]   Pressman, R. S., *Making Software Engineering Happen: A Guide for Instituting the Technology,* Prentice-Hall, 1988.
[RUB92]   Rubin, K. S. and A. Goldberg, "Object Behavior Analysis," *CACM,* vol. 35, no. 9, pp. 48-62.
[RUM91]   Rumbaugh, J., M. Blaha, M. Premerlani, W. Eddy, and W. Lorensen, *Object-Oriented Modeling and Design,* Prentice-Hall, 1991.
[SHL88]   Shlaer, S. and S. Mellor, *Object-Oriented Analysis: Modeling the World in Data,* Prentice-Hall, 1988.
[TOP93a] Topper, A., D. Ouellette, and P. Jorgensen, *Structured Methods: Merging Models, Techniques, and CASE,* McGraw-Hill, 1993.
[TOP93b] Topper, A., "Object Technology and COBOL," *Object Magazine,* March/April 1993, pp. 54-58.
[WIR89]   Wirfs-Brock, R. and B. Wilkerson, "Object-Oriented Design: A Responsibility-Driven Approach," OOPSLA'89 Conference Proceedings, *SIGPLAN Notices*, October 1989, pp. 71-76.
[WIR90]   Wirfs-Brock, R., Wilkerson, B., and L. Wiener, *Designing Object-Oriented Software,* Prentice-Hall, 1990.
[X3J93]   X3J4.1 Technical Report, March 10, 1993.

Chapter 3

Object-Oriented Concepts and Terminology

How does the concept of an object and classification relate to analysis, design, and programming? What deliverables are required from object-oriented analysis and design to successfully implement a solution using an object-oriented programming language? How are object-oriented techniques different from traditional structured techniques? How do the concepts of object persistence and classification fit into a database management system (DBMS)?

The philosophies and principles of object-oriented development are based on the work of many individuals over the past 30 years. Many of these people have written about using objects in programming, design, analysis, and other areas (i.e., DBMS). One problem in learning about object technology is the diverse set of terminology and concepts that apply to the different technologies.

Prior to discussing specifics about object-oriented development, I will define the concepts and principles of sound software engineering. This is followed by a thorough discussion of object concepts and terminology. Finally, I will introduce and evaluate the example problems in light of an object-oriented perspective.

3.1 Introduction

Object-Oriented Analysis (OOA) is a process of analyzing or modeling the requirements for a system using objects, attributes, and relationships. Traditional OOA techniques identify system components (objects), their relationships, and behaviors in an object model.

Object-Oriented Design (OOD) is a process of translating or specifying a physical software structure that is composed of reusable components (objects) that communicate via messages built from the object model defined in Analysis. OOD delivers an object specification to programming and must consider existing objects for reuse in the completed software product.

Object-Oriented Programming (OOP) is a process of creating programs using collections of self-sufficient objects with encapsulated data and behavior that interact with each other via messages. A critical aspect of OOP is inheritance, which allows objects to share constructs with other objects. Class libraries make object-oriented programming a building-block process.

<u>*Object-Oriented Programming Languages*</u> (OOPLs) support the concept of classes, objects, methods, inheritance, encapsulation, and message passing. Optional features that OOPLs might support include multiple inheritance, dynamic binding, and polymorphism. While true OOPLs exist, some traditional languages have been extended to support some concepts of object-orientation.

In the programming phase, objects act differently from procedural modules in that they are event- or message-driven and autonomous. A collection of objects is assembled together to carry out the required functionality for a system with an application or operating system object often serving as the starting point. Unlike procedural systems, however, there is no inherent hierarchy of control in an object-based application. Also, systems built with objects pass control back and forth based only on messages sent, not any defined control flow or sequence.

Procedural programs, on the other hand, are composed of subroutines or functions that can receive control only from higher up in the hierarchy, often, from a main routine. Objects, from a conceptual perspective, work in parallel and receive control from other objects, perform the operations requested, then pass control (via another message) to other objects.

Building object-based applications becomes a process of assembling the required objects and establishing message passing to elicit the required operations. Objects also can execute and behave differently based on the context in which they receive messages. For instance, the ATM example in this chapter describes a keyboard object that collects keystrokes and passes the appropriate information back to the ATM controller. This keyboard object can collect the ID number for a bank customer, a transaction type, or an amount, and send an appropriate message back depending on the context in which it is called. The ATM controller, in this case, simply sends the appropriate message to the keyboard controller to elicit the appropriate response.

Object-oriented applications exhibit behavior common in declarative languages rather than in procedural languages. Under object-oriented development, you declare the classes and objects, their attributes and methods, how they interact and their interfaces. However, existing OOPLs are more procedural than declarative because their implementation of objects and methods is similar to traditional subroutines (e.g.., C++). This is definitely the case with object-oriented COBOL, which is a modified version of COBOL that supports objects, messages, and inheritance.

Common concepts of procedural programming include top-down, sequential processing, separate data structure and procedure sections, passed parameters, and applications under program control. Few of these concepts, however, exist in object-oriented programming.

OOPLs include support for abstract data types (ADTs), which are extensions to the existing simple data types in most programming languages. In COBOL, the simple data types are defined in the PICTURE clause and include numeric (PICTURE 9) or alphanumeric (PICTURE X). The numeric data types can be further specified as zoned decimal (USAGE IS DISPLAY), binary (USAGE IS BINARY or COMP-1), floating point (USAGE IS COMP-2), packed decimal (USAGE IS COMP-3), or table index (USAGE IS INDEX). Depending on the USAGE clause, different operations can be applied against these data types. These operations are supported by the COBOL compiler, and there are distinct differences in how the numeric data types actually are implemented on the different hardware environments.

There are similarities between traditional COBOL and object-oriented COBOL. For example, the VALUE clause and the 88 levels in a data definition represent definitions of specific domains of data elements or fields and restrict the values that are used in the data element. Likewise, subroutines are similar to methods in objects and in OOCOBOL individual procedure divisions are associated with each object.

3.2 Principles of Software Engineering

Over the years, several important contributions have been made to the field of software engineering to improve the products and process. Many of these ideas have been practiced informally by most in the software development community and are based on sound, engineering principles. I present these principles here to help you better understand the benefits of object-oriented development and the reasons behind the development and evolution of object technology. These principles are:

- Use a formal method
- Divide and conquer

- Abstraction and generalization
- Hierarchical ordering and partitioning
- Hiding complexity
- Modularity
- Incremental, iterative development

3.2.1 Use a Formal Method

Most of the software development that has occurred over the past 50 years has been <u>adhoc</u> or chaotic. Very few software applications have been developed using a formal process or method, and the result is poor software quality, overdue software delivery, and expensive maintenance.

Many studies have shown that using a formal development method improves the overall quality and productivity of software engineers, and makes the development process easier to estimate, plan, manage, and coordinate. Using a formal development method with defined artifacts or deliverables also leads to work products (models, specifications, requirements, prototypes, etc.) that can be used in maintenance to lower the cost of evolving systems.

What I mean by "formal?" Simply, a formal development process or method is one that satisfies four criteria:

- It is written down, defined, or documented
- It is taught to new development staff
- It is used extensively by all or most development staff
- It can be measured.

If a method of development meets these four criteria, it can be considered "formal." The reasons for formalizing a development process are based on the criteria themselves.

If a development process is documented, it can be learned easily by others. If it is documented, it also can provide a shared view of the development environment — something often lacking in most software development organizations. This shared view of software engineering facilitates consistency of the products created and the process used. Once a development process is defined, it can be managed and information can be collected to help estimate and plan future projects. Without a formal process that is widely used by most developers, a plan for future development is only an educated guess.

Also, if a process is defined, it can be evaluated for possible improvement, both in the deliverables or artifacts created and the process itself. Watts Humphrey and others at the Software Engineering Institute have defined a five phase process maturity model that is based on defining and improving the software engineering process using quality improvement techniques.

At a basic level, any defined software development method consists of three components, which together satisfy the criteria specified for formal development: *techniques, representations, and notations.*

Techniques represent the "how" of formal software development. They consist of the practices, philosophies, and sound engineering methods that have evolved over the past 50 years. Many of these techniques are described in the following sections and stem from the experience of creative individuals developing complex software. Techniques or methods have a focus or orientation and provide guidelines for developers in analyzing, designing, programming, testing, and managing software engineering.

Because techniques have a defined set of tasks, roles, responsibilities, and deliverables, they satisfy the first and second criteria of formal methods. They help to document or define a development process, and they can be taught to new developers.

Techniques often call for the creation of *representations,* or deliverables, as part of the development process. These representations can take a variety of forms but are created to help communicate, understand, and verify the outcome of the development process. Example representations include data or process models, executable specifications, requirements documents, or design specifications. As the development process includes more people, takes more time, and reflects increased complexity, it must be understood by everyone involved or there will be errors or oversights that will be expensive to fix in maintenance.

Representations reflect the underlying structure or behavior of software systems, but *notations* or diagrams are the physical implementations of these representations. While a data model might be a representation of the data structures in a system, an entity-relationship diagram is a specific notation that has defined symbols and connections that reflect the nature of the model. There can be a variety of notations for representations (for example, a process decomposition diagram or a structure chart), which might reflect the hierarchical structure of a system. Example notations include data flow diagrams, action diagrams, flowcharts, or structure charts.

Representations and notations help satisfy the third and fourth criteria of a formal development process. The diagrams or notations help developers understand what other team members have created and ensure that there is consistency between the members. Because the representations are delivered as part of the development process, they also can be measured and tracked.

3.2.2 Divide and Conquer

Perhaps the oldest and most effective principle of software engineering is to solve difficult, complex problems by dividing or decomposing them into a set of smaller, independent but related problems. The resulting smaller problems then are much easier to understand, solve, and manage. Once these smaller problems have been addressed and solved, the resulting larger problem can be solved by integrating the smaller portions. Decomposing a problem into subproblems allows complexity to be controlled and composition allows subproblems to be integrated into a whole.

Decompose: to separate into constituent parts or elements, or into simpler compounds.
Compose: to form by putting together; to form the substance of.
[Webster]

...intelligent decomposition directly addressed the inherent complexity of software by forcing a division of a system's state space.
D. Parnas [PAR85].

Software or systems analysis often proceeds by dividing or decomposing a problem into smaller problems, thus reducing the overall complexity of a system. One important question when using decomposition is what are the criteria to be used to decompose a problem? There are several guidelines or methods for decomposing systems:

Functional decomposition begins by defining the functionality of a system (i.e., what the system does), then for each major statement of function, decomposing them down into lower levels of functionality.

Data decomposition divides a system based on its underlying data structures. Data that is used together is grouped together, and data that is isolated is separated.

Object decomposition works by identifying and decomposing major objects or abstractions in the problem domain, where objects represent tangible entities that exhibit well-defined behavior.

Decomposition has dominated software development thinking and practice for several years but has its own limitations. Performing a good decomposition, for example, requires that people doing the decomposition have a very complete knowledge of the problem being decomposed. Anything less than complete understanding probably will result in an imperfect decomposition. In addition, decomposition can be arbitrary, especially functional, because in many cases system functions can not be discretely partitioned without adversely affecting the overall functionality of the system.

Perhaps the biggest drawback to using decomposition is the problem of putting the system components back together when they are finished. Once divided, the pieces must be put back together to form a coherent whole. Composition uses combination to build a larger system from existing components. When this occurs, the interfaces between the components in the decomposition often are the weak link. If the interfaces are not clearly defined, followed, and tested upon component completion, integrating the pieces at the end of the process can be disastrous.

Analysis: separation of a whole into its component parts; an
examination of a complex, its elements, and their relations.
Synthesis: the composition or combination of parts or elements
so as to form a whole; deductive reasoning.
[Webster]

Analysis and synthesis are closely related to decomposition and composition, respectively, which were just discussed. Analysis most often is seen as breaking down a problem into lower-level problems and further breaking down these until "manageable" problems are reached (i.e., decomposition).

Synthesis is exactly the reverse process: when you synthesize, you put pieces together to make a larger whole. All engineering disciplines, especially software engineering, prosper when there is a sequence of alternating cycles of analysis and synthesis.

One view that helps people to understand the differences and similarities of these concepts is to consider analysis as a discovery process that has as its goal a complete understanding of the problem. Synthesis, on the other hand, is a development process that builds something from what already is understood.

If developers have a poor or incomplete understanding of what is required, the chances that they can build something new that will satisfy the requirements are slim.

3.2.3 Abstraction and Generalization

Abstract: disassociate from any specific instance; expressing a quality apart from an object.
Generic: relating to or characteristic of a whole group or class.
Abstraction: to simplify a problem or system by focusing on those aspects of the system which are relevant, and de-emphasizing those aspects which are not.
Generalization: to examine a group of things (objects) looking for similarities and differences upon which to base a new generic or idealized thing (class).
[Webster]

Unable to master the entirety of a complex object, we chose to ignore its inessential details, dealing instead with the generalized, idealized model of the objects.
D. Parnas [PAR83].

Conceptually, each step in the software development process is a refinement in the level of abstraction of the solution domain. Software engineering moves from high-level requirements in analysis to low-level modular units in design to code-level units in implementation.

Several types of abstraction are available, including procedural, data, and object. Procedural abstraction works from a high-level view of system functionality down to lower levels that map to individual procedures or processes. Data abstraction allows developers to represent something in various levels of detail, based on the data structures used.

Another type of data abstraction is an abstract data type (ADT), which specifies the characteristics of a structural or behavioral property that a collection of entities or objects share. For example, a data abstraction for a deck of cards would be defined as a pair of values, which can be of four different types — hearts, diamonds, spades, or clubs — and contain 13 different values — from ace through king. The cards can be organized into classes, by their type as well as by their value.

Abstract data types represent data structures that map to the abstractions in the problem domain. Object abstraction combines data structures with operations that can be applied to those structures. In the example of a deck of cards, you might have operations to Shuffle, Deal n Cards, etc. These operations would be part of the ADT for your deck of cards and would be defined alongside the data structures themselves. Using ADTs, you can extend the power of the programming language to support data types that are user defined. More on this ADT example in chapter 5.

Data abstraction extends the expressiveness of algorithmic formalizations into the realm of components with data structure aspects.
D. Parnas [PAR83].

Generalization allows modules to be defined with generic parameters that represent different types or classes. At compile or run time, different instances of the operations or methods are used for the different types. Generalization allows similar things to be generalized into a high-level abstraction with shared data structures or methods.

3.2.4 Hierarchical Ordering and Partitioning

Hierarchy: a graded or ranked series.
[Webster]

Another principle that helps deal with complexity in software development is to arrange the components of a problem or system into a hierarchy so that they can be better understood. A hierarchy is a ranking or ordering of abstractions. Different types of hierarchies can be used in software development, including functional, data, and classification.

Hierarchical partitioning allows a problem to be represented by function, information (data), or a combination of the two. In this manner, the problem or solution domain can be described or designed at one level, prior to moving down to the next level of detail. This approach typically is used in conjunction with decomposition, but the two concepts can be used separately as well.

Functional hierarchies are partitioned based on the actions taken by each component in the hierarchy. In analysis, functional hierarchies can be used to decompose a system based on what it does. In design, a functional hierarchy can be used to structure a system based on the functions of the system. Data hierarchies are organized on the data structures in the system, and components represent groups of higher-level structures.

Classification represents the organization of objects based on similarities and differences in data structure and operation. Several types of classification relationships are available, including inheritance, "kind of," and "part of." Inheritance classification is the ordering of classes of objects such that lower-level objects or classes inherit similar data structures and operations from higher-level classes.

Also, by organizing objects into groups of related abstractions, you come to explicitly distinguish the common and distinct properties of different objects, which further helps you to master the inherent complexity.

3.2.5 Hiding Complexity

When analyzing, designing, or programming a computer system, you can hide nonessential information from external units so that they know only what they need to accomplish their goal. In this fashion, you can limit the impact of future changes on units that interact. System details that are likely to change independently should be kept hidden from other modules, and only assumptions that are not likely to change should be included in any module's interface.

Information hiding is a principle that seeks to hide data structures and operations from outside units. These units often are called *black boxes*. To use an existing black box, there is no need to understand the details or the internal specifics of how the box works, only what the box does and how to use it.

By using information hiding, it should be possible to change the implementation of a module without knowledge of the implementation of other modules and without affecting the behavior of other modules. It also should be possible to make a major change to a system as a set of independent changes to individual modules. Changes to implementations should not directly affect changes to the interfaces of the modules.

3.2.6 Modularity

The principle of modularity allows a program to be designed and built from autonomous and independent units. *Modularity* allows complex programs or systems to be managed more intellectually by human beings. Modularity also leads to an ease of understanding by anyone that did not create the original component. Each module should be simple enough so that it can be understood fully, and any software engineer should be able to understand the responsibility of a module without understanding it's internal design.

Ideally, a module should represent a single function or object and should provide the services required of that function or object completely. At a basic level, a module also is a computational unit. The concept of modularity stems from the use of black boxes in engineering to build complex systems. A black box has specific inputs, outputs, and functions and supports the concept of information hiding discussed earlier. As described, each black box (or module) should solve one well-defined piece of a problem and should be as independent as possible.

A corollary to modularity is that, with an increasing number of modular units, the interfaces or interactions between the units grows as well. That is to say that more modular units also mean more definition of interaction, and potentially more complexity of interaction, between units.

To follow up on the concept of modularity, modular units should be functionally independent such that each unit addresses a specific function or requirement and has as simple an interface as is possible when viewed by external units. Independent units also lead to easier maintenance because the effects of modification are limited, the propagation of errors is reduced, and the reusability of the units is increased.

To be used, modular descriptions must be created using the concept of information hiding (described previously) and described with:

- The roles played by each individual module
- The hidden details of the module
- The services provided by the module

Two measures of the quality of a modular unit are cohesion and coupling. *Cohesion* is a measure of the strength of functional association or dependence of processing activities, usually within a single module or subsystem. *Coupling* is the degree of dependence of one module on another, specifically a measure of the chance that a defect in one module will appear as a defect in the other or the chance that a change to one module will necessitate a change to the other.

3.2.7 Use an Incremental, Iterative Development Process

Experience suggests that designing complex systems requires an iterative, incremental process. Numerous organizations have attempted to subject their staff to a sequential, waterfall-like process with sometimes disastrous results.

Several studies of software developer behavior suggest that people work at different levels of abstraction and on different aspects of a project at any point in time. Attempting to force an arbitrary set of steps that begin and end, and a set of deliverables to be created and not allowed to evolve, leads to errors and added complexity in the development process.

Several popular design methods have evolved over the past 30 years to address the complexity of systems. These include structured design, data-oriented design, and object-oriented design.

Function-oriented design refers to a technique that uses functional partitioning and hierarchical organization in a top-down fashion, with special emphasis on reduced coupling and strong cohesion. Structured design seeks to design a system based on black boxes that are placed together in a hierarchy of control with minimized interfaces between the modules.

Data-oriented design uses the structure of inputs and outputs to define the architecture of a system. These methods require study of the organization of data structures prior to defining the functionality of a system.

Object-oriented design is a method of translating or specifying a physical software structure that is composed of reusable components (objects) that interact via messages. Object-oriented design delivers an object specification to programming and must consider existing objects for reuse in the completed software product.

Along with these methods, several design heuristics have emerged. In design, you use refinement or elaboration to define more and more detail for each component, and you quit refining when what remains are details that can be expressed in terms of actual program code or statements. In design, you always strive to develop data structures that will be simple and stable over the life of the system.

3.3 Terminology

Prior to describing a process for developing software using objects, messages, inheritance, etc., you must define your terms and concepts. While some of these terms have general acceptance in the industry, others are subjective depending on whether you are describing a OOPL, an OODBMS, or an OOA/D method. The sidebar beginning on page 76 contains a description of general terms as defined by the Object Management Group.

According to Grady Booch [BOO89], an object is an entity that:

- Has state
- Is characterized by the actions that it suffers and that it requires of other objects
- Is a unique instance of some (possibly anonymous) class
- Is denoted by a name
- Has restricted visibility of and by other objects
- Can be viewed either by its specification or by its implementation

A *class* is a group or category of things (objects) that all share the same functions and data. Classes also are called *abstract data types*. Classes describe a set of objects via their external properties and not their representation. Classes are abstract, generic, and not physical things.

Classification is the process of organizing objects as conceptual "things" that share similar characteristics and behaviors. Through classification, objects that are similar can be grouped into related groups. Generalization is the process of idealizing specific objects based on common characteristics and behaviors.

Inheritance is a property that allows child objects to reuse data and functions from parent objects. As a son or daughter might inherit their eye or hair color from their mother or father, objects inherit characteristics and operations from their parent class. *Multiple inheritance* allows an object to inherit from more than one parent, while *single inheritance* restricts inheritance to a single parent.

Objects are instances of classes that represent abstractions in the problem or solution domain. An object incorporates a data structure and the operations on the data structure in a physical entity. Objects restrict or protect access to their data structures and do not allow changes to the content of their data by external agents (i.e., other programs or objects). Objects also hide complexity and the details of their data structures and operations from external agents.

Object *methods* are simply procedures or operations that reside in an object and determine how the object will act when it receives messages. Methods are similar to program subroutines but are implemented differently from subroutines or functions in a traditional procedural programming language.

Encapsulation is a philosophy of combining data structures and operations into an object. Objects hide their data structures (information hiding) and methods from outside programs or objects. Because of this hiding, outside programs do not need knowledge of the data structures or implementation of operations to use the services of the object. This leads to minimizing the impact of changes to associated objects. Data structures inside an object can not be modified by outside objects or programs.

In an object-oriented approach, objects communicate via *messages*. These messages are the only acceptable means of objects interacting. An example of a message might be a user object requesting that a specific book be checked out to them in the library system. Messages cause objects to change states or instance values. Message passing allows objects to have autonomy that is not available in other methods or languages and allows objects to be created separately, then integrated together once they are built.

Information hiding refers to operations (methods) that are carried out by objects but are hidden from other objects. Because of information hiding, objects can be modified or enhanced without changing the way that they are used by other objects. Objects can be thought of as black boxes that can send and receive messages without any knowledge of other objects underlying data structures or mechanics.

Polymorphism results when a single message causes different actions when received by different objects. For example, a circle object and a square object might both receive a "draw" message, but each will perform a separate and different function upon receiving this message. In a similar fashion, one object might respond to a message in a different manner depending on the context in which the object is acting at the time. In this way, messages and object behavior can be context dependent.

A *class library* is a collection of generic classes that can be adapted (inherited) and tailored for a new application. Through the use of class libraries, common abstractions and code can be reused across many applications.

Persistence is the permanence of an object or the period of time that space is allocated and available for the object in memory. Persistent objects live even after the program that creates them terminates, while temporary objects cease to exist once the program that creates them terminates.

Binding refers to the mechanism for associating the address of a called procedure with a caller; *static binding* occurs at compile and link time while *dynamic binding* occurs at run time.

Garbage collection is the automatic destruction of unreferenced or unused objects by the operating system or the programming language and the return of their memory to the available pool.

3.4 Concepts and Principles

As you begin to understand objects, classes, methods, and messages, you need a framework of concepts and principles on which to base your understanding. The following sections introduce the concepts involved in object-oriented development and include examples for discussion purposes.

In object-oriented development, the world is composed of objects, including their properties and behavior. Objects are grouped into categories (called *classes*), and all objects can be categorized in this manner. This form of categorization is "classification," which involves organizing objects as conceptual things with similar characteristics or properties and behaviors. An object can be simple or composite (i.e., composed of other individual objects).

Objects can be combined to create more complex objects. As objects change, their state changes. When this change occurs, this is termed an *event*. All objects can act on and are acted upon by other objects. Instance variables or fields are the characteristics of an object that can change. Object-oriented development is based on the following concepts [WAN89]:

Data abstraction — Defining the behavior of an object instead of its representation; the behavior of an object is encapsulated in its methods, which have access to the state of an object and can change that state.
Independence and persistence — Objects will exist even if their creator dies or is terminated; objects are the only entities allowed to change their own state and can not change other objects' states.
Message passing — Objects can communicate with other objects only via messages; a message can cause an object to behave a certain way by invoking its' method.
Homogeneity — Because everything can be represented as an object, messages and instance variables or variables also can be considered as objects.
Classification by inheritance — Objects can be grouped into classes or object types, and all objects in a class will have the same instance variables and methods and respond to the same messages.

3.4.1 What is an Object?

Object: something that is or is capable of being seen, touched or otherwise sensed; something physical or mental of which a subject is cognitively aware; a thing that forms an element of or constitutes the subject matter of an investigation or science; a noun or noun equivalent denoting in a verb constructions that on or toward which the action of a verb is directed.
[Webster]

Objects are entities or things around us that have characteristics (attributes), communicate with other objects (messages), and have predictable behaviors (methods). An instance of an object exists when the object possesses all the attributes of a specific thing. As children, we all knew how to identify things (objects) based on their similarities and differences.

Objects control or protect their data structures and don't allow them to be modified by outside programs or objects. This eliminates any possible corruption by outside objects and eliminates the need for outside programs to know about or understand the data structures inside the objects. Objects can use other objects services without having knowledge of their inner workings.

3.4.2 Object Attributes and Properties

Objects are composed of characteristics, attributes, or instance variables with a specific set of values and properties. Each of these attributes can be considered as a class with the values allowed being the domain of the attribute. Object attributes are different from traditional record fields or data elements in that they can have complex domains. Traditional table columns or data elements have primitive or simple data types (i.e., integer, real number, string, etc.). Object attributes can contain complex structures, including nonlinear data types (video, audio, graphics, etc.), and can decompose to become other objects or classes of objects.

Attributes: variables of an object that change over time and help to define its properties, also called *data* or *states*.

Object properties or behaviors are defined as the set of methods or operations (procedures) that can change the state of the object. Object states map to changes in attribute values, and these states represent the valid life of the object. Object states can be changed only by the methods inside the object, not by external objects. Requests to change object state are passed as messages to objects.

3.4.3 Object Behavior and Operations

Objects can be characterized or classified based on their attributes or their behavior. Both forms of classification are useful in object-oriented analysis, design, and programming. Attributes define what an object *is*, while behaviors define what an object *does*. Behaviors are observable aspects or states of an object over time.

3.4.4 Object Lifetimes and Interactions

All objects are created, perform some function or service, and can be saved or deleted. Objects can be persistent or transient. Persistent objects outlive the program that creates them, while transient objects are stored only in memory and are deleted when an application program ends. Persistent objects must be stored somewhere and managed (see OODBMS).

Objects also interact or collaborate with other objects to perform specific system functions. When objects interact, one object initiates the interaction and the other participates in the interaction. Objects can have different roles or responsibilities within a system, sometimes acting as initiators and sometimes as participants.

3.4.5 Object Messages

Objects can be viewed as black boxes, with their implementations hidden from outside objects. In this sense, the information that they maintain is hidden from outside objects, along with their implementation of methods. This is called *information hiding*. Objects can request services from other objects using messages. Messages act as the interface to all objects and are specified for every object that is created. Messages that are not understood by objects are ignored.

Object messages support the concept of clearly defined interfaces that restrict the operations that are available and limit the impact of future change on objects that interact. With clearly defined interfaces between objects, software products can be designed, built, and tested separately, then combined or integrated at a later date. This helps allow different groups to develop classes and objects without having to worry about the resulting objects working together when they are finished.

Message passing allows objects to have autonomy that is not found in other languages or methods. This autonomy allows objects to be created separately, perhaps by different groups, then brought together at a later time. Assuming messages are defined and do not change, objects can interact loosely with limited impact on each other if their underlying data structures or implementations change.

3.4.6 Object Composition

Complex objects can be built from simpler objects, thus providing another way of hiding complexity and implementation details from other objects that collaborate with them. This facilitates building software in layers and in increments and allows design details to be put off on some objects until more information is gathered on the objects that they must interact with.

3.4.7 Object Types

There is much in the literature to suggest that objects in a software system can take on generic roles and responsibilities or be classified into different groups based on their behavior. Wirfs-Brock, Kerth, Coad/Yourdon, Shlaer/Mellor, and Booch have all offered their views on object types or roles, while Meyer has described the generic classes of objects in the Eiffel Libraries. These views are described here, along with a summary of how these issues relate to the concepts of objects in development.

According to Wirfs-Brock [WIR92], objects can be characterized based on their behavior into the following groups:

- Controlling — objects that perform a cycle of action.
- Coordinating — objects that act as managers of client requests and services.
- Structuring — objects that maintain relationships between objects.
- Informational — objects that hold values for objects.
- Service — objects that perform a single operation or activity on demand.
- Interface — objects that support communication between system objects and external systems or users.

Kerth [KER91] identifies the following roles that objects play:

- System domain — objects that interface the system with the programming environment.

- Application domain — objects that contain knowledge of the problem domain and coordinate objects in the system to accomplish a desired objective.
- Foundation — objects that act as workers, hide information about data structures, external devices, etc. from application and system objects.
- Informational — objects that contain small pieces of information and are passed from object to object as parameters.
- Human-Interface domain — objects responsible for interacting with the user.

According to Coad/Yourdon [COA90], there are four types of management objects:

- Interface/Presentation — objects that manage interaction with the user and the look-and-feel of the application.
- Control/Computation — objects that manage control in the application and decision making.
- Data Management — objects that manage data structures, both internal and external to the application.
- Application — objects found in the problem domain that are not implementation specific.

The Shlaer/Mellor method [FAY93] identifies five basic categories of objects:

- Tangible objects — represent something physical in the problem domain.
- Roles — represent the purpose or assignment of a person, piece of equipment or organization.
- Incidents — represent events.
- Interactions — represent a transaction or contract between objects.
- Specifications — represent rules, standards, or quality criteria.

Shlaer/Mellor [SHL88] also identify four basic domains for a software system:

- Application — the objects that reflect the key abstractions in the problem domain.
- Service — objects that provide generic services (i.e., data access, communication, etc.).
- Architecture — the objects that reflect the design of the system (i.e., client/server, etc.).
- Implementation — the objects that support the implementation (i.e., OOPL, DBMS, etc.).

Booch [BOO91] also describes groups of classes (class categories) and subsystems as collections of logically related components in analysis and design. Booch defines class categories as organizations of logically related classes. Subsystems in a Booch module diagrams resemble class categories in class diagrams, but represent logical related modules and facilitate reuse at the design and implementation level. Subsystems are layered in a "part of" or aggregation hierarchy where higher-level subsystems incorporate the functionality of lower-level subsystems.

Meyer [MEY90] discusses the role of classes or generic objects that cover seven distinct areas:

- Kernel — classes for basic system needs, including handling arrays and strings, I/O, exception handling, access to command line arguments, and arithmetic conversions.
- Support — classes for browsing, persistent object storage and retrieval, debugging and testing of classes, access to internal object structures, string pattern matching, and memory management.
- Data structures — classes implement fundamental data structures, including lists, trees, stacks, queues, hash tables, and others.
- Lexical — classes support lexical analysis.
- Parsing — classes support development of parsers and compilers.
- Winpack — classes support window-based applications that run in a character-based environment (i.e., terminals).
- Graphics — classes that support windows, menus, mouse input, and geometric figures.

The organization of the [Eiffel] libraries is not arbitrary. In particular, the architecture of the Data Structure Library is the direct result of an ongoing theoretical effort to provide a general taxonomy of the fundamental data structures of computer programming.
Meyer [MEY90].

As you identify and define objects in analysis, design, and implementation, you should consider the roles and responsibilities of objects, as well as the types specified previously. You also can look for specific objects that manage other objects in the problem or solution domain, and classes and class structures consisting of the base types offered by Meyer and others.

3.4.8 What is a Class?

A class is a generic type of thing, while an object is an instance or a specific occurrence of a thing. Thus the use of the term 'instantiation,' as in an object is instantiated — an instance of the class is created. Classes can not be instantiated; an instance of a specific class can be created only as an object of that type.

Classes represent abstract concepts and really are only models of the characteristics and properties of a specific object. Classes also are called *types*, from the evolution of abstract data types, and are generalizations of specific objects. Classes are related to objects via the instance-of (or is-a) relationship in a classification hierarchy where the class is the parent and the object is the child.

3.4.9 Class and Object Relationships

Classes and objects can be related or associated in a number of different forms. Two common associations between classes and objects are aggregation and generalization. *Aggregation* refers to the grouping or combining of attributes, objects, or classes to make up a composite class or object. Classes and objects are composed of attributes, so there is an aggregation relationship between each class or object and its attributes. Likewise, classes or objects themselves can be composed of other classes and/or objects using an assembly or whole/part relationship.

Generalization and *specialization* relationships exist between each object and its parent class or classes. The class is the generalization of the object (i.e., its parent) while the object is the specialization of the class (its child). Instance relationships are synonymous with generalization/specialization relationships.

3.5 Example Problems

I will present two example applications to illustrate the OOA/D techniques and OOCOBL programming discussed. Using these examples, I will show how the results of an object-oriented analysis, design, and implementation might look and discuss the issues in such a development process. My goal here is not to provide correct representations of these problems, but rather to articulate the mechanics of the methods and tools that I recommend in actual problem domains.

The library problem represents a typical management information system (MIS) that manages data structures, access to these structures, and provides a level of security and extensive reports. The automated teller machine (ATM) system is a good example of a reactive system that has somewhat simple data structures and limited functionality but must handle a graphical user interface (GUI) and event-driven behavior.

3.5.1 The Library Problem

The library problem is very popular in software engineering literature. It has been a conference problem at several major national and international conferences [WIN88], the Software Engineering Institute uses it in selected curriculum modules, it has been extensively studied in the literature [HUR91], and various CASE vendors use it as a demonstration problem. The Jackson design advocates claim it is the "best example" for their method [CAM86] and a very formal specification is given in [KEM85].

Consider a small university library system with the following required transactions or functions:

1. Add a copy of a book to the library.
2. Remove a copy of a book from the library.
3. Check out a copy of a book from the library.
4. Return a copy of a book to the library.
5. Get the list of books in the library written by a particular author.
6. Get the list of books currently checked out by a particular user.
7. Find out which user most recently checked out a particular copy of a book.

Within the library system, there are two types of users: library staff and ordinary users or borrowers. Transactions 1, 2, 3, 4, 5, and 7 are restricted to library staff only, while ordinary users can use transaction 6 to find out which books they currently have checked out.

Finally, there are three additional constraints on the library system:

A. All copies of books in the library either must be available for checkout or must be checked out (i.e., no reserve books).
B. No copy of a book can be both available for checkout and checked out at the same time.
C. An ordinary user can not have more than a predefined number of books checked out at one time (i.e., there is a set borrow limit).

In a software development project for the library problem, a first step would be to express the given requirements in written form. In the process of reexamining the stated requirements, it is likely that some flaws or unspecified issues in the original narrative description would be discovered. Some examples of outstanding issues for the library problem might include:

D. How does the library system differentiate between staff and ordinary users?
E. What is the "predefined maximum borrowing limit" for a user? How is this information entered?
F. Regarding transaction 5, what does "in the library" mean? The possibilities are: "available for checkout" (i.e., physically in the library) or "either available for checkout or checked out" (owned by the library).
G. Transactions 6 and 7 suggest data structures which, over prolonged system use, will grow very large. How will these structures be managed by the library system?
H. Where do library books come from? Where do they go when they are removed?

Based on these issues, an additional requirement for the library system was specified:

8. Modify the library system to archive the list of books checked out to a specific user and the list of users that have checked out a book when these lists contain 100 entries.

In addition, when designing possible solutions to the library problem, there are a number of details that should be addressed including:

I. How will the library system be implemented? As a mainframe-based, screen-oriented system? As a PC-based system?
J. What type of file or database support is available for implementing the library system? Will a database be used?
K. How will security for the library system be implemented?
L. What external systems should the library interact or interface with?

3.5.2 The Automated Teller Machine Problem

Automated teller machines (ATM) are common occurrences and are good examples of interactive systems. Like the Library problem from the previous section, the ATM has become a common example used to describe or compare object-oriented development methods. Several excellent descriptions of object-oriented solutions to the ATM problem are described in [RUM91], [WIR92], and [LUB92].

One essential characteristic of interactive systems is that they are event driven, and these events can occur in any order. An ATM system has a very strong control component, exhibiting context-dependent behavior, and only minimal process and data components. As such, it is a nice complement to the more traditional Library problem. The ATM system description follows:

An ATM system processes transactions against valid accounts in a bank. Accounts are assigned by the bank and numbers are given to customers as they open accounts. An eight-digit personal account number (PAN) is assigned to every bank customer. Individual bank accounts (checking, saving, etc.) are created with a two-digit suffix added to the PAN. If customers attempt to access an account that does not exist, they receive an error message.

ATM transactions supported include balance inquiry, which simply prints the current account balance, withdrawals, which allow debits to account balances, deposits, which allow deposits to be entered but not immediately processed, and funds transfers, which allow funds to be moved among existing customer accounts. Deposits are not processed directly by the ATM system but are batched together and processed by bank tellers on the next business day. Current account balances do not reflect deposits made at the ATM except on the following business day.

The ATM communicates with bank customers via the 16 screens shown in Figures 3.1 and 3.2. Using a terminal with features as shown in Figure 3.3, ATM customers can select any of four transaction types: deposits, withdrawals, balance inquiries, and funds transfers, and these can be done on several types of accounts, including checking, savings, money market, etc.

When a bank customer arrives at an ATM station, screen S1 is displayed. The bank customer accesses the ATM with a plastic card encoded with his or her personal account number (PAN), which is a key to their account file, containing the customer's name, password and account information. If the customer's PAN matches the information in his or her account, the system presents screen S2 to the customer. If the customer's PAN is not found, screen S4 is displayed, and the card is kept.

At screen S2, the customer is prompted to enter his or her personal identification number (PIN). If the PIN is correct (i.e., matches the password in the customer account), the system displays screen S5; otherwise, screen S3 is displayed. The customer has three chances to enter their PIN correctly; after three failures, screen S4 is displayed, and their card is kept.

From screen S5, the customer selects the desired transaction, then the system displays screen S6, where the customer chooses which account the selected transaction will be applied to.

If a balance inquiry is requested, the system prints the current account balance and displays screen S14. If a sensor detects that the transaction receipt tape is gone, the system displays screen S16 and updates a field in the Terminal Control File. When this occurs, the system stays in the out-of-order status until a service technician fixes the problem.

If a deposit is requested, the status of the Deposit Envelope slot is determined from a field in the Terminal Control File. If no problem exists, the system displays screen S7 to get the transaction amount. If there is a problem with the deposit envelope slot, the system displays screen S16. Once the deposit amount has been entered, the system displays screen S13, accepts the deposit envelope, and processes the deposit. The deposit amount is entered as an unposted amount in the local ATM file, and the count of deposits per month is incremented. Both of these (and other information) are processed by the master bank (centralized) system once per business day. The system then displays screen S14 and prints a receipt.

If a withdrawal is requested, the system checks the status (jammed or free) of the withdrawal chute in the Terminal Control File. If jammed, screen S16 is displayed, otherwise, screen S7 is displayed so that the customer can enter his or her withdrawal amount. Once the withdrawal amount is entered, the system checks the Terminal Status File to see if it has enough money to dispense. If it does not, screen S9 is displayed; otherwise the withdrawal is processed. The system checks the customer balance (as described in the Balance request transaction), and if there are insufficient funds, screen S8 is displayed. If the account balance is sufficient, screen S11 is displayed and the money is dispensed. The withdrawal amount is written to the unposted local ATM file, the account balance is updated, and the count of withdrawals per month is incremented. The balance is printed on a transaction receipt, and after the cash has been removed, the system displays screen S14.

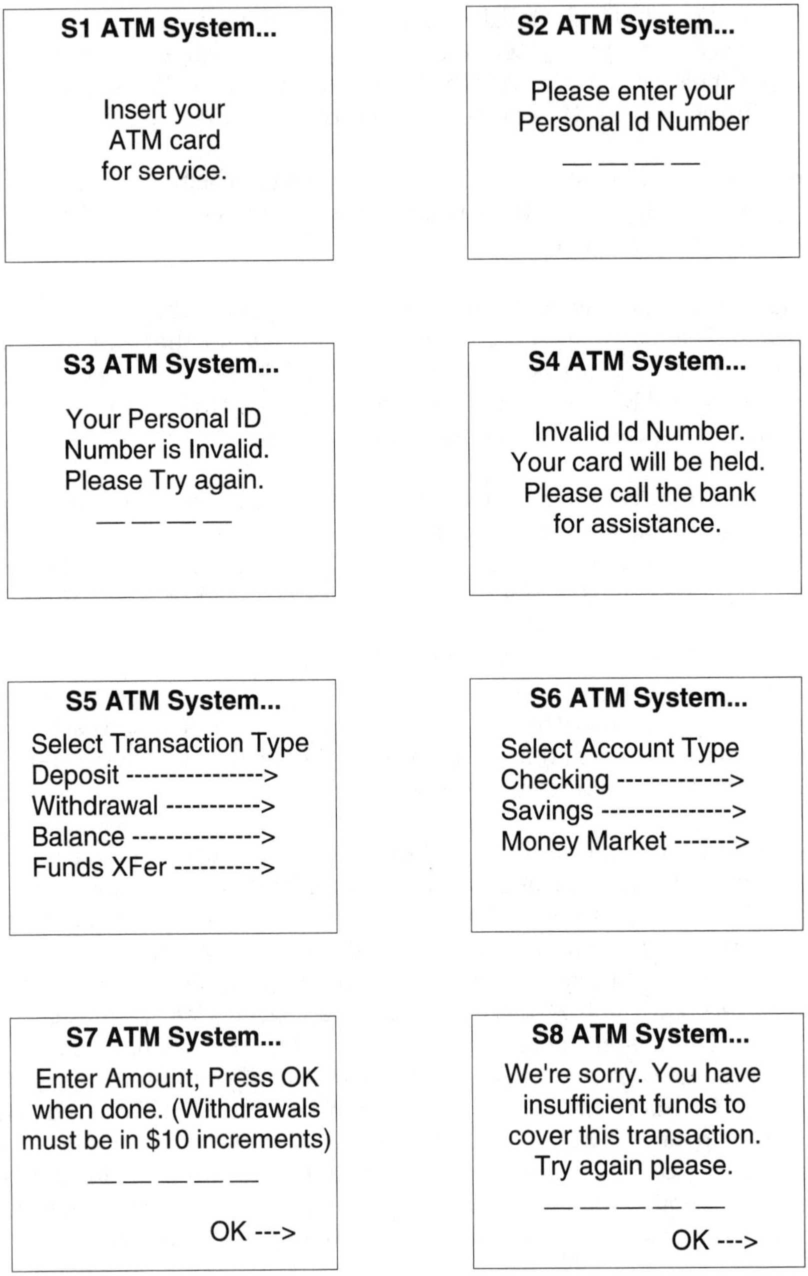

S1 ATM System...

Insert your
ATM card
for service.

S2 ATM System...

Please enter your
Personal Id Number

— — — —

S3 ATM System...

Your Personal ID
Number is Invalid.
Please Try again.

— — — —

S4 ATM System...

Invalid Id Number.
Your card will be held.
Please call the bank
for assistance.

S5 ATM System...

Select Transaction Type
Deposit ---------------->
Withdrawal ----------->
Balance --------------->
Funds XFer ---------->

S6 ATM System...

Select Account Type
Checking ------------->
Savings --------------->
Money Market ------->

S7 ATM System...

Enter Amount, Press OK
when done. (Withdrawals
must be in $10 increments)

— — — — —

OK --->

S8 ATM System...

We're sorry. You have
insufficient funds to
cover this transaction.
Try again please.

— — — — —

OK --->

Figure 3.1
ATM screens.

Chapter 3 Object-Oriented Concepts & Terminology   71

```
┌─────────────────────────────┐   ┌─────────────────────────────┐
│      S9 ATM System...       │   │      S10 ATM System...      │
│                             │   │  Please select account      │
│   We're sorry. We don't     │   │  to transfer funds into.    │
│   have enough cash on       │   │   Checking ------------>    │
│   hand to cover your request│   │   Saving --------------->   │
│   Another transaction?      │   │   Money Market ------>      │
│              Y -->          │   │   Other ---------------->   │
│              N -->          │   │                             │
└─────────────────────────────┘   └─────────────────────────────┘

┌─────────────────────────────┐   ┌─────────────────────────────┐
│      S11 ATM System...      │   │      S12 ATM System...      │
│                             │   │                             │
│   Your balance is being     │   │  Please select account      │
│   updated. Please take      │   │  to transfer funds into.    │
│   Money from Dispenser.     │   │   Money Market -------->    │
│                             │   │   Loan ------------------>  │
│                             │   │   Mortgage ------------->   │
└─────────────────────────────┘   └─────────────────────────────┘

┌─────────────────────────────┐   ┌─────────────────────────────┐
│      S13 ATM System...      │   │      S14 ATM System...      │
│                             │   │   Your Account Balance      │
│   Please put Envelope       │   │   is printed on your        │
│   into Deposit slot.        │   │         Receipt.            │
│                             │   │   Another Transction?       │
│                             │   │              Y --->         │
│              OK --->        │   │              N --->         │
└─────────────────────────────┘   └─────────────────────────────┘

┌─────────────────────────────┐   ┌─────────────────────────────┐
│      S15 ATM System...      │   │      S16 ATM System...      │
│                             │   │                             │
│   Thank you for using       │   │   We're sorry. This         │
│   the ATM system. Please    │   │   ATM is temporily          │
│   take your card and        │   │   out of service.           │
│        receipt.             │   │                             │
│                             │   │   Please try again later.   │
└─────────────────────────────┘   └─────────────────────────────┘
```

Figure 3.2
ATM screens - continued.

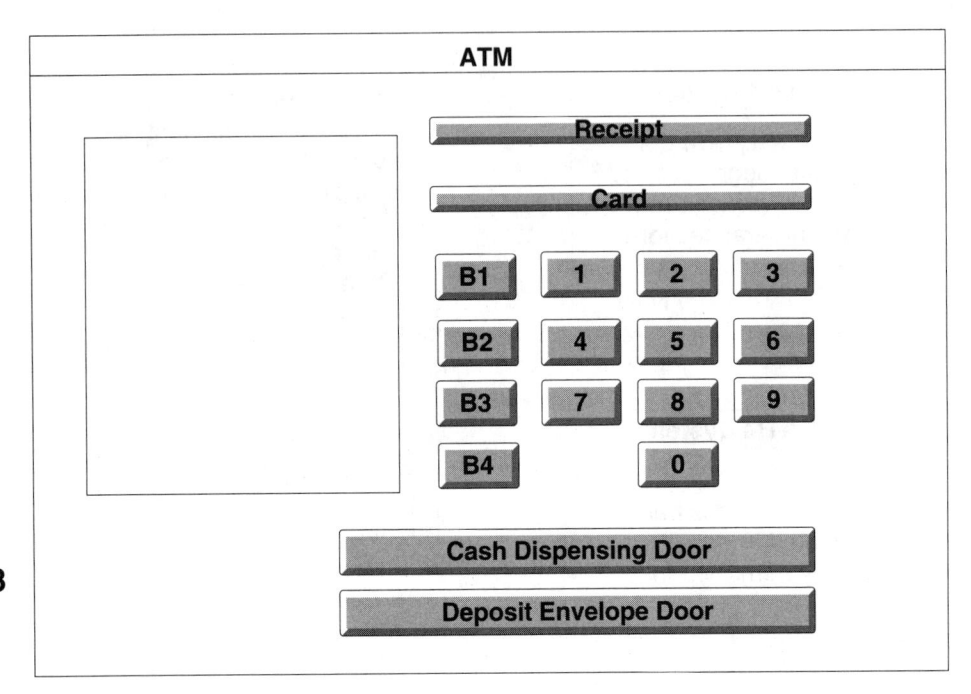

Figure 3.3
ATM user interface.

If a funds transfer is requested, screen S7 is displayed and the amount to be transferred is entered. As with the withdrawal transaction, if the amount requested is greater than the amount available in the account, screen S8 is displayed and appropriate action is taken. After the balance is verified, screen S10 is displayed and the account to which the funds will be transferred is entered by the bank customer. If selected, other account options are displayed on screen S12, which allow funds to be transferred into special accounts, including mortgages, loans, and lines of credit. The account from which the funds are transferred is debited, the account into which the funds are transferred is credited, and a withdrawal and deposit transaction are posted to the local ATM file. Screen S14 is displayed, and a receipt is printed.

When an "N" is entered in screen S14, the system presents screen S15 and returns the customer's ATM card. Once the card is removed from the card slot, screen S1 is displayed. When a "Y" is entered in screen S14, the system presents screen S5 so that the customer can select additional transactions.

There is a surprising amount of information "buried" in this system description. For instance, if you read it closely, you can infer that the terminal only contains $10, $20, $50, or $100 bills (see screen S7). This textual definition probably is more precise than what usually is encountered in practice. I have deliberately tried to keep this example simple to eliminate verbose discussion of the system.

As with the Library problem, the problem statement raises a plethora of questions. For example, is there a fixed withdrawal limit? What keeps a customer from taking out more than his actual balance if he goes to several ATM terminals? There are lots of "start up" questions: how much cash is initially in the machine? How are new customers added to the system? These, and other "real world" refinements, are eliminated to maintain simplicity.

As with most software projects, the ATM problem statement does not provide all the information that you might want in designing and implementing a solution for the bank. Some example issues that are unresolved pertaining to the ATM system include:

A. What bank functions are available to the ATM system? How does the ATM system interact with the external bank files and functions?
B. What time constraints are in place for the ATM system? For instance, if a person is in the middle of a transaction, then does not respond to a prompt from the ATM within 3 minutes, how should the system respond? Should it keep the card? Allow more transactions?
C. How are the ATM status's set to determine if the various hardware components are working? For instance, how is the withdrawal chute status set to Jammed? How is it reset?
D. How does the ATM system respond to requests to transfer funds into the same account from which they are drawn (i.e., transfer from savings into savings)?
E. Future ATM transactions might include Debit card withdrawals, autopayment of selected bills (i.e., phone, gas, electric, water, taxes, etc.), remote access (via a network of ATMs), and even automatic funds transfer for periodic payments (estimated taxes, etc.). How can the ATM system be designed to limit the potential changes of these types of functions in the future?

One method that I used in the development of the ATM system was to prototype the user interface portion under a graphical user interface (GUI). The resulting interface is shown in Figure 3.3. Using this approach, I was able to develop a working version of the interface that simulated the ATM hardware environment, define interfaces to the ATM systems, then modifiy the system to support the actual physical environment when the system was delivered.

3.6 References

[BOO89] Booch, G., "What is and what isn't Object-Oriented Design," *American Programmer*, vol. 2, nos. 7-8, Summer 1989.

[BOO91] Booch, G., *Object-Oriented Design with Applications*, Benjamin/Cummings, 1991.

[CAM86] Cameron, J. R., "An Overview of JSD," *IEEE Trans. on Soft. Eng.*, vol. SE-12, no. 2, Feb. 1986, IEEE Computer Society Press, pp. 222 - 240.

[COA90] Coad, P. and E. Yourdon, *Object-Oriented Analysis*, Prentice Hall, 1990.

[FAY93] Fayad, M.E., L. J. Hawn, M. A. Roberts, and J. R. Klatt, "Using the Shlaer-Mellor OOA Method," *IEEE Software*, March 1993, pp. 43-55.

[HUR91] Hurwitcz, M., "Health Food for Programmers," *LAN Magazine*, May 1991, pp. 138-152.

[KER91] Kerth, N. L., "A Structured Approach to Object-Oriented Design," OOPSLA '91.

[KEM85] Kemmerer, R. A., "Testing Formal Specifications to Detect Design Errors," *IEEE Trans. on Soft. Eng.*, vol. SE-1, no. 1, January 1985, pp. 32 - 42.

[LUB92] Lubars, M., G. Meredith, C. Potts, and C. Richter, "Object-Oriented Analysis for Evolving Systems," *proceedings of the Intl. Conference on Software Engineering*, May 11-15, 1992.

[MEY90] Meyer, B, "Tools for the New Culture: Lessons Learned from the Design of the Eiffel Libraries," *CACM*, vol. 33, no. 9, pp. 68-88.

[PAR83] Parnas, D., P. C. Clements, and D. M. Weiss, "Enhancing Reusability with Information Hiding," *ITT Proceedings of the Workshop on Reusability in Programming*, 1983.

[PAR85] Parnas, D., "Software aspects of Strategic Defense Systems," *CACM*, vol. 28, no. 12, p. 1328.

[RUM91] Rumbaugh, J., M. Blaha, W. Premerlani, F. Eddy, and W. Lorensen, *Object-Oriented Modeling and Design*, Prentice-Hall, 1991.

[SHL88] Shlaer, S. and S. Mellor, *Object-Oriented Systems Analysis: Modeling the World in Data*, Prentice-Hall, 1988.

[WAN89] Wand, Y, "A Proposal for a Formal Model of Objects," *in Object-Oriented Concepts, Databases, and Applications*, W. Kim and E. Lochovsky, eds, ACM Press, 1989.

[WIN88]   Wing, J. M., "A Study of 12 Specifications of the Library Problem," *IEEE Software*, July 1988. pp 66 - 76.
[WIR92]   Wirfs-Brock, R., "Responsibility-Driven Design," *SCOOP*, vol. V, no. 3, 1992, pp. 8-9.

What is Object-Oriented?

One problem with object technology is the lack of standards for terminology and concepts in the industry. Discussing objects, messages, inheritance, etc. can be confusing when each person has a different understanding of what each of the terms means. To some extent, the terms used will be different depending on the subject matter. For example, the concept of an object is different as it is applied to a specific OOPL vs. an OODBMS.

In this sidebar, I will summarize the work done to date in defining common terminology for object technology. Various papers have been published in technical journals on this topic, and much debate has occured, but a common set of definitions and concepts for object-oriented development still is missing.

One attempt to provide the industry with a standard set of definitions of terminology is provided by Alan Synder of SunSoft who proposed these definitions to the Object Manager Group (OMG). The core concepts of object-orientation as described by Synder [SYN93] include:

- Objects explicitly embody some *abstraction* from the problem domain.
- Objects *provide services* that their clients might request; data that can be modified by a client via a service is called state.
- Clients issue requests and are not concerned with the details of how the operation is performed — by isolating clients from the details of an object's implementation, you can change how the object is implemented without having to modify all clients that use that service (*information hiding*).
- Objects *encapsulate data and services*, and clients cannot directly access or manipulate data associated with an object.
- Requests identify operations as an entity that denotes a service
- Requests can (but don't have to) identify objects and objects can be identified directly and reliably.
- New objects can be created as needed.
- Operations can be generic and a service can have different implementations for different objects (*polymorphism*).
- Objects can be classified in terms of their services or in terms of the interfaces that they support (*classification*).
- Objects can share a common implementation — when they do, they will have identical data formats and share executable code; each object has its own unique copy of data.
- Objects can share partial implementations using classification.

Terminology

Object — an identifiable entity that plays a visible role in providing a service that a client can request; services are defined independently of the form of data or the algorithms used to implement the services.

Operation — an identified service for an object.

Encapsulated object — an object that can be accessed only by issuing requests.

Embedded object — when an existing system (program, module, etc.) is wrapped with appropriate code to implement an interface.

Request — identifies an operation and includes parameters; when a request is issued, a binding process determines the actual code to be executed and the data that the code will access.

Generic operation — has different implementations for different objects (polymorphism).

Interface — describes the ways that an object can be used, including a set of potential requests that identify the object as a parameter (some OOPLs describe an interface by omitting implementation-oriented information, like procedure bodies, and cannot be instantiated).

Interface hierarchy (classification) — when objects that share interfaces are grouped into a hierarchy as a form of classification; interface hierarchies classify objects according to their client-visible behavior or their services.

Typed OOPL — types constrain the possible parameters of a request and characterize the possible result values; object types can be defined by interface or implementation or by both.

Dynamic binding — the selection of code to perform a requested service made at the time that the service is requested.

Static binding — the selection of code to perform a requested service made before the services actually is requested.

Object implementation — an executable description of how to perform the set of services associated with an object.

Single (implementation) inheritance — permits an object to be defined in terms of a single existing object.

Multiple (implementation) inheritance — permits an object to be defined in terms of more than one object implementation.

These definitions emphasize object identification, the concept of a generic operation, distinctions between services (interfaces) and implementations, and between classification and construction.

Other Attempts to Define Object-Orientation

Stefik and Bobrow [STE86] define two fundamental concepts of object-orientation — message sending and specialization — along with classes. Wegner [WEG87] and [WEG89] defines object-oriented programming languages as those supporting objects, classes, class inheritance, and information hiding (encapsulation). Wegner also includes strong typing, concurrency, distribution and persistence in true OOPLs. Thomas [THO89] defines four concepts of object-orientation: encapsulation, message passing, classification, and binding (static and dynamic). Wand [WAN89] defines a formal model of objects that is based on object interactions. Booch [BOO89] defines object-orientation in terms of four major elements: abstraction, encapsulation, modularity, and hierarchy; and three minor elements: typing, concurrency, and persistence.

Until a concensous is reached in the industry, terminolgy for objects and related technology will continue to be a question of context and perspective. As you consider a migration to object technology you first must wrestle with the issue of what you mean and what is represented when you say "object-oriented development."

References

[BOO89] Booch, G., "What Is and What Isn't Object-Oriented Design," *American Programmer*, Vol.2, Nos.7-8, Summer 1989.

[STE86] Stefik, M. and D. Bobrow, "Object-Oriented Programming: Themes and Variations," *AI Magazine*, Winter 1986, pp. 40-62.

[SYN93] Synder, A., "The Essence of Objects: Concepts and Terms," *IEEE Software*, January 1993, pp. 31-42.

[THO89] Thomas, D., "What's in an Object?," *Byte*, Mar. 1989, pp. 231-240.

[WAN89] Wand, Y., "A Proposal for a Formal Model of Objects," in *Object-Oriented Concepts, Databases, and Applications*, W. Kim and E. Lochovsky, eds, ACM Press, New York, 1989, pp. 537-559.

[WEG89] Wegner, P., "Learning the Language," *Byte*, Mar. 1989, pp. 245-253.

[WEG87]   Wegner, P., "Dimensions of Object-Based Language Design," *SIGPlan Notices*, vol. 22, no. 12, December 1987, pp. 168-182.

Chapter 4

An Object-Oriented Life Cycle

I will begin this chapter with a discussion of various models of software development life cycles (SDCLs) so that organizations can begin to think about software development as a formal process. By definition, any organization that develops software anywhere follows some development process, whether it is defined or not, and that process can be broken down into stages or tasks, so software life cycles are inevitable.

The original SDLC, the waterfall model, was comprised of discrete steps that proceeded in sequence, one following the other. Under this view, deliverables from one phase dropped down into the next phase, thus the term, *waterfall life cycle*. Alternatives to the waterfall SDLC include the popular spiral (defined by Barry Boehm), prototyping, iterative, and object-oriented.

An object-oriented development life cycle (OODLC) includes iteration and evolution throughout, delivering work products at various points in the process. Object-oriented development also combines design, coding, and unit testing of work products (i.e., classes) and requires analysis of available reusable components in design prior to developing "new" components from scratch. All of these factors impact the software development life cycle and must be considered when developing object-oriented software.

4.1 Introduction

Software development life cycles (SDLCs) have been around for many years, with the original waterfall model, the spiral model, and various other versions of the development process described and used over the past 30 years. SDLCs define the stages or phases, tasks, and deliverables or work products that are created as part of the software development process. Generally, SDLCs focus at a very high level, and some have used the term *software process* to describe the lower-level tasks and deliverables.

One simplistic view of software development phases is shown in Figure 4.1. This view, which was offered by Pressman [PRE88], divides the development life cycle into three basic overlapping phases or stages:

- *Definition*, which defines what a system will do.
- *Development* of a solution, which defines how the system will be implemented based on the environment.

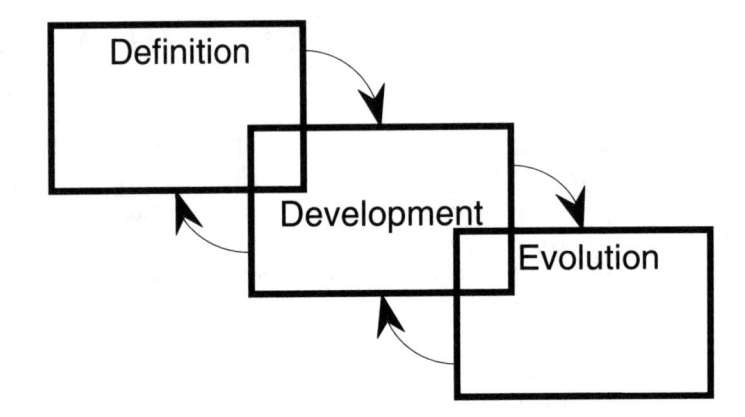

Figure 4.1
Simplified software development life cycle.

- *Maintenance* (or evolution), which represents change to the software product over its useful life.

One benefit of this view is that it clearly delineates the phases and also shows the inherent overlap between the stages. Definition describes in detail what a system will do without any implementation considerations. Development takes the definition of what the system will do (from Definition) and, considering the implementation characteristics of the system, creates a proposed solution that includes automated components. Maintenance includes both definition and development, but for changes to the system once it becomes operational. These phases are intertwined, and developers often move between them as a project progresses.

Definition, for example, might overlap Development and include aspects that describe how the system will be implemented. Specified requirements might cause additional questions to be asked that pertain to implementation issues, which might result in changes to the requirements. Likewise, solutions recommended in development might cause evaluation of requirements based on the cost and time to deliver. Maintenance represents the combination of definition and development based on changes to the system.

Software development is not a linear process and thus should be considered from an iterative or evolutionary perspective. Organizations that delineate between the activities of definition and development find exceptions that must be considered for successful development of quality systems. In the discussion that follows on development life cycle models, keep these factors in mind.

4.2 Traditional Software Development Life Cycles

In the past, traditional development life cycles have been based on management concerns about delivery of work products and have included specific beginning and ending sequences for tasks. For instance, in the traditional waterfall life cycle, analysis proceeds design, which proceeds programming, etc. Key to these life cycles is the concept of separate analysis, design, and coding, delivery of artifacts or work products at the end of each phase, checkpoints for continuation, and delivery of the final product (i.e., the software system) in one massive implementation effort.

In this section, I will explore two popular software development life cycles before introducing one that has been modified for object-orientation.

4.2.1 The Waterfall Life Cycle

In 1970,. W. W. Royce presented a paper [ROY70] describing what we now know as the waterfall model of software development. The name comes from the popular way of drawing the phases of the model as cascading downward, as shown in Figure 4.2. Because this model is the basis for most of the other models, I will discuss it in detail and use it as a basis of comparison for the other life cycle models.

Systems Investigation and Planning (**Planning**): This phase involves the initial request for the system, investigation, preliminary interviewing, cost/benefit analysis, and the planning and scheduling of the resources for the proposed system.

Deliverables: System scope document
General system requirements document
Cost, benefits, time, and expected impact on external systems
Business plan (Optional)
Plan for next phase (resources)

Systems Analysis (**Analysis**): This phase usually involves defining the scope of the proposed system, modeling any existing system components, and defining the data or information needs of the system. Typical subtasks include interviewing end-users, reviewing existing input and output documents and procedures, defining the data collected and reported on, and modeling the existing data and process requirements of the system.

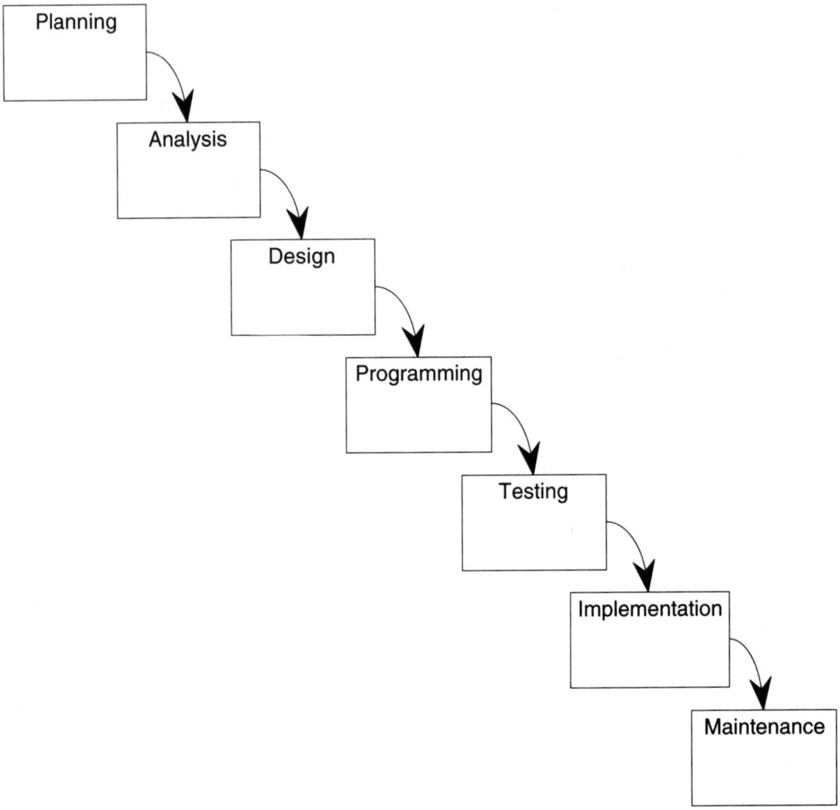
Planning
Analysis
Design
Programming
Testing
Implementation
Maintenance

Figure 4.2 Waterfall life cycle.

Deliverables: Detailed requirements document
User interface document
Data, process, and control models
Screen, menu, and report layouts
Data structure definitions

Systems Design **(Design)**: The design step can be further broken down into data or database design and process or system design. The data design usually determines the physical (hardware) constraints and performance issues related to how the information is structured and accessed. The process design often can involve breaking down a system into its subfunctions or modules and creating descriptions of the logic and processing to be achieved in each.

Deliverables: System architecture document
Module description documents
Physical data structure design document
Test plan and procedures

Programming: The programming phase involves taking the design specifications and transforming them into the appropriate source and executable code for the chosen programming language.

Deliverables: Program code (source and executable)
File/database descriptions or table definitions

Testing: Often considered as part of the Programming phase, this step involves determining whether the programs (and the entire system) meet the functional requirements and correctly perform the actions required.

Deliverables: Unit test verification documents
Integration test verification documents
System test verification document

Implementation: The process of placing a system, including the source code, executable code, JCL, and documentation into a production state, including converting existing data files, performing any final quality control, and initializing the system.

Deliverables: Documentation
Job control/execution statements

Maintenance: The process of supporting, enhancing, and fixing a system from the time, it is placed into production until it is replaced or phased out.

Deliverables: Change request
Impact analysis reports
Cost/benefits analysis document
Modification schedule/plan

While the waterfall SDLC is convenient for management, it typically is difficult to follow because of its reliance on completion of a task before beginning the next. Studies suggest that good software engineers often move from analysis to design, then return to analysis, and work at a variety of different levels of abstraction during a normal development project. In addition, waterfall SDLC projects often suffer from the inability to modify requirements following analysis, and reluctance to change aspects of the system in design and programming and experience massive manpower loading in the latter phases (i.e., programming, testing, etc.).

4.2.2 The Spiral Life Cycle

The spiral model developed by Barry Boehm [BOE88] is a blend of evolutionary development and prototyping (Figure 4.3). The main contribution of the spiral model is that, before any work is done, a risk analysis and a cost/benefit analysis are performed. The spiral model shows development activities proceeding through four quadrants.

In the first quadrant, the focus is on determining the objectives of the project, identifying available alternatives, feasibility, primary constraints, etc.

In the second quadrant, the focus shifts to evaluating the alternatives and identifying risks for each alternative. Alternatives are chosen to reduce the risk of the project, and the focus shifts to developing prototypes of the system and verifying the next level of the project.

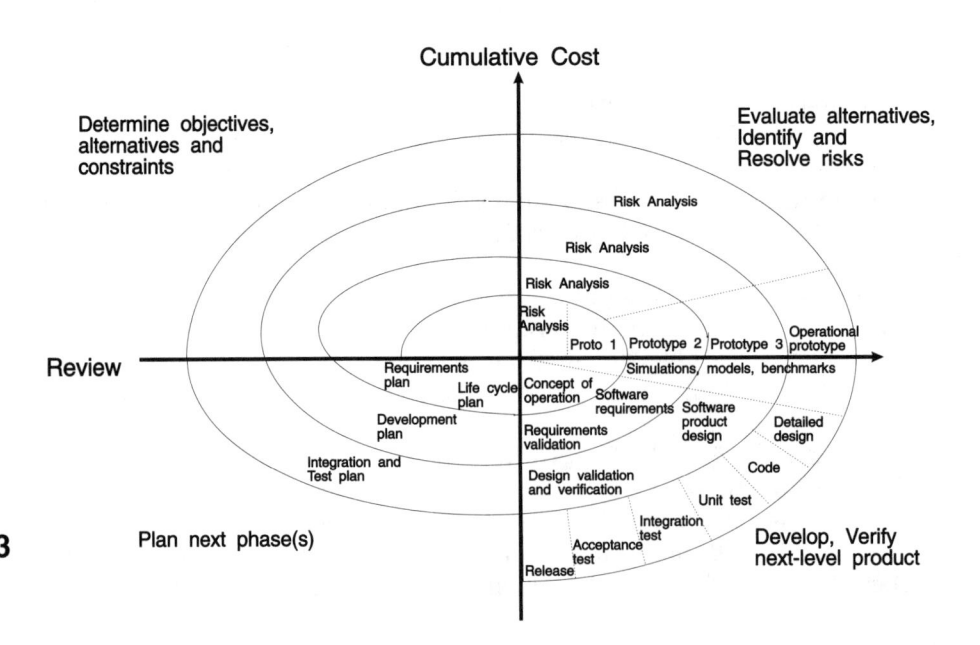

Figure 4.3 Spiral life cycle.

Each circuit around the spiral has a different focus but culminates in a review followed either by commitment to the next round or rework of portions completed during the round just completed. During the first round, the high-level risks, mainline alternatives, and constraints lead to a go/no-go decision on a project. A commitment to proceed with the next round includes development of a concept of operations to assure that all parties share a common view of the project and to identify more specific risks.

The second circuit around the spiral is similar in function to the first but represents a level of more detail. From this point on, the spiral model echoes the phases of the waterfall model. The third trip is dedicated to high-level requirements, while the fourth covers preliminary design. The succeeding trips around the spiral can be used to produce a build sequence for the finished application.

Notice that the spiral model makes extensive use of rapid prototyping and emphasizes the identification of risks and alternatives. This framework is flexible enough to permit the incorporation of desirable features of many of the life cycle models that I have discussed. One concept that has been embraced by the industry from the spiral model is the idea of evolving artifacts or work products and the use of prototyping throughout the development process.

4.3 Life Cycle Issues in Object-Oriented Development

Object-oriented development requires a re-evaluation of the issues that defined the life cycles described earlier. Because of the nature of object-oriented development, the deliverables created, the changing role of developers, and the use of prototyping and iteration in the process, traditional life cycles don't adequately support object-oriented development.

In this section, I will discuss the specific aspects of object-oriented development that are different from traditional development, then introduce an SDLC for objects in the next section.

4.3.1 Evolution in Software Development

Evolve: to undergo evolutionary change.
Evolution: a process of change in a certain direction; a process of continuous change from a lower, simpler, or worse to a higher, more complex, or better state.
[Webster]

Software development involves a series of tasks with specific work products or artifacts produced at various stages. One basic tenant of software engineering is that these artifacts or work products evolve over time. Requirements specifications are never complete but represent a working definition of the system under study at a point in time. Requirements change, and so must a requirements specification document if it is to accurately reflect the system under study. Likewise, design specifications change as different constraints and decisions are made. Program code ultimately must be made static so that executable code can be generated, but applications often are modified once they are released.

All development artifacts — including requirements, design specifications, and code — evolve and change over the life of a system, so evolution is inevitable. The evolution of the software development artifacts, including the system itself, is at the core of object-oriented development.

In an object-oriented software development life cycle (OOSDLC), work products or artifacts evolve and change as the project progresses. This represents problems from a configuration management perspective, both in maintaining and controlling versions of work products and in communicating updates to team members. Change management must be part of any object-oriented development effort and must track changes to the evolving work products. Documentation — in the form of printed reports, diagrams, and notes — must be made available to all team members so that they can be kept up to date on the status of each work product.

Change by itself is not beneficial, but change towards improvement is. Work products in an OOSDLC change as more information is gathered or more is learned about the system, and change is geared towards including more functionality in the system. Artifacts in an OOSDLC are evolving constantly, and this can lead to problems in communication between team members and managing versions of the artifacts.

4.3.2 Prototyping

Prototype (noun): an original model on which something is patterned; an individual that exhibits the essential features of a later type; a standard or typical example; a first full-scale and usually functional form of a new type or design of a construction (as an airplane).
Simulation (noun): the act or process of simulating; a sham object; the imitative representation of the functioning of one system or process

by means of functioning of another; examination of a problem often not subject to direct experimentation by means of simulating device.
Simulate (verb t): to assume the outward qualities or appearance of, usuually with the intent to deceive; to make a simulation of (as a physical system); syn see ASSUME.
[Webster.]

As Bernard Boar so appropriately said [BOA84]: "If a picture is worth a thousand words, an animated model [prototype] is worth a thousand pictures."

Prototyping involves the creation of a simulation or working model of a system prior to development of the actual system. Prototypes can be evolutionary, where they become the finished system, or throw-away, where they are built to discover something about the system under study. In both cases, a prototype allows developers and users to experiment with ideas before building a complete, functional system.

Problems with traditional requirements specification techniques often cause errors or bugs in the finished system after it is delivered. In many cases, the cause of these errors can be directly related to errors in the specification of requirements for the system. Prototypes can provide a more visceral form of requirements specification to users than traditional, paper-based models and specifications created with structured techniques.

With a prototype, the user can exercise the system just as though it already were operating in his or her own environment and thereby provide vital feedback to the developer on the suitability of the specification. Also, a prototype is a model of a system represented in a form already familiar to users. Prototypes, unlike traditional paper-based models, also are easier to modify and enhance, and this encourages changes in the requirements and specifications throughout the development process. A prototype can help to clarify the impact of design decisions prior to generating a large amount of rework. In addition, a prototype can be easily understood by users and developers alike, can describe in detail the functionality of a system, and can encourage refinement of functionality down to a very low level earlier in the development process.

Studies with prototyping techniques have found that, for users, exercising a prototype was easier than using paper models and systems created from a prototype were more likely to meet user requirements [GOM81]. Feedback from building a prototype also has proven to be extremely valuable in developing the finished system. Studies also have shown that prototyping tends to produce a smaller software product with roughly the same functionality, requiring less effort [BOA84].

Prototyping can produce higher productivity as measured by user satisfaction per person-hour, an improved human-machine interface (delivering something that works), and a reduced deadline effect at the end of the project. Experimental results suggest that prototyping increases the actual utilization of an information system by the users. Furthermore, user satisfaction with the information systems delivered is higher for prototyped systems than for systems developed using traditional techniques [ALA91]. Field and laboratory observations suggest that prototyping makes communication between users and designers relatively easy and conflict-free. Given the expressive nature of the prototype, it is not hard to understand how it can be effective in bridging the communication gap between developers and users.

Before committing to using a prototype as part of a development process, it is important to decide what the objective of the prototype will be. A basic question that should be answered by both developers and users is, "What do we expect to learn from developing a prototype, and how will this help us create better software?" There are different types of prototypes and, likewise, many different reasons for building a prototype. The two basic types of prototype are a *throw-away* prototype, which is used to validate the user requirements by modeling the behavior of the system, and an *evolutionary* prototype, which is refined repeatedly until it becomes the final product.

These two types, while similar, have very different purposes. A throw-away prototype is built to help define the requirements for the system prior to a traditional development process, while an evolutionary prototype is part of a traditional development effort and must include practical design considerations. When finished, a throw-away prototype is discarded, while an evolutionary prototype becomes the finished system. The implication in creating an evolutionary prototype is that design decisions must be made with an awareness of a real-world system and all the restraints imposed on the implementation environment.

Davis [DAV92] suggests that these prototypes be used for very different types of problems and help to define different types of requirements. While I don't necessarily agree that throw-away and evolutionary prototypes are orthogonal, I do see benefit from both under the right circumstances. Davis also suggests combining the two types of prototypes into what he calls "operational prototyping."

Prototyping in object-oriented development occurs at all stages — Analysis, Design, Coding, Testing, and Implementation. As I have already shown, the work products that are created as part of the object-oriented development process evolve and change, so the use of prototyping to determine which functional aspects of a system are correct and how these aspects should work ais a critical part of the process. If you are using an OOPL, for instance OOCOBOL, than prototyping becomes part of the design, test, and implement process. As classes (or objects) are defined, they are coded, tested, then released into a production state. The project proceeds by defining other objects or classes in the problem domain.

4.3.3 Iteration and Incremental Development

Iterate: to say or do again or again and again.
Iterative: involving repetition; relating to or being a computational procedure in which replication of a cycle of operations produces results that approximate the desired result more and more closely.
Increment: to increase especially in quality or value; something gained or added.
[Webster]

Iteration can be used at various points in the SDLC and allows work products (deliverables) to be reviewed and validated prior to moving on to other tasks. Iterative development tends to go hand-in-hand with prototyping, but the two also can be used separately. The key to iteration is the refinement of work products throughout the development process. To iterate without any progress is meaningless.

Object-oriented development lends itself to exploration of alternative designs, and often is used together with prototyping. *Iterative development* calls for reviewing a work product prior to moving on to the next phase. Iterative development means repeating tasks or stages but does not specify that progress has been made during these repetitions.

Incremental development is development by adding to work products such that something is gained and progress is made toward the eventual product. Again, incremental development typically is associated with prototyping and involves the development of a system in increments or parts. The process of incremental development represents adding or increasing functionality to a system, but any incremental process must conclude at some point, and object-oriented development is no different.

Iterative development involves repetition, generally from design and coding through testing and delivery. As work products — classes or subsystems — are completed, they must be tested and evaluated for quality assurance and reusability. This is part of the design and implementation process and the fact that this process occurs iteratively must be recognized and managed.

Iterative development must be controlled by considering how modifications in analysis, design, coding, etc. will affect each aspect of the system. Iterations and parallel development teams (artifacts) present many challenges to project managers, including document versioning, iteration planning, and presentation of incremental changes to system artifacts.

Adele Goldberg had the following observations on two years of object-oriented projects [GOL93]:

- Incremental integration is the key difference in how a project that used object technology must be managed.
- The critical cultural change that is required is that incremental results are incrementally tested and incrementally released, and this adds complexity to the process.
- Maintenance is mixed with development.
- Prototyping seems endless but is a learning exercise.
- Reuse often means that systems include functionality that is not required, which can increase time and resources.
- Reuse does not decrease the amount of testing required.
- Some developers want to distribute a subsystem for use by others as soon as it has passed unit test — this adds management complexity to the process.

4.3.4 Conflict of Class Design vs. Application Design

Any object-oriented development project faces a dilemma as the project moves from design into coding and testing: Should more time be spent developing reusable components or getting the system up and running? Unfortunately, the answer to this questions is "yes."

Object-oriented design is composed of two different sets of tasks: system or application design and class/object design. These tasks have different steps and goals. Iin application design, you want to create a design for the interacting objects that will operate in the proposed environment and satisfy the stated requirements; in class/object design, you seek to develop reusable components that will be generic enough to be used in future projects. These goals often are in opposition and can cause management problems in any OOSDLC.

Because one goal of object-oriented development is to acquire or build a library of reusable components, the task of creating reusable classes must be balanced against designing and coding classes to complete the requirements of the system under study. These two goals of object-oriented design are competitive and often result in scheduling problems. Organizations that cannot justify staff whose goal is to identify potentially reusable components must struggle with the additional effort to generalize classes in the design phase.

An ideal approach to this dilemma would be to have a group of staff dedicated to reuse. These staff would be charged with identifying, collecting, and making available reusable components and encouraging reuse throughout the organization. While this might be impractical in some organizations, failure to provide incentives for reuse will result in little or no reuse. I put off more discussion on the issue of reuse until chapter 12.

4.4 An Object-Oriented Software Development Life Cycle

David Taylor [TAY93] has suggested a simple, four-step OOSDLC:

1. Design a model of the business activity
2. Construct classes to support the model
3. Assemble methods for the completed classes
4. Add interfaces to solve business problems

Perhaps the best treatment to date of the issues involved in defining an OOSDLC are covered in papers by Hendersen-Sellers and Edwards [HEN90] [HEN93a] [HEN93b]. The first paper compares traditional SDLCs with the tasks common to object-oriented development and proposes a framework for an OOSDLC. The second and third papers describe a fountain model for object-oriented development and discuss the issues involved in adopting this approach.

In their papers, Hendersen-Sellers and Edwards point out that an OOSDLC contains both top-down and bottom-up views, because analysis often occurs in a top-down fashion, while design follows both approaches, and construction is bottom-up, because systems are built from predefined components that are assembled into a finished system. A generic OOSDLC described by Hendersen-Sellers and Edwards is shown in Figure 4.4 and includes the following steps:

1. Requirements specification — This phase includes review of the requirements and an analysis of these requirements to specify a high-level object model.

2. Identification of objects and services — This phase seeks to identify and further define the classes, objects, attributes, and operations found in the prior phase. In some cases, this also would include specification of object behaviors. It is important to remember that, at this point, no attempt is made to specify the underlying details of each object in terms of its implementation.

3. Establish interactions, services rendered and required by each object — This phase seeks to define messages passed between objects and the services that they will provide to other objects. Object responsibilities and behaviors are defined in terms of interfaces, and at this point in the process, two major types of interaction or association are defined: association and aggregation. A third type of association, generalization, can be defined or postponed until the Design phase.

4. Merge OOA results into OOD (identify and use any available reusable components) — This step defines each object in more detail and seeks to reuse any available classes in the Reuse Library.

5. Design internal details — Concurrently with the prior step, the internal structure of each object is designed and objects are decomposed into more primitive objects. In some cases, client/server and contractual relationships are defined at this point, and following this step, groups of classes or objects can be further developed using the process shown in Figure 4.5. Every attempt is made to use existing classes in the Reuse Library in this phase. The classes and objects defined here are implemented, tested, and delivered. In design, associations and aggregation relationships are mapped to client/server relationships.

6. Analyze class hierarchies — This step reevaluates the available classes in an iterative process, seeking to modify the hierarchies to best suit the goal of reuse in design. The generalization of objects is used to create classes, and attributes and operations are placed within the hierarchies so as to increase potential reuse. The overriding principle of this task is to determine whether an object represents one or more abstract data types.

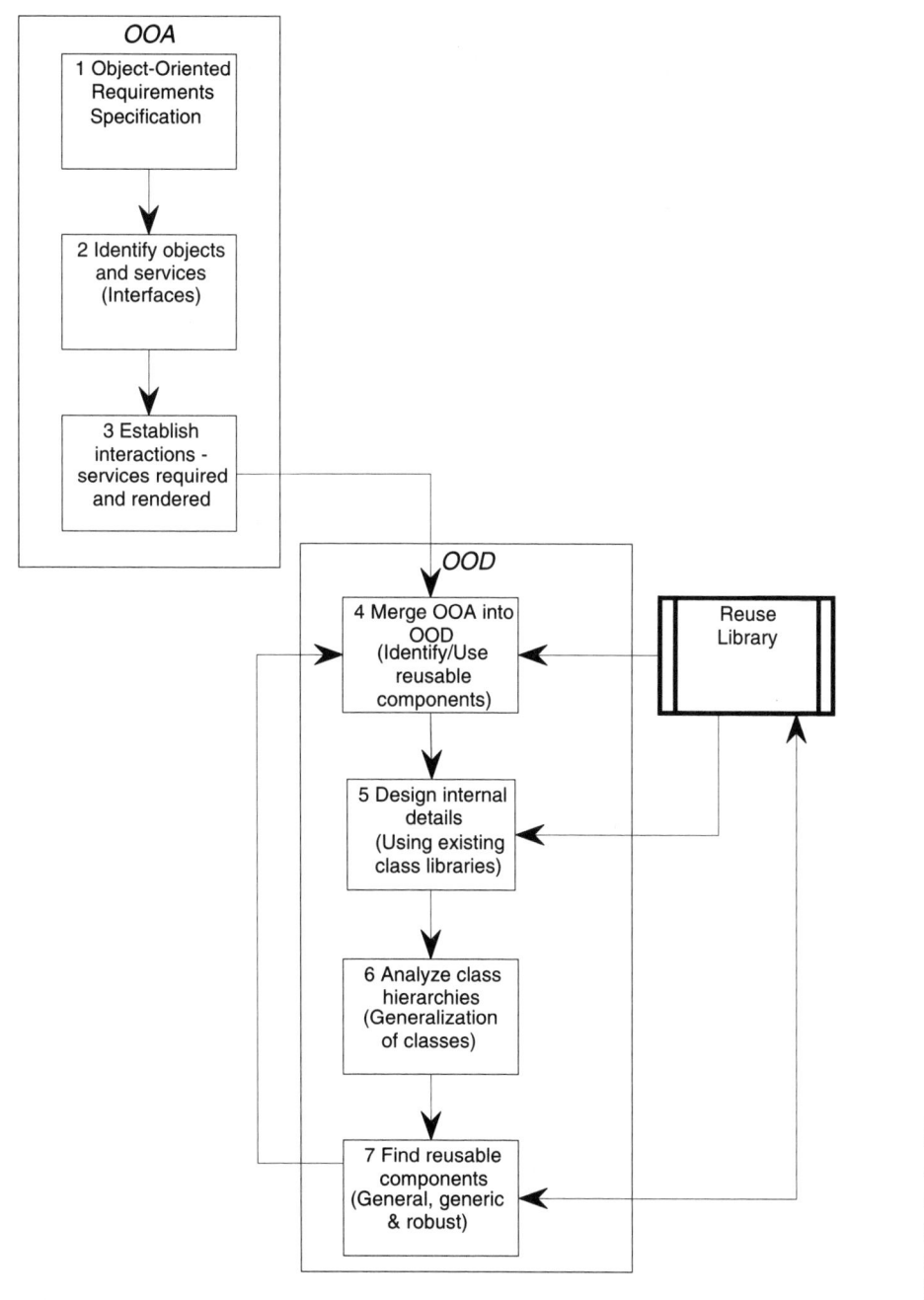

Figure 4.4 An object-oriented software development life cycle.

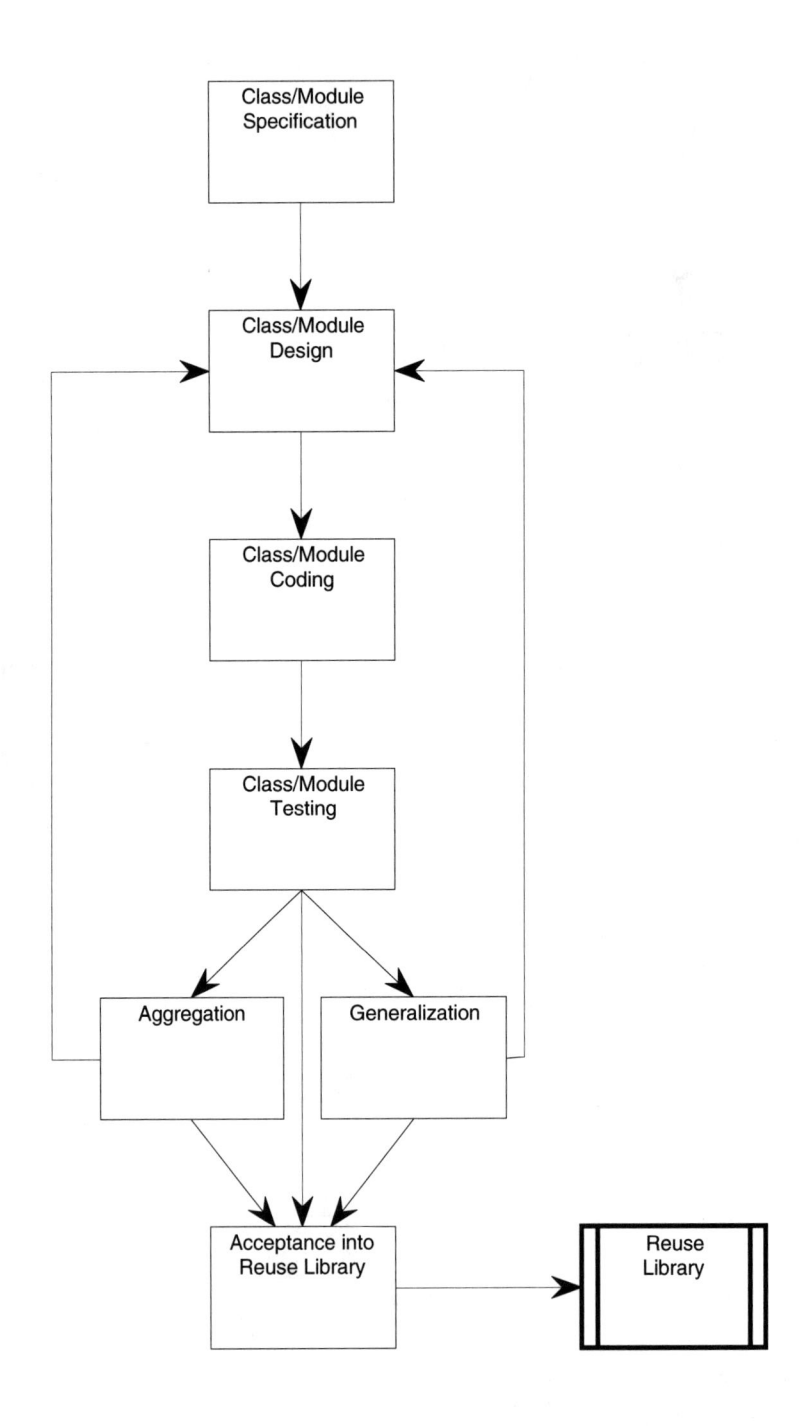

Figure 4.5
Class or module development.

7. Find reusable components — Using aggregation and generalization, this phase reconsiders each defined object and class for potential reuse in other applications. For a component to be reused, it must be general, generic, and robust. Prototyping can be used to provide feedback from users as to the system under development. The goal of this phase is to populate the Reuse Library, and this task can be assigned to a specific group or person responsible for reuse.

Hendersen-Sellers and Edwards point out that phases 4 through 7 of their OOSDLC are iterative, and there must be a balance between top-down concerns for application development against bottom-up issues in class/object design and construction. The process of designing classes or groups of classes, turning them over to a programming team that will implement them, then testing each prior to accepting them is shown in Figure 4.5.

Henderson-Sellers and Edwards do an excellent job of showing how reuse and domain analysis can be integrated into an OODLC and offer a Fountain model OOSDLC (Figure 4.6) that might replace the waterfall and spiral models described in section 4.2.

Artifacts or work products in an OOSDLC are developed and delivered in parallel, unlike in a traditional SDLC. This represents a serious challenge to project managers because these artifacts must be coded and tested while other products still are being analyzed and designed. Also, because one objective of any OOSDLC is to deliver reusable components, every project must consider and contribute to the pool of reusable classes. Cost estimates for each work product must be created in the requirements and feasibility study and updated in analysis and design.

Roles and irresponsibilities in object-oriented development are significantly different from traditional software development. Where as traditional software development requires analysts, designers, coders, testers, quality assurance, and maintenance staff, object-oriented development is best staffed with class designers, class implementors, system architects, and programmers.

Tasks in an OOSDLC vary in their duration and, unlike traditional software engineering, might undergo a number of iterations before a stable set is developed. For example, analysis progresses until a stable object model is defined, when generalization, verification and validation can be undertaken for the system. Henderson-Sellers and Edwards recommend that object models should be created for each major subsystem. I will look more closely at managing an OOSDLC in chapter 12.

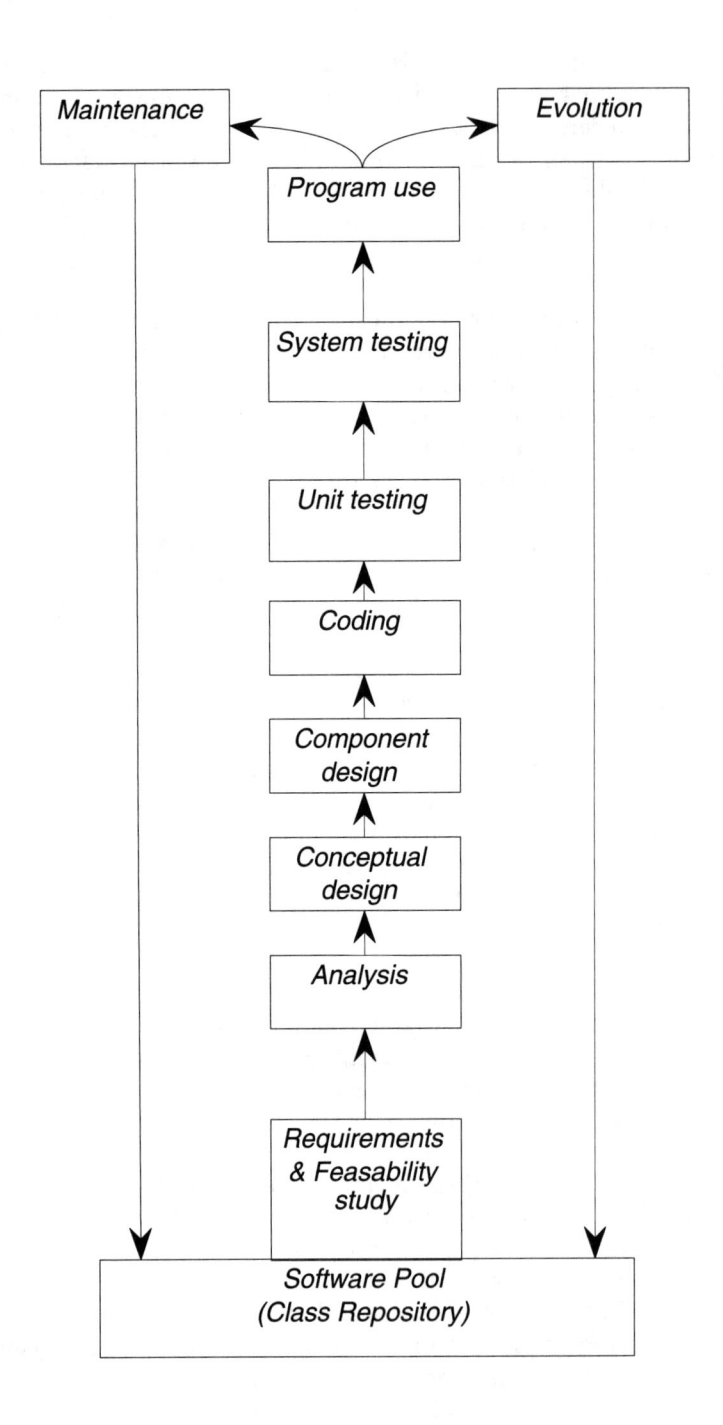

Figure 4.6
The fountain model OOSDLC.

4.4.1 Object-Oriented Analysis

The OOA process delivers an object model that defines the objects, classes, relationships, attributes, and operations that were abstracted from the problem space. This model should be complete and consistent across objects and classes and should define the instance variables or attributes used by objects. While some OOA techniques often use traditional data models to specify objects and classes, others use informal techniques for object identification. As you will see in chapter 6, a list of objects, attributes, and operations also can be extracted from a textual description of a system by identifying the nouns and verbs in the text.

In chapter 6, I will also explore some of the popular methods for object-oriented analysis, and using our two example problems, I will describe an OOA process. Popular OOA methods fall into two distinct groups: those that begin by looking for data structures in the problem domain and those that look for object responsibilities and behaviors in the problem domain. Booch even has suggested that a traditional structured analysis can be used to identify potential classes, objects, and messages [BOO91].

Recalling the work of Hendersen-Sellers and Edwards, you can include tasks for domain analysis in your OOA phase to help identify reusable components at that level. Another task that is often completed in an OOA phase is defining the architecture for the system and the interaction between domains. I will investigate this process in more detail in chapter 6.

4.4.2 Object-Oriented Design

Unlike traditional design, object-oriented design (OOD) begins by analyzing the existing design components (in a reusable library) to determine which can be adapted to support the system under study. This is a dramatically different approach from traditional design where developers effectively begin design with a clean slate and design a solution from scratch.

Obviously, if object-oriented design is to take advantage of reusable components, one of the tenants of object-oriented development, the components must have been developed already and be available for reuse or extension. This begs the question about how reusable components are defined, stored, searched, and accessed, which I will cover in chapter 14.

OOD requires that a clean, well-partitioned architecture is defined in analysis. The resulting structure must be based on this architecture and the objects and interactions defined in OOA. In OOD, systems of objects are gathered into partitions, which serve as the unit of distribution on control. A design architecture defines how objects are plugged into modules or subsystems.

The OOD process delivers an object specification that defines how the objects will be constructed, which classes will be defined, how the objects will communicate and interact, and the dynamic behavior of the objects throughout their life. OOD must consider the role of existing classes and objects in the design of a new system and also must consider the limitations of the chosen OOPL in implementing the solution. Dynamic and static aspects of objects and classes should be specified in OOD, and the design process typically is iterative and evolutionary in nature. OOD must balance the issues and goals of application delivery and the identification and use of reusable components.

OOD might require several different types of iteration, including rapid iteration at the lower levels, slower iteration at the management levels, and virtually non-iterative at upper management and customer levels. OOD also is closely intertwined with programming in a Design/Build/Test/Deliver process as shown previously in Figure 4.5. As classes are designed, they are coded, unit tested, and delivered. This allows components to be designed and built quickly and used in the composition of the system. I will look at this relationship between OOD and programming in more detail in chapters 7 and 8.

4.4.3 Object-Oriented Programming

Under the object-oriented paradigm, programming is a process of assembling objects to support the functionality for a system. Problem domain objects are mapped to solution domain objects in implementation and typed languages are used to create objects and methods that communicate via messages. Unlike traditional procedural programming, objects act in an asynchronous manner, and can only interact via the passage of messages.

Object-oriented programming (OOP) has been described as programming the differences, since existing classes of objects are reused and extended or changed to create new systems. Where existing objects do not support the data structures or methods for a new system, they can be extended to add these features. This leads to a view of software development that considers each new system in terms of how it is similar and different from existing system components.

Many OOP languages (OOPLs) are available from a variety of vendors, and each has its strengths and weaknesses. Prior to reviewing these OOPLs in depth, I need to establish some common functions or concepts for all OOPLs. At the very least, an OOPL should provide support for class definition, inheritance, encapsulation, and message passing. Optional features that OOPLs might support include multiple inheritance, polymorphism, dynamic binding, and garbage collection.

There are two distinct types of OOPLs: true and hybrid languages. *True OOPLs* were created to specifically support object-oriented concepts and provide the best support for these constructs. *Hybrid OOPLs* are traditional procedural languages that have been extended to support object-oriented constructs. Example true OOPLs include Actor, Eiffel, and Smalltalk, while example hybrid OOPLs include C++, CLOS, Objective-C, and Object-Oriented Pascal. Figure 4.8 compares several popular OOPLs based on common characteristics. I will look more closely at OOCOBOL in chapter 8.

4.4.3.1 Comparing Object-Oriented Programming Languages

Even though I will be describing OOCOBOL as a OOPL in this book, there are other, equally viable OOPLs that can be used together with or in place of OOCOBOL. Figure 4.7 represents the prominant OOPLs available and showing their operating environments, vendors, and a comparison of features.

Smalltalk — Smalltalk, the original OOPL, was defined as part of the Xerox PARC by Alan Kay and was extended by Adele Goldberg and Dan Ingalls of Tectronix. In Smalltalk, everything is an object, and the only way to have an operation performed is by sending a message. An object is a collection of private data and methods (operations) that act on that data. Methods are public to all inheriting objects. Because everything is an object, there is consistency throughout the Smalltalk environment. Also, Smalltalk is an interactive environment, with an interpreted language that is tightly coupled with the operation environment. Smalltalk also includes editors, linkers, browsers, debuggers, and extensive class libraries.

Smalltalk is a typeless language (no type checking) that supports single inheritance and provides automatic support for garbage collection so that the system determines the existence of each object. While this makes programming in Smalltalk less complex, it also causes costs in machine resources (i.e.,

	Ada	**C++**	**CLOS**
Platforms	Many	Many	HP, Sun, Apollo & VAX
Vendor	Alsys	AT&T Borland IBM Microsoft	Luicd, Inc. Franz
Features:			
Instance Variables	Yes	Yes	Yes
Instance Methods	Yes	Yes	Yes
Inheritance	None	Multiple	Multiple
Binding	Static	Both	Both
Class Variables	No	Yes	Yes
Class Methods	No	Yes	Yes

	Eiffel	**Objective-C**	**Smalltalk**
Platforms	Unix VAX	Next Intel486	Many
Vendor	Interactive Software Engineering	Stepstone Next	ParcPlace Digitalk Envy Enfin
Features:			
Instance Variables	Yes	Yes	Yes
Instance Methods	Yes	Yes	Yes
Inheritance	Multiple	Single	Single
Binding	Dynamic	Both	Dynamic
Class Variables	Yes	Yes	Yes
Class Methods	Yes	Yes	Yes

FR = Future Release

Figure 4.7
Comparing OOPLs.

performance problems), which can prohibit Smalltalk from being used for time or resource-critical systems.

Smalltalk is an excellent language for building graphical applications and encourages prototyping. Once developed, these GUI-based applications can be redeveloped in traditional languages or left in Smalltalk. Smalltalk also is a pure object-oriented language that cannot be subverted and is an excellent teaching tool for procedural programmers to learn object-oriented concepts.

Eiffel — Eiffel was developed by Bertrand Meyer of Interactive Software Engineering and supports the concepts of object, class, method, message, subclass, and inheritance. Eiffel is one of the few OOPLs that support multiple inheritance and, like C++, is statically typed (for type checking) and dynamically bound.

Eiffel includes sophisticated exception handling that supports preconditions and postconditions for methods, along with assertions that check all instances of a class for the same constraints. Eiffel also includes automatic garbage collection and a mature development environment with browser, editor, and configuration management built in. Eiffel libraries have been developed by ISE and others, and there is a C code generation capability in the EiffelBench product from ISE.

Eiffel has been placed into the public domain, and used extensively for commercial software development, and there now is a non profit organization, the International Consortium for Eiffel, that controls the evolution of the Eiffel language.

C++ — C++ was developed by Bjarne Stroustrup of AT&T Bell Labs and supports the definition of data types (classes) and methods (operators and functions) on these data types. C++ provides control operators on these data types including operator overloading, constructors, and destructors.

Operator overloading is supported in C++ and allows new objects to be used with + and - operators. Constructors and destructors are available within C++ to dynamically establish instances of classes (objects) automatically. While this does not replace the need for garbage collection, it reduces the need for this facility. C++ also supports multiple inheritance.

Classes in C++ are defined using the *Class* operand which replaces the *Struct* command, and all methods in a Class are private unless defined otherwise. Class constructs that are defined as private are restricted to methods within the class, while protected constructs are restricted to subclasses. Methods in a Class can be of two types: friend or member. *Friend methods* are conventional C functions, while *member methods* are linked directly to classes.

C++ supports static and dynamic binding (virtual functions) within a defined inheritance hierarchy. This makes C++ a very attractive choice for all types of software, including time- and resource-restricted systems. Also, because C++ is a superset of the C language, organizations can move slowly into C++ without loosing their investment in C expertise. This also can lead to problems if staff do not accept and adopt object-oriented concepts over time.

Objective-C — Objective-C was developed by Brad Cox of Stepstone and now is a prominent language because of the NeXT computer. NeXTStep includes Objective-C as part of its development environment, and many software-ICs now are available for the NeXTStep environment.

Objective-C supports dynamically bound objects and classes and adds single inheritance to the C language. Cox took the concepts found in Smalltalk and developed C-based constructs for the language, including a new definition for classes, a new object data type, and a new message expression type.

Each class in Objective-C consists of two files: the interface and the implementation. The *interface* defines what generally is available to users of the class and includes the name, parent class, instance variable declarations, and method declarations. The *implementation* file defines the actual method definitions.

Objective-C has extensive class libraries (Cox calls them software-ICs) that implement basic data structures and GUIs. NeXTStep includes an interactive development environment, similar to Smalltalk, that also is tightly coupled with the NeXT operating system.

Object-Oriented Pascal — Object-Oriented Pascal (OOPascal) first was used by Apple for the Macintosh computer and now is available on the IBM PC. Under OOPascal, classes are similar to records with the addition of a new reserved word "object," which allows for the creation of classes that inherit methods and data types.

OOPascal supports static and dynamic binding in a similar fashion to C++, using virtual methods, and also includes constructors and destructors (like C++).

Ada — Much debate is underway as to whether Ada is an OOPL, and a new standard (9X) is planned that will address some of these issues. Ada has many useful features that encourage software composition but provides limited support for classification in its current standard (Ada 83).

Ada is a strongly typed language that supports static inheritance through derived types. Ada binds all items at compile time (static binding), and all data types must be explicitly declared. Ada packages can provide new features and an interface for the consumer and supplier of the services and can provide an encapsulation mechanism by allowing features to be defined without having to specify the implementation details underneath the interface.

Within Ada, access types are pointers but can be used to provide dynamic binding by programmers if needed. Ada doesn't support subtypes or derived types and thus does not support full inheritance. A proposed standard for Ada, 9X, should support true inheritance in the future.

CLOS — Common Lisp Object System (CLOS) is a set of object-oriented extensions to the Lisp language and is descended from New Flavors and Common Loops. CLOS supports objects, classes, methods, subclasses, and inheritance. Messages in CLOS are replaced with generic function calls, and CLOS supports multiple inheritance.

All aspects of CLOS can be customized as needed, and the language supports post- and precondition methods for classes. CLOS has been used for AI or Knowledge-Based applications and language development but has not been widely used for traditional applications.

4.4.3.2 Class Libraries

Several powerful class libraries now are available for many operating environments and OOPLs, most of which are written in C++. To take advantage of OOP, developers must understand how specific class libraries are organized.

Most class libraries come in source code format, and storage and retrieval must be incorporated into the object-oriented development environments. Browsers display class information in a bubble and can be used to traverse through the related classes — between parents, ancestors, clients, suppliers, etc.

Class libraries must be continuously enhanced and restructured to best fit the changing needs of the clients that use them. Areas for class library improvement include:

- Apply methods of abstraction to improve the consistency of the classes.
- Provide better indexing and retrieval facilities for classes.
- Provide uniform mechanisms for each class.
- Combine classes into frameworks (reusable components).
- Extend the GUI classes to support new/better hardware/software features.
- Develop more specialized classes for specific types of software.

4.4.4 Object-Oriented Testing

Once software has been designed and produced, it must be tested to ensure it satisfies the original requirements and does not contain any errors or bugs. Two terms that often are used in the process of testing software are: *testing*, the systematic execution and examination of all portions of a system to ensure it performs as it was specified or designed; and *debugging*, the process of correcting known system errors.

Testing is closely related to requirements specification and tracking, because all of the requirements for a system can be used in the testing phase to ensure that the system meets the original need. As requirements are collected, they can be used to prepare test plans and test cases for the various system components. Once a test plan is developed, the test cases are used to verify the accuracy and correctness of the system before it is accepted into production.

The overall goal of software testing is to locate those faults that will have the most significant impact on the use of the software and those that can be found within a reasonable amount of effort. Testing should be an important part of any Quality Assurance function in the development process.

There are several different types or levels of testing, including:

- *Unit* — testing individual modules, programs, or subsystems to ensure that all functions have been verified and all data have been entered and processed correctly.
- *Integration* — testing modules or subsystems where there are interfaces to ensure that components work together correctly.
- *Regression* — testing portions of a system that have been tested previously but were modified.
- *Validation* — testing the application to confirm that all requirements

have been satisfied.
- *System* or *acceptance* — testing the complete application to ensure that it works as designed and accepting the system into production.

Object-oriented components (classes and subsystems) don't map to the concepts of centralized testing that are used in traditional COBOL applications. Testing in object-oriented development represents a significant change from traditional development, primarily because of the nature of the system components and their delivery throughout the life cycle.

What is required in object-oriented development is a different approach to testing that focuses on the system components and their interactions. As you already have seen, the process of delivering classes involves design, coding, and unit testing each component prior to acceptance. The unit in this case is the class or subsystem, and you generally begin by testing all of the primitive classes using the specification of the class for test case data.

For instance, acceptance criteria for unit testing classes might include all methods tested, all states tested, all transitions tested, and all paths followed. Also, incremental testing of class structures is required to verify component quality up and down the hierarchy. Integration testing (testing instances of classes that work together), polymorphism, and dynamic binding also affect testing of object-oriented systems, in addition to the following special considerations:

- Inheritance provides a natural guide to reusing test cases.
- Information hiding makes writing test drivers more difficult.
- Multiple entry points make testing harder to manage.
- Interfaces are well-defined and should be explicit.
- Polymorphism and dynamic binding expand the range of possibilities for interclass testing.

4.4.5 Estimating, Planning, and Managing Object-Oriented Development

The process of planning, estimating, and managing an object-oriented development project represents additional challenges to those organizations adopting object technology. As you already have seen, an object-oriented development life cycle is substantially different from a traditional development effort.

Scheduling resources, planning tasks and deliverables, measuring project progress, estimating cost and time, etc. all require different methods and techniques from traditional COBOL development. In addition, the evolving work products, the reuse of components for each project, and the metrics for object-oriented development — effort, cost, time, complexity, reused code, etc. — all represent changes that management must incorporate into the software engineering process. I will cover these topics in more detail in chapter 12.

4.4.6 Object-Oriented Maintenance

As with every other aspect of software engineering, maintaining an object-oriented software product is significantly different from that of a mainframe-based COBOL application. The problems faced by maintainers of software designed and implemented with objects and messages must not be overlooked when adopting object technology.

Managing and tracking relationships between components (inheritance and messaging), version and configuration management for classes and objects, and managing reuse are all new facets of object-oriented maintenance. Managing class libraries of reusable components represents its own challenges, but I will cover maintenance of object-oriented software in chapter 10.

4.5 Roles and Responsibilities of Staff

In addition to the changes in the development life cycle, the work products created, and the requirements for managing and tracking deliverables, an object-oriented development approach requires different roles and responsibilities for development staff.

Booch [BOO91] and others have suggested that object-oriented development requires recasting the roles and responsibilities that developers, managers, and clients play in the software process. Traditional software engineering positions — such as programmers, analysts, and designers — must be replaced with new positions. Examples of the roles and responsibilities in an OOSDLC might include:

- *System Architects* — Senior developers who design and develop architectures for the organization.
- *Class Designers* — Less senior developers who create and maintain the class hierarchy, with the goal of maximizing reuse.
- *Class Implementors* — Junior developers who select from the available

classes and implement as objects to satisfy the needs of an application.
- *Application Programmers* — Programmers who take the results of the objects defined by the Class Implementors and assemble them using in OOCOBOL to satisfy the needs of the application.

In general, an object-oriented approach requires that software developers adopt a product culture — focusing on product quality, fitting the process to meet the product, and working on building teams of egoless developers — as well as changes in the focus and techniques used. Remember that prototyping in an object-oriented project becomes part of analysis, design, and build/test and that there must be a focus on system architecture (i.e., assign a team whose responsibility is to set and maintain a technical vision of the product throughout development).

Object-oriented development requires at least three different areas of focus or review by teams or groups:

Architecture — These people are generalists and application domain specialists who perform top-level design, including identifying major classes, and provide a conceptual and technical vision for the project; ideally, this group consists of 4 to 10 people who all understand the product and business.

Application designers — Usually organized around business/functional lines, these developers consume reusable components (classes) and build applications from them; they also work with class designers to develop, build, and improve specific classes and methods.

Class designers — These people actually own the classes, and develop and manage them and usually are responsible for testing and improving the classes.

4.6 References

[ALA91]   Alavi, M., "An Assessment of the Prototyping Approach to Information Systems Development," *Software Engineering Benchmark Handbook*, Applied Computer Research, Phoenix, 1991, pp. 91-100.

[ARA89]   Arango, G., "Domain Analysis: From Art Form to Engineering Discipline," *ACM SIGSOFT* (Soft. Eng. Notes), vol. 14, no. 3, May 1989.

[BER91]   Bersoff. E. H. and A. M. Davis, "Impacts of Life Cycle Models

	on Software," *CACM*, vol. 34, no. 8, pp. 104-117.
[BOA84]	Boar, B., T. Gray, and T. Seewaldt, "Prototyping vs. Specifying: A Multiproject Experiment," *IEEE Trans. on Soft. Eng.*, vol. 10, no. 3, 1984, pp. 39-44.
[BOE88]	Boehm, B. W., "A Spiral Model of Software Development and Enhancement," *IEEE Computer*, vol. 21, no. 5, May 1988, pp. 61-72.
[BOO86]	Booch, G., "Object-Oriented Development," *IEEE Trans. Soft. Eng.*, SE 12, 3, February 1986, pp. 211-221.
[BOO91]	Booch, G., *Object-Oriented Design with Applications*, Benjamin-Cummings, 1991.
[BOO93]	Booch, G., *Object-Oriented Design with Applications*, second edition, Benjamin-Cummings, 1993.
[CAM86]	Cameron, J. R., "An Overview of JSD," *IEEE Trans. on Soft. Eng.*, vol. SE-12, no. 2, Feb. 1986, IEEE Computer Society Press, Washington D.C., pp. 222 - 240.
[COA90]	Coad, P. and E. Yourdon, *Object-Oriented Analysis*, Prentice-Hall, 1990.
[DAV92]	Davis, A. M., "Operational prototyping: A New Development Approach," *IEEE Software*, September 1992, pp. 70-77.
[DEC92]	de Champeaux, D., "Toward an Object-Oriented Software Development Process," *HP Laboratories Technical Report*, November 1992.
[GOL93]	Goldberg, A., "Wishful Thinking," *Object Magazine*, May-June 1993, pp. 87-88.
[GOM81]	Gomaa, H. and D. Scott, "Prototyping as a Tool in the Specification of User Requirements," *Proceedings of the Fifth Intl. Conf. on Software Engineering*, IEEE Computer Society, pp. 333-342, 1981.
[HAR92]	Harrold, M. J., J. D. McGregor, and K. J. Fitzpatrick, "Incremental Testing of Object-Oriented Class Structures," *Proceedings of the Intl. Conference on Software Engineering*, May 11-15, 1992.
[HEN90]	Henderson-Sellers, B. and J. M. Edwards, "The Object-Oriented Systems Life Cycle," *CACM*, vol. 33, no. 9, pp. 143-159.
[HEN93a]	Henderson-Sellers, B. and J. M. Edwards, "The 'Fountain' Model," *Object Magazine*, 3(2), July-August 1993, pp. 71-79.
[HEN93b]	Henderson-Sellers, B. and J. M. Edwards, "The O-O-O Methodology for the Object-Oriented Life Cycle," *SIGSOFT*, vol. 18, no. 4, October 1993, pp. 54-60.
[HUR91]	Hurwitcz, M., "Health Food for Programmers," *LAN*

	Magazine, May 1991, pp. 138-152.
[JEA90]	Jean, C. and A. Strohmeier, "An Experience in Teaching OOD for Ada Software," *ACM SIGSOFT*, vol. 15, no. 5, pp. 44-49.
[MCG93]	McGregor, J. D., "Testing Object-Oriented Systems," Proceedings of Object World '93, February 1-4, 1993.
[PRE88]	Pressman, R., *Software Engineering: A Beginner's Guide*, McGraw-Hill, 1988.
[ROY70]	Royce, W. W., "Managing the Development of Large Software Systems: Concepts and Techniques," *Proceedings of WESCON*, August 1970.
[TAY93]	Taylor, D., "A Development Life Cycle for Object Technology," *Object Magazine*, January-February 1993, pp. 18-24.
[WIN88]	Wing, J. M., "A Study of 12 Specifications of the Library Problem," *IEEE Software*, July 1988. pp 66 - 76., IEEE Computer Society Press, Washington D.C.

Chapter 5

COBOL Considerations in Object-Oriented Development

Unlike other programming languages, COBOL represents some challenges when the concepts of objects, messages, and inheritance are applied. COBOL, a product of the early software engineering community of the 1950s, has evolved to include support for many popular design and programming concepts over the past 40 years. In the first chapter, I explored the history of the COBOL language and the factors that affected its evolution to support object-orientation.

In this chapter I will look at COBOL as an object-oriented programming language and the changes in the COBOL 97 standard to support objects and messages. I will delve into more detail on the history of COBOL, its use over the years for applications development, the traditional development environment for COBOL, and the language constructs. I also will look at COBOL data structures and types, file structures, and organizational issues before considering modern software engineering practices — including abstract data types, inheritance, message passing, and classification — and their role in COBOL development. I use the deck of cards example that was introduced in previous chapters to highlight the new concepts in object-oriented development in COBOL.

I also will investigate the role of analysis and design in traditional COBOL development, CASE tools, prototyping, reusable COBOL components, client/server and distributed systems development with COBOL. I will conclude the chapter with a review of the OOCOBOL standard, its syntax, the concepts that it encompasses, and the status of the standard at the time this book was published.

5.1 Introduction

As COBOL matures as a programming language, the uses of COBOL change. The early uses of COBOL included traditional business systems development and maintenance, and the language was created with an eye toward ease of application understanding. This resulted in the English-like format and syntax for COBOL that helped make it more maintainable. COBOL applications, when developed correctly, can be easier to maintain than those built using other languages, especially assembler and C, which also are closer to the operating environment.

COBOL traditionally has been viewed as a language for developing management information systems (MIS) or business applications. Originally, COBOL was structured to support batch sequential processing with large numbers of records as input and output. The SORT and REPORT facilities in COBOL were added later to make batch transaction processing easier. COBOL's strengths over other alternative programming languages, such as C or Pascal, include its support for files and databases, its ease of understanding and maintenance, its widespread support on most major computer platforms, and its evolution to support sound software engineering concepts.

Over the years, COBOL has been used to develop all types of software, including some nontraditional MIS applications. In the past few years, we have seen COBOL described as a tool for building client/server, distributed, and even GUI applications. COBOL, like any other programming language, continues to evolve to support the needs of the software engineering community.

There are several major movements, some of which I have described in previous chapters, that are affecting the changes to the COBOL language we all know and love. These include a movement towards distributed systems, graphical interfaces, reusable components, and from simple data types to abstract or complex data types. I will focus in this chapter on the latter item, having covered the other topics in more depth in other chapters.

Traditional COBOL development was geared around simple, fixed data types and structures. The earliest COBOL applications were developed to support numeric and alphanumeric data types stored in sequential data stores (i.e., tapes). As more sophisticated storage mechanisms evolved, COBOL added support for indexed sequential and random or keyed access to these structures. These mechanisms evolved to include external database management systems (DBMS), and COBOL supported these storage capabilities via the CALL construct. Interestingly, the data types supported in these storage mechanisms did not change, other than to support a broader range of numeric data.

In the past few years, computer applications have expanded to support more diverse data types, including variable data such as graphic images, animation, audio, and video. These complex data structures are difficult (if not impossible) to support in a traditional COBOL application, because the language provides no inherent support for these data types. What is required for COBOL to support these data types is object orientation. Abstract data types which were introduced in chapter 3 and included in the COBOL-97 standard, provide direct support for these variable data types.

5.1.1 History

Originally developed by the Conference on Data Systems Languages (CODASYL), COBOL was defined and described first in 1959. The ANSI and CODASYL standard for COBOL, COBOL 68, included the IDENTIFICATION, ENVIRONMENT, DATA, and PROCEDURE divisions and allowed for extensions to the language by COBOL compiler vendors. As a result, there were many differences in how COBOL compilers worked based on the original COBOL 68 standard.

Software in the 1960s was mostly batch-oriented transaction processing with simple data types and tape-based files. The COBOL 68 standard reflects this in its support for multiple tape reels, sequential processing and access, and commands to close tapes with and without rewinding them. Also included in the COBOL 68 standard are commands GO TO, ALTER n TO PROCEED TO m, and GO TO n DEPENDING ON m. These commands map very nicely to the types of control structures used in assembler, where the processing logic changes depending on the input to the program. Anyone who has ever tried to debug or test a program that contains ALTER or GO TO n DEPENDING ON m commands has found this process to be tedious and difficult, but these commands were included in COBOL to ease the transition from Assembler.

The COBOL 68 standard also included commands for sorting records, examining string variables, searching tables, and generating reports. With the standards that followed, COBOL 68 closely matched the principles of software engineering that were dominant at that time. Early COBOL applications also reflected the simple data types and sequential processing prevalent during the 1960s.

In 1974, a revised standard for COBOL was produced that did not immediately achieve success in the industry because most vendors didn't move quickly to support it. IBM, the major mainframe vendor at the time, did not release support for the COBOL 74 standard on their System/370 series computer until 1977. COBOL 74 introduced support for multi-tape files, indexed access to disk files, a new COMMUNICATION DIVISION, a PROCEDURE DIVISION

USING a data area, and a CALL command. These features were added to support some of the emerging concepts in software engineering, including re-entrant code, modular code, and random access to large data stores (i.e., disk-based).

The next standard, COBOL 85, is widely used in the IBM community (sold generically as COBOL II on IBM machines) and incorporated support for popular structured programming concepts introduced in the late 1970s. Included in this standard was support for nested programming, a CASE statement, global and local data structures, CALLs to external modules by content or reference, and common programs or subroutines. Other modifications to the COBOL language introduced in the 85 standard included changes to the way the PERFORM statement worked and modifications to file I/O.

The proposed standard for COBOL in the 1990s is the ANS COBOL 97 standard expected to be released before the end of the century. This standard will incorporate, among other things, objects, classes, encapsulation, and inheritance into the COBOL language. These extensions are being added to allow COBOL application development to take advantage of the benefits of object-orientation. As I already have shown, OOCOBOL also will support the abstract or complex data types now common in software, including audio, video, and graphics, as well as layering of software and reusable components.

At the time this book was written, the standard had been defined within the ANSI X3J4 committee and was supposed to be available for public comment in 1995. The only available OOCOBOL product in 1994 was the Micro Focus Object COBOL Option, which supported a subset of the ANSI standard, although IBM has plans to release an Object COBOL product by early 1995. As a result, the examples in this book are syntactically consistent with the ANSI X3J4 OOCOBOL standard but were not compiled using the initial version of the Micro Focus product. Micro Focus plans to support the ANSI X3J4 standard in a future version.

5.1.2 Existing COBOL Applications

Any discussion of a new COBOL standard must take into consideration the large base of existing applications developed with previous versions of COBOL compilers. Estimates range from 100 million to 1 billion lines of COBOL in existence in the early 1990s. Many of these COBOL applications were developed prior to the general acceptance of structured methods, and many are executing under COBOL 74 standards. Other COBOL applications that still are being supported were created in the 1960s and include ALTER GOTOs, GO DEPENDING ON, and other nightmarish forms of assembler-like programming.

A traditional COBOL development effort during the 1970s and 1980s might have included an analysis of user need, design of program structure using flowcharts, and direct coding in COBOL. These COBOL applications might contain some semblance of documentation; however, in many cases, the documents were not modified as the COBOL programs that they represent were changed over the years. The promise of ease of understanding of COBOL programs only works when they are built in a standard format and include sufficient internal documentation to explain the purpose of each section. Unfortunately, many existing COBOL applications consist of programs that were not developed with these factors in mind and include spaghetti code throughout.

The structured revolution of the 1970s brought with it an acceptance of top-down programming, single entry/exit to modules, and independence of function. Studies showed that maintenance of COBOL was easier when programs were developed in a structured format. With the structured programming of the 1980s, COBOL application development changed to include some data and function modeling during analysis, structured design resulting in a partitioned program described in a structure chart, and the use of pseudocode to describe the functions in a COBOL subroutine. The COBOL applications developed during this period reflect a hierarchical structure that includes PERFORM UNTIL/THRU statements, absence of GOTO commands, and in some cases, CALLs to common external routines.

Unfortunately, many of the COBOL applications developed during the 1980s also suffer from lack of documentation, nonstructured architectures, and special assembler subroutines to increase system performance or reduce system size. It is not uncommon to find organizations that rewrote their own versions of VSAM and CICS routines and interface their COBOL applications with these routines.

One potential solution to the general lack of documentation for existing COBOL programs are the reverse engineering programs described in chapter 11. These products attempt to automatically recover some design specifications from existing COBOL applications. Many of the existing reverse engineering products capture data structure or database definitions and program structure but not program logic. Even without support for program logic, these reverse engineering tools still offer benefits to organizations that must maintain or change legacy systems built 15 or 20 years ago by programmers no longer with the organization. I will look in more detail at legacy systems and OOCOBOL in chapter 11.

5.2 COBOL as a Software Engineering Tool

For COBOL to move from its role as a programming language used for batch and character-based online applications to one that supports all types of software development, it must evolve to support the concepts prominent in software engineering in the 1990s. Developers of applications with OOCOBOL must struggle to learn the concepts of object-orientation (as described in chapter 3) and apply them to COBOL applications development.

For this transition to occur, COBOL itself must change, and those responsible for developing and maintaining COBOL applications must change as well. Luckily, COBOL programmers can use their existing expertise and knowledge to ease the transition to object-oriented development as described in subsequent chapters. Existing COBOL concepts also can be carried forward into this brave new world of object-oriented development. Figure 5.1 describes some COBOL concepts that apply to object-oriented development and are covered in more detail in the following sections.

Recalling the discussion of software engineering principles in chapter 3, COBOL must support new concepts including abstraction and generalization, information hiding, encapsulation of data structures and operations, generic classes of objects that interact via messages, and an incremental and iterative development process. The challenge for COBOL developers is to learn to use these new techniques and incorporate them into the applications built during the 1990s. The OOCOBOL standard provides support for all these concepts and allows COBOL applications to be built using these principles.

5.2.1 Data Types

In COBOL, you define data structures (01 level) in the DATA DIVISION that consist of fields or data elements. These data elements or fields all must be of a specific data type allowed in COBOL (example data types = integer, real, string, etc.). You can construct very complex data structures using combinations of data elements with repeating fields, group, and elementary items, but the lowest-level fields or elements must be of the types supported by the COBOL compiler.

Old COBOL Concept	Object-Oriented Concept
COBOL data types	Classes or abstract data types (ADTs)
Data structures	Encapsulation of data & methods
Subroutines/Functions	Class/Object methods
Hierarchical structures (structure chart)	Class hierarchy (classification)
Graphical representations of models and specs (DFD, ERD, structure chart)	Graphical representations of objects (Class, object, module diagrams)
Functional decomposition	Object decomposition
COBOL Compiler, Editor, Linker	Object-oriented development environment

Figure 5.1 COBOL concepts and object-orientation.

COBOL was developed with two simple data types that were common in other programming languages at the time. These data types include numerics (i.e., PIC 9) and alphanumerics (PIC X) or strings. The numeric data types can be further subdivided into integer, real, and COMP. These are defined in the COBOL language syntax and are supported by the COBOL language vendors. While the actual storage of these data types might vary with individual COBOL implementations, the basic data types are supported in all of the COBOL products.

After a variable or field is defined in a COBOL program (in the DATA DIVISION) as a specific data type, you can manipulate it in the PROCEDURE DIVISION in memory using the standard COBOL verbs. The COBOL compiler manages the different types of operations that are performed based on the type of data you use.

For instance, you can define a numeric field in COBOL to be binary (COMP), floating point (COMP-1 and COMP-2), or even packed decimal, and when you use the COBOL commands ADD, MULTIPLY, or SUBTRACT, the compiler inserts the proper assembler commands to ensure that it works correctly regardless of the data type that you use. Even though each of these operations will vary depending on the type of data that you use, the compiler allows you to use these commands generically without having to deal with the details of each data type. In this sense, COBOL directly supports simple data types and operations on these types within the framework of the language.

COBOL data types also can be defined with a specified range or domain of possible values for each type. For example, you could define a set of possible values for a data element or field in the DATA DIVISION using the VALUE clause and 88-level entries. Using this method, you can specify that a field only contain the values in these entries and include references to these entries in the PROCEDURE DIVISION. In this manner, you can define the range of possible values that your data elements can contain and use this range in your programs. By using this approach, you can specify within your COBOL program the domain of values that each data type can hold.

Remembering the discussion of abstract data types (ADT's) in chapter 3, ADTs can be considered as extensions of simple data types or as complex data types. ADTs represent abstractions of data structures and operations beyond the simple types described previously (i.e., integer, real, etc.). Object-oriented development uses classes to define these complex data types (or ADTs) in the same way that COBOL already supports simple data types. ADTs can be built from simple data types and can have operations specified for their values. Using ADTs, you can extend the data types allowed in COBOL and also specify the legal operations or commands that can be executed on these data types.

Concerning the example I introduced in chapter 3, consider an ADT that maps to a deck of playing cards. The deck holds 52 cards of values from 2 to 10, and Jack, Queen, King, and Ace. Four suits of cards are allowed — hearts, diamonds, clubs, and spades — with each suit including values for cards from Ace to King. The physical implementation of this deck of cards might be a collection of cards or an array of alphanumeric values, say from 1C (i.e., one of clubs) through AS (Ace of spades). You might choose to represent this as a data type defined as follows:

Card; value = { 2,3,...King,Ace }
Suit; value = { Clubs, Diamonds, Hearts, Spades }
Deck of Cards = Collection of 52 Suit of Card

Given this definition of a data structure for a card deck, you can begin adding operations to your ADT. Example operations or services provided by the Deck of Cards might include Create, Shuffle, Deal n card, Cut the cards, etc. The key to the concept of an ADT is that you can define the data structure as shown previously in combination with the operations on the data. For example, you might define the following operations:

- Deck of Cards.Create — creates the collection of 52 cards with the proper values (i.e., Ace of Hearts ... King of Spades).
- Deck of Cards.Shuffle — organizes the collection of cards in random order.
- Deck of Cards.Deal (*n*) — selects the next *n* cards from the top of the deck.

Notice that I used the convention *ADT.Operation* to define the procedures or methods for the card deck. I will continue to use this convention as I move into the OOCOBOL realm. Once I have defined the ADT for the Deck of Cards, I can consider implementing it in OOCOBOL. I would define a class called Deck_Of_Cards with the data structure and operations described earlier.

5.2.2 Data Structures

As already stated, one of the major strengths of COBOL as a development tool is its inherent support for external data structures or files. The FILE SECTION allows external data structures of any type to be defined and accessed directly in COBOL using the READ and WRITE verbs. All the popular file access mechanisms — indexed sequential, random, sequential, and dynamic — are supported in the DATA DIVISION of any COBOL program via the ORGANIZATION IS and ACCESS IS statements.

Conceptually, files are collections of common or similar data types. Records in files are occurrences of data that can be represented using a file definition and record layouts. The physical file, which is external to the COBOL program, consists of records of the same or similar types (i.e., transactions, master records, etc.). Access to these files can be via a number of mechanisms, including keyed access via pointers into the file or offset to records, sequential access by record number, or random access to a DBMS via record keys.

COBOL file definitions must reference or contain only valid data type definitions that map to the COBOL record types in the WORKING STORAGE section. COBOL FD and 01 record descriptions describe the data structures and can contain multiple record types for the file, with simple data types defined as variables or attributes of each record type.

COBOL files can be physical occurrences of records in a file, as in sequential or indexed files, as rows in a table with the fields as the columns (relational view), as occurrences of records in a set with data fields or variables (network view), or as parent/child records in a DBMS (hierarchical view). Regardless of the access mechanism used, all COBOL data structures must be defined in the WORKING STORAGE.

Those COBOL applications that reference or access external DBMS data structures must contain DDL statements processed by a precompiler and translated into FD, 01, and WORKING STORAGE data structures in the DATA division, and CALL commands in the PROCEDURE DIVISION. In a sense, these data structures are defined externally to the COBOL program and are loaded into the programs' working storage section by the external routines that access them. In this case, data structures used by COBOL programs actually are managed and accessed by external programs (i.e., DBMSs).

One philosophy built into COBOL, and most other procedural programming languages, is the separation or data from processing. The fact that every COBOL program always has separated the DATA from the PROCEDURE divisions is consistent across all previous versions of the language. All other popular procedural programming languages — including Pascal, C, PL/1, RPG, and Fortran — provide similar separations of data structures from the operations that act upon them.

As you begin a migration to an object-oriented version of COBOL, you must accept that this separation of data and procedure is no longer valid. In OOCOBOL, you *encapsulate* or join together the processing with the data structures. Together, the encapsulated data structure and procedures are called an *object*. Data structures in an OOCOBOL program cannot be separated from the operations that act on them.

In many cases, COBOL programs INCLUDE files or copy books that represent common definitions of data structures stored externally to the programs themselves. In a similar fashion, OOCOBOL programs reference external files that define the classes and objects to be used in an application. External class and object definitions are loaded into the COBOL program at compile or run time in a similar fashion to INCLUDE files or copy books.

Figure 5.2 pictorially shows the structure of an OOCOBOL class. Notice that a class contains its own WORKING-STORAGE SECTION and can contain its own private methods in a PROCEDURE DIVISION. Also notice that objects can be specified within the class definition and contain their own WORKING-STORAGE SECTION, as well as methods. Figure 5.3 is an extract from an OOCOBOL class definition for the Deck Of Cards ADT described above.

5.2.3 Program Structure

A traditional COBOL program contains four major divisions as shown in Figure 5.4, including IDENTIFICATION, ENVIRONMENT, DATA, and

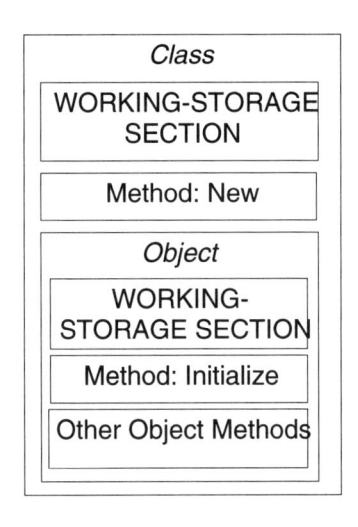

OOCOBOL Syntax

Class Structure	OOCOBOL Syntax
Class	
WORKING-STORAGE SECTION	CLASS-ID. ClassName.
Method: New	METHOD-ID. New.
Object	OBJECT-ID. ObjectName.
WORKING-STORAGE SECTION	
Method: Initialize	METHOD-ID. Initialize.
Other Object Methods	

Figure 5.2 OOCOBOL class structure.

PROCEDURE. These divisions represent the major areas of any COBOL program, and in previous versions — and up through COBOL-85 — they must appear in the order shown.

Of these four, the IDENTIFICATION and ENVIRONMENT divisions are compiler or operating environment specific and provide support for program identification, date compiled, and file control parameters. The IDENTIFICATION division has only one required paragraph, the PROGRAM ID, with all the other entries being optional. The two major paragraphs of interest in the ENVIRONMENT division are the CONFIGURATION and INPUT-OUTPUT sections.

The CONFIGURATION section includes commands for SOURCE and OBJECT-COMPUTER, as well as SPECIAL-NAMES. The INPUT-OUTPUT section supports FILE- and I-O-CONTROL, where access to files is defined from the hardware-specific viewpoint.

Most of the time spent developing and maintaining COBOL programs is in the remaining two areas, the DATA and PROCEDURE divisions. Of these, the DATA division describes all the data structures or information that the COBOL program will be using. Within the DATA DIVISION, there are sections for file descriptions (FILE SECTION), record descriptions (WORKING STORAGE SECTION), parameters shared with other programs or the operating system (LINKAGE SECTION), and reports (REPORT SECTION). Any data structure or data element used in a COBOL program must be defined in the DATA DIVISION and must have a valid data type associated with it.

```
              IDENTIFICATION DIVISION.
              CLASS-ID.        Deck_Of_Cards IS PERSISTENT
                               INHERITS CharacterArray.
              ENVIRONMENT DIVISION.
              DATA DIVISION.
              WORKING-STORAGE SECTION.
              01  Deck_Of_Cards.
                  03  Suit                    PIC X.
                       88    Hearts                      VALUE "H".
                       88    Clubs                       VALUE "C".
                       88    Dimonds                     VALUE "D".
                       88    Spades                      VALUE "S".
                  03  Value                   PIC X.
                       88    Ace                         VALUE "A".
              * Values 2 through 9 are represented as values '2' through '9'.*
                       88    Ten                         VALUE "T".
                       88    Jack                        VALUE "J".
                       88    Queen                       VALUE "Q".
                       88    King                        VALUE "K".
                  03  Deal_Status             PIC 9(4) COMP-5.
                       88    Dealt                       VALUE 1.
                       88    Not_Dealt                   VALUE 0.
              01  Card                        PIC XX.
              01  Next_Card                   PIC XX.
              01  Card_Deck                   Usage Object Deck_Of_Cards.
              01  Deck                        Usage Object Reference.
```

Figure 5.3 Deck of Cards class data division.

The PROCEDURE DIVISION represents all the functions, logic, or processing that will occur in a COBOL program. The COBOL standards support different PROCEDURE DIVISION commands, but at a basic level, each command can be of two types, PARAGRAPH or SECTION names, or valid COBOL commands or operations. Any COBOL PROCEDURE DIVISION can be subdivided into a variety of paragraphs and/or sections that can be executed (performed) in any sequence. Each PARAGRAPH or SECTION in a COBOL program represents a logical grouping of operations.

As you move towards an OOCOBOL environment, you will find the lines separating the DATA and PROCEDURE divisions blurring. Recalling the

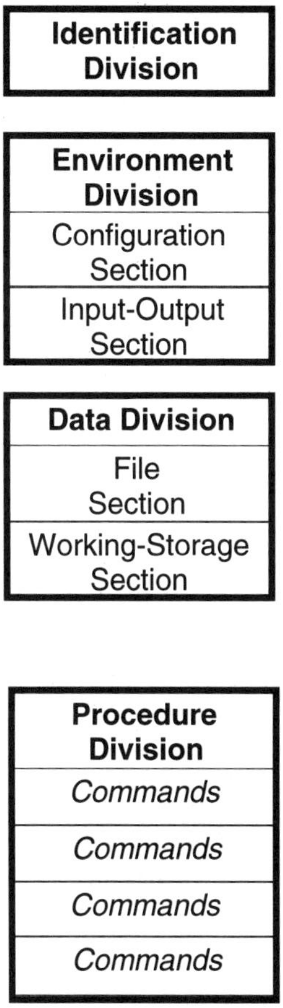

Figure 5.4 Traditional COBOL program structure.

definition of encapsulation, in OOCOBOL you bring together the data structures that represent abstract classes with the operations on those data structures into an object. An OOCOBOL object contains both DATA and PROCEDURE Divisions in a single definition.

5.2.4 Program Calling Hierarchies

There are two specific COBOL commands that allow for the transfer of control in a program: the PERFORM and CALL verbs. The PERFORM verb is used when control is transferred to an internal subroutine, while the CALL command is used when control is passed to an external routine. The COBOL PERFORM command supports a variety of control mechanisms, including

THRU, VARYING, and UNTIL, which dictate the conditions under which the subroutine is executed and when control is returned. When the PERFORM command is used, the subroutine is executed until the condition of completion is reached, and control returns to the next COBOL verb following the PERFORM statement.

The CALL verb works in a similar manner to the PERFORM command but allows external programs or subroutines to be executed from within a COBOL program. The format for the CALL command is, CALL x USING y, where x is the subroutine called and y contains any variables passed between the subroutine and the calling program. Any CALLed subroutines must define the data structures passed in their LINKAGE SECTIONs. A hierarchy of calls can be built using the PERFORM and the CALL commands to implement a structure where higher-level programs call lower-level routines. Figure 5.5 shows the two different types of subroutines in a traditional COBOL program.

In an OOCOBOL program, you define classes and objects externally to the COBOL programs that call them. These class and object definitions contain methods or operations that are similar to subroutines or functions defined in a traditional COBOL program. These methods or operations in an OOCOBOL program are defined in the same way that SECTIONS and PARAGRAPHS are specified in a traditional COBOL program. However, unlike traditional COBOL subroutines, object methods are called in a fashion similar to external subroutines (i.e., using the COBOL CALL command) and not using the PERFORM verb for internal subroutines.

Two new commands in the COBOL 97 standard that I will discuss in the following sections are CREATE, which creates an instance of an object, and INVOKE, which calls an object method.

After the class and methods for the Deck of Cards has been defined and compiled, you can create an instance of it and use it in a COBOL program. Prior to using an instance of the Deck of Cards, you must create an instance of the object using the CREATE verb, which has been added to the COBOL 97 standard. Using the deck of cards example, you might write a program that creates and invokes the deck using the following OOCOBOL command:

CREATE Deck of Cards

Another more practical approach to creating objects would be to place a method in the Deck of Cards class that creates an instance of that object. For example, invoking the method "New" results in creation of a Deck of Cards

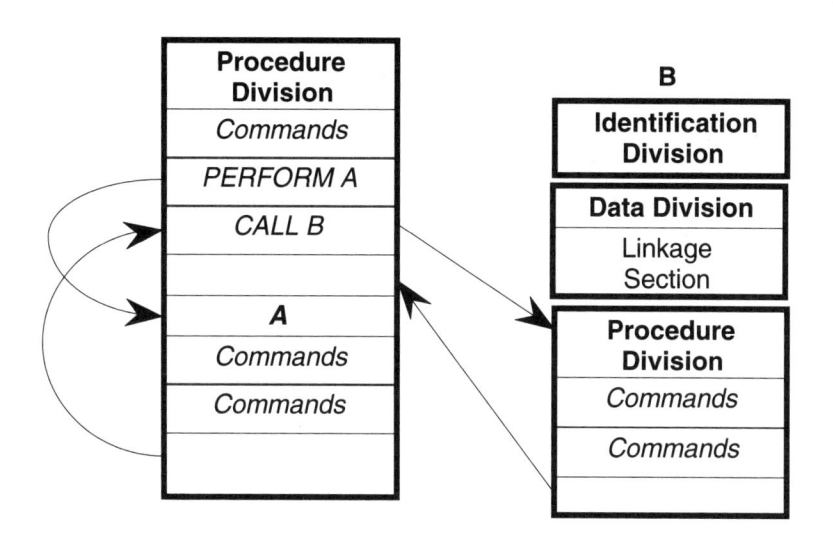

Figure 5.5
Traditional COBOL subroutines - internal and external.

object with each cards' Deal_Status set to 0 (or Not_Dealt). When called, the New method returns a deck in the Deck_Of_Cards data structure.

Continuing with the example of a deck of cards, Figure 5.6 represents some of the methods associated with the Deck of Cards class defined in Figure 5.3. Notice that I have operations for each function or service provided by the class, along with the method "New" that I described earlier. Also notice that the Deck of Cards is not persistent (i.e., is deleted after the program that creates it stops executing) and that it inherits from the class CharacterArray.

To use the Deck of Cards, you must invoke or call one of its methods after you create an instance of it, in a similar fashion to calling an external subroutine in traditional COBOL. In OOCOBOL, object methods are called using a new verb, INVOKE, with the following format: INVOKE n m USING y RETURNING z, where n is the object name, m is the method or operation name, y contains the parameters passed to the object, and z are the parameters returned by the object. An example of invoking the shuffle method for our Deck of Cards follows:

```
INVOKE DECK_OF_CARDS SHUFFLE
    USING Card_Deck
    RETURNING Deck_Of_Cards.
```

Object-Oriented Development in COBOL

```
IDENTIFICATION DIVISION.
CLASS-ID.       Deck_Of_Cards IS TRANSIANT
        INHERITS CharacterArray.
* Class definitions from Figure 5.3 go here *
METHOD-ID. "New".
LOCAL-STORAGE SECTION.
01 TEMP         USAGE OBJECT REFERENCE.
LINKAGE SECTION.
01  THE_DECK    USAGE OBJECT REFERENCE.
01  DECK_REF    USAGE OBJECT REFERENCE.
PROCEDURE DIVISION
        USING DECK_REF
        RETURNING THE_DECK.
    INVOKE Super "new" RETURNING The_Deck.
    INVOKE The_Deck "Initialize".
    EXIT PROGRAM.
END METHOD "New".

METHOD-ID. "Initialize".
WORKING-STORAGE SECTION.
01 SIZE    PIC X(4) COMP-5.
PROCEDURE DIVISION.
    MOVE 52 TO SIZE.
    INVOKE sortedcollection "ofReferences" USING SIZE
    RETURNING thecollection.
    EXIT PROGRAM.
END METHOD "Initialize".

OBJECT-ID. Cards INHERITS Deck_Of_Cards.
PROCEDURE DIVISION.
METHOD-ID. Shuffle IS PUBLIC.
* Shuffle - organizes the collection of cards in random order.
PROCEDURE DIVISION USING Deck_Of_Cards
        RETURNING Deck_Of_Cards.
    ...
END METHOD Shuffle.
END OBJECT Cards.
END CLASS Deck_Of_Cards.
```

Figure 5.6 Methods for Deck of Cards.

The Shuffle method is called to reorganize the cards into a random order before dealing them out in a game. The method is passed a reference to the Card_Deck data structure in the class and returns the new deck in the correct order for dealing.

To actually deal cards from the deck, you invoke the Deal method as follows:

INVOKE CARDS DEAL 1
      RETURNING NEXT_CARD.

In this case, the cards are dealt one at a time until there are no more cards available (i.e., all cards contain a status of Dealt) or each player has received the correct number of cards. For instance, if there are 5 players playing straight poker, each player is dealt five cards, one card at a time. In this case, the deal method is invoked five times for each player for a total of 25 cards dealt.

Looking beyond the syntax for creating or invoking objects, I now will focus on the way that object-oriented COBOL programs are structured or architected and how these programs differ from traditional COBOL applications.

5.2.5 Program Design

In traditional COBOL applications, programs are designed and built following the principles of structured design and programming. These principles partition the functions of a program into modules or subroutines where control is passed from top to bottom in a hierarchy. Using a process called *functional decomposition*, a developer might model the functions of a system using data flow diagrams (DFDs) in analysis, then translate those DFDs into a structure chart in design, and finally translate each module in a structure chart into a paragraph or section in a COBOL program.

DFDs and structure charts are visual representations of the data flow between processes defined in analysis and modules defined in design. A structure chart represents the hierarchy of modules in a program based on function, with data passed between modules shown as couples. In structured design and programming, the focus is on reduced coupling and strong cohesion between modules, modules with a single purpose, and minimized interfaces between modules. An example of a simple COBOL structure chart is shown in Figure 5.7.

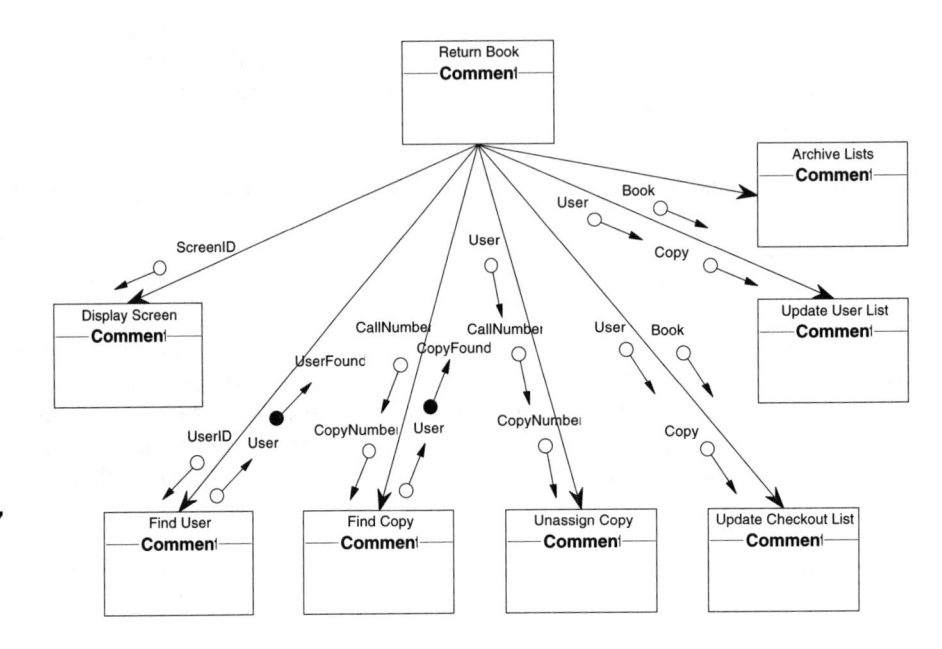

Figure 5.7
Simple structure chart.

In object-oriented programming, you partition COBOL programs into discrete objects that perform specific functions and control private data structures. Using OOCOBOL, you seek strong cohesion and reduced coupling amongst classes, and you build a controlling mechanism for the objects to interact within the application. In building OOCOBOL applications, you apply a different technique, *object decomposition*, to build a collection of objects that interact via messages to perform the functions for a specific subsystem.

In OOCOBOL, instead of a functional hierarchy of control, you have a classification hierarchy and object interactions that are represented in design using object and module diagrams. Also in design, you specify how objects interact using messages and how services can be requested between objects. An example of a Booch object diagram for the Deck of Cards example is shown in Figure 5.8. I will delve into more detail on the Booch design representations in chapter 7 and on OOCOBOL in chapters 8 and 9.

5.2.6 Development Environments

Initially targeted at mainframe computers, COBOL has moved onto all of the major development platforms including the PC — DOS, Windows, and OS/2

— and Unix. Micro Focus even offers a version of COBOL for the Apple Macintosh computer. Figure 5.9 describes some popular COBOL development products, along with the COBOL standards supported, and the environments that they operate in.

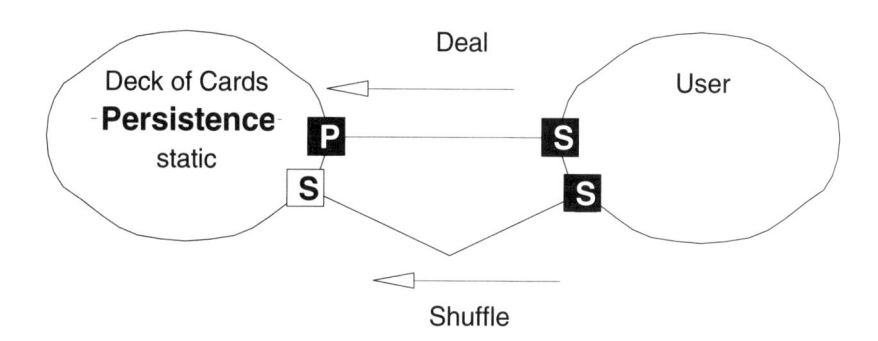

Figure 5.8 Deck of Cards Booch object diagram.

A typical COBOL development environment includes an editor, a compiler, and a linker. OOCOBOL development requires a different set of integrated tools used to build and maintain object-oriented systems. An object-oriented development environment (OODE) typically is offered with an OOPL, such as the Object COBOL Option from Micro Focus, and includes the following components:

- Class libraries: a set of generic objects, containing variables and methods, that perform specific functions.
- Frameworks: a set of application-specific class libraries developed for a specific category of applications, like a GUI.
- Browsers: programs that permit navigation through class libraries and show relationships between classes (inherits), messages, methods for a class, variables, senders of a message, implementors of a message, and the actual code that implements a method.
- Editors: programs that allow OOPL code to be created, modified, and extended in an interpreted environment.
- Inspectors: allow examination and editing of an object's instance variables.
- Profilers: analyze a methods performance (i.e., show where the method spends its time) and trace messages and their action in a system.
- Debuggers: control the execution of a running program and allow data structures to be examined and modified.
- Incremental compilers and linkers: support repetitive compile and link steps and include affected objects and methods.

Vendor, product & phone number	COBOL standards supported	Development platforms supported	Deployment platforms supported
AcuCOBOL - AcuCOBOL-85 (619) 689-7220	COBOL 85	PC (DOS and Windows)	DOS, Windows, and Unix
Computer Associates - CA-Realia II Workbench (516) 342-5224	COBOL 74 and 85	PC DOS and Windows	IBM MVS, VM, PC DOS, Windows and OS/2
DEC COBOL	COBOL	DEC VAX/VMS, Ultrix and OSF/1	DEC VAX/VMS, Ultrix and OSF/1
Hewlett Packard - COBOL (303) 229-3800	COBOL 85	HP/UX	HP/UX X Widows System version 11
IBM - COBOL and COBOL II (800) IBM-DIRECT	COBOL 74, 85 and 97*	IBM MVS, VSE, VM, AIX and OS/2	IBM MVS, VSE, VM, OS/400, AIX, and OS/2
Liant Software - RM/COBOL-85 (800) RM COBOL	COBOL 74 and 85	PC DOS, OS/2, and Unix	PC DOS, OS/2 and Unix
MicroFocus - COBOL Workbench (415) 856-4161	COBOL 74, 85 and 97*	PC (DOS, Windows and OS/2), Unix, and Macintosh	IBM MVS, VM, OS/400, PC DOS, Windows and OS/2
MBP - Visual COBOL (800) 231-6342	COBOL 74 and 85	PC DOS, Windows, OS/2, Unix and DEC VAX/VMS	DOS, Windows, OS/2, Unix and DEC VAX/VMS
Unisys - COBOL	COBOL 74 and 85	A Series and U Series	A Series and U Series

* support for the proposed OOCOBOL standard in an optional product

Figure 5.9 COBOL products available.

- Configuration management tools: manage the objects, classes, and methods and control modification to them; track changes, identify affected objects, etc.

Examples of object-oriented development environments include NeXTStep (Objective-C), ObjectCenter (C++), and ObjectWorks (Smalltalk).

NeXTStep from NeXT is a popular and sophisticated OODE that includes a window server, a workspace manager, an application kit, and an interface builder. A NeXTStep application is created by building a user interface, defining or enhancing the underlying objects and their behavior, and implementing the objects. Within NeXTStep, the central object that provides an application structure is Application, which contains an event-loop that processes GUI messages.

ObjectCenter from CenterLine provides a set of tools that includes static and run-time error detection, debugging, incremental linkers, and graphical browsers for classes, data structures, projects, and cross references between code and variables. Objectworks from ParcPlace includes incremental compilers and linkers, source code browsers, class browsers, debuggers for source code, and an object inspector.

5.3 Developing OOCOBOL Applications

As I already have shown, traditional COBOL application development involves some basic requirements definition, followed by design of the system — which might include database design, screen layout definitions, etc. — then the actual programming. If CICS is used, a screen development effort might include modeling and specifying the flow of control between screens, common program function key assignments, etc.

A traditional COBOL development effort might follow the waterfall development life cycle described in chapter 4, or might include prototyping. In some cases, COBOL development might follow a structured development technique, perhaps structured design or even structured analysis, and result in a structured programming solution. Most likely, COBOL development is done using an *ad hoc* approach to software production and follows no formal development process.

Recalling the basic principles of software engineering from chapter 4, object-oriented development in COBOL represents a significant change from the traditional way of development COBOL applications. As you develop OOCOBOL solutions, you draw on the principles of software engineering developed over the past 40 years and make use of the practices that have proven to reduce maintenance costs and improve software quality.

These practices include the use of a formal development method, supported by a set of notations, guidelines, and automated tools. As you develop applications in OOCOBOL, you also must strive to add to your existing library of reusable components. You follow the heuristics of sound software engineering in using information hiding, decomposition, abstraction, generalization, and an iterative, incremental development process.

In the sections that follow, I'll identify issues to be considered as you progress through your object-oriented development effort for COBOL. Specifically, I will address issues including analysis and design, CASE tool support, prototyping, class library use, and other OOCOBOL implementation factors. I will introduce these issues in preparation for a more detailed discussion of object-oriented development in the next four chapters.

5.3.1 Analysis and Design for OOCOBOL

As you move to object-oriented development in COBOL, you take a different approach to the development process, not only in the programming phase, but in analysis and design. Remembering the discussion on object-oriented analysis and design in chapter 4, you will begin the development process by defining the requirements for our system and reviewing these requirements with the users. Once the requirements have been specified, and hopefully documented in some form, you can use any number of methods to identify potential classes, objects, attributes, methods, and messages in the problem domain.

I will discuss the process of object-oriented analysis in more detail in the next chapter, but your goal in analysis is to create an object model that reflects your understanding of the key abstractions and mechanisms in the problem domain. This object model will consist of the classes, objects, attributes, methods, and messages required for the domains under study. As you examine the problem domain, you also will seek to identify and classify reusable components and to use prototyping to help your users better understand the system that you plan to deliver.

From the object model, you consider available reusable components that can be used to implement a system that supports the requirements specified. In object-oriented design, you begin by looking at the classes you already have to see how they can be modified or extended and mapped to those required for our application. As you find reusable components, you refine them, describe their interaction with other objects in more detail, design their internal mechanisms, and package them into a design specification. I will look at the process of object-oriented design and popular methods in chapter 7.

5.3.2 CASE Tools

Throughout the development process, you need to collect, describe, communicate, and manage your findings somewhere. In most cases, you would choose to use a set of automated tools to manage and control the resulting work products or artifacts created.

CASE tools support formal development methods by automating the collection and management of the artifacts that result when these methods are applied. Traditional CASE tools support function- or data-oriented methods, such as DSSD, Information Engineering, or Yourdon Structured Design. OOA/D CASE tools work in a similar fashion but support techniques for object-oriented development. A partial list of available OOA/D CASE tools is shown in Figure 5.10.

For those organizations that already are using traditional methods and CASE tools, the major CASE vendors currently are not supporting object-oriented development techniques. At press time, none of the major CASE vendors, including Knowledgeware, Texas Instruments, Andersen Consulting, Bachman, CGI, and IBM were not supporting any of the OOA/D methods in their tool sets. The one exception to this is Intersolv, which has released support for selected OOA/D methods in their Excelerator product set.

One question that comes to mind when considering OOA/D CASE support is: What functionality should these products support? The following list describes some generic requirements for OOA/D CASE tools:

- Notational support (diagrams, symbols, connections, etc.)
- Textual specifications for classes, objects, attributes, methods, etc. (templates)
- Syntax checking for notations and specifications

Product & Vendor	Platforms	OOA/D Methods
Atriom from Semaphore	IBM PC (Windows)	Booch, Martin/Odell & OOMT
BOCS from Berard Software Engineering	IBM PC (Windows & OS/2)	EVB (Berard)
Excelerator II OOA/D from Intersolv	IBM PC (Windows & OS/2)	ObjectOry, Martin/Odell, Rumbaugh & RDD
MacAnalyst & MacDesiger from Excel Software	Macintosh	Booch, Coad/Yourdon, OOMT & Shlaer/Mellor (OOA)
ObjectMaker, CGen & AdaGen from Mark V Systems	IBM PC (Windows), Macintosh, Unix (Sun & HP/Apollo), and VMS	Bailin, Booch, Buhr, Coad/Yourdon, Colbert & OOMT
ObjectOry from Objective Systems	IBM PC (Windows) and Unix (DEC, HP, IBM and Sun)	ObjectOry (Jacobson et al)
ObjectPlus & ParadigmPlus from Protosoft	IBM PC (Windows & OS/2) and Unix (Sun, HP/Apollo & IBM)	Booch, EVB, Fusion, HOOD, and OOMT
ObjectTool from Object Intl.	IBM PC and Unix (Sun)	Coad/Yourdon
OMTool from Martin Marietta Advanced Concept Center	IBM PC (Windows) and Unix (Sun & HP)	OOMT
Paladian Design tool from Paladio Software	IBM PC (Windows)	Booch
PowerTools from ICONIX	Macintosh	Booch, Coad/Yourdon, OOMT, ObjectOry & Shlaer/Mellor (OOA)
Rose & Insight from Rational	IBM PC (Windows & OS/2) & Unix (IBM & Sun)	Booch
Select OMT from Select Software Tools	IBM PC	
System Architect from Popkin Software & Systems	IBM PC (Windows & OS/2)	Booch, Coad/Yourdon & Shlaer/Mellor (OOA)
Teamwork from Cadre Technologies	IBM PC (Windows & OS/2), Unix (Sun, HP/Apollo & IBM) & VMS	HOOD, OOMT & Shlaer/Mellor (OOA & RD)
TurboCASE from StructSoft	Macintosh	Shlaer/Mellor (OOA & RD)

Figure 5.10 Some OOA/D CASE tools.

- Multiple-view/update support - static, dynamic, internal and external - for models and specs
- Repository support including multi-user access, security restrictions, requirements tracking, object management, configuration management, etc.
- Verification checking, including cross-diagram, completeness and consistency checking
- Integrated browsers, inspectors, incremental compilers, etc.
- Class/object tracking for reuse management
- Object-oriented and structured support
- GUI prototyping support
- Generation or assembly of classes/objects from specifications
- Incorporation of external class libraries into the repository (Reverse Engineering)

In the examples, I will use the Coad/Yourdon OOA method and the Booch OOD method, supported by a Windows-based CASE product from Popkin Software and Systems. System Architect is used in all our examples primarily because it provides sound CASE support at a reasonable price. System Architect 3.0 supports both object-oriented and traditional structured methods, user-defined repository elements, has a GUI prototyping facility, a SQL-based reporting language, and retails for under $1500.

5.3.3 Prototyping and OOCOBOL

As I introduced in chapter 4, prototyping provides an excellent method for gaining insight into the functional requirements of users. Prototyping also helps users better understand a software system, because it is delivered in a format that they already are familiar with, and this helps them provide more detailed information on requirements earlier in the development process.

As I also showed in chapter 4, any object-oriented SDLC can incorporate prototyping in analysis, design, and programming as a tool for delivering portions of the application in increments. Recalling the discussion on object-oriented design, you take a subset of the application, perhaps a subsystem, design it fully, including the key interfaces with external subsystems, then implement it in OOCOBOL, unit test it, and deliver it to the user community for their review. In this fashion, each subsystem is delivered as a working prototype of portions of the entire application over a period of time. As each new subsystem is delivered, it must be integrated with previously delivered subsystems, and a final system acceptance test is required before the application is considered complete.

If you are developing an application for a graphical environment, perhaps under Windows or OS/2 Presentation Manager, you might choose to take advantage of available GUI development tools in building our prototypes. While these products often allow design and generation of only the user interface portion of an application, they can be used during analysis and design to create external views or prototypes of the system. These types of GUI prototypes help define perhaps the most important aspect of a system, the user interface, earlier in the development process.

I will discuss GUI prototyping tools in more detail in chapter 9. One possible GUI prototyping product that works well with an existing OOCOBOL compiler is Dialog System from Micro Focus. For instance, the ATM example might incorporate a user interface developed separately in Smalltalk or Dialog System. Using one of these products, you could build the graphical components of the ATM, design their underlying functions and behavior, then deliver this portion as a subsystem that interfaces with the ATM. More on this approach in chapter 9.

5.3.4 Other Issues for OOCOBOL Development

In addition to the issues that I have covered in this chapter, there are many additional factors that must be considered before programming in OOCOBOL. While I will cover the majority of these issues in detail in chapters 8 and 9, I will introduce some of the factors here for consideration.

Because objects can be created dynamically in OOCOBOL using the CREATE command, should you allow any program that uses an object to create it in this fashion? As already mentioned, you also could provide each class with a base method, "New," which creates an instance of the object and returns it for initialization. Recall that you also can reference objects as data types in the COBOL DATA DIVISION, but if you do, you need to associate the objects that you create with them to the data elements. Objects can be dynamically created and associated with data elements that reference the objects by calling the New method and passing the data element name.

Another factor to be pondered is how external data structures can be used within OOCOBOL programs. The OOCOBOL standard includes support for intrinsic data types that map to traditional data elements (i.e., PIC X and PIC 9). This is important because intrinsic data types can be used in COBOL files while class data types cannot. Remember that OOCOBOL programs can continue reading and writing files using the old COBOL commands. Consider the issue of SQL DBMS access in an OOCOBOL program. In chapter 9, I will use an example — the library problem — to show how a RDBMS can be used to store and retrieve objects. I chose to use SQL to store and manage access to instances of Books, Users, and Copies in their methods.

As you build applications in OOCOBOL, you also must decide whether to use static or dynamic binding of objects and methods. For simplicity of learning, I recommend that all OOCOBOL programs use the static binding provided in the language. Recalling the discussion of these binding types, you can bind objects with their methods at compile time using the USAGE OBJECT option. To bind objects and methods at execution time, you would use the USAGE UNIVERSAL option.

Finally, you should consider using existing classes in OOCOBOL. I postpone a complete discussion on classes in OOCOBOL until chapters 7, 8, and 9, but the COBOL 97 standard as it is defined in 1994 does not contain any definition of available classes. Given the need in object-oriented design for good reusable classes, you can hardly make the case for reuse without a library of components available.

5.4 The Evolving OOCOBOL Standard

At the time that this book was being written, the OOCOBOL was being developed by X3J4 but still was undergoing change. At the same time, Micro Focus made available a working OOCOBOL product that allowed development under DOS, Windows, and OS/2. While Micro Focus was a key player in the X3J4.1 committee, the standard that results from public comment might be significantly different from the one defined at the time this book was written.

As a result of this, I have chosen to provide our examples in compliance with the existing (i.e., as of May 1994) OOCOBOL standard. The OOCOBOL standard probably will change, and the Micro Focus COBOL product that currently supports object-orientation already is different from the standard as it exists. One basic difference between the OOCOBOL standard and the Micro Focus product is in their support for inheritance. The Micro Focus Object COBOL Option does not support multiple inheritance in its initial version (1.5) while the draft committee standard does support it.

The X3J4.1 COBOL committee consisted of representatives from industry and vendors of COBOL products created in 1989 to investigate object-orientation for the COBOL language. The X3J4.1 committee included members from the following corporations:

- American Express
- Computer Associates
- Hewlett-Packard
- Hitachi Software Engineering
- IBM
- Micro Focus
- Microsoft
- Unisys

At the time this book went to publication, there were several unresolved issues in the COBOL 97 standard including support for object persistence, garbage collection, and class libraries.

Perhaps the most important aspect of the OOCOBOL standard that still is undefined is in the area of class library support. As this book went to press, the X3J4 committee identified several types of classes as critical for OOCOBOL development, including collections, callbacks, file access, persistence, exceptions, intrinsics, string manipulations, and non-COBOL interfaces. Additional classes that might be pursued in the future by the X3J4 committee include memory allocation, GUI, report generation, networking and communication, and intrinsic functions.

5.5 References

[OBI94a] Obin, R., *Extract from X3J4.1 Meeting 7 Minutes*, Micro Focus, 1994.
[OBI94b] Obin, R., *Full Revision Working Paper WR-730.2*, Micro Focus, 1994.
[OBI93]   Obin, R., *Object-Oriented Features Summary* (version 4), Micro Focus, October 7, 1993.
[X3J93]   X3J4.1 Report, *Object-Oriented Extensions to COBOL*, March 10, 1993.

Chapter 6

Object-Oriented Analysis

Analysis, as I described it in chapter 4, is the process of defining a system in sufficient detail, usually delivering a textual document written by or with the help of the eventual users of the system completely. During analysis, you seek to understand the system. Using the simplified SDLC in Figure 4.1, Analysis is synonymous with Definition.

With an object-oriented approach to analysis, you seek to model the system under study using objects and messages. An object model results from this analysis, which describes the key abstractions and mechanisms in the problem domain.

There are a variety of methods described by books, and papers and taught in workshops for performing an analysis using objects. In this chapter, I will introduce the concepts of modeling systems using objects, review popular object-oriented analysis (OOA) methods, discuss the Coad/Yourdon OOA method, which I used for the example problems, and any issues in applying this method. I will conclude by covering the movement from OOA to object-oriented design.

6.1 Introduction

Object-oriented analysis is the process of analyzing or modeling the requirements of a system with objects and messages. Traditional OOA methods identify system components, their relationships, attributes, and behaviors.

As with any analysis, the purpose of OOA is to thoroughly understand the problem domain. Remembering the simple development life cycle that I introduced in chapter 4, analysis is concerned with fully defining the problem domain. One probable outcome of OOA is an object model, which will define and describe the classes, objects, attributes, and services or operations in the problem domain.

Remembering the discussion in chapter 3 of a formal development process, the outcomes of the OOA phase also are used to communicate, verify, and track the development process. A manager, for instance, might run a variety of reports in a CASE tool to verify that all classes, objects, attributes, and services have been fully defined and satisfy the stated system requirements. The diagrams or notations that I will be using in the OOA examples also help to communicate the structure and behavior of the systems to everyone involved.

The object model might have many distinct views or perspectives, depending on the problem domain. For instance, if you are working on a reactive or real-time system, the dynamic view of an application might be of great interest to you. Likewise, if you are building a system that will use distributed computing and a graphical user interface (GUI), you might need to study the user interface and develop a prototype to define in more detail the user interface requirements for the system. In other cases, you can define a static, dynamic, and functional view of the classes and objects in the problem domain. Different OOA methods call for different object model contents, but, this phase generically should deliver an object model [HOL91] describing:

- Classes and relationships between classes
- Class operations or methods
- Constraints on classes, methods, and relationships
- Class behavior
- Rationale for each abstraction or mechanism (how, when, where, and why)
- Traceability back to the user requirements

When you consider relationships in OOA, you consider how the classes and objects in the problem domain can be associated or related. As with traditional data modeling, there are a variety of different types of relationships in an object model. These include *inherits (generalization)*, *uses*, and *part-of (aggregation)*. Coad/Yourdon call these relationships *structures*; others use the terms sup/supertypes or abstract data types (ADTs).

While notations vary between OOA techniques, some type of class/object diagram represents pictorially the objects and classes in the problem domain with supporting textual information stored about each class and object in a dictionary or repository. Additionally, dynamic information about objects can be represented using finite state machines or object life history diagrams. At the lowest level in the object model, definitions of the services of each object and the interactions between the objects should be described in a diagram or textual specification.

An object model has four major elements: abstraction, encapsulation, modularity and hierarchy. Three minor elements of the object model: typing, concurrency and persistence.
G. Booch [BOO89].

The primary purpose of the object model is to communicate to both humans and machines the functionality of the system using a defined method. To be effective, an object model must have a formal basis that supports it (including vehicles for verifying its content, completeness, and consistency), a method that allows it to be created (identification of parts, partitioning, etc.), and diagrams or notations that can facilitate communication of its structural and behavioral representations.

Regardless of the method or approach that you use in analysis, you should always be cognizant of the overlap between the tasks in analysis and design. Many authors have written about the blending of analysis and design, and it is difficult to know for any project at which point analysis ends and design begins. In most cases, the OOA/D process will be iterative and evolutionary, such that what you learn early in the process will need to be modified as you move forward into design and implementation.

Remembering the discussion in chapter 4 about prototyping and iteration, the OOA phase will deliver definitions of classes and objects that then can be further defined in the context of the implementation environment in the OOD phase. Also remembering that OOA/D can be accomplished by diverse groups that need understand only the interface between objects or domains, you can have ongoing tasks of OOA, OOD, OOP, testing, and implementation at any time. These issues represent challenges to managers in the areas of communication between team members and changing object model components.

6.2 Identifying Objects, Classes, Attributes and Operations

Because the goal of OOA is to develop a model of the objects, attributes, and relationships in the problem domain, I must begin with a discussion of identifying key abstractions and mechanisms. There are many tools and techniques available for identifying problem domain components, each with their own strengths and weaknesses. What are some guidelines or practices that you might use?

In this section I will investigate several methods for finding classes and objects, which often is the most difficult part of object-oriented development. In practice, you might find that a combination of the methods described in this section helps you gain an adequate understanding of the problem domain that you need prior to proceeding into design.

Booch [BOO91] offers advice on finding key abstractions, which he believes involves two separate, but related tasks: *discovery* and *invention*. Discovery is the process of recognizing the abstractions used by domain experts, while invention involves creating new classes and objects that are required for design and implementation of a solution.

6.2.1 Data Modeling

Many popular OOA/D methods use traditional data or information modeling techniques to help find potential objects and classes. Because data structures form the basis for objects and classes, you could use abstract data types to begin to classify the problem domain into appropriate subject areas. Mapping entities in a data model to objects or classes in an object model is a convenient approach but not without its drawbacks. By using entity-relationship diagrams (ERDs), you can help to identify entities, potential classes and objects, attributes, and relationships, and this can be a first step in the object identification process.

Of the popular OOA methods, Shlaer/Mellor, Coad/Yourdon, Booch, and Rumbaugh recommend or use some form of data or information modeling to create an initial list of potential classes, objects, and attributes. In the case of Shlaer/Mellor, Coad/Yourdon, and Rumbaugh, the information model is the object model, with some slightly different relationships represented and notations used.

Some in the industry have criticized the use of data models for finding classes and objects because this approach does not recognize generalization and aggregation relationships. Also, data models can not represent or support the concept of encapsulation and focus only on the attributes of objects, and not their behavior. This can lead to basing inheritance structures based on common attributes and not on behavior or services.

One interesting study [SHA93] compared data or information modeling methods with those that focus on object collaboration and responsibilities and found:

The responsibility-driven method (RDD) was shown to produce a design that was much less complex than that produced by the data-driven method. In particular, the responsibility-driven design exhibited much greater cohesion of classes and much less coupling between them.

6.2.2 Domain Analysis

Domain: a sphere of activity or interest; field.
[Webster]

Domain analysis (DA) is another popular technique for identifying classes and objects for the problem space. DA is a process where experts in the problem area are interviewed and information is collected from them with the hope of specifying the subject area in depth. In most cases, the results of these interviews are used to build a domain model that contains all of the key abstractions of the problem domain. DA relies on the ability of domain experts to identify the objects, functions, and relationships in the problem space and of the analysts to define and represent these definitions in model form.

One goal of DA is to identify and structure information for reusability. In this sense, DA is a process by which information is identified, captured, and organized for reuse. Secondarily, DA seeks to develop and evolve an information infrastructure for organizational reuse.

By using DA, organizations can identify common features for specific domains, select and abstract the objects and operations that characterize those features, and create procedures that automate those procedures.
R. Prieto-Diaz [PRI90].

Prieto-Diaz has defined a four-step domain analysis methodology that consists of the following tasks:

- Acquire domain knowledge: define the scope and identify sources of knowledge
- Functional analysis: identify major functional components, relationships, and propose a generic architecture
- Identify objects and operations: perform an analysis of the vocabulary searching for nouns, verbs (objects and functions), and relationships, define standard descriptions of components
- Define domain models: develop a common architecture, map the component descriptors to the proposed architecture, refine, and update the architecture as needed

At a generic level, domain analysis is composed of three simple steps that are iteratively applied:

- Identify reusable components
- Using abstraction and generalization, classify these components for reuse
- Catalog the components in a reuse library

Domain analysis is not without its own weaknesses, including its requirement for modeling the domains first, followed by application development, and a lack of standard notations for domain models.

6.2.3 Informal Analysis of Textual Requirements Documents

Grady Booch [BOO89] on identifying objects:

Read the specification of the software that you want to build. Underline the verbs if you are after procedural code, the nouns if you aim for an object-oriented program.

Another technique for finding potential classes, objects, attributes, and operations is to examine a written (textual) description of the problem domain and extract the nouns and verbs. Nouns in the problem description can be considered as potential classes, objects, or attributes, while verbs can be potential operations or services of objects.

Deciding which nouns will be modeled as classes, objects, or attributes is subjective and sometimes difficult. Using a prototype to facilitate communication with potential users of a system can help developers to derive or identify the key abstractions. The prototype helps users of the system to understand how it will behave, and they can describe in detail changes to the prototype based on abstractions or mechanisms that are missing.

As with data modeling, some in the industry have criticized the use of textual documents as a source for potential classes and objects because the inference is that these documents accurately reflect the problem domain and are mostly unambiguous. Adelle Goldberg and Kenny Rubin have stated their feelings along these lines in [RUB92]:

In addition, this approach (using nouns to identify objects or classes) has a strong bias toward the tangible aspects of a problem. Tangible objects are often important to recognize and capture. However, just as often, the conceptual objects have significant influence on the structure of the analysis results.

6.3 Popular OOA Methods

There are many popular formal methods for analysis that model the problem domain using objects, messages, and inheritance. Some of these are documented in books and taught in formal workshops, while others are described in technical papers or used by consulting organizations. As with other development methods, OOA techniques vary in their philosophy, notation, representation, and process.

Some of the more popular OOA methods are shown here:

- Coad/Yourdon
- Martin/Odell (PTech)
- Object Behavior Analysis
- Object-Oriented Modeling Technique
- Shlaer/Mellor
- Synthesis

In this section, I will review some of the more popular OOA methods before describing the one that I chose to use for the example problems so that the reader can become more familiar with alternative methods of analysis using objects. I also will provide a sidebar at the end of chapter 7 comparing OOA/D methods.

6.3.1 Shlaer/Mellor OOA

Sally Shlaer and Steven Mellor have defined techniques for object-oriented analysis and design and described them in their books [SHL88] [SHL92]. Their OOA technique is loosely based on the previous work of Paul Ward and Mellor in real-time structured analysis. The Shlaer/Mellor OOA approach uses the same notations as the Ward/Mellor method, but with a very different focus: instead of focusing on the control behavior of a system, Shlaer/Mellor focus on the information collected and used by a system. Their design method incorporates recursive design and their notation uses modifications to traditional structure charts.

The steps in the Shlaer/Mellor OOA method include:

1. Analyze the problem domain by defining domains and subsystems by decomposing the problem domain into conceptually distinct domains.
2. Build an information model that identifies the objects, relationships, and attributes, along with the multiplicity and conditionally specifications.

3. For each active object in the information model, create a state model (state-transition diagram or STD) that contains all of the potential states in the object's life cycle and the events that cause transitions from one state to another.
4. Create an object communication diagram (OCD) that illustrates all of the object state models and communication between objects. For each action create a data flow diagram (DFD) that shows all the processes for the action, and the data flows among the processes and data stores.
5. For each state transition in the STDs, create a DFD and describe the processing that causes the state to change using process specifications. Processes in the DFDs can create events that appear in the STDs.
6. Generate reports from the diagrams in the form of an objects/attributes list, an event list, and a relationship list. Each object in the information model becomes a data store in a DFD.
7. State the boundaries of the system — the imaginary line between the abstract system and the portion outside the system. This distinction should be based on external events that cross this boundary.
8. Create an external event list.
9. Create a functional requirements document and back this document up with the abstract system models created in the Systems Analysis phase.

Shlaer/Mellor Notation

A. *Domain charts* are used to describe the different domains in the application.
B. *Information structure diagrams* are entity-relationship diagrams where each entity is an object and relationships indicate class and object connections in the form of inheritance and instantiation.
C. *State transition diagrams* (STDs) are built for each object depicting their life cycle in states.
D. *Object communication diagrams* (OCDs) are data flow diagrams where object states are shown along with communication between objects. OCDs describe the processing that causes an object state to change using process specifications.

6.3.2 Object-Oriented Modeling Technique (OMT)

Rumbuagh, Blaha, Premerlani, Eddy, and Lorensen of General Electric defined a technique for OOA/D that is similar to the Shlaer/Mellor method in its use of notations and techniques. Both methods begin by building a model of the objects and classes in the problem domain — Shlaer/Mellor call theirs an Information Model, while Rumbaugh *et al* call theirs an Object Model. [RUM91].

Both Rumbaugh and Shlaer/Mellor use an ERD to represent object models and attach finite state machines for the objects and/or classes to model the life of the object or its time-dependent behavior. Rumbaugh *et al* prefer Harrel's Statecharts, while Shlaer/Mellor use state transition diagrams to represent the dynamic aspect of their model. Both Shlaer/Mellor and Rumbaugh also use data flow diagrams to depict the functional aspects of a system.

The Rumbaugh object model notation allows objects and classes to be shown, allows support generalization/specialization connections, and supports part of/aggregation connections between classes and objects. OMT also supports instantiation connections with an instantiation relationship, and messages with propagation of operations.

OMT provides limited design support with OOD actually performed as part of OOP and design issues that should be addressed are defining an architecture (i.e., transaction driven vs. event driven, DBMS vs. flat file, etc.) and adding minor additional details to the existing object models to support object design.

OMT Notation

A. *Object Models* (entity-relationship diagrams) represent the objects and relationships.
B. *Statecharts* show the dynamic behavior or the life cycle of an object.
C. *Data flow diagrams* depict the functional aspects of an object.

6.3.3 Object Behavior Analysis (OBA)

Adele Goldberg and Kenny Rubin of ParcPlace have described an object-oriented development method in a CACM paper [RUB92]. Their method, Object Behavior Analysis (OBA), models systems as collections of interacting objects, with each object having its own defined set of behaviors and attributes.

OBA focuses on the behaviors of system components, especially on which objects initiate actions and which only participate in behaviors. OBA also seeks to identify and model contractual relationships between objects whenever an objects agrees to provide services to another object. In this case, the object that is responsible for invoking the service of the other object is the initiator, while the service provider is the participant.

OBA consists of five basic tasks:

1. Define the context of the system for analysis.
2. Understand the problem domain by focusing on object behaviors.
3. Define objects based on their behaviors.
4. Classify objects and their relationships.
5. Model the dynamics of the system.

OBA is an iterative method with multiple entry points that can be accomplished in parallel. OBA can also be proceeded by data modeling, enterprise modeling, or domain analysis, which can identify basic objects or entities.

OBA Notation

A. *Scripts of use scenarios* that identify the initiator, the action performed, the participant, and the service delivered. Tables, spreadsheets, or text used to represent these scripts.
B. *Glossaries of object collaborations* (for initiators and participants) that define the parties involved, their definition, role, and other information. These glossaries are developed for objects, services, attributes, and states, and are similar to the simple data dictionaries that often are used in structured methods.
C. *Object modeling cards* that define objects, classes they inherit from, attributes, services, contractual relationships, and references to other artifacts.
D. *Object relationship diagrams*, which define the contractual and organizational relationships between objects. Alternative notations can be used to represent these relationships, from Booch, Coad/Yourdon, OOMT, etc.
E. *System and Object life cycle diagrams*, primarily in the form of Statecharts, action diagrams, petri nets, or state-transition diagrams.

6.4 Coad/Yourdon Object-Oriented Analysis

Another popular technique for Object-Oriented Analysis and Design is from Peter Coad and Ed Yourdon. The Coad/Yourdon OOA/D approach is defined in their books [COA91] and [COA92] and is similar to the Shlaer/Mellor and OMT methods described earlier. I have chosen to use the Coad/Yourdon OOA method for the example problems to explain the OOA process using the Library and ATM problems.

Coad and Yourdon define object-oriented as objects, classification, inheritance, and communication with messages. Their approach to development is based on information and semantic data modeling, and concepts of object-oriented programming languages (i.e., generalization and aggregation).

Their method is based on identifying objects and attributes, classification and assembly structures, and message, between objects. Coad/Yourdon define objects as instances of something interesting in the problem space, and these objects can be classified by their behavior.

6.4.1 Introduction

The Coad/Yourdon method is strongly oriented towards a data view of the application domain. This approach is appropriate for applications that have strong or complex data structures, including the Library problem, but might be inappropriate or inadequate for applications that have weak or simple data structures but complex behavior, such as the ATM problem.

One overriding principle of the Coad/Yourdon method is that there are several different views or levels of an object model. The five views in the Coad/Yourdon method reflect the levels of abstraction in the problem domain and include classes and objects, attributes, subjects, structures, and services. As we build an object model, you continue to specify more of the details of the model at these different levels. The five views also must be integrated and verified for completeness and consistency when the object model is complete, and a CASE tool can help make this process more practical and efficient.

The Coad/Yourdon method also uses a modeling notation that probably is very familiar to most COBOL programmers: a modified entity-relationship diagram (ERD). The ERD has been used extensively over the years to represent the data or database structures for systems and should be recognizable to most COBOL developers. The ERD consists of symbols for entities and connecting lines for relationships that represent the associations between entities.

6.4.2 Technique

The tasks in the Coad/Yourdon Object-Oriented Analysis method are shown in Figure 6.1 and include:

Flow diagram

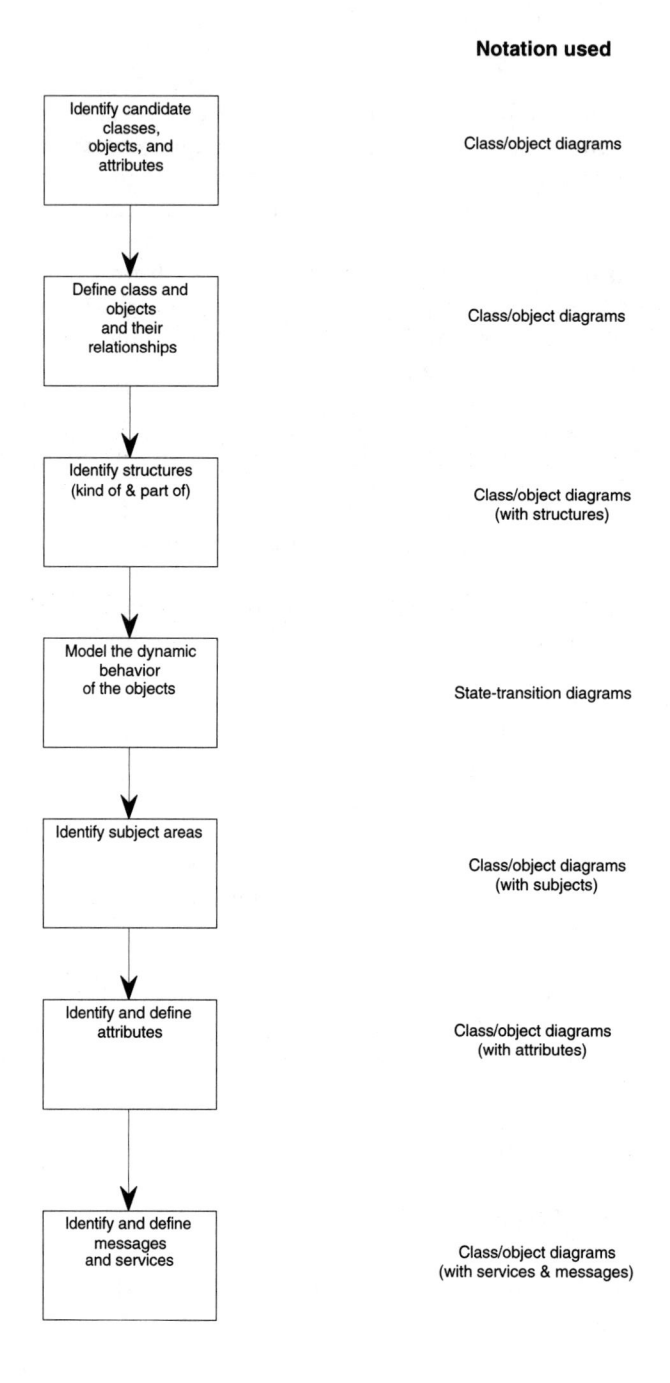

Step	Notation used
Identify candidate classes, objects, and attributes	Class/object diagrams
Define class and objects and their relationships	Class/object diagrams
Identify structures (kind of & part of)	Class/object diagrams (with structures)
Model the dynamic behavior of the objects	State-transition diagrams
Identify subject areas	Class/object diagrams (with subjects)
Identify and define attributes	Class/object diagrams (with attributes)
Identify and define messages and services	Class/object diagrams (with services & messages)

Figure 6.1
Coad/Yourdon OOA/D life cycle.

1. Identify classes and objects using an object layer ERD.
2. Define class and object relationships using an object layer ERD.
3. Identify structures using a structure layer ERD.
4. Model the dynamic behavior of the objects using STDs.
5. Define subjects using a subject layer ERD.
6. Define attributes (and instance connections) using an attribute layer ERD.
7. Define services (and message connections) using a service layer ERD; Coad/Yourdon define two types of messages or interactions: between a user of a system and the system and between objects in the system.

6.4.3 Representation and Notation

The outcomes of the Coad/Yourdon technique are the representations, in this case an object model, consisting of definitions of classes, objects, attributes, relationships, etc., and the notations used are those specified by Coad/Yourdon. These notations define a five-layered object model including:

A. Subjects: mechanisms for controlling which portions of a model are considered by the developer at a given time; subjects are similar to domains as defined by Shlaer/Mellor and others.
B. Classes/objects: abstractions of data structures and exclusive processing on the data.
C. Structures: manage complexity and inheritance; two primary forms of structure are inheritance classification (*generalization / specialization*), which show class and member relationships, and assembly (*aggregations*), which show whole/part relationships.
D. Attributes: data elements or instance variables (fields).
E. Services: operations performed by objects.

6.5 Sample Problem Discussion

As a first step in your analysis, you should consider the problem domain of the systems under study. In the first example, the Library is part of a larger domain, that being a university. As with all universities, you would include systems that support faculty, staff, students, administrators, etc. While it is not specified in the problem description, you might have to consider the interaction of the Library system with other, external systems. These might include student information systems, financial systems, billing systems for library services, or even administrative systems that manage staff and faculty information.

One tool that can help you consider the higher-level abstractions, including subsystems, in the Library problem is the Shlaer/Mellor domain chart. Remembering the description of this diagram in section 6.3.1 I will use this notation in the examples. Figure 6.2 shows the resulting Shlaer/Mellor domain chart for the Library system. The figure shows that the *Library system* interacts with several domains, including a *User Interface*, *Reporting*, and *List Services*, as well as the *Software Architecture* for the system. *User Interface* and *List Services* interact with the *Operating system* while the *Reporting* system interacts directly with the *Software Architecture* and the *User Interface*. The *Software Architecture* must work closely with the *Operating system*, the *Network*, and the *Programming language* used to implement the system.

By splitting the reporting, user interface, and list services from the library application domain, you allow for future flexibility and insulate the library system from the implementation of these services. For example, you might choose to implement the software architecture on a variety of operating environments, including DOS, Windows, and OS/2, all supported on a LAN. If you separate the library domain from the user interface, you are able to provide generic services to the library, such as displaying screens, collecting and verifying input, etc. This supports the concept of software layering and defining specific interfaces between subsystems.

As you move into design, you need to further define the interfaces between the library system and other university systems, including student and staff management, to verify library users and staff, etc. These are discussed in the next chapter. You also need to be more specific about the implementation of your system as you move into design, to address issues such as language used (in this case, OOCOBOL), DBMS used, networking protocol, etc.

Another factor that you should consider at the beginning of your development effort is the type of classes and objects that exist in our system and their place in the respective domains. Recall the discussion of this issue in chapter 3 (section 3.4.7) and consider mapping each object type to a specific domain or layer of the library application.

Another consideration at this point in the development is the type of application the library system represents. A library system basically is a transaction processing system where users check out books and return them and you report on the results. As such, your choice of objects should reflect the strong data view that exists in the library domain.

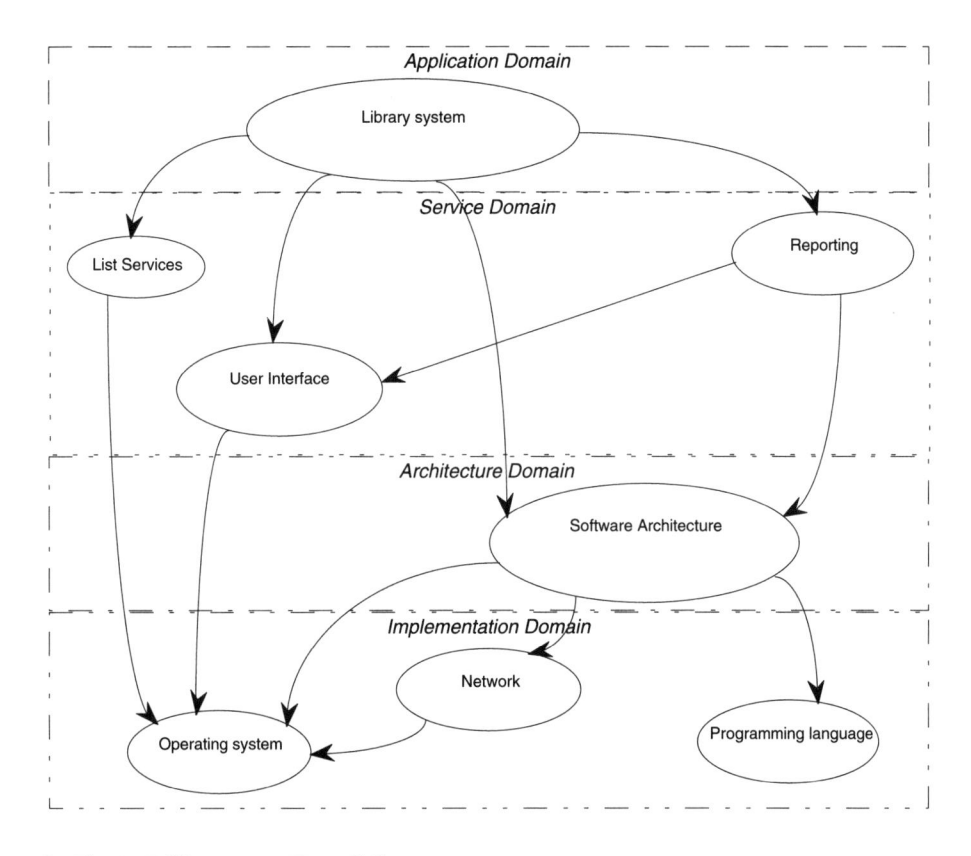

Figure 6.2
Library system - Shlaer/Mellor domain chart.

6.5.1 Library Problem

The Library problem is a simple system that might be best implemented using a relational DBMS and a 4GL; however, for the purposes of this book, I am using OOCOBOL and discussing the constraints on accessing database tables in the design and implementation chapters. I also will assume that a Local Area Network (LAN) will support the Library system and that the operating environment will be DOS, Windows, and OS/2.

CICS and DB2 will be used for external staff/student access (in external systems), and you will be expected to interface with these systems. The system can be implemented on a Unix server with LAN access provided via the different PC environments, DOS, Windows, and OS/2. As an alternative, you might choose to implement the system using CICS for OS/2 (letting CICS manage the library transactions), or an online transaction processing (OLTP) system and SQL on a file server.

Using the textual description of the requirements for the library system, you can identify potential key abstractions and make these objects or classes. Figure 6.3 shows initial candidate objects, attributes, and operations for the Library system. Some obvious candidates include Books, Users, Staff, Copies, Authors, ListofBooks, and ListofUsers. Further reviewing the description, you also might associate attributes with each of these objects and operations or services that each object might supply to other objects in the problem domain.

As you evaluate the library system, you also might find issues that are not clearly resolved, as I demonstrated in chapter 4. Some of these issues might lead you to make choices in analysis that you might later regret in design. You also made several assumptions based on missing or incomplete information. These assumptions include:

- More than one copy of a book might be available in the library.
- Each copy of a book must be uniquely identified within the library.
- An implementation-specific security system will be available during the design phase to address the issue of restricting access to library transactions by user type.
- The library system will be implemented using a data structure that supports keyed or indexed access to data.
- The archive process will be handled by batch (offline) components of the library system. These components will not be addressed in Analysis.

As you continue with your analysis, you might develop a prototype of the library system and allow library staff to provide feedback on the system and its functionality. For example, I built a prototype of the library system, including screens and menus, to facilitate the understanding of the system. I will look more closely at this prototype when I get into design (chapter 7), and I also will examine whether you should use CICS as the terminal controller and transaction processor, OS/2 Database Manager or DB2 as the database, etc.

As part of this process, you begin to identify current and future needs of the library system and to begin generalizing about the candidate objects that were identified in Figure 6.3. After much discussion, I classified the objects into groups using three distinct types of relationships: *association*, *kind of* (generalization), and *part of* (aggregation). Figure 6.4 shows the resulting classes, objects, and relationships for the library system. For example, a Book is a kind of library Media, and a Book contains Authors and Copies.

Objects	Attributes	Operations/services
Book	Title, Publisher	Add, Delete, Print
User/Staff	Name, ID, Password, BorrowLimit, Staff	Add, Delete, Print, SetBorrowLimit
Copy	Number, DateOut, DateIn	Checkout, Return
Author	Name	Add, Delete, Print
ListofBooks	Title, Name, DateOut, DateIn	Add, Delete, Print
ListofUsers	Name, Title, DateOut, DateIn	Add, Delete, Print

Figure 6.3
Library system - candidate objects, attributes, and operations.

The final objects, attributes, and operations include some obvious and some not-so-obvious abstractions. For instance, I chose to separate Library Staff from Library Users and defined two different objects that inherit from a class called People. Why make each a different object? For one reason, the requirements specify that there are two types of users and that I must differentiate between these types. By creating two different object types I satisfy this requirement. For another, the two types of people, although similar, represent significantly different abstractions in the overall Library problem. Figure 6.5 represents the final objects, attributes, and services for the Library problem.

Looking at the library system, consider the issue of object composition and collaboration. For instance, as I mentioned previously, Author is included as part of the Book object. This view supports many authors for each book. I could have chosen to make Author a separate object with an association to Book but instead embedded it within Book. The Book object is composed of many Authors, so I show this as a *part-of* relationship between Book and Author. Also, Copy is included as part of the Book object for the same reason (i.e., there can be more than one copy of a book available).

The Book object also contains additional attributes that are needed to satisfy the requirements but are not specified in the document. For instance, DateDueBack is needed to support future overdue fees, and CallNumber is needed to support assumption #2: each copy of a book must be uniquely identified.

Figure 6.4
Library system - objects, classes, and relationships.

Class	Objects	Relationships
Media	Book	Kind of (generalization)
	Video Tape	Kind of
	Record	Kind of
Person	Library User	Kind of
	Library Staff	Kind of
	Faculty	Kind of
	Student	Kind of
List	ListofBooks	Kind of
	ListofUsers	Kind of
ListOfBooks	Book	Part of (aggregation)
	User	Part of
Book	Author	Part of
	Copy	Part of
Book	User	CheckedOut (association)
Book	User	Returned (association)
Book	ListOfBooks	Returned (association)
Book	ListOfUsers	Returned (association)

One approach that might help you would be to build a data model of the library system to help identify objects and attributes. Given this approach, you probably would find entities including Book, User, Staff, Author, etc. This approach is limited, however, because it typically identifies only the physical abstractions of the problem domain and tends to classify objects based on their attributes alone, not their behavior. If there were a data model already in use for the library system, you definitely would use it in conjunction with the Coad/Yourdon method to better understand the problem domain.

Concerning attributes, I added additional fields, including DateOut and DateIn to the Book object to satisfy the functionality of checking out and returning books. Whenever a Book is checked out, the program collects the date that it was checked out, and when it is returned, the program collects that date as well. This allows you to determine if a book is returned past its due date and to calculate a late fee in this case.

Notice that I also have specified an object named Copy and that it contains the services for checking out and returning a book. I did this to allow the model

Object	Attributes	Operations/Services
Book	Title, CallNumber, Author, Copy	Add, Remove, Print
Author	Name	Add, Remove, Print
Copy	DateOut, DateDueBack	Checkout, Return, Print
Library User	Name, ID, Password, BorrowLimit	Add, Remove, Print, UpdatePassword
Library Staff	Name, ID, Password, BorrowLimit EmployeeType, DateHired	Add, Remove, Print, UpdateBorrowLimit
ListOfBooks	Title, DateOut, DateDueBack, Name	Add, Archive, Print
ListOfUsers	Name, DateOut, DateDueBack, Title	Add, Archive, Print

Figure 6.5
Library System - Final objects, attributes, and operations.

to represent the relationship established between a copy of a book being checked out and the user that checked out the book. When a book is checked out, the CheckedOut relationship is established, and when the book is returned, the relationship is broken. When a book is not checked out, there is no relationship with a user and the book is available for checkout. Your implementation must support this type of association between Book, Copy, and Library User.

Library Staff and Library Users are specialization's of a class called People. Taking this approach, you will find that all people have common attributes and operations that you can model. Common attributes for People might include Name, Address, Password, UserID, and BorrowLimit. UserID might be an integer that is assigned by the Library system whenever a new user is added, while BorrowLimit might be the same for all library users. Common services for People might include Add, Delete, Print, and UpdatePassword.

Recognize that you could extend this view to include additional people who, at some future time, might use the library, including university faculty, administrators, alumni, etc. Because you have defined the generic attributes and services for all people the library might be concerned with, you might not need to modify the definition of People based on future changes. Figure 6.6 shows the generalization for library people with the objects, attributes and services using the Coad/Yourdon notation. In the figure, fields listed equals attributes, while operations listed equals services.

By making Library Staff a specialization of People, you can add the service UpdateBorrowLimit to allow them to change the number of books that can be checked out at any time by a user. I also created a new abstraction in the library example, the Listof construct, for Users and Books. This abstraction is convenient for satisfying the requirements for reports and queries (requirements #5, 6 & 7). Using this approach, you can create a generalization List and define common attributes — Name, Title, Date Out, Date Due Back, and Date In — as well as services — Add, Archive, and Print — where archiving satisfies requirement 6.

Finally, I also have created a generalization or class called Media, which is a generalization of Books, Video Tapes, Records, etc. This allows me to define common attributes and services for any current or future type of artifact available from the library (perhaps including CDs, Video Games, Magazines, etc.). Each type of library Media has a Title, DateOut, DateIn, and DateDueBack, along with services to Add, Remove, Checkout, Return, and Print each. Notice that CallNumber was not included in the Media class because not every library artifact will require this field to uniquely identify it in the library. For example, there can be more than one copy of each video available for checkout, but these will not have CallNumbers like books. Figure 6.7 represents the structures for media class and its children using the Coad/Yourdon notation.

As you continue defining the object model, you must consider the operations or services for each object. Add, Delete, and Print can be generic services that all objects encapsulate, but you also must define any additional services to support the functionality of the library system. For instance, you need to define whether a Book or a User contains the Checkout and Return services. If you allow each User to have the Checkout/Return services, you place the responsibility with the User object. If you place the service at the Book object, this object controls the status of each book (i.e., whether it is checked out or not). We decided to place Checkout and Return in the Book object because these operations directly affect and should control the relationship between a Copy of a book and a User.

```
            ┌─────────────────────┐
            │      People         │
            │─── Fields ──────    │
            │      Name           │
            │      Address        │
            │      Password       │
            │      BorrowLimit    │
            │─── Operations ──    │
            │      ModifyPassword │
            └─────────────────────┘
```

```
  ┌──────────────────┐         ┌──────────────────────┐
  │   Library User   │         │    Library Staff     │
  │─── Fields ───    │         │─── Fields ───        │
  │    Name          │         │    Name              │
  │    UserID        │         │    UserID            │
  │    Address       │         │    Address           │
  │    Password      │         │    Password          │
  │    BorrowLimit   │         │    BorrowLimit       │
  │─── Operations ── │         │    EmployeeType      │
  │    AddUser       │         │    DateHired         │
  │    FindUser      │         │─── Operations ───    │
  │    PrintUser     │         │    AddStaff          │
  │    RemoveUser    │         │    Checkout          │
  └──────────────────┘         │    FindStaff         │
                               │    ModifyBorrowLimit │
                               │    PrintStaff        │
                               │    Return            │
                               └──────────────────────┘
```

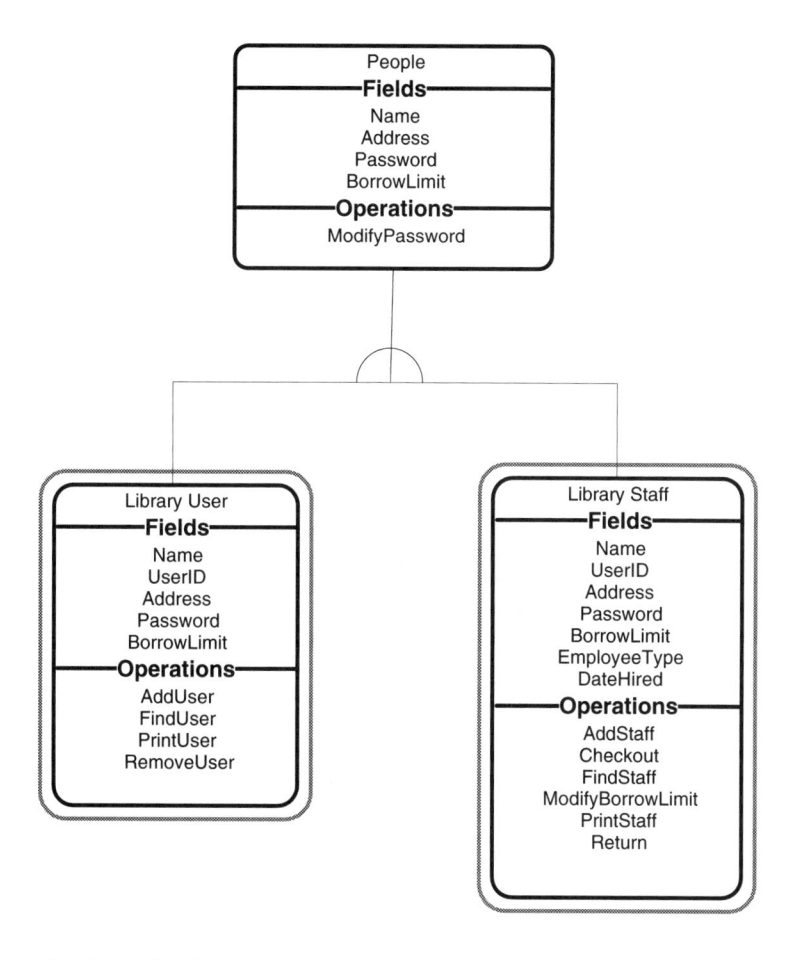

Figure 6.6
Generalization of library users and staff.

As you look at the Library system, you will find that there are only a few messages sent based on the associations between objects. The association between Book and User, Checkout, can be implemented in a variety of ways, with the Book sending a message to User, the User sending message to Book, or even the Library Staff sending a message to the Book. As you look at these objects, you should consider which object (Book or User) instigates the communication. In this case, I chose to have the Library Staff send a message to the Book with the User and Copy specified, because in my view the Library Staff will be responsible for checking out the physical books. This physical representation maps well to the abstraction in our model under this scenario.

Consider a library that has an electronic system for making sure books are not removed from the library unless checked out. This system, for example, could include metal detectors at each door into or out of the library, and check for books by attaching some kind of metal object or tag to each book. In this case, if a book is to be checked out, the library staff would remove the object or tag to not set off the metal detector as the user exits the building.

The only other message in the Library problem is when a Book is returned. As with the Checkout, I specified that, when a Book is returned, the Library Staff sends a message to the Book. When the Book receives this message, it notifies the ListOfBooks and ListOfUsers, then removes the association between the Book and the User (established when the Book was checked out).

Remember the requirements; you need to support archiving the lists when they contain 100 entries (requirement #8). I have chosen to have the List of objects (Users and Books) determine when an entry is added, if the list contains 100 entries. If it does, it archives the list and resets it to 0 entries.

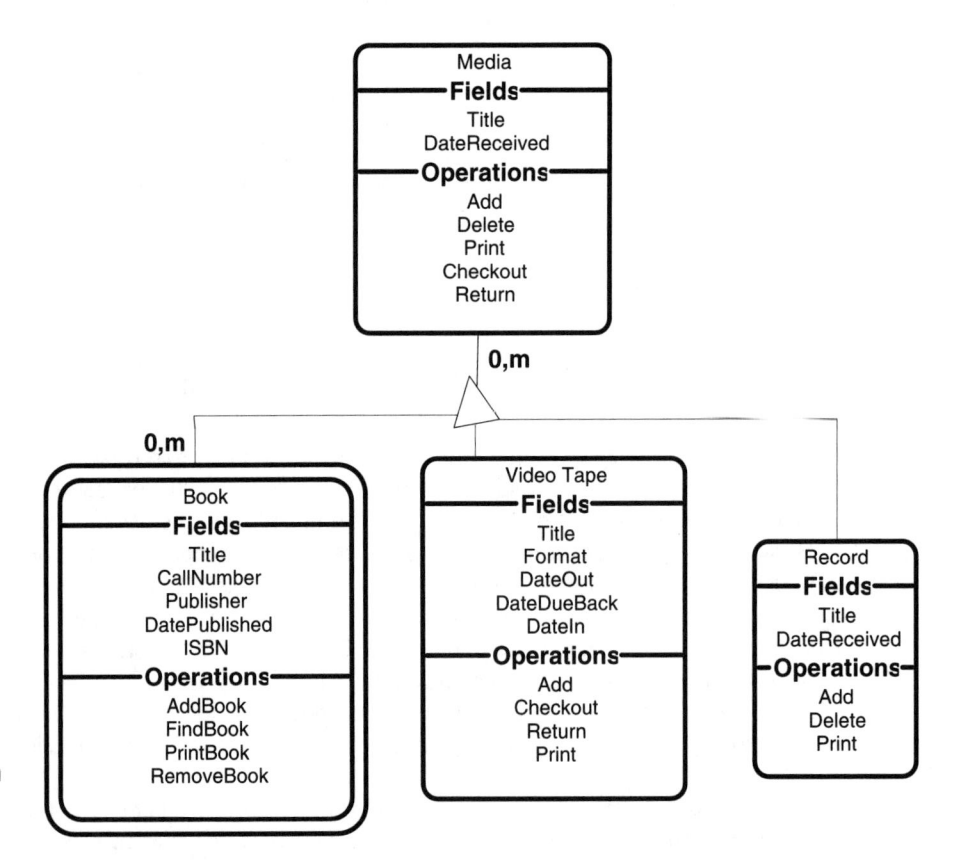

Figure 6.7 Generalization of Library Books.

The completed object model for the library system is shown in the Coad/Yourdon diagram in Figure 6.8. The object model is described in more detail in section A.1, which includes definitions of the classes, objects, attributes, services, and messages in the Library domain. As a result of the OOA for the Library problem, I have identified several reusable components for future projects, including classes for Media (a generalization of Books), People (a generalization of Users), and ListOf.

6.5.2 ATM Problem

Prior to attempting to define the problem domain for the ATM system, I need to review the requirements document and further investigate the outstanding issues identified in chapter 3.

In the second example, the ATM system, you probably have to consider systems external to the ATM. Given that ATMs are simply part of a larger banking system and that ATM transactions are different forms of traditional bank transactions, you would need to review any information available on these external systems.

The bank domain includes additional views that are not part of the ATM system, including account management, reporting, financial services, etc. Taking a global view of the banking environment, you must consider bank services to customers, current legacy systems (Bank accounts, Transactions, etc.), and future services (debit cards, etc.) as part of any analysis process for the ATM system.

Figure 6.9 represents a Shlaer/Mellor domain chart for the ATM system. This figure shows that the *ATM system* interacts with *Bank Services*, the *User Interface*, the *ATM log*, and the *Software Architecture*. *Bank Services* interacts with the *Network*, while the *User Interface* interacts with the *Operating system* and the *ATM log* interfaces with the *Software Architecture*. The *Software Architecture* interacts with the *Operating system*, the *Network* and the *Programming languages* used to implement the system.

Splitting the domain as shown allows for flexibility and layering of the ATM system to support future banking services and keep the system insulated from the physical environment as much as possible. In the next chapter, I will define more specifically the interfaces between the *ATM* system and the *Bank Services*, *User Interface*, *Software Architecture* and the *ATM log*.

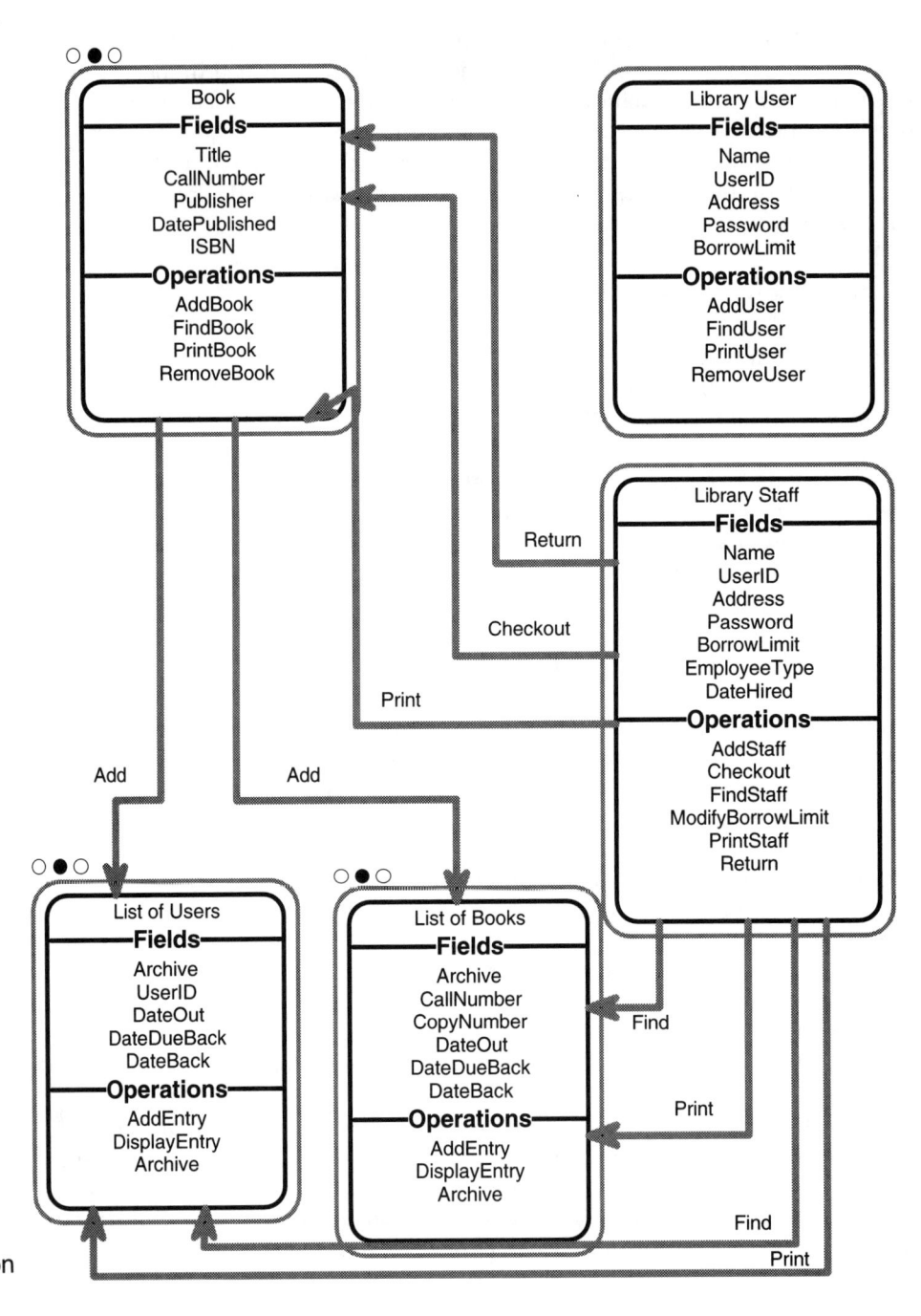

Figure 6.8
Library system - Coad/Yourdon diagram.

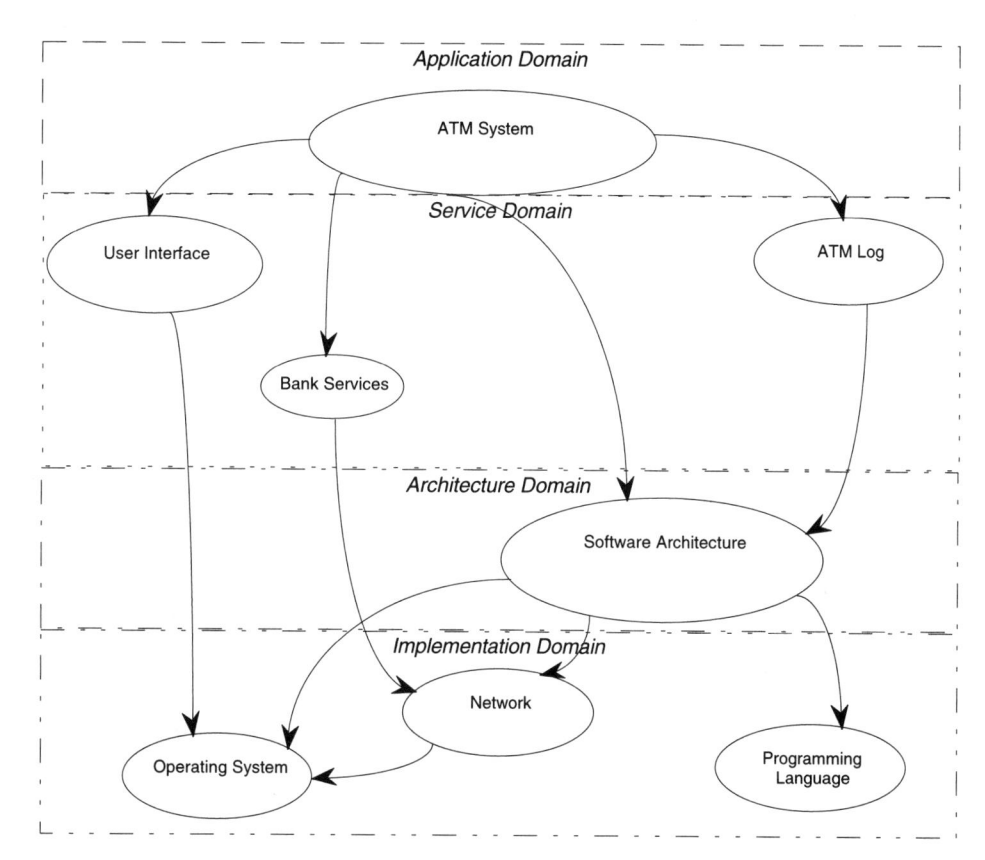

Figure 6.9
ATM system - Shlaer/Mellor domain chart.

As you consider the ATM problem, one thing that immediately should come to mind is the strong dynamic behavior in the system. The ATM system is considered to contain context-sensitive behavior (i.e., different transactions — withdrawal, deposit, etc. — require different keypad entries, and the system must respond to stimuli based on the state that it is in at the time). This view should be represented and well understood as you analyze the ATM system if we are to be successful in designing a workable solution. The layout and screens for the ATM system was described in chapter 3.

After reviewing the ATM textual requirements document, I might identify potential key abstractions in the problem domain as shown in Figure 6.10. Several critical components can be identified and defined for the ATM system, some are derived directly from the requirements description and representing physical components — including Card, Withdrawal chute, Receipt printer — while others are logical representations — including Transaction, Account, etc.

166   Object-Oriented Development in COBOL

Objects	Attributes	Operations/Services
Checking Account	AccountNumber, Name, PIN, Balance,	Open, Close, Print
Savings Account		Open, GetCard
Card	Name, PIN	ActivateCard, DeactivateCard
Balance/Deposit/Withdrawal Transaction	Amount, Date, Type	Apply
Deposit slot	Status	Check, Open, Close
Withdrawal chute		DispenseCash
Card slot		Accept, EjectCard
Receipt printer		Print
Local ATM file		
Master ATM file	Amount, Date, Type	Apply transactions
Customer	Name, ID, Password, etc.	

Figure 6.10 ATM system - candidate objects, attributes, and operations.

You might want to consider the concept of an ATM session mentioned in the document describing the ATM system. Under this view, a bank customer interacts with the ATM in a session that constitutes a banking transaction. Given this view, each of the ATM screens would map to a step in the session, with predefined inputs allowed at each point and actions taken as a result of each selection. This approach maps the control structure of the ATM system into an object that could represent the behavior of an ATM session in the design phase.

Another possible view of the ATM system might be to consider the problem in terms of several, distinct states (not simply as screens) that map to bank transactions. An example of this view might lead to the states and transitions shown in Figure 6.11. Notice in this diagram that I have identified three initial states, *Waiting for ATM card*, *Waiting for PIN*, and *Waiting for transaction*, a middle set of states that correspond to the ATM transactions (*Balance, Deposit, Withdrawal,* and *Funds Transfer*), and a final state that closes the ATM session.

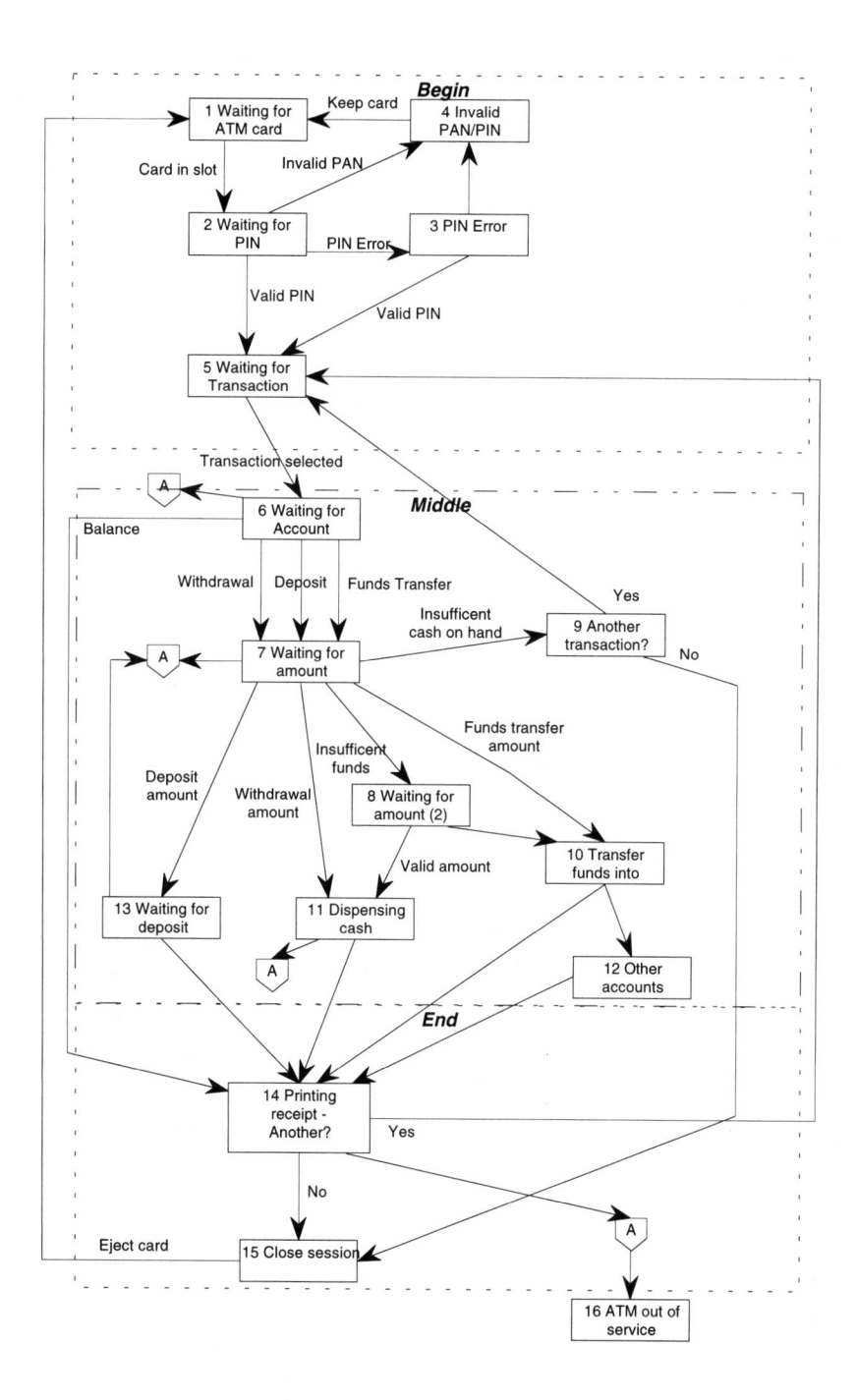

Figure 6.11 ATM system - states and transitions.

Following up on this view, you might choose to consider the ATM system as simply a transaction collection system, where customers enter information, which is stored in the ATM log. This approach might lead to the creation of a data model. From this model, you might identify ATM Transaction, Account, User Interface, and ATM entities as candidate classes. Using this approach I specified the classes, objects, and relationships shown in Figure 6.12 and the final objects, attributes, and services shown in Figure 6.13.

As you define each object and class, consider which attributes are required. Notice that I added Date and Time to the ATM for audit purposes. I also have added the attribute CashOnHand to help determine when the ATM is empty or has insufficient cash available. In design, you might choose to calculate (beginning amount - each transaction) this value or to store it, but this decision is not required in analysis.

I also have added Dispense Amount to signify the amount of cash to be dispensed. This field would be sent to the User Interface, which manages the physical hardware for the ATM. The User Interface also would require a

Class	Objects	Relationships
Account	Saving	Kind of (generalization)
	Checking	Kind of
Transaction	Balance inquiry	Kind of
	Withdrawal	Kind of
	Deposit	Kind of
Hardware	Deposit slot	Kind of
	Withdrawal chute	Kind of
	Card slot	Kind of
	Printer	Kind of
Hardware	Controller	Part of (aggregation)
	Mechanical	Part of
ATM	ATM UI	ATM Session (association)
ATM	Account	Verify PAN/PIN (association)
ATM	Account	Debit (association)
ATM	ATM File Manager Log	ATM Transaction (association)

Figure 6.12
ATM system - final classes, objects, and relationships.

Object	Attributes	Operations/services
ATM	TerminalID, Date, Time	ATMSession
Account Manager	AccountNumber, PIN, Type, Balance	VerifyAccount, DebitAccount, CreditAccount
ATM File Manager	TransactionType, Account, Amount, Date/Time, Balance	LogTransaction
ATM User Interface	Status of slots [Card, Deposit, CardInSlot, Withdrawal, Receipt], CashAvilable, Date, Time	EnterPIN, EnterPAN, etc.

Figure 6.13 ATM system - final objects, attributes, and operations/services.

keyboard and screen buffer to store the keystrokes that are entered and the screens displayed by the ATM.

One important issue in your analysis is where services will reside in the ATM system and which messages will be sent between objects. For example, each Account in the ATM system will include basic services including Open, Close, Debit, Credit, and Print Balance. Likewise, each ATM transaction will include Create, Log, and Print services.

Remembering that the ATM system has context-dependent behavior (with specific keyboard entry at each point), I have chosen to disperse the behavior between the ATM hardware and the ATM User Interface. In the future, you might want to make the ATM system more user-friendly by allowing the CANCEL key to exit from any screen. This might add complexity to the dynamic model of the ATM system but would make the system easier to use and less rigid.

Because the ATM system is a reactive system, you probably would want to define the dynamic behavior of the system in terms of the states and transitions. If you took a simplistic approach, you might assign each screen or panel of the ATM system to a state. Another approach might be to assign certain aspects of each ATM session, say the beginning, middle, and end, to different states as I have shown in Figure 6.11.

This would allow you to keep common states or transitions in a single dynamic view and might help to coordinate the interaction between the ATM and the hardware. Under this view, the overall ATM session is considered as a transition from initial (i.e., waiting for a card), to account and password entry (validating the transaction), to accepting the type of account, transaction, and amount (as applicable), with each different transaction requiring its own set of states and transition, terminating in the print receipt and eject card task, which return the machine to its initial state.

Notice, when you take this approach, that you identify common states and transitions for the ATM system and that these are indicated using the dashed lines in the diagram. I do this to point out the goal of viewing the problem domain in terms of common behavior. In the next chapter, I will follow up on this view and discuss how the common behavior in the ATM system can be used to design a solution to maximize reuse and flexibility.

As you investigate the ATM system, you will come to view several generalization/specializations in the problem domain. For instance, Bank Accounts share common attributes — including Number, Type, Balance, Customer, and Date Opened — and services — Open, Close, Credit, Debit, and Print Balance. Given this view, Savings, Checking, and Money Market accounts are specialization's of the Account abstraction. Figure 6.14 represents the Coad/Yourdon notation for the bank account classes and objects.

Likewise, bank account Transactions share common attributes — including Type, Account Number, Balance, Amount, Date, and Time — and services — including Log. With this view, Withdrawals, Deposits, and Balance Inquiries are defined and funds transfers are a composition of a withdrawal followed by a deposit. Figure 6.15 shows the Coad/Yourdon notation for the banking transactions.

Also in the ATM system are different kinds of hardware, including Deposit slot, Withdrawal chute, Card slot, Printer, etc. As you evaluate these hardware components, you will find that their compositions are similar and that they include a controller and some mechanical parts. As a result, I have defined an Interface controller that works with the various hardware components and handles all the details of that communication.

Composition and collaborations in the ATM system are dynamic and complex. For instance, the interaction between the User Interface (UI) and the hardware represents a variety of messages and components. The UI is further composed of the following objects with the attributes shown:

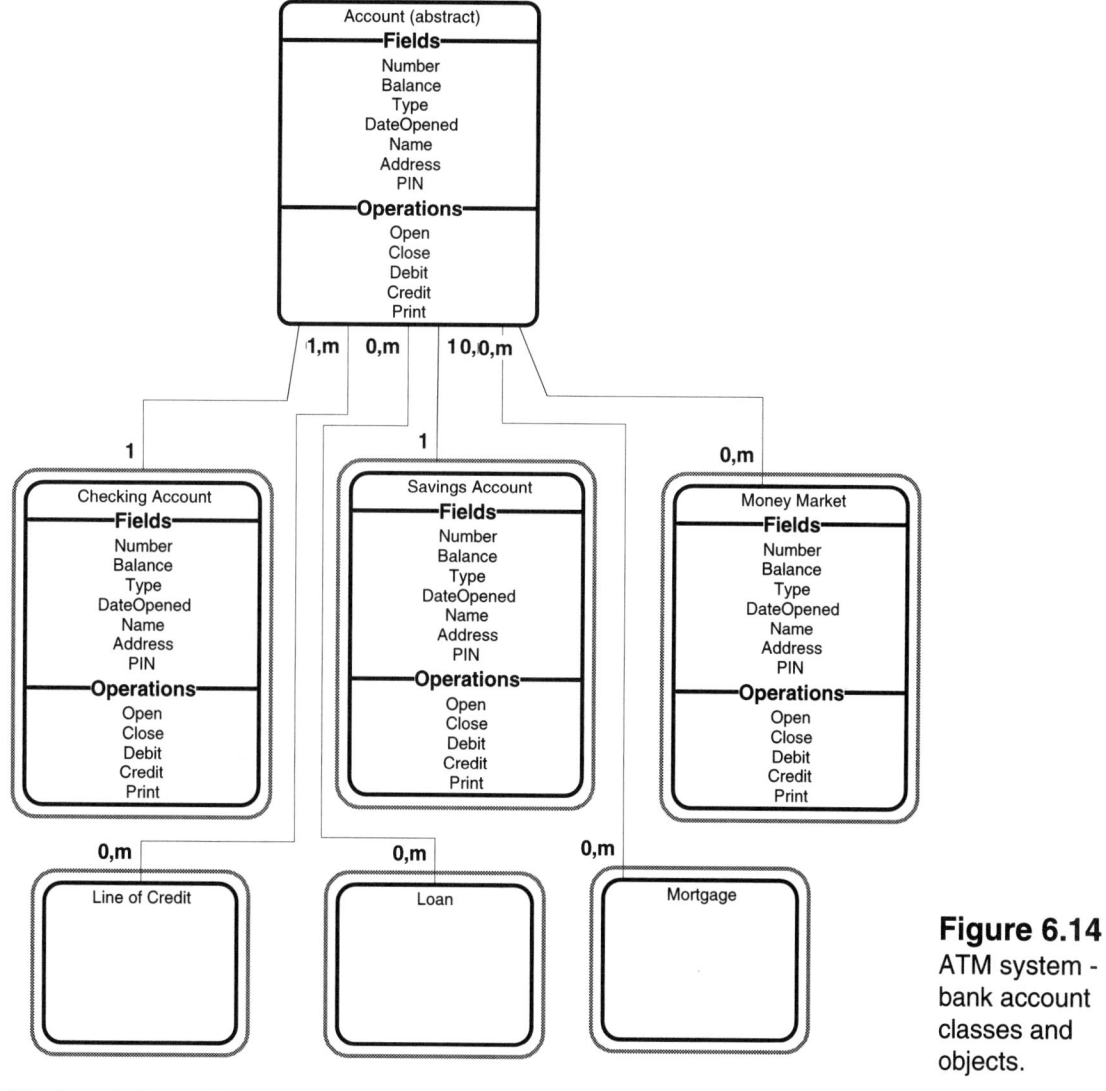

```
                    ┌─────────────────────┐
                    │  Account (abstract) │
                    │ ──── Fields ────    │
                    │   Number            │
                    │   Balance           │
                    │   Type              │
                    │   DateOpened        │
                    │   Name              │
                    │   Address           │
                    │   PIN               │
                    │ ── Operations ──    │
                    │   Open              │
                    │   Close             │
                    │   Debit             │
                    │   Credit            │
                    │   Print             │
                    └─────────────────────┘
```

Figure 6.14 ATM system - bank account classes and objects.

Account (abstract) with Fields: Number, Balance, Type, DateOpened, Name, Address, PIN; Operations: Open, Close, Debit, Credit, Print.

Relationships (1,m / 0,m / 1 0,0,m) to:

- **Checking Account** (1) — Fields: Number, Balance, Type, DateOpened, Name, Address, PIN; Operations: Open, Close, Debit, Credit, Print.
- **Savings Account** (1) — Fields: Number, Balance, Type, DateOpened, Name, Address, PIN; Operations: Open, Close, Debit, Credit, Print.
- **Money Market** (0,m) — Fields: Number, Balance, Type, DateOpened, Name, Address, PIN; Operations: Open, Close, Debit, Credit, Print.

Subclasses (0,m each):
- **Line of Credit**
- **Loan**
- **Mortgage**

Keyboard Controller   KeyboardBuffer
CRT Controller   ScreenBuffer
Card Slot Controller   CardInSlot, PAN
Desposit Slot Controller
Withdrawal Chute Controller   CashAvailable,
                                   DispenseAmount
Receipt Tape Controller   Receipt [AccountNumber,
                                   TransactionType, Amount,
                                   Date, Time]

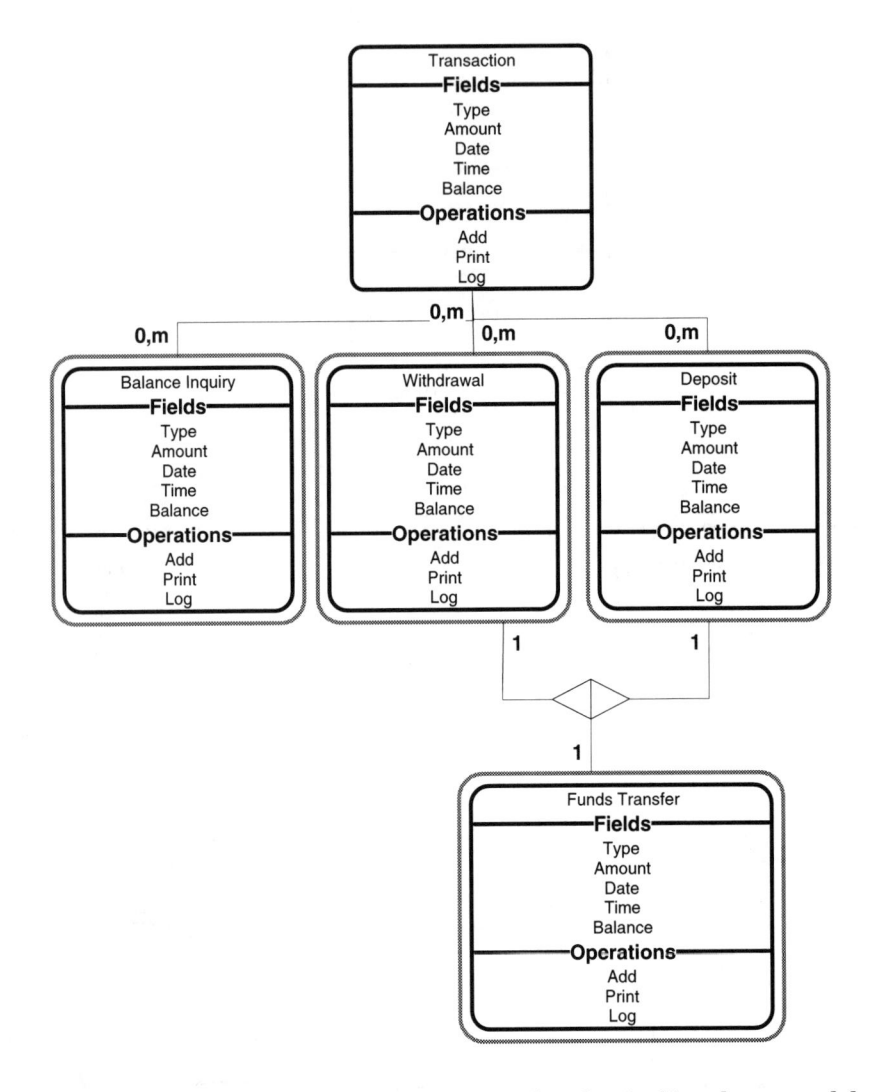

Figure 6.15
ATM system - account transaction classes and objects.

```
                        Transaction
                        ─Fields─
                          Type
                          Amount
                          Date
                          Time
                          Balance
                        ─Operations─
                          Add
                          Print
                          Log
```

```
   Balance Inquiry        Withdrawal           Deposit
   ─Fields─              ─Fields─             ─Fields─
     Type                  Type                 Type
     Amount                Amount               Amount
     Date                  Date                 Date
     Time                  Time                 Time
     Balance               Balance              Balance
   ─Operations─          ─Operations─         ─Operations─
     Add                   Add                  Add
     Print                 Print                Print
     Log                   Log                  Log
```

```
                        Funds Transfer
                        ─Fields─
                          Type
                          Amount
                          Date
                          Time
                          Balance
                        ─Operations─
                          Add
                          Print
                          Log
```

This view allows the User Interface to access the physical hardware and deal directly with each hardware component. The ATM system simply interfaces with the User Interface and uses messages to request services such as keyboard input, screen display, cash dispensing, etc.

You might choose to view the ATM object as a financial transaction (i.e., a class of objects that perform a particular financial transaction) or as an abstraction of banking services. Given this view, the ATM object could be given a controlling role in the system. With this approach, the ATM object collaborates with a User Interface to present a greeting, display menus, messages, print receipts, etc. The ATM object also would collaborate with an ATM log object to log each transaction and with a bank account object to retrieve and verify account, password (PIN), and current balance. It might be impractical for security reasons to allow the ATM object to update an account balance, so it probably will have to collaborate with the bank account object to request a balance update on a withdrawal or funds transfer.

I have chosen to use the Coad/Yourdon method and notation for the examples, so I ended up with the object model shown in Figure 6.16, which is further described in section A.1. Following this method, I defined the key abstractions as Account Manager, ATM File Manager, ATM, and User Interface. The User Interface is required to satisfy the requirement that the system appear as shown in chapter 3. As an outcome of the OOA for the ATM problem, I have

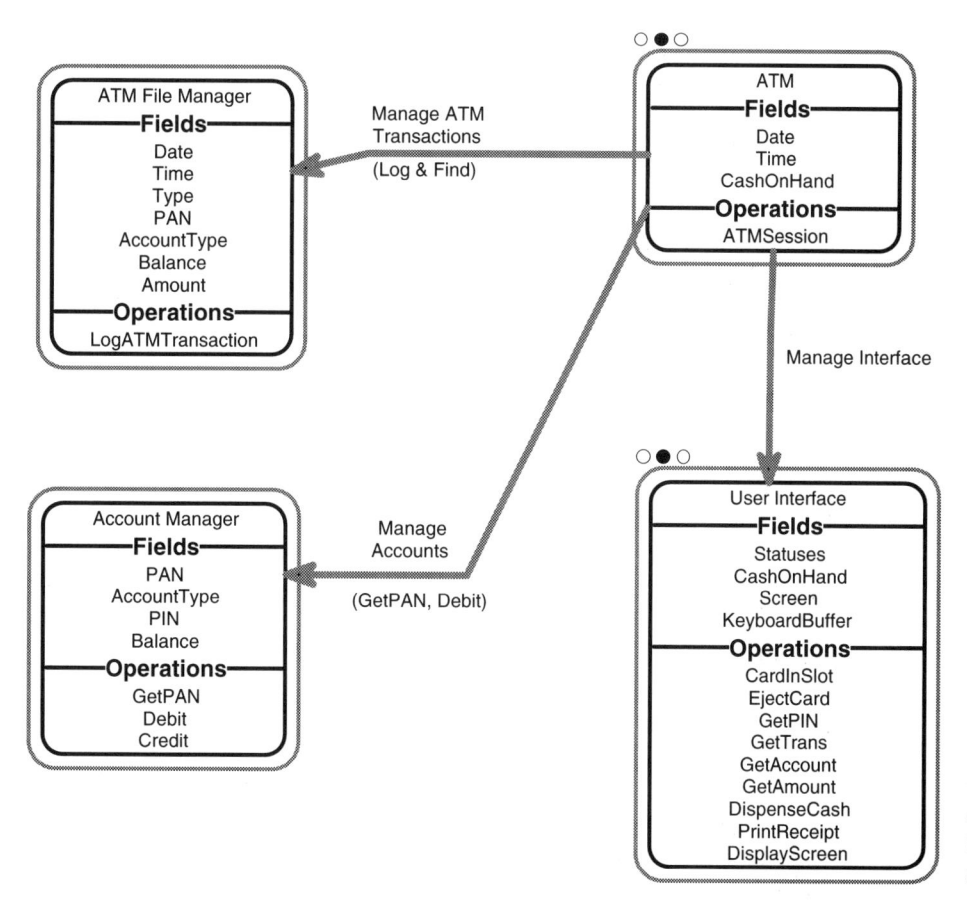

Figure 6.16
ATM system - Coad/Yourdon diagram.

defined several potentially reusable components, including Accounts, Transactions, and hardware constructs.

In defining the ATM system, you might choose to build a prototype to help you better understand the system and its behavior. Assume that the bank is interested in making the ATM system as user-friendly as possible, so they have installed a prototype ATM system in one of their banks to collect customer feedback. Further suppose that, from this feedback, the bank manager has asked you to include functionality to allow customers to cancel out of any ATM screen and return to the prior screen. This would allow someone to proceed forward with a transaction, then back out to a specific level and try another transaction. How would this added functionality impact your view of the ATM system? I will investigate this issue in more detail in the next chapter. A prototype of the ATM user interface is shown in chapter 3 and in section A.1, along with the definitions of the classes, objects, attributes, services, and messages for the ATM system.

Other issues that might have an impact on the evolution of the ATM object model include whether the bank's existing computer system (perhaps these systems are mainframe-based) can be integrated with the new ATM system, how their legacy systems can be made to act like objects, and what types of security should be incorporated into the ATM system. I will investigate some of the these issues in subsequent chapters.

As I mentioned in chapter 3, I chose to develop a working prototype of the ATM system in Windows. I built the ATM user interface using the GUI painting facility in my CASE tool, System Architect. An alternative method would be to build a prototype of the ATM user interface in Smalltalk. This would serve several purposes: you could verify the look and feel of the user interface, you could verify the behavior of the interface, and you also could design and build the ATM system to interact with the interface, thus reducing the reliance of the ATM on its hardware systems. This last consideration might allow you to adopt the ATM system to future hardware components (for example, speech recognition equipment) without having to redesign the entire ATM system. I will investigate this option in the next two chapters.

6.6 Moving from OOA to OOD

Once you have completed the object model for your systems, you release them to a design group that will be responsible for creating an object specification for the programmers. OOD will delve into more detail and will include iterative design, code, test, and implement tasks. I will examine these issues in more detail in the next chapter.

An issue that I have not yet covered is requirements traceability, or documenting and tracing the functional requirements for a system throughout its development. The idea of tracking requirements is simple: if you document the requirements for a system, you also can track the deliverables (models, specifications, code, etc.) that are created in the development process that satisfy those requirements and prove to users that you are not overlooking any system functions.

For example, you can define the requirements for both of the example systems, either using a CASE tool that supports requirements objects or by using an external document management system. Once the requirements are stored, you can reference them in the definition of the deliverables in your CASE tool (if they are stored outside the tool) or associate them with the deliverables themselves (if they are stored in the tool). Following this process, you can run reports or queries that show where each functional requirement has been satisfied in each stage of development. For example, you could associate the class/object ListOfUsers with requirement #8 to indicate you have a component in your model that satisfies this requirement. Figure 6.17 represents a report that identifies requirement #8, defined as Version 2 Requirement #8, and its associated deliverables.

Requirements associated with diagram symbols
Page   4
Name
Description
    Name   Type
Maintain Book List By User Version 2
Requirement #8
Record user and book information in the UserList data store as the book is returned to the library. The list will be used to query the books borrowed by a user.

List of Users	Class/Object
Maintain Book List By User	Document
Unassign Copy	Process
Update User List	Module
Version 2	Requirement

Figure 6.17
Requirement and associated deliverables.

Some CASE tools allow functional requirements to reference other requirements, so using these tools, you can build a hierarchy of requirements, starting at a high level of abstraction and decomposing down to a low level. This allows you to associate the appropriate level of requirement with its corresponding component in your development process. My CASE tool, System Architect, has this facility, and I have built a document structure in the product that reflects the requirements for the Library and the ATM system. These diagrams and textual specifications are described in the Appendix.

Another consideration as you complete your analysis is the possible reuse of prior OOA project deliverables. If you accept that object models contain generic abstractions in the problem domain, you might find that there are common objects or classes across different domains in an organization. The idea is that abstractions and mechanisms might appear in more than one problem domain in an organization, and if so, you can reuse these abstractions and mechanisms in those domains.

Remembering the review of Domain Analysis, you might end up reviewing previously defined object models before you analyze other problem domains or subject areas looking for potential reusable abstractions. If you find common abstractions, you can begin your OOA process for that domain by using the class, object, attribute, and operations defined for those abstractions.

6.7 References

[ARA89]   Arango, G., "Domain Analysis: From Art Form to Engineering Discipline," *SIGSOFT Engineering Notes*, vol. 14, no. 3, May 1989.

[BOO89]   Booch, G., "What is and what isn't object-oriented design," *American Programmer*, Vol.2, Nos.7-8, Summer 1989.

[BOO91]   Booch, G., *Object-Oriented Design with Applications*, Benjamin/Cummings, 1991.

[COA91]   Coad, P. and E. Yourdon, *Object-Oriented Design*, Prentice Hall, 1991.

[COA90]   Coad, P. and E. Yourdon, *Object-Oriented Analysis*, Prentice Hall, 1990.

[HOL91]   Holibaugh, R., "Object-Oriented Modeling," *Addendum to the Proc. of OOPSLA '91*, pp. 73-77, 1991.

[PRI90]   Prieto-Diaz, R., "Domain Analysis: An Introduction," *ACM SIGSOFT*, vol. 15, no. 2, pp. 47-54.

[RUB92]   Rubin, K. and A. Goldberg, "Object Behavior Analysis," *CACM*, vol. 35, no .9, pp. 48-62.
[RUM91]   Rumbaugh, J., M. Blaha, W. Premerlani, F. Eddy, and W. Lorensen, *Object-Oriented Modeling and Design*, Prentice-Hall, 1991.
[SHA93]   Sharble, R. C. and S. S. Cohen, "The Object-Oriented Brewery: A Comparison of Two Object-Oriented Development Methods," *ACM SIGSOFT*, vol. 18, no. 2, April 1993, pp. 60-73.
[SHL92]   Shlaer, S. and S. Mellor, *Object Life Cycles: Modeling the World in States*, Prentice-Hall, 1992.
[SHL89]   Shlaer, S. and S. Mellor, "An Object-Oriented Approach to Domain Analysis," *ACM SIGSOFT*, vol. 14, no. 5, 1989, pp. 66-77.
[SHL88]   Shlaer, S. and S. Mellor, *Object-Oriented Systems Analysis: Modeling the World in Data*, Prentice-Hall, 1988.
[WIR89]   Wirfs-Brock, R. and B. Wilkerson, "Object-Oriented Design: A Responsibility-Driven Approach," *In Proc. of OOPSLA '89*, pp. 71-75.
[WIR90]   Wirfs-Brock, R., B. Wilkerson, and L. Wiener, *Designing Object-Oriented Software*, Prentice-Hall, 1990.

Chapter 7

Object-Oriented Design

Again referring to the simplified SDLC discussed in chapter 4, design is concerned with development of a solution, given the constraints of the operating environment and a model of system functionality defined in analysis. A simplified view of the difference between analysis and design is that analysis defines "what" a system will do, while design defines "how" it will be done.

Your goal in OOD will be to take the object model created in OOA and, based on some environmental or implementation decisions, develop a solution that can be implemented in OOCOBOL. Perhaps the most significant restraint on OOD is the focus on reusing any existing components (objects) that are available for the solution domain.

Remembering the discussion on the intertwining of OOD and OOP, I will look closely at the process of designing, building, then unit testing each class or subsystem in this chapter. I will pay special attention to the reuse of OOCOBOL classes, the data structures used in OOD, and their implementation in the OOCOBOL language. Because of the relationship between design, code, and unit test, this chapter will be closely tied to the next chapter which will describe creation of the actual OOCOBOL code for each class designed.

7.1 Introduction

Object-oriented design is a process of translating or specifying a physical software structure that is composed of reusable components (objects) built from an object model defined in Analysis. OOD delivers an object specification to programming and must consider existing objects for reuse in the completed software product.

OOD takes the object model created in Analysis and transforms it into an object specification based on the implementation details of the solution domain. Objects must interact via messages. Some objects will be decomposed into component objects, and this information is defined in the object specification. Architectural design decisions should be made in OOD along with object and class design (hierarchies, inheritance, etc.) and object packaging. Much of OOD will be dependent upon the OOPL used and the limits on the programming language.

In this case, I am using the Booch OOD method and creating the deliverables specified in this approach. The Booch method consists of specific tasks, roles, responsibilities, and calls for the creation of an object specification as a representation of the structure and behavior of the system. In the case of the Booch method, a series of notations or diagrams will be created to help communicate and verify the structure and behavior of the system during design.

Remembering that construction in an object-oriented development life cycle is a process of assembling existing objects to meet the needs of the problem domain or system under development, to describe an object, you must specify its attributes, its behavior, and its relationship with other objects in the target programming language. To use an object, the data structures and operational details don't need to be understood.

Implementation issues must be considered in OOD including data access, GUI, class libraries, and distributed processing. If a system is to be implemented in a client/server environment using Windows or OS/2, you must determine if there are class libraries available that can provide reusable components for presentation and data access. Where possible, you should reuse purchased classes and reduce your overall development effort accordingly. A key task in OOD should be identifying and adopting or extending reusable components.

Developing reusable components is in direct opposition to the task of application development, and you must recognize this issue and plan for it. For example, if your goal is to create reusable components, then you must seek to generalize any classes or objects that you design. This effort requires time and energy, usually on the part of a staff person or group, maintaining a repository of reusable components. To achieve reuse, you also must provide incentives for reuse in our organization. Many studies show that most developers reuse only what they have developed themselves, so you need to provide a process or procedure for searching for reusable components and rewards for reusing these components on new projects. I will cover reuse in more detail in chapter 13.

Another factor to consider as you progress through design is the intertwining between analysis, design, programming, and testing in object-oriented development. Recalling the discussion of an object-oriented development life cycle, the outcome of OOA (the object model) will represent your understanding of the problem domain at a point in time and to a specific level of detail. This is the basis for your OOD process and the specification of the objects and messages that make up the solution domain.

Following the design of the objects and modules, you begin programming a subset of the system, perhaps a set of integrated modules or subsystems, then unit test and deliver them. Once you have delivered these modules or subsystems, you return to the analysis and design process to work on other aspects of the system. Prototyping can be used throughout this process to help users understand and communicate to you the exact behavior of the system or to test out the subsystems you have developed.

As you design, create, and test classes and subsystems, you must remember that these components will evolve as you move forward in the application development process. One key aspect of this process is configuration management and documentation of the classes and subsystems after design.

The process of object-oriented design is the antithesis of cookbook approaches. As we will see, object-oriented design is more of an incremental, iterative process, in which the products of design gently unfold over time.
G. Booch [BOO91].

7.2 Using Object Models

In OOD, you take the object model that was defined in OOA and refine it based on your implementation environment. This process involves some generic tasks as well as some that are specific for an implementation in OOCOBOL.

Regardless of the implementation environment, the objects in the model should be generalized into classes and you must use every opportunity to look for potentially reusable components throughout OOD. In the case of the example problems, I already have begun to generalize the objects into classes that share attributes and behaviors. As I progress through OOD, I will review the classification hierarchy for possible changes that will promote more reuse in this or later projects. In some cases, you might want to have a staff person responsible for class hierarchy management and another person who manages the library of reusable components.

Once you begin using a class hierarchy whenever a class is modified, especially a higher-level class, you must consider the impact of the change on any lower-level classes that inherit from the parent. Moving attributes or methods (operations) higher in a classification hierarchy makes them more applicable to other applications, but there are trade-offs to doing so. This brings me to some guidelines for managing class hierarchies to maximize reuse.

The _Law of Demeter_ states that methods of a class should not depend in any way on the structure of the class, except the immediate (top-level) structure of their own class, and each method should send messages to objects belonging to a very limited set of classes only. This law leads to the development of loosely coupled classes, whose implementation secrets are hidden and encapsulated. The danger in developing loosely coupled classes is that they might not fully exploit the commonality that exists in the problem domain. The opposite approach, tightly coupled classes, leads to difficulty in understanding what a class does without looking at all the classes it inherits from or uses.

In [BOO91], Booch suggests guidelines for building classification hierarchies. _Inheritance_ relationships are appropriate if every instance of B also can be viewed as an instance of A, while _using_ (or aggregation) relationships are appropriate when every instance of B simply possesses one or more attributes or characteristics of A. Booch further suggests:

- Keeping all operations primitive within a given class, so that each class exhibits a small, well-defined behavior.
- Separating methods that do not communicate with one another.
- Grouping together behaviors in a single method if it leads to a simpler interface, but balancing this against larger more complicated methods.
- Separating out behavior across methods to keep methods simpler, but balancing this with more complicated interfaces.
- Balancing the contracting between objects — too much contracting leads to fragmentation, while too little leads to large, unmanageable modules.
- Declaring methods for objects in the class or in class utilities supported in the OOCOBOL.
- When creating utility classes, keep them primitive and reduce the coupling among classes.

When assigning methods to classes, he recommends considering:

Would this method be more useful in other contexts?
Will this method be difficult to implement?
How related are the class and the method under consideration?
Does the method implementation depend on the internal details of the class?

When making choices of representation for a class or an object in a programming language, Booch recommends:

- Relationships with cardinality of n require collection classes.

- Relationships with cardinality of "0" or "1" are implemented with a pointer or reference to an object.
- Consider computing a value vs. storing the value in an object.
- Visibility and information hiding are competitive concepts and must be balanced in design.

This last issue is very important as you consider how each class will interact and view classes it communicates with. Because you goal is to create loosely coupled classes, you need to balance the benefits of information hiding in classes with their ability to interact with those classes they collaborate with.

In addition to these generic OOD techniques, you need to make special considerations for the OOCOBOL development environment, with its available class libraries. As you design the example systems, examine the existing OOCOBOL classes for application or extension. You also can include multiple inheritance, garbage collection, the concept of a factory for objects in the example problems, because these features are all defined in the current OOCOBOL standard.

7.3 Reuse of Existing Design Components

Most reuse that occurs in object-oriented development is at the level of source code. When an organization purchases a class library, they receive a library of source code definitions for classes that can be instantiated. There generally is no design representation for these code-level components in the class library. One reason for this is that there are not yet any *de facto* standards for design representations (i.e., notations) that all class library vendors accept or support.

While not yet available for use with OOCOBOL, some CASE tools support design representations that do map to commercially available class libraries. Rational, for example, provides the Booch Components as an optional product to be used with their ROSE CASE tool. These components, typically delivered only as source code in a class library, are delivered in the ROSE repository and are available to designers as reusable modules or subsystems in Booch's notation.

Another approach to making class library components available to designers would be to manually document the contents of the classes in a CASE tool. While this approach might lead to higher levels of reuse in design, it also would require a significant effort to capture the design representation and an ongoing one to maintain the design representation when the library changes.

An alternative approach that organizations can use to capture design information from their existing systems is to use reverse engineering or design recovery products to analyze existing source code for potential classes and reusable components. Design recovery represents one method of recovering design information from existing systems. Any legacy system that has a defined data model has potential candidate classes, attributes, and objects that can be extracted out. I will look more closely at this process in chapters 10 and 11.

Application frameworks, if available, can be considered to provide specific functionality and used in the OOD process. Examples include the Microsoft Foundation classes or the Object Windows Library from Borland. However, for a component to be reused, it must be easily found and have a description or specification that defines the semantic and syntactic meanings of its components. At a minimum, the design specification for a reusable component should describe what functions it performs, what information it contains, what its interface is, and how it can be used. In addition, an example of the component used in an application can help developers understand how the component functions.

All reusable components must be classified and accessible to developers so they can locate them as they are needed. There are many studies that describe good classification structures and tools for reusable components, including [PRI87] and [POD92]. The role and responsibility for describing, categorizing, and managing these reusable components can be the job of a reuse group. I will delve into more detail on reuse in chapter 12.

7.4 Reuse of Existing Programming Constructs

The primary reason that most developers don't reuse software components is because they can't find a potential module to reuse. This holds true whether you are looking for reusable components in design or in construction (i.e., programming). If you expect to make use of reusable components, in this case programming constructs, you must be aware they exist and what functions they perform.

In the case of OOCOBOL, you must investigate the available class libraries delivered with the compiler and, whenever you are charged with coding a class, begin by finding any existing classes that might share the data structures or operations that you are looking to implement. Knowing what available classes are in the OOCOBOL library will result in reuse of these classes in applications but requires that designers study these libraries before designing solutions.

As an example of how you might design an object from the OOCOBOL class libraries, return to the example of a Deck of Cards that I introduced in chapters 3 and 5. A deck or collection of cards includes 52 with the value pairs {Ace of Diamonds, 2 of Diamonds, ... Queen of Hearts, King of Hearts}. Understanding that any design offers a multitude of choices, you examine the Deck of Cards example for discussion purposes.

One thing that becomes apparent as you consider this example is that the Deck of Cards actually is a set of 52 unique elements or items with a predefined pair of values. This is a bounded set of elements, that is fixed in size, and there are no duplicates allowed in the set (i.e., you don't allow for 2 Ace of Spade cards in the deck). An alternative design would be to have two different collections of cards — one that represents the cards available to be dealt and the other representing those already dealt. In this case, the Deal method simply moves cards from one collection to the other, while the Shuffle operation moves all the cards into the collection available for dealing.

Without delving into too much detail on the OOCBOL classes, you can consider any of OOCOBOL collection classes for the Deck of Cards ADT, including Bag, CharacterArray, VSet, Dictionary, OrderedCollection, or SortedCollection. Given these considerations, you might choose not to use a Bag class for the Deck of Cards, because a Bag can include duplicates. You also might ignore the Dictionary class, because it supports a pair of data elements — one for a key and the other for the actual data — and you do not require keyed access to the Deck of Cards.

You might use the VSet class for are Deck of Cards, because it allows unordered sets and does not allow duplicates, or the CharacterArray class with a pair of data elements (for instance XY, where X=2 through 10, J, Q, K, A and Y= C,D,H,S) stored in sequence. You also might choose to implement the Deck of Cards using either the OrderedCollection or the SortedCollection class. The OrderedCollection allows elements to be placed in a list on a first-in-first-out (FIFO) format, such as for a stack or queue, where the list can grow dynamically, while the SortedCollection stores elements in ascending or descending sequence.

One consideration that you should make in your design of the Deck of Cards is how you will support the Shuffle operation. Remember that the Shuffle operation organizes the deck of cards in random order, so you must consider an operation for your Deck of Cards that matches this function. If you cannot find one, you have to define your own and extend one of these classes to include it. One possible design for the Shuffle operation would be to add a third element to the Deck of Cards and store the card deck in order as follows:

Deck of Cards = Collection of 52 Suit of Card + OrderValue (1..52)

When the Deck of Cards.Shuffle operation occurs, the OrderValue field is assigned a random number from 1 to 52 with no two cards having the same OrderValue. This ensures that the cards will be dealt in their OrderValue. When the Deck of Cards.Deal n Cards occurs, it simply extracts the next n cards in ascending OrderValue. For this to work, you need to implement the Deck of Cards as either an OrderedCollection or, a SortedCollection, where the cards are kept sorted by OrderValue.

I now will examine the design differences between the available collections that I am describing. If you use a collection that allows duplicates, you must provide your own mechanism (operation) to make sure no duplicate cards are in your deck. However, you could easily do this when the deck of cards is created because you can assign the card values in sequence. You do need an ordered collection if you are to use the sorting mechanism described earlier, but you don't need a collection that prevents duplicates, so you can eliminate a VSet or CharacterArray because they are not ordered.

This leaves OrderedCollection, which would require that the cards be reordered every time you shuffle the cards, or SortedCollection, which does not. Another design issue in the card deck is whether you will have to reorganize the collection every time you shuffle them or if there is another way to design the data structure to limit the movement of the cards within the deck. One approach, which would eliminate the need to reorganize the deck of cards when the shuffle operation occurs, would be to use two collections in the ADT: one that represents the cards and their values and one that represents the order of the cards to be dealt.

For example, you could use the structure described earlier where each card is an entry in a stack or memory-based array with values reflecting the card and its suit (array PIC XX[52]). You could have a second array, also containing 52 entries, that would reference the cards in the other array in the order that they should be dealt (array PIC X[52]). The index to this second array could be used to represent the order of the cards, and the value in the second array could be the card (index to the first array).

A better design might be to have the Deck of Cards.Deal method deal cards in random order when the Deck of Cards.Shuffle method is performed first. Under this design, the deck of cards is implemented as an array of 52 items with an additional field indicating if the card already has been dealt (a boolean field that is either true — the card has been dealt and can't be dealt again until the cards are shuffled — or false — the card can be dealt).

In this design, the cards could be dealt in ascending order by value (i.e., Ace of Hearts, 2 of Hearts, 3 of Hearts ... Queen of Spades, King of Spades) or in random order by simply having the Deck of Cards.Deal method generate a random number between 1 and 52 and dealing that card if it hasn't already been dealt. If the card already has been dealt, the process continues until a random card is found that hasn't been dealt yet. Once a card is dealt, the boolean value is set to true and that card is ignored by the Deal method until the deck is reshuffled.

The strength of this design is that it doesn't require any changes to the order in which the cards are stored in the array. The functionality for Shuffle is implemented via the added field (Dealt) and the Deal method. When the DeckofCards.Shuffle method is executed, the dealt field for all the cards in the deck is set to false allowing them to be dealt in any order.

Using this approach, you could use the CharacterArray class to store the data (i.e., card values, suit, and dealt field) for the array. After careful consideration, I will create an implementation for the Deck of Cards in the next chapter.

7.5 Popular OOD Methods

As with the OOA methods described in the previous chapter, there are a variety of design techniques that create or specify a system design using objects and messages. Of these, I'll review the following popular methods prior to discussing the Booch method that I will use for the example problems.

- Booch
- Object-Oriented Structured Design (OOSD)
- Responsibility Driven Design (RDD)
- Shlaer/Mellor - Recursive Design
- Synthesis

A sidebar beginning on page 221 compares popular OOA/D methods in more detail.

7.5.1 Shlaer/Mellor Recursive Design

OOD under the Shlaer/Mellor approach uses Recursive Design and the object-oriented design language (OODL) [SHL90]. OOA/Recursive Design involves five steps:

1. Partition the system into domains (OOA)
2. Analyze the application and service domains (OOA)
3. Specify the architectural domain
4. Map the architecture to the implementation domain
5. Map the application to the architecture and services.

Within Recursive Design, there are two separate but related views of an application: System design and Program design. System design defines which programs are required and how they communicate and strategies for sharing data and managing program control. Program (or object) design defines which components map to which programs, how the components interact, and how data and control are managed by components. The key distinction between system and program design is in the level of control. Systems manage many threads of control, while programs manage a single thread of control.

Shlaer/Mellor Notation

An *inheritance diagram* shows inheritance relationships between classes in a class hierarchy with public and private inheritance indicated. The inheritance diagram is derived from the Information Structure diagram created in OOA.

A *dependency diagram* shows invocation and friend relationships between classes, including data coupling and dependencies between classes and modules.

A *class diagram* represents an external view of each class and illustrates the details of the interface for the class, including visible operations.

A *class structure chart* (a modified structure chart) shows the internal structure of each class, including public, private and protected operations, data couples, exception propagation and handling, and polymorphism.

Inheritance diagrams represent classes in an inheritance hierarchy, while dependency diagrams show interactions between classes. At a lower level, class diagrams represent the external view and class structure charts describe the internal view of each class. Class dependency diagrams represent invocations and data structures defined within a class structure chart.

7.5.2 Synthesis (Page-Jones and Weiss)

Design in Synthesis [PAG91] is composed of the following tasks:

1. Assign each object class to a physical processor (processor-communication diagram) showing the interprocessor communication requirements in content and in physical form
2. Establish all software services, including GUI/Windows services, DBMS managers, stacks, queues, bags
3. Declare software packages (package communication diagrams) using partitioning by periodicity, performance, use of the program, geography, processor capability, processor capacity or operating environment. In these diagrams, nodes represent programs and connections represent intertask communication requirements
4. Design class internals (method-structure diagrams)
5. Construct programs in an OOPL.

Synthesis Notation

Central to Synthesis is the unified object notation (UON), which is a superset of Larry Constantine's structured design notation. UOM is composed of seven basic views: external views of object modules, interface views of object modules, class definition (or object interface) diagrams, class hierarchy (or inheritance) diagrams, object communication (or neighborhood) diagrams, and object internal (or method structure) diagrams.

The *object module external view* is used to show objects without their internal or interface information. The object module interface view shows an object with its supported methods and distinguishes between class and instance methods.

Class definition diagrams provide the external interface or abstract definition of the features of a class that are available in a normal way to external clients. These diagrams show messages (and their elements) being passed between classes and defined as a list of formal object names with the object couple.

Class hierarchy diagrams depict subclass/parent directed relationships, highlighting tightly coupled relationships and single or multiple inheritance.

Object communication diagrams show the interaction of selected objects through message passing. These diagrams show only the methods of each object that are called into play by the messages shown and events are drawn and labeled.

Object internal diagrams show the internal or detailed design of an object module. These diagrams are derived from a structure charts but have been extended to handle object oriented concepts including message passing, hierarchy of components, class and instance variables, etc.

7.5.3 Object-Oriented Structured Design (OOSD)

Anthony Wasserman, Peter Pricher, and Robert Muller of Interactive Development Environments (IDE) have developed a technique for design [WAS89] that combines aspects of traditional structured design (SD) with object-oriented design (OOD). IDE is a CASE tool vendor that markets Software Through Pictures.

Object-Oriented Structured Design (OOSD) is an architectural design method that integrates a top-down method of design, popularized by Yourdon/Constantine, with a bottom-up OOD approach, based on the work of Booch and Buhr. IDE claim OOSD can support traditional structured designs as well as object-oriented designs. OOSD does not provide a detailed procedure for developing the design, only a notation for representing the result.

At a very basic level, OOSD supports the creation of a hierarchy of objects and uses functional decomposition of a system with an orientation towards classes of objects.

OOSD Notation

OOSD includes a modification to the structure chart with a set of symbols for modules in a system. The *object-oriented structure chart* (OOSC) adds notations for objects, classes, methods, visibility, instantiation, exception handling, hidden operations, generic definitions, inheritance, and concurrency.

7.5.4 Responsibility Driven Design (RDD)

Responsibility-Driven Design (RDD) is described in [WIR90] by Rebecca Wirfs-Brock, Brian Wilkerson, and L. Wiener. RDD is based on object-oriented development experiences within Tektronix with the Smalltalk language.

RDD models an application as a collection of objects that collaborate to discharge their responsibilities. The RDD method focuses on what actions must be accomplished and which objects will accomplish them. Responsibilities represent a means of apportioning work amongst objects within an application and RDD focuses on the knowledge an object maintains (data) and the actions an object performs (services).

Responsibilities also represent the publicly available services defined by objects. The responsibilities of an object are all the services that it provides for all objects that communicate with it. Under RDD, the designer looks for classes of objects and builds a model of the key classes that will fulfill the overall design objectives.

The goal of RDD is to develop a pattern for distributing the flow of control and sequencing of actions among collaborating objects and to understand how each object accomplishes its tasks. Also, this method seeks to preserve encapsulation, maximize reuse, and minimize the complexity of a class methods and information structure. The authors of this method recommend constructing simple interfaces to objects whenever possible.

The RDD tasks include:

- Discover the classes required to model the application
- Determine what behavior the system is responsible for, and assign these responsibilities to specific classes
- Determine what collaborations must occur between classes of object to fulfill those responsibilities.

RDD Notation

RDD uses *index cards* to represent classes (also called Class or CRC cards) that consist of text describing the class name, super/subclasses, responsibilities and collaborations.

Class specifications (data dictionary) describe more detail on each class, including related hierarchy and collaboration graphs, a general description of each class, and its contracts and methods.

Collaboration graphs display collaborations between classes and subsystems, with contracts shown and paths of collaboration between them. Subsystems are defined as a set of classes collaborating to fulfill a common set of responsibilities. A large application is made less complex by identifying subsystems within it and treating those subsystems as classes.

Hierarchy diagrams represent inheritance relationship in a latticelike structure or a hierarchy. Subsystem cards and specifications also can be used to represent opportunities for abstract superclasses.

I prefer a model with moderately intelligent, collaborating objects over one with intelligence concentrated into just a few objects. I much prefer a distribution of control over a concentration of power.
Wirfs-Brock [WIR93].

7.6 Booch Object-Oriented Design

In his books, Grady Booch describes a technique for the design and implementation of systems using an object model and specification. Booch defines an object as a model of a real world entity that combines both data and operations on that data. These objects, once identified, are the basis for the modules of a system or set of related objects.

In his early books, Booch created notations that represented the constructs of the Ada language and derived a set of objects from a specification and informal design. The early Booch notation shows dependencies between the Ada packages and tasks that implement the objects. Later Booch books describe a more generic OOD approach with an architecture diagram based on the earlier work [BOO91]. Booch has recently updated his method as described in [BOO93] to incorporate some of the concepts and notations from other popular object-oriented methods.

7.6.1 Introduction

Grady Booch uses object decomposition and iterative design with prototyping in his object-oriented design method. The booch method consists of the following steps:

1. Requirements Analysis
2. Domain Analysis
   - 2.1 Identify classes and objects at a given level of abstraction
   - 2.2 Identify semantics for each class and object
   - 2.3 Identify relationships among these classes and objects
3. Object-Oriented Design (See Figure 7.1)
   - 3.1 Define initial architecture and prototypes
   - 3.2 Define the logical design
     - 3.2.1 Define the data structures
     - 3.2.2 Define data types

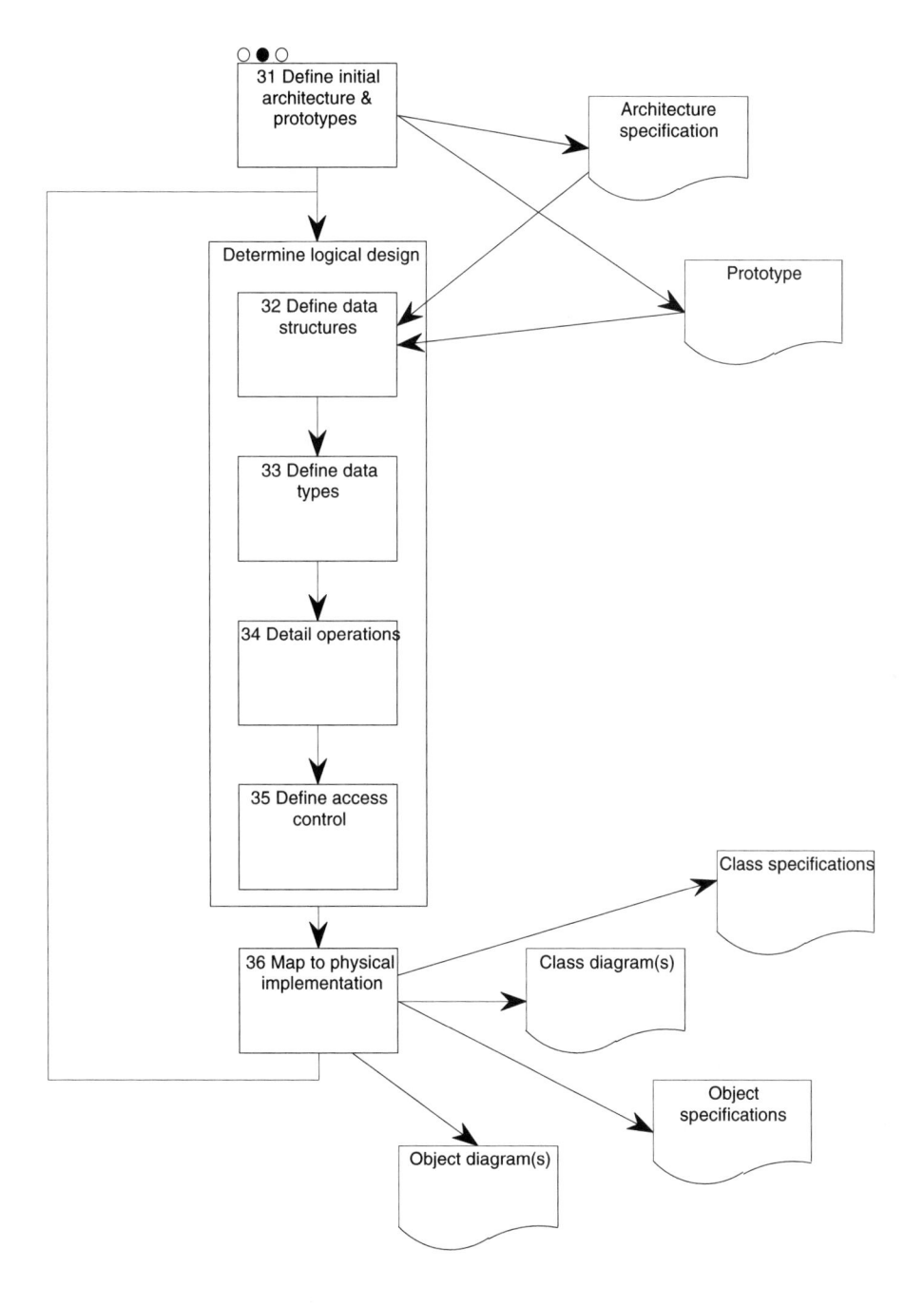

Figure 7.1 Booch object-oriented design tasks.

             3.2.3   Define operations
             3.2.4   Define access control
     3.3   Map the resulting design to physical implementations
             3.3.1   Make design decisions concerning the representation of
                     the classes and objects defined (i.e., decide how its
                     behavior should be implemented)
             3.3.2   Allocate each class and object to a module
     3.4   Refine the design and return to 3 as required
4.   Implement the classes and objects
5.   Return to 1 for each lower level of abstraction
6.   Modification tasks — add, change classes, subsystems, etc.

Because I have chosen to use the Coad/Yourdon OOA method (described in the previous chapter), I can skip steps 1 and 2 of the Booch method. These steps deliver work products similar to those created in the Coad/Yourdon method, including a list of key abstractions and mechanisms, a system charter (or requirements document), class and object diagrams, attributes, services or operations, and class and object specifications. I generically call this the object model and described it in the Appendix. Because I have created these in the OOA process, I reference them in this chapter and you are welcome to review them in the Appendix.

Also notice that the expected deliverables or representations from the OOD process include an architectural specification (including Booch process and module diagrams), a prototype, Booch class diagrams and specifications, and Booch object diagrams and specifications. As I review the example problems, I will discuss the deliverables created and their evolution as I move into implementation.

7.6.2 Technique

One critical aspect of the Booch method is determining when the OOD process is completed. Booch suggests several criteria that can be used to halt the OOD process. These include when there are no new key abstractions or mechanisms, when the classes and objects that are defined can be implemented by composition from existing reusable components, when all operations have been assigned to appropriate classes, and/or when each operation has been fully analyzed.

Booch recommends using prototyping to define the problem domain and address subsets of requirements for the system. Information collected during the prototyping process is fed back into the OOA/D process. Booch also suggests the use of object scenarios to represent the behavior and interaction of objects at various levels of abstraction. Booch uses object diagrams for this purpose, and you can select the objects defined in the Coad/Yourdon class/object diagram as your initial objects.

7.6.3 Representations and Notations

The Booch method includes four basic representations or views and six notations, some of which are optional. The Booch OOD method includes the following notations:

A) *Class diagrams* and specifications or templates represent key abstractions in the problem domain and their mechanisms.

B) *Object diagrams* and specifications or templates represent logical instances of generalizations in the class diagram.

C) *Process diagrams* represents the context of the system and its interaction with external systems.

D) *Module diagrams* represent visibility and packaging of classes and objects into modules.

E) *Timing* or *state-transition diagrams* (optional) represent dynamic behavior of classes and objects.

Booch class diagrams map to the class/object view in the Coad/Yourdon OOA method described in the previous chapter. Some of the Coad/Yourdon structures, especially the whole/part structures, represent the *uses* or *contains* relationship in the Booch class diagram notation. Booch also supports a wider set of class relationships, including *inherits* and *instantiates*, which map to the generalization/specialization structures in the Coad/Yourdon notation.

The class category symbol in the Booch class diagram can be used to show category visibility, which represents an encapsulated name space between classes that might have private, exported, or imported visibility. Class categories are layered using a "kind of" hierarchy.

Likewise, Booch object diagrams resemble the service view of the Coad/Yourdon notation. In fact, if your CASE tool supports both the Coad/Yourdon and the Booch method, you might be able to translate your existing Coad/Yourdon diagrams into Booch diagrams.

The Booch process diagram represents the context for the system and its interaction with other systems or hardware components. The symbols in the process diagram include:

- *Processor*: a CPU capable of executing software applications
- *Device*: any hardware device that interacts with a processor (examples: disk, terminal, printer, CRT, etc.)
- *Connection*: a physical connection between a CPU and an attached device

The default attributes for the processor are name, description, characteristics, processes, and scheduling. Characteristics can represent the manufacturer of the CPU, its model number, its memory, etc. Each processor can have allocated to it one or many processes that will execute at the CPU. A list of processes can be supplied and provide a reference to each process in the encyclopedia.

Processor scheduling can be one of five types: *manual*, which means a human must schedule processes; *cyclic*, which means control passes between processes based on a fixed processing time; *executive*, which implies that some algorithm controls the schedule; *preemptive*, which represents a priority system for use of the CPU; and *nonpreemptive*, which allows processes to execute until they relinquish control of the CPU.

The Booch module diagram represents the architecture of the system. These diagrams, however, are tied to the packaging constructs in the Ada language and have little value outside this language. Booch recommends using the subsystem symbols in non-Ada environments, and I use these constructs in the example problems. In fact, the subsystems in the Booch module diagram map closely to the domains in the Shlaer/Mellor diagrams that you created in chapter 6.

7.7 Problem Discussion

As in Analysis, I will proceed with the review of the two example applications, the Library problem and the ATM system. As I already have mentioned, I used prototyping in the development of both systems, and learned a lot about these systems by studying real-world example systems. I will begin the discussion by looking at the architectural designs of both systems before describing each in more detail.

Using the Booch method, you start by defining the context for each system, represented in a process diagram. In the case of the Library system, I defined the process diagram in Figure 7.2. Notice in this representation that the Library system interfaces with CRTs or terminals, which also might be PCs connected on a LAN, and the University system, which maintains student information, financial information, etc. For example purposes, the Library system is a simple, centralized DBMS with workstations or PCs that can access or update the Library data via the LAN. Printers also mighy be attached to specific PCs to allow reports to be printed in this configuration.

The Booch process diagram for the ATM system is shown in Figure 7.3. Notice that the ATM system interacts with the ATM User Interface and the Central Bank computer. The ATM User Interface works with the ATM hardware, specified as the Card reader, Deposit slot, Withdrawal chute, Receipt printer, Keyboard, and CRT. The ATM User Interface handles all the details of sending screens, receiving keyboard input, dispensing cash, opening and closing the various slots, etc. This design insulates the ATM system from the physical details of any particular ATM machine and the bank functionality (i.e., account management).

The other aspects of the architecture for the example systems, including the module diagrams and the prototypes created, are described in subsequent sections.

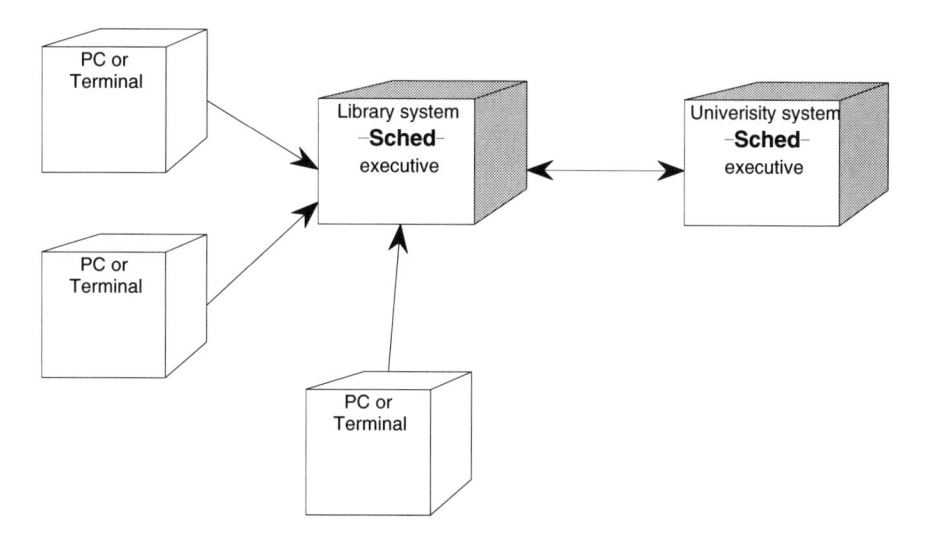

Figure 7.2
Library system - process diagram.

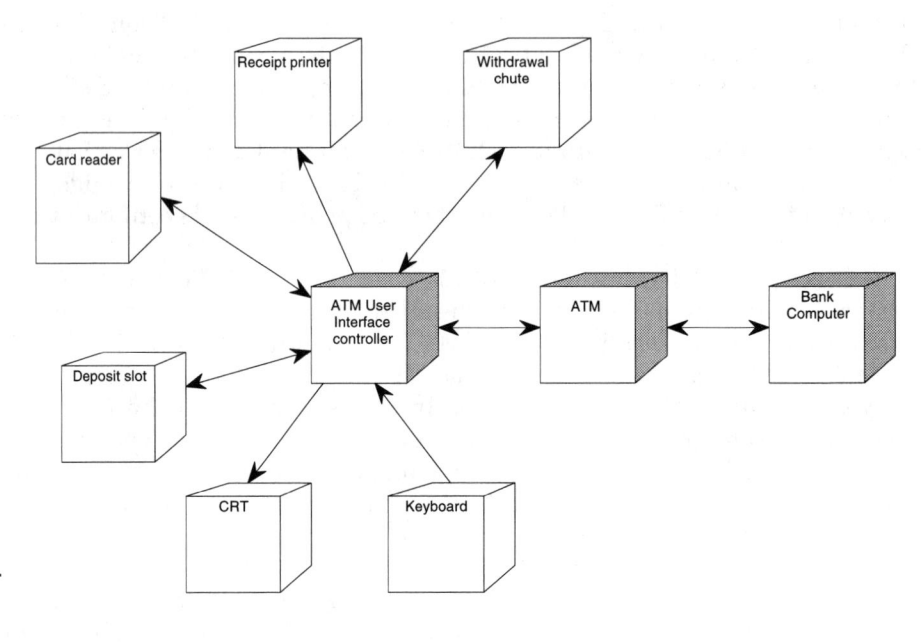

Figure 7.3
ATM system - process diagram.

7.7.1 Library Problem

The assumptions that were made during Analysis that must be addressed in design:

1. More than one copy of a book may be available in the library.
2. Each copy of a book must be uniquely identified in the system.
3. An implementation-specific security system will be available during the design phase to address the issue of restricting access to library transactions by user type.
4. The Library system will be implemented using a data structure that supports keyed or indexed access to data.
5. The archive process will be handled by batch (offline) components of the library system. These components were not addressed in Analysis.

Initial considerations for the Library problem include what tools you will use for prototyping, for managing the presentation of data (i.e., the user interface), which database or file system you will use to store the data, and if you should consider using CICS as a transaction processing system.

Building a prototype of the library system was quite easy and included the menus, screens, and reports for the system. I used a Windows-based CASE tool (System Architect) to define the screens and menus for the Library system instead of a GUI development tool, primarily because I felt that the user interface portion of the application already was well understood. Figure 7.4 shows the Library Signon screen as a Windows dialog box. As a result of the creation of the prototype, I have specified other screens and menu structures, which are described in section B.1.

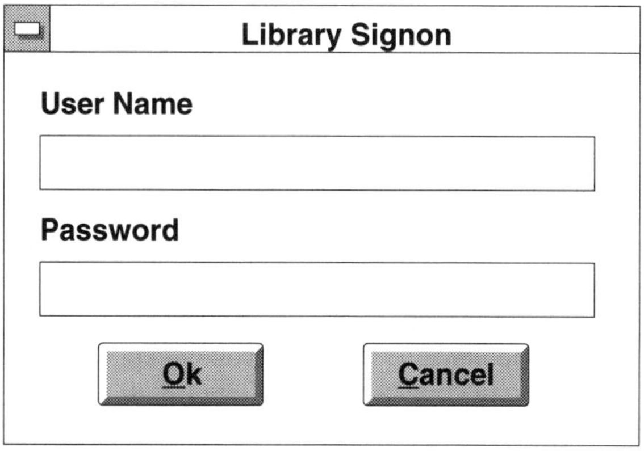

Figure 7.4
Library system - signon dialog box.

Notice that I created a signon screen for everyone accessing the library system. This was to support the security restrictions in the requirements document. In this design, when a user signs onto the system, they must specify their user ID and their password. When they are signed on, the system determines if they are a library user or a staff person and provides the correct menu of options for each.

To keep the Library problem simple but authentic, I chose a relational database management system (RDBMS) as the storage mechanism for most of the library data structures. I could have decided to use persistent objects, perhaps in a Dictionary, for storage of the book, user, staff, etc. If I had, I would have to address the issue of relationships between user and copy, etc., and I felt this would have clouded the issue of OOCOBOL development unneccessarily. I did decide to implement the Lists in the example problem using OOCOBOL collections, which are described later.

For simplicity, I assumed that the implementation of the Library system would be on a file server with a SQL-based DBMS, perhaps DB2/2, OS/2 Database Manager, Sybase, or something similar. Given this assumption and using the relational notation defined by Codd [COD70], I defined the basic tables of the Library problem as:

- Book (<u>Call Number</u>, Title, Publisher, Date Published, ISBN, Author Name)
- BookAuthor (<u>Call Number</u>, <u>Author Name</u>)
- BookCopy (<u>Copy Number</u>, <u>Call Number</u>)
- User (<u>User ID</u>, Name, Address, Borrow Limit)
- Staff (<u>User ID</u>, Name, Address, Borrow Limit, Employee Type, Date Hired)

Notice that I created the BookAuthor table to satisfy requirement #5 (provide a list of books by author). This table is created or updated whenever a new book is added to the library system and simply creates a tuple for each author of the book. Also notice that the BookCopy table reflects the concept of many copies of a book being in the library (see assumption #2). When a new book is added, the Library Staff must specify the number of available copies. The system then creates a table consisting of the Call Number and a unique Copy Number for each available copy.

In addition to these basic tables, I defined another table in the Library system:

- CheckedOut (<u>Call Number</u>, <u>Copy Number</u>, <u>User ID</u>, Date Out, Date Due Back)

The CheckedOut table is created when a user checks out a specific copy of a book and exists until the book is returned. When a book is checked out, the Book, Copy, and User tables are selected and joined to create the CheckedOut table. When this table is created, the date that the book was checked out and the date it is due back are stored. When the book is returned, the entry in the table is removed.

Remembering the exclusion of the Listsof object, I chose to implement these as references to permanent objects managed by OOCOBOL. Whenever a book is checked out by a user, an association is made between the User and the Book and Copy, which satisfies requirement #6 (CheckedOut table). Requirement #7 requires a permanent store of the books checked out to a user and those users that have checked out a book in the past. These Lists are required because, when a Book is returned, the association between the Book, Copy, and the User is removed.

In the design, the library data structures map to RDBMS table entries described in section A.2. Notice that the Book structure contains a field for ListOfUsers and that the User contains a field for ListOfBooks. Also notice that these fields have a new data type, USAGE OBJECT, which specifies that the collections are part of these data structures. This represents a reference to an object (in this case, a collection or List of Users or Books) that is included in the table entry of each Book and User. Each Book and User table will contain a field for the reference to the Lists.

Implementation choices for these Lists include any of the OOCOBOL collection classes. As I evaluated these classes, I focused on the characteristics of the Lists and their behavior. The two Lists being designed, List of Books and List of Users, might contain duplicate entries and are stored in the order that they are placed into the List. You might want to design these Lists with indices to allow quick access to each entry; however, with a maximum of only 100 entries in each List, you will not be severely penalized if you choose not to index them.

If you chose to order or sort these Lists, you could use the OrderedCollection or the SortedCollection classes in the OOCOBOL libraries. One approach might be to order the Lists by the date that a book was checked out so that you could display the Lists in ascending order by date. If you choose not to order the Lists, you would exclude the Bag class because it is used primarily when there are numerous duplicates and you do not expect many duplicates. I chose the CharacterArray for both of the Lists because this class stores strings as objects and allows indices and instances of different size. I defined both classes, List_Of_Books and List_Of_Users, to inherit from the generic Listof class utility, which itself inherits from the CharacterArray class.

The behavior of the List objects is the same and begins with initializing them as empty collections (i.e., no entries). When a book is returned, the operations performed are as follows:

Book is returned: 1) Table CheckedOut is searched for the correct User, Book, and Copy
2) A data structure is built from this entry with the following information: User ID, Call Number, Copy Number, Date Out, Date Due Back, and Date Back
3) The entry in CheckedOut table is removed
4) An Add message is sent to the List of Books along with the data structure built in step 2
5) An Add message is sent to the List of Users with the data structure built previously.

List of Books: 1) The entry is added to the list
2) If the list is full (i.e., contains 100 entries), the archive operation is executed, which copies the list to the archive data store, then initializes it.

Once the data structures have been defined, I will begin looking at the data types for the Library system. The complete COBOL data structures and types for the Library system are described in section A.2.

Another option for the Library system would be to use some form of transaction processor (TP), perhaps CICS, to manage the library transactions. I chose not to use CICS or any other TP environment because most of these are not yet integrated into the OOCOBOL environment and would represent significant effort to make them work with OOCOBOL applications. The defined architecture for the Library system is represented in the flowchart in Figure 7.5.

Returning to the design of the library system, I will review the classes and objects from analysis focusing on their data structures and operations. As part of this process, I will convert our Coad/Yourdon diagram to Booch class diagram. One nice feature of my CASE tool (System Architect) is that it allows me to copy the Coad/Yourdon class/object symbols into a new Booch class diagram and transform the symbols into the Booch clouds. Once you have placed the classes in the Booch diagram, you must define each class and specify its relationships in the System Architect encyclopedia. I have modified the System Architect encyclopedia to map more directly to the OOCOBOL environment by including attributes for data elements (fields) that map to COBOL data types.

Key abstractions in the Library problem are shown in the class diagram in Figure 7.6 (carried forward from the Coad/Yourdon diagram in chapter 6) and include Book, Library User, Library Staff, List of Users, and List of Books. Not shown at this level of abstraction is the decomposition of the Book class showing that it contains or uses two other classes: Author and Copy. This correlates to the definition that I gave previously of the RDBMS tables for Book.

As I look at services in the library system, I will focus on the collaboration and responsibilities between the objects. For example, you will find that there are definite responsibilities between a book and a user, a book and a list, a book and a staff, etc. Whenever a book is checked out, the staff object sends a message (Checkout) to the book object with the User ID, the Call Number, and the Copy Number. The Book object then establishes the relationship between

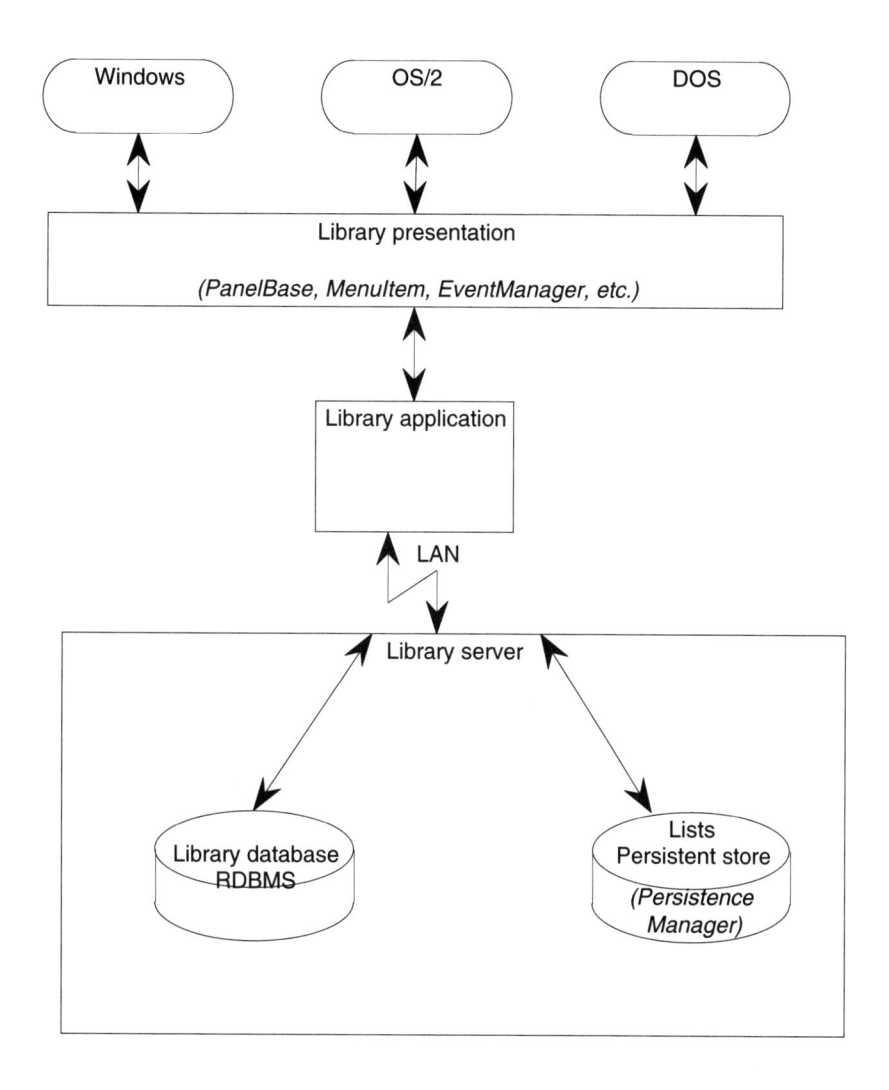

Figure 7.5
Library system - architecture diagram.

the Book, Copy, and the User in the relational table.

In the RDBMS implementation, a table would be created that would join the Book, Copy, and User tables and include the fields DateOut, DateDueBack, etc. If you used an indexed file to manage the Book, Copy, and User structures, an association would be made between the Copy and the User. Each Copy is associated with its Book (owner) when they are added to the file, so this operation must include the establishment of this association.

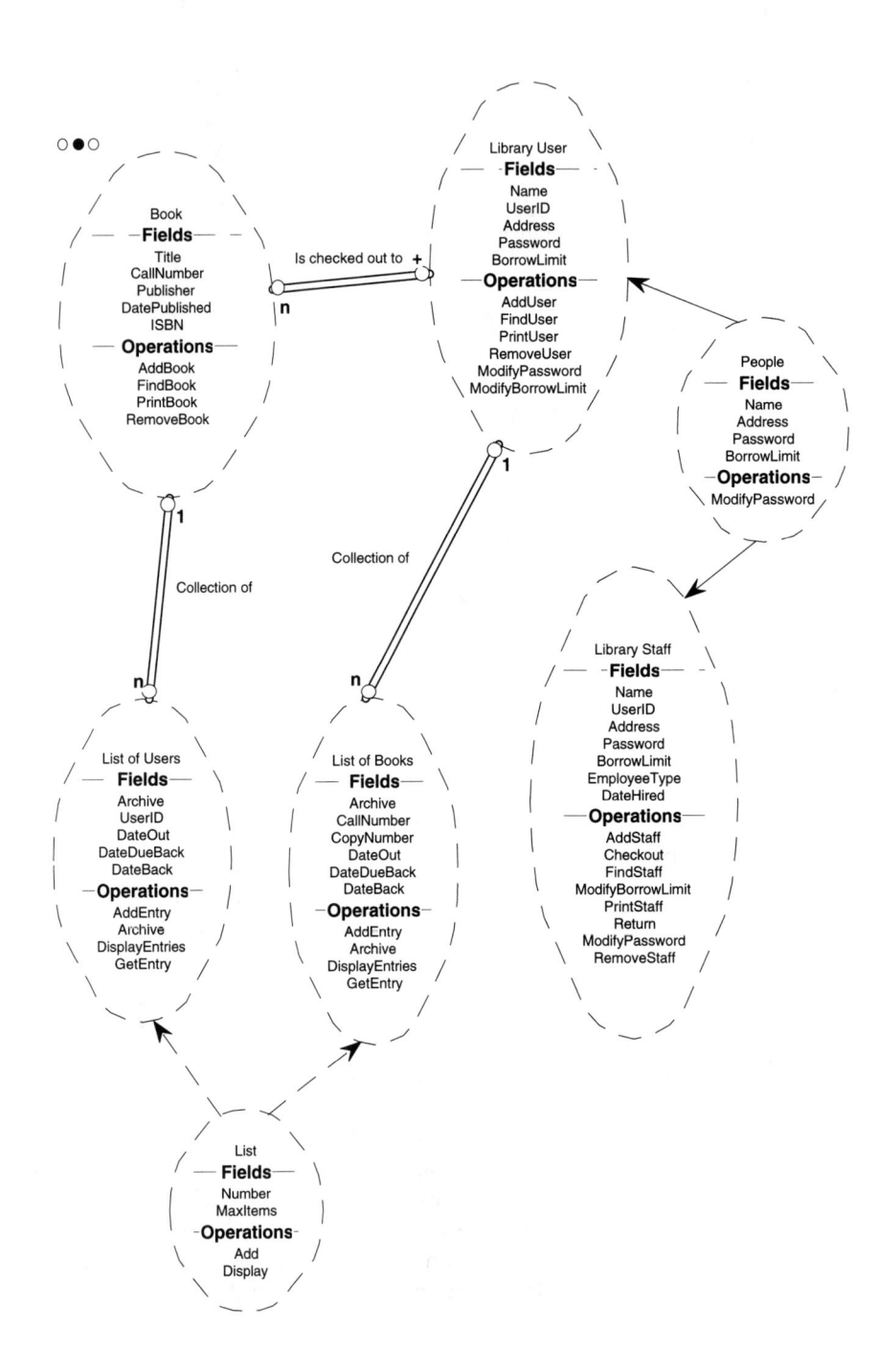

Figure 7.6
Library system - class diagram.

One notation that helps define the operations and collaborations for objects is the Booch object scenarios diagram. In these diagrams, you begin by picking a service, say Checkout, and identifying the sequence of operations for all the objects involved in the collaboration. In this case, you begin by having the Library Staff object send a message to the Book object requesting that the Copy of the book be checked out to the User specified. The book object verifies that the copy is not already checked out to someone else, then makes the association with the User. Some notification could be made back to the Staff object to indicate the book now is checked out to the user, perhaps returning the Date Due Back.

Looking at the Return operation, you will see that the Library Staff object sends the message Return to the Book object, which in turn collects the Date Returned, breaks the association between the Book, Copy, and User, then sends a message to both the List of Books and the List of Users to add the entry to their collections. Figure 7.7 represents the scenario for returning a Book using the Booch notation.

Given this scenario, you determine which objects require access to which data structures. In this case, the Book and Copy objects need access to the User structure to make the association whenever a book is checked out and to remove it when a book is returned. Also, because the Library Staff object can update a User's borrow limit, it will need access to the User data structure. The List structures are part of the Book and User objects, so these objects should have access to the List structures.

An additional factor in the implementation is how the Library objects — Book, User, and Library Staff — will interface with the RDBMS. For example, as you define each Add operations, you must specify that, when a object is added, an entry is placed into the appropriate table. You also need to perform any necessary formatting, verification, etc. required for the data to be stored in the table correctly.

Given this definition, the PDL for the Add Book operation might look something like this:

Book.Add
    Verify that the book doesn't already exist in the system
    If the book already exists,
        notify the staff of the exception
    Else,
        Add the Book table entry

Object-Oriented Development in COBOL

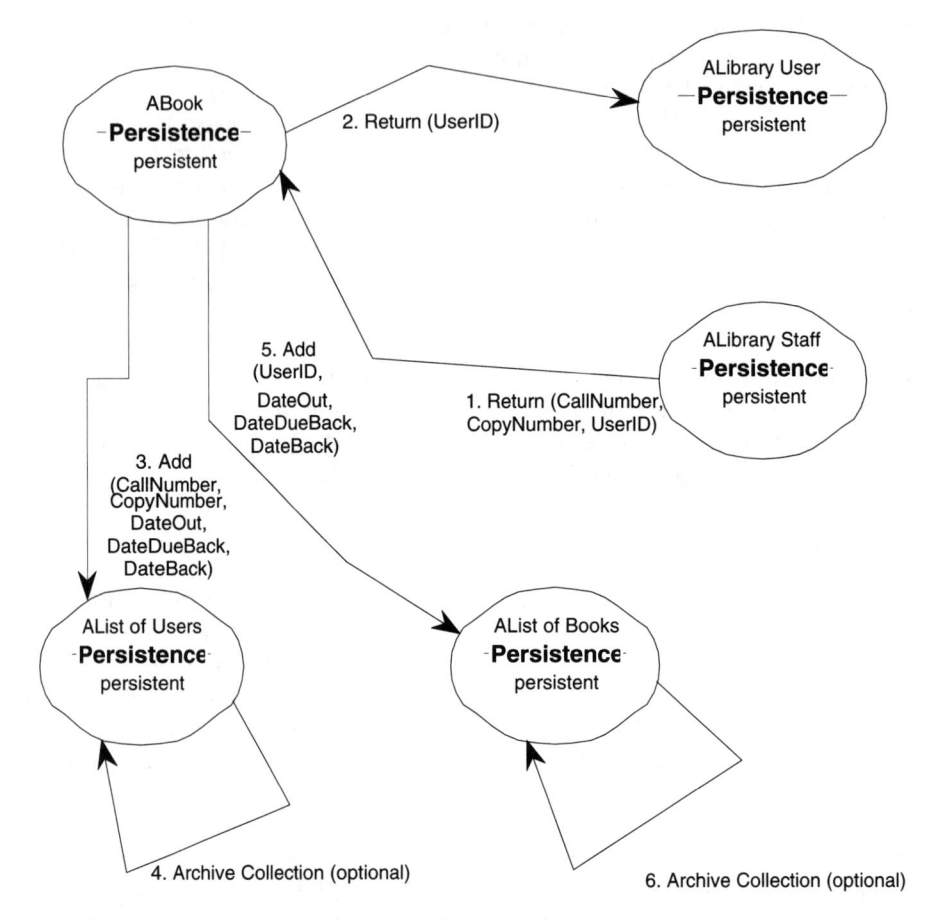

Figure 7.7
Library system - return book object scenario diagram.

[Diagram showing object interactions:
- ABook (Persistence, persistent)
- ALibrary User (Persistence, persistent)
- ALibrary Staff (Persistence, persistent)
- AList of Users (Persistence, persistent)
- AList of Books (Persistence, persistent)

Messages:
1. Return (CallNumber, CopyNumber, UserID)
2. Return (UserID)
3. Add (CallNumber, CopyNumber, DateOut, DateDueBack, DateBack)
4. Archive Collection (optional)
5. Add (UserID, DateOut, DateDueBack, DateBack)
6. Archive Collection (optional)]

Add the BookAuthor entries for the required authors
Add the BookCopy entries for the required copies
Initialize the List_Of_Users collection to 0 entries and set Archive to false

Likewise, any Find operations must be mapped to SQL commands to locate the correct Book, User, Copy, etc., and any CheckoutBook operation must map to the correct SQL JOIN commands. The Print operation for the tables would simply display the fields on the screen or on an attached printer. The Remove operations would have to verify the correct book, copy, or user, then remove any associated table entries for BookAuthor, BookCopy, and CheckoutBook.

Now that you have designed the objects, including their data structures, data types, operations, and access control, you need to document the architecture and map it to an OOCOBOL implementation. The first step is to review the library domains as defined in chapter 6, then consider designing subsystems accordingly.

The resulting Booch module diagram for the Library system is shown in Figure 7.8. Notice that I have specified five basic subsystems for the Library, University Interfaces, List Services, Data Access, and Network Facilities. Again assuming that the system will be implemented on a LAN with the Library files managed on a server, you specify the Data Access subsystem which manages the persistent data structures (Book, Copy, User, etc.); the List Services, which manage the Lists of Users and List of Books and access to these lists; the University Interfaces, which support access to other University systems; and the Network Facilities, which manage the communication over the LAN. The Appendix describes the resulting object specification and diagrams in more detail.

Another issue that you might consider when building the Library system is what existing legacy systems you will need to interface with in the future. These might include a student information system, financial system, or even an administration system. As I designed the Library system, I considered interfacing with the student information managed by the university. An additional requirement that would require this interface would be for the system to add any overdue book fines to each students' invoice at the end of each semester. While I do not delve into the details of how this interface could be built, I will look more closely at these issues in chapter 11.

7.7.2 ATM Problem

The ATM system is much different from the Library system in its design because it represents a reactive environment with a sophisticated, context-sensitive user interface. Before I consider a design for the ATM system, I will state the assumptions I made in building this system. In this case, I indicated that I would be using Windows as the GUI for our ATM system, storing the ATM transactions in a permanent data store (file), and interfacing with an existing banking systems.

As I built a prototype of ATM user interface, I found that I could simulate the interface in Windows using a dialog box. Figure 3.4 showed the Windows user interface and includes buttons for the keyboard, a text screen, etc. Obviously,

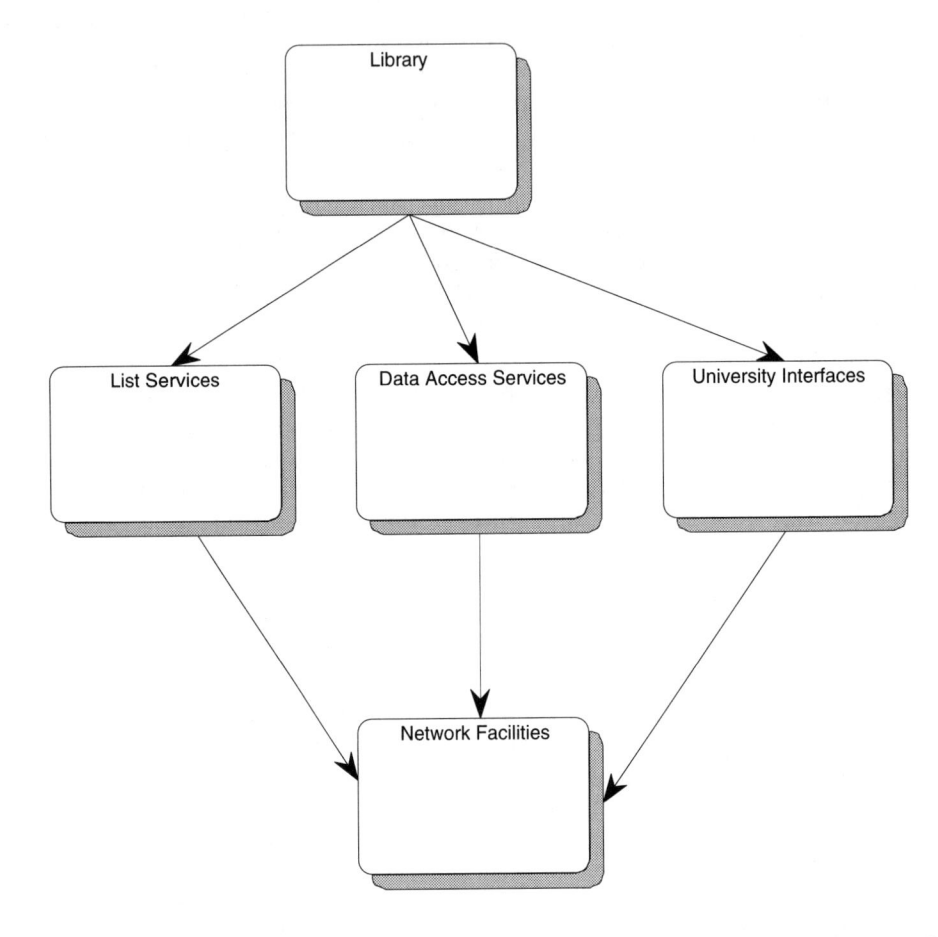

Figure 7.8
Library system - module diagram.

[Diagram: Library module at top connects down to List Services, Data Access Services, and University Interfaces, which all connect down to Network Facilities.]

I could not implement the withdrawal, deposit, or the card slot, but I defined icons to represent these physical components to make the prototype more realistic.

As I discussed in the previous chapter, you might choose to build a Smalltalk implementation of the UI, then let that portion of the system manage the input and output for the ATM. Micro Focus provides a product for interfacing OOCOBOL and Smalltalk/V applications, called Co-Link/V, and Digitalk also sells a product, PARTS, that also can be used to integrate COBOL applications with Smalltalk GUI front-ends.

I will begin by reviewing the classes in the ATM object model and converting them to the proper Booch notation. Like the Library system, I first convert the

Chapter 7 Object-Oriented Design 209

Coad/Yourdon class and objects into classes as shown in Figure 7.9. The key abstractions (from OOA) include ATM, ATM File Manager, ATM User Interface, and Account Manager. The ATM class includes one copy of the Account Manager and ATM User Interface classes. The ATM also interacts with the ATM File Manager class via the ATM Session. The ATM User Interface contains a display screen, keyboard, Card slot, Deposit slot, withdrawal slot, and receipt printer.

As I define the classes, you will notice the strong collaborations and responsibilities between the ATM and its subsystems. As with the library system, one powerful tool for understanding and designing these collaborations is the

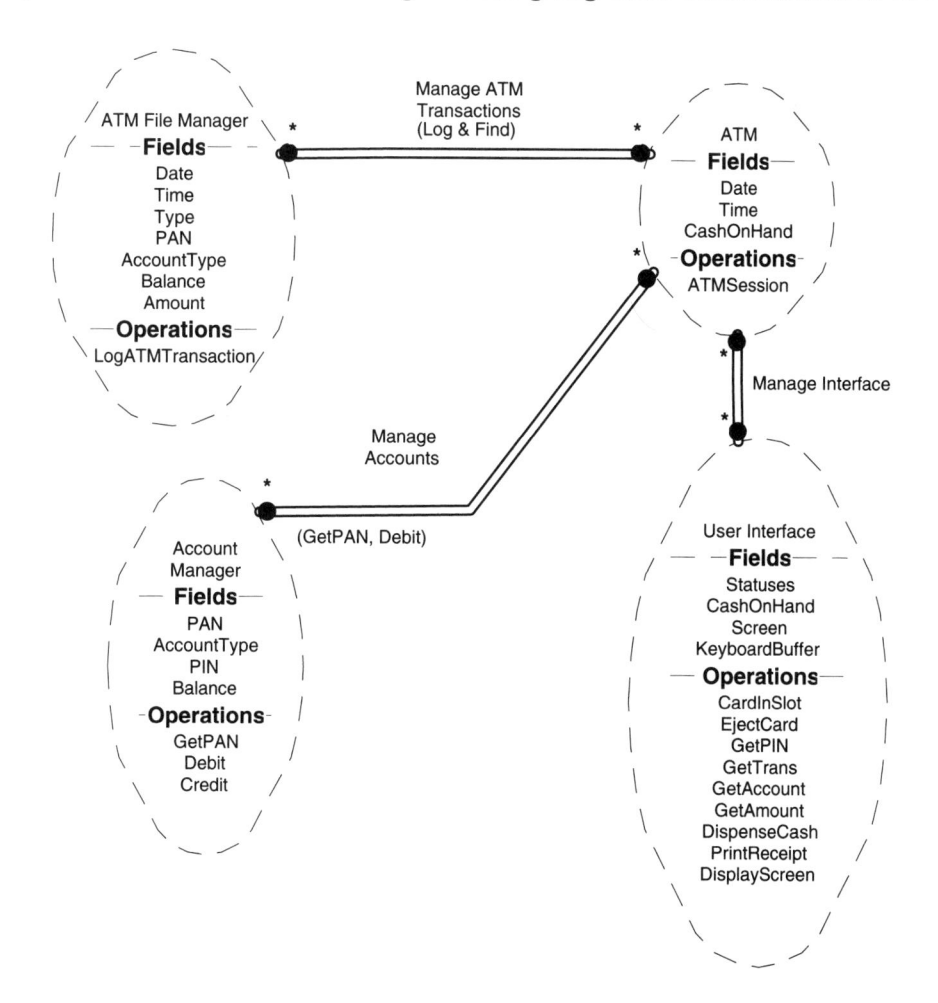

Figure 7.9
ATM system - class diagram.

Booch object scenario diagram. Figure 7.10 represents the scenario for beginning an ATM session, while Figure 7.11 represents the scenario for ending an ATM session. Both of these diagrams map to the state-transition diagram that I created in the previous chapter.

Using these scenario diagrams, you can define, in detail, the collaborations and responsibilities for the ATM system. In this case, I defined object scenario diagrams for five collaborations: Begin Session, Withdrawal, Deposit, Funds Transfer, and End Session. Notice that I did not define a scenario for the Balance Inquiry transaction. This is because a Begin and an End session together support the functionality of this transaction and all validated transactions includes printing a receipt.

As you define these collaborations, you will find the key responsibilities are between the ATM and the ATM UI. If you take only these key collaborations, you can identify the following interactions:

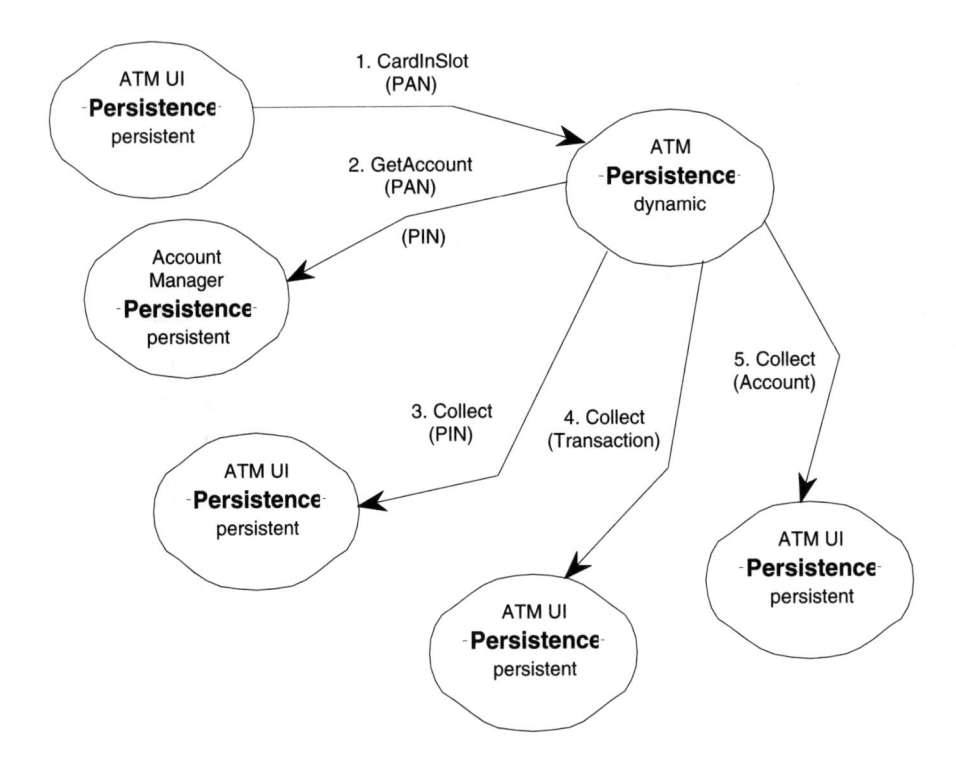

Figure 7.10
ATM system - begin session object scenario diagram.

Chapter 7 Object-Oriented Design   211

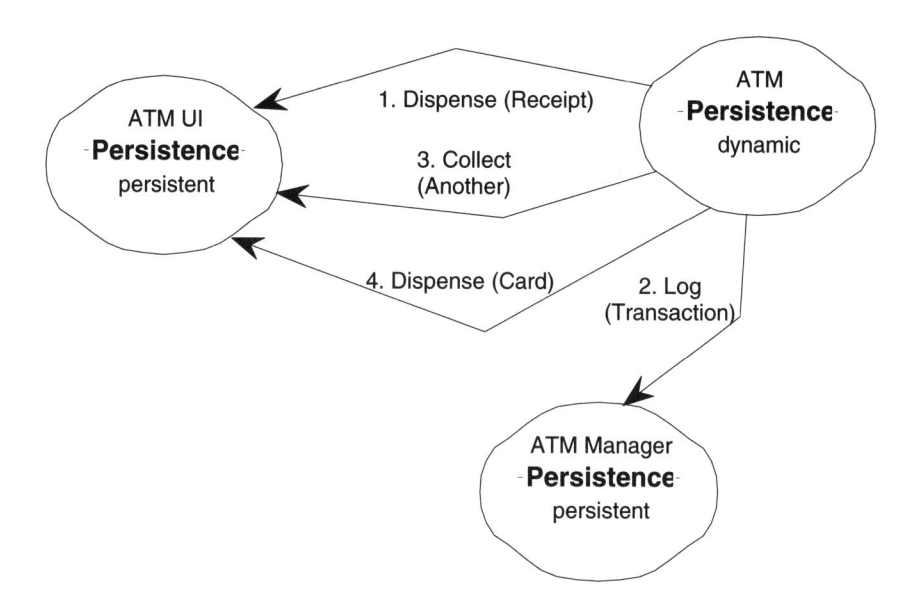

Figure 7.11
ATM system - end session object scenario diagram.

(Diagram: ATM Persistence dynamic → 1. Dispense (Receipt) → ATM UI Persistence persistent; ATM → 3. Collect (Another) → ATM UI; ATM → 4. Dispense (Card) → ATM UI; ATM → 2. Log (Transaction) → ATM Manager Persistence persistent)

Message	Parameter	From	To	Next action
(Initial)	-	-	-	Waiting for a card
CardInSlot	PAN	UI	ATM	Verify Account
GetPIN	PIN	ATM	UI	GetTransaction
GetTrans	Transaction	ATM	UI	GetAccount
GetAccount	Account	ATM	UI	GetAmount(Nonbalance)
GetAmount	Amount	ATM	UI	Dispense (Withdrawal)
AnotherTrans	Answer	ATM	UI	EjectCard
EjectCard	-	ATM	UI	Back to initial state

One approach to a design for the ATM would be to define the interactions between the ATM and the user interface (UI) based on a small set of generic collaborations with the ATM acting as the client and the UI as the server. Figure 7.12 shows the client/server relationship between the ATM and the UI using RDD notation (described in section 7.5.4) In this sense, the collaborations can be generically grouped into two requests: Collect or Dispense. A Collect request made by the ATM to the UI can be used to get the PIN, transaction type, account, amount, deposit, or another transaction, while a Dispense request can be used for cash (as in the withdrawal transaction), printing a receipt, and ejecting the card when the session is over.

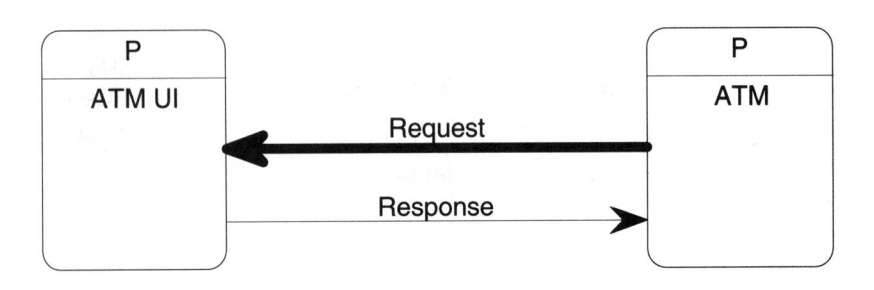

Object-Oriented Development in COBOL

```
┌─────────┐                              ┌─────────┐
│    P    │                              │    P    │
│         │◄──────── Request ────────────│         │
│ ATM UI  │                              │  ATM    │
│         │────────  Response ──────────►│         │
└─────────┘                              └─────────┘
```

Request:
Collect: PIN
Transaction
Account
Amount
Deposit
Another
Dispense: Cash
Receipt
Card

Response:
PIN
Transaction
Account
Amount

Another (Y|N)
Exception*

Figure 7.12
ATM system - ATM and UI client/server relationship.

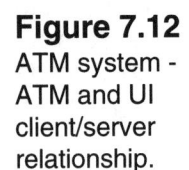

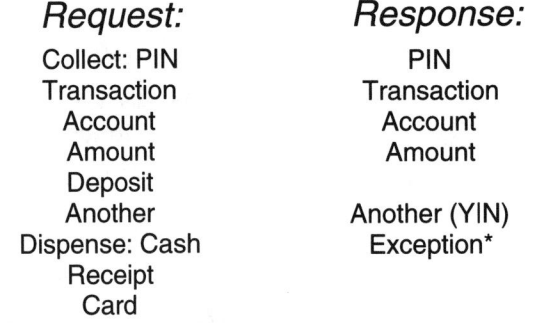

If you choose this approach, you must add a third collaborations between the ATM and the UI, Card in Slot, to handle the initial message sent from the UI to the ATM. Together, these three collaborations make the interface between the ATM and the UI much simpler and allows you to specify all the interactions required for the ATM to manage a bank transaction or session.

As you review the ATM object model, you will recognize that the data structures in the system are fairly simple. You also will realize that the functional characteristics of the ATM system are tied directly to the control flow of the transaction. Different transactions require different fields and different actions. Using the object model from OOA, you can identify some common characteristics of all ATM transactions.

For example, each ATM transaction begins with the same set of screens (1 through 6) and ends with the same set of screens (14 and 15). Beyond this, there is little in common in the ATM system except the flow of control for the different transactions. I will begin by considering the collaborations and responsibilities of the ATM system and possible design trade-offs.

One design for the ATM system would be for the ATM to delegate responsibility for collecting customer information to each ATM Transaction by creating it and passing it a list of accounts for the customer. The ATM then would tell Transaction to perform the transaction selected by the customer, and the Transaction would collect the account, amount, etc., then collaborate with the Account Manager to perform the actual transaction.

This approach gives each transaction type a simple client interface and allows the ATM to have visibility over bank customers. Also, the ATM can ask the customer for common data — PIN, transaction type, account, and amount — then pass this information to the Transaction object. Under this scenario, a Transaction also would be responsible for logging itself and printing a receipt. A Transaction obviously would need to collaborate with the Account Manager object to perform the actual update and might need to return an exception condition if the requested action could not be performed so that ATM would know how to respond to the customer.

This design allows the ATM object to cycle through transactions without knowing (or caring) about what happens within each. By empowering Transaction to gather the information that it needs, it must collaborate with more objects within the context of its goals. While this makes it harder to reuse Transaction objects within the ATM system, it might allow wider reuse of these objects outside the ATM system (i.e., within the larger Bank domain). This approach might allow reuse of the Withdrawal and Deposit Transaction objects in other areas of the bank, such as regular bank processing by clerks, etc.

An alternative design would divide responsibilities in the ATM differently. For example, the ATM would collect customer information (PAN, PIN, transaction, account, amount, etc.), then create a Transaction object and tell it to perform the bank account update or inquiry necessary to accomplish the transaction. The ATM then would log the resulting transaction and print the receipt. In this design, the Transaction object encapsulates the ATM-specific behavior by performing transactions. A Transaction also might create a Bank Transaction object to perform the actual update/inquiry from the bank account. As with the previous design, a Transaction object would collaborate with the Account Manager to perform the actual update.

As you consider the responsibilities and collaborations in the ATM system, you will come to realize that the control view of this application is the dominant or most important view. Following this, the ATM data structure should reflect that and our design should be built around the control view.

Bertrand Meyer in his paper [MEY87] suggests another possible design for the ATM system along these lines. The approach that he proposes can be used for any interactive system which progresses through a series of states (or in this case, screens), each with a predefined pattern of behavior. His design is as follows:

1. The system displays a screen and a series of options for the user
2. The user selects an option via the keyboard
3. The answer is verified by the system, and a message or screen is displayed if an invalid option is selected
4. The resulting answer is processed by the system, and a transition is made to the next logical state in the system.

Meyer introduces the law of inversion in his design to place the operations for the system into the data structure that represents the states and transitions. Because in an interactive system, the data structure is used by all states and transitions, this is a good candidate for an object-oriented design. Meyer goes on to suggest ways of using inheritance and abstract data types to implement a solution based on this approach.

I chose to design the ATM system along the lines of the design proposed by Meyer with some minor modifications. For instance, I used the concept of a state and transition data structure (in Meyer's case, it takes the form of a two-dimensional array) to define the behavior common to every ATM session. Remembering the state-transition diagram I created in the previous chapter, I built an object, calling it ATMState, that defines the behavior of the ATM system. When you design this object, you defer defining the details of the individual states until you design each ATM transaction. Given this approach, you would define five possible states for an ATM session, including Begin session, Withdrawal, Deposit, Funds Transfer, and End session.

Following this approach, you also would design an object, perhaps calling it ATM Session, that would use the ATMState object to process the states and transitions of the system. This structure would be a two-dimensional array, containing the valid states and transitions for the ATM. Each state would have a basic method, Do, that performs the following operations:

1. Display screen (n)
2. GetInput(Answer)
3. Process (Answer) [Transition to the next appropriate state]

Given this design approach, I would have a data structure for the ATM state as shown in Figure 7.13. The data structure actually is a two-dimensional array with its index referencing the screen number (from 1 through 16 for the ATM system) and the values representing the next screens or states. Notice that the states defined in Figure 7.13 correspond to the states that I defined in the state-transition diagram in chapter 6. Given this design, the ATM simply allows a bank customer to progress through the valid ATM states and performs specialized operations at selected states as required.

For example, under this view, the ATM would perform the following operations in state 14 — printing a receipt and asking if another transaction will be processed:

1. Print receipt (via ATM UI)
2. Log ATM Transaction (via ATM File Manager)
3. Display screen 14 (via ATM UI)

Once the ATM UI prints the receipt, it collects the answer to the question: "Another Transaction?" (screen 14). This answer is passed back to the ATM state via the Request/Response collaboration between the ATM and the UI, which then transitions to the next state (i.e., screen 15 [close the ATM session] if the answer is "No," or screen 5 [waiting for a transaction to be selected] if the answer is "Yes"). Following the first scenario (no more transactions), the ATM would perform the following operations in state 15:

1. Eject the card (via ATM UI)
2. Display screen 15 (via ATM UI)

Following this scenario, once the ATM UI indicates that the card has been taken, the ATM transitions to the next state, in this case 1 (Waiting for another card). Every state in the ATM system can be processed using the common method (Do), and the behavior of the system is based on the states in the ATM data structure. This places the structure of the system in its data as recommended by Meyer and fits in nicely with the collaborations that I described previously between the ATM and the UI.

In addition to the ATM state data structure in Figure 7.13, I defined additional data structures and types as shown in section A.2. Notice that I have data structures for bank accounts, ATM transactions, the ATM itself, and the User Interface. In this case, the data structures are fairly simple, with the exception of the ATM, which contains the control structure described earlier.

Object-Oriented Development in COBOL

State/Screen	Next State/Screen				
1	2	0	0	0	0
2	3	4	5	0	0
3	4	5	0	0	0
4	1	0	0	0	
5	6	0	0	0	0
6	7	14	0	0	0
7	8	9	10	11	13
8	10	11	0	0	0
9	5	16	0	0	0
10	12	14	0	0	
11	14	0	0	0	0
12	14	0	0	0	0
13	14	0	0	0	0
14	15	5	0	0	0
15	1	0	0	0	0
16	16	0	0	0	0

Figure 7.13
ATM system - ATMState data structure.

Given the definition of the major ATM state operations described previously, I will focus on the additional methods in the ATM. Returning to the scenario diagrams described previously, you will find that you need operations to effect the collaborations and responsibilities in these diagrams. For example, I defined the ATM UI operations Card in Slot, Collect, and Dispense. The Account Manager contains operations for GetAccount, GetBalance, Debit, and Credit, while the ATM File Manager contains a single operation: LogTransaction. Each of these operations, their messages, and parameters are described in section A.2.

Data structure access control in the ATM system is fairly simple. For example, the Account Manager has private access to all bank accounts, the UI has private access to the ATM hardware, and ATM Manager has access to the ATM Transactions.

The final deliverable from our OOD is the Booch module diagram. The ATM module diagram is shown in Figure 7.14 and includes subsystems for the ATM, User Interface, Account Manager, and ATM File Manager. Given the nature of the ATM system, the Account Manager allows bank accounts to be accessed via their number and manages all account services while the ATM File Manager maintains a log of ATM transactions in a persistent data store.

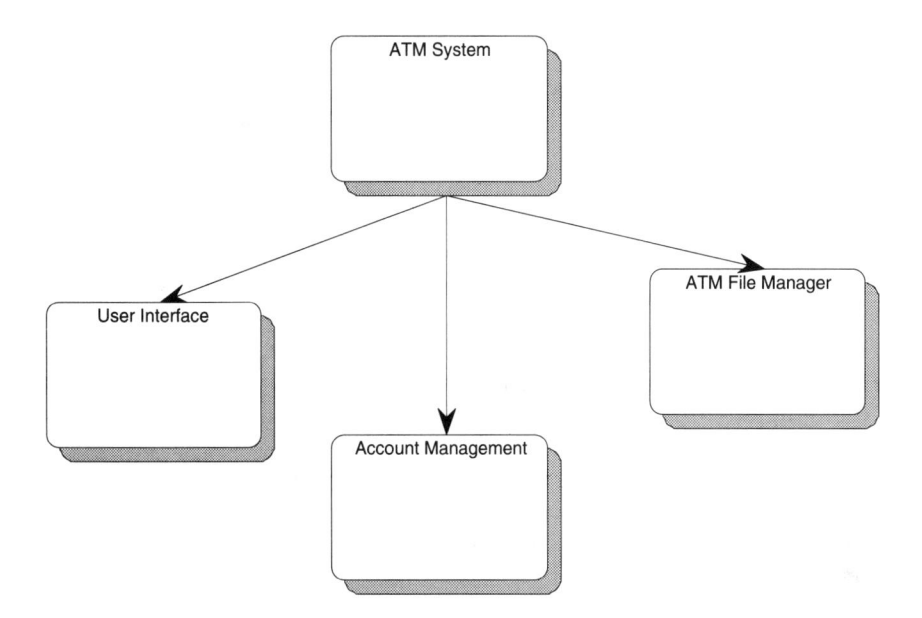

Figure 7.14
ATM system - module diagram.

The most interesting subsystem in the ATM problem is undoubtedly the User Interface, which manages interaction between the ATM and the bank customer.

Section A.2 describes the resulting object specification in more detail.

7.8 Moving from OOD to OOP

After you have completed the object specifications for the example systems, you are faced with the task of creating OOCOBOL implementations of the classes, objects, etc. Recalling the discussion on object-oriented SDLCs in chapter 4, you probably would not complete the specification of each subsystem for these examples prior to beginning implementation in OOCOBOL. Rather, you would probably deliver specifications for objects in subsystems gradually over time, using the incremental approach described in chapter 4.

One view of this method might be to deliver the User Interface subsystems for each example for implementation, followed by other subsystems. As the User Interface subsystems are built, they are unit tested, and the interfaces between the subsystems are described in detail. You can return to Shlaer/Mellor domain chart and verify the nature of the interfaces between subsystems matching this representation against the Booch module diagrams.

Designing an object-oriented solution requires full knowledge of the available classes in the class libraries. For this implementation in OOCOBOL, Micro Focus has delivered a fairly limited set of classes primarily modeled after those found in Smalltalk. Of these classes, you will be interested especially in the collection and GUI classes in the next two chapters.

I could have chosen to use the Micro Focus Dialog System (DS) for the user interface of the library system, but I did not. Using DS would insulate the library system from the deployment environment, and DS supports DOS, Windows, OS/2, Macintosh, Unix Motif, etc. The reason that I chose not to use DS in this case was because the OOCOBOL product does not currently support DS in the OOCOBOL class libraries. This would have meant a design of the complete user interface for the library system in DS, with an interface to the OOCOBOL application. I felt the benefits of using DS (i.e., interoperability) were overshadowed by the lack of support for the product in the OOCOBOL libraries. Micro Focus has indicated its plans to incorporate some of DS into a future OOCOBOL product set but has not given an expected delivery date.

Another approach to designing the presentation portion of the Library system would be to develop it in a GUI tool or Smalltalk and interface it with the application itself. In this case, I decided to build the Library system using the OOCOBOL presentation components in the Micro Focus class libraries. These classes support DOS (with an optional extended memory manager from Micro Focus), Windows, and OS/2 and should evolve in the future to support the Dialog System product described earlier. I will discuss the implementation of the presentation portion of the Library system in more detail in chapters 8 and 9.

7.9 References

[BOO93]	Booch, G., *Object-Oriented Design with Applications*, second edition, Benjamin/Cummings, 1993.
[BOO91]	Booch, G., *Object-Oriented Design with Applications*, Benjamin/Cummings, 1991.
[BOO90]	Booch, G. and M. Vilot, "A First Look at Object-Oriented Design," *C++ Report*, 2, 2, February 1990, pp. 11-13.
[BOO86a]	Booch, G., *Software Engineering with Ada*, Benjamin/Cummings, 1986.
[BOO86b]	Booch, G., "Object-Oriented Development," *IEEE Trans. Soft. Eng.*, vol. SE-12, no. 2, February 1986, pp. 211-221.
[COD70]	Codd, E.F., "A Relational Model of Data for Large Shared Data Banks," *CACM*, vol. 13, no. 6., June 1970.
[MEY88]	Meyer, B., *Object-Oriented Software Construction*, Prentice-Hall, 1988.
[MEY87]	Meyer, B., "Reusability: The case for Object-Oriented Design," *IEEE Software*, vol. 4, no. 2, March 1987.
[PAG91]	Page-Jones, M. and S. Weiss, *Synthesis: Object-Oriented Systems Development*, Wayland Systems course notes, 1991.
[POD92]	Podgurski, A. and L. Pierce, "Behavior Sampling: A Technique for Automated Retrieval of Reusable Components," *proceedings of the Intl. Conference on Software Engineering*, May 11-15, 1992, pp. 349-360.
[PRI87]	Prieto-Diaz, R., "Classifying Software for Reusability," *IEEE Software*, January 1987, pp. 6-16.
[SHL90]	Shlaer, S. and S. Mellor, *Real-Time Recursive Design*, Project Technology course notes, 1990.
[WAS89]	Wasserman, A. I., P. A. Pircher, and R. J. Muller, *Concepts of Object-Oriented Structured Design*, Interactive Development Environments, 1989.

[WIR90]   Wirfs-Brock, R., B. Wilkerson, and L. Wiener, *Designing Object-Oriented Software*, Prentice-Hall, 1990.
[WIR93]   Wirfs-Brock, R., "Stereotyping: A Technique for Characterizing Objects and their Interactions," *Object Magazine*, November-December 1993, pp. 50-54.

Comparing OOA/D Methods

When comparing object-oriented techniques, it is helpful to look carefully at the objectives of analysis and design in the object-oriented paradigm. Object-oriented Analysis (OOA) techniques share as their goals identifying a correct set of objects, their attributes, and operations and any relationships between objects. The resulting object model serves to explain the behavior and structure of the problem domain in object-oriented terms.

Likewise, object-oriented design (OOD) techniques refine candidate objects into classes, define message protocols for all objects, define data structures and procedures and map these to an object-oriented programming language (object specifications). Several techniques for OOA/D have been proposed and are being used to some degree within the industry. The outcome from OOD, an object specification, must include sufficient detail about the objects, messages, and interfaces to support creation of a solution in an OOPL.

The Booch method (used in this text) is more focused on design, but has been used effectively with traditional structured analysis techniques, object-oriented analysis techniques, data modeling, and informal requirements specification techniques. Some have criticized the Booch approach as ignoring requirements definition and lacking in non-Ada design representations.

Critics of the Shlaer/Mellor approach argue that it is really just a rehashed use of the structured analysis with a focus on information modeling instead of control modeling. Similar arguments can be made for the Coad/Yourdon, OOMT, OOSD, Synthesis, and Martin/Odel methods. These techniques do not support key object-oriented concepts including message passing, inheritance, and encapsulation in the analysis phase. The resulting object specifications often reflect a functional modularity rather than a structural and behavioral modularity of objects. In this respect, these methods are very similar to structured analysis/design and their results can suffer from some of the same problems often observed in using these echniques.

OOD methods can be compared on the basis of the process used to design data structures, the level of detail provided in their notations, and the level of detail describing the design process. Some OOD methods that combine traditional function-oriented concepts including cohesion and coupling with others deal more exclusively with class design or object interactions.

Some object-oriented techniques, including Object-Oriented Structured Design (OOSD) from Interactive Development Environments and Synthesis, are modifications to traditional functional techniques with some object-oriented concepts added. One benefit to using these techniques is that they support both a functional and an object-oriented perspective. While these techniques might serve to help organizations move toward OOA/D methods in an evolutionary fashion, they also retain some of the problems and drawbacks associated with the functional techniques.

Many object-oriented techniques are geared toward DOD and Ada development, including HOOD, MOOD, and Ray Buhr's approach. Buhr has developed an OOD technique that is similar to the Booch technique and also is aimed at Ada development, with inspiration from Structured Design techniques and an orientation towards objects, graphical notation and a conceptual model. The Buhr technique combines some aspects of Structured Analysis and Structured Design techniques and uses Structure charts along with Ada structure graphs (ASGs). One drawback to using the Buhr (as well as the Booch) approach is that it is very closely tied to the Ada language.

Still other object-oriented methods — including Responsibility Driven Design, Object Behavior Analysis, Object-Oriented Analysis and Specification, and Object-Oriented Software Engineering — focus most of their efforts on object interactions and behavior and provide few details on identifying and classifying objects, attributes, and methods. While these methods provide good techniques for specifying the behavior of objects in the solution domain, they assume an intuitive understanding of the problem domain that rarely exists in real-world development.

In the past few years, several technical journals have included articles that compare OOA/D methods, including [BUL92], [FIC92], [KAR93], [MON92], and [PAG92]. Some of these papers compare only OOA/D methods, while others compare traditional development methods with object-oriented techniques. Still other papers — such as [FAY94], [FAY93], [HIN94], and [SHA93] — report on experiences of organizations applying specific OOA/D methods.

Generically speaking, OOA/D methods can be compared in a variety of ways including:

- Notation/Representation [TOP93] — Analysis and Design representations and notations used.
- Focus or area of initial interest [FOW92] — Data-driven vs. event-driven vs. scenario-driven.

- Processes [MON92] — OOA/D processes supported, representations, and complexity.
- Common Tasks [FIC92] — Method characteristics, including relationships, tasks, partitioning, etc.
- Resulting object models and specifications [SHA93] — Their complexity, support for encapsulation, etc.

Each of these will be reviewed in the following sections.

Sharble and Cohen

Boeing Computer Services (BCS) reported in a technical journal [SHA93] on their experiences with two popular object-oriented development methods. The paper discussed projects that used object-oriented metrics from [CHI91] to compare the results of two different object-oriented methods for software development. The paper is interesting for a number of reasons: it is the first actual comparison of object-oriented methods based on the same problem; it is the first published use of metrics for object-oriented development; and the findings presented suggest that there are substantive differences in the philosophies of the object-oriented methods that affect the outcomes in terms of the complexity and cost of enhancement of the resulting systems.

Sharble and Cohen compared two prominent object-oriented methods: Responsibility Driven Design (RDD), which was described by Wirfs-Brock, Wilkerson, and Wiener and the Shlaer/Mellor method. The Shlaer/Mellor method shares many philosophical points with the Coad/Yourdon method, as well as the Object-Oriented Modeling Technique (OOMT). BCS has had extensive experience with these methods and even teach their use within the Boeing organization.

The Sharble and Cohen comparison focused on two essential viewpoints of these object-oriented methods: the internal and external views of objects and classes. These views are compared in Figure 1, where RDD is Responsibility Driven Design. The metrics used by Sharble and Cohen were those described by Chidamber and Kemerer [CHI91] and include the following with their corresponding numbers in the table:

- Weighted methods/class (1)
- Depth of inheritance tree (2)
- Number of children (3)
- Coupling between objects (4)
- Response for a class (5)
- Lack of cohesion in methods (6)

Sharble and Cohen added three additional metrics that were measured:

- Weighted attributes/class (7)
- Number of tramps or extraneous parameters (8)
- Violations of the Law of Demeter - minimizing coupling between classes (9)

The results of the comparison of these metrics for the methods are shown in Figure 1.

Monarchi and Puhr

Monarchi and Puhr [MON92] compared a variety of OOA/D methods based on a common set of tasks and representations. The results of their comparison are shown in Figures 2 and 3. As part of their study, Monarchi and Puhr also developed a typology for comparing methods and identified several areas for improvement in the existing OOA/D methods, including :

Metrics	(1)	(2)	(3)	(4)	(5)	(6)	(7)	(8)	(9)
RDD	71	19	13	20	127	21	44	0	0
Shlaer/Mellor	130	21	19	42	293	64	64	0	40

- The RDD produced less complex systems than the Shlaer/Mellor approach.
- The Shlaer/Mellor approach seemed to lack support for the principle of encapsulation.
- Focusing on an object's responsibilities seems to provide a natural grouping of data and operations
- Describing objects in terms of responsibilities leaves internal details unspecified until very late in the design process, and this discourages formation of other objects that are dependent on that detail.
- Describing objects in terms of their data structures requires that internal details be specified earlier in the design process, and this encourages the formation of highly interdependent objects that have high coupling and low cohesion.
- Responsibilities provide a complete basis for inheritance and allow for better expression of the principle of classification.
- RDD exhibited much greater cohesion of classes and much less coupling between them.
- RDD produced a better organized inheritance hierarchy with greater potential for reduced redundancy.

Figure 1
Sharble/Cohen results and observations.

- Models that synthesize static and dynamic aspects of an object-oriented system at different levels of abstraction
- A clear definition of what layers and views are important for representing and designing an object-oriented system and a means of integrating and balancing these views
- Evaluation models for OOA/D methods that can measure the quality of the analysis and design process.

Fichman and Kemerer

Another paper that compares methods in some detail is from Fichman and Kemerer [FIC92]. Fichman and Kemerer studied and compared function-oriented, information-oriented, and object-oriented methods with a focus on how these methods are similar and different. While their paper did not cover all of the OOA/D methods or include data-oriented techniques, it did offer some interesting thoughts on how traditional functional methods compare with object-oriented techniques. The results of the Fichman and Kemerer study are shown in Figure 4 and 5.

A functional decomposition of systems violates encapsulation because operations can directly access a multitude of different entities and are not subordinated to any one entity; this view is the antithesis of the object-oriented view. Fichman and Kemerer [FIC92].

Martin Fowler

According to Martin Fowler, OOA/D methods are based on three views:

Behavioral view: Separate finite state machines for each class; behavior of the entire system vs. individual objects or classes (subsystems). Object collaborations must be described using some higer-level notation. In real-time systems, threads of control must be specified. Procedure-based, state-based (state-transition diagrams statecharts), mechanism-based (timing, etc.), and event-based (whole system dynamics).

Data structure view: Types of object relationships — associations, sub/supertypes, and aggregation. Object types — entity (data), interface, and control objects. Derived from data modeling and includes attributes and operations.

OOA/D Process support	Bailin	Booch	Coad/Yourdon	Meyer	OOMT	Shlaer/Mellor	Wirfs-Brock & Wilkerson
1 (a) Identification of: Semantic classes	☒	☒	☒	☒	☒	☒	☒
Attributes		☒	☒		☒	☒	
Behavior	☒	☒	☒	☒	☒	☒	☒
Relationships: Generalization		☒	☒	☒	☒	☒	☒
Aggregation		☒	☒		☒		☒
Other		☒			☒	☒	☒
1 (b) Placement of: Classes			☒				☒
Attributes			☒				
Behavior	☒	☒		☒	☒		☒
1 (c) Specification of: Dynamic behavior		☒			☒		
2 (a) Identification of: Interface classes			☒				
Application classes							
Base/Utility classes					☒		
2 (b) Optimization of classes		☒	☒	☒	☒		☒

Figure 2 Monarchi and Puhr comparison.

Sidebar: Comparing OOA/D Methods 227

Representation & Complexity Management	Bailin	Booch	Coad/ Yourdon	Meyer	OOMT	Shlaer/ Mellor	Wirfs-Brock & Wilkerson
3 (a) Static View: Objects	☒	☒	☒	☒	☒	☒	☒
Attributes		☒	☒	☒	☒	☒	
Behavior	☒	☒	☒		☒	☒	☒
Relationships: Generalization		☒	☒	☒	☒	☒	☒
Aggregation		☒	☒		☒		
Other		☒			☒	☒	
3 (b) Dynamic View of: Communication		☒	☒				☒
Control/Timing		☒	☒		☒		
3 (c) Constraints on: structure		☒	☒		☒	☒	
dynamic behavior		☒			☒	☒	
4 (a) Structural complexity		☒	☒	☒	☒	☒	☒
4 (b) Behavioral complexity							☒
4 (c) Static structure		☒	☒				☒
Dynamic behavior							

Figure 3
Monarchi and Puhr comparison - continued.

Method Characteristics	Bailin Object-Oriented Requirements Specification (OORS)	Coad/Yourdon OOA	Shlaer/Mellor OOA
Identification/ classification of entities	Entity- relationship diagram (ERD)	Class/Object diagram	Information structure diagram (ISD) [ERD]
General-to-specific and whole-to-part relationships	ERD	Class/Object diagram (Structure layer)	ISD
Other Entity Relationships	ERD	Class/Object diagram (Structure layer)	ISD
Attributes	Not supported	Class/Object diagram (Attribute layer)	ISD
Large-scale model partitioning	Domain-partitioned ERD	Class/Object diagram (Subject layer)	Domain chart; subsystem communication access, and relationship models
States and transitions	Not supported	Object-state diagram; Service chart	State model (STD)
Detailed logic for functions/ services	Not supported	Service chart	Action DFD and Process Specification
Identification of exclusive services	Entity-DFD	Class & Object diagrams (Service layer)	State models & Action DFD
Entity communication (via messages or events)	Entity-DFD	Class and Object diagrams (Service layer)	Object communication model; Object access model

Figure 4
Fichman and Kemerer comparison.

Method Characteristics	Booch Object Oriented Design	Object-Oriented Structured Design (OOSD)	Responsiblity Driven Design (RDD)
Hierarchy of modules (physical design)	Module diagram	Structure chart (modified)	Not Supported
Data definitions	Class diagram	Structure chart	Class specification
Procedural logic	Operation template	Not supported	Class specification
End-to-end processing sequence	Timing diagram	Not Supported	Not Supported
Object states and transitions	State-Transition diagram (STD)	Not Supported	Not Supported
Definition of classes and inheritance	Class diagram	Structure chart	Hierarchy diagram
Other class relationships (instantiates, uses, etc.)	Class diagram	Structure chart	Class specification
Assignment of operations/ services to classes	Class diagram	Structure chart	Collaboration graph; class specification
Detailed definition of services/ operations	Operations template	Not Supported	Class specification
Message connections	Object diagram and template	Structure chart	Collaboration graph

Figure 5
Fichman and Kemerer comparison - continued.

Architectural view: Functional decomposition — entities are created, accessed, and deleted by processes (DFDs) or object decomposition — describing how objects and architectural components communicate with each other; defining object levels with objects and messages shown. Describing visibility how classes and subsystems are able to use the interfaces (services) of other components. Contracts between objects (collaborations) and visibility at different levels in the architecture. Define subsystems (groups of related classes with high coupling), visibility between components, and messaging.

Fowler identifies three basic types of OOA/D methods:

- *Data-driven* — Associations and operations are defined first; focus is on identifying and defining objects and attributes, then on their services; identify types, generalizations, associations and aggregations, identify operations (state models), and develop architecture.
- *Event-driven* — Events are identified and traced through the system to define its behavior.
- *Scenario-driven* — Responsibilities or collaborations between objects are the focus of these methods, with attributes defined later in the process; identify scenarios, determine classes and relationships (based on use of system).

Based on these three groups, Fowler classifies popular OOA/D methods as follows:

- Booch — data-driven, using object decomposition in design
- Coad/Yourdon — data-driven, simple but limiting
- OOSE (Use-case) — scenario-driven, object types in design
- Martin/Odell (Ptech) — event-driven, rehashed IE with object-flow diagrams (architecture)
- Rumbaugh (OMT) — data-driven with some focus on dynamic behavior, useful for both OO and non-OO deployment
- Shlaer/Mellor — data-driven with some focus on dynamic behavior, focus on recursion and automated translation of Object models into design/implementations
- Wirfs-Brock — scenario-driven, with focus on responsiblities (oriented towards Smalltalk)

Fowler makes the following recommendations when selecting OOA/D methods:

- Data-driven methods are similar, differences are primarily notational; use multiple and dynamic classification (Rumbaugh and Martin/Odell).
- Event-based modeling is superior for the whole system, statecharts should be used as notation Use object decomposition (not functional decomposition) with contracts.
- Data-driven methods can be difficult to scope, while scenario-driven methods can embed the current thinking; use events and data together.
- Tailor method whenever necessary and reconsider available methods/tools every few months.

References

[BUL92]	Bulman, D., "An Objective Survey," *Embedded Systems Programming*, vol. 5, no. 3, 1992, pp. 20-31.
[CHI91]	Chidamber, S. R. and C. F. Kemerer, "Towards a Metrics Suite for Object-Oriented Design," *OOPSLA '91 proceedings*, SIGPLAN Notices, 26 (11), Oct. 1991, pp. 197-211.
[FAY93]	Fayad, M.E., L.J. Hawn, M.A. Roberts, and J.R. Klatt, "Using the Shlaer-Mellor OOA Method," *IEEE Software*, March 1993, pp. 43-52.
[FAY94]	Fayad, M. E., W. Tsai, M. A. Roberts, L. J. Hawn, and J. W. Schooley, "Adapting an Object-Oriented Development Method," *IEEE Software*, May 1994, pp. 68-76.
[FIC92]	Fichman, R. G. and C. F. Kemerer, "Object-Oriented and Conventional Analysis and Design Methodologies," *IEEE Computer*, October 1992, pp. 22-39.
[FOL92]	Fowler, M., "A Comparison of Object-Oriented Analysis and Design Methods," *Object World 93' proceedings*, July 1993.
[HIN94]	Hines, K. and B. Sanders, "Communications Systems Design with Object-Oriented Analysis/Recursive Design," *Object Magazine*, March-April 1994, pp. 68-71.
[KAR93]	Karam, G. M. and R. S. Casselman, "A Cataloging Framework for Software Development Methods," *IEEE Computer*, February 1993, pp. 34-46.
[MON93]	Monarchi, D. E. and G. I. Puhr, "A Research Typology for Object-Oriented Analysis and Design," *CACM*, vol. 35, no. 9, pp. 35-47.
[PAG92]	Page-Jones, M., "Comparing Techniques by Means of Encapsulation and Connascence," *CACM*, vol. 35, no. 9, pp. 147-151.

[SHA93]　　　Sharble, R. C. and S. S. Cohen, "The Object-Oriented Brewery: A Comparison of Two Object-Oriented Development Methods," *ACM SIGSOFT*, vol. 18, no. 2, pp. 60-73.

[TOP93]　　　Topper, A., P. Jorgensen, and D. Ouellette, *Structured Methods: Models, Techniques, and CASE*, McGraw-Hill, 1993.

Chapter 8

Programming in Object-Oriented COBOL

Object-oriented programming is not like traditional COBOL programming, because you begin by taking the object specification (from OOD) and examining the library of existing classes for reusable components. Given a specification of a data structure and the operations on that data (i.e., the behavior of the class), you can consider how objects can be derived from the existing classes in our libraries.

OOP is intertwined with OOD, and you also must strive to rethink and re-evaluate the classification structure of the libraries as you implement the objects to improve reuse. OOD provides you with a description of the classes, objects, messages, and methods or operations and a class hierarchy to draw from when implementing a solution in OOCOBOL. In OOP, you delve into more detail concerning the implementation of each class and work at a lower level of abstraction than you did in OOD.

Once you are finished with the design of classes or subsystems, you create programs that represent the abstractions in the programming language. In this case, OOCOBOL supports the concepts of objects, classes, messages, and inheritance and provides a set of reusable classes for implementation as objects. In our case, these classes are delivered with the Micro Focus OOCOBOL product. OOP also is intertwined with testing, and as you move through this phase you alternate between coding, compiling, linking, and testing each program or subsystem.

As I introduced in the previous chapter, creating reusable classes also is one of the expected outcomes of OOP. Assuming you start with a set of reusable classes from a class library delivered with OOCOBOL, you still must strive to expand the set of reusable components in OOP.

8.1 Introduction

All OOPLs support the basic concepts of objects, but some support more of the specifics than others. True OOPLs were developed from the group up to support these concepts, while hybrid OOPLs are traditional procedural languages that have been extended to support some or all of the concepts. At a minimum, any OOPL should support encapsulation, inheritance, message passing, polymorphism, and some form of binding between objects and their methods. Additional support might include multiple inheritance, overloading, method combination, garbage collection, and interfaces.

In chapter 4, I described the popular object-oriented programming languages and their features. I also compared these languages based on a common set of constructs that all the OOPLs support. OOCOBOL, as it is currently defined, supports the constructs described in chapter 4 and will include many features not found in other OOPLs.

OOCOBOL programming, like other object-oriented development, requires that programmers understand the available classes before beginning their coding efforts. They must find reusable classes, methods, and messages that might satisfy the object specification document in the libraries available or create new classes if none exist. As they create these objects in OOCOBOL, programmers must always reconsider the design of the software along with the classification hierarchy. Reuse must be a duel goal for OOCOBOL programmers along with delivery of a functioning software system.

Generically, OOCOBOL programming involves the following tasks:

1. Study the object specification (from OOD) and review the existing class library.
2. Locate relevant classes in the library that match the behavior and/or data structures specified in the object specification.
3. Derive or create subclasses from these classes as needed to satisfy the object specification.
4. Add or modify classes, class/object methods (operations), or fields (attributes) as needed.
5. Reorganize the classification hierarchy as needed to improve reuse.
6. Compile the OOCOBOL programs to create the necessary objects and messages.
7. Test the OOCOBOL programs to ensure that they meet requirements and work correctly.
8. Return to step 1 and begin working on other components.

Using the two example problems, I will review the Library and ATM systems, looking closely at the objects required and their interaction. In the case of the Library problem, I will focus specifically on the creation of the Listof objects, along with the User, Library Staff, Book, and Copy objects, then integration of these into a finished system. In the case of the ATM system, I will begin by working on the User Interface, then the Account Manager, ATM, and the ATM Transaction Manager, finally integrating these components into the eventual system.

Prior to examining the example problems and how I plan to implement them in OOCOBOL, I will look at the ANSI COBOL 97 standard, its syntax and structure, implementation issues, the structure of the Micro Focus OOCOBOL class library, and additional development items.

8.2 ANSI COBOL 97 Standard

The proposal for object-oriented COBOL (OOCOBL) has identified several important features to be supported, which are described later. As you read about these features, keep in mind that they still are under discussion and might change they eventually are implemented. A lengthy public review of the OOCOBOL standard (over 2 years) will be required before the standard is accepted by the ANSI.

OOCOBOL supports the concepts of classes, objects, and inheritance, along with several other features, including interfaces for classes, method prototypes, multiple inheritance, factories, dynamic and static binding, conformance, polymorphism, and garbage collection.

Key to the notion of OOCOBOL is the concept of an object/class having an interface that defines only the services available, not the implementation of those services. This separation of interface from implementation is critical to the concept of object-oriented development and is not found in most other OOPLs. Method prototypes can be defined for objects and can be defined inside or outside the class. Methods in OOCOBOL are recursive, and data defined within a method is local to that method. Classes in OOCOBOL can inherit from multiple classes and also can inherit from multiple interfaces.

Factories are introduced in OOCOBOL and support shared object data, dynamically created objects, and public and provide methods for all objects of a specific class. OOCOBOL will support static binding and type checking, but a special object type, Universal, allows objects to be ignored by the compiler (this supports the concept of dynamic or late binding). *Conformance* is a property that allows an object to be used when another object is expected. Conformance in OOCOBOL is based on interfaces, thus allowing existing objects to be modified to include new features without adversely affecting existing implementations. Through conformance, polymorphism is supported in OOCOBOL.

OOCOBOL also supports garbage collection and automatic memory management. Existing COBOL systems can be compiled with only minor changes and Intrinsic objects can be used to support existing COBOL data types (i.e., records and files). Object methods can be compiled separately from their object/class and factory definitions. In addition, independent methods (i.e., methods not associated with a specific object/class) can be defined inside any standard COBOL construct. Objects accessed through their interface are allocated dynamically.

In short, OOCOBOL as it is proposed today, looks very promising as a powerful object-oriented programming language. Obviously, much work still is required by implementors of the OOCOBOL standard in the areas of class libraries, syntax checking, etc., but the promise of object-oriented development in COBOL is close to realization.

8.2.1 Defining Classes and Objects

Recalling the discussion of OOCOBOL in chapter 5, classes and objects must be defined using the correct COBOL 97 syntax. As I reintroduce this syntax, refer back to section 5.2. In OOCOBOL, each class and object is defined using the structure shown in Figure 8.1. Class and object definitions are placed into separate files in a similar fashion to copy books or include files in traditional COBOL and are compiled separately from the OOCOBOL programs that use them.

The OOCOBOL standard uses the following format to define a class:

CLASS-ID.   ClassName IS [PERSISTENT | TRANSIENT
                           {COLLECTABLE}]
        INHERITS ClassName ClassName ...

Classes can be defined as persistent or transient, with transient objects managed by the garbage collection facilities in the COBOL compiler and run-time environment. Persistent objects should be managed by some object management system. The current version of the Micro Focus OOCOBOL compiler does not support transient objects, and all objects, even those defined as TRANSIENT COLLECTABLE, are persistent. The Micro Focus command, "OOPSuspend," makes every object that is a descendant of the class Base PERSISTENT. The developer is responsible for deleting or finalizing any objects that are not persistent.

CLASS-ID. ClassName.	*Define the name of the class.*
WORKING-STORAGE SECTION.	*Data storage for the class*
	— local or private to the class.
METHOD-ID. "new".	*Define the method "new"*
	inside the class
END METHOD "new".	*definition itself.*
OBJECT.	*Define the other object*
WORKING-STORAGE SECTION.	*methods and data.*
METHOD-ID. "initialize".	*Define the specialized object*
END METHOD "initialize".	*methods.*
[Other method definitions]	*Other methods...*
END OBJECT.	*Signify the end of the object*
END CLASS ClassName.	*and class definition.*

Figure 8.1 OOCOBOL syntax.

Under the Micro Focus OOCOBOL product, another call, "OOPSResume," brings in all previously stored objects for activation. Objects that are descended from the PersistenceManager class can be manipulated directly, whereas the other objects are managed by Micro Focus. Notice that classes can inherit from one or more other classes. The current version of the Micro Focus OOCOBOL compiler does not support multiple inheritance.

The OOCOBOL standard uses a simple command to define an object: OBJECT. I uses a similar format for each method in a class:

METHOD-ID. MethodName.

Following the definition of the object, its data, and methods, there are required end statements. For example, each method must end with:

END METHOD MethodName.

Each object must end with an END OBJECT command. Likewise, every definition of a class must end with an END CLASS statement:

END CLASS ClassName.

8.2.2 Referencing Objects in OOCOBOL

After objects have been defined, they can be created and referenced in OOCOBOL. I will begin by introducing two ways that objects, once created, can be referenced in COBOL. In the same way that data values can be referenced by COBOL fields, objects can be referenced by fields. The COBOL 97 standard contains a new USAGE type, OBJECT, that supports object references.

There are several different ways to reference an object in OOCOBOL, and both use the USAGE OBJECT command in the COBOL 97 language. The first method allows objects to be referenced dynamically at run time, while the second option references a single class of objects also at run time. The syntax for the first options is:

```
01    DataName           USAGE OBJECT REFERENCE.
```

This approach allows objects to be referenced dynamically at run time, and the type of object can be different (i.e., the field can reference any class of object). When this syntax is used, the field name (DataName) contains a handle for the object.

The syntax for the second option is:

```
01    DataName           USAGE OBJECT REFERENCE ClassName.
```

This represents a static reference to an object created at run time. The object is specified by the name in the command (i.e., the field can reference only an object of the type or class specified — ClassName). Another method used for simple COBOL data types is:

```
01    DataName           USAGE INTRINSIC OBJECT.
```

Objects can be passed via references to them between programs. In this sense, the fields that contain references to objects are passed as parameters between methods or programs. Given these data elements:

```
01    DataName           USAGE OBJECT REFERENCE ClassName.
01    OtherDataName      USAGE OBJECT REFERENCE.
```

An example of a method with an object reference that is passed as a parameter is:

```
INVOKE ObjectName MethodName USING DataName
       RETURNING OtherDataName.
```

In this example, MethodName is passed the object referenced by DataName and returns an object referenced by OtherDataName. Objects can be passed in the same way data elements can be, via the LINKAGE SECTION and with the USING and RETURNING phrases.

8.2.3 Creating and Using Objects in OOCOBOL

Objects can be created in a variety of ways in OOCOBOL, including via the CREATE command provided in the COBOL 97 syntax or dynamically via the "new" method in the Micro Focus Base class. The OOCOBOL standard for creating an instance of an object is:

CREATE ObjectName.

The OOCOBOL standard for using an object method is:

INVOKE ObjectName MethodName
    USING DataStructure1 DataStructure2 ...
    RETURNING Variable1 Variable2 ...

An alternative mechanism for creating objects within the Micro Focus Object COBOL Option is to use the "new" method in the Base class as follows:

INVOKE SUPER "new" RETURNING lsnew.

This creates an instance of any object of type Base returned as the variable Isnew. Once an object has been created, it must be initialized using an "Initialize" method in the class definition. The "Initialize" method should create any data structures required (i.e., collection, bag, array, etc.) and perform any user-defined initialization processing. An example of an "Initialize" method might look something like this:

METHOD-ID. "Initialize".
PROCEDURE DIVISION.

    MOVE 0 to NextUserID.
    EXIT PROGRAM.

END METHOD "Initialize".

8.3 Implementation Considerations

There are some obvious issues that you need to consider when implementing a system using object-oriented COBOL. These include whether a GUI will be used, data access, operating environment, existing class libraries, etc. As I review the object specification for the example systems, you will need to consider what types of data structures and access mechanisms will be required or available for each problem. Before I consider the example problems, I will return to the discussion of our Deck of Cards example from chapter 3, 5, and 7 to consider how you might implement it in OOCOBOL.

Figure 8.2 represents one possible implementation of the Deck of Cards class data structure in OOCOBOL. Notice that I have used the design approach where the deck consists of 52 items in a CharacterArray with the following fields:

- Suit — Indicates the suit of the card (H=Hearts, C=Clubs, D=Diamonds, or S=Spades)
- Value — Indicates the value of the card (A=Ace, 2=2 ... J=Jack, Q=Queen, or K=King)
- Dealt — Indicates whether the card has been dealt since the last shuffle operation {0 = available, 1 = already dealt}

The data structure for the deck of cards consists of the fields:

- Suit: PIC X {H | C | D | S}
- Value: PIC XX {2..10 | J | Q | K | A}
- Dealt: PIC X {0 | 1}

Given this implementation, I built a class with some of the methods shown in Figure 8.3. These methods were introduced in chapter 5 and include:

- *new* — Creates an instance of the DeckofCards object.
- *Initialize* — Initializes the DeckofCards by assigning the values and suits for the cards and setting the Dealt field to false.
- *Shuffle* — Resets the Dealt field of each card to false.
- *Deal (n)* — Deals the next *n* cards from the deck in random order.

By building objects around data structures, and inheriting methods that are common to all users of the structure, we can inherit the states and defer definitions of any methods that vary in the application.

```
CLASS-ID.       CardDeck
                INHERITS Base.

WORKING-STORAGE SECTION.

77 NumberofCards                     Value 52.
01 nil                    OBJECT REFERENCE EXTERNAL.
01 SelectionMethodName PIC X(30)     Value "SelectCards".

METHOD-ID. "new".
LINKAGE SECTION.
01 ADeckofCards        OBJECT REFERENCE.

PROCEDURE DIVISION RETURNING ADeckofCards.

    INVOKE SUPER "new" RETURNING ADeckofCards.
    INVOKE ADeckofCards "Initialize".
    EXIT PROGRAM.
END METHOD "new".

OBJECT.
WORKING-STORAGE SECTION.
01 DeckofCard-Storage.
    03    ACollection          OBJECT REFERENCE.
    03    OtherCollection      OBJECT REFERENCE.
    03    SortTtyle            PIC X.
        88    CmpOrdValue         Value "O" "o".
    03    CurrentSuit          PIC X.
    03    CurrentSuitlen       PIC S9(9) COMP-5.
    03    CurrentCard          PIC XX.
    03    CurrentCardlen       PIC S9(9) COMP-5.
    03    CurrentDealt         PIC X.
        88    Dealt               Value "1".
        88    NotDealt            Value "0".
    03    CurrentPrdValen      PIC S9(9) COMP-5.
```

Figure 8.2 Portions of the deck of cards class data.

Object-Oriented Development in COBOL

```
METHOD-ID. "Initialize".
****************************************************************
*     This method initializes the array of cards.
****************************************************************
WORKING-STORAGE SECTION.
01  Work-Area.
    03    i                PIC 99.
    03    j                PIC 99.
    03    Index            PIC 99.
    03    TmpValue         PIC 99.
01  ASize                  PIC 9(4) comp-5.
PROCEDURE DIVISION.
    MOVE 52 TO ASize.
    INVOKE CharacterArray "ofReferences" USING ASize
        RETURNING ACollection.
    Perform Init-Suit
    Varying i from 1 by 1
    Until i = 4.
    EXIT PROGRAM.
Init-Suit.
    Perform Init-Value
    Varying j from 2 by 1
    Until j = 14.
Init-Value.
    Case i = 1: suit = "H".
    Case i = 2: suit = "C".
    Case i = 3: suit = "D".
    Case i = 4: suit = "S".
    Index = i + j.
    Suit[Index] = suit.
    TmpValue = j.
    Case j = 14: TmpValue = "A".
    Case j = 11: TmpValue = "J".
    Case j = 12: TmpValue = "Q".
    Case j = 13: Tmpalue = "K".
    Value[Index] = TmpValue.
    Dealt[Index] = "0".

END METHOD "Initialize".
```

Figure 8.3
Portions of the deck of cards class methods.

B. Meyer [MEY89].

8.4 Reuse of Micro Focus OOCOBOL Classes

Remembering the goal of building applications from reusable components, I will begin by studying the Micro Focus class library for potential objects in the examples. Unfortunately, the existing Micro Focus class library is fairly limited and supports only basic object types.

The Micro Focus Object COBOL Option classes that are delivered in version 1.5 include:

- *Base* — A generic or superclass for all classes that handles the default behavior for methods (i.e., error handling, persistence, etc.).
- *Behavior* — An object that represents a class, the instances of which also are classes.
- *Clipboard, Callback, etc.* — These classes provide specific functions or manage specific O/S resources including the clipboard, callbacks to routines, etc.
- *Collection* — Classes that manage collections of items, like bags, queues, stacks, etc.
- *Cversion* — Called by the Micro Focus object-oriented runtime to if the correct version of the class library is running.
- *DelegateManager* — Manages message forwarding to objects when the original object does not understand the message (used internally).
- *Dependent* — Manages the notification of changes/deletions to all dependents of an object.
- *Event* — An instance of this class is passed as a parameter whenever an application receives notification of an event taking place.
- *EventManager* — Manages all panel events for GUI environments.
- *ExceptionManager* — Manages all exception handlers.
- *Font* — Font manages fonts.
- *GuiBase* — A generic or superclass for all Micro Focus GUI classes, responsible for event management, etc.
- *Intrinsic* — Manages all basic (intrinsic) COBOL data types (PICTURE).
- *Keybrd* — This class manages keyboard functions including function keys, etc.
- *MenuItem* — Menu and window graphic elements (Windows, DOS, and OS/2).
- *Mouse* — The mouse class manages all mouse manipulations.
- *Nilobject* — The Nilobject is invoked whenever an object is invoked with a nul reference.

- *PersistenceManager* — Supports the saving and loading of persistent objects.
- *TextObject* — Another class used internally to manage details of text items drawn in windows.

As you already have seen, collections are used to store groups of elements, and there are a variety of different collection classes with subtly different purposes and functions. Figure 8.4 represents the class hierarchy for the Micro Focus OOCOBOL collection classes. For example, Ordered Collections have elements that are kept in a predefined order, like those used for stacks, queues, etc. Sets are collections of elements without duplicates, while Dictionaries store a set of associations or links between some key data and the actual data itself. A SortedCollection maintains its elements in ascending or descending order by key. I will examine the collection classes in more detail later in this chapter as I build the example programs.

The PersistenceManager allows for the storage and management of objects that are permanent or exist after they are created in an external object store. For example, all of the objects in the ATM example are Persistent, while all the Library objects, except the Listof objects, are temporary and are physically stored in SQL tables. The Listof objects are managed by the collection class and referenced in the Library SQL tables but exist as persistent objects.

Other major Micro Focus classes and possible uses can be explored outside the scope of the example problems. For example, the Micro Focus Clipboard class allows data to be written and read from the system clipboard, while the Dependent class allows objects to be associated with other objects and managed together so that, when one object changes, the other object is notified. The ExceptionManager class manages all exception handlers or callbacks for errors, while the Mouse class manages mouse movements, clicking, dragging, ect. Finally, the Intrinsic class allows simple COBOL data types (i.e., PIC X, PIC COMP, etc.) to be accessed and managed in OOCOBOL programs.

In the next chapter, I will focus more on the Micro Focus GUI classes, including EventManager, MenuItem, CallBack, and GuiBase.

At this point, you should state your assumptions about how you will implement the OOCOBOL classes. I will use the Micro Focus preferred approach of creating and initializing the objects in the OOCOBOL programs. For each of the example problems, I will assume that every object is an instance of some class that itself is a child of the Base class. This allows you to assume that every

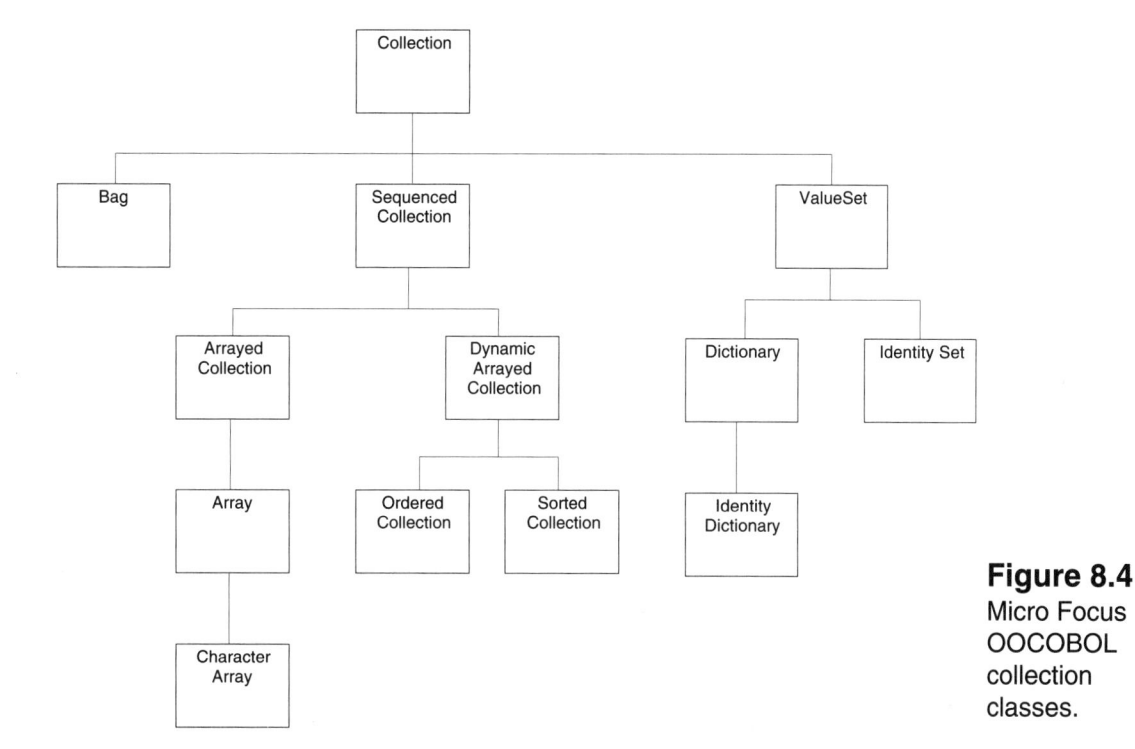

Figure 8.4 Micro Focus OOCOBOL collection classes.

object that you define will have a "new" method, which you will use to create instances of the object at run time, and an "Initialize" method, which you will be responsible for supplying when user-defined initialization is required. The "new" method always creates an instance of the object, then calls the "Initialize" method. As of early summer 1994, the ANSI X3J4 committee was considering eliminating the "CREATE" verb from the COBOL 97 syntax.

I also assume that some instances of objects require the use of the COBOL 97 FACTORY concept, which allows you to define class-level values for specific data elements or fields. I assume that these FACTORY structures will contain their own "Initialize" methods, which will be responsible for managing access to these shared data areas. More on the use of this FACTORY concept when I discuss the ATM example.

Finally, a note about the Micro Focus class libraries themselves. Class libraries must be continuously enhanced and restructured to best fit the changing needs of the clients that use them. The Micro Focus class library is no exception and likely will change over time. During the beta test period for the Object COBOL product, the libraries changed several times. You must recognize this and carefully consider your choices of classes as you implement your example solutions. Areas for class improvement include:

- Applying methods of abstraction to improve the consistency of the classes
- Provide better indexing and retrieval facilities for classes
- Provide uniform mechanisms for each class
- Combing classes into frameworks (reusable components)
- Extend the GUI classes to support new/better hardware/software features
- Develop more specialized classes for specific types of software.

For [reuse] to occur, the components must be atomic, or treated as such, so that composition can be accomplished without much change.
C. Jette and R. Smith [JET89].

8.5 OOCOBOL Products Available

Micro Focus currently offers the only true OOCOBOL product released in the summer of 1994. Other COBOL vendors that have committed to the COBOL 97 standard include IBM, DEC, HP, Unisys, and Computer Associates. The only question remaining is when these vendors will provide their own implementations of the COBOL 97 standard in their compiler products.

8.5.1 Micro Focus Object COBOL Option

Micro Focus delivers a development environment with many of the facilities that were described earlier in their Object COBOL Option to the Workbench version 1.2. The OOCOBOL environment is shown in Figure 8.5, and in its initial version, supports 16- and 32-bit compilers for DOS, OS/2, and Windows and provides support for a subset of the current draft OOCOBOL standard.

Included in the OOCOBOL package are class libraries, a class browser, an OOPS run time environment, examples, and an interface to Smalltalk. Most of the Micro Focus OOCOBOL effort has been geared around codevelopment with the Smalltalk language, and many of the features in the OOCOBOL Workbench mimic those found in popular Smalltalk environments.

8.5.2 Other COBOL Products

In addition to Micro Focus, PC-based versions of COBOL compilers that support the ANSI 74 and 85 standards are available from a variety of vendors.

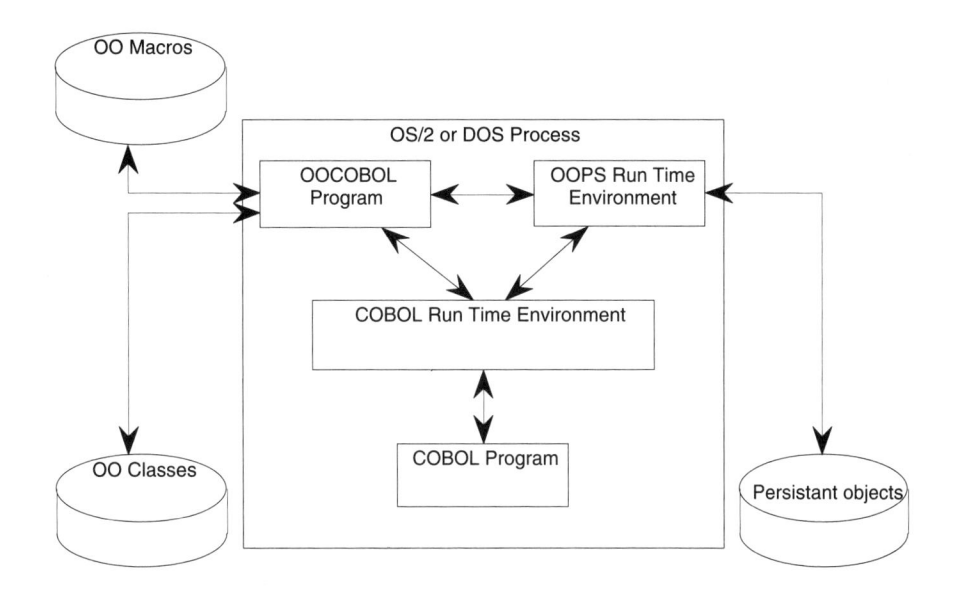

Figure 8.5
Micro Focus OOCOBOL development environment.

[Diagram: OS/2 or DOS Process containing OOCOBOL Program ↔ OOPS Run Time Environment, both connected to COBOL Run Time Environment, which connects to COBOL Program. External storage: OO Macros, OO Classes (connected to OOCOBOL Program), and Persistant objects (connected to OOPS Run Time Environment).]

While these products do not currently support the proposed COBOL 97 standard and object-orientation, they do deliver GUI-based development tools and many have indicated plans to support the OOCOBOL standard in the future.

IBM has announced their plans to deliver an Object Oriented COBOL product in early 1995 which will run on their MVS and OS/2 platforms and supports the proposed COBOL 97 standard. IBM was unable to deliver more information on their forthcomming OOCOBOL product prior to this manuscript being completed.

Computer Associates offers the CA-Realia II Workbench, a COBOL development environment that supports the Realia COBOL compiler. Additional options for the Realia product include CICS, IMS, and VSAM support. Included with the Realia Workbench are an editor, the compiler, a source-level debugger, and an integrated development environment.

MBP Software and Systems Technology has Visual COBOL, a Windows-based development product that supports the ANSI COBOL 85 standard. MBP also offers a Btrieve file manager, a GUI screen painter, a source-level debugger, and an editor.

Liant Software offers RM/COBOL-85, along with RM/CO*, a COBOL development environment: RM/PANELS, a Windows and DOS screen management facility; RM/CodeBench; RM/GRAFS; RM/plusDB; and RM/COMPANION, a menu-driven report writer. RM/CO* includes a project management facility, source-code editor, and a source-level debugger in an integrated development environment.

Acucobol sells AcuCOBOL-85, which is available for IBM PCs running under DOS. Hewlett Packard offers their own COBOL-85 product for the HP/UX operating environment, while DEC offers COBOL-85 support for their VMS and Ultrix environments, Unisys offers COBOL-85 compilers for their A, B, and U series machines.

8.5.3 Netron/CAP

Unlike Micro Focus, Netron offers a COBOL code assembly tool that supports many of the concepts of object-oriented development. Paul Bassett [BAS91] has described a method, and many organizations have successfully used Netron/CAP, for developing COBOL systems in an object-oriented manner. Netron/CAP is based on the concept of a "frame" as the dominant component in software development and is similar to OOPLs in that these frames are combined to form working systems.

While the concept of the frame is prominent in artificial intelligence circles, Netron uses the term to mean "adaptive subassemblies." These subassemblies can be combined at many levels of abstraction and can support functionality across a wide variety of operating environments. Frames are assembled into whole programs to satisfy specific problems.

Within Netron/CAP, frames are implemented as a mixture of COBOL code and meta commands and Bassett compares frames to classes. Netron/CAP is delivered with an extensive library of reusable frames that support screen-based I/O, DBMS I/O, screen definition, query reporting, etc.

Frames within Netron/CAP are used in a "same-as, except" system of data and function types similar to encapsulation in traditional OOPLs. Netron/CAP programs are composed of generic frames with specific parameters applied to tailor them for specific use. Netron/CAP supports multiple inheritance through this "same-as, except" concept but allows programs to be built using frames with the differences specified to enable complexity to be hidden.

Netron/CAP frames are assembled in a hierarchy with generic or application-independent frames at the bottom of the hierarchy and application-specific frames at the top of the hierarchy. Within Netron/CAP, generic data structures can be specified with their methods in a separate frame and these frames later can be combined to form a single package, not unlike the class construct in all OOPLs.

In a sense, a Bassett frame hierarchy is similar to a class hierarchy in a traditional OOPL. Netron also provides wrapper frames that hide functionality to further encourage reuse. Frames support multiple inheritance through their "same-as, except" capability and their components (data structures and methods) also can be modified or removed at any level within the hierarchy. Netron/CAP frames actively adapt, rather than passively inherit, their characteristics from their parents. These adaptable frames allow complexity to be hidden in the same fashion as OOPLs, thus allowing them to be developed using object-oriented design methods. Netron also offers a reusable code manager, along with a catalog and browse facility to support reuse at many levels.

Frame templates can be developed within CAP for subroutines, copybooks, macros, documentation, and objects, and Netron already supports popular workstation operating environments, including Windows, OS/2, and Motif. As Netron continues to accumulate extensive experience with frames, the product will evolve to support more of an object-oriented flavor in the future. Netron already offers an alternative to the plans for OOCOBOL that is available today and is supported by a wide variety of software applications.

8.6 Sample Problem Discussion

In considering the two example problems, you can make some assumptions about the implementation environments of both systems. Some of these assumptions are made in the spirit of allowing these examples to mimic most of the properties of traditional computer systems, while others help make these problems more interesting.

Because I am are using the Micro Focus COBOL product in a GUI environment (Microsoft Windows), I can build the example applications in a variety of ways. One method would be to define the classes interactively using the Micro Focus Class Library Browser. Using this approach, you would create new class definitions as descendents of superclasses and create the COBOL code for the objects, data structures, and methods by selecting options from the Library Browser menu.

An alternative approach would be to use a text editor to create the example class definitions in .CBL files, then compile them using the Micro Focus COBOL compiler. You might choose to use the Micro Focus Editor, or you might use an alternative editor or word processor to create these COBOL files. If you were operating in a non-GUI environment, you still could use the Micro Focus Editor that runs under DOS or any editor of our choice, but you would not be able to load the classes dynamically using the Class Library Browser as described previosly.

For purposes of the examples, I will use both these methods. The first example, the Library problem, will use the Micro Focus COBOL editor to create the class definitions. I then will compile these files using the Micro Focus compiler.

The second example, the ATM system, will use the Class Library Browser to define the classes interactively. I chose this approach for several reasons: the ATM example is a GUI-based example, and you should be comfortable with the graphical environment prior to developing for it; the Micro Focus Object COBOL Option includes an example class for bank accounts that I will extend to fit this example; and the Class Library Browser is common to other OOPL environments, especially Smalltalk, and is a powerful tool for interactive software development.

As I discuss each problem, recognize that I have omitted a detailed discussion of the issues of implementing these problems in a GUI, because chapter 9 will address these issues. For this reason, I limit my discussion to non-GUI items.

8.6.1 Library Problem

This version of the library problem will be implemented using a local area network of PCs with workstations available at specific collection points in the library. The library system will interface with other, mainframe-based systems, including the student information system and the financial systems for the university. Also, the Library system will be implemented using a RDBMS, so the principle data structures will be implemented as relational tables.

As you implement the Library system, you are faced with a plethora of options. For example, you could use IBM's CICS and OS/2 Database Manager for presentation and data access in the OOCOBOL application. You also could use Micro Focus Dialog System for presentation and any popular SQL-based RDBMS for the data access. Regardless, you must decide on a management

```
IDENTIFICATION DIVISION.
CLASS-ID.        Book IS TRANSIENT COLLECTABLE
                 INHERITS Base.
ENVIRONMENT DIVISION.
DATA DIVISION.
WORKING-STORAGE SECTION.
01  Book.
    03    CallNumber            PIC X(32).
    03    Title                 PIC X(60).
    03    Publisher             PIC X(60).
    03    DatePublished         PIC 9(8).
    03    ISBN                  PIC X(16).
    03    ListOfUsers           USAGE OBJECT REFERENCE.
01  Copy.
    03    Copy_ID.
          05    CallNumber      PIC X(32).
          05    CopyNumber      PIC 99.
    03    DateOut               PIC 9(8).
    03    DateDueBack           PIC 9(8).
01  Author.
    03    AuthorBook.
          05    CallNumber      PIC X(32).
          05    LastName        PIC X(30).
          05    FirstName       PIC X(30).
```

Figure 8.6
Library class data.

mechanisms for the RDBMS and non-RDBMS data structures (i.e., your Lists). Figure 8.6 represents portions of the Library data structures.

As I already stated, you goals in OOP are to support the functionality of the Library system using OOCOBOL and an RDBMS on a LAN. For this to occur, you map the Library objects to Micro Focus classes and review the classes for application in this example problem. In the Library system, the majority of the objects are stored externally in SQL tables. For this reason, you map the Book, Copy, Author, User, and Staff objects to the Base class and define them as TRANSIENT, which means that they are not kept by OOCOBOL following the termination of the program that creates them. Under the ANSI COBOL 97 standard, this means the objects are created in memory but are stored externally in a SQL DBMS and are reloaded each time they are used.

As a result, you have the following mappings from the Library problem to the Micro Focus classes:

- Book: Base — Transient [SQL database table]
- Copy: Base — Transient [SQL database table]
- Author: Base — Transient [SQL database table]
- User: Base — Transient [SQL database table]
- Staff: Base — Transient [SQL database table]
- CheckedOut: Base — Transient [SQL database table]
- List of Users: OrderedCollection — Persistent
- List of Books: OrderedCollection — Persistent.

While I chose to use SQL as the DBMS for storage and access to the basic Library data, I also could have defined these as persistent Dictionary objects. A Dictionary stores key and data pairs or associations in a fixed sized data store. The design trade-offs for doing so include managing the associations and relationships among the various objects, such as between Users and Books, and supporting group data structures. You could have used intrinsic associations for group data items, but this approach might prove too complicated and you need keyed access to these structures. In some cases, as with the User, you need both primary and secondary keys based on UserID and UserName.

```
METHOD-ID. FindUser.
* Returns specific user information by UserId, or if not found,
* by UserName.  If still not found, returns exception condition.
PROCEDURE DIVISION USING UserID RETURNING User.
    SELECT * FROM USER WHERE User_ID = UserID.
    If User_ID NE UserID
        SELECT * FROM USER
         WHERE User_Name = UserName.
        If User_Name NE UserName
            THEN PERFORM EXCEPTION-CONDITION.
    MOVE User_Name to UserName.
    MOVE Password to UserPassword.
    MOVE BorrowLimit to UserBorrowLimit.
    EXIT PROGRAM.
END METHOD FindUser.
```

Figure 8.7
SQL commands in the FindUser method.

Because SQL tables are used, the RDBMS manages the storage and retrieval of the data structures and you simply can build the SQL commands into the appropriate object methods. For example, the User Find method is shown in Figure 8.7 and contains SQL commands to locate the correct User via the UserID or UserName value in the SQL table.

Of the data structures in the Library problem, the two Lists — List of Users and List of Books — are built as OrderedCollections as previously described in Chapter 7. As you review the OrderedCollection class methods, you will find that you have only to construct the list data in a string and specify the ordered field, which in the case is the DateOut to use these classes. The OrderedCollection class includes methods to initialize the collection, set the size, add, find, and remove elements, determine the capacity, etc.

These Lists actually are referenced as part of other objects — Book contains list of authors and Users contain list of books. Each book copy is its own unique row in the BookCopy table and is associated with a user when they check out a book. Book and User table entries contain references or pointers to these collection objects. When a book or user is added to the system, the methods must create an instance of OrderedCollection for the List and store the handle for the object in the appropriate table entry.

One question that came up as I built my Lists was whether they actually are fixed-sized lists or variable-sized lists. Consider that the List of Books and Users should never contain more than 100 entries and therefore is fixed in size. Whenever a List of Books or Users contains exactly 100 entries the List is archived and reset to 0 entries. In this sense, the List of object is very much like a stack. Another question concerns the need to expand the size of the list in the future and how you might accomplish this.

To satisfy the requirements to print out the lists of users or books, you can use a report writer or utility program to ask for the call number (if the list is of users who have checked out a book) or the user ID (if the list is of books checked out to a user), then print the contents of the List associated with the object found. Printing a list of books by author can be accomplished by writing a SQL query against the BookAuthor table.

Another issue to be decided is how you will implement the shared data elements in the Library system. These include the next User ID, default Borrow Limit, etc. I chose to use an OOCOBOL factory for storage and management of these common values. In the class definition for the User, I define a factory data element, NextUserID, and a method, GetNextUserID, which increments the NextUserID field and returns the result to the Add method of the User object.

Finally, I should review the Base class methods for any items of interest. As I do, you will see that every object contains a method "new," Name, which returns the name of the class; Description, which returns a description of the class; and Equal, which determines if another object is equal to this. The Base class contains no attributes because you supply your own data elements when you create subclasses. Excepts from the Library User class methods are shown in Figure 8.8.

8.6.2 ATM Problem

The automated teller machine system represents an interesting architecture, because there could be many ATMs scattered around a local area all serviced by different bank offices. Ideally, each ATM would be physically connected to a bank office, but you also might decide to place ATMs in nonbank offices, including malls or shopping centers, office parks, or even in theatre complexes.

The ATM system should be able to handle distributed processing for bank transactions if you make some assumptions about the ATM transactions. For instance, you might specify that any withdrawal transaction will be processed by the nearest bank office — perhaps connected by phone lines — while deposits will be batched and processed by a specific bank office — perhaps wherever the account is held — the following business day.

Portions of the ATM class data structures, which were described in the previous chapter, are shown in Figure 8.9.

Mapping ATM Objects to Micro Focus classes results in the following:

- Account: Base — Transient vs. Dictionary — Persistent (?)
- ATMTransaction: OrderedCollection — Persistent
- ATM Session: Base — Transient
- ATM UI: GuiBase (discussed in next chapter).

An interesting question is whether the ATM objects are transient or persistent. Accounts are external to the ATM system and should be considered as TRANSIENT, like most of the Library objects. You could build the Account object as a Dictionary of value pairs — stored by Account Number — that is persistent. You can implement the Account class using any mechanism for

```
IDENTIFICATION DIVISION.
CLASS-ID.        Book IS TRANSIANT COLLECTABLE
                 INHERITS Base.
* Class definitions for Book here *
METHOD-ID. "new".
WORKING-STORAGE SECTION.
01  TEMP         USAGE OBJECT REFERENCE.
LINKAGE SECTION.
01  Book         USAGE OBJECT REFERENCE.
01  Book_REF     USAGE OBJECT REFERENCE.
PROCEDURE DIVISION USING Book_Ref RETURNING Book.
    INVOKE Super "new" RETURNING Book.
    INVOKE Book "Initialize".
    EXIT PROGRAM.
END METHOD "new".

METHOD-ID. "Initialize".          /* For Factory */
* Initialize Book class by creating the SQL table and indexes *
WORKING-STORAGE SECTION.
01  SIZE               PIC 9(4) COMP-5.
PROCEDURE DIVISION.
    CREATE TABLE BOOK
         PRIMARY KEY CallNumber.
    CREATE TABLE COPY
         PRIMARY KEY Copy_ID.
    CREATE TABLE AUTHOR
         PRIMARY KEY AuthorBook.
    CREATE INDEX XBOOK
         ON BOOK (CallNumber).
    EXIT PROGRAM.
END METHOD "Initialize".

OBJECT.
PROCEDURE DIVISION.
METHOD-ID. Add.
* Add - creates the entry in the Book table with the proper values.
```

Figure 8.8
Portions of the Library class methods.

```
IDENTIFICATION DIVISION.
CLASS-ID.        Account IS TRANSIENT COLLECTABLE
                 INHERITS Base.
ENVIRONMENT DIVISION.
DATA DIVISION.
WORKING-STORAGE SECTION.
01  Account.
    03    Number                        PIC 9(8).
    03    Type                          PIC XX.
          88    Checking                      VALUE "CK".
          88    Saving                        VALUE "SV".
          88    MoneyMarket                   VALUE "MK".
          88    LineOfCredit                  VALUE "LC".
          88    Mortgage                      VALUE "MG".
          88    Loan                          VALUE "LN".
    03    FirstName                     PIC X(30).
    03    LastName                      PIC X(30).
    03    Address.
          05    Street                  PIC X(30).
          05    Street_2                PIC X(30).
          05    City                    PIC X(30).
          05    State                   PIC XX.
          05    Zip_Code.
                07    Zip_5             PIC 9(5).
                07    Zip_4             PIC 9(4).
          05    Phone_Number.
                07    Area_Code         PIC 999.
                07    Phone_3           PIC 999.
                07    Phone_4           PIC 9(4).
    03    Balance                       PIC S9(6)V99.
    03    PIN                           PIX 9999.
    03    DateOpened                    PIC 9(8).
```

Figure 8.9
Portions of ATM class data.

testing purposes because accounts are external objects managed by another application (i.e., Account Manager) and support basic services such as GetPAN, GetBalance, Credit, Debit, etc. The existing Account Manager system is COBOL-based CICS and IMS. In chapter 10, I will review a process of wrapping this existing Bank Account system to interface with the ATM system.

ATM session data is transient (i.e., deleted after each ATM Transaction is logged to the file). ATM Transactions are persistent, and I have chosen to use the OrderedCollection class for them. These transactions actually contain values — PAN, PIN, Date, Time, etc. — and are stored permanently in an ATM Log file. I chose to store them as PERSISTENT OrderedCollections ordered by Date and Time. The ATM UI is persistent because the hardware statuses, cash on hand, etc. must be maintained over the course of the life of the ATM. There is no stated need to retrieve the ATM transactions although you might want to add functionality to print them at the end of each business day.

Finally, the ATM User Interface is not covered in this chapter but is described in chapter 9. In that chapter, I will cover GUI design and implementation issues and review the objects and classes available in the Micro Focus library for Windows and OS/2 PM support. Excepts from the ATM system class methods are shown in Figure 8.10.

8.7 Testing OOCOBOL Programs

Once you have delivered your OOCOBOL programs, they must be tested. Recalling the discussion of an OOSDLC in chapter 4, you can begin by unit testing the subsystems that you deliver. As each subsystem is delivered, it is unit tested, then as more subsystems are built and delivered, they are integration tested against the other subsystems. The key aspects of the example problems that should be thoroughly tested during this phase are the interfaces that support the services for each subsystem.

In the case of the Library system, you test the Library subsystem by entering values for books, authors, and users. You can verify the accuracy of the data by running SQL queries against the RDBMS tables once the data has been loaded. You perform functional tests on the Library subsystem by viewing and updating data, performing the checkout and return function, and running the reports. Recalling the initial requirements for the Library system, you can expect to perform at least the following tests: add a copy of a book, remove a copy of a book, check out a copy of a book to a user, return a copy of a book, generate a list of books in the library written by a particular author, generate a list of books currently checked out by a particular borrower, find out which borrower most recently checked out a particular copy of a book, set the borrow limit for a user, and verify that only library staff can do most of these functions.

For the ATM system, you could unit test the ATM with or without the User Interface by simply generating messages and verifying the outcome. Changes

```
IDENTIFICATION DIVISION.
CLASS-ID.         Account IS TRANSIANT COLLECTABLE
                  INHERITS Base.
******* Class definitions for Account here *********
METHOD-ID. "new".
WORKING-STORAGE SECTION.
01  TEMP                USAGE OBJECT REFERENCE.
LINKAGE SECTION.
01  Account             USAGE OBJECT REFERENCE.
01  Account_REF USAGE OBJECT REFERENCE.
PROCEDURE DIVISION USING Account_Ref  RETURNING
Account.
    INVOKE Super "new" RETURNING Account.
        INVOKE Account "Initialize".
        EXIT PROGRAM.
END METHOD "new".

METHOD-ID. "Initialize".         /* For Factory */
*  Initialize Account class by setting the Account Number, balance,
and date. *
WORKING-STORAGE SECTION.
01  SIZE         PIC X(4) COMP-5.
PROCEDURE DIVISION.
    COMPUTE Next_Account_Number + 1 TO Number.
    MOVE 0 to Balance.
    MOVE Current_Date to DateOpened.
    EXIT PROGRAM.
END METHOD "Initialize".

OBJECT.
PROCEDURE DIVISION.
METHOD-ID. Add.
*  Add - creates the Account entry with the proper values.
PROCEDURE DIVISION USING Account RETURNING Balance.
    MOVE Balance to Balance.
    EXIT PROGRAM.
END METHOD Add.
```

Figure 8.10
Portions of the ATM class methods.

in the values of the ATM during the session, verification of account information, and logging of transactions can all be checked in this fashion. In addition, you can use a prototype of the ATM UI to simulate interaction with the ATM (i.e., pushing buttons, progressing through the ATM session, etc.) and verify the interface between the UI and the ATM.

You also should test the interface between the ATM and the Account Manager to ensure that accounts can be found and balances verified. You might want to build a small sample account file to test the interface. You can test the ATM File Manager by storing ATM Transactions as persistent objects and writing a utility program to print out these objects following an ATM session.

Once the subsystems have all been delivered, unit, and integration tested, you should perform a system or application test to make sure that all of the original requirements have been satisfied. If your CASE tool supports requirements tracking, you can verify that all functional requirements have been satisfied by running these reports. Each system requirement should be supported in the object model, in the object specification, and in the finished system, and users should sign-off on the delivery of these systems prior to acceptance.

8.8 References

[BAS91]	Bassett, P., "Engineering Software for Softness," *American Programmer*, 1991, pp. 1-15.
[BAS87]	Bassett, P., "Frame-Based Software Engineering," *IEEE Software*, July 1987.
[BIG89]	Biggerstaff, T. J. and A. J. Perliss, *Software Reusability: Concepts and Models,* and *Applications and Experiences*, Vols. 1 & 2, ACM Press and Addison-Wesley, 1989.
[JET89]	Jette, C. and R. Smith, "Examples of Reusability in an Object-Oriented Programming Environment," *in Software Reusability*, vol. II, Addison-Wesley, 1989.
[MEY89]	Meyer, B., "Reusability: The CASE for Object-Oriented Design," *IEEE Software*, vol. 4, no. 2, March 1987.

Chapter

9

Building GUI Applications in Object-Oriented COBOL

As more and more applications are ported to PCs and LANs, the need to support graphical user interfaces (GUIs) is becoming essential in COBOL development and maintenance. OOCOBOL provides some powerful features that make the migration to GUIs easier and more flexible.

Also, as more organizations look at a migration to client/server or distributed systems, GUIs will continue to support more of the functionality of these applications. As you already have seen, older systems that were mainframe-centric had very little presentation logic or user interface functionality. Newer client/server applications might have very demanding or complex presentation logic, including sophisticated editing and rule checking, and require transaction processing in a distributed environment.

As applications move toward graphical environments, developers must understand an event-driven model of programming and deal with asynchronous processing and message passing. This event-driven view lends itself very nicely to an object-oriented perspective, because you can encapsulate the data structures and operations into generic classes that manage the GUI components. OOCOBOL provides an excellent vehicle for this migration and allows for the development of reusable GUI classes that manage these details.

9.1 Introduction

Throughout the 1960s and 1970s, 3270-based CRTs were the input/output vehicle of choice for most of the IBM systems developed. Likewise, the VT100 terminal provided a similar function for the DEC world. Early Unix systems also shared this text-based terminal interface. With the advent of the PC in the 1980s, the 3270-type interface was moved to a dedicated workstation but not significantly changed. Many existing systems developed in the 1980s and even 1990s still incorporate character-based, block-oriented input and output devices as the interface of choice. From this viewpoint evolved the use of menus, keyboard navigation, and function keys to support special processing.

With the advent of the graphical user interface (GUI) in the 1980s, popularized by the Apple Macintosh, more and more software applications development groups began considering the form and content of the interaction of the computer with the client. With this development came the realization that software could have a user-centric viewpoint. A PC or a workstation can support a graphical environment, with a pointing device (most often a mouse or trackball) used to identify an object to be manipulated, thus making it easier conceptually for a non-technical user to work with computer systems. The WIMP (Windows, Icons, Menus, and Pointing device) interface has changed the way that people view computing and continues to gain acceptability in the applications software market. With millions of copies of Microsoft Windows sold, the software industry continues to move towards a graphical, more user-centric viewpoint in the future.

GUIs bring to application software much power and flexibility but also much complexity and difficulty in dealing with the events and messages that drive the interface. Environments such as Microsoft Windows, IBM's OS/2 Presentation Manager, HP's NewWave, and NextStep include graphical elements that provide consistency of display and interaction, a common conceptual model of human-machine interface, and the ability to arrange and interact with several software applications on a virtual desktop, all of which are available at the movement of a mouse or other pointing device. The challenge for software developers is to better support the GUI environments and rethink the way that systems are developed to incorporate this user-centric viewpoint.

Many existing applications are being reengineered to take advantage of the power of the workstation and distributed or client/server processing, and the GUI is playing a large role in this conversion process. However, traditional character-based applications require a significant change in thinking prior to conversion to a GUI environment. In many cases, the application itself might need to be redesigned around the interface to improve the productivity and efficiency of the user.

As user interfaces evolved and became more powerful and flexible, software developers spent more time understanding the system from the user standpoint and dealing with the complexities of graphical environments. The move away from mainframe-based applications to client-server applications signals the end of the dumb user interface. Existing CASE products often provide little, if any, direct support for developing sound user interfaces and have taken only first steps towards supporting GUIs in their products. Other, more powerful alternatives represent a better investment for software developers, including GUI painters, visual object-oriented programming languages (OOPLs), and user interface (UI) class libraries.

While some estimates suggest that the user interface represents between 20% and 40% of an application, developers must remember that the presentation portion is the most important component if only because it is the part that users interact with on a regular basis. There is no doubt that with the widespread acceptance of GUIs in the future, the interface will represent a more significant percentage of an application, perhaps as much as 70% of the total application.

Several GUIs now are available on a variety of hardware platforms and provide a user-friendly facility for interaction with the computer. A GUI can be characterized as having windows, icons, dialog boxes, and a mouse or some other input device (touch screen, tablet, etc.). Underneath, GUIs support windowing, imaging, an Application Programming Interface (API), and a framework for application development that encourages a common software representation.

The first GUI was developed at the Xerox PARC along with Smalltalk, and this led to the first popular graphical environment, which was developed at Apple Computer for the Lisa. This environment was later copied and extended for the Macintosh, which became the first widely used graphical computer operating environment. Early in its development, Apple realized they could encapsulate the complexity of the GUI into classes of objects.

Apple saw that GUIs exhibit object-oriented behavior and that their inherent complexity could be managed and controlled using OOP techniques. In a similar manner, from the user perspective, a GUI represents visual objects that resemble real-world objects found on an actual desktop. Printers look like printers, file folders look like folders, and the trash can looks like a trash can. The mouse (or some other device) is used to select and perform operations on the GUI objects that can be directly manipulated by the user. This conceptual model maps nicely to the user view of real world objects (i.e., files, printers, folders, etc.).

9.2 Popular Graphical User Interfaces

The Apple Macintosh was the first commercially successful GUI environment. The Macintosh had a WIMP interface and allowed logical abstractions of the desktop to be replicated on the computer screen. The Macintosh, for example, included a trash can into which files could be deposited to be deleted. This metaphor led to much greater acceptance and use of the Macintosh by nontechnical people.

Based on the success of the Macintosh, Microsoft developed Windows for the DOS PC marketplace. While the original Windows versions were relatively unsuccessful, version 3.*x* has sold over 10 million copies. The market for Windows applications subsequently has outpaced those for DOS applications, and several research groups are predicting Windows will be the *de facto* operating environment for the 1990s.

OS/2 was IBM's answer to the Macintosh graphical environment, and Presentation Manager delivered on the promise of the desktop metaphor. IBM went beyond Microsoft and Apple with their release of OS/2 version 2.0 that included the Desktop Workplace, an object-oriented desktop environment. IBM and Apple both are working on a further evolution of this graphical environment in the Taligent operating system planned for 1995.

For the Unix market, OSF/Motif is becoming the graphical standard. While there are alternatives (most notably OpenLook from Sun), Motif has captured the majority of the marketplace in the early 1990s. The Next environment, which was originally developed for the Next computer, has evolved to support Intel 80486-based computers and includes its own graphical standards. While this graphical revolution took place on the desktop, very few mainframe-oriented operating environments have adopted the GUI.

9.3 GUI Applications

The most notable difference between the graphical interfaces on the PC or workstation and those developed for the mainframe or minicomputers is the *event-driven behavior* of the GUI environment. Under Windows or OS/2 PM, the user controls the flow and behavior of the application, not the application program. Under traditional mainframe-oriented applications, the COBOL program dictates the flow of control and the actions taken, often in a specific sequence. In this fashion, older COBOL programs execute in a linear or serial fashion, with the program directing the actions that occur and the order in which they occur.

In a GUI environment, the user of the application decides how and when specific actions will be undertaken. In this sense, any GUI application is *user-centered* so that the user initiates and controls all the actions for the application and can choose to reduce the application to an icon (or make the application wait) while they do something else entirely. When the application program needs information from the user, it must display a dialog box or window requesting the information. However, the user can close the window or dialog box, move on to some other task, or even close the application entirely. This represents a major philosophical difference in how GUI applications are designed and built.

GUI applications are *message-based*, while traditional mainframe COBOL applications are sequential or program-based. In a GUI application, an event or message indicates that something has happened in the environment and that the application program might need to respond to this event. Within each GUI environment, the operating system manages passing messages and responding to events, while the application program must be prepared to respond properly to whatever events occur. Any GUI application must consider and account for these messages as part of its normal processing.

GUI applications also must be prepared to *respond to asynchronous external events* or requests from outside their scope or environment. One example of this is when a Windows or OS/2 PM application is printing to the standard printer and an error occurs. The application must notify the user of the error and ask for direction immediately. This type of message cannot be ignored or disregarded by the user. This adds another level of complexity to a GUI application not found in traditional MIS programs.

Another key concept of a GUI application is that it can exhibit *modal processing*. Modal processing requires that the user respond to the request prior to selecting another task or activity. In effect, a modal dialog box freezes the rest of the GUI application until it is concluded or resolved.

9.3.1 Architecture of a GUI Application

Another difference between traditional COBOL applications and GUI applications is in their structure. Every GUI program shares a common structure or architecture, because the application interacts with the GUI in the same fashion, regardless of its function. As can be seen in Figure 9.1, a GUI application begins by initializing itself, any instances of objects, then the main window for the application. Following this initialization, the program sets up an infinite loop to process messages received from the GUI environment. As various menu options or dialog boxes are displayed and information is collected, the program responds accordingly. Messages must be received by the correct portion of the program and appropriate action taken.

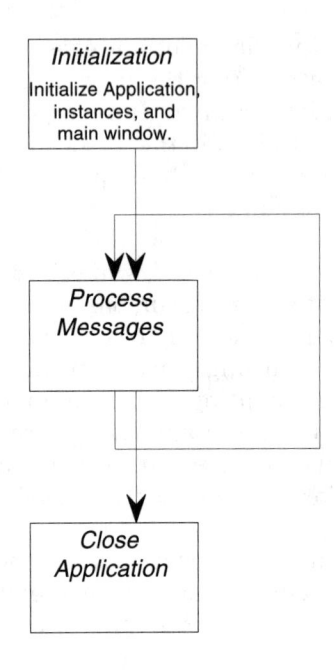

Figure 9.1
Generic GUI application flow.

[Diagram: Initialization (Initialize Application, instances, and main window.) → Process Messages (loop) → Close Application]

A COBOL program that executes in this type of environment might contain the following generic structure and logic:

MAIN SECTION.

Perform Initialize-Application.
Perform Initialize-Window.

Perform Message-Loop
Until   EXIT,
         CLOSE,
OR   WM_DESTROY.

Perform Close-Application.
Perform Close-Window.

STOP RUN.

If the user of the application selects Exit or Closes the main window, the application terminates; however, prior to doing so, it must close the main window and the application itself and return environment resources (memory, devices, etc.) to the control of the operating system. Only upon successful completion of these actions can the GUI application terminate.

Both MS Windows and OS/2 Presentation Manager (PM) support a class structure for their windowing systems. The primary object in both of these environments is the window, which acts as the central object in the GUI environment. Any events that affect a window must be handled by that window. The window responds to each event based on the methods that are defined. Within the GUI environment, main windows can spawn child windows, which can spawn other child windows, etc. Any child window has the same properties as its parent window and usually must be drawn within the parent window space.

Windows have handles that are used to manipulate them, and when a window is created, the O/S returns the handle to the application program. Every object in the GUI has as its first parameter its handle, and the syntax of the GUI functions are object-based. Messages created specify which operations or methods are to be performed.

For example, OS/2 PM has over 100 general-purpose messages and over 150 special-purpose messages for dialog boxes, scroll bars, etc. Within presentation manager, messages can be categorized into four main types:

- Input — Generated in response to keyboard or mouse input.
- System — Generated in response to programmed events or system interrupts.
- Control — Support two-way communication between windows and other GUI objects.
- User — User-defined to convey data after a predefined event occurs.

When GUI applications are developed, the programmer must anticipate which messages will be received and which code will execute to handle each message. For example, when a dialog box is placed on the screen, various control messages could be received for list boxes, push-buttons, radio buttons, etc. Other messages cause a dialog box to close or terminate.

GUIs also contain components or graphic items that are built or used in a specific order or hierarchy. For example, a standard GUI application might have the following hierarchy of components:

Main Window with menu options (Application)
    SubWindow with menu options (Subsystem)
        Dialog box(es)
    Other SubWindows (Subsystems)
        Other dialog boxes
    Application-level dialog boxes (Menu options)
        ...

These GUI components must be initialized and displayed in the correct order, with the lower-level windows or dialog boxes overlaying the main window. Whenever a request is made to close a higher-level GUI component, any lower-level components must be closed and disposed of first.

Figure 9.2 shows an example application hierarchy for a GUI program. Notice that the highest level component in the GUI is the Application, followed by the Main Window, etc. Also notice that the Main Window contains a Menu, which itself contains SubMenus and Menu Items, and that the Main Window also can contain child Windows — also called *dialog boxes*. This structure or hierarchy represents the logical elements of any GUI application and these items must be created and destroyed in the proper sequence for the application to function correctly.

9.3.2 Components of GUIs

All GUIs have a common set of components of facilities including:

- An *API*, which provides a set of programming language constructs allowing the developer to define how the application will control the environment.
- A *windowing system*, which allows multiple applications to be running on a single monitor.
- An *imaging model*, which defines how fonts and graphics are displayed and manipulated on the screen.
- An underlying *operating system*, which manages the files, devices, resources, etc.
- A set of *tools and frameworks* for extending the interface and creating applications.

Figure 9.3 shows these components for Windows and OS/2 PM environments. While the GUI environments are similar, they have different mechanisms and architectures underneath. Figure 9.4 represents the architecture of Microsoft Windows 3.*x* while Figure 9.5 shows the architecture for OS/2 2.*x* Any Windows or OS/2 application must recognize the architectures of these environments and interact appropriately with the GUI components.

Getting back to the sequence or logic of a GUI application, Figure 9.6 shows a default or generic logic for a Windows application. The Windows program begins by initializing itself, processing messages until the user has indicated that he or she wants to exit or close the application, then closes the application.

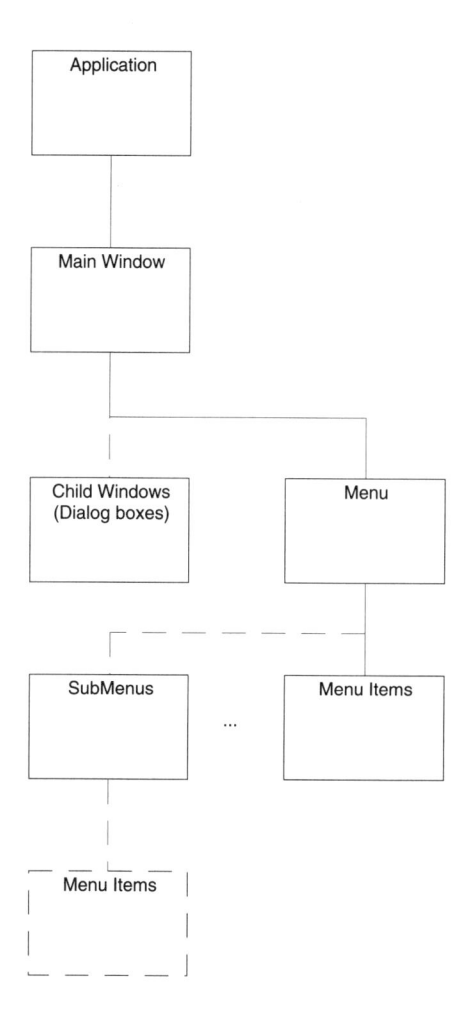

```
                    ┌─────────────┐
                    │ Application │
                    │             │
                    └──────┬──────┘
                           │
                           │
                    ┌──────┴──────┐
                    │ Main Window │
                    │             │
                    │             │
                    └──────┬──────┘
                           │
                ┌──────────┴──────────┐
                │                     │
        ┌───────┴───────┐      ┌──────┴──────┐
        │ Child Windows │      │    Menu     │
        │(Dialog boxes) │      │             │
        │               │      │             │
        └───────┬───────┘      └──────┬──────┘
                │                     │
                │ - - - - - - - - - - │
        ┌───────┴───────┐      ┌──────┴──────┐
        │   SubMenus    │      │ Menu Items  │
        │               │ ...  │             │
        │               │      │             │
        └───────┬───────┘      └─────────────┘
                │
        ┌ ─ ─ ─ ┴ ─ ─ ─ ┐
        │  Menu Items   │
        │               │
        │               │
        └ ─ ─ ─ ─ ─ ─ ─ ┘
```

Figure 9.2
GUI component hierarchy.

Also notice that the Process Message logic loops through getting the next Windows message, determining if there are additional message to process (if not, the application is closed), translates the message, then dispatches a response message back to Windows. The Process Message procedure must contain or reference a Window procedure that examines Windows messages and a default procedure for the application. Example Windows messages include *Create, Destroy, Close, Quit, Scroll, Paint*, etc. Figure 9.7 shows a similar logical structure for an OS/2 PM application. Notice how similar the logic and flow is to the Windows program described earlier.

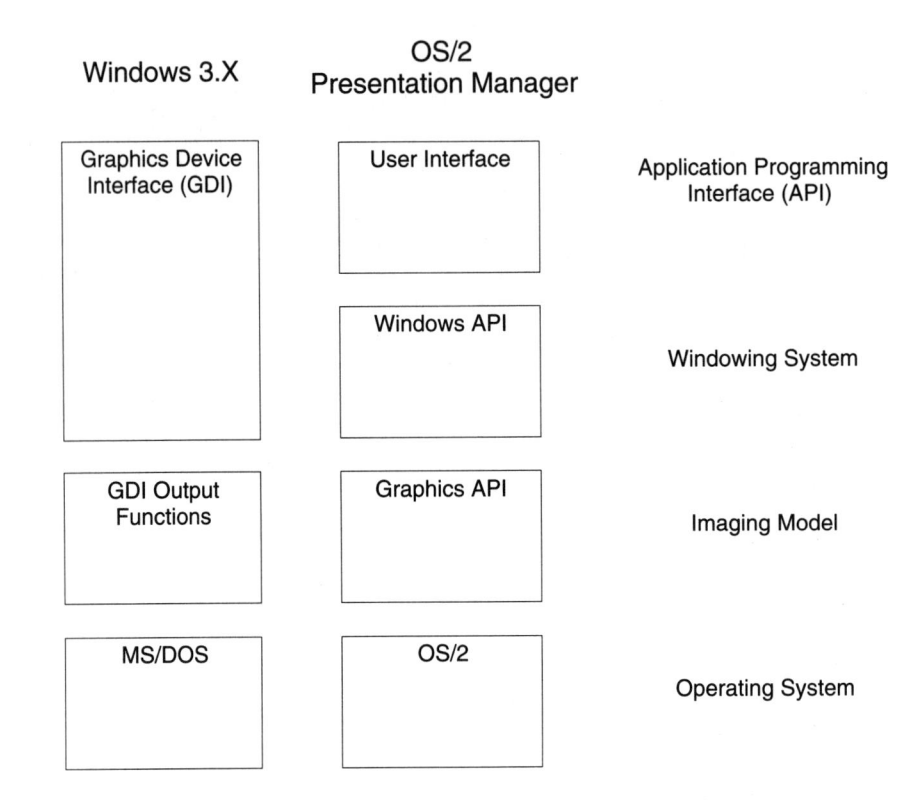

Figure 9.3
Windows and OS/2 PM GUI components.

```
                    OS/2
Windows 3.X    Presentation Manager

Graphics Device     User Interface      Application Programming
Interface (GDI)                              Interface (API)

                    Windows API         Windowing System

GDI Output          Graphics API        Imaging Model
Functions

MS/DOS              OS/2                Operating System
```

One outcome of the evolution of GUIs and the Smalltalk language is the use of OOPL class libraries to specify the behavior of the GUI itself. A class hierarchy is defined for the GUI that includes windows, dialog boxes, icons, etc. and their variables and behavior. Smalltalk, the first GUI development environment, includes the Model/View/Controller (MVC) class mechanism, which represents the components of the GUI and their interaction.

A GUI class library, when available, includes the set of components or widgets that can operate in the GUI. GUI events are handled by predefined methods and messages are passed to the objects where they can be processed by the application program. Popular GUIs include Windows, OS/2 Presentation Manager, OSF/Motif, OpenLook, DECWindows, NextStep, and the Macintosh.

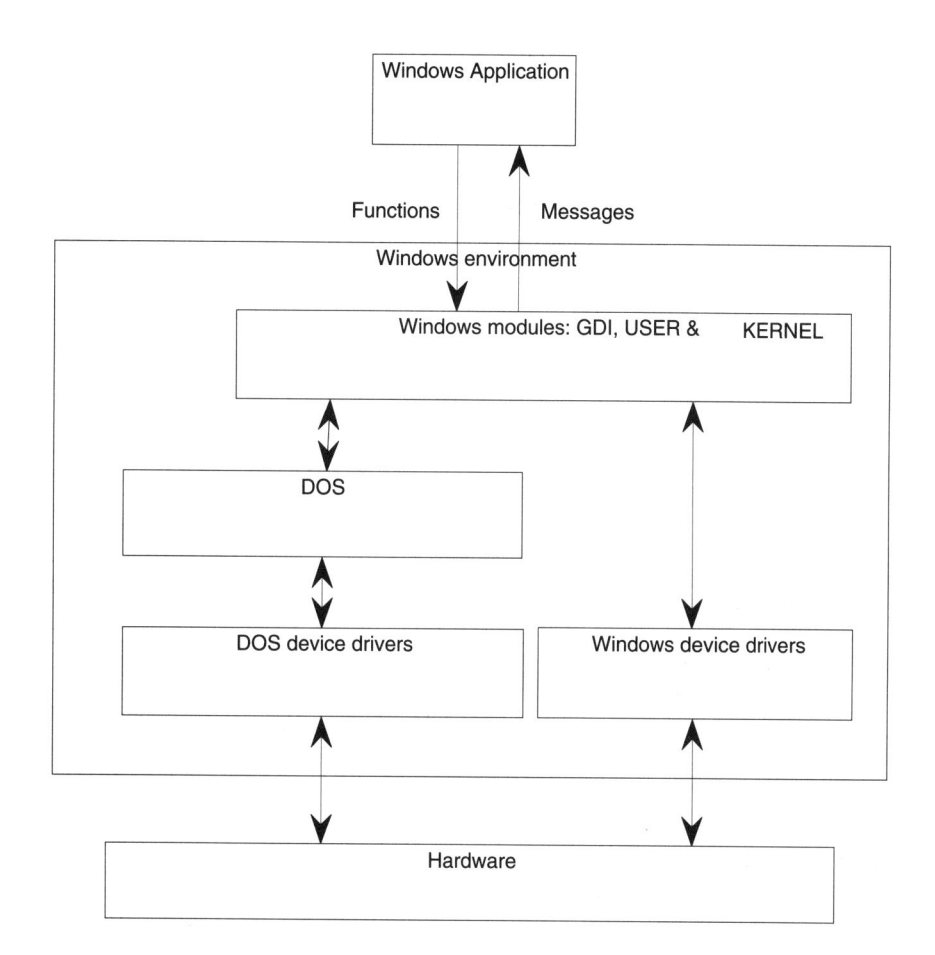

Figure 9.4 Windows architecture.

9.3.3 Behavior of GUI Applications

As you have seen, one basic difference between traditional COBOL applications and GUI applications is that COBOL programs usually are controlled by the flow of logic in a single program, while GUI applications are controlled by the user of the application. Traditional COBOL programs have a hierarchy of control or flow that begins in the PROCEDURE division and runs till the STOP RUN or GOBACK command is encountered.

Mainframe COBOL programs also process information in a sequential fashion, usually reading in transactions, locating data from a database or file,

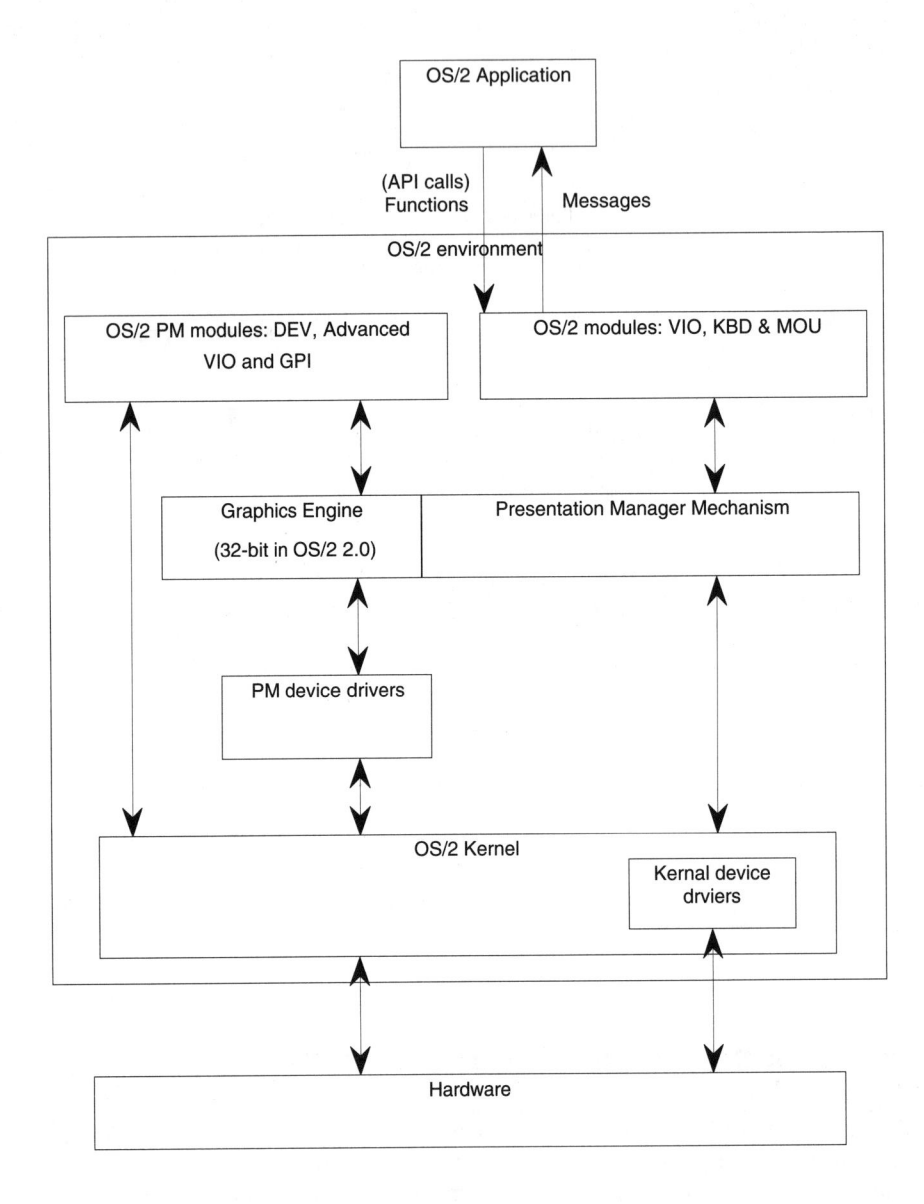

Figure 9.5
OS/2 architecture.

updating or printing the contents of these structures, then moving on to the next record. This sequential mode of processing has even been carried forward into online CICS COBOL programs.

For example, CICS programs typically process information in sequence, allowing the user to enter values for fields on a screen map, then doing some

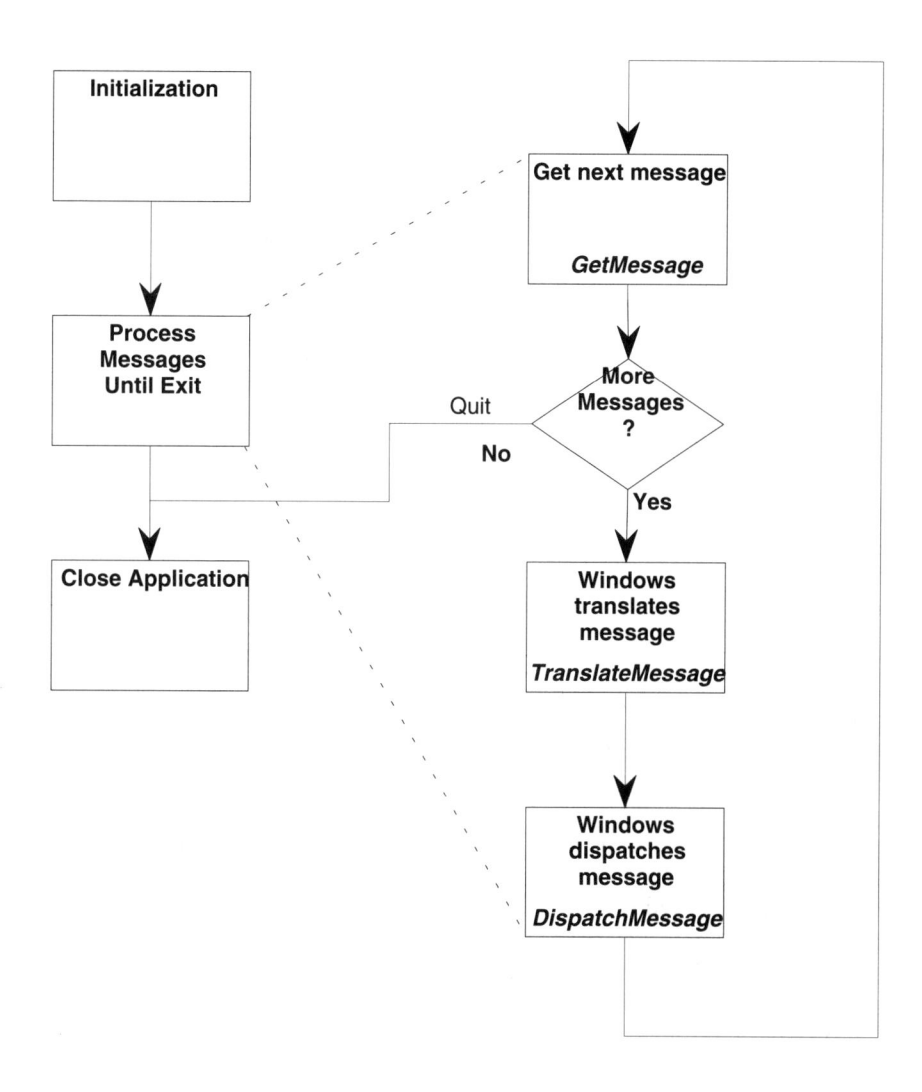

Figure 9.6
Windows application flow.

editing of the input data before updating the file or database table. Other online transaction processing systems use similar processing logic to manage access and updates to files or database structures.

In a GUI environment, there usually is no prespecified order or flow of control for the data input to an application. Likewise, there might not be a predefined sequence or hierarchy of processing that occurs for each transaction. While

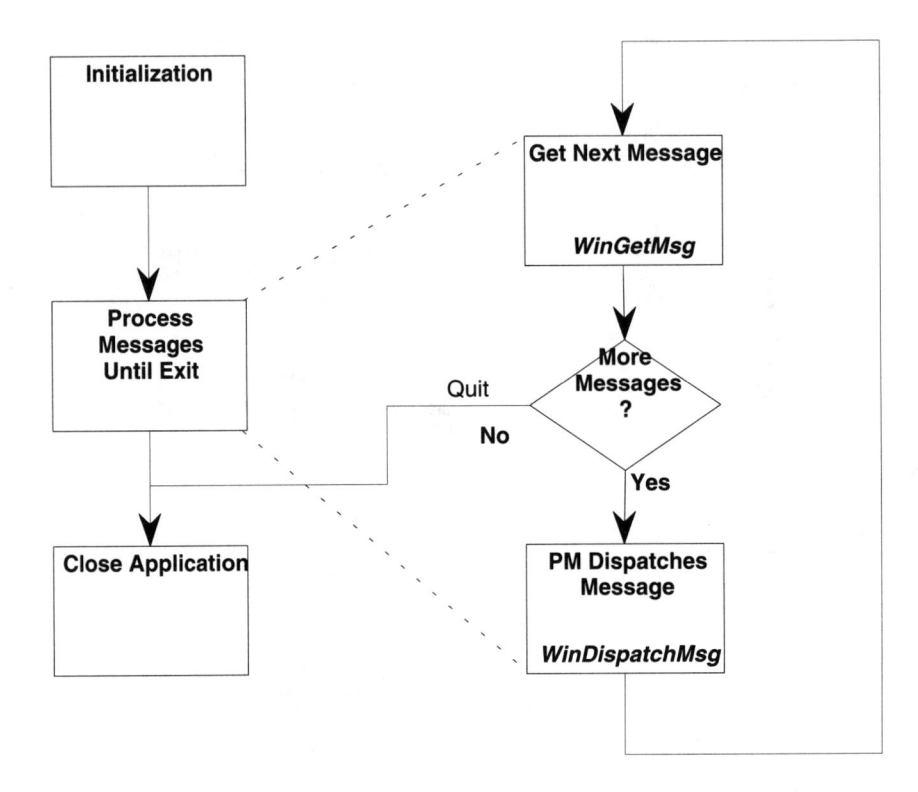

Figure 9.7
OS/2 Presentation Manager application flow.

some GUI applications might force the user to follow a mainframe-centric transaction-oriented view, most powerful systems in Windows or OS/2 operate in a user-specified order of control. If the user chooses to begin entering information, perhaps looking through records or tables for a specific entry before updating the item, they can do so. Likewise, the user might decide to begin entering transactions, but then minimize the application and begin working on a completely different application, before returning to the first program to continue. In some cases, the first program can be closed prior to completing all the transactions or even the current transaction.

This user-driven behavior of GUI applications is dramatically different from traditional COBOL programs where the program behaves in a predefined fashion and always processes each transaction to completion before moving onto the next. GUI applications also must contend with asynchronous events or actions that occur outside their own domain but affect them. For example, a GUI application might be processing transactions and printing them when the printer is taken offline for some reason (maybe they need to change the paper feeder). When this occurs, the program will be notified by a message sent from the GUI environment that the printer is no longer available. Any recovery processing must be defined in the application if it is to continue to process transactions correctly.

GUI applications also can work in a pseudo-concurrent environment and can have multiple tasks or threads of control running at any given time. For example, a banking application might begin accepting a transaction while also beginning a thread of control to submit a batch of previously entered transactions to a remote system for processing. Once the batch of transactions has been processed, the GUI application will be notified (again using a message or event) and must terminate the thread of control before returning to the transaction being entered.

COBOL programmers that are building GUI applications must learn and understand the behavior of their GUI environment, the available resources and components (icons, windows, dialog boxes, buttons, etc.), and the environmental factors (available memory, disk access, remote processing, etc.) and account for the asynchronous processing that can occur in these environments.

9.4 Developing GUI Applications

How does developing a user interface fit into the larger process of developing software? Any software development life cycle (SDLC), regardless of whether it targets a GUI, client/server, or mainframe-based transaction-oriented system, must address the issue of the interface with the user. All software is developed for someone, and neglecting the needs of that someone in the development process is a prescription for failure.

Many popular development methods now incorporate joint development tasks (i.e., facilitated sessions or JAD sessions) in the software engineering process, and many in the industry have discussed the benefits of these sessions in other articles (see *American Programmer*, vol. 4, no. 1). Many other techniques incorporate the use of a prototype in the development process, which can improve the overall user interface. Both of these methods can improve the resulting system and address the perspective of the user early in the development process.

When a graphical environment is the deployment environment for an application, special consideration must be given to the process of designing and building the user interface. Figure 9.8 shows an example design process for

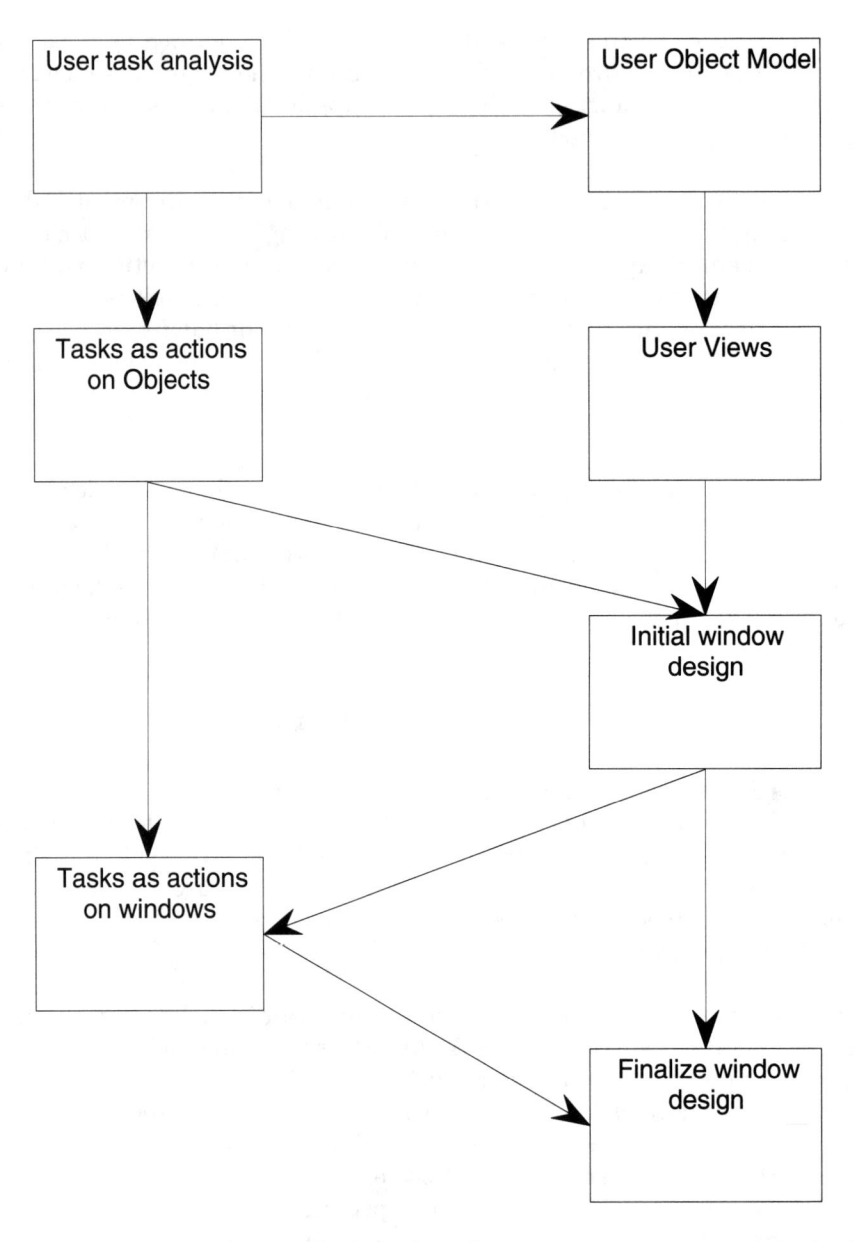

Figure 9.8
GUI design process.

a GUI environment from [CAM92]. Graphic operating environments, including Windows and OS/2, represent a challenge to developers in terms of the creation and management of graphical components, user views, and graphical design. As with any other development tool, GUIs can be used to develop usable, efficient applications or can be used to develop cumbersome, complex applications that have little value.

GUI development should rely on the creation and evolution of a prototype to ensure that the final user interface meets the ascetic and functional needs of the users. Regardless of whether a GUI is used or not, user interface development is an iterative process. User interface development also should be supported with tools and methods that capture the user perspective. Creating a prototype of a user interface can help facilitate this development process and allows the user to modify the interface prior to delivery of the final system. The appearance, function, flow, and navigation of a software application must be considered when building any type of computer system.

Nongraphical interfaces also must be considered during the development process because not all systems are created to run in a GUI environment. Character DOS, Unix, and mainframe-based systems must work with textual information, support scrolling, online help, and keyboard navigation. Development tools and methods for these systems must address these issues. Pen-based systems represent even more of a challenge, by providing a pointing device similar to a mouse, a graphical environment, and support for character recognition.

Using a keyboard for navigation in applications has been studied extensively, but most of the major user interface development tools ignore the keyboard for navigational purposes. At the IBM T. J. Watson Research Center, researchers have developed a tool that supports keyboard navigation using application graphs. The ITS development environment described in [UKE93] supports abstract operations such as filling in forms, selecting among choices, manipulating lists, and reading text, all with the keyboard as the input mechanism.

Others have experimented with the use of color to highlight and improve understanding in development environments [OBE92]. Using color in the display of textual information represents another powerful vehicle for communicating with the user. As more applications begin to examine work flow and user interaction in more detail, issues such as task relationships, completion criteria, context-sensitive help, and error handling must be addressed. Future computer applications must be flexible in their user-interface, perhaps supporting pens for written input or even a microphone for spoken input.

The popularity of SQL and RDBMS in the market has led to more applications that must interact with SQL-based DBMS, supporting the data access portion of an application. Popular 4GLs, including Oracle, Ingres, Informix, and Ramis, have evolved to support GUIs and distributed DBMS access, but many are not portable across platforms or databases. These products provide benefits to organizations that already are committed to using these databases and want to develop applications for GUI environments.

In the future, the role of designing the user interface will gain more significance in the development life cycle, as more focus is placed on the user perspective. Powerful tools and methods for designing and delivering sophisticated user interfaces will enable this movement towards user-centric systems.

The process of designing and building a GUI-based application involves several tasks or activities that will be described in more detail in section 9.8. Generically, these tasks include:

1. Build the user interface portion of the application (screen layout/design)
2. Create the resources for the UI defined in step 1 (dialog boxes, menus, etc.)
3. Specify the user of the resources in the programming language
4. Compile the programs and resources (i.e., the GUI application)
5. Build the application by linking together the resources and program(s).

9.4.1 Issues for GUI-based Development

What new or outstanding issues must be addressed as developers create user-centric systems? Many in the industry have described the problems and possible remedies for developing sophisticated user interfaces for computer systems. Also, many excellent resources are available that detail experiences building powerful user interfaces.

Roger Pressman [PRE92] has identified several models of human-computer interaction that should be considered when developing a computer application. These include a design model, which represents the procedural aspects of a system; a user model, which defines the profile of the userl a system perception model, which is internal to each user; and a system image model, which maps the user's understanding of a system to the use of the system itself. Pressman suggests developing user interfaces with consistency of presentation, providing meaningful feedback, verifying nontrivial destructive actions, providing easy reversal (i.e., undo) of actions taken, limiting the amount of information to be memorized, being more efficient and forgiving of mistakes, providing online help, and using simple action verbs or short verb phrases when interacting with users.

Knowing the type of user that will be interacting with a system is critical to creating a workable interface. Pressman identifies the following categories or types of software users:

- Novices — Those with little or no semantic knowledge of the application or computer usage in general.
- Knowledgeable, intermittent users — Those with some knowledge of the application, but low recall of syntactic information required to use the system.
- Knowledgeable, frequent users — Those with good knowledge, often thought of as "power users" of a system.

Beyond studying or defining the user, other considerations for interface development should be addressed, including basic design issues, human-computer interaction issues, and following existing standards for user interaction.

Donald Norman [NOR88] suggests that a good design, whether it be a user interface or an appliance, should include the following qualities:

- Visibility — So that users can tell what is going on and what their options are at each point in the process.
- A good conceptual model — So users will have a comfortable cognitive model when using a computer application.
- Good mappings — So users can determine how the system will respond to their actions, how the controls and states will act, and what is visible in the system following each action.
- Feedback — So users can see the result of their actions immediately and are provided with appropriate feedback.

In the area of human-computer interaction, developers must understand the relationships between the computer software, the human using the software, and the tasks to be carried out by the human. Defining the user provides a basis for understanding their cognitive, perceptual, and social viewpoint. Defining the tasks helps to identify common or basic structures that are repetitive or memorized. Work flow, now a popular term used in designing user interfaces and systems, refers to the definition of the flow of paper or tasks to perform a specific business function. By integrating the work flow into a computer system, you allow the user to follow the process they already are comfortable with in performing their assigned tasks.

User interface design guidelines are available for a variety of platforms. The most notable of these is common user access (CUA) defined by IBM under their system application architecture. IBM has established two sets of CUA guidelines the Basic Interface Design Guide (BIDG) for nonprogrammable and programmable workstations and the Advanced Interface Design Guide (AIDG) for programmable workstations. The BIDG supports presentation using the object-action style (i.e., selecting the object before the action to avoid modal processing), keyboard navigation, and full-screen panels (with command areas, message areas, and function key areas) accessed sequentially via menu-driven or command-driven interfaces. The ADIG supports both graphical and object-oriented interfaces (i.e., the OS/2 Workplace shell) using action bars, pulldown and popup menus, function key assignments, messages and commands, keyboard and mouse interaction, field and group identifiers, contextual, extended, and an index for online help. Under the OS/2 Workplace shell, for example, applications appear as icons and can be associated with actions and other applications using common protocols.

The user model in CUA represents a customizable workspace organized around user-relevant objects. This model supports user tasks against the objects (i.e., copy, open, move, etc.), and the user's focus is on the objects and their actions, rather than on the actions available for all objects. This object-sensitive viewpoint helps all types of users understand the available actions for each object in the workplace [ART90].

9.4.2 Developing Good GUI Applications

A well-designed GUI application doesn't just happen, it must be designed and built with an eye towards the issues described in the previous sections. A successful GUI application should incorporate appropriate controls, graphical elements, and follow sound GUI development guidelines.

GUI applications can include a variety of graphical elements, including windows, subwindows, menus, submenus, dialog boxes, icons, and bitmaps. In some cases, a GUI application consists of a single main window or dialog box, as is the case for the Windows or OS/2 PM calculator or character maps. In other cases, a single main window is used along with a variable amount of text or data displayed in a window under a set of menu options. The Windows Write and Notepad applications are examples of this type of GUI program.

GUI applications consist of many different types of windows, including a main window with menus and submenus, child windows, and dialog boxes. Prior to looking in more detail at the process of developing GUI applications, I will review some basic terminology and guidelines for these applications.

The main window for a GUI application is called the *application window*, which usually contains a resizable frame and a title bar. This window should have a control-menu box and include minimize and maximize buttons. If the main window is a dialog box, it will not contain a maximize button but still should have a control-menu box and a minimize button. The application window is called the *parent window* and may contain *child windows*.

Child windows that allow for text or data to be displayed and edited are called *document windows*. Document windows can be tiled or cascaded under the application window, should be able to be reduced to icons, and should always stay inside the main window. Additional child windows can be created as needed under the document window. All child windows can be resized, maximized, or minimized, and when a child window is maximized, its title should be appended to the main window title. When a child window is closed, its parent window is redrawn and receives control.

Under main or child windows, a series of menus and submenus can be used to allow access to different program functions. Windows' menus are built in a hierarchy, with menu options sometimes exploding to submenus with additional options. Menus contain options or submenus that themselves contain options or submenus, etc. Figure 9.9 shows a simple GUI menu hierarchy. When the user selects a menu by clicking on it, the options available should be displayed. This continues down the menu hierarchy until all options have been displayed and an option or menu item has been chosen.

Dialog boxes allow an application program to request information from the user or offer a series of options for selection. Dialog boxes should have a minimize button, and a menu bar and can be of three types: modeless, modal, and system modal. *Modeless boxes* stay visible until they are closed, regardless of the action taken. When a modeless dialog box appears, the user can use other functions in the application without having to respond to the request. *Modal boxes* require that the user respond, then click on the OK or CANCEL

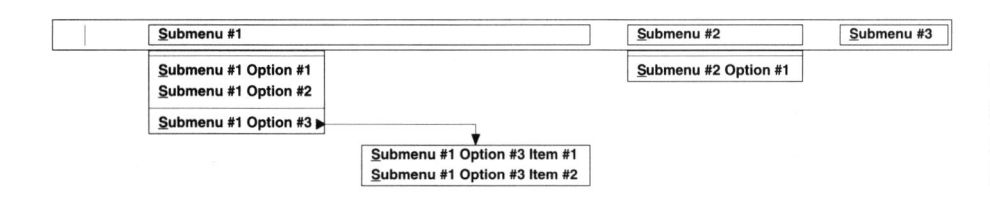

Figure 9.9
Simple GUI menu hierarchy.

button before proceeding. *System modal boxes* should be used only when a response is required because some problem needs immediate fixing. These boxes do not allow any other action to be taken in the GUI environment until the dialog box is closed.

Within dialog boxes, a number of *controls* can be used, including command buttons (OK, CANCEL, etc.), radio buttons, check boxes, list boxes, text boxes, static text fields, and group boxes. Figure 9.10 represents an example dialog box with selected controls. *Command buttons* describe a command or action that will be carried out when they are pressed. Most dialog boxes contain an OK and a CANCEL button, at a minimum.

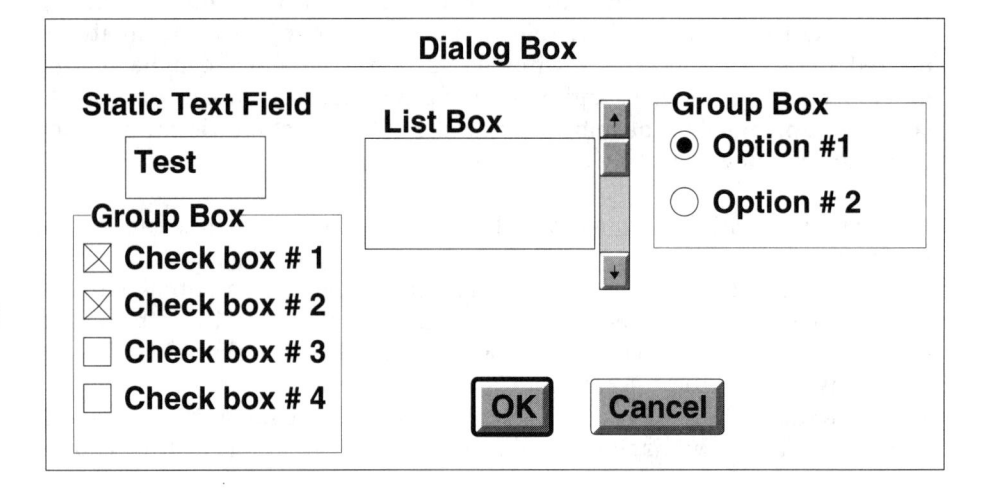

Figure 9.10 Windows dialog box with common dontrols.

Radio buttons represent selection of a single choice from a limited set of options. When a radio button is pressed or turned on, any other radio buttons in the group are turned off. Radio buttons represent an either-or option and should be used when the number of choices is limited to four of five options. *Check boxes*, on the other hand, represent a series of options that can be selected in combination. Check boxes contain an X when they are selected to indicate that they have been checked. Clicking on a radio button or check box changes its state.

List boxes display a column of choices, often with a scroll bar to the right or above, to allow more options to be displayed and selected. By default, list boxes allow a single option to be selected from a list, but this can be reset to allow multiple options to be selected at one time. *Combo boxes* are list boxes that allow the user to type their own option if the correct one isn't listed.

Text boxes allow the user to type or enter information using the keyboard. Text boxes can be single- or multiple-line. Static *text fields* are labels for buttons, check boxes, etc. and simply describe the controls in a dialog box. *Group boxes* allow related controls (radio buttons, check boxes, etc.) to be enclosed within a lined box to represent associated information.

Views represent a logical picture of physical data displayed in a window. When a window contains data or text that is displayed for editing or viewing, as is the case in any file display or edit program, the data is viewed in chunks. A viewer program or class allows data to be displayed or edited in chunks, based on the size of font used and the window size, by sliding the scroll bar up or down.

9.4.3 GUI Development Tools

When considering GUI development, there are a number of user interface development tools available that support presentation environments and data access as described earlier. Popular presentation environments include character DOS, Microsoft Windows, IBM's OS/2, Apple's Macintosh, character Unix, and the more popular Unix graphical environments including Motif and OpenLook. Other factors to consider include support for middleware components, in the form of remote procedure calls or APIs, non-SQL data access support, and support for non-GUI environments.

Several different types of GUI development tools are available and these products can be generically categorized into the groups that are described in the following paragraphs:

GUI design prototyping tools — including CASE:W, Gpf, TeleUSE, Interface Architect, Builder Xcessory, iXBUILD, and Easel — allow a user interface to be designed, built, and tested prior to incorporation into a functioning application system. Some of these products support prototyping of the interface, while others allow editing and some logical processing of data collected on the workstation. The benefits of these products include the ability to build powerful interfaces, supporting various UIs, and managing some of the complexity in the UI environment. The drawbacks of these products include a lack of integration with middleware and data access portions, portability across platforms, and limited value for non-GUI applications. Some of these products are evolving to include better SQL support to improve their data access component.

GUI-based 4GLs — including Powerbuilder, Progress, Uniface, and SQLWindows — allow a GUI application to be built with limited functionality, generally for SQL-based systems, and suffer from the same limitations as the GUI prototyping tools. The benefits of these products include a powerful GUI development environment, SQL access, and emerging support for middleware standards. The drawbacks of these products include a lack of complete integration with middleware, portability across platforms, non-SQL support, and proprietary languages for representing business logic.

GUI-aware CASE tools — including IEF, ADW, Excelerator, and APS — allow applications to be designed and generated from CASE tools. These products simply are enhanced versions of traditional CASE tools and often do not support message-based, asynchronous processing in GUIs..

Visual OOP environments — including Parts, VisualWorks, Visual Basic, Visual C++, ObjectVision, and Enfin — object-oriented programming environments that allow systems to be built in Smalltalk, Basic, or C++ from reusable components provided by the vendors. With these products, GUI applications can be assembled from these components, often for SQL-based systems. The benefits of these products include support for the object-oriented development paradigm and reuse of pre-existing development components. The drawbacks of these products include a lack of integration with middleware, limited support for DBMS (especially for non-SQL data access), portability across platforms, operating performance, and support for non-GUI environments. The sidebar on page 301 describes popular visual OOP products.

GUI class libraries — including ObjectWindows, CommonView, zApp, C++/Views, Synchorworks, Galaxy, Component Workshop, Foundation Classes, and XVT — allow OOPL-based applications to be created from reusable GUI classes in external libraries. The benefits of these tools include reuse of code and portability across a variety of environments, including non-GUI platforms. The drawbacks of these products include their complexity and a lack of integration with middleware. As the CORBA standard evolves and more vendors support it, the middleware integration issue for the object-oriented products might be resolved.

Several GUI prototyping tools now are available that allow developers to build GUI interfaces by placing objects on the screen and defining basic characteristics. In this fashion, a GUI application can be developed in an interactive fashion, often with a working prototype of the GUI portion of the application acting as a standalone component.

Once created, the GUI prototype includes the necessary variables, methods and message handling logic to support the GUI. Some of these products provide OOPL constructs, while others generate procedural language constructs. Many of these products support standard DBMS access and update (SQL-based) and support a variety of GUIs for PC, Macintosh and Unix systems.

Example GUI prototyping tools include CASE:Windows/PM, ObjectVision, Visual Basic, 3-in-1, and AppMaker. Some vendors have decided to offer GUI development tools that incorporate class libraries and OOEs. Examples include Parts from Digitalk, VisualWorks from Parcplace Systems, ViewCenter from CenterLine, Envy/Developer for OS/2 and Windows from Object Technology Intl., and Galaxy from Visix Software.

9.4.4 Class Libraries in GUI Development

As you already have seen, class libraries can be used to hide the details of implementation for a specific GUI environment and can be instantiated into GUI applications. Through information hiding, encapsulation, and inheritance, GUI class libraries can be purchased and used to build graphical applications. The data structures, events, and collaborations required in the GUI are hidden in the classes in the library.

Class libraries can be very beneficial to GUI development but also require extensive research and use before developers are able to quickly identify and use the individual classes. Learning a complex GUI class library can take anywhere from three to six months. Once developers understand the key abstractions in a GUI class library, learning the specific details of a competitive library or GUI environment will take less time.

All the popular GUI environments now have commercially available class libraries, usually delivered in C++ code, that can be used in GUI application development. In this section, I introduce three popular GUI class libraries and review an upcoming set of classes for the Taligent operating environment, as well as the Micro Focus GUI classes and development tools.

The Microsoft Foundation Library (MFL) represents Microsoft's view of the components in a Windows GUI environment. The MFL represents the base classes for Windows GUI development and was designed to improve speed and reduce size, provide a transition from Windows to MFL, and be easily extensible. MFL allows Windows API calls to be called as classes and was developed by a team of 25 Microsoft engineers [FIS92].

The MFL was designed in a bottom-up fashion and provides a thin but practical class library. In the MFL, Windows objects are placed within a container that provides member functions for all Windows objects. This container doesn't cache object states, which allows them to be directly mapped to the Windows API. Critical MFL design issues were object creation/destruction, message processing, and code size and complexity.

Borland has developed and markets their own class library for Windows and OS/2 PM called the ObjectWindows Library (OWL). A class hierarchy of the OWL is shown in Figure 9.11. Design goals of ObjectWindows included support for the Windows event-driven environment with message handling, reduced length of Windows start-up code, conformance with standard UI guidelines, and support for full access to Windows APIs [URL92].

Next and Sun offer another version of a set of GUI components that originally were tied directly to the Next computer but are now offered on a variety of Unix platforms, including Intel 80486-based systems, Motorola 68000, PowerPC, Sun Sparc, and HP RISC environments. Sun and Next have defined their own object-oriented O/S, called OpenStep, which will include the NextStep desktop, object frameworks, and distributed object management on top of the Unix operating system. A partial representation of the NextStep GUI class hierarchy is shown in Figure 9.12 [AND93].

IBM and Apple have their own plans for future operating environments and are working on developing the frameworks under the Taligent name. HP recently has joined IBM and Apple and plans to support the Taligent operating environment in their future products. Taligent consists of frameworks or class libraries for applications that allow the operating system services to be available to applications, along with development tools for C, C++, and Smalltalk. Taligent will operate on the Mach kernel developed at Carnegie Mellon Univsity.

9.5 CICS is an Event-Driven Environment

CICS, the popular IBM mainframe terminal control system, represents an environment very similar in functionality to the GUIs described earlier. An example of a CICS COBOL program is shown in Figure 9.13. For instance, mainframe COBOL programs must interface with CICS in a similar fashion to the way COBOL programs interface with Windows or OS/2 on the PC. In a CICS COBOL program, an interface (i.e., set of data structures) is defined in the DATA DIVISION for sending and receiving messages from CICS, and the PROCEDURE DIVISION uses the LINKAGE SECTION to pass informa-

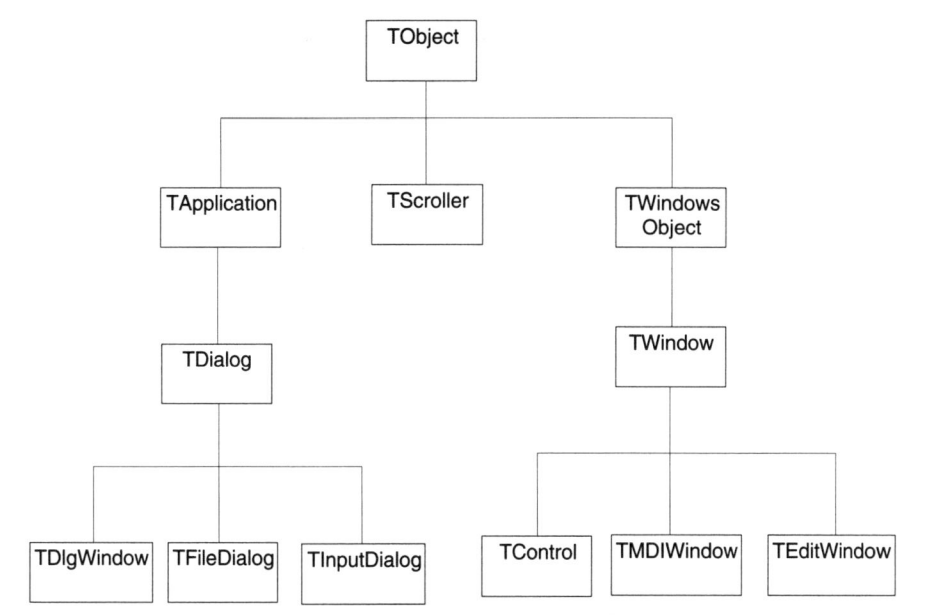

Figure 9.11
Partial ObjectWindows library class hierarchy.

tion back and forth. GUI-based applications also must share data structures with the operating environment, including handles for windows and dialog boxes, icons, bitmaps, etc.

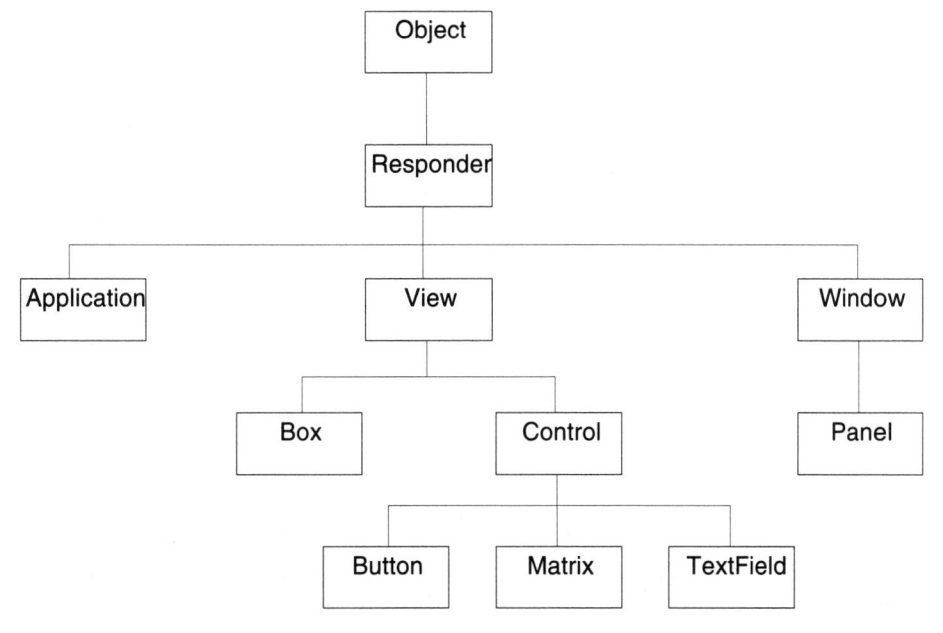

Figure 9.12
Partial NextStep class hierarchy.

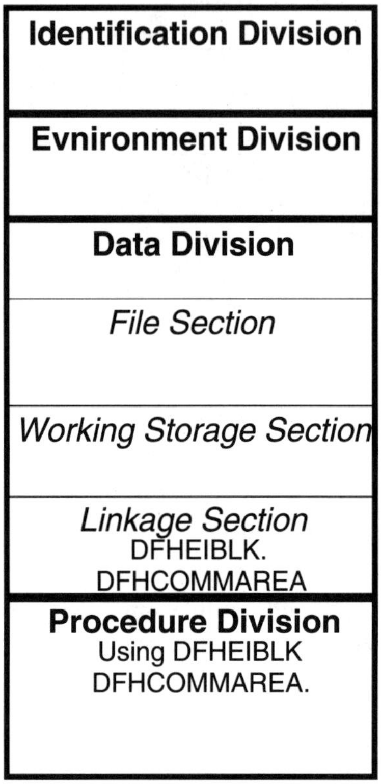

Figure 9.13
CICS COBOL program structure.

```
┌─────────────────────────────┐
│   Identification Division   │
├─────────────────────────────┤
│    Evnironment Division     │
├─────────────────────────────┤
│       Data Division         │
│  ┌───────────────────────┐  │
│  │     File Section      │  │
│  ├───────────────────────┤  │
│  │ Working Storage Section│ │
│  ├───────────────────────┤  │
│  │    Linkage Section    │  │
│  │      DFHEIBLK.        │  │
│  │      DFHCOMMAREA      │  │
├─────────────────────────────┤
│     Procedure Division      │
│       Using DFHEIBLK        │
│       DFHCOMMAREA.          │
└─────────────────────────────┘
```

Under the mainframe scenario, CICS manages all screen elements and controls, allowing the user to page forward or backward, skip or tab through the fields, and press any special function keys (F1 — F12) to request specific operations. In this sense, CICS acts as the presentation manager for 3270-type terminals and insulates the COBOL program from the mechanics of the interface. In a similar fashion, OS/2 PM and Windows manage the graphic components, along with the user interaction, and insulate GUI applications from these details.

Also, CICS applications must deal with special processing requirements, perhaps via function keys that perform certain functions, abend processing, or when they process online transactions in a nonsequential way. Windows and OS/2 PM applications also must respond to external events or exceptions in the same fashion. Figure 9.14 shows the relationship between CICS and a CICS application. Notice how similar the relationships are between the presentation environments in GUIs and in CICS.

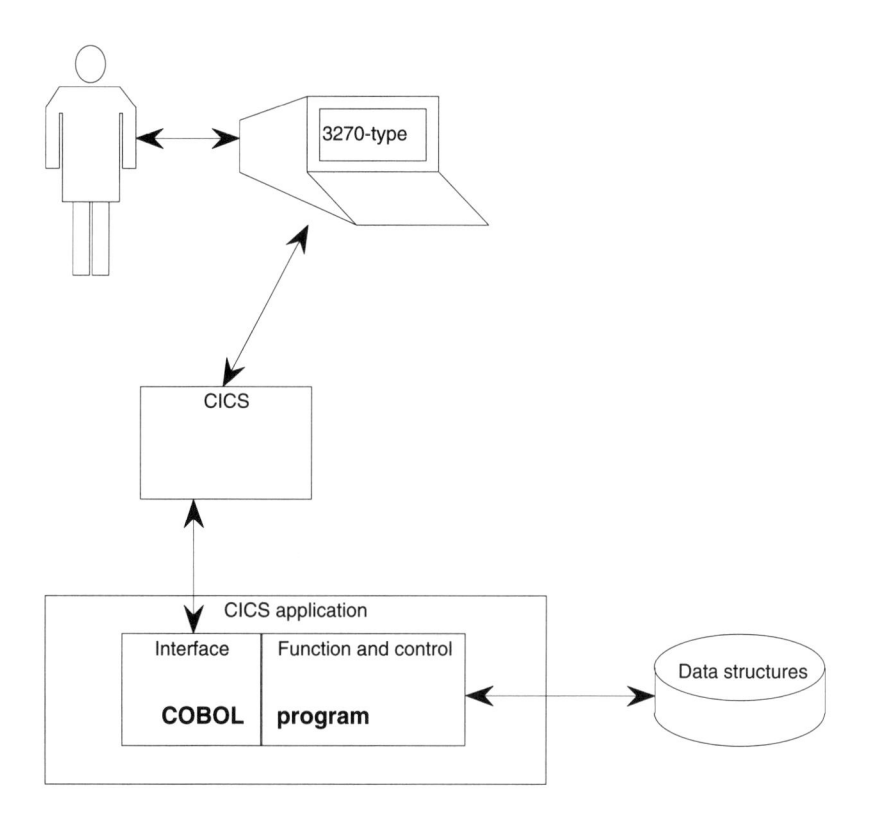

Figure 9.14
CICS Application Structure.

9.6 Client/Server Issues for GUI Development

Most users of a computer application can describe their system only by how it behaves from their vantage point. The user interface (UI), or that portion of an application that acts as a buffer between the user and the application itself, represents the most important aspect of a system from the user standpoint. When a system has a poor user interface, it often is virtually unused, whereas a system that has an excellent user interface empowers and improves the productivity of the user. However, the user interface often is overlooked when management information systems (MIS) are developed in corporate America, and most of the interfaces of the monolithic systems in use today are poor.

Early systems had a definite system-centric perspective and provided little benefit in the area of user interface. As databases and systems evolved throughout the past 30 years, this system-centric viewpoint has been carried forward by MIS organizations. All software systems consist of three distinct portions or functions: *human or user interface, middleware,* and *DBMS or data access* (see Figure 9.14). Some applications might contain simplified user interfaces or mix middleware with data access, while others might have combined user interfaces and middleware. Middleware is a term now generally used in conjunction with client/server or distributed systems that represents the portion of an application supporting the underlying logic or business rules and any required communications with remote systems. Applications are moving towards more sophisticated middleware components as distributed or client/server systems gain prominence.

As middleware evolves, the focus in development expands to include the presentation of information. By and large, the dominant user interface throughout the early years of computing was the character-based, terminal-oriented interface. The original user interface was a single line on a telex machine, and the interface itself was dumb (i.e., providing no help to the user in its operation). From the telex evolved the cathode ray tube (CRT) with its 24 lines of text scrolling from the bottom up. For the majority of its lifetime, the CRT provided a similar user interface (i.e., the character-based textual format described previously).

In 1989 a group of software vendors and user organizations gathered to form the Object Management Group (OMG), which was chartered with defining standards for interoperability between applications across heterogeneous networks. As of 1992, the OMG had over 200 organizations as members and a staff of less than 10 people.

Key to the work of the OMG is promoting an architecture that combines distributed processing with object-oriented technology. The Object Management Architecture (OMA) should help to solve many industry problems related to cooperative processing (client/server) and portability across multiple hardware and software problems. The full OMA specification was published in 1992.

At its most basic level, OMA defines a standard means for creating, preserving, locating, and communicating between objects in a network. OMA simply defines the layers of interfaces and services that allow objects to communicate.

OMA does not suggest standards for programming languages or tools to support development of object-oriented software and the standards defined will be independent of networks, protocols, and operating systems. The OMA consists of four components: the Common Object Request Broker Architecture

(CORBA), Object Services, Common Facilities, and Application Objects. Application objects can be applications or pieces of applications. Object services provide basic utilitylike objects that can be called on to establish communications and perform housekeeping functions. Common facilities are functions that are common across applications, such as printing or error reporting. CORBA often is shortened to Object Request Broker (ORB).

The ORB is the underlying interface that links the other pieces together. ORB specifies the information to be presented when one object is communicating with another object using the Interface Definition Language (IDL), an OMB-developed language with roots in C++, or using dynamic invocation. The ORB allows objects to communicate dynamically, adding and removing objects while running, and also specifies features for managing interobject messages.

Within the ORB is the ORB Core, the dynamic invocation interface, the IDL stubs interface, the IDL skeleton, the object adapter, and the interface repository. The ORB maintains the interface repository, which specifies the location of each object and how it can be invoked. More on distributed object management systems and support for the ORB in chapter 14.

The OMG now publishes a bimonthly newsletter, *First Class*, which is available to members and nonmembers. The OMG also has established special interest groups (SIGs) for Analysis and Design, Class Libraries, OODBMS, and other areas.

9.7 OOCOBOL GUI Considerations

Another option for developing OOCOBOL applications for different user interfaces is Micro Focus Dialog System. This product represents a user interface development environment that insulates COBOL programs from the details of managing the interface. Dialog System supports most PC or workstation environments for graphic and character interfaces, including DOS, Windows, OS/2, and Unix (Motif and character mode).

Dialog System also allows existing 3270-based applications to be run under DOS and OS/2 text mode via emulation of graphical objects. Dialog System manages all graphic elements, including icons, buttons, windows, and dialog boxes and provides interfaces to the different events and functions in the graphical environment. Dialog System is designed to behave in a similar fashion to CICS, with a data and control block passed to and from the COBOL program that deals with the data structures internally. Dialog System also supports CUA and SAA for IBM platforms.

Micro Focus also offers Transaction Manager, which supports an online transaction processing (OLTP) facility for COBOL programs. Another Micro Focus product that facilitates client/server computing is the Application to Application Interface (AAI) middleware that supports synchronous remote procedure calls, asynchronous message passing, and message queue processing. AAI supports a variety of platforms, including DOS, Windows, OS/2, AIX, OS/400, MVS/CICS, MVS/Batch, TSO, CICS/VSE, and SCO Unix.

The Micro Focus OOCOBOL classes are being looked at by the ANSI X3J4 committee for acceptance as foundation classes for the COBOL 97 standard. While the Micro Focus OOCOBOL classes are simple, they represent a good starting point for base classes for the OOCOBOL language. Micro Focus plans to allow Dialog System to be used as a screen painter in the future that will generate to the GUI classes. Micro Focus also is examining Transaction Manger and the AAI products for extension to OOCOBOL class libraries in the future.

Delivered with the Micro Focus Object COBOL Option in the class library are the Panels version 2 classes, which support GUI development. Figure 9.15 represents the GuiBase classification hierarchy. Like Dialog System, Panels supports GUI applications for Windows 3.x, OS/2 PM, and Motif, along with DOS and OS/2 character mode. Panels provides an API interface to non-OOCOBOL programs, along with data items, records, error codes, events, and objects or graphic elements. The main Panels data structure is P2E-Parameter-Block, and Panels errors are returned as 78-level statuses (e.g., P2-NO-ERROR, P2ERR-BAD-FUNCTION, etc.). Panels events come from gadgets (buttons, entry fields, list boxes, menu options, etc.), the keyboard, or the mouse and must be managed by objects or callbacks in a console controller.

To use panels, you must copy PAN2LINK.CPY into the WORKING-STORAGE SECTION of your COBOL program. To use the panels error codes, copy PAN2ERR.CPY into the WORKING-STORAGE SECTION. Panels maintains resources in a side file that defines the environment the COBOL program operates in, gadgets, and references to the physical resources.

Panels supports objects (also called gadgets) and their management in a graphical environment. These objects can include icons, bitmaps, buttons, dialog boxes, entry fields, the keyboard, the mouse, etc. Panels menu options are defined as callbacks in a controller class that manages the functions for each option. These callbacks receive control when the menu option or GUI object is selected by the user. The class EventManager initializes Panels, receives all events, and dispatches them to their appropriate object/method.

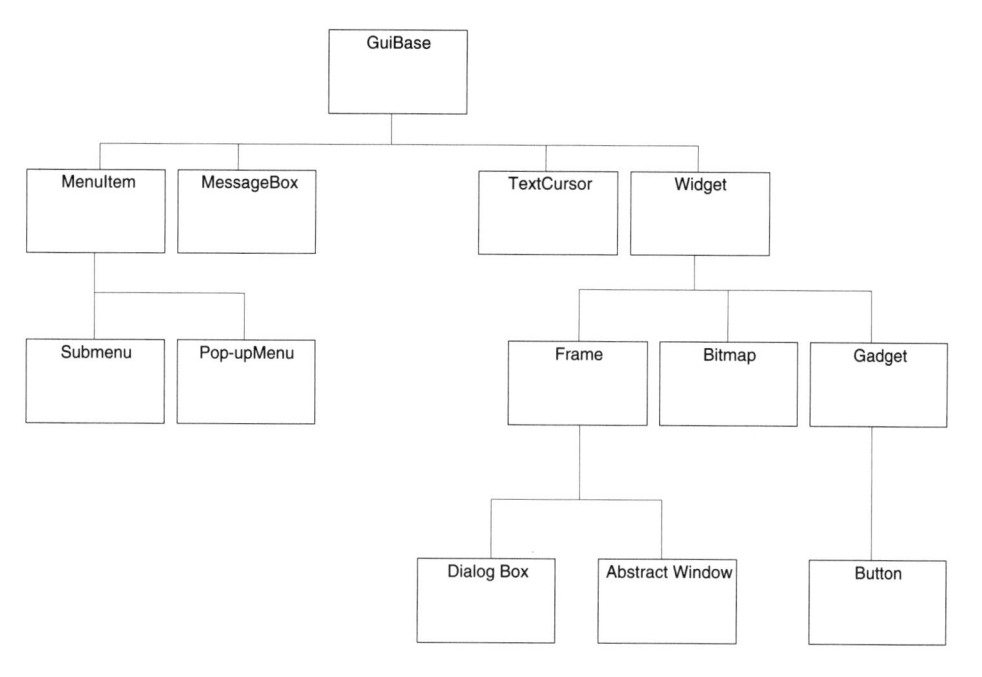

Figure 9.15
Micro Focus GuiBase - GUI class hierarchy.

The dispatch method translates the event and decides which object should receive the message. Classes for GUI components (i.e., windows, dialog boxes, buttons, etc.) manage their own messages and events.

The class CallBack stores messages that can be invoked later, and the message "invoke" is sent to a CallBack to invoke the messages stored (maximum message size is 30 characters). CallBack manages messages and events for MenuItems and objects. The class MenuItem receives selected events that are associated with a callback. All GUI objects, including buttons, windows, icons, bitmaps, etc. are called *widgets*. Some GUI objects, including buttons, list boxes, scroll bars, etc., are *gadgets*, which are a subclass of widgets.

Widgets represent a class of the panels objects that have dimensions in a GUI environment. All widgets have attributes x, y, width, and height, and the widgets class provides an interface for accessing and updating these attributes. Subclasses can override update methods that are not appropriate for selected objects.

Gadgets are an abstract class of widgets that can be placed in dialog boxes or windows. Positioning coordinates for gadgets specify the position of the top left corner of the gadget in units of the environment. Console controllers manage components, menu options, and views of an application. Views, as described earlier, simply are windows that display application data with scroll bars.

As with other OOCOBOL objects, Panels objects are referenced in a data field that must be supplied whenever the object is used. When object events are returned by Panels, they include the identifier, the handle, and the handle of the ancestor window to which the object is a descendent. As events are received by each object method, they perform their function and exit. Recall the discussion of the hierarchy of GUI components in section 9.3.1. Higher-level objects — such as windows, menus, or dialog boxes — have descendent or child objects, such as buttons, scroll bars, etc. Messages received by the lower-level objects are passed onto the any higher-level objects that are affected.

The logic for a GUI application that uses the Micro Focus Panels classes consists of a main program, which controls the application; a GUI controller, which manages the events and actions selected by the user; and application objects, which actually perform the functions of the system. The structure of these programs is shown in Figure 9.16.

A typical GUI problem creates an instance of GUIController, initializes the application objects, and sends the message "Go" to the controller to start the application. When the application terminates, any persistent objects are stored using the "OOPSSuspend" command. A class ConsoleControlle often is used to support a character-based environment, which has its own callback methods, while a class GUIController supports GUI environments. An instance of the Controller is created dynamically in the main program depending on the operating environment.

When the Controller is created, it is initialized with callbacks for menu options, and the "Go" method starts processing events and continues until the application is closed or the user exits. When the user selects the exit option or closes the application, the "close" method is given control and invokes the event manager "terminate" method. Callbacks and methods in the Contoller map to methods in the application objects. For example, a callback to a view method calls the View method in the application object, which retrieves the data and displays it. A simple example of a panels GUI program is shown in Figure 9.17.

Chapter 9 Building GUI Applications in Object-Oriented COBOL

Figure 9.16 Panels GUI program structure.

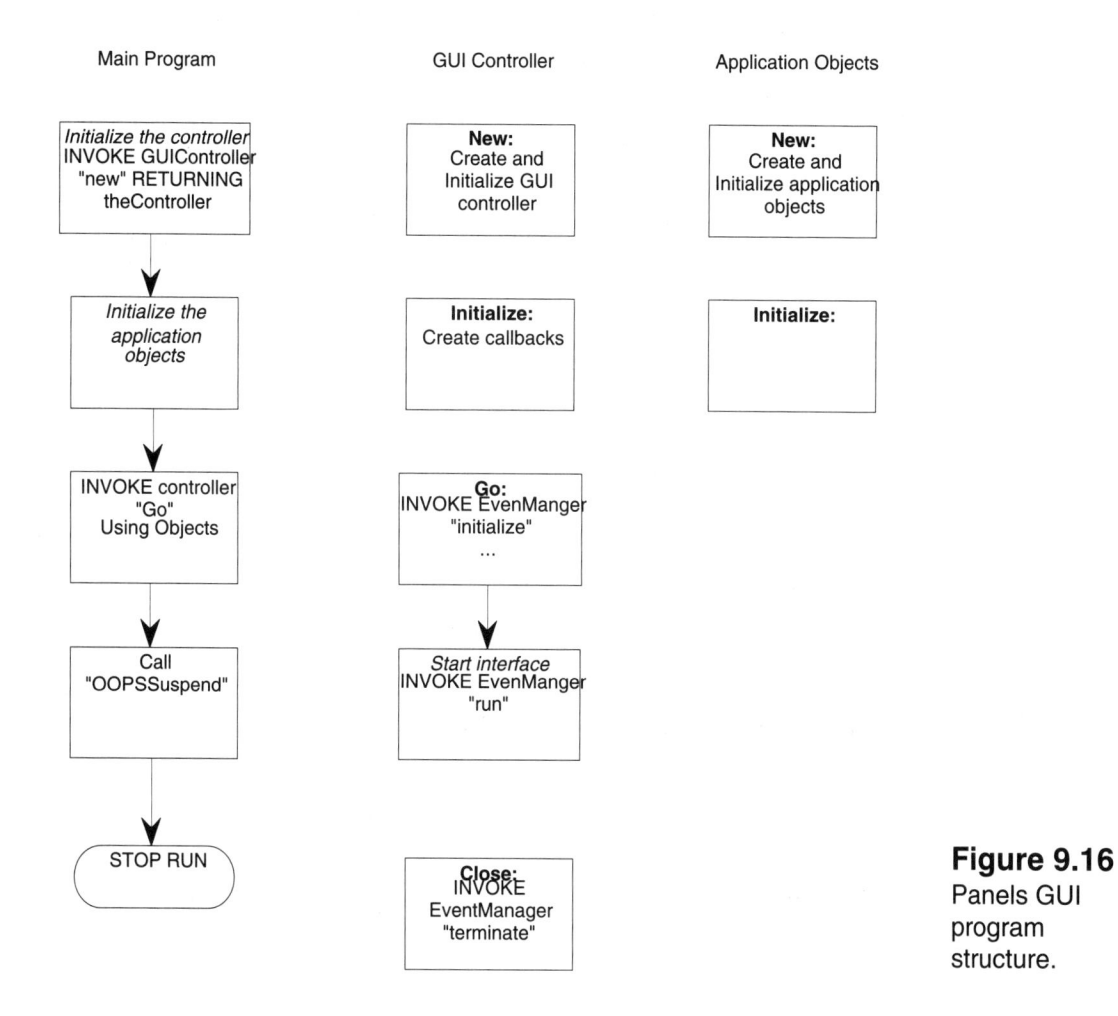

9.7.1 Library Problem

The Library system is intended to be delivered in a diverse PC-based environment, with support for Windows, DOS, and OS/2 screens and reports. The Library database resides on a server that will be accessible via requests over a LAN.

The Library signon screen is shown in chapter 7 and is a dialog box with two text entry fields — one for the UserID and one for their password — and two command buttons — OK, and CANCEL. This signon dialog box accepts the

```
MAIN-PROCESS SECTION.

    INVOKE EventManager "initialize"   { Initialize and Register
                                         the application }
    INVOKE Window "create"             { Create Windows }
    INVOKE aWindow "setEvent"
    INVOKE aWindow "showMenus"   { Build and Display menu }
    INVOKE aWindow "show" { Show Initial Window/Dialog box }
    INVOKE EventManager "run"          { Get first event }
    PERFORM PROCESS-EVENT THRU
        GET-NEXT-EVENT
        UNTIL Close.
    INVOKE EventManger "terminate"   { Terminate Panels }
    STOP RUN.

PROCESS-EVENT SECTION.

    Evaluate event-type
        CASE Event-Type 1
            Process event 1
        ...
    End Evaluate
```

Figure 9.17 Example Panels program.

UserID and password and, if the user is library staff, presents the menu for staff. If the user is not staff, they are presented with the library user menu. Figure 9.18 represents the Windows menu structure for library staff.

The Library screens also can be represented as Windows dialog boxes, Figure 9.19 is the GUI screen for checking out books. Notice that I built these screens as dialog boxes that do not contain menu options but can be minimized, maximized, or closed. Also notice that most of the fields are implemented as simple text entry fields, with the exception of the Author, which is a list box.

I could have used Dialog System from Micro Focus, or any other GUI development tool, to design and build the Library user interface. I decided that, because Dialog System is not yet integrated into the Micro Focus Object COBOL Option and specifically supported with the class library, I would use the Panels classes along with MenuItem and CallBack.

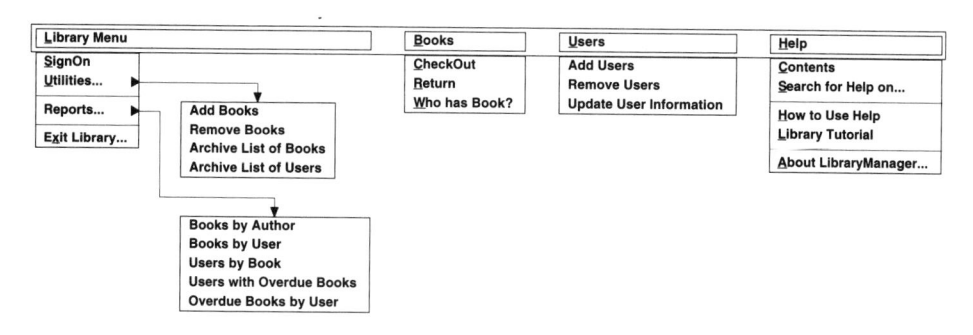

Figure 9.18
Library staff menu structure.

9.7.2 ATM Problem

The ATM is a highly interactive system, with GUI buttons, keyboard, and screens. As I have described in previous chapters, I designed the ATM system with a separate user interface (UI) subsystem. The ATM UI interfaces with the ATM subsystem and is a dialog box without any menu options or a control menu. Because the ATM UI can not be closed, I do not include a control menu with minimize, maximize, or close options.

Figure 9.19
Library checkout book screen.

The ATM UI dialog box includes command buttons — one for each number (0 through 9) and for the four buttons — a list box for the screen display, and simulations for the card reader, cash dispenser, withdrawal chute, and receipt printer. Because you actually cannot have the hardware objects in the GUI, you need to model them with buttons that can be pressed to simulate their use.

Another option you might have used for the ATM system would be to build the UI portion in Smalltalk. Smalltalk is a powerful GUI development environment and can be easily integrated with Micro Focus COBOL applications. Using this approach also would allow you to have one team developing a prototype of the UI in Smalltalk while another team performed a parallel development on the other ATM subsystems. I chose not to use this approach because I wanted to implement the entire ATM solution in OOCOBOL.

9.8 Future User Interface Development

The future of user interfaces will include object- and task-oriented operating environments, more powerful and elaborate GUIs, pen-based and voice-based input, and the convergence of online help with expert systems and computer-based training.

With the plans of IBM, DEC, Apple, HP, and Microsoft, future operating systems will provide even more powerful user interfaces. There is no question that providing users with a consistent visual structure, interaction style, reversibility (undo), window model, and object-action approach has benefit. Future user interfaces will be object-oriented, including NextStep, NewWave, Taligent, and Cario. These interfaces will represent applications or programs as icons (objects) that will closely resemble and behave like the real world objects that they represent. These icons also will be dynamically linked, and this will allow documents or files to contain dynamic references to external programs and data structures.

In addition, online, context-sensitive help will be merged with the ideas of workflow analysis to form an integrated user environment. Work has been under way on a number of these issues, including performance support systems (PSS) described in [GER91]. Future software applications might also include hypertext-based guidance systems that will answer questions, direct users, and facilitate improved productivity. HyperNews, developed in the late 1980s at the Turing Institute [RUD92], represents a marriage of Hypermedia with a Postscript graphic model (News) and artificial intelligence languages (Lisp and Prolog).

In the future, portable user interface applications will be generated for all environments, including DOS, Windows, OS/2, Macintosh, Unix (Motif, OpenLook and character), MVS, VMS, and other platforms. For example, one application could be specified along with its user interface and tools could support generated systems for all these environments, plus various file and database structures. As tool vendors extend their support for these environments, they also will address the issues of integration with middleware and remote databases discussed earlier. True client/server systems with efficient partitioning of parts (for instance, presentation on workstation, DBMS on server, middleware on application servers) will result from the evolution of these products.

Moving beyond GUIs to next generation user interfaces (including speech recognition, handwriting recognition, intelligent interfaces, and visual and virtual reality systems) also will change the nature of the user interface. Pen-based and voice-based systems already are available, although in primitive form, and will continue to mature as the technology changes.

As we approach the year 2000, there is no doubt that more and more software applications will be built from a user-centric perspective with a powerful user interface. Developers that refuse to accept this change in viewpoint will be left behind and end up supporting the existing character-based systems developed in the 1970s and 1980s.

9.9 References

[AND93]   Anderson, G. H., "Developing a Custom Trading Application in NextStep: A Case Study," *Object World '93 (June 1993) proceedings.*

[ART90]   Artim, J. M., J. M. Hary, and F. J. Spickhoff, "User Interface Services in AD/Cycle," *IBM Systems Journal*, vol. 29, no. 2, pp. 236-249.

[CAM92]   Cameron, J., "New Ingredients for an Object-Oriented Method," *Object Magazine*, September-October 1992, pp. 64-67.

[EGE92]   Ege, R. K. and C. Stary, "Designing Maintainable Reusable Interfaces," *IEEE Software*, November 1992, pp. 24-32.

[GER91]   Gery, G. J., *Electronic Performance Support Systems*, Weingarten Press, 1991.

[GUT93]   M. Guttman, J. A. King, and J. Matthews, "A Methodology for Developing Distributed Applications," *Object Magazine*, January-February 1993, pp. 55-59.

[FIS92] Fisher, L., "Experience Report - Constructing a Class Library for Microsoft Windows," *OOPSLA '92 (October 1992) proceedings*, pp 37-38.

[NOR88] Norman, D. A., *The Psychology of Everyday Things*, Basic Books, 1988

[OBE92] Oberg, B., and D. Notkin, "Error Reporting with Graduated Color," *IEEE Software*, November 1992, pp. 33-38.

[PRE92] Pressman, R. S., *Software Engineering: A Practitioner's Approach*, third edition, McGraw-Hill, 1988.

[RUD92] Rudolf, J., and C. Waite, "Completing the Job of Interface Design," *IEEE Software*, November 1992, pp. 11-23.

[UKE93] Ukelson, J. P., J. D. Gould, and S. J. Boies, "User Navigation in Computer Applications," *IEEE Trans. on Soft. Eng.*, vol. 19, no. 3, pp. 297-306.

[URL92] Urlocker, Z., "ObjectWindows: A Technical Overview," *Borland Language Express*, vol. 1, no. 2, pp. 11-13.

Visual Object-Oriented Programming Tools

As object-oriented programming evolved, several vendors of OOPL products saw an opportunity to deliver visual tools for technical and nontechnical staff to allow software applications to be assembed from pre-existing components. Visual OOP tools represent a combination of traditional OOP languages (usually Smalltalk or Basic) along with visual icons or symbols that represents classes of objects available for use.

The idea behind visual programming is to put powerful programming tools in the hands of nonprogrammers and allow them to design and generate their own applications. The theory behind this idea is that users of a software application know what they require, so why not let them develop their own computer solutions? The problem with this approach has always been developing sophisticated programming tools that nontechnical people can use easily. Another related problem is insulating non-technical staff from any implementation specific details related to programming structure and performance.

A normal visual programming environment includes a visual language, a rapid prototyping tool for the user interface, and a set of existing components that represent common application functions. Critical to the success of any visual programming tool is a set of symbols or icons that represent these common functions and a mechanism for assembling these constucts into working software applications.

For a review of the technical issues involved in deploying visual programming tools, see the October 1990 issue of the *IEEE Transactions on Software Engineering*.

Product	Vendor	Environment	Language	Cost
Component Workshop	Component Software	Macintosh	C++	$2,500
Dialog System	Micro Focus	DOS, Windows, OS/2 and Unix	COBOL	$1,250
Enfin	Easel Corp.	OS/2 and Windows	Smalltalk	$4,000
GeODE and Developer Pro	Serious Corp.	Sun SPARC, Macintosh, OS/2, and Windows	Smalltalk-based	$5,000 and $1,500
Layout	Objects	DOS	C	$500
Object/Designer	ImageSoft	Windows	C++	$300
ObjectVision	Borland	OS/2 and Windows	C++	$150
PARTS Workbench	Digitalk	OS/2 and Windows	Smalltalk	$2,000
VisualAge	IBM	OS/2	Smalltalk	$2,500
VisualBasic	Microsoft	Windows	Basic	$200 - $500
Visual Objects	Computer Associates	Windows	Clipper	$300
VisualWorks	ParcPlace Systems	Macintosh, Windows and Unix (OpenLook and Motif)	Smalltalk	$3,000 - $5,000
VzCreate	VZ Corp.	OS/2	C++	$600
WindowsBuilder	Cooper and Peeters	OS/2 and Windows	C	$1,000

Maintaining Object-Oriented COBOL Applications

Chapter 10

After software is delivered, it must be allowed to evolve over the years to continue to satisfy the needs of the users who paid for it to be created. The process of maintenance includes removing defects or errors in the system, adding new functions or data structures, improving the performance of the system, and accommodating any new technologies (i.e., hardware and software) that are introduced after the system is placed into production. Most organizations spend up to 60% of their maintenance effort just trying to identify where a bug or error is in an application.

Many estimates place the cost of a system expended in maintenance at over 50% and perhaps as high as 80% of the total system cost. This means that maintenance undoubtedly is the phase of software development where the majority of the time and resources are spent. This also means that the maintenance phase represents the largest potential are for improvement. Some estimates place annual expenditures for maintenance at $70 billion [EDE93].

Capers Jones of Software Productivity Research (SPR) estimates that there currently are over 2 billion lines of COBOL code in use worldwide, over 2 Million active COBOL programmers worldwide, and over 375,000 programmers maintaining COBOL applications in the United States [JON92]. He also estimates that there are twice as many COBOL programmers as C programmers in the United States.

In this chapter, I will review maintenance, the tasks and activities involved, types of maintenance requests, strategies, and object-oriented maintenance issues. I will finish the chapter by looking at the two example problems and reviewing potential changes. As I cover maintenance, I will focus on the issues unique to object-oriented systems and how these systems are different from traditional systems.

10.1 Introduction

Maintenance: the modification of a software product, after delivery, to correct faults, to improve performance or other attributes, or to adapt the product to a modified environment.
IEEE STD 1219-1993 [IEE93].

Traditional COBOL maintenance involves a variety of tasks, from reviewing existing programs and documentation to locating an error in an old program and from searching for a field or variable in a collection of programs to modifying a program to add new functions. Basic COBOL maintenance can be difficult and frustrating, especially if there isn't sufficient documentation or design information available. This process is made harder when COBOL programs share data structures and there are functional dependencies between programs across a system.

OOCOBOL maintenance includes the same tasks as those in a traditional COBOL environment with the addition of other tasks to improve reuse and migrate non-OOCOBOL applications to OOCOBOL using the strategies described in Chapter 12.

One potential benefit of OOCOBOL is that the resulting objects, classes, etc. will be easier to extend or modify because they will incorporate information hiding. What this means is that OOCOBOL programs that encapsulate data structures and that operations or methods can be modified without adversely affecting other objects that interact because those objects don't need to know or understand the implementation details of the object.

Maintenance is a microcosm of traditional software development. It includes all the tasks in development, planning, analysis, design, programming, and testing but involves systems that already are operational. Software systems by their nature evolve and change and might operate 30 years or more after they are implemented. As organizations look to reduce their costs, software systems must be operational longer and must be extensible to support new features and new hardware/software environments.

At the heart of the maintenance process is the change or maintenance request. A user often submits a request for change or modification to an existing system that starts the process. In most cases, this request is in the form of a document describing the change. In some cases, change requests might come from the technical staff (for example, when a new operating system or database system is implemented) or even from within the development group (when a new system is to be implemented that must interface with an existing system).

The average Fortune 100 company maintains 35 million lines of code and adds 3.5 million new lines a year just in enhancements, updates, and other maintenance. That doesn't count new development.
K. Melymuka [MUL91].

10.2 Maintenance Tasks

A process model for maintenance had been defined by the IEEE and is shown in Figure 10.1. The maintenance process includes the tasks that are described in the following paragraphs.

Identify the problem / modification, classify and prioritize it. When a request for modification or change is submitted, it is classified based on its type (see section 10.3). It is prioritized based on the available resources, estimated time to complete, impact, and outstanding requests. Change requests, for example, might be placed into a queue to be reviewed and prioritized by subject area or time to complete. Higher priority requests can be processed quickly, while lower priority requests might be kept in the queue until resources are available.

Analyze the item. The change request is analyzed to determine where the change should be made in the affected system. If the request is a *corrective* modification (i.e., an error), then determine where the error is occurring and why. If the request is for an *enhancement*, analyze the potential impact of the change on the system and any related systems.

As with traditional development, this stage is concerned with discovering or learning as much as possible about the requested change so that a determination can be made as to how to proceed. This phase also defines the nature of the change and its impact on the system. Impact analysis is a critical task in this phase and helps estimate the cost and affect of a change on the working system.

Design a solution. With a good understanding of the problem, you can begin to design the requested change by producing a list of action items that describe the change in terms of code and design documentation. If you have available documents, models, or specifications, you might begin by reviewing these to determine what alternative design options you have and their cost and benefit. This phase of maintenance is much like the design phase of the development life cycle.

Implement the change. Once the change has been designed for the system, you can introduce the changes into the production system. This involves programming the solution, either by modifying existing code or by deleting or inserting new code, unit testing the code to make sure it works correctly, then documenting the changes.

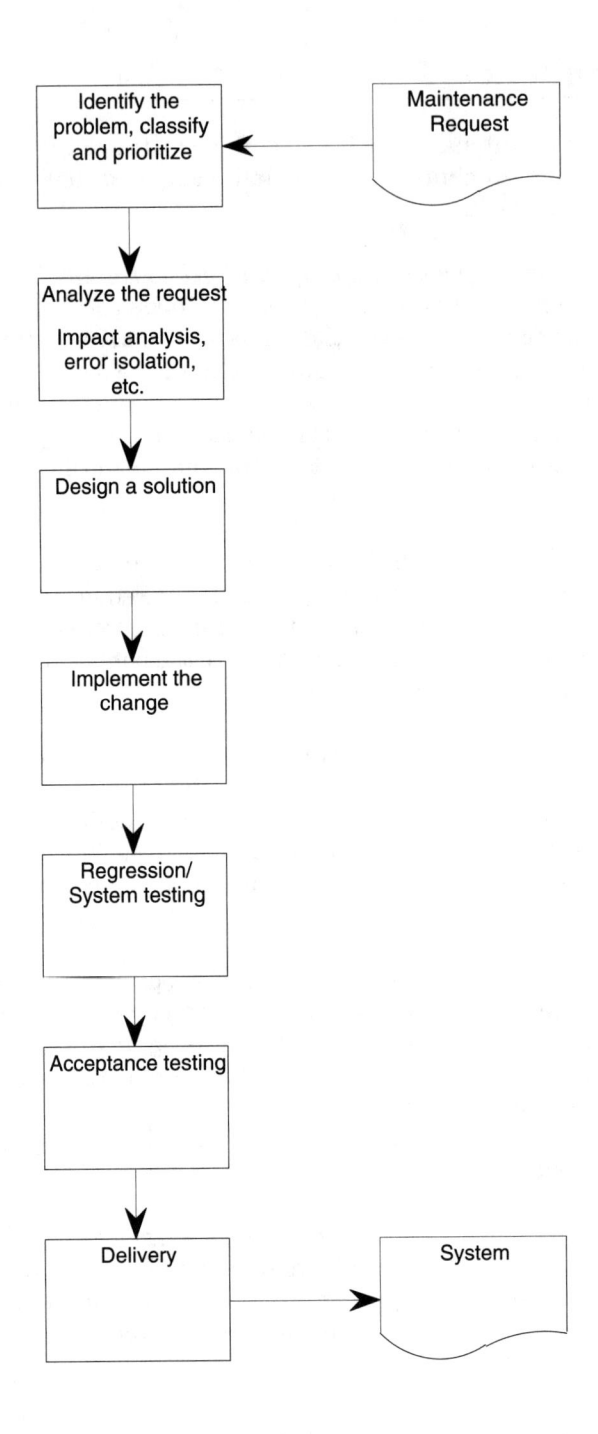

Figure 10.1 IEEE STD-1219-1993 maintenance process.

Regression/system testing. Following coding and unit testing, you must test the system to determine whether the change was successful. If not, you must return to the second step and try again. Regression testing allows you to test portions of the system to ensure that you have not caused any ripple effects (i.e., any unforeseen changes in the functionality of the system that might have been caused inadvertently by the change).

Acceptance testing. The users test the system to determine whether the change was introduced successfully. If not, return to the second step. Once the system has been accepted, you must place it into a production status as you did when you delivered the initial system.

Deliver the system. The final maintenance task is to deliver the modified system into production.

10.3 Types of Maintenance

Maintenance means different things to different people. To a user of a system, maintenance means fixing the system when it is broken, while to a maintenance programmer, it might mean changes in the requirements for the original system. As a result, maintenance is difficult to characterize because its definition is so subjective.

For purposes of this discussion, maintenance shall be synonymous with evolution of a system from the point that it initially is implemented and deployed untill it is retired or replaced. When you look at maintenance in general, you can identify at least four basic types of maintenance tasks or actions [SWA76]:

- Corrective — diagnosis and repair of *errors* in a system in production.
- Adaptive — modifications to a system in production to properly *interface* with a changing environment (either hardware or software).
- Perfective — changes in the *functional requirements* of a system already in production.
- Preventive — *improving* a system based on anticipated future needs (maintenance costs, complexity, reliability, security, etc.).

Figure 10.2 represents the results of a study by Lientz and Swanson [LIE80] of 487 software engineering organizations and the percentage of maintenance time spent on each of the types of maintenance described previously. Notice their results suggest that most maintenance is perfective or involves changes

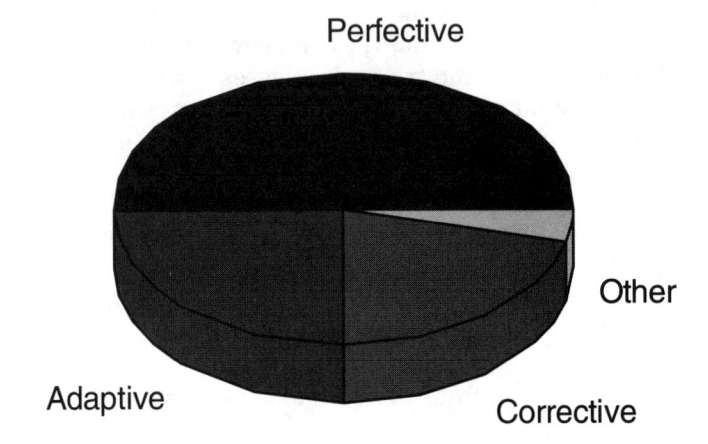

Figure 10.2
Distribution of maintenance types.

[Pie chart showing maintenance types: Perfective, Adaptive, Corrective, Other]

to the original functional requirements supporting the notion that getting a clear, concise definition of requirements is the key to delivering a good working system.

Several excellent resources are available on maintenance of software. Pressman [PRE92] suggests differences between structured and unstructured maintenance, cost of maintenance and controlling the maintainability of software and describes in detail a maintenance organization and tasks. Figure 10.3 represents a set of tasks to determine the type of maintenance request and how to process it.

10.3.1 Measuring Software Maintainability

Possible metrics of software maintainability proposed include Halstead's software science measures [HAL77], information flow, and cyclomatic complexity [MCC76]. Grady [GRA87] suggests that the number of modules affected by a change, defect rates, module stability (i.e., changes to modules over time), and module complexity can all be measures of software maintainability.

At a minimum, software maintainability is related to several important characteristics, including understandability, complexity, modularity, support for information hiding, and reusability. Each of these factors can affect the maintainability of a software system.

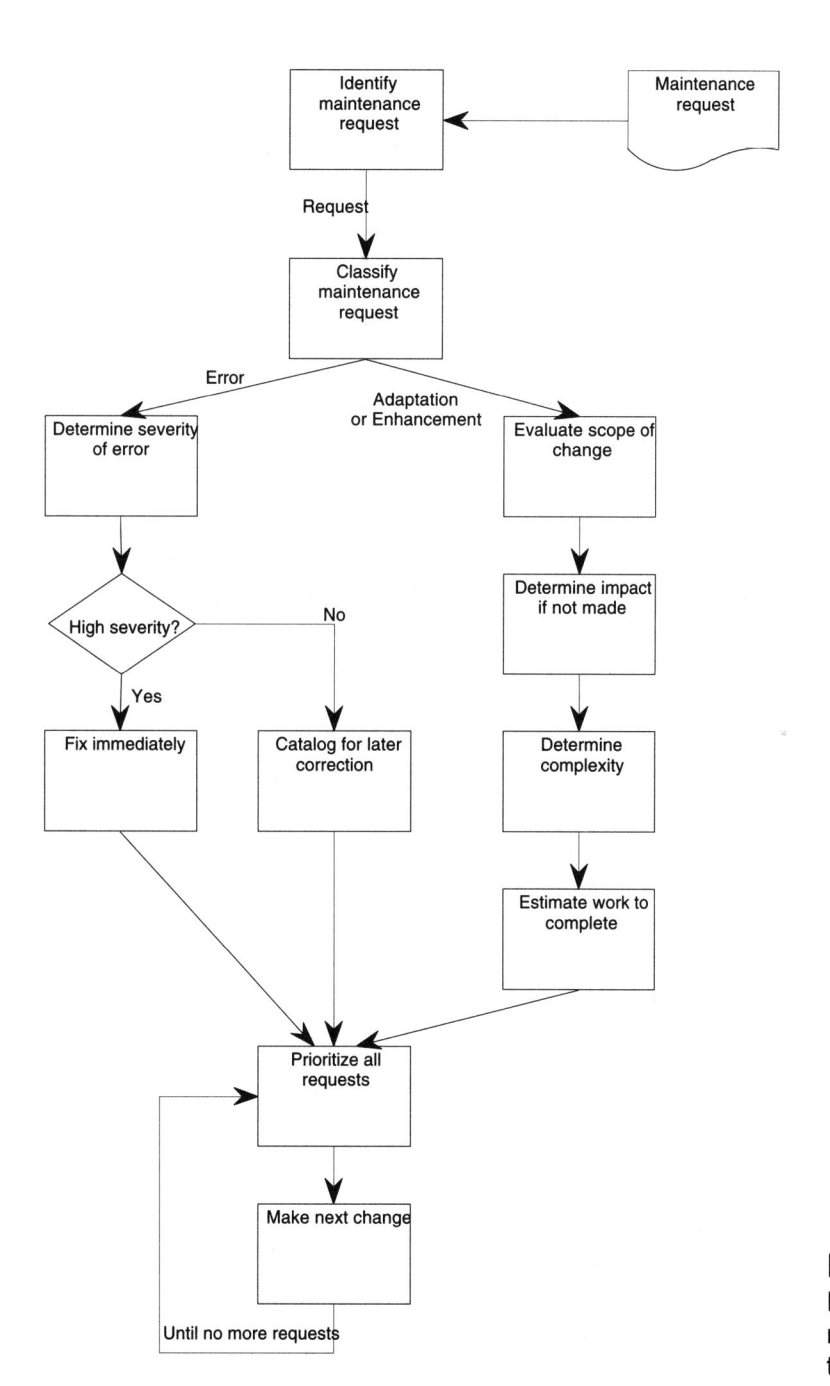

Figure 10.3 Determining maintenance types.

For many years, advocates of structured programming have claimed that modular programs were easier and less costly to maintain than nonmodular programs. The basis for this hypothesis was that nonmodular programs (i.e., programs that don't have a top-down structure of small modules with low coupling and high cohesion) were more complex and thus harder to understand and change than modular programs. Recently, a technical paper [BAN93] reported findings at a large MIS site that confirm these observations.

In this study, over 18 million lines of COBOL code were studied for a large banking institution to determine if modular programs were less complex and thus easier to maintain than unstructured code. The average size for the application systems in this environment were over 225,000 lines of COBOL code, and the average maintenance project took over 1,000 hours to complete and added or modified over 5,000 lines of code.

The results of this study proved that increased software complexity significantly decreased the overall productivity of software maintenance. Specifically, this study found that 25% of the overall cost of maintenance and up to 17% of the total system cost could be cut by reducing the complexity of software by using modularity. The complexity measures used in this study were average module size, average procedure size, and branching complexity or GOTO statements. As a result of this study, Banker *et al* suggest using a cost model shown in Figure 10.4 to estimate maintenance costs.

Another interesting study was done to determine where organizations indicated that they had the most problems with maintenance [ZEP92]. Figure 10.5 summarizes the results of this study.

10.3.2 Cost of Maintenance

As you consider the factors that affect software maintainability, you also must consider the cost of maintenance over the life of a system. Belady and Lehman [BEL72] suggest the following formula for measuring or estimating the cost of software maintenance :

Cost of maintenance = $E + K(c - d)$

where E = effort or productivity of maintenance staff
K = a constant
c = software complexity
d = degree of familiarity with the system

```
┌─────────────────┐   ┌─────────────────┐   ┌─────────────────┐
│   Module size   │   │  Procedure size │   │    Branching    │
│   (LOC/module)  │   │  (LOC/procedure)│   │ (flow of control│
│                 │   │                 │   │    of GOTO)     │
└────────┬────────┘   └────────┬────────┘   └────────┬────────┘
         │                     │                     │
         └─────────────┐       ▼       ┌─────────────┘
                       ▼               ▼
┌─────────────────┐   ┌─────────────────┐
│ Project factors │   │    Software     │
│ (hours, function│   │  comprehension  │
│ points, LOC,    │   │                 │
│ skill, method,  │   └────────┬────────┘
│      etc.)      │            │
└────────┬────────┘            │
         │                     │
         └──────────┐   ┌──────┘
                    ▼   ▼
              ┌─────────────┐
              │   Software  │
              │ maintenance │
              │   project   │
              │    costs    │
              └─────────────┘
```

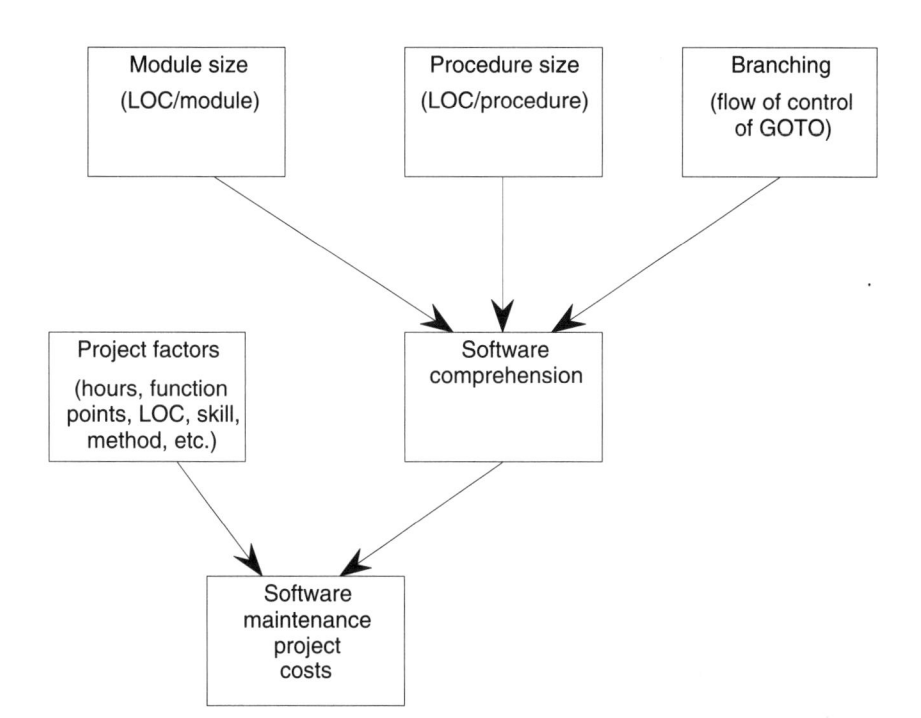

Figure 10.4
Maintenance project cost model.

Percentage of Sites Reporting Problems

	Serious	Regular	Occasional
Missing source code	1%	5%	68%
Inconsistent data	4%	18%	51%
Resistant object code	4%	9%	31%
Unstructured code	7%	26%	44%
Poor documentation	11%	36%	39%

Figure 10.5
Reported maintenance problems.

Pickard and Carter [PIC93] suggest an approach to using design metrics (i.e., structural or cyclomatic complexity) as predictive measures of maintenance over the life of a system. Figure 10.6 indicates a framework for collecting and using these metrics in the life cycle. As part of their study, Pickard and Carter evaluated 57 COBOL programs for which there was no design documentation and attempted to show a correlation between design metrics and maintainability.

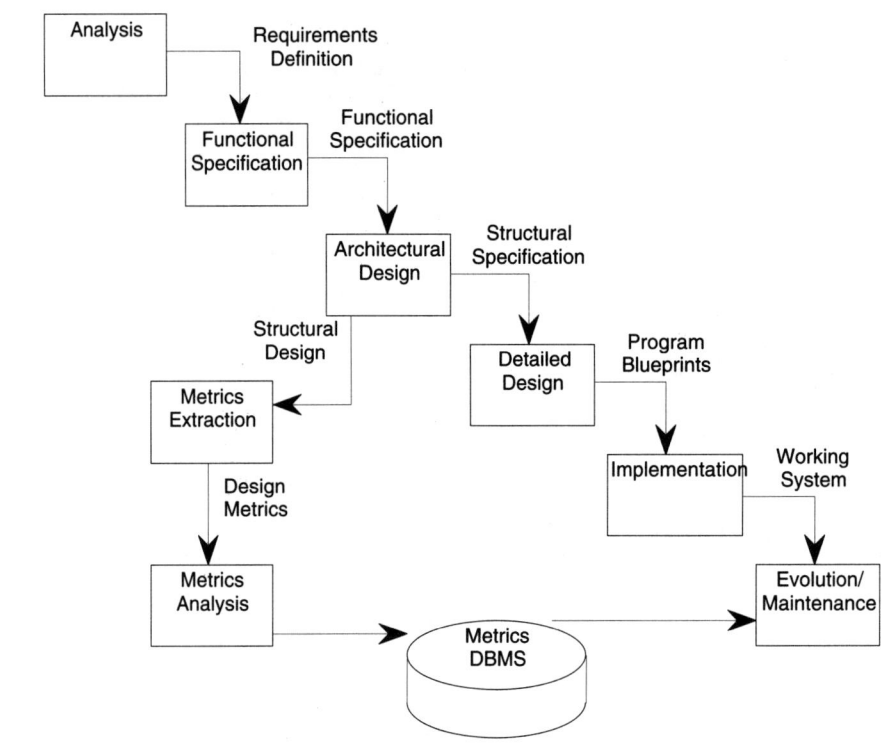

Figure 10.6
Using design metrics to predict maintainability.

10.4 Maintenance Strategies

There are five basic strategies typically associated with maintaining or enhancing existing systems. These are described in the following paragraphs.

Replace existing programs with programs that use newer technologies (i.e., IMS — DB2) or retire programs that are no longer used. This implies a normal evolution from legacy systems to new systems that replace them. The new development might consider the existing system or might begin with a totally new development project that starts with a new requirements specification. Replacing existing systems represents the most expensive option or alternative.

Example: When systems are replaced, their functionality must be duplicated and they must be removed from production and replaced. While this is the most costly of the activities, it also is the approach taken taken by most companies.

Reformat or reorganize the program source code by inserting indentation and renaming variables and procedures so that they conform to standards and conventions. Because much time is spent trying to figure out what existing systems do, formatting these systems can improve their readability and understanding and improve the maintenance process.

Example: A COBOL program that has variable names such as SWITCH_1 or COUNT_10 or programs that contain run-on code are very difficult to understand for a novice or anyone that didn't write the program.

Restructure the program source code (i.e., making the code more structured) for documentation purposes. As done previously, this process begins by examining existing unstructured code and applying structured programming constructs to the code without loosing any functionality. The reason for restructuring is for easier maintenance.

Example: Programs that have multiple GOTOs or complex IF statements can be very difficult to follow and studies have shown that unstructured code is more difficult to maintain than structured code.

Re-engineer (i.e., redesign or re-architect) the source code by adding functions or procedures without changing the functionality of the system. This process involves changing some implementation details of an existing system, perhaps the DBMS or programming language, without changing the functionality of the system.

Example: Most older programs, those written prior to the advent of structured concepts, tend to have calls to I/O routines scattered throughout and do not attempt to consolidate common functions in any way. In many cases, if common routines can be setup for I/O and screen handling, the maintenance of these programs becomes easier over time.

Reverse engineer or automatically translating the existing program source code and data structure definitions into logical specifications or diagrams so that the overall system structure and functionality are documented. This process takes the existing implementation deliverables (i.e., code, JCL, and data structures) and determines what the structure and behavior of the system is. This is followed by population of a CASE repository with the resulting information.

Example: When an existing IMS application must be overhauled or replaced, some products can take the existing database definitions and create a logical data model with attributes and relationships intact. If you lose any of the systems structure in this process, the resulting system will not duplicate the one that you are replacing.

Of these five strategies, the most promising is reverse engineering, because it allows existing systems, for which there often is little if any useful documentation available, to be used to create specifications and models automatically. An example reverse engineering process is shown in Figure 10.7. Many reverse engineering products currently are available and are discussed in more detail in the next chapter.

Reverse engineering, while powerful in concept, is not without its own drawbacks. Tom McCabe, architect of the essential and cyclomatic complexity measures, has identified a life cycle for reverse engineering that deals with identifying redundant and reusable software components [MCC90]. Figure 10.8 represents the life cycle that McCabe proposes, which includes the following tasks:

- Identify and eliminate redundant code before reverse engineering it
- Identify reusable code before reverse engineering it
- Find all occurrences of related routines/functions
- Restructure existing code
- Modularize complex modules
- Identify error-prone modules
- Verify the correct implementation of design specifications

10.5 OOCOBOL Maintenance

One way to better understand the types of maintenance on a system developed using OOCOBOL would be to make actual changes to a system that you already have built. Because I have built two applications, the Library and ATM systems, I will use these examples to help describe the maintenance process. Each of these applications will be modified as specified later, and I will review the impact of these modifications and the types of tasks required to make these modifications.

While there haven't been many studies comparing maintenance of object-oriented and procedural systems, one study [HEN93] found that object-oriented code requires fewer modules and sections to be edited, fewer lines of code to be changed, and fewer new lines of code to be added. This study further found that a system built with an object-oriented programming language produced fewer changes in source code and the changes required were more localized.

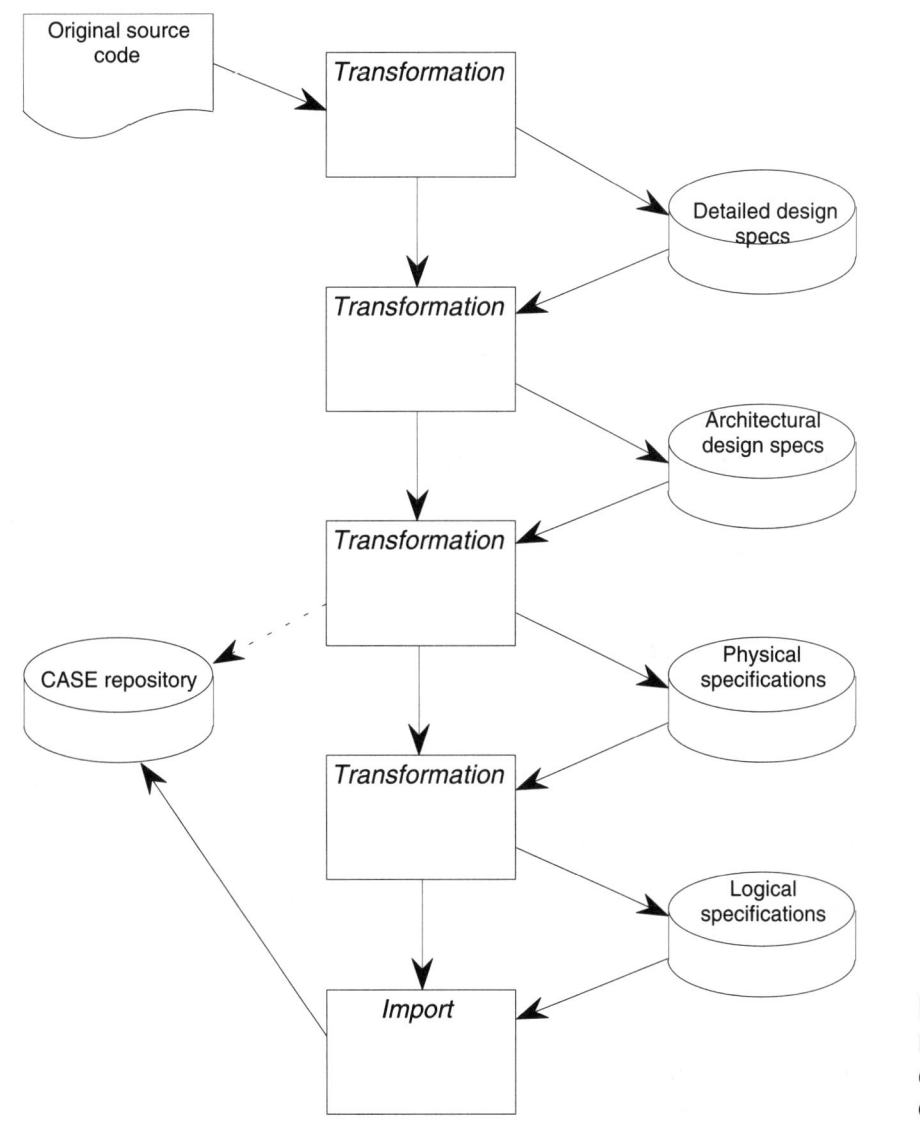

Figure 10.7
Reverse engineering life cycle.

The Henry and Humphry study was conducted on 24 students enrolled in a software engineering course over a 22-week period. The two programming languages used were C and Objective C, and the application that was modified consisted of around 4,000 lines of code.

Figure 10.8
McCabes' maintenance life cycle.

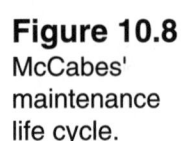

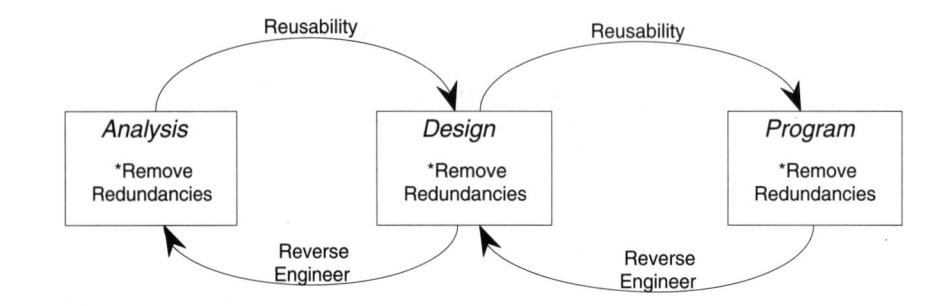

Another study done by Wayne Haythorn of an ATM system [HAY94] written in C++ looked at three different development approaches: functional decomposition (FD), object-based (OB), and polymorphic object-oriented (OO). The resulting ATM system was modified to determine the impact of the proposed changes on each system. Figure 10.9 shows the results of the study listing each type of change and the amount of code modified under each approach. Of the three methods used, the third view (polymorphic object-oriented) had a significantly lower level of complexity in its modules and resulted in less overall modified code for each maintenance request. Interestingly, the object-based development method resulted in higher levels of modified code for three of the seven changes, with slightly lower levels for the other four.

Haythorn also compared the percentage of total code that was required to be understood for each type of change and compared the results as shown in Figure 10.10. Notice that, in almost every case, the percentage of code that must be understood to make a change is higher for a system created using functional design than either object-based or object-oriented. One exception, the change to support rush hours, resulted in a lower percentage for functional design than for object-based or object-oriented. Also notice that object-

Type of change	FD	OB	OO
Add type of tellor	64%	56%	28%
Multiple queues	45%	54%	10%
Customer can leave queue	39%	43%	19%
Transaction types change	75%	56%	28%
Rush hours	6%	17%	11%
Varying the number of tellers	23%	26%	10%
Cash machines and phone	89%	100%	52%

Figure 10.9
Comparing modified code by type of change.

oriented development represents up to half the required code be understood than functional or even object-based for some changes.

10.5.1 Library Problem

As I look at maintenance, I will consider the two example problems that I developed solutions for in OOCOBOL and examine how these applications might change. In this section, I will introduce four requests for modification or change to the Library system. The first three modifications will be discussed in detail in this section while the third will be discussed in the next chapter. Following these, I will look at changes to the ATM system in the same light.

Change request #1

Modify the library system to implement a two-week loan period and to apply a late fee of $ .50 per day for any books returned after the due date.

Discussion: This request is clearly a change in functional requirements or a new functional requirement. Recalling the object model and specification, this request will impact the Checkout and Return methods of the Library Staff object. To support the two-week loan period, you must modify the Checkout method to calculate the value of the DateDueBack as the current date + 14 days. To support the $.50 late fee, you need to modify the Return method to calculate the late fee as follows: (DateBack - DateDueBack) * .5 If the result is 0, this is the late fee. This raises another question: what do you do with the late fee? Should you store the late fee in one of the SQL table — perhaps in the User table — or in one of our Lists — probably the ListofBooks?

Change request #2

Modify the library system to mail out a notice every week to any user who has an overdue book if they have not returned them within a week of their due date. Consolidate each notice to save on mailing costs and only send out one notice to each user, regardless of how many overdue books they might have checked out.

Discussion: This also is a new requirement for a report or notice to be printed every week of the users that have late fees for overdue books. This change requires a new List of Users with late fees that is associated with each Book. Modifying the Return method could result in the following logic:

1. Calculate the number of days a book is returned past the due date.

2. If the book is overdue, calculate the late fee.
3. Send a message to the ListofLateUsers to add this user. This list should contain the UserID, DateDueBack, DateBack, and late fee.
4. Every week, a report can be run that reads the ListofLateUsers for each book, locates the UserName and Address, and prints a notice.

Change request #3

Modify the library system to keep track of the number of overdue books that each user has over a period of time. Store this total with the other user information on file and display it in the appropriate screens and reports.

Discussion: This request also can use the List object in the Library system to store a collection of the books returned late by a specific user. You could create a ListofOverdeBooks and associate it with the User. In a similar fashion to change request #2, you could modify the Return method to store the number of overdue books in the User object and modify the User screen and reports to print out this information.

Change request #4

Modify the library system to send a message to the student financial system indicating those users that have overdue fees. These overdue fees should be added to any outstanding funds that students owe the university. For example, at the end of each semester, the financial system sends out invoices to each student covering their course fees, room and board, etc. for the upcoming term. It would be very easy to have these invoices include any overdue fines that students have on library books.

Discussion: This last request requires that you interface the Library system

Type of change	FD	OB	OO
Add new types of tellors	76%	70%	32%
Support multiple customer queues	58%	51%	23%
Customer can leave queue	41%	27%	20%
Transaction types change	87%	73%	49%
Rush hours	4%	16%	9%
Varying the number of tellers	36%	33%	32%
Diversion of resources	28%	38%	18%
Cash machines and phone	87%	81%	41%

Figure 10.10
Percentage of total code that must be understood for a change.

with an external system, in this case the university financial system. While this task might be outside the scope of what I can accomplish in this chapter, I will be looking at strategies for interfacing with non-object-oriented legacy systems in the next chapter. I will postpone further discussion on this change request until chapter 11.

10.5.2 ATM Problem

I also have a modification request for the ATM system that has a direct impact on the system functionality. As with the library system, prior to making the change, you must determine what impact the requested change will have on the ATM system.

Change request #1

Modify the ATM system to allow bank customers to cancel or back out of an ATM session up until the system has dispensed cash (via a withdrawal), collected a deposit, or transferred funds between accounts. To support this added functionality, a new button (CANCEL) will be added to the ATM user interface, and when this button is selected, the user will be returned by the system to the previous screen.

Discussion: This change request makes sense and can be applied easily to the interface between the ATM UI and the ATM. Recalling the design of the ATMState table, you can progress back through this table by storing the current state in a field in the ATM UI and branching to that state when the CANCEL button is pushed. Further information is required to implement this change request.

In the case of the ATM system, a bank customer can cancel out of their session up until screen 11 or 14. Once the bank customer has taken their withdrawal or their printed receipt, they cannot cancel the transaction. For example, assume a bank customer has progressed through screen 10 of the ATM system but suddenly decides that he or she have entered an incorrect account type. At screen 10, he or she can press the CANCEL button and return to the previous screen (in this case, 7).

If you evaluate the modifications to the ATM system to support the CANCEL button and its functionality, you soon will realize that you have to change the ATM user interface (to add the new button), change some of the screens (to signify that the CANCEL button is available), and change the ATM state-transitions to support the CANCEL function.

Change request #2

Modify the ATM system to allow support for new ATM transactions, including remote debit requests from gas stations, convenience stores, utility companies, and other banks or savings institutions.

Discussion: This request is a natural extension to the ATM functionality, and many banks now offer debit cards and features such as these for their accounts. Because you have built the ATM with an eye towards future bank transactions, you can easily modify it to accept these new transactions. An example of how this would be accomplished would be to reuse the existing withdrawal and deposit transactions to support credits and debits to accounts. For example, you might create a new set of ATM transactions for the new functions with the withdrawal and deposit as parent classes.

Change request #3

Modify the ATM system to allow direct deposits to the bank account during regular business hours.

Discussion: This change requires a tighter interface between the ATM and the Account Manager subsystems. Recalling the initial constraints, I assumed in designing the system that deposits would not directly change the balance of an account but would be batched and updated the following business day. If this requirement changes, the impact on the ATM system is slight, because you need modify only the service provided by the Account Manager and the request made by the ATM.

10.6 General Object-Oriented Maintenance

As you review the change requests for the example systems, along with the work of Haythorn and others, you will see that maintaining object-oriented systems is significantly different from maintain traditional systems. Studying maintenance of object-oriented systems will help you better understand the types of tasks and activities required and the tools and methods needed to support these tasks.

A research team at Florida/Purdue Software Engineering Research Center and Bellcore have been studying the impact of object-orientation on maintenance [WIL92]. Their findings indicate that dynamic binding complicates tracking dependencies between components in an object-oriented system, and this can adversely affect maintenance. The type of dependencies that can exist in an object-oriented system and must be tracked for maintenance include: class-to-class, class-to-method, class-to-message, class-to-variable, method-to-variable, method-to-message, and method-to-method.

Wilde and Huitt suggest that browsing tools should support each of these types of relationships to facilitate maintenance of object-oriented systems. For example, a calling hierarchy could be viewed as a hierarchy of methods; however, because of dynamic binding, the hierarchy would be difficult to create, and there often is no main method in a system like a main program in a traditional system. Wilde and Huitt go on to recommend that class-uses-class relationships should be used for understanding an object-oriented system and development environments should support alternative clustering methods for browsing.

Tasks, roles, and responsibilities of staff in maintaining object-oriented systems differ from traditional MIS. Recalling the discussion of the roles and responsibilities of object-oriented development in chapter 4, you expect the following tasks will be performed by staff:

- System Architects — Maintain the software architectures for the organization.
- Class Designers — Maintain the class hierarchy with the goal of maximizing reuse throughout the organization.
- Class Implementors — Review available classes and implement objects to satisfy the needs of a change request.
- Application Programmers — Assemble the classes created or modified by the implementors using OOCOBOL.

10.6.1 Configuration Management Issues

As you saw in previous chapters, managing relationships in an object-oriented system is a challenge. Bersoff and Davis [BER91] identified several problems for configuration management systems regarding software reuse. They suggest strategies including maintaining a list from each reusable component (or class) to all implementations in systems so that any changes can be tracked forward to affected systems, notifying users of reusable components when they change, keeping track of different versions of a class, and maintaining interface details for all classes.

Wilde, Huitt, and Matthews [WIL93] suggest strategies for managing classes, including using dependency analysis to understand an object-oriented system, separating class specifications from implementations to take advantage of information hiding, tracing program dependencies via an inheritance tree in maintenance, and keeping the number of methods smaller to decrease the number of relationships that a maintainer must understand. They also report several new types of problems maintaining object-oriented code, including dynamic binding and polymorphism, which result in difficulty understanding how objects execute, and cooperating objects, which require deciphering groups of classes to understand their behavior.

I will cover configuration management in more detail in chapter 12.

10.6.2 Maintaining Class Libraries

Managing a class library involves many different tasks and problems [NIE93], including inadequate inheritance structure, missing abstractions, overly specialized classes, and deficient object modeling may impair the reusability of a class library.

To improve class libraries, the following maintenance tasks can be undertaken:

- *Class tailoring* — Implementing specialized or optimized versions of a method for a class instead of the ones provided in the superclass.
- *Class surgery* — Modifications to the class library with an eye towards classification consistency; before any modifications can be made to the library, the impact of the change must be determined and evaluated.
- *Class versioning* — Keeping track of different versions of implementations of a class (role of the OODBMS to support this).
- *Class reorganization* — Identify and add missing abstractions, making classes more general, increasing modularity, etc.

Classes can be in several types of relationships, has-a (part-of), is-a (kind-of), or message passing.

A software application can be considered as a group of classes that work together to provide some function, accessible through a public protocol. Managing and maintaining class hierarchies [BOO93] involves the following actions:

- Adding new classes to the library
- Changing the implementation of a class

- Changing the representation of a class
- Changing the interface of a class
- Reorganizing the class hierarchy.

10.7 References

[AN87]	An, K. H., D. A. Gustafson, and A. C. Melton, "A Model for Software Maintenance," *Proceedings of the Conference on Software Maintenance* (1987), pp. 57-62.
[BAN93]	Banker, R. D., S. M. Datar, C. F. Kemerer, and D. Zweig, "Software Complexity and Maintenance Costs," *CACM*, vol. 36, no. 11, November 1993, pp. 81-94.
[BAS84]	Basili, V. R. and B. Perricone, "Software Errors and Complexity: An Empirical Investigation," *CACM*, vol. 27, no. 1, (1984), pp. 52-52.
[BEL72]	Belady, L. and M. Lehman, "An Introduction to Growth Dynamics," *Statistical Computer Performance Evaluation*, W. Freiberger, ed., Academic Press, 1972, pp. 503-511.
[BER91]	Bersoff, E. H. and A. M. Davis, "Impacts of Life Cycle Models on Software," *CACM*, vol. 34, no. 8, pp. 104-117.
[BOO93]	Booch, G. and M. Vilot, "Simplifying the Booch Components," *C++ Report*, June 1993, pp. 41-52.
[HAY94]	Haythorn, W., "What is Object-Oriented Design?," *JOOP*, March-April 1994, pp. 67-77.
[EDE93]	Edelstein, D. V., "Report on the IEEE STD 1219-1993: Standard for Software Maintenance," *ACM SIGSOFT*, vol. 18, no. 4, October 1993, pp. 94-95.
[GRA87]	Grady, R., "Measuring and Managing Software Maintenance," *IEEE Software*, vol. 4, pp. 35-45, 1987.
[HAL77]	Halstead, M., *Elements of Software Science*, North Holland, 1977.
[HAR82]	Harrison, W., K. Magel, R. Kluczny, and A. DeDock, "Applying Software Complexity Metrics to Program Maintenance," *IEEE Computer*, vol. 15, pp. 65-79, 1982.
[HAY92]	Haythorn, W., "Defensive Analysis to Capture Potential Change," *Proceedings of the OOPSLA '92 conference*, pp. 115-121, 1992.
[HAY94]	Haythorn, W., "What is Object-Oriented Design," *JOOP*, March-April 1994, pp. 67-78.
[HEN93]	Henry, S. and M. Humphrey, "Object-Oriented vs. Procedural Programming Languages: Effectiveness in Program Maintenance," *JOOP*, June 1993, pp. 41-49.

[HUN93] Hunscher, D., "Stories from the Frontlines: Managing Object-Oriented Development in an Engineering Environment," *Object Magazine*, January-February 1993, pp. 75-78.

[JON92] Jones, C., "Hopper's Legacy: Innovation, Education," *IEEE Software*, March 1992, p. 95.

[KEF93] Keffer, T., "The Design and Architecture of Tools.h++," *C++ Report*, June 1993, pp. 28-33.

[KOR86] Korson, T. D. and V. K. Vaishnavi, "An Empirical Study of the Effects of Modularity on Program Modifiability," *Empirical Studies of Programmers*, E. Soloway and S. Iyengar, eds., Ablex, 1986.

[LEJ92] Lejter, M., S. Meyers, and S. P. Reiss, "Support for Maintaining Object-Oriented Programs," *IEEE Trans. Soft. Eng.*, vol. 18, no. 2, pp. 1045-1052.

[LIE80] Lientz, B. and E. Swanson, *Software Maintenance Management*, Addison-Wessley, 1980.

[MCC76] McCabe, T., "A Complexity Measure," *IEEE Trans. Soft. Eng.*, December 1976, pp. 308-320.

[MCC90] McCabe, T., "Reverse Engineering, Reusability, Redundancy: The Connection," *American Programmer*, vol. 3, no. 10 (October 1990), pp. 8-14.

[MEL91] Melymuka, K., "Managing Maintenance: The 4000-pound Gorilla," *CIO*, vol. 4, no. 6, pp. 74-82, March 1991.

[NIE93] Nierstrasz, O. and X. Pintado, "Class Management for Software Communities," *CACM*, vol. 33, no. 9, pp. 90-103.

[PIC93] Pickard, M. M., and B. D. Carter, "Maintainability: What is it and How do We Measure it?" *SIGSOFT*, vol. 18, no. 3, pp. 36-39.

[ROM87] Rombach, D., "A Controlled Experiment on the impact of Software Structure on Maintainability," *IEEE Trans. Soft. Eng.*, vol. SE-13, no. 3, pp. 344-354, 1987.

[PRE92] Pressman, R., *Software Engineering: A Practitioner's Approach*, third edition, McGraw-Hill, 1992.

[SWA76] Swanson, E. B., "The Dimensions of Maintenance," *Proceedings of the 2nd Intl. Conf. on Software Engineering*, IEEE, October 1976, pp. 492-497.

[WIL92] Wilde, N. and R. Huitt, "Maintenance Support for Object-Oriented Programming," *IEEE Trans. on Soft. Eng.*, vol. 18, no. 12, December 1992, pp. 1038-1044.

[WIL93] Wilde, N., R. Huitt, and P. Matthews, "Maintaining Object-Oriented Software," *IEEE Software*, January 1993, pp. 75-80.

Chapter

11

Wrapping Applications as Objects

One serious drawback to using object-oriented development for MIS applications is it doesn't help the old, legacy systems that still must be maintained. Many of these systems include pre-COBOL 74 code that might not support structured programming and might include ALTER GOTO or GOTO DEPENDING ON statements. Existing DBMS systems also might require controlled access to data structures, and questions of how these will be handled in OOCOBOL remain largely unanswered.

One technology that is showing promise in the area of maintaining existing COBOL systems is "wrapping" them as objects. The idea in wrapping existing applications is to define the data structures accessed by legacy systems and establish a set of operations that can be applied to those data structures. When this is accomplished, the existing systems appear from the outside to be objects that can receive requests and provide services just like any other objects. It makes no difference if the objects were developed using an OOPL or in traditional procedural programming languages as long as they provide services via a clearly defined interface.

While the benefits of wrapping applications are obvious, the challenges of wrapping existing legacy systems as objects might hinder their use in practice. Because most existing systems were not developed with an eye towards encapsulation, services, and formal interfaces, they must be modified to support an object-oriented view. Most existing applications also do not have adequate design specifications and are difficult to comprehend and modify.

In this chapter, I will introduce the concepts of object wrapping, discuss the options available for wrapping applications, goals and strategies, constraints, and report on experiences of organizations that have wrapped legacy systems. I also will cover reverse engineering (introduced in the previous chapter) in more detail, provide a partial list of available products, and discuss the use of GUI development and visual OOP tools to wrap existing applications. The experience section is limited because wrapping applications is a relatively new concept and there are few actual reports on object wrappers.

11.1 Introduction

An *object wrapper* is an automated component that provides an object-oriented interface to an existing system but still maintains the old implementation.

Wrapping existing systems as objects represents a strategy that organizations can use to migrate to object technology but must be considered in the larger picture of overall systems maintenance as described in the previous chapter. Maintaining systems, as previously defined, involves a variety of tasks, strategies, and requests for change, and object wrapping offers some benefits in specific areas of maintenance.

Wrapping applications provides a specific, formal interface for them that external programs can use to request services and brings the outward appearance of object-orientation to these existing systems. Systems that have specific interfaces are thought to be "wrapped" as objects if they can communicate by sending and receiving messages. Existing mainframe-based teleprocessing programs can be modified to support message-based programming with links to client applications on workstations. In some cases, macro languages and visual OOPL environments can be used to wrap existing applications with little modification to the existing system.

Many organizations are investigating wrapping as a tool to help them move towards client/server systems and many have had success in converting existing COBOL programs to support intelligent DBMS access. Because the majority of these systems are mainframe-based, there is a need to capture the data access and update components and isolate these from the user interface portions and the transaction processing functions. However, issues — including coordinating data, supporting security and integrity, and tracking and fixing bugs in wrapped systems — must be addressed prior to successfully adopting this approach.

Wrapping applications as objects supports the concepts of encapsulation, information hiding, messaging, and software layers. By wrapping system functions and data structures as objects and providing protocols for service requests, these legacy systems can benefit from these software engineering concepts. Wrapping existing systems should be done only when you have a clear vision of what benefits you will receive and what the associated costs will be.

When you consider the use of object wrappers in maintenance, you should recall the discussion in the previous chapters about the distinct portions of any application — presentation, functions or logic, and data access — and which portions that you will be focusing on in the wrapper. You might need to make significant changes to the application functionality for a legacy system, and this will dictate a very different approach to object wrapping than changes to the presentation or data access portion. Likewise, if you expect to make substantive changes to the entire application (i.e., all portions), than the wrapper approach you select might be quite different.

You also need to define your goals in using an object wrapper. If your goal is to migrate an existing system to object technology, than you expect to eventually replace the system with an object-oriented version. If, on the other hand, you plan to reuse portions of the existing system but have no short-term plans to replace it, then you have very different expectations for the wrapper.

11.2 The Concept of an Object Wrapper

The term object wrapper first was used by Dietrich of IBM [DIE89] and has been subsequently described in detail by Ian Graham. Most of the wrapping strategies described in this chapter come from the work of Graham as reported in *Object Magazine* [GRA92] [GRA93a] [GRA93b] [GRA93c] [GRA93d].

Wrapping existing applications involves defining their data structures and establishing a set of operations and services that can be requested by outside systems. An object wrapper can be used to provide an object-oriented interface to an existing system that still can maintain its old language, data structures, and functionality. Wrapping existing systems as objects is useful for adding the concepts of object-orientation to complex but stable legacy systems and allows organizations to create new objects when new features are required using an object-oriented approach.

The process of object wrapping requires building an abstraction, in the form of design specifications or models, for the existing system. Any existing application can be considered as an object having operations that map to the functions performed. These functions can be accessed via a command line, form, programming library, or GUI. The application must be wrapped to give it the outside appearance of an object. The wrapper defines the implementations of operations that are defined in the interface class representing the application. These operations will use existing functions to respond to requests for services.

The size and complexity of the wrapper will depend on the functionality of the application. For systems that operate from a command line, the wrapper might take the form of a script. For applications that use a screen interface, the wrapper might consist of code that reads and writes data from the screen. An implementation class definition for the wrapped system will provide information about how the object can be activated, its location, and its polices of use. The wrapper receives messages from external objects or systems, translates them for the legacy system, and decodes and formats the output for return to the requester. Figure 11.1 shows a logical representation of an object wrapper for a DBMS application.

One method for wrapping legacy systems is to capture or extract the data structures and functions in specification form to use as a basis for building an object wrapper. Before a system can be wrapped as an object, its functionality and data structures must be well understood. Two representations are essential for program understanding: structure and function. The *structure* of an application defines the hierarchical relation of the physical components of a system, while the *function* describes the functionality provided by the system.

To accomplish this, you first must view the wrapped application as providing definite services to external systems and the wrapper as a means of providing communication with the existing system. Typically, this wrapper provides access to the data in the legacy system, and a message must be sent to the

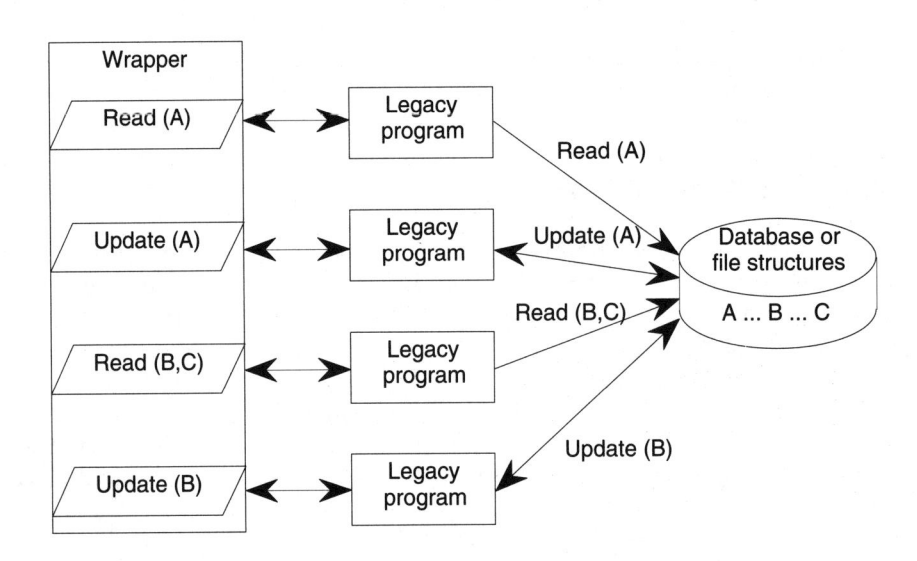

Figure 11.1
Example object wrapper for legacy system.

wrapper requesting any information. For example, an existing CICS COBOL application that consists of several programs, a menu, and screens can be wrapped so that object methods are defined for each menu option, and parameters passed for the required fields.

11.3 Benefits of Object Wrappers

The potential benefits of object wrappers for legacy systems are described in the following paragraphs.

Migration of existing systems to object-orientation — Object wrappers allow organizations to realize the benefits of object-orientation by making their legacy systems appear as objects from the outside. By wrapping these systems as objects, they can be viewed and used externally as objects that provide services via clearly defined interfaces. Wrappers also allow the organization to continue migrating to object technology without ignoring their existing systems.

Reuse of data and functions in existing systems — By defining and specifying the data structures and operations of legacy systems, this information can be considered in the same manner as classes or objects in an object-oriented system and can be reused in other systems. Once data structures and services are defined, they can be integrated into future systems as reusable components. Organizations that have a significant investment in business logic and complex processing can reap the benefits of these systems without loosing their initial investment. If you plan not to replace the existing system and are looking only for potential reusable components, than your expectations and strategy will be significantly different.

Movement toward client/server (GUI as a front-end to legacy systems) — Wrapping existing mainframe systems as objects also allows organizations to take a step toward client/server applications, because defining the data structures and services can be a first step in isolating the presentation of the information from these functions. With clearly defined services, these legacy systems can be migrated to GUI and/or distributed environments, where front-ends can be designed and built to interface with these services. For example, mainframe-based legacy systems can be migrated to Unix SQL servers on a LAN, with their functions or logic as RPCs. This view also supports the software layers approach described in previous chapters and the use of middleware in client/server applications.

Enhance existing systems using an incremental approach — without continuing to change large, monolithic systems, organizations can modify them using a wrapper approach to include new functions or features, which are implemented as objects and methods. Using this approach allows an organization to move in increments towards object technology without having to rewrite their old systems. As new functionality in object-oriented systems takes over for the legacy system, the old system can be phased out or disabled.

Reduced complexity of existing systems based on redesign and redevelopment of the most costly or complex functions/programs as objects — Organizations can identify those modules or programs that are the most complex and error-prone and model, redesign, and reimplement them in OOCOBOL. This approach can reduce the cost of maintenance, because these programs/modules are most likely the cause most of the errors or problems in maintenance.

11.4 Types of Object Wrappers

Object wrappers, by their very nature, will be designed, built, and implemented differently depending on the type of system that they are developed for. Many organizations build object wrappers for mainframe-based, online file and database entry and update systems, such as CICS IMS applications. Other organizations require a GUI front-end or are using a RDBMS and moving towards SQL-based file servers. Still other organizations are expending most of their maintenance resources finding and fixing bugs or errors in a small percentage of their existing systems. Some organizations might be looking for reuse of key functions or data structures in their legacy systems and are not planning on replacing them anytime soon.

The nature of the requirement for a wrapper will dictate the type of wrapper used. A number of different styles or types of object wrappers have been proposed [GRA93b], including those described in the following paragraphs.

Handshake: Where a wrapper carries duplicate data between a legacy system and a new object-oriented system keeping both copies up to date and synchronized. This approach requires duplicated live data, so there will be problems with data integrity and security and double the storage requirements, etc., and this approach generally is not beneficial for migration to object technology or reuse.

Borrow: Where an old system is wrapped so that messages can be received by it and data can be borrowed from the legacy system for use in other systems.

This data, once borrowed, will be invalid after a period of time, or an update mechanism must be built into the wrapper to support the handshake type described previously. This approach requires that existing data be copied to new objects as it is used, it is difficult to manage updates to the data after it has been borrowed, and there are questions about when the old data and system can be eliminated.

Take-over: This wrapper migrates the data in an existing system to an object-oriented system, manages access to the new data, and provides the functionality of the old system. The existing system must be defined in terms of its data structures and functions, and a new object-oriented system eventually must take over these functions for this approach to work. This approach requires that the data must be migrated to the new object-oriented system and that questions about the data integrity, the cost, and whether the object wrapper will have to send messages to external objects, which adds complexity to the wrapper, must be considered.

Translation: This method uses a traditional object-oriented analysis (OOA) to identify classes, objects, attributes, and operations in the old system and to translate them into an object-oriented design and implementation. This approach, which is a subset of the take-over one in the previous paragraph, requires good object models, a translation strategy, and a lengthy and costly development process to build the new system, including staff training, tool and method acquisition, etc. The translation approach can use *reverse engineering* tools to build models and specifications for the existing system. The translation option partition portions of the existing data structures with related functions and encapsulate them into new objects.

Data-centered translation: A subset of translation approach that uses data structures as the focal point for translating the system as described in the previous paragraph. Because most of the reverse engineering tools that are available focus on data structures or files, this approach is the one most often used in translation.

These different types of object wrappers might share similarities, or even overlap in their purpose, but they generally are used for different reasons and with different goals and objectives. Factors that affect the choice of which strategy to use include system type, structure, and availability of documentation. For example, GUI front ends typically perform a handshake or borrow function, while the take-over and translation strategies require more complex wrappers and more detailed information on the existing system.

11.5 Strategies for Wrapping Objects

As previously stated, object wrappers can be beneficial as another tool for maintaining existing systems and migrating to object technology. Wrapping systems as objects can be accomplished using a variety of methods and tools, including reverse engineering or design recovery tools, GUI front-ends, and CASE repositories. In this section, I will provide a map of the different types of wrappers based on recommendations from [GRA93c] for the use of the wrappers in maintenance. Figure 11.2 represents recommendations for the use of wrapper strategies mapped to the goals of wrappers that were described in section 11.1.

In general, object wrappers work best for mature, stable systems that can be frozen from significant change until they are rebuilt using object technology. In most cases, object wrappers should be considered as a short-term solution and should not be expected to support extended functionality over an extended period of time. When the goal of an object wrapper is reuse, the wrapper can support system functions for the life of the legacy application, but this assumes that the existing system satisfies existing needs and is stable. In general, wrappers allow organizations to incrementally migrate to object-oriented development, but they usually cannot be used to postpone this migration forever.

The wrapper strategies can be considered in terms of the portions of applications that they are best suited for supporting or migrating. For example, the

Reason/ Strategy	Migration to object-orientation	Reuse of components	Extension to existing system	Front-end with additional functions (GUI)	Reduce existing system complexity
Handshake	N	N	N	N	N
Borrow	N	Y	Y	Y	N
Take-over	?	N	N	N	N
Translation	?	N	Y	Y	?
Data-centered translation	Y	N	Y	Y	Y
Reverse engineering	Y	Y	Y	Y	Y

Figure 11.2 Strategies for wrapping Objects.

first three options — handshake, borrow, and take-over — often are used for wrapping the data access part of a system, while the translation option typically is used for migration of entire systems to object technology. The handshake strategy often is used when there is little or no overlap in data between the old and the new system or when the goal of the wrapper is reuse.

The borrow strategy is well suited for reuse, system extension, and GUI front ends but not for migration, because it might require changing the functionality of the old system. As with the handshake option, borrowing data can be beneficial when there is a clear split between the old and new system functionality.

The take-over method is a questionable strategy except for migration to object technology, because it allows incremental replacement of existing systems with objects and messages. The borrow and take-over strategies have significant technical drawbacks, which will be described in later sections. All three of these options — the handshake, borrow, and take-over — might not be suited for eventual replacement of the legacy system, because they require significant up-front effort, which is difficult to recapture in any subsequent object-oriented development effort.

The translation strategy, while costly, represents the best option for migration, extension, and GUI front ends. The complexity of the data management portion of the legacy system will dictate how practical it is to translate the system. For example, translation works well when the existing system was built using functional decomposition, because objects can be encapsulated from the entities in the data model and the functions in the DFDs.

Reverse engineering represents the best approach but requires automated tools and support from a maintenance group. One approach is to use reverse engineering tools to import existing system data or file structures, create a data model, and use a CRUD matrix to map functions to data (i.e., the data-centered translation strategy). The primary consideration here is the complexity of the data model and the type and structure of the code in the system.

In some cases, reverse engineering tools can support automated migration from one DBMS or file structure to another. For example, the Bachman Reengineering Product Set supports migration from VSAM or IMS to DB2. With this approach, the product identifies all the programs and functions that access the data structures so that they can be changed to use the new file access mechanisms. This approach generally works best when the application being migrated doesn't have overly complex functionality.

Wrappers developed to support a GUI interface or intelligent front-end can add new functions that were built using a GUI development tool. The exception to this approach is when the existing system has a strong data centered view or when the benefits of migration are large enough to justify building a complex wrapper (i.e., the take-over or translation strategy). One approach would be to wrap the presentation portion of the application using a GUI development tool, perhaps Micro Focus Dialog System, then migrate the data access portion using translation, and finally reengineer the application logic using a traditional object-oriented analysis, design, and implementation approach in OOCOBOL.

As you consider maintenance of existing systems, you will find that corrective maintenance tasks are usually not appropriate for object wrapping, while preventative, adaptive, and perfective requests can be accomplished using a wrapping strategy. For example, if your goals are migration to object technology and extension of an existing system, you can change the functionality of the system with a focus on objects and messages. One method for this type of conversion would be to take the data-centered translation approach, capture the data structures in an object model, develop and implement a borrow wrapper that interfaces with the legacy system, then extend the system by adding new objects that interact with the wrapper.

If on the other hand, your goal is to reuse existing legacy system components, then your approach will be quite different. For those legacy systems that are not being replaced and already contain complex functional or business logic that can be reused, you can use reverse engineering tools to capture models and specifications, which can be used in maintenance. Once these components have been identified and captured, they can be placed into a reusable components library for use on other projects.

11.6 Wrapper Methods and Tools

As organizations undertake their wrapper development efforts, they have a variety of methods and tools available that can help them. While some of these tools provide automated support for the development effort, much manual work still is required to ensure consistency and completeness of the wrapper.

Data access or DBMS wrappers often use reverse engineering tools to identify entities in a file system or database. Because file and database structures are static and often defined in copy books or schemas, these structures can be captured easily and used to create data models. When entities are identified using this approach, two types of objects are found in most legacy systems: domain objects, which are stable and generic and represent persistent aspects of the application, and application objects, which represent variable (by time, place, etc.) aspects of the system. It is important to recognize the different types and treat them differently with respect to migration to object technology.

For example, one approach might be to wrap all domain objects together into a single interface, while another would be to wrap portions individually. The former approach might not work for complex data structures, while the latter might work well for systems with isolated domains. The role of the OMG CORBA standard in the use of these types of wrappers for distributed systems will be beneficial when all development tools support the standard. More on distributed systems and the OMG in Chapter 14.

11.6.1 Design Recovery and Reverse Engineering

A formal approach to software engineering creates a number of artifacts, work products, or deliverables as part of the development process. In this formal development life cycle, work products are created at each stage of the development process and these deliverables help to define and communicate the complexities of the software product at various stages of development. For example, consider a development method that creates data, process and control models in the requirements specification phase; application and database design specifications in the design phase; and actual source code and file/database structures in the coding phase. These deliverables can be used to help understand the resulting software system once it is in an evolution or maintenance phase.

Unfortunately, many organizations have not been using formal software development methods, and many existing legacy systems do not have corresponding specifications or models that represent accurate system structure or behavior. Without specifications or models for these systems, maintenance is often is hazardous, difficult, and time-consuming and any change made might cause a ripple effect in the system. For instance, a change to a data element that is used in several programs can lead to errors or bugs in different parts of a system.

As a result of missing or incomplete specifications, many maintenance staffs spend the majority of their time simply trying to figure out what their existing systems are doing. One set of products that holds much promise in helping organizations better maintain and enhance existing systems are *reverse engineering tools*.

Reverse engineering, as defined in the previous chapter, is an automated process of creating design specifications and, in some cases, models of an existing implementation of a software system. The process involves evaluating existing source code and database structures and creating specifications that represent aspects of these systems in a CASE repository. Reverse engineering is the opposite of forward engineering where design specifications are used to create source and executable code. Another term that often is used and is synonymous with reverse engineering is *design recovery*.

Some aspects of reverse engineering are easier to implement than other types because of the nature of deriving specifications from existing systems. The process of extracting file and database structure information from existing systems now is available from a variety of CASE tool vendors. A partial list of reverse engineering or design recovery products are listed in Figure 11.3.

The process of reverse engineering or design recovery actually is simple and straight forward. Recalling Figure 10.7 in the previous chapter, reverse engineering consists of the tasks described in the following paragraphs.

Data from existing systems (for which there is insufficient or incomplete specifications or models) are exported to source files prior to using the reverse engineering tool. These files might contain database schemas or file definitions for various systems, including VSAM, DB2, Oracle, Informix, as well as screen definitions (i.e., 3270-based screens, etc.).

Within the reverse engineering tool, the source file from the previous step is selected and the product populates the target CASE Encyclopedia from the information in the source files. In the case of a database schema, an entity-relationship diagram is created with attributes, entities, access paths, indexes and relationships. In the case of 3270-based screens or menus, maps are defined in the encyclopedia with the layouts and fields.

Once these design specifications and models are loaded into the CASE tool, they can be modified and used to maintain and regenerate new systems. The process of reverse engineering the specifications and models saves considerable effort that would be required to capture the same information manually without reverse engineering. Also, once the specifications and models are captured in the CASE tool, reports and documentation can be produced to help facilitate the maintenance process.

Product and Vendor	Source Code Supported	Platforms Supported
Application Browser from Hypersoft Corp.	COBOL	IBM PC/DOS and VAX/VMS
COBOL/Structuring Facility from IBM	COBOL	IBM System/370 MVS & VM
Excelerator for Design Recovery from Intersolv	COBOL, IMS, and CICS/BMS maps	IBM PC/DOS & OS/2
InterCASE Reverse Engineering from InterPort	COBOL, C, BMS & MFS maps	IBM PC/DOS, VAX/VMS, Unix and IBM System/370 MVS
PM/SS from Adpac	PL/1, IMS/DL1, CICS, and VSAM	IBM System/370 MVS
ProDoc from Scandura	Ada, C, COBOL, Pascal, and FORTRAN	IBM PC/DOS
Q/Auditor from Eden Systems	COBOL & PL/1	IBM PC/DOS and System/370 MVS & VM
RE-SPEC from Software Products & Services	FORTRAN & Pascal	IBM PC/DOS, VAX/VMS, Unix, and IBM/370 MVS
Reengineering Product Set from Bachman	COBOL, VSAM, ISAM, IDMS, and DB2	IBM PC/DOS and OS/2
RevEnge from Alben Software	C	IBM PC/DOS
Reverse DBMS from Chen & Associates	VSAM, IMS, ADR, IDMS, DataCom DB, etc.	IBM PC/DOS
SuperCASE SCI from Advanced Technology Intl.	FORTRAN	VAX/VMS

Figure 11.3
Available reverse engineering tools.

When an existing system is reverse engineered, the resulting design specifications can be used to build a replacement system using object orientation or to facilitate building an object wrapper for the system. In either case, the resulting documentation also can help your staff maintain the legacy system in the future. Data structure definitions can be used to identify potential classes, objects, attributes, and relationships in existing systems, while program structure and logic can be used to identify methods and services.

Marijana Tomic of IBM describes experiences using COBOL Structuring Facility and an object-oriented re-engineering process [TOM94]. This paper discusses an approach that focuses on modularization of COBOL programs by replacing single large compilation units with a functionally equivalent collection of smaller units. Two approaches to this process are described in the paper, including a data-centered and an object-oriented modularization method, along with the problem of COBOL aliases in the process.

11.6.2 Capturing Classes/Objects from Legacy Systems

Another approach to migrating legacy systems to object-orientation is to recover potential classes, objects, and methods from existing systems. Systems built using functional design methods typically have high data coupling between modules. When extracting potential classes and objects from these systems, data structures that represent related entities normally are grouped together because they tend to be used or modified together. Examining the aggregate data structures in these systems can help detect the presence of potential objects and classes.

A subprogram's parameters also can help identify objects. If a subprogram is passed different parameters on different invocations, the actual parameters might contain different objects belonging to a class and part of the subroutine can form methods of the class. The tasks of finding local and global objects is hindered by the nature of programming. Data structures can be defined locally or be shared by many programs or modules.

When a data model is available or captured via a tool, it can be the basis for an object model, as described in chapter 6. The functional model, if available, can be used to identify methods and messages, but the models must be integrated to support encapsulation. Also, when a 3270-based system is wrapped, the function keys can be mapped to GUI events and managed by macros or visual development tools such as Microsofts' Visual Basic or Asymentrixs' Toolbook.

A recent OOPSLA workshop [FRA93] compared wrapping applications to reverse engineering them. Based on their own experiences, the workshop members recommend that organizations evaluate how they can capture and maintain artifacts from their existing systems, re-engineer their systems using an incremental approach, and begin by focusing on a portion of the system. They reported that re-engineering was less risky than wrapping systems. The members identified a series of steps in a re-engineering process for a legacy system, as shown in Figure 11.4, which include those described in the following paragraphs.

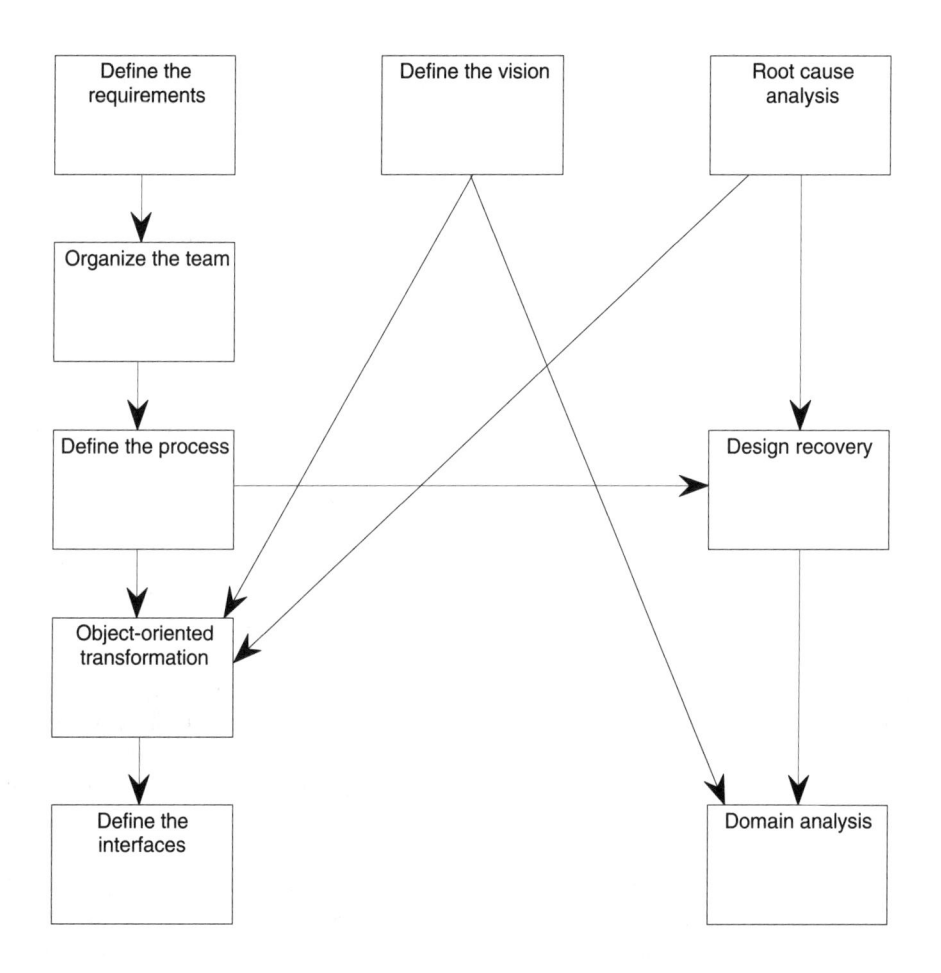

Figure 11.4
A re-engineering process.

Define the vision for the re-engineering process. Educate the team members, managers, and users about the process, its goals, tasks, objectives, and expected results.

Define the requirements for re-engineering. Make sure that you are solving the correct problem, identify constraints on the process, existing hardware, system interdependencies, performance, market-window, costs, etc. Specify the requirements and review them for agreement by all interested parties.

Organize the team. Form, organize, and educate the re-engineering team in the methods and tools used. Establish a team leader who has responsibility and authority to oversee the process and manage the results.

Define the re-engineering process. Specify the methods and tools that are required for the effort, identify the roles and responsibilities of staff, deliverables, etc.

Transform systems to object orientation. Goals of the re-engineering effort should be making the system more maintainable, developing models and specifications for the existing software, analyzing the domain, identifying classes and objects, etc. Automated tools combined with manual effort can result in object models and specifications, as well as documentation for the existing system.

Define the interfaces. Technical and business decisions should be captured in an enterprise-wide model of the application domains. Focus on the interfaces between subsystems in the legacy system and specify these interfaces in a repository or formal document reviewed by all parties.

Perform root-cause analysis. Identify undesired properties of the legacy system within the re-engineering project, and eliminate redundancies, error-prone modules, integrity problems, etc.

Recover design specifications. Recover design specifications from any available documents as well as from the existing system using available automated tools and manual effort. The goal should be to identify the structure of the systems, along with the data and functions that are supported so that an integrated set of models can be built.

Analyze the domain. Identify business models from the legacy system or develop object wrappers to enable reuse of the system, including functionality and data access. The goal of domain analysis, as described in Chapter 6, is to identify key abstractions and mechanisms in the problem domain for possible reuse in other domains.

Another interesting approach to reverse engineering object-oriented components from existing systems is described by Ong and Tsai [ONG93]. They have built a prototype of a semiautomatic process to examine aggregated data structures in legacy systems and detect the presence of objects and classes. Their automatic class/object extractor can be used for migration to object technology, identification of reusable or redundant components, and specification of wrapper objects in legacy systems. While their approach focused on FORTRAN systems, they are working on improving the process and supporting other languages in the future.

The Ong/Tsai approach identifies classes and object based on the assumption that data structures that are related usually are grouped or used together. They identify potential classes and objects by looking at groups of data structures and parameters passed between subroutines. They also suggest focusing on included files or copy books as a starting point for classes or objects and on subroutines as sources for methods or operations. In the application of their process to a large FORTRAN system (18,000 lines of code), they extracted 70 potential classes and found 20 distinct classes.

11.6.3 Object Wrapping Tools

As organizations investigate their options and strategies for object wrappers, they should recognize that there are a variety of tools available, from simple, inexpensive GUI development products (such as Visual Basic) to complex, expensive reverse engineering products that can be beneficial. Any acquisition of these tools should be done with an eye towards the cost of the tools, the training required, and the expected benefits. In this section, I will discuss a few of the more practical object wrapper tools on the market to give readers a flavor for the types of products available.

Digitalk PARTS Wrappers

Digitalk offers several products under their parts assembly and reuse tool set (PARTS), including PARTS COBOL and CICS Wrappers, that can be used to wrap existing COBOL CICS programs as objects. The PARTS Wrappers use a Smalltalk interface wrapped around the existing COBOL CICS code, and most of the users of the Digitalk PARTS Wrappers have used them to build a GUI around an existing COBOL CICS application. In PARTS, all components are considered to be objects, with clearly defined interfaces and messages that can be passed back and forth.

The CICS Wrapper allows CICS applications to be compiled on the PC under OS/2, identifies the linkage section for data used in the program, and builds PARTS components that activate this data. However, the process is not without problems, including mapping the control, integrity, and security features in a CICS application as objects and messages.

The COBOL Wrapper allows existing COBOL systems to be compiled and linked in Micro Focus COBOL and to create a DLL with the COBOL subprograms, which can be called by other PARTS components. The PARTS COBOL Wrapper generates a PARTS message for each COBOL subprogram, maps the COBOL data structures into PARTS events and messages, and creates a buffer of linkage section data to be used as arguments for calls to the COBOL subprograms.

IBM's System Object Model

IBM offers System Object Model (SOM) and Distributed SOM as a possible product for object wrapping and plans to introduce COBOL bindings in 1994. SOM is an operating system interface that allows objects to communicate regardless of which language they were created in or which platform they are operating on. DSOM supports the OMG CORBA standard and lets objects communicate over a LAN or WAN environment. Existing legacy systems can be wrapped as objects using SOM or DSOM bindings that allow them to be viewed externally as objects that support services via messages.

Currently, IBM offers SOM and DSOM language bindings for C and C++ only but plans to support COBOL in the coming year. Micro Focus also has announced plans to support SOM and DSOM objects in a forthcoming version of their Object COBOL Option. IBM offers a SOMobjects Developer Toolkit for $365 (OS/2) and $585 (AIX), which includes a SOM compiler and class libraries.

VOOP Tools

Various other products can be used for object wrapping, most notably the GUI development tools and visual object-oriented programming language (VOOP) environments. Of these, Micro Focus Dialog System (DS) supports the capture of CICS BMS mapsets or IMS MFS format screens that can be used to generate GUI front ends. With this approach, existing character-based 3270 screens can be imported into DS, rebuilt for a GUI environment (such as Windows or OS/2 PM), and a Host Connect Facility will manage the interface between DS and the 3270 commutations software. The DS data access facility supports a variety of data structures, including Btrieve, DB/2 OS/2 Database Manager, and XDB for OS/2. Using a data-centered translation approach, an existing DB/2 database could be migrated to OS/2 and the CICS screens and functions could be ported into DS.

Any of the other VOOP tools described in the previous chapter also can be used for object wrapping, primarily for SQL-based data access. Examples include Visual Age from IBM, Visual Object from Computer Associates, and VisualWorks from ParcPlace. Visual Age supports VSAM, IMS, and DB/2 data access under OS/2. Visual Object supports SQL and open database connectivity (ODB) data access under Windows NT and OS/2. VisualWorks supports Oracle and Sybase data access, along with access to 48 other databases via the EDA/SQL gateway, under Windows, OS/2, System 7 (Macintosh), and several flavors of Unix.

11.7 Rationale for Wrapping Applications

Given all these strategies, types, methods, and tools for object wrapping, when is it best to use an object wrapper? To answer this question, I will reintroduce the benefits of object wrapping (from section 11.3) and discuss each type of wrapper and potential products that might be used to support these types.

To *reuse* existing system components, you can use reverse engineering tools and domain analysis, followed by an OOD and OOP process if you plan to replace the system. Reusable components can be identified in the existing system with the help of reverse engineering tools; however, before these components can be used, they must be checked for redundancies against other components as described by McCabe's life cycle in the previous chapter. If you plan only to reuse, and not replace, the existing system, then the system data structures and functions should be documented in a repository or reuse library so that they can be found when needed. If you plan to replace the existing system but reuse some or all the components, the resulting data structures and functions can be encapsulated into objects, and a traditional OOD/OOP process follows this step.

To *migrate* to object technology, you can borrow, handshake, take-over or translate the data, then later use an object-oriented development life cycle (i.e., OOA, OOD, and OOP) to transfer portions of the application into objects and messages. One approach would be to use the data structures identified as initial objects and classes, migrate or take-over the data, followed by the presentation portion (using a GUI front-end), then migrate the application logic.

To *enhance* or *extend* existing systems in increments, you could borrow or handshake the data, then translate or take-over it, and implement any changes in increments using an OOD/OOP process and tools. For example, you might take an existing VSAM CICS application, use the handshake or borrow strategy to build a data access wrapper, translate the data into a SQL-based database with a GUI front-end, then make any additional changes in the GUI development environment. Complex business logic could be kept on the mainframe until the migration to SQL, when it would have to be replicated in the GUI development tool or as object methods.

To add an intelligent front-end or GUI to an existing system or *migrate to client/server*, you probably would borrow or handshake the data, then develop and maintain the functionality in a GUI tool in a similar fashion to the one described earlier. Distributed systems standards, including DCE and CORBA, should support better interfaces and remote access in the future.

To *reduce complexity* of an existing legacy system, you can isolate the presentation, application logic, and data access in the system, then use reverse engineering to identify modules or programs with the highest levels of complexity. Once identified, these modules or programs could be redesigned and built to reduce their complexity, with or without the help of automated tools (i.e., restructuring tools).

Of the strategies introduced in section 11.5, the translation approach has proven successful on several projects. The results of the translation are an object-oriented description of an existing system. Because reverse engineering products still are quite limited, Grahm suggests the following strategy for wrapping existing applications:

1. Build an object wrapper that communicates using object-oriented components and *borrow* the data in the legacy system.
2. Perform an Object-Oriented Analysis on the legacy system and create an object model. If reverse engineering tools are available, use them to document the system and identify potential classes, objects, attributes, and methods. This step was covered in more detail in the previous chapter.
3. Use the *translation* strategy to migrate the application to object-orientation. Take the object model built in step 2, perform an object-oriented design, followed by an implementation in OOCOBOL.

Wrapping existing applications, while beneficial, is not without drawbacks or limitations, as identified in [DIE89]. These constraints include those described in the following paragraphs.

Object-wrapper developers are not free to choose the best representation for the problem in object-oriented terms because they must keep the existing system operational. This can lead to wrappers that are a bad mix of unstructured CICS COBOL and objects and messages. The resulting wrapper can be difficult to maintain and of little value in the migration to object technology.

Developers must expose the existing system's functionality or protect it from change; usually this means only allowing read-access to the system's data (i.e., borrow) and requires that the existing system be studied in depth to define its functions. Building an object wrapper requires a detailed understanding of the existing system, and this can be a costly effort when there is little or no useful documentation for the system. Failure to completely understand a system when a wrapper is built might result in a wrapper that is invalid or incomplete and of little practical use.

An object wrapper must preserve the state of the data in production systems, which includes security and integrity. This often is difficult to do without massive redundancy of data and functionality. Existing systems that have security and integrity constraints must have wrappers that enforce the same functions and features or the data can be compromised. Redundant security and integrity functions can lead to inconsistencies between the existing system and the wrapper.

Garbage collection and memory management must be synchronized with the legacy system so that, when objects are created and destroyed, they are added or deleted from the existing system. This synchronization problem is similar to the previous replication problem, but pertains more to the question of what happens to data when it is added or removed from a legacy system. System performance issues can make this an even more difficult problem.

In addition, any attempt to reuse existing software components must be undertaken with consideration for the GIGO rule: Garbage in equals garbage out. If an existing legacy system has erroneous, incomplete, or inaccurate data, this data will not be fixed automatically by the wrapper. If data needs to be corrected and the wrapper is responsible for doing so, this adds complexity to the wrapper and brings up issues of synchronization of data between the legacy system and the wrapper. The overriding consideration for GIGO is the cost of fixing this data versus the cost of keeping it the same.

While object wrappers can be beneficial when used in the right circumstances, they are not without their own limitations or drawbacks, many of which I already have discussed. These include limited reverse engineering support for business logic; difficulty understanding complex code; consideration of special subsystems (i.e., replacements for VSAM or CICS written in assembler); code, data, and functional duplication; integrity; security; and synchronization.

This leads to a final question regarding object wrappers: When is to not a good idea to use an object wrapper? As you already have seen, object wrappers can be beneficial for solving specific maintenance problems. Not all problems can be solved by wrapping an existing system as an object. Certain types of legacy systems might not be suited for object wrappers. For example, dynamic legacy systems (i.e., systems that change dramatically over a short period of time), systems that have complex data management portions, and systems that offer little of value for reuse are all types that might not benefit from object wrappers.

11.8 Example Problem

Recalling the Library problem, you received a modification request (#4) in the previous chapter to wrap the existing system so that it can send a message to the student financial system indicating those users that have overdue fees. These overdue fees should be added to any outstanding funds students owe the university.

Discussion: This change request requires that you interface the Library system with an external system (in this case the university financial system). To wrap the existing system, you first must identify your goals, examine the strategies for wrapping, and discuss practical issues related to implementing a wrapper for this purpose.

Assuming that your goal in this endeavor is to eventually migrate the student financial system (SFS) to object technology and perhaps enhance the system using an incremental approach, you probably would initially use the handshake approach, followed by the take-over or translation method.

If you use the handshake method, you would have to define the data required, which in this case is the student data (Id, name, and amount overdue), as well as the service provided, in this case a message can be sent from the Library system to the SFS requesting that their account be debited with the amount overdue. Following this, you would review the SFS to find out how a students' financial data can be modified, what security and integrity constraints are in place, and what exception conditions might occur if a request is invalid. Possible exception conditions include invalid or unregistered student, unauthorized request, etc. Any object wrapper you build must take into consideration possible exceptions and account for changes to the amount due over time.

While it is impractical to spend too much time here guessing about how this request actually might be resolved, I provide it simply as a vehicle for discussion purposes.

11.9 Case Studies in Wrapping Applications

As organizations apply object wrapping to their legacy systems, they can benefit from the experiences of others who have used wrappers themselves. While there are not a large number of experiential reports on the use of object wrappers in the literature, the following three studies describe in some detail experiences with object wrapping.

Citicorp

Citicorp has over 100 million lines of COBOL code in their legacy systems and has been wrapping their applications for several years. Developers at Citicorp identified objects and relationships between objects business services and discovered that finding the objects was difficult because the technology was immature. They also found that wrapping was not very beneficial because it did not remove or resolve outstanding technical issues (i.e., integrity, security, synchronization, etc.).

They used the following wrapping process:

1. Perform a top-down analysis (i.e., structured or functional decomposition) of their business areas and identify subject areas, classes, an architecture and framework, etc.

2. Perform a bottom-up business process analysis (BPA) or reverse engineering of their existing systems using objects as active participants. Study the interaction of objects, and which objects are in rich terms, identify large-grained objects that encapsulate business behavior, and find where these services are performed in the legacy system.

3. Create an outside view of each object and define its interface along with any new business objects, then implement these as wrappers for the legacy system.

4. Build a hierarchy of business objects (i.e., a framework) and test it against the actual business systems to ensure that it supports all the key functions and mechanisms.

As a result of this process, Citocorp staff built several sets of models, including:

- Structural — representing the relationships between objects
- Functional — representing how each works (this model turned out to be much more complex than the structural model)

- Business — using BPA and reverse engineering tools, looking at communications, work flow, etc.

Citicorp found that there were many difficult technical issues for wrapping legacy systems, and the implementation of services still held them back. They also found that they could overlay legacy systems with wrappers only when they understood how the business actually works. This required significant analysis of the existing business functions.

Deere & Company

Deere and Company placed a message-based front-end on some of their existing applications that allowed them to migrate their mainframe-based systems towards client/server. Originally, Deere and Company had a plan to construct an enterprise-wide runtime object model that allowed logical access to all their objects, but they subsequently have scaled back this effort to look at key problem domains as starting points for wrapping.

The object wrappers developed at Deere and Company were written in C++ but incorporate a variety of object technology, including Enfin, PARTS, and VisualWorks. Developers built a logical object model with late binding for their parts system and related data stores in their existing functional model to transactions and images (i.e., take-over). The object wrapper has knowledge of the internal structure of the data, receives requests, retrieves the data (regardless of where it is or in which format it is stored), and returns the data to the requester. Raster and vector data are stored separately but are provided by the wrapper at run time.

The initial wrapper system was developed for an engineering imaging system to help identify reusable parts. Developers did not create an API for each object but are considering this approach in the future to allow other systems to access the data by looking at the data flows in the functional model. The functional model existed for the parts system, in a CASE repository or, in some cases, in paper-form, and the object model was built from these models.

Deere and Company created their own object tool kit to support late binding, polymorphism, and dynamic creation of objects in their wrapper. Developers found the technical problems were not well understood when they began the wrapper project, and there was insufficient support for languages and tools available. Developers plan to build a big, deep enterprise-wide object model for their systems in the future but recognize that this will take significantly longer. Their next project will incorporate geometric data from their existing systems into the wrapper [BOZ91].

EDS

EDS developed wrapper code that could be shared across multiple applications based on shared entities, attributes, and functions. Their legacy systems manage a group of related concepts, each of which was represented as wrapper objects.

EDS built legacy access code to create and populate wrapper objects from the existing data (i.e., the borrow strategy), update the existing data when appropriate, and translate messages sent to the wrapper into function calls or commands for the legacy system.

EDS staff identified three ways of providing wrappers to existing systems:

- Via direct database access, where data in existing systems is accessed, but not updated, and presented to outside objects (i.e., borrow).
- Via terminal emulation, where data can be accessed and updated via an interface that manages edits and controls access to existing data (i.e., handshake).
- Via application programming interfaces (APIs), where messages are received and translated into appropriate function calls in the existing system (i.e., take-over).

All three wrapper options require mapping the existing data structures or database entities to the objects, identifying functions (services) provided, and translating these services into requests and messages [CUM94].

11.10 References

[BIG89]	Biggerstaff, T. J., "Design Recovery for Maintenance and Reuse," *IEEE Computer*, vol. 22, no. 7, pp. 30-49, 1989.
[BOZ91]	Bozman, J. S., "Wrapping Code Can Save Time," *ComputerWorld*, May 12, 1991.
[CUM94]	Cummins, F. A. and M. H. Ibrahim, "Wrapping Legacy Applications," *First Class*, vol. IV, issue II, pp. 10-20.
[DIE89]	Dietrich, W. C., L. R. Nackman, and F. Gracer, "Saving a Legacy with Objects," *Proceedings of OOPSLA '89*, N. Meyrowitz (ed.), Addison-Wesley, 1989.

[EWA93] Ewald, A. and M. Roy, "Why Object Technology is Good for Systems Integration," *Object Magazine*, January-February 1993, pp. 60-63.

[FRA93] Fraser, S., "Re-Engineering Design Trade-offs in a Legacy Context," *OOPSLA '93 conference proceedings*, pp. 115-117.

[GRA2] Grahm, I., "Interoperation: Reusing Existing Software Components and Packages," *Object Magazine*, November-December 1992, pp. 36-37.

[GRA93a] Grahm, I., "Interoperation: Reusing Existing Software Components and Packages," *Object Magazine*, January-February 1993, pp. 22-24.

[GRA93b] Grahm, I., "Interoperation: Reusing Existing Software Components and Packages," *Object Magazine*, March-April 1993, pp. 25-26.

[GRA93c] Grahm, I., "Interoperation: Reusing Existing Software Components and Packages," *Object Magazine*, May-June 1993, pp. 26-28.

[GRA93d] Grahm, I., "Interoperation: Reusing Existing Software Components and Packages," *Object Magazine*, July-August 1993, page 36.

[GRA91] Grass, J. E., "Design Archaeology for Object-Oriented Redesign in C++," *proceedings of the TOOLS5 conference*, Prentice-Hall, 1991.

[JAC91] Jacobson, I., "Re-Engineering of Old Systems to an Object-Oriented Architecture," *proceedings of OOPSLA '91*, pp. 340-350.

[ONG93] Ong, C. L. and W. T. Tsai, "Class and Object Extraction from Imperative Code," *JOOP*, March-April 1993, pp. 58-68.

[REI91] Reiss, S. P., "Tools for Object-Oriented Redesign," *proceedings of the TOOLS5 conference*, Prentice-Hall, 1991.

[SNE92] Sneed, H. M., "Migration of Proceduraly Oriented COBOL Programs to Object-Oriented Architecture," *proceedings of the Conference on Software Maintenance*, Nov. 9-12, 1992, pp. 105-116.

[TOM94] Tomic, M., "A Possible Approach to Object-Oriented Reengineering of COBOL Programs," *ACM SIGSOFT*, vol. 19, no. 2 (April 1994), pp. 29-34.

Managing Object-Oriented COBOL Development

Chapter 12

Managing any software engineering effort requires technical as well as cultural or people skills. Because software engineering is a social process, much of managing software development relates to understanding, motivating, and guiding people. Traditional software management involves several distinct tasks, including setting goals, assigning resources, planning tasks, tracking progress, monitoring deliverables, etc.

Managing an object-oriented development project represents a dramatic change from traditional software engineering management. As you have seen in other chapters, object-oriented development involves new and interesting twists on a typical application project. These include the use of prototyping and iteration, evolution of work product, the duel goals of reuse and application delivery, different methods of estimation and planning, as well as new metrics and project management goals.

In this chapter, I will look at the task of managing software engineering in general and specifically at the changes required to manage an object-oriented development project. I will begin by introducing some strategies for managing reuse, estimating and measuring object-oriented development, and managing the results of the effort.

12.1 Introduction

Manage: to direct; to control; to carry on; to cope with. *n.* the act of managing; administration.
Webster's.

Prior to delving into the unique aspects of an object-oriented development project, I will begin by looking at the roles and responsibilities of a project manager on a traditional software engineering effort. Managers are charged with directing or controlling the software engineering process, establishing the goals of the project, assigning tasks to staff, tracking the status of the project, as well as providing whatever resources are required to successfully complete the project.

In a simplistic view, a software development manager is responsible for the tasks that are described in the following paragraphs.

Setting goals and standards and providing a vision for the project: The manager of any software engineering project must establish a clear, unified vision of the project for all staff involved, including their individual roles and responsibilities, the tasks that they will undertake, expectations on them, etc. Any social activity that requires interaction and cooperation of a group of people must have established responsibilities and tasks as well as a clear picture of each person's role. For an object-oriented project, the goals are delivering a quality software product that meets the customer's needs plus contributing to the library of reusable components for any subsequent projects. These goals also must be considered in light of any time, cost, and productivity expectations that are placed on the project by outside sources. Managers also establish and coordinate the use of formal methods, tools, standards, and procedures within the project and oversee any changes in these areas.

Planning the project: A secondary task or responsibility for managers of software engineering projects is to plan the tasks, resources, sequence, dependencies, deliverables, etc. to ensure that the resulting software product meets the customer's needs and is delivered in an acceptable timeframe given the resources available. This typically involves estimating the work that will be required, assigning staff to specific tasks, defining formal mechanisms for communication between staff members, reviewing the work products throughout the project, etc. For an object-oriented project, metrics and estimation models that work for traditional software engineering projects do not work well. For example, basing estimates on the number of lines of code (LOC) produced per day does not reflect the use of reusable components in object-oriented development. New measurements and estimation tools must be employed for object-oriented projects to ensure that they are planned correctly.

Tracking the progress of the project: A software engineering manager also must know at all times what the current status of the project is so that he or she can report to higher-level managers on progress and make any changes that are required to keep the project on track. For an object-oriented project, this represents a serious challenge, because the work products that are created evolve over the life of the project and it is difficult to know when these products finally are completed. As part of this process, a project manager must compare the effort expended on the project to the plan, make changes in the plan as required, and monitor task completion.

Manage all the resources required to complete the project: Managers are responsible for allocating tasks to staff, as well as any additional resources required — including money, more staff time, tools, training, etc. — as needed to keep the project on schedule. The principle factor in these tasks is anticipating and dealing with uncertainty and risk. Good project management often is based on sound estimation and tracking tools and methods. With the technical skills that are required to perform these tasks, a good manager also must be a leader and have sound people management skills. In many cases, a good manager also is a good technical person, who understands the problems and issues in software engineering and can account for them in practice.

As part of the project planning process, staff must be assigned responsibilities and tasks must be scheduled based on estimates of the effort to complete each phase. In addition, dependencies between tasks, sharing deliverables among staff, and tracking the work products all must be coordinated by management. A project that is completed on-time or ahead of schedule is one that strives to maintain accurate controls on the project, the deliverables, and resolve any outstanding problems.

[F]ormal methods and tools used by management as the basis for sizing, planning, estimating, and tracking major software projects often are close to nonexistent. In company after company, projects are sized by guesswork and estimated by manual, seat-of-the-pants methods.
T. C. Jones [JON94].

12.2 Challenges for an Object-Oriented Project

As you already have seen, an object-oriented development effort is substantially different in structure, methods, tools, roles and responsibilities, and effort from a traditional MIS project. Those managers who are responsible for overseeing an object-oriented project must go through a learning process themselves so that they can accommodate these changes and still meet their project constraints.

In this section, I will review the ways that an object-oriented project is different from a traditional project, and look at available tools and methods that can help managers address these issues.

12.2.1 Evolution and Iteration

A distinctive difference between traditional projects and an object-oriented project is in the software engineering life cycle, the tasks, and the deliverables that are created. Recalling the discussion of an object-oriented development life cycle in chapter 4, the process includes iteration through analysis, design, programming, and testing, with delivery of work products at each point that represent portions of the final system. This iterative nature calls for dramatically different tools and techniques to manage the process.

Booch calls this phenomena *round-trip gestalt design*, while Shlaer/Mellor use the term *recursive design*. Regardless of the name, object-oriented development involves incremental design and delivery of subsystems, and this represents change from traditional sequential development life cycles. This evolutionary approach also creates substantially different requirements for unit and integration testing, which must be incorporated into any estimates and plans for the project.

In addition, ensuring that team members are knowledgeable about the status of work products and the overall project requires formal and informal communications on a regular basis. Team members should be encouraged to use peer-to-peer communication to remain current on the status of work products, and managers should schedule regular reviews of the work products at various points in the object-oriented life cycle. These points might include in analysis (during requirements specification and after identification of classes, attributes, and services), in design (whenever class details are defined, interfaces are changed, or subsystems are completed), as well as in programming (when subsystems are implemented or changed) and testing (following unit and integration testing of subsystems).

A document management system and a CASE repository can help facilitate this team communication and support changes to the work products during analysis and design, while a configuration management system can be used to manage changes to the actual programming code.

12.2.2 Prototyping

As you saw in chapter 4, prototyping is the development of working models of a system delivered to users early in the development process to elicit requirements and specifications. In an object-oriented development environment, work products become prototypes of the subsystems and evolve over time to become the finished system. This form of prototyping includes delivery of pieces of the system (subsystems) that work with interfaces that are defined. These subsystem prototypes become the finished system following system integration and acceptance testing. The evolution of work products in an OOSDLC represents challenges for managers in the areas of version control, tools support, communication, formal reviews, measurement, and estimation.

Prototyping, as it is used in an object-oriented development project, begins early in the process, usually in design, and continues through coding, testing, and implementation. As with other prototyping methods, the working subsystems that are delivered to users must be allowed to change over time as more information is collected, and managers and staff should not fight requests for change in the prototype during development.

As subsystems are implemented, they should be delivered to users and a formal mechanism should be in place to capture change requests and process them as the project proceeds. When a subsystem is deemed acceptable by users, it still must be integrated with subsequent subsystems when they are delivered, and this process might require additional changes.

How can a manager estimate the amount of effort required and the time to complete an object-oriented project given these difference? Later in this chapter, in section 12.6, I will look more closely at estimating object-oriented projects and dealing with these issues. In the next section, I will cover the difficult issue of managing reuse in software engineering.

12.3 Managing Reuse

Perhaps the most challenging aspect of any object-oriented development effort is the dual goals of delivering a working application but also delivering reusable components for use in subsequent projects. In chapter 7, I reviewed the problems inherent in meeting both these goals. In this section, I will look more closely at reuse in general.

I will begin by defining software reuse, the types of reuse possible, the required organizational structure to support reuse, classification schemes to organize and identify reusable components, principles of design for reuse, prohibitors to reuse, potential benefits of reuse, a reusability framework, and experiences of organizations that have implemented reuse.

12.3.1 Introduction

Reuse: the re-application of previously developed components used to develop new systems.
Software reuse: the use of existing software components to construct new systems.

Software reuse, long a goal of software engineering, seeks to reduce the overall cost of developing new systems by using components (models, designs, or even code) from previously developed systems. The cost of systems developed with reuse is calculated as:

Cost of new system = cost of new components developed + cost of tailoring existing components from previous systems

While many organizations have labored to include reuse over the years, very few (if any) have achieved any significant level of reuse outside the laboratory. There are many reasons for this, including failure to address cultural or people issues, failure to encourage and reward reuse, limited availability of reusable components, and failure of the existing tools and methods to support adequate levels of reuse.

Software work products can be reused at all stages of the software development life cycle, including source code, design specifications, models (requirements), prototypes, and architectures. As I evaluate component reuse, I will define the different types of reuse, the organizational structures required to support reuse, issues of classification and identification of reusable components, principles of design for reuse, factors that prohibit reuse, a framework for reuse, and experiences of organizations that have achieved some level of reuse.

Types of reuse include:

- *Opportunistic* — Reuse is conducted at an individual level; no procedures for reuse exist, and libraries contain components that originally were not designed for reuse; predictions of less than 25% increase in productivity that often will payoff in 2 to 5 years.
- *Compositional* — Reuse of existing components for building new systems based on well-established collections, efficient library systems and standard interfaces; estimates of up to 40% productivity improvements and payoff in 3 to 5 years.

- *Generative* — Reuse at the design specification level; time to payoff is short (1 or 2 years) with productivity improvements of 60% to 90%, depending on the domain, but the domain of the generators is narrow.
- *Black-box* — Reuse of software components without any modifications, reuse unit interactions by means of standard interfaces (i.e., via object-oriented programming languages); productivity improvements of up to 30% with time to payoff under 24 months.
- *White-box* — Reuse of components by modification and adaptation; productivity can improve up to 60% with a 3 to 5 year time to payoff.

Ruben Prieto-Diaz has written extensively on software reuse [PRI91a] [PRI87]. He recommends a strategy for implementing software reuse that is incremental, as shown in Figure 12.1. A reuse program requires an organizational structure and a collection of support tools aimed at fostering, managing, and maintaining the practice of reusing software.

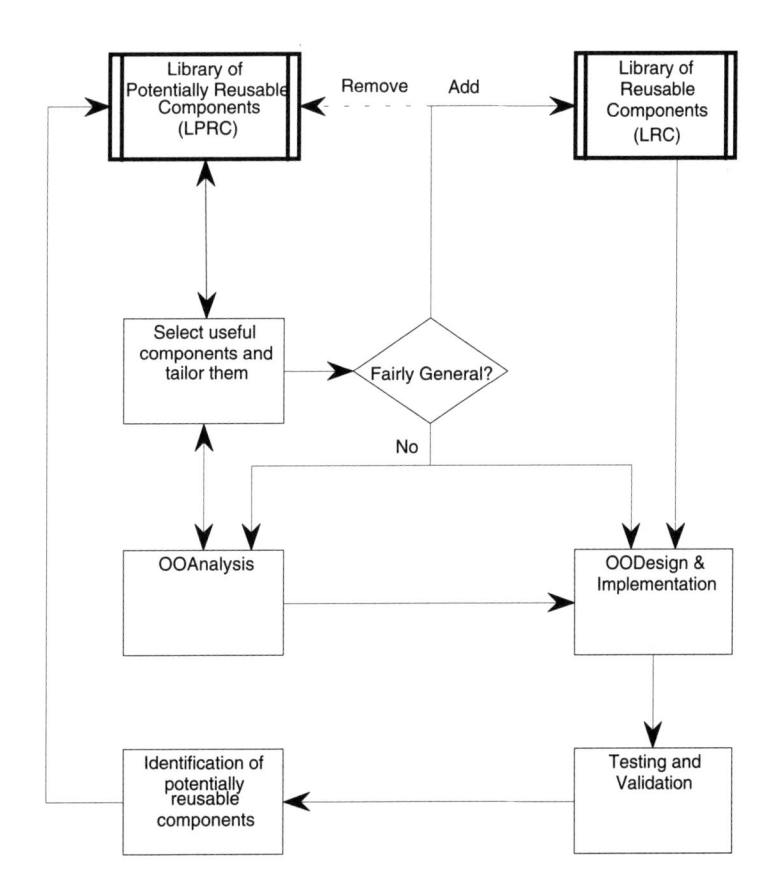

Figure 12.1
An incremental ruese program.

Implementing a software reuse program as shown in Figure 12.1 involves analyzing existing systems to select potentially reusable components, defining a classification scheme for components, and using an automated library to maintain the components. When this approach is used, every attempt should be made to identify potentially reusable components at all levels of the software engineering process, from analysis through implementation, and across all domains.

12.3.2 A Reuse Organizational Structure

Most organizations that have attempted to adopt reuse have found that the principal problems are not technological but involve unwillingness to address the most important issues influencing software reuse: *managerial* (organizational, motivational, and financial), *economic* (cost/benefit, cost/estimation, pricing, contracting, and support), *legal* (copyright, liabilities, responsibilities, etc.), *cultural*, and *social*. I will look more closely at these issues in a subsequent section.

One approach would be to establish a reusable library team that is to be consulted on each project and looks for potential components for reuse. This team also looks for possible new components to add to the library. To this end, Henderson-Sellers and Pant [HEN93] suggest a life cycle for reuse as described in Figure 12.2.

The two-library reuse model begins by placing any project-specific classes into a library of potentially reusable components (LPRC). A new project thus progresses through the normal object-oriented development process as shown, then an additional step is added: Identification of potentially reusable components. This step is undertaken with the help of the library team and simply places any components that might be reusable from the project into the LPRC as shown.

As a first step in each new project, the classes in both the LPRC and the library of reusable components (LRC) are evaluated to identify classes that can be reused. If there are classes that can be reused, then and only then are these classes generalized and moved into the LRC by the library team. This two-library reuse model is both economical and practical, because it places the cost of generalization on the project that gains the benefit of reuse and prevents over generalization (i.e., generalization of all components, even those that will not be reused).

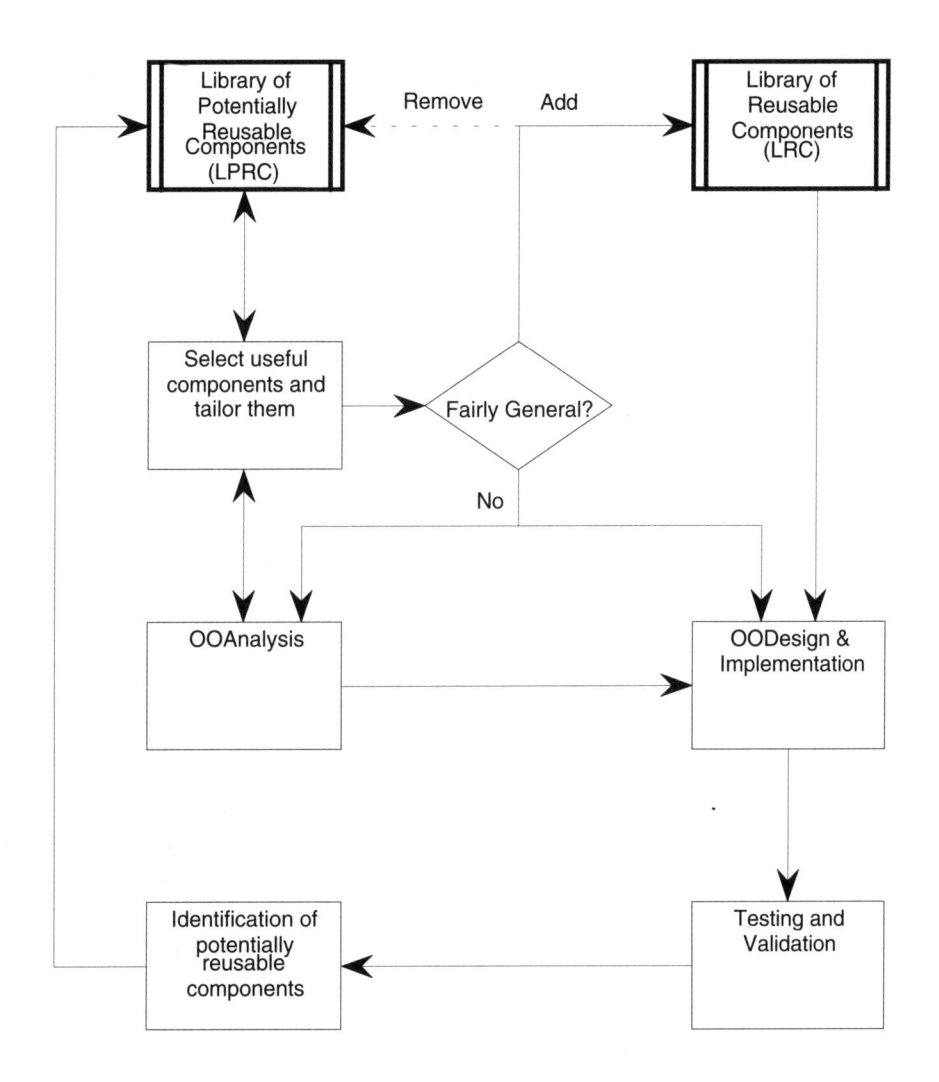

Figure 12.2
A two-library reuse model.

A library management group also can be considered as an asset management group, because each reusable component is an asset of the organization, and provides initiatives, funding, and polices for reuse within the organization. This group might consist of a librarian, who collects, procures, updates, and distributes reusable components (i.e., manages requests for reusable components) and a reuse support center, which assists and trains staff in finding and using components.

Perhaps the best treatment to date on large-scale reuse has been the four-year Software Reuse Project at the Nippon Telegraph and Telephone Corporation (NTT) described in [ISO92]. This study, which involved over 100 software engineers and over 1 million lines of code for C and PL/1 systems, found that the software reuse activity requires a reuse organizational structure and flow as shown in Figure 12.3.

The results of the project showed that the reuse ratio (size of reused module divided by the size of the program developed) stabilized at around 17% after the four-year period. This study also found that the reused module size stabilized after four years at 500 lines of code. Further study results indicate:

- Over the four-year period, ongoing projects used more modules from other projects — up to 60% at the end of the period.
- The usage of the reuse library improved — average reuse frequency increased from .18 in the first year to .28 in the fourth year.

Method	Component Developers	Description
Ad hoc	Single development group	Select candidate components and modify them for reuse; informal communication used to notify developers of the available components
Cooperative design	Two (or more) development groups	Find common functions for two (or more) applications and design them to meet mutual needs; formal communication between groups required
Domain Analysis	Special reuse team	Analye a domain or subject area, identify common functions, and develop reusable components; requires formal communication between the reuse team an other groups

Figure 12.3
Reuse methods, roles, and approach.

- The ratio of modules reused at least once per year stabilized at .2 (or 20%).
- The reuse library grew steadily to around 800 modules.

This study identified the following as impediments or prohibitors to software reuse:

- Inadequate reusable modules — the initial investment in acquiring or constructing this library is prohibitive
- No direct benefit to developers
- Uncooperative staff in projects — too busy to reuse
- No benefit to outside developers to reuse
- Slow response to maintenance needs
- Unreliable modules
- Poor documentation
- No standards for development process
- Performance degradation
- Unpredictable benefits

Figure 12.4 describes an organization and activity flow for reuse groups as defined in the NTT project. McGregor and Sykes also report on barriers to

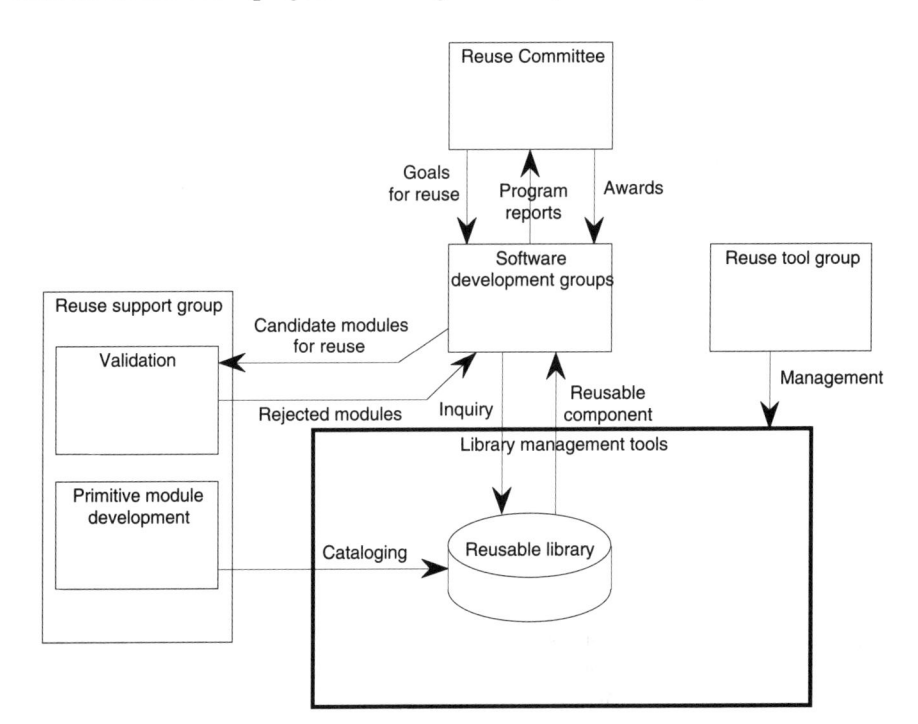

Figure 12.4 Reuse organization and activity flow.

reuse [MCG91]. Their findings suggest the following:

- An organization's bottom line is an initial barrier to reuse
- Communication within large, complex organizations is a continuing barrier to reuse
- Component integration is dificult
- Component design is or should be application dependent
- Components can be validated only in context
- Large libraries of components are difficult to maintain and learn to use

12.3.3 Classification Schemes

Prieto-Diaz and others suggest using a classification scheme based on facets and using a thesaurus for vocabulary control and to help clarify concepts. For each component in the library, you define its function, class, and domain. These then can be used to identify each component by defining the name as the function performed + class + application domain.

One suggestion for cataloging and classifying objects is given in [HEN92] and uses a natural-language, full-storage, free-text retrieval. Their approach defines the following characteristics for each reusable component :

Library name
    Cluster or category name
        Class name
            Class services/features: state/data and behavior/functionality
        Superclass name(s)
        Classes required as suppliers of services to this class
        Related entries
        Synonyms for this class
    Facet category
Language
Date created
Version
Size in bytes
Source or Author
Vendor
Cost $

Related entries: 1) Classes required as aggregate components (Whole/part relationships)
                            2) Other relevant notes on this class

Specifying reusable components so that they can be reused requires defining their inputs, outputs, and computational characteristics, as well as defining their behavior and class or environment in which they are meaningful. For each component, I might define a prolog and an epilogue for interfacing with the object, along with a computational nucleus composed of a functional overview, interface syntax and semantics, dependencies and characteristics, and perhaps an example use.

Populating and organizing the reuse library is by far the most difficult task in reuse. Existing systems might provide artifacts or work products that can be used in other systems. Reverse engineering holds promise in design capture but might reveal only structure and components, not why design decisions were made, and might reflect an implementation bias in existing systems.

Reuse-oriented programming is defined as: object-centered design (modules/classes/types and not just procedures/functions as components) + careful separation of abstract behavior from implementation detail + disciplined use of programming constructs to support local certifiability (component-wise reasoning) of program behavior. Achieving reuse involves designing and implementing software solutions with specific goals and responsibilities. These principles are as follows:

- Strive to reuse black-box components, not source code
- Identify, encapsulate, and specify commonalties and variabilities
- Separate specification of the abstract interface from implementation
- Do not allow a client to break a component's abstraction
- Extend component behavior by addition only, not by modification

Good planning reduces the loss of human problem solving by reducing redundant and dead-end work, by enhancing communication, and by helping groups select environments that support higher productivity. Any work product (an explicit, physical result of a work activity) that makes problem solutions readily accessible to later projects is a good candidate for reuse.

Reuse should complement automation, not compete with it. Time spent reusing work products that are not generated automatically is time well spent. Build reusable parts for local expertise and buy reusable parts for outside expertise. Maintenance is itself a form of reuse-with-replacement process. Modular reuse strategies should take a divide-and-conquer approach that supports both the design of new, highly reusable systems and the analysis of existing, potentially reusable systems.

The defining characteristic of good reuse is not the reuse of software per se, but the reuse of human problem solving.
B. Barnes and T. Bollinger [BAR91].

12.3.4 A Reusability Framework

OOPLs provide class libraries that provide an approach to reusability but a reusability framework requires components developed internally. All OOPLs come with a set of reusable components (or classes) that can be reused or tailored, but these classes often are generic (i.e., containers) or specific to a presentation environment (i.e., Windows or OS/2 PM). Organizations that hope to achieve some substantive level of reuse also must develop or acquire their own domain-specific reusable components to add to those provided with the OOPL.

Features that impact reusability and extensibility include inheritance type and mode (selection or nonselective), information hiding, genericity, polymorphic assignment, dynamic binding, abstract classes, overriding and renaming methods, and constructors. Additional factors to consider for reuse include visibility and interface features (i.e., public versus private) of class methods, data representation, instance variables, exclusion of methods, availability of methods, same-named methods, and naming conflicts of methods.

Three different types of reuse are compared in this chapter, along with the developers of the reuse unit and a description of the reuse process itself. Each method calls for a different organizational group or person to create the reusable components and specific lines of communication to facilitate reuse of these units once they are created.

Regardless of the method of reuse used, for reuse to occur there must be communication between the developers (or producers) of components and the users (or consumers) of those components. Formal lines of communication and procedures should be established to provide time and resources for identifying, using, and creating reusable components.

While OOPLs include support for classification based on inheritance, formal methods and procedures are required to reuse classes. Inheritance represents an is-a relationship between components, and a derived class is a specialization of a base class. Dynamic binding is one of the features in an OOPL that supports polymorphism. Genericity or parameterized polymorphism and overloading are other approaches to reusability in a OOPL.

12.3.5 Prohibitors to Reuse

Issues that can prohibit reuse include economic incentives that work against reuse (i.e., the added cost and time to generalize, locate, etc.), the "not-invented-here" syndrome, difficulty in retrieving components, and lack of management commitment to reuse (i.e., avoid the "next project can do it" syndrome). Other barriers to reuse include lack of discipline, lack of a training culture, and overall confusion in the software process on the part of developers.

Factors that prohibit reuse from a technical perspective include complexity, single-threadedness, invisibility, difficulty of replication, lack of representation of design for reuse, lack of a strategy for optimizing reuse (reuse is a multiorganizational issue and requires a critical mass of components before any real benefit is realized), and the initial cost of developing or acquiring reusable components, that might be high.

When these obstacles are overcome, the potential benefits of reuse can be substantial. A partial list of benefits to software reuse are listed here:

- Cost and time to market can be reduced
- Software can be taken off the critical path
- Software quality can be improved
- New features can be easily integrated into software
- A common look-and-feel can be used

12.3.6 Experiences with Reuse

Raytheon reports an average of 60% reused COBOL code in new systems and a net increase in productivity of 50% over a period of six years [LEN84]. NASA conducted an internal study and foudn that 42% of their ada code was reused on the third project [COO90]. NEC reported a six-fold productivity improvement and an almost three-fold quality improvement from reuse [MAT82]. GTE Data Services reported 14% reuse in the first year of their project and predicts 50% reuse within six years [PRI91b].

Virginia Technical University conducted an experiment to determine if object-oriented development improved productivity through reuse [LEW92]. Their results indicated that there is a balance between the power of generality, encapsulation, class hierarchies and inheritance, and abstraction.

They identified four levels of reuse for a component : completely reusable, reusable with slight modification (less than 25%), reusable with major modification (greater than 25%), and not reusable. Twenty-one students were used in groups to track the amount of reuse along with productivity improvements, which were measured in runtime errors, time to fix errors, etc.

Their findings indicate that:

- Object-oriented development does promote higher productivity.
- Object-oriented development improves productivity when staff are moderately or strongly encouraged to reuse.
- Reuse promoted high productivity regardless of the language used.
- The extent of productivity improvement was higher for object-oriented development than for procedural development.

Several reports of experience with reuse are given in [GRI92]. HP has established a Corporate Software Reuse Program and has measured quality improvements ranging from 3 to 10 times less defect density with reused code. IBM created its Reuse Technology Support Center and has been developing reuse metrics for several years, including source lines of code (SLOC), reused SLOC, SLOC reused by others, development cost, development defect rate, and error repair rate. From these, other metrics can be calculated, including reuse percentage, reuse cost avoidance, and reuse value added.

Motorola created a Reuse Working Group, which is over four years old. This group has worked with engineers to improve reuse but has found that substantial management support is required because developing reusable software takes more time than not reusing.

A reuse management facility (RMF) was developed by NCR for their COOPERATION product. The RMF stored, sorted, indexed, and retrieved development information. It supported similarity matching, proximity searching, fuzzy matching, and topical searching [KIN93].

A separate effort to evaluate how CASE repositories facilitate software reuse was conducted at two major institutions: First Boston Corporation and Carter Hawley Hale Information Services [BAN93]. The authors found that, contrary to expectations, the overall level of reuse didn't grow with a larger pool of reuse candidates, that familiarity was an important factor in reuse, and that the pool of familiar objects dictated the level of overall reuse in these organizations. This research also showed that over 60% of the reuse was attributed to developers reusing their *own* products.

This research also found that the top 5% of developers accounted for creating over 50% of the reusable components and that organizational barriers and disincentives prohibited reuse. The conclusions reached from this study were that domain analysis plays a critical role in designing for reuse, that initial levels of reuse were 35% at both sites, and that final reuse by some developers was as high as 75%. Figure 12.5 shows a revised model of reuse as described in the First Boston and Carter Hawley Hale study.

Others have attempted to quantify the cost and benefit of reuse including [MAR92] and [GAF92]. Of these, Margono and Rhoads from Computer Sciences Corp. (CSC) used a model of reuse economics based on the work of the Software Productivity Consortium (SPC). This model calculates the cost of delivering a software product as equal to the cost of developing new software plus the cost of reusing existing software.

CSC split their software products into categories based on their size, complexity, reactive characteristics, availability, reliability, interactiveness, and extensibility. Their results found that the cost of creating reusable software was twice the cost of developing nonreusable software due to overhead. This is consistent with the findings of the U.S. Army Information System Software Center [RAY91].

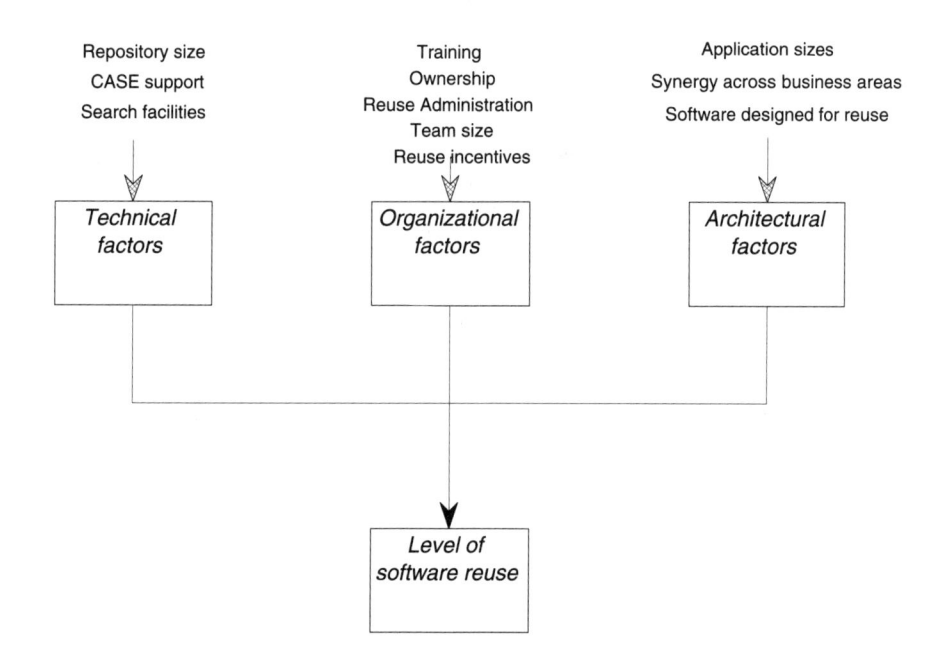

Figure 12.5
A model of software ruese.

CSC also found that the cost of software developed with reuse must include the cost of the producer of the reusable components and the cost of the consumer of those components, that a monitoring group is critical to establishing reuse, that reuse should be considered in the early phases of software development (including analysis and design) and that the maintenance cost of reuse is difficult to measure.

Several important observations on reuse can be made from these and other case studies and are summarized here:

- Management support is mandatory
- Organizational structure for reuse must be in place
- Incremental program development is required with reusable components
- Success, both financial and organizational, depends on strong incentives for reuse
- Domain analysis was performed in most cases

12.4 Planning for Object-Oriented Development

Object-oriented projects require a different work-breakdown structure than is typical. They also require a development approach that is either iterative, incremental, or some combination of the two.
M. Pittman [PIT93].

As you saw in section 12.2, planning an object-oriented project represents another change for managers. The typical project planning tasks — estimating, assigning resources, tracking deliverables, etc. — are different in an object-oriented project, and new methods and tools must be used when these projects are planned. In a typical MIS project, the system is decomposed by functions that are used to estimate the work required. In an object-oriented project, the system is decomposed into classes and interfaces, so estimates of the effort required must be based on the number and complexity of the classes.

Estimation of object-oriented projects can be accomplished using a variety of methods and tools. Matthew Pittman has written on the subject of estimating and planning object-oriented projects [PIT93]. Pittman offers the diagram of staff and plan shown in Figure 12.6 as a fine-grained planning and tracking approach to object-oriented projects.

Notice in this diagram that the project manager creates and maintains the project plan, makes adjustments based on work products that are delivered throughout the project, works closely with the project leader and the team members in guiding the process, and reports back to upper management on progress. The project leader takes the project plan, assigns work products to staff, monitors the progress of efforts, completion of work products, etc. and reports back to the project manager. Developers are assigned work products to be completed, objectives, etc. and regularly turn in progress reports to the project leader, turn completed work products over to quality assurance, etc.

Pittman reports that an object-oriented project can be estimated using one of three approaches: by analogy, where previous projects (which might or might not have been object-oriented) are used as a basis for new projects; by metrics, where estimates are based on measures of the project compared with metrics collected on previous projects; or by method, where a formal planning method is used.

Of the three methods, estimates by analogy are most common method but also most inaccurate unless an organization has had extensive experience with previous object-oriented development efforts. Estimating by metrics requires measurements of size, complexity, etc. that fit object-oriented development, collections of metrics from previous projects, plus some mechanism for

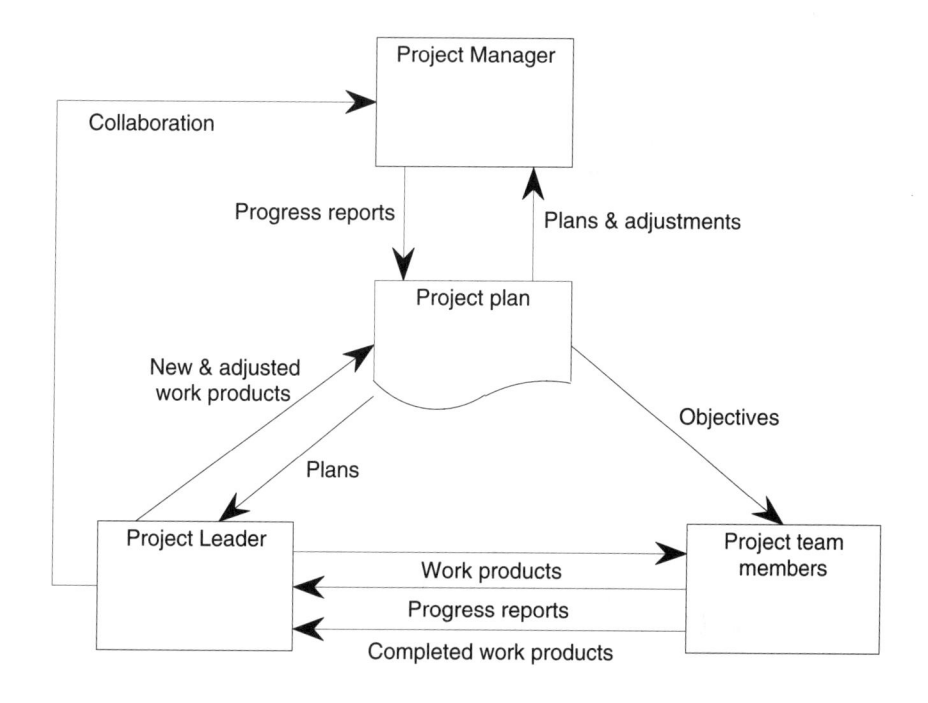

Figure 12.6 Object-oriented work products and project plans.

quantifying project scope. Estimates based on formal methods, such as COCOMO, must make adjustments for object-oriented development. Pittman suggests that any COCOMO plan be adjusted as follows: 80% of Analysis/Design in up-front incremental analysis and the remaining 20% of design across all other increments, 50% of test to acceptance of the final product and the remaining 50% of test across all other increments.

Milestones for an object-oriented project include acceptance of deliverables in formal and informal reviews, completion of work products or documentation, or demonstrations and reviews of working prototypes. These milestones can be planned and estimated for each major subsystem in a project, and if required, for each class and service identified in the early phases of the project.

Once a project has been estimated, it must be planned given the available resources. Staff and resource allocation is different from traditional development given the tasks that are required and the roles and responsibilities defined in chapter 4. Grady Booch suggests that more resources are required in object-oriented design, that fewer resources are required for object-oriented programming, testing, and implementation, and that object-oriented projects typically require as much or slightly less than a traditional project. Booch suggests these observations be made following the learning curve for object technology adoption.

In addition, staff skills, roles, and responsibilities are different in an object-oriented project (see chapter 4) and any initial project must consider the learning curve and cultural change required of the staff. Object-oriented projects often use smaller groups or teams of staff, with specific subsystems used as work products, and each team given responsibility for a subsystem. When an object-oriented development project is planned, it should include appropriate staff to finish the work products in time and within budget.

An example object-oriented project structure for a medium-sized system might look something like this (the numbers in parentheses indicate the number of people assigned):

- Manager — Responsible for overseeing the project, assigning resources, reporting progress, etc. (1)
- System Architects — Design and develop architectures for the application, one as the project leader. (1 or 2)
- Class Designers — Create and maintain the library of reusable components. (3 or 4)

- Class Implementors — Select and implement classes as objects. (4 or 5)
- Application Programmers — Assemble the components into subsystems in the programming language. (4 or 5)

Pittman offers advice for tracking work products in an OOSDLC. He recommends that work products be small enoughthat project tracking can be based on completed packages, that projects use well-defined completion criteria (such as testing a class's public protocol, testing that a class's behavior, peer reviews, reworked estimates, assessment of reuse, progress updates, and sign-off on final products) and that work products be completed by developers in a serial manner.

Pittman also suggests that managers of object-oriented development efforts must track fine-grained work products of short duration. He suggests using work products that take only two or three days to complete, because this allows ample time for feedback and changes to the plan when work products take longer than expected.

12.5 Measuring an Object-Oriented Project

One challenge in planning, estimating, and managing an object-oriented development project is measuring the process and the work products. The traditional measures of software projects — lines of code or function points — have little value in an object-oriented effort. Remembering that one goal of object-oriented development is to reuse as much existing information as possible, the new lines of code have little meaning unless they are combined with reused lines of code.

Prior to looking at possible metrics for object-oriented development, I will define some basic concepts of software measurements. There are many possible measures of a software development project, including size, effort, complexity of the resulting system, cost, number of errors or defects, and maintenance effort or cost. Most MIS organizations use few (if any) formal metrics of software outside the cost — in linear months and in effort. There are several excellent resources on the subject of software measurement and planning, including [BOE81] [GIL88] [GRA87] [JON86] [PAG85] [SHO83].

Two basic measures of any software project are the time to deliver the product, which is based on developer productivity, project size, familiarity with the tools and methods, etc. and the quality of the resulting product, which is based on user satisfaction, number of changes to the system, etc. Of these two basic types of measures, effort or time appear to be the most widely used, often are inaccurate, and focus on the process, while quality seems to represent more of a user-perspective and focus on the product.

Measuring developer productivity is difficult, mostly because organizations currently are not measuring productivity, so there is nothing to measure against, but also because different developers, given the same problem, will come up with different solutions. In this sense, productivity is almost like measuring apples against oranges. For those organizations that choose to measure it, productivity in an object-oriented project can be measured by counting the classes in logical and physical design that are completed and working, the stability of the classes as the project progresses, or the stability of the key interfaces in the system.

Measuring software quality involves the work products delivered. In an object-oriented project, these include the classes, subsystems, and the final system. Work products can be evaluated for quality at various points in the project, via internal (i.e., developer) and external (i.e., user) reviews. For any type of measurement to work, it must be accurate and based on quantifiable attributes of the product or process. Recently, several important contributions have been made in the area of metrics for object-oriented products.

Chidamber and Kemerer of MIT have defined the following as possible metrics for object-oriented development [KEM91]:

- *Weighted methods/class* — Helps to define the complexity of an object. The number of methods and the complexity of the methods involved is an indicator of how much time and effort are required to develop and maintain the object.
- *Depth of inheritance tree* — A measure of how many ancestor classes potentially can effect a class. It is useful to have a measure of how deep a particular class is in the hierarchy so that the class can be designed with reuse of inherited methods.
- *Number of children* — A measure of how many subclasses are going to inherit the methods of a parent class. It also gives an idea of the potential influence that a class has on the design. If a class has a large number of children, it might require more testing of the methods.
- *Coupling between objects* — A count of the number of noninheritance-related couples with other classes. Excessive coupling between objects outside of the inheritance hierarchy is detrimental to modular design and prevents reuse. This measure is useful to estimate how complex the testing of the various parts of the design will be.

- *Response for a class* — The response set is a set of methods available to the object. Because it specifically includes methods called from outside the object, it also is a measure of communication between objects. If a large number of methods can be invoked, the testing and debugging of the object becomes more complicated.
- *Lack of cohesion in methods* — Uses the notion of degree of similarity of methods — fewer disjoint sets implies greater similarity of methods. Cohesiveness of methods within a class is desirable, because it promotes encapsulation of objects.

Grady Booch has identified five measures or metrics for determining if a given class or object is well designed [BOO91]. *Coupling* is in regard to classes and objects but must be considered against inheritance. Weakly coupled classes are good, but inheritance (tightly couples superclasses and their subclasses) helps to exploit reuse. *Cohesion* measures the degree of connectivity between the elements of a single class or object. *Coincidental cohesion* occurs when unrelated abstractions are placed into the same class. *Functional cohesion* occurs when the elements of a class all work together to provide some well-bounded behavior.

Sufficiency represents how well a class captures enough characteristics of the abstraction to permit meaningful and efficient interaction. *Completeness* refers to the interface of the class and balances sufficiency. Whereas sufficiency implies a minimal interface, a complete interface is one that covers all aspects of the abstraction. A complete class exists when the interface is general enough to be commonly used by any client. *Primitiveness* relates to the operations in a class or object, and operations should be as primitive as possible. An operation is primitive if you can implement it only through access to the underlying representation.

Others in the software engineering community also have described potential metrics for object-oriented development. T. Kraemer of Hewlet-Packard defined metrics for object-oriented development by life cycle phase [KRA89] as follows: analysis, cumulative engineering months; design, number of object classes designed and months to design, number of methods designed and months to design each; coding, number of object classes coded, months to code, number of methods coded, months to code, and compile and link success rates; and testing, defects found and resolved, cumulative defects vs. cumulative Q/A hours, defect find rate, estimated Q/A hours remaining; and unresolved defects.

David Taylor also has proposed possible metrics for object-oriented development for predicting resource requirements for projects. He has identified possible metrics [TAY93], including the number of methods/class, number of component objects/class, number of messages/class, number of collaborators/class, number of parameters/class, ratio of public to private methods/class, and mean and variance of messages/method, objects/method, parameters/message, component objects, methods total, and objects receiving messages, among others.

Sam Adams of Knowledge Systems Corp. has proposed four levels of software metrics: project, component/application, class, and method. Others have taken existing or proposed metrics and extended them. For example, Steven Bilow of Tektronix has extended McCabe's cyclomatic complexity measure for object-oriented components. Automated support for metrics is available in the Metrics for Object-Oriented Software Engineering (MOOSE) from Belcore.

12.6 Configuration Management Issues

Managing an object-oriented project also means managing changes to the work products. Configuration management or change control are terms that often are used to describe the control of change to the outcome of a software engineering effort (i.e., the software itself). In this section, I will review some basics of configuration management techniques and tools prior to discussing the unique aspects of managing change to an object-oriented software product.

Software configuration management (SCM) usually consists of four basic tasks or activities [BER80]: *identification* of components, storage, and access to work products including systems, subsystems, baselines, etc.; *control* creates and enforces procedures for changes to the baseline; *status accounting* records all activities against the work products so that they can be re-created; and *auditing* supports reports and checks against the work products for consistency and completeness.

A baseline is a milestone in the development or deployment process that is marked by the delivery of one or more configuration items where approval is required through a formal technical review. Configuration control represents the procedures for creation and change of work products — who can change them, when, etc. Configuration auditing reports on the status of work products, who last changed them, when they were changed, impact analysis, etc. In theory, configuration management can be applied to work products throughout the development process. In practice, a typical MIS organization might use configuration management only for to the finished product (i.e., the source and executable code for the system). In most cases, the SCM maintains the relationships between the source and executable code.

With a procedural software product, each program is captured in source code format, usually in a production library. From this production library, an executable version of the program is created using a compiler and linker. Any required subroutines or called programs are compiled or linked with the executable code as needed. Different versions of the source and executable code might be maintained in separate libraries, and changes to the system normally must be made using a predefined procedure.

Relationships that must be maintained in a traditional MIS application relate only to the program-to-modules or subroutines that are used and required at compile or link time. These programs and modules, or subroutines, must be kept in sync, and any changes to one must be reflected in the other. You can consider this relationship as a parent (i.e., main program) to child (i.e., subroutine or module) that is kept by the SCM.

With an object-oriented product, the relationships that must be tracked are different. These issues were discussed in some detail in [BER91]. With a software solution assembled from classes that communicate via messages, cross-references must be maintained between classes and their children, classes and their methods, and classes that interact via messages. The relationship between a parent class and its children might represent a one-to-many pointer from the class to all the objects or subclasses that inherit from it. Likewise, each child in the inheritance relationship must be considered whenever a change is made to its parent class.

Object-oriented products create difficult problems for SCMs, including how to support multiple authors that each own a changed version of the same parent class, how to manage ownership of classes across domains, and how to fix bugs in higher-level classes when they have a large number of children. Any SCM used to support an object-oriented project must address these issues.

In short, the traditional concepts of configuration identification, configuration control, and configuration auditing practices do not seem to work well for reusable software.
E. H. Bersoff and A. M. Davis [BER91].

Cataloging and tracking reusable components represents yet another function that can be considered as part of the SCM system or as a separate aspect of object or reuse management. These functions often are the responsibility of the reuse group or team and should include the following items:

- *Cataloging* — Managing the creation and use of components, including access and updates, and uniquely identifying each component; also supporting browsing and search methods that promote reuse.
- *Concurrency* — Multiple execution threads, synchronization, and communication and concurrency control through message-passing or an OODBMS.
- *Distribution* — Global object naming, remote message-passing, or method invocation.
- *Security* — Ownership of objects, "access rights," or permission to invoke an object's methods.
- *Transaction management* — Access and update to classes/objects.
- *Version management* — Management of versions of classes/objects over time.

12.7 Quality Assurance Issues

Returning the issue of software quality, many organizations have found that quality assurance (QA) can be beneficial in delivering software that meets the user's needs. Many organizations have instituted total quality management (TQM) initiatives that incorporate quality assurance as a critical part of the software engineering life cycle. QA often involves establishing standards and metrics for quality, creating a QA staff responsible for implementing and tracking quality standards, incorporating QA reviews in the development life cycle, and providing staff with training in quality improvement methods and techniques.

Perhaps the most widely used method in QA ais the peer review, which allows work products and documentation to be reviewed formally within the development group throughout analysis, design, programming, testing, and implementation. These internal reviews might take the form of structured walkthroughs or joint application design (JAD) sessions. Along with the peer reviews, formal user reviews should be included in the object-oriented development process for key abstractions and mechanisms with subject matter experts.

Subsequent reviews or walkthroughs can be performed internally, with users, and with QA staff to review module and process diagrams for the systems' physical architecture. As work products are created or modified in the development process, team members and affected users should review these products (often in the form of diagrams, specifications, or working components) for acceptance. Likewise, when a new class is ready for submission into the library of reusable components, QA staff, developers, and class designers should review them and get sign-off prior to adding them to the repository.

Additional aspects of QA include testing, both at the unit level and the system level, and formal measurements of quality throughout the life cycle. Concerning testing, the granularity of the units that are tested is different in object-oriented development (classes vs. programs), along with who tests the components (class implementors and programmers in unit testing and class designers in integration and system/subsystem testing). A separate Q/A group also can be directly involved in system-level acceptance tests and should perform follow-up evaluations with users on the quality of the system.

As I discussed in section 12.6, quality metrics can be quantitative (such as defects per 1000 lines of code, cost to fix defects vs. cost to develop the system, and percentage of changes made to code after the system is implemented, etc.) or qualitative, including user satisfaction with the system after delivery, stability of the system and classes over time, major changes to the system, etc.

12.8 References

[ALH91] Al-Haddad, H. M., K. M. George, and M. H. Samadzadeh, "Approaches to Reusability in C++ and Eiffel," *JOOP*, September 1991, pp. 34-45.

[BAN93] Banker, R. D., R. J. Kauffma, and D. Zweig, "Repository Evaluation of Software Reuse," *IEEE Trans. on Soft. Eng.*, vol. 19, no. 4, April 1993, pp. 379-389.

[BAR91] Barnes, B. H. and T. B. Bollinger, "Making Reuse Cost-Effective," *IEEE Software*, January 1991, pp. 13-24.

[BER91] Bersoff, E. H. and A. M. Davis, "Impacts of Life Cycle Models on Software," *CACM*, vol. 34, no. 8, pp. 104-118.

[BER80] Bersoff, E. H., et al., *Software Configuration Management*, Prentice Hall, 1980.

[BIG84] Biggerstaff, T. J. and A. J. Perliss, ed., "Special Issue on Reusability," *IEEE Trans. on Soft. Eng.*, vol. SE-10, no. 5, September 1984.

[BIG87] Biggerstaff, T. J. and C. Richter, "Reusability Framework, Assessment, and Directions," *IEEE Software*, vol. 4, no. 2, March 1987, pp. 41-49.

[BIG89] Biggerstaff, T. J. and A. J. Perliss, *Software Reusability: Concepts and Models,* and *Applications and Experiences*, Vols. 1 & 2, ACM Press and Addison-Wesley, 1989.

[BOE81] Boehm, B. W., *Software Engineering Economics*, Prentice-Hall, 1981.

[BOO91] Booch, G., *Object-Oriented Design with Applications*, Benjamin/Cummings, 1991.

[COO90] Coomer, T. N., J. R. Comer, and D. J. Rodjak, "Developing Reusable Software for Military Systems - Why it is Needed and Why it isn't Working," *ACM SIGSOFT*, vol. 15, no. 3, pp. 33-38.

[CUR83] Curtis, B., "Cognitive Issues in Reusability," Workshop on Reusability in Programming, *ITT Programming*, September 1983, p. 192-197.

[GAF92] Gaffney, J. E. and R. D. Cruickshank, "A General Economics Model of Software Reuse," *proceedings of the Intl. Conference on Software Engineering*, May 11-15, 1992, pp. 327-337.

[GIB91] Gibson, E., "Flattening the Learning Curve: Educating Object-Oriented Developers," *JOOP*, February 1991, pp. 24-28.

[GIL88] Gilb, T., *Principles of Software Engineering Management*, Addison-Wesley, 1988.

[GRA87] Grady, R. B. and D. L. Caswell, *Software Metrics: Establishing a Company-Wide Program*, Prentice-Hall, 1987.

[GRI92] Griss, M., *proceedings of the Fifth Annual Workshop on Software Reuse*, Hewlett-Packard, October 26-29, 1992.

[GUT92] Guttman, M. K. and J. R. Matthews, "Managing a Large Project: CASE Study of a Long-Term Project at NCR," *Object Magazine*, November-December 1992, pp. 75-78.

[FRE83] Freeman, P., "Reusable Software Engineering: Concepts and Research Directions," in *Workshop on Reusability in Programming*, ITT Programming, September 1983, pp. 2-16.

[FRE87] Freeman, P., "A Perspective on Reusability," *in Software Reusability*, Computer Society Press of the IEEE, 1987, pp. 2-8.

[HEN92] Henderson-Sellers, B. and C. Freeman, "Cataloguing and Classification for Object Libraries," *ACM SIGSOFT*, vol. 17, no. 1, pp. 62-64.

[HEN93] Henderson-Sellers, B. and Y. R. Pant, "Adopting the Reuse Mindset Throughout the Life Cycle," *Object Magazine*, November-December 1993, pp. 73-75.
[HEW89] "Product Development using Object-Oriented Software Technology," *Hewlett-Packard Journal*, August, 1989, pp. 87-100.
[HOP91] Hopper, J. W., *Software Reuse: Guidelines and Methods*, Plenum Press, 1991.
[HSI93] Hsian-Chou, L. and W. Feng-Jian, "Software Reuse Based on a Large Object-Oriented Library," *ACM SIGSOFT*, vol. 18, no. 1, 1993, pp. 74-80.
[HUN93] Hunscher, D., "Stories from the Frontline: Managing Object-Oriented Development in an Engineering Evironment," *Object Magazine*, January-February 1993, pp. 75-78.
[ISO92] Isoda, S., "Experience Report on Software Reuse Project: Its Structure, Activities, and Statistical Results," *proceedings of the Intl. Conference on Software Engineering*, May 11-15, 1992, pp. 320-326.
[JON84] Jones, T. C., "Reusability in Programming: A Survey of the State of the Art," *IEEE Trans. on Soft. Eng.*, vol. SE-10, no. 5, 1984, pp. 488-493.
[JON94] Jones, T. C., "Software Management: The Weakest Link in the Software Engineering Chain," *IEEE Computer*, May 1994, pp. 10-11.
[JON86] Jones, T. C., *Programming Productivity*, McGraw-Hill, 1986.
[KEM91] Kemerer, C. and S. Chidamber, "Towards a Metrics Suite for Object-Oriented Design," MIT Sloan School of Management. 1991.
[KIN93] King, J. A., S. J. Olds, and J. D. Stuber, "Reuse Management Facility," *Object Magainze*, March-April 1993, pp. 72-74.
[LAN84] Lanergan, R. G. and C. A. Grasso, "Software Engineering with Reusable Designs and Code," *IEEE Trans. on Soft. Eng.*, vol. SE-10, no. 5, 1984, pp. 498-501.
[LEN89] Lenz, M., H. A. Schmid, and P. F. Wolf, "Software Reuse through Building Blocks," *IEEE Software*, July 1989, pp. 34-42.
[LEW92] Lewis, J. A., S. M. Henry, D. G. Kafura, and R. S. Schulman, "On the Relationship between the Object-Oriented Paradigm and Software Reuse: an Empirical Investigation," *JOOP*, July/August 1992, pp. 35-41.
[LOR91] Lorenz, M., "Real-World Reuse," *JOOP*, November/December 1991, pp. 35-39.

[LUB88] Lubars, M. D., "Wide-Spectrum Support for Software Reusabiltiy," *Software Reuse: Emerging Technology*, Will Tracz, ed., CS Press, 1988, pp. 275-281.

[MAR92] Margono, J. and T. E. Rhoads, "Software Reuse Economics: Cost-Benefit Analysis on a Large-Scale Ada Project," *proceedings of the Intl. Conference on Software Enginereing*, May 11-15, 1992, pp. 338-348.

[MAT82] Matsumoto, M., "SEA/I: Systems Engineer's Arms for Industrial Production and Support of Application Programs," *proceedings of the 6th Intl. Conference on Software Engineering*, September 1982, pp. 39-40.

[MCG91] McGregor, J. D. and D. A. Sykes, "A Paradigm for Reuse," *American Programmer*, vol. 4, no. 10, pp. 31-39.

[MCI69] McIlroy, M. D., "Mass Produced Software Components," *Software Engineering Concepts and Techniques*, paper presented at the 1969 NATO Conference on Software Engineering, pp. 88-98.

[PAG85] Page-Jones, M., *Practical Project Management*, Dorset House, 1985.

[PIT93] Pittman, M., "Lessons Learned in Managing Object-Oriented Development," *IEEE Software*, January 1993, pp. 43-53.

[PRI93] Prieto-Diaz, R., "Status Report: Software Reusability," *IEEE Software*, May 1993, pp. 61-66.

[PRI91a] Prieto-Diaz, R., "Making Software Reuse Work: An Implementation Model," *ACM SIGSOFT*, vol. 16, no. 3, 1991, pp. 61-68.

[PRI91b] Prieto-Diaz, R., "Implementing Faceted Classification for Software Reuse," *CACM*, vol. 34, no. 5, May 1991, pp. 88-97.

[PRI87] Prieto-Diaz, R., "Classifying Software for Reusability," *IEEE Software*, January 1987, pp. 6-16.

[RAY91] Raymond, G. E. and D. M. Hollis, "Software Reuse Economics Model," *proceedings of the Eighth Annual Washington Ada Symposium*, 1991, pp. 141-155.

[REE93] Reed, D. R., "Perspective: The Engineering Manager," *Moving from C to C++*, SIGS Publications, pp. 10-11.

[SHO83] Shooman, M. L., *Software Engineering: Design, Reliability, and Management,* McGraw-Hill, 1983.

[SOL83] Soloway, E. and K. Ehrlich, "What do Programmers Reuse? Theory and Experiment," *Workshop on Reusabiltiy in Programming*, ITT Programming, September 1983.

[SPC93]   *Reuse Adoption Guidebook*, Software Productivity Consortium, Tech. Report SPC-92051-CMC.
[TAY93]   Tayler, D. A., "Software Metrics for Object Technology," *Object Magazine*, March-April 1993, pp. 22-28.
[TRA92]   Tracz, W., "Domain Analysis Working Group Report: First International Workshop on Software Reusability," *ACM SIGSOFT*, vol. 17, no. 3, 1992, pp. 27-34.

Migrating to Object Technology

Chapter 13

Any organization that seeks to adopt a new development approach — whether it be with object technology, CASE, or any other technology — must recognize the potential impact of that technology on its staff and existing environment. Failure to consider and plan this migration process will result in a loss of any significant benefits from the technology, regardless of what has been promised by the technology vendors. Some in the industry have suggested that organizations must be mature before they can benefit from the introduction of new development technology or formal methods, and there are a number of models of the software engineering process that can be used to define and improve the process.

Any attempt to adopt new technology must consider the potential impact of the technology on the organization, its staff, and management practices. Software engineering is a social endeavor — involving people with diverse background and expectations — and requires a shared view of the process by everyone. Managing software engineering projects requires dealing with social and technical issues, and automated tools and formal methods can help define and improve the process if applied wisely. I suggest taking a holistic view of software engineering and considering the role and impact of change on the processes and people involved before attempting to adopt object technology.

In this chapter, I will look at the process of adopting object technology and the scope of this process. I will review the effect migration to new technology has on staff and management, the three basic components of any software development process, the role and type of process models available, a software process improvement strategy, training and education for this migration process, and experiences of organizations that have adopted object technology. I also will provide a strategy for adopting object technology in general, and OOCOBOL specifically, in a traditional MIS environment.

13.1 Introduction

One way to consider a migration to object technology is to view the process as an incremental one involving many steps. Peter Wegner of Brown University has defined three different levels of object-orientation that can be helpful when considering this transition. You will find that these three views or levels can be achieved if planned and managed accordingly in a short period of time (perhaps nine months to a year) and can provide a slow, even migration path to full use of object technology.

Object-based development supports the concepts of objects and messages as a means of communication. This view is a first-step in the migration process and represents the modeling, design, and implementation of object-based systems or applications that are composed of objects (encapsulated data and process) that interact or collaborate via messages.

Class-based development supports the concepts of object-based development with the addition of generic objects or classes. Using the incremental migration process described previously, an organization might move from an object-based perspective to a class-based perspective by beginning to identify generic objects or abstract data types (ADTs) from the pool of objects in applications that already have been built or are under development. The process of generalization can be applied slowly to existing and new systems so that a pool of classes can be defined.

Object-oriented development supports the class-based approach but adds the concept of classification by inheritance. This final stage represents the use of objects and messages, ADTs and generalization, and inheritance based on attributes and properties or behaviors. At this level, reusable components can begin to be classified and reused using inheritance relationships.

Along these lines, Kerth and Andreason reported on their experiences managing a successful transition to object technology [KER93]. While I will examine other experiences migration to object technology later in this chapter, I will review the Kerth/Andreason report here as a basis for the transition to object-oriented COBOL.

Kerth and Andreason identify five basic stages of object technology transition:

1. *Assimilating* the literature — reading literature, researching, etc.
2. *Experimenting* with objects on small projects and groups.
3. *Building* large systems of objects in teams.
4. *Standardizing* the use of object technology.
5. *Optimizing* resources around object technology.

These stages are shown in Figure 13.1 along with the capabilities or focus of each stage, the tasks required of developers and managers during these stages, and the impact the use of object technology at the stage has on the

Stages	Capabilities and Focus	Developer Tasks	Manager Tasks	Impact on Software Process
Assimilating	Interest & Enthusiasm	Read, study, learn, discuss	Provide training and resources, think about the big picture, allow staff to experiment, etc.	None
Experimenting	Few developers building systems rapidly	Learn languages, notations, object think, etc.	Encourage exploration and team building, develop a vision of adoption, etc.	Incremental process, standard life cycle
Building	Improving the systems built	Select tools (OOPLs, OOA/D methods, etc.), learn about reuse, incremental development, etc.	Manage object-oriented development, improving quality and the software process	Modifications to existing methods, tools, etc., configuration management, project planning, etc.
Standardizing	Several projects use object technology, experiences become part of software culture	Select a common method, tools, procedures, etc. and understand when not to use object technology	Identify and implement metrics, measure, refine efforts, etc.	New life cycle standards, work products, reviews, etc.
Optiminzing	Using object technology to improve the process	Focusing on reuse across projects and domains	Establish different groups to define, build, deliver, and support software	Reuse of internal and external components as part of software process

Figure 13.1 Stages in the transition to object technology.

overall software process. Later in this chapter, I will examine other views on technology adoption, not specific to object technology.

13.2 A Strategy for Adopting Object-Oriented COBOL

While it is impossible to provide every software engineering organization with a blueprint for successful adoption of object technology, I can recommend a series of tasks that should be performed when considering adoption to help improve the chances of success. The remaining sections of this chapter address many of the issues that can prohibit successful adoption of object technology, along with observations and recommendations from organizations that have adopted object technology. This information is provided to help organizations deal with the difficulty inherent in changing their software engineering process to incorporate OOCOBOL and objects.

In this section, I will provide a generic, but hopefully appropriate, list of tasks that organizations should undertake as they migrate to OOCOBOL. Figure 13.2 represents a flowchart of these tasks. I suggest that these tasks be assigned to a group of staff in the organization with a manager or executive as the sponsor of the adoption process and that these tasks be performed with the insight and consideration of everyone involved in the software engineering process. Organizations that undertake this adoption process also should plan on a long-term commitment to change and quality improvement and to a five-year strategy for adopting OOCOBOL.

There is one assumption that I make as I provide these recommendations: OOCOBOL will be the chosen implementation environment. These tasks, therefore, assume that the resulting development environment will include OOCOBOL as the programming language of choice.

Assess the current software engineering environment. As a first step in any change process, the current state of software engineering should be defined in sufficient detail to identify problems and items for improvement. Typically, this assessment involves asking some basic questions about the way that software is developed in the organization, surveying the staff on their skills, documenting the use of methods and tools, and presenting an assessment report to management for their review.

Pressman [PRE88], Humphrey [HUM89a], and others [TOP93] have covered this topic in sufficient detail to allow organizations to have a basis for performing this task. The SEI, along with other organizations, also can perform and train staff for an assessment.

Select OOA/D methods and formalize the development process. Once an organization has defined its existing software engineering environment and identified areas for improvement, it can begin to look at tools and techniques for formalizing and improving the process. Existing staff skills can be a guide to selecting appropriate methods, as can application domains and implementation environments. The task of choosing an appropriate formal development method is not trivial and involves extensive research.

When considering OOA/D methods, use any available resources, including comparisons in technical journals, experiential reports of organizations that

```
          ┌──────────────┐
          │ Assess current│
          │   software   │
          │  engineering │
          │  environment │
          └──────────────┘
                 │
                 ▼
            ┌──────────────┐
            │Select OOA/D  │
            │ methods and  │
            │formalize the │
            │ development  │
            │   process    │
            └──────────────┘
                   │
                   ▼
              ┌──────────────┐
              │   Identify   │
              │Environment   │
              │   Issues     │
              └──────────────┘
                      │
                      ▼
                ┌──────────────┐
                │Identify,     │
                │evaluate, and │
                │select OOA/D  │
                │   tools      │
                └──────────────┘
                        │
                        ▼
                  ┌──────────────┐
                  │Adopt OOA/D   │
                  │Methods and   │
                  │   Tools      │
                  └──────────────┘
                           │
                           ▼
                    ┌──────────────┐
                    │Use OOCOBOL as│
                    │an object-based│
                    │  language    │
                    └──────────────┘
                              │
                              ▼
                      ┌──────────────┐
                      │Use OOCOBOL as│
                      │a class-based │
                      │  language    │
                      └──────────────┘
                                 │
                                 ▼
                         ┌──────────────┐
                         │Use OOCOBOL as│
                         │an object-    │
                         │oriented lang.│
                         └──────────────┘
                                     │
                                     ▼
                               ┌──────────────┐
                               │ Re-evaluate  │
                               │   software   │
                               │  engineering │
                               │   process    │
                               └──────────────┘
```

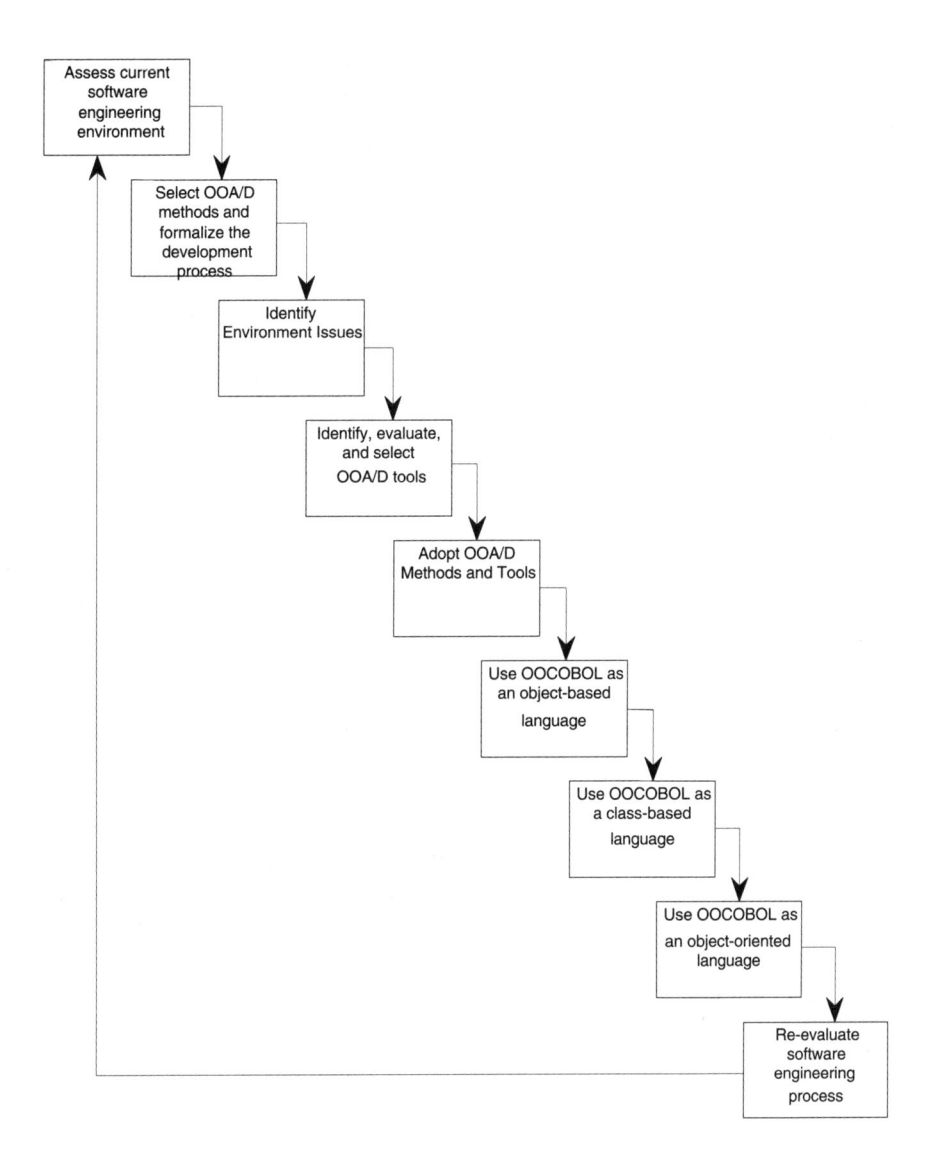

Figure 13.2 A strategy for adopting OOCOBOL.

have adopted specific methods, and the sidebar at the end of chapter 7, which compares some popular object-oriented techniques. Published comparisons of OOA/D methods also are available from SIGS Publications and the Object Management Group (OMG). Also helpful are journals and magazines that cover object technology, including *Object Magazine*, *Journal of Object-Oriented Programming* (JOOP), and *Report on Object Analysis and Design* (ROAD).

Identify environment issues. Concurrent with the evaluation of methods, organizations should identify any specific implementation issues that can impact their choices of methods and tools. Issues — such as the implementation hardware and software, required DBMS, teleprocessing support, networking, and GUI — should be considered whenever methods and tools are evaluated. These implementation factors should be weighed against any future changes in these items given the long-range perspective taken in adopting object technology.

Identify, evaluate, then select OOA/D tools. After careful consideration, an organization can begin to identify and evaluate automated tools to support OOCOBOL development. These tools might include traditional development products — such as CASE tools, configuration management, project management and estimation, metrics — as well as object-oriented tools, including class libraries and browsers.

One caution for those organizations that plan to evaluate these products: do so with a pilot project and don't purchase them without using them on an actual project. Many organizations see a slick product at a conference or in a demonstration and purchase the product for use only to find out that it will not work in their environment, either for technical or cultural reasons. Without using any tool on a real project, organizations will never know whether the product helps or hinders their software engineering efforts.

Adopt OOA/D methods and tools. Once methods and tools have been evaluated, recommendations can be made regarding which OOA/D techniques and supportive tools should be purchased and adopted. Simple buying training and tools does not guarantee successful use of these products on real projects. Any organization that adopts methods and tools must provide training for all staff, should consider using mentors to encourage and support the adoption process, and also should provide a culture where change can be fostered. I will cover the issue of cultural change in more detail later in this chapter, but organizations should anticipate a 12 to 18 month learning curve for adoption of any formal method or technique.

Use OOCOBOL as an object-based language. To begin the migration to full use of object-orientation, I suggest that organizations take the approach described in section 13.1. This approach takes a slow, incremental view of object technology adoption beginning with the use of objects (encapsulations of data structures and operations), clearly defined interfaces, and messages in an *object-based* perspective.

Existing and new applications can be analyzed, designed, and even implemented with this object-based view as a first step to full object-orientation. Using the methods described in chapters 6 and 7, an organization can produce object models and specifications that are mapped to a implementations in OOCOBOL with objects, messages, and clearly defined interfaces between subsystems.

Look at generalizations of objects. After migration to an object-based perspective, organizations can begin looking for generalizations of their objects as classes in their application domains. Once objects have been defined on previous projects and in existing systems, these objects can be considered for generalization into classes. Using the concepts of abstraction, aggregation, and generalization, staff can begin to view their development efforts in terms of interfaces and services provided by classes that exhibit the same behavior and attributes as specific objects. This is referred to as a *class-based* view in section 13.1.

Begin building or extending a class library using inheritance. After more projects have been developed with a class-based perspective, you staff will be in a better position to begin looking for reusable components. Recalling the discussion of reuse in chapter 12, any attempt to implement large-scale reuse must include tools and techniques for measuring and rewarding reuse within the organization. Reusable components can be acquired in the form of class libraries or created for selected application domains and, using OOCOBOL, can be organized into hierarchies based on inheritance.

Movement to an *object-oriented* development environment that supports objects, classes, messages, and reuse requires technical, managerial, and cultural properties in a software engineering process. Using OOCOBOL, organizations can use the class libraries provided by the compiler vendor (such as those in the Micro Focus Object COBOL Option), purchase them from other vendors, or concentrate on populating their own libraries.

Re-evaluate methods, tools, etc. for improvement. A final step in the migration to OOCOBOL is to determine if the adoption of methods, tools, and language components have improved the software engineering process. For any quantifiable improvement to be shown, measurements must be taken prior to the adoption process and afterward so that any differences can be identified and measured. Regardless of whether the adoption of OOCOBOL improves an organization's software development process or not, the organization should perform a follow-up evaluation and might be required to make additional changes to enhance or improve the process in the future.

13.2.1 Scope of Change

As previously mentioned, any attempt to migrate to object technology must consider the change that is required to make this transition. The scope of this change is broad, potentially affecting everyone in the organization that works with software. Any change also must consider the roles and responsibilities of staff, their existing skills, the tools and methods used, and the measurements and metrics that drive the process. Management must understand the potential impact of introducing object technology to their staff and provide the required support and resources to be successful

In my experience, the scope of change involved in adopting object technology is broad and is often underestimated. Failure to involve all affected parties early and throughout the migration process dramatically increases the likelihood of failure. Managing expectations and providing staff with an environment for change are key issues to improving the success of any adoption process. Providing sufficient training to developers and managers also is key to successful migration to object technology.

Prior to attempting a transition to any new technology, the organizations must make commitment at the highest levels, even above the software engineering managers, to provide whatever resources are necessary to successfully adopt a new approach to software development. A transition to object technology requires executive sponsorship, along with the understanding and acceptance of users of the eventual software products. Some organizations try to implement change by management edict, which often results in failure. A more practical approach is for management to set some general software engineering goals — perhaps to improve overall software quality — and establish a long-term plan for achieving these goals. Following the development of the plan, management must guide the migration process and support their staff in making the transition to object technology.

Organizations often underestimate the cost associated with transitioning to object technology. Most experiential reports indicate that the cost of training staff will be the most expensive aspect of adoption, followed by the tools and infrastructure required to support object-oriented development. Any organization undertaking a migration to object technology also should understand the inhibitors to cultural change: the not-invented-here syndrome, lack of adequate training and support, lack of a clear view of software engineering, and failure to convince staff of the benefit of object-oriented development.

Another factor that often prohibits successful adoption of object technology is the misled view that the migration process can occur quickly. Those organizations that have been successful report that the time to achieve change might take up to 5 or even 10 years. As with other software development technologies, object-oriented development can provide substantial benefits if those involved have a valid timeline for achieving these benefits.

Later in this chapter (see section 13.7) I will look more closely at the experiences of those organizations that have made or still are making the transition to object technology to review their observations and recommendations. This information is vital to anyone involved in the transition because it highlights the actual experiences of organizations that have been through the process.

13.2.2 Software Production Framework

Many organizations have tried and failed to implement formal software development methods and automated tools. In my experience, problems most often occur in organizations that bring in technology and try to force a rigid, formal development process without considering the cultural and organizational impact of this adoption on their staff and clients.

I recommend that organizations take a holistic view of software development, and we offer the term *software production framework* (SPF) as a definition of all the organizational, technical, and cultural aspects of software engineering. In my view, the SPF includes all the components commonly described or written about, including the software engineering triad, software development life cycles and notations, as well as the interrelationships and roles and responsibilities of staff within the organization. Figure 13.3 describes the SPF along with its components and the affected organizational levels, from top to bottom.

Software development life cycles (SDLCs), as described in chapter 4, define a series of tasks and activities for software production and the sequence and dependencies between these tasks. Generally included in any SDLC are stages for planning, analysis, design, programming, testing, and maintenance. SDLCs focus on the highest organizational level, deal with the role of development in the organization, and provide a schedule for software development and maintenance. Some SDLCs are linear, while others are iterative or evolutionary, allowing for cycles of activities or tasks with feedback loops built in, and deal with organizational and high-level management issues.

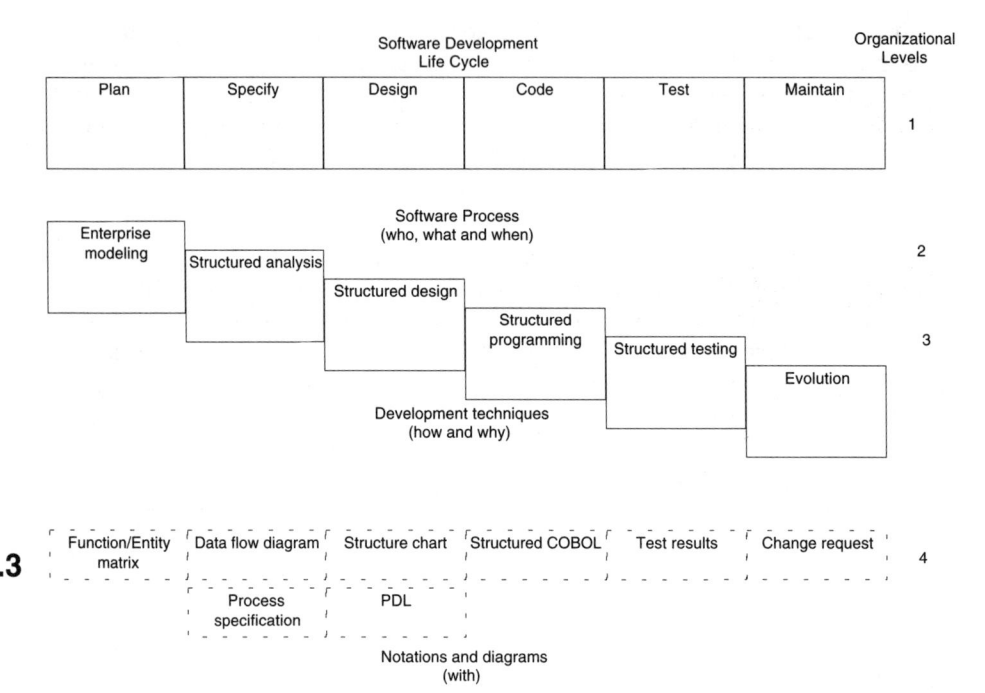

Figure 13.3
A software production framework.

A software process defines the roles, responsibilities, staff dynamics, and management tools and techniques for software development and maintenance. Software processes focus at the development organization or group level but might include other stakeholders in the development process, such as clients, quality assurance staff, and auditors. Software processes deal with interaction and staff control issues and provide the who, what, and when of a development process. Who does what when in software production is addressed by the software process.

Software process models help organizations understand and potentially improve the process that they use to develop software by allowing them to quantify, study, and analyze their process using standard symbols and notations. Several types of software process models are available, including the Software Engineering Institute (SEI) Software Process Maturity Model [KEL89], the TAME Goal Oriented Approach [OIV92], system dynamic models [ABD91], and quality improvement models [CLA91]. I will review these and other software process models in more detail in section 13.3.

Formal development techniques provide specific tasks, methods, and representations (or deliverables) for the creation of software product artifacts throughout the development process. Techniques focus at the project team level and describe group-related activities that require communication, standard methods and procedures, and a shared view of the development process and the products created. Automated tools, including CASE tools, can support techniques and the representations that they require. Techniques support specific tasks within the SDLC and software process and provide the how and why of the process, where how a task is accomplished and why it is necessary are defined by the technique.

Notations and diagramming tools define the actual content of the representations used in the techniques and provide standard symbols and notations for each deliverable or artifact. Notations are aimed at the lowest level within the organization, individual developers, and provide guidelines for describing the artifacts called for in the development technique. Notations describe the with for the technique's how. In other words, the development techniques describe how a task is accomplished, but the notation describes with what specific tool the representation is created.

Another term that commonly is used in reference to software production is *methodology*, which actually means the study of methods. The generally accepted use of this term maps methodology to a specific SDLC, a software process, and some particular techniques and notations. Commercially available methodologies usually include specific stages, tasks, roles and responsibilities, development techniques, and supporting notations and diagrams.

A holistic view of software production should include all of these perspectives, and should consider the development staff and the different levels. For instance, software process, and by implication software process improvement, is focused at the middle management level of an organization, and any attempt to define or study an existing process should begin at this level. Likewise, adopting new development techniques will affect development staff and project organization and should be considered from this vantage point first.

Some organizations might choose to adopt a software process improvement view. Other organizations might want to develop or acquire a methodology to address all the aspects of the SPF in a single decision. Still other organizations might choose to focus directly on the adoption of formal development techniques and automated tools.

13.2.3 Software Engineering Triad

One view that supports the relationship between software development process, methods, and tools is the concept of a software engineering triad described in [TOP93]. This concept, shown in Figure 13.4, represents the three basic components of any software development environment and their relationships. The three components — process, methods and tools — are interrelated, and there are strong relationships among the elements.

I begin by offering a definition of *software process*:

A social activity, highly creative in nature, that is conducted in an environment of limited resources and produces a series of representations (or deliverables) of an intangible product, "software."

Formal development techniques represent the "how" of software process. I prefer the term *technique* to its more popular rivals (software development methodology, software development methods, structured methods, etc.) because it carries some of the connotations of craftsmanship with it. In a sense, software development techniques have been passed down from older developers to newer ones, not unlike other methods used by other craftsman.

My definition of *formal technique* is:

The use of an engineering, disciplined approach to developing software that typically can be characterized by five criteria: it (the technique) is written down, repeatable, teachable, measurable, and automatable.

Techniques that are used but not taught, are not written down or measured, or are practiced by only a certain individual in an organization cannot be considered "formal techniques" as we have defined them and cannot be automated with a set of popular tools.

For the purposes of this book, I define *Computer-Aided Software Engineering (CASE)* to be:

The automation of formal techniques, notations, and methods for the development of software.

At a very basic level, CASE tools automate a specific technique. Ideally, a CASE tool should not hinder, but enhance, the use of techniques and provide verification checking and automated support for the routine, mundane aspects of applying the technique to a large project.

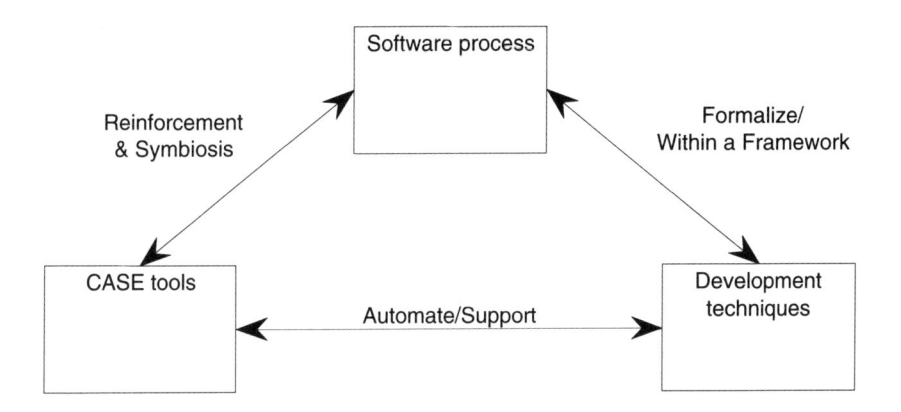

Figure 13.4 The software engineering triad.

With over 300 CASE products currently available, it is becoming increasingly difficult to determine which tools actually match the definition that I use and which do not. Future CASE products will provide support for object-oriented techniques, and with the movement towards tool integration, selecting CASE products should be easier.

As you have seen, developing software is a social process that involves three related components: a process, techniques, and automated tools (CASE). A software process defines the tasks, deliverables, and resources that are used to produce software, or the who, what, and when. Techniques are the how and why of software process, and there is a wide variety of popular development methods or techniques. CASE tools make using techniques practical for medium- to large-sized projects and define with what notations development staff will communicate.

Organizations that develop software without fully understanding or considering each of those components, or the overall framework of software production, cannot realize the promise of improved software quality and developer productivity. By realizing that software development is a group activity, involving people with differing views and backgrounds, organizations can begin to focus on the critical issues of software production.

13.3 Software Process Modeling

Within the software development industry, many organizations have found it useful to apply the notations and techniques that are used to develop software to model the software development process itself. A software process model must, at a minimum, answer the following questions:

- What tasks make up the process?
- Who performs these tasks and what artifacts are created or used?
- How are these tasks actually performed (i.e., development techniques)?
- What relationships exist among the stakeholders involved in the process?

By far, the most popular software process model created to date is the software process maturity model (SPMM) developed by the SEI. This model consists of five levels of maturity that a software engineering organization can be at based on their software process, use of methods and tools, and management practices.

The software process models described in this section include process maturity, system dynamics, continuous quality improvement, goal-oriented, and common-sense management. Taken together, they provide a comprehensive picture of the software process.

13.3.1 Software Process Maturity Model

Figure 13.5 describes the SPMM defined by Watts Humphrey [HUM89A] [HUM90]. This view also is widely taught and used by the SEI at Carnige Mellon University. The basis for the SPMM is the observation that organizations can be at one of five possible levels of software maturity — from initial or *ad hoc* to optimized. These five levels correspond to an organization's ability to manage and improve software engineering.

The SPMM levels are:

- *Initial* (or ad-hoc) — Where an organization has no defined software process, does not regularly use project planning or estimation, and software development is very informal.
- *Repeatable* — Organizations at this level still have a mostly *ad hoc* software engineering process, but the process is used by everyone and backed by management; software projects are estimated and measured based on previous projects and no attempt to improve the process is possible.
- *Defined* — Organizations at this level have formally defined their process, and it is accepted and used by everyone involved; the process is used for its own merits and is qualified by management.
- *Managed* — The software engineering process of organizations at this level is not only defined, as in level 3, but is measured, with data collected used to modify the process; the process at this level is directly related to software quality measurements.

Characteristics

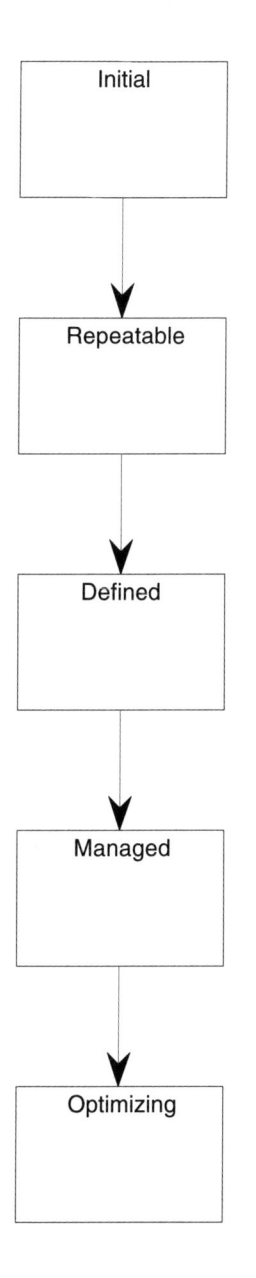

Initial — No defined process, no use of project planning or estimation (Ad-hoc or seat-of-the-pants)

Repeatable — Ad-hoc process, used and backed by management. (Know the ropes)

Defined — Formally defined process that is understood and accepted by everyone. Process is used for its own merits and is qualified but not quantified.

Managed — Measured software process, where data are collected and used to modify the process. Process is related to software quality.

Optimizing — Software process is under measured control, weak spots are identified and modified or fixed.

Figure 13.5 The software process maturity model.

- *Optimized* — The ultimate software maturity, organizations at this level can improve the process via measured control; weak spots in the process are identified and fixed.

The SEI works with organizations to help them identify where they are in the SPMM and show them how they can improve their process. As defined by SEI, software process improvement can take years and requires fundamental and extensive change to corporate culture. SEI recommends that the first step toward improving the software process is assessing the state of the current environment and defining it formally.

13.3.2 Models of Roles and Activities

Modeling the various roles and responsibilities of the stakeholders in the software development process also brings insight into the software process. The mainline roles for software production are software development, testing, project management, and maintenance. Secondary roles include software quality assurance, configuration management, auditing, and possibly process and reuse management. These roles are conducted by people, and this is a point where a data modeling technique is applicable.

Aoyama [AOY87] offers an object-oriented view where work products are objects and the methods associated with an object correspond to tasks or activities. In the object-oriented view, a review object, for example, would have scheduling, preparing, conducting, and reporting as associated methods or services. Aoyama emphasizes that his object-oriented view is explicitly static, and he prefers a Petri net model to describe process dynamics.

13.3.3 Models of Interactions/Communication

When you consider the dynamics of the software process, the real-time metaphor becomes very useful. Consider the myriad of interactions and communications among roles and activities on a software development project. You can easily imagine long feedback loops, situations where deadlock might occur, and so on. How do/should you represent such interactions? In her book on project management, Zells maintains that much of the reason that project estimates are so unreliable is that so many activities are never identified and, hence, never scheduled in the first place [ZEL90].

13.3.4 Models of System Dynamics

System dynamics is an industrial engineering term that recently has been applied to the software process [ABD91]. System dynamics uses feedback loops to model control systems, especially where the item being controlled is a social activity. Abdel-Hamid's main contribution is to highlight the fact that software project management, like software process, is a nonlinear activity. When the output of a subsystem changes (increases or decreases), the successor subsystems are affected.

In their book, Abdel-Hamid and Madnick explore many feedback cycles, quantifying them with industry studies where they can. One of the contributions is that they "test" their model against widely held beliefs (I probably should dignify them by calling them "hypotheses"), such as Brooke's law (adding people to a late project makes it later). Their model supports many of these scenarios.

13.3.5 Models of Continuous Quality Improvement

Other organizations, including AG Communication Systems (AGCS), a joint venture between GTE and AT&T, have found a quality management perspective and an orientation towards continuous process improvement to be effective in process modeling [CLA91]. AGCS has developed the quality management process model shown in Figure 13.6 and uses it to drive a continuous improvement of their development process.

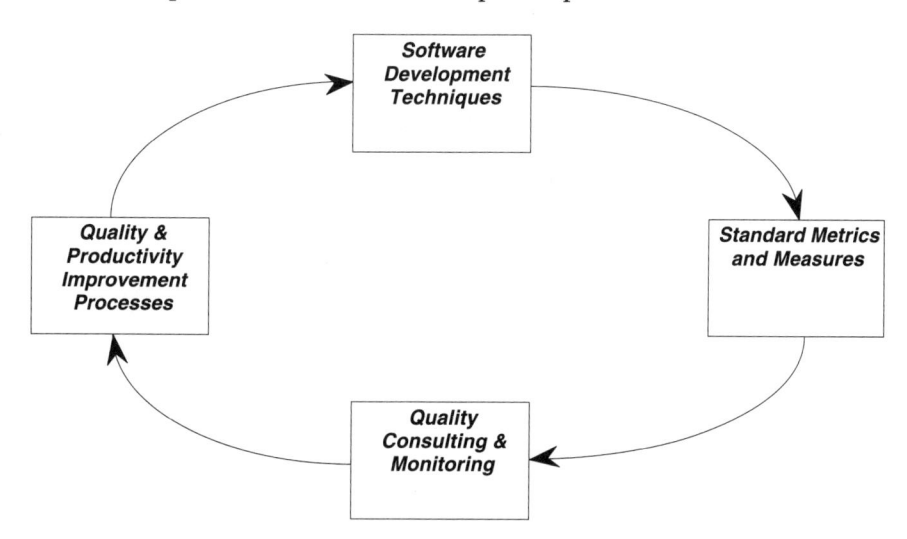

Figure 13.6 Continuous quality improvement.

AGCS has used software metrics extensively to affect change in its software process and has instituted quality consultants to help improve the quality of the process and the product. Within AGCS, these quality consultants develop and monitor quality plans, monitor and consult on the metrics that are used, conduct post-mortems on projects completed, lead regular quality council meetings, and focus on continuous process improvement.

AGCS has found that establishing a software engineering process improvement group and a quality council helps it keep focused on the concept of continuous improvement. AGCS also reports that a critical aspect of its success in improving quality is the use of metrics within the larger scope of continuous improvement.

13.3.6 Goal-Oriented Models

The TAME project [OIV92] includes a model of software processes that has an object-oriented meta-model and uses a goal-oriented approach. TAME uses a Goal/Question/Metric paradigm, which is geared towards improving the software development process. A Quality Improvement paradigm establishes project and organizational goals, a mechanism for measuring progress against these goals, and an approach to building software measurements and applying them against these goals.

Within TAME, an experience factory collects the experience of software developers and includes two types of knowledge: descriptive knowledge, which describes the "how" of software development, and procedural knowledge, which includes experience in setting goals, answering questions, and collecting empirical data.

Under the TAME approach, a Goal Question Metric Program is used to define and interpret software goals, which include a purpose and a perspective for each goal. The purpose of a goal represents the process or product used, and the perspective represents the measurable aspects of the end result and the point of view of the stakeholders involved.

13.3.7 A Common-Sense Management Model

Another model of software processes that has been proposed is the common-sense management model (CMM) [YEH91]. CMM proposes a model that can guide management in process modeling away from parts of the process to a three-dimensional view of software development.

The CMM includes activities, which define the phases of development and are sequential; communication structures, which define explicit communication channels for all stakeholders involved; and an infrastructure, which supports long-range goals of continuous quality improvement. The resulting model, called Cosmos, supports separation of concerns, co-evolution of artifacts, evolutionary prototyping, tangible definitions of artifacts, and continual improvement.

Within Cosmos, there is a two-level process hierarchy that includes control, to allow coordination and management of process and project functions, and execution, which supports specific tasks or activities. Key to the Cosmos view is the support for explicit communications between stakeholders and an infrastructure to support the creation and evolution of software development artifacts.

13.4 Software Process Improvement

One approach to improving the software engineering process is to apply total quality assurance to the process as described in [TOP93]. Using this approach, organizations follow a blueprint for adopting technology that helps to define and improve their software engineering methods and techniques along the lines of a quality improvement initiative. This approach consists of four basic steps.

Model the existing software process. Before any form of process improvement can begin, the status quo must be understood. Whatever the existing process is, it must be documented so that it can be used as a point of reference for process improvements.

What modeling form is appropriate for describing an existing process depends on how well the existing process is defined. If the process is at the Initial or Repeatable maturity levels, as defined by the SEI SPMM, it probably is sufficient to record the life cycle model in use, then do the best to make a PERT chart of the typical activities. This will be very rough, because there probably are many interactions and communication paths that simply are not remembered.

Measure the software process. Once new tools and techniques have been successfully introduced, by definition the process has been changed. The Measured and Optimizing levels of SEI process maturity require a process group to continuously monitor the process and to recommend changes. Process groups identify process metrics that are tailored to an organizations process and goals, then they gather data for these metrics. Process metrics are more difficult to identify than product metrics. I will relate one such process metric here.

Product and process metrics tend to be self-fulfilling prophesies. If people know how they will be judged, they will conform to those expectations. Suppose, for example, that your employer announces that your salary increment is directly tied to how frequently you wear a blue shirt to work. Buy blue shirts and wear them everyday! The key to effective process metrics is that they must encourage desired behavior. For a more useful example, suppose you posit a metric that reflects reviewer effectiveness: number of discovered errors (by severity) per hour of preparation time.

Improve the software process. By changing the process and measuring the results, the software engineering process can be improved. When this occurs, the process and products must be measured to ensure that changes are improvements and not detriments. Using the models described previously, the process can be modified, measured, and improved or optimized.

Evaluate the process and begin again. Once the software engineering process has been defined, measured, and improved, the whole cycle begins again so that further improvements can be made. Organizations that continue through this cycle several times might find that they are at a level consistent with the optimized maturity of the SEI's SPMM.

13.5 Training and Education

Perhaps the most challenging aspect, and the most expensive, of any cultural change is the role of training and education of your staff. As with other cultural changes, migrating to object technology involves changing basic aspects of the development environment and process. Without adequate training and an opportunity for your staff to learn a "new" way, the migration process cannot succeed. Those organizations that have made or are making the transition to object technology report universally that the most important criteria is sound staff training.

When considering developing a training plan for your staff, consider their existing skills and expertise. Developers who have experience in functional programming will be required to change their perspective, while developers with little or no prior experience in procedural programming are much more likely to accept object-oriented concepts.

There are several experiential reports in the literature on training staff in object-oriented development, including [CON93], [COO94], [DSO93], [GIB91], [LOV93], [MCK93], and [WIE93]. C. Thomas Wu [WU93] recommends a three-stage, bottom-up method for teaching object-oriented programming:

1. Using a small, simple example, explain and illustrate the syntax and semantics of an OOPL, without discussing inheritance, polymorphism, etc.
2. Using the same example, introduce the concepts of reuse, abstraction, encapsulation, and polymorphism.
3. Using the same example, introduce the full concepts of object-orientation, including classification, inheritance, etc.

Based on the experiences of organizations that have adopted object technology, I suggest the following recommendations for training developers in object technology.

- *Programmers* ~ Introduction to OOPL — Introduces the basics of object-oriented programming without classification, inheritance, etc.
  ~ Hands-on programming (1 month) — Allows the programmers to experiment with the concepts of object-orientation on pilot projects.
  ~ OOA/D methods — Introduces the concepts of objects, messages, encapsulation, etc. from a modeling and design perspective, using a formal OOA/D method.
  ~ Intermediate-level programming — Applies the concepts of objects, messages, etc. on small, prototype-oriented projects.
  ~ Application development — Covers objects in the development life cycle, reuse, etc.
  ~ Prototype to product — Covers the issues of prototyping and the design, code, test, and implement phases.

- *Designers* ~ Introduction to OT — Introduces the concepts of object-oriented development.
  ~ OOA/D methods — Introduces the concepts of objects, messages, encapsulation, etc. from a modeling and design perspective, using a formal OOA/D method.
  ~ Project management for OT — Covers objects in the development life cycle, reuse, etc. from the perspective of managing the process.
  ~ Selecting applications for OT — Determines which applications can benefit from object technology, areas for potential reuse, etc.
  ~ Mentoring to build OOA/D skills — Develops the skills needed to teach others about object technology.

- *Managers* ~ Introduction to OT — Introduces the concepts of object-oriented development.
  ~ OOA/D methods — Introduces the concepts of objects, messages, encapsulation, etc. from a modeling and design perspective, using a formal OOA/D method.
  ~ Project management for OT — Covers objects in the development life cycle, reuse, etc. from the perspective of managing the software process.

13.6 Technology Transition Strategies

Along with the experiences of those organizations cited in the case studies, others in the industry have written on the subject of technology transfer as it relates to CASE and software development techniques. When reviewing the results of these efforts, there are some common findings that surface and point to several viable strategies for the technology transfer process.

Five major models for technology transition have been identified, including breadth of impact of change, organizational maturity, levels of learning a new technology, diffusion of innovation, and mutual adaptation. Each of these views will be discussed in more depth in the following sections.

13.6.1 Barb Bouldin

Barbara Bouldin has written on managing the cultural change that is required to make the transition to software development techniques and CASE [BOU89]. Bouldin's view is that the breadth of impact of change must drive the technology transition process. Bouldin spent several years at AT&T as a change agent for CASE and structured methods and has identified a life cycle for implementing change along with several key factors to successfully managing this change. These factors include:

- Providing information in familiar terms to everyone.
- Listening effectively, brainstorming, and developing a basic game plan.
- Planning intermediate deliverables.
- Not using edicts and involving users and staff early and throughout.
- Building on what already is effective.
- Avoiding excessive ambition.
- Managing everyone's expectations.
- Implementing without disruption.
- Keeping everyone involved.
- Performing periodic reviews and sign-offs.

13.6.2 Roger Pressman

Roger Pressman also has written on the process of making the transition to software development techniques and CASE [PRE88] and introduced the Software Engineering Life Cycle (SELC) shown in Figure 13.7 for this transition. Pressman's approach involves five basic steps:

1. Assessment — Assess where the organization is in its software development environment and identify strong and weak points in the process. Pressman recommends that organizations perform a software engineering audit or detailed assessment of their current development environment prior to moving forward with CASE and development techniques.
2. Education — Educate everyone involved in the methods, techniques, and tools to be used or already available.
3. Selection — Select any new techniques and/or tools that can help improve the software development process.
4. Installation — Install selected techniques and tools.

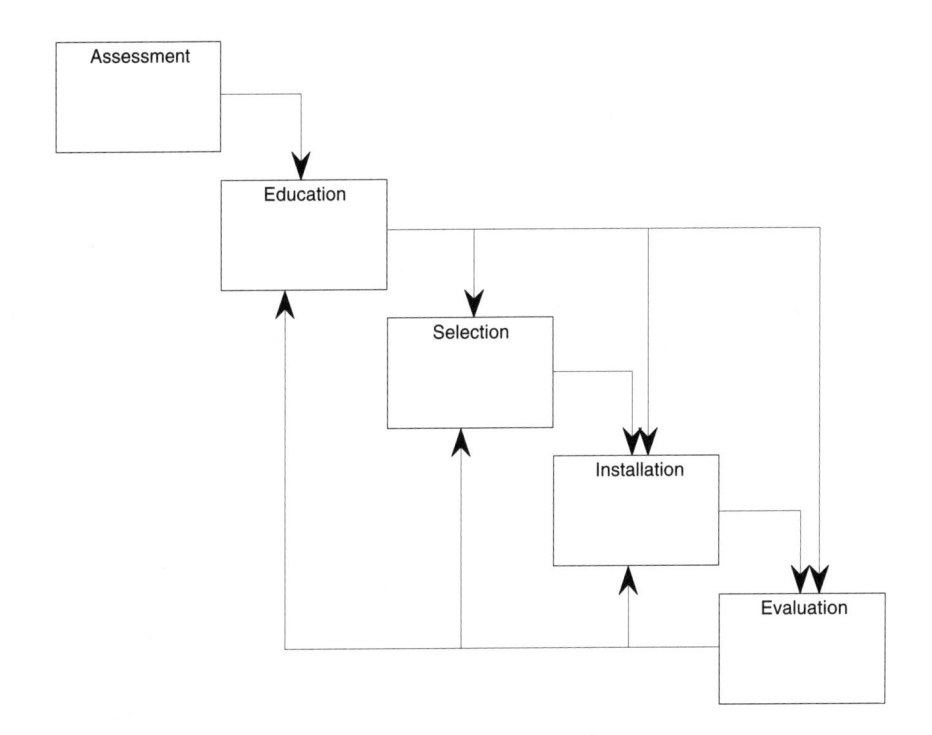

Figure 13.7 Pressman's Software Engineering Life Cycle.

5. Evaluation — Evaluate whether the software process has been improved by the tools and techniques installed and how the process can be further improved with other tools and techniques.

Pressman strongly suggests, as others do, that a SELC is a repetitive process that doesn't stop once techniques and tools have been successfully implemented. This view is shared by the total quality management (TQM) initiatives and the focus on continuous process improvement.

13.6.3 Watts Humphrey

Watts Humphrey, while at the SEI at Carnegie Mellon University, pioneered the SPMM and has written about it in [HUM89a]. This model has generated much discussion in the industry and is evolving within the SEI.

The SPMM has been widely used by organizations to determine whether they are ready for CASE and software development techniques. Humphrey also has identified a life cycle for improving and controlling the software process itself. Humphrey pioneered the concept of a defined software process, considering the product or outcome of the process (the software itself) the same way that one would that of a manufacturing process. Quality standards should be established to define the product, software. Evaluating the process for quality improvement can be done with software process models like the SPMM. Measuring the process can help identify ways of improving the process.

Phil Crosby has identified stages of quality management maturity that represent the views of management in an organization that are related to the concepts of quality and the process of improving quality of a product or service. Taken together, Crosby's levels of quality awareness present a goal-directed view of software process improvement. Humphrey and the SEI recommend that a software process assessment be the first step in defining a software process. SEI provides training and consulting for five-day assessment sessions to their clients.

13.6.4 The J Curve

The J curve, shown in Figure 13.8, identifies seven stages of software engineering expertise that explain the changes that occur when developers are introduced to development techniques and as they acquire expertise with these techniques. These stages are:

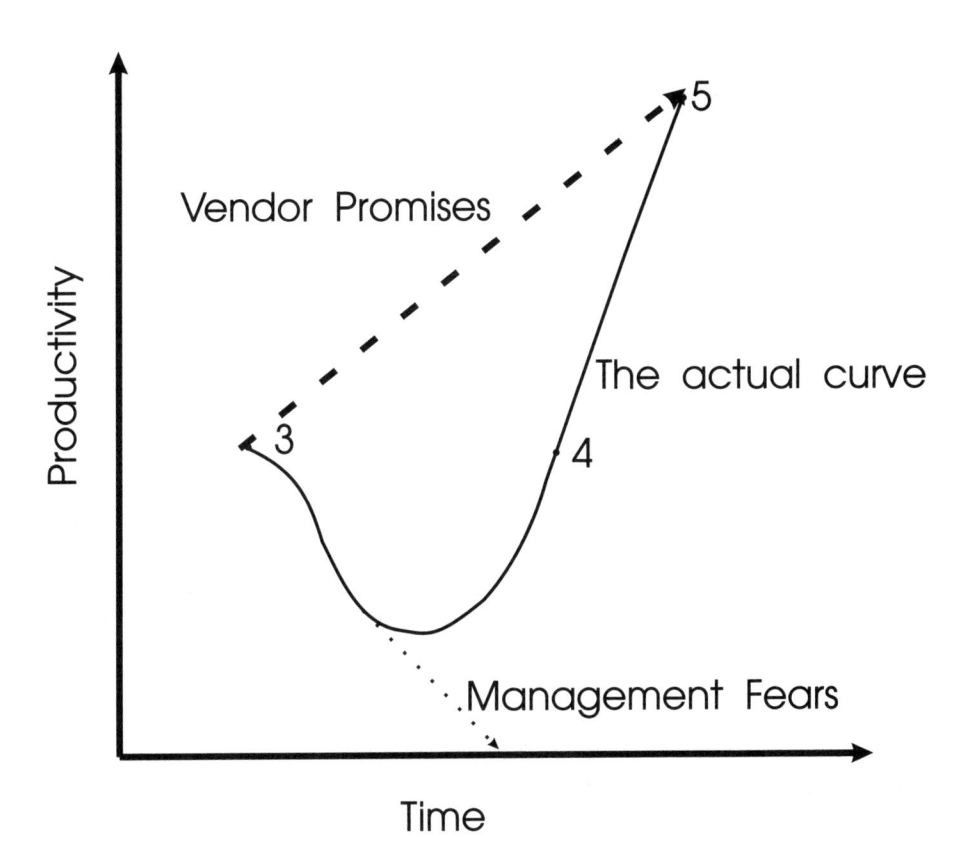

Figure 13.8
The J curve.

- Stage 1: *Innocent* people have never heard of software engineering methods and have no knowledge of their applicability. Stage 1 people might be blissfully unaware of any problems or a perceived "software crisis."
- Stage 2: *Exposed* people have heard of software engineering methods through colleagues, magazine articles, or whatever and believe that these methods have some relevance to them and their jobs.
- Stage 3: *Apprentice* people have been through a seminar or tutorial on software engineering methods and have a broad, superficial understanding of the methods themselves. However, stage 3 people have no practical experience applying the methods on real-world problems.
- Stage 4: *Practitioners* actually have used software engineering methods seriously at least once. They know about the tough parts and how to make the methods work; however, at this stage, the methods are not always second nature. Additional guidance often is required with stage 4 people to ensure productivity.

- Stage 5: *Journeymen* (or *Journeywomen*) use software engineering methods regularly and naturally in their day-to-day work. Once at this stage, staff members typically are more productive and rarely need any advice or guidance on using the methods.
- Stage 6: *Experts* are thoroughly conversant with software engineering and know the rules so well that they even know when to break them to achieve better results. They often are found training others in software engineering methods.
- Stage 7: *Researchers* are at the leading edge of software engineering practices and often are called upon to write books, give papers, and speak on software engineering methods. They discover new ideas and advance the state of the art in software engineering.

The J curve focuses on the transition from learning about development techniques to using them regularly and effectively. When presented with the J curve, many software engineering managers ask if there isn't some way to avoid going through the curve. The answer is "yes," but only by hiring software engineers that already have been through the curve, and this still doesn't solve the problem of getting those developers who have not been through the curve up to speed.

13.6.5 Alternative Views on Technology Transition

The J curve is similar to other observations that have been made about the process of learning new concepts. Bloom's taxonomy often is used by educators to describe levels of mastery of forms of knowledge or experience. These levels of knowledge, to a certain extent, parallel the levels of expertise described by the J curve. The process of acquiring knowledge is directly applicable to any technology transition process, because your staff must accept knowledge or expertise to begin effectively using new tools or techniques.

Inexperienced developers often focus on the notations used in the method, whereas experienced developers focus on the technique (process) used and the representations. Beginning developers tend to view the problem domain in terms of the symbols and terminology of the notation, whereas experienced developers view a system and its essential nature as represented by the notations within the method. The process of learning how to see the "forest for the trees" when using a formal method is a critical stumbling block to effectively using these methods.

Experienced developers often use the representation and technique to help them ask questions about the system and think about the problem, whereas beginning developers tend to spend their time defining terms and drawing diagrams, forgetting that the diagrams are simply a means of better understanding the problem and not an end in themselves.

This view of focusing on different aspects of the methods described in this text can help organizations prepare for and deal with the cultural change that is required to learn new ways of developing software. Technology transition often is the problem that organizations that fail to implement tools and techniques successfully do not address adequately.

The SEI has undertaken the Transition Models Project, which is demonstrating and studying the process of adopting software engineering technologies. SEI advocates the development of capability for planning and implementing technology transition within its customer base through a technology receptor function (TRF). TRF includes management oversight, work groups tracking and evaluating technology, pilot projects for new technologies, and a core group of planners who coordinate and report on implementation projects.

Staff at the Consortium for the Management of Emerging Software Technologies (COMSOFT) have defined a framework for technology transfer that includes a search of all relevant literature, knowledge engineering to validate the knowledge in the literature, basic research to address gaps in existing knowledge, and an advanced knowledge delivery vehicle based on hypertext and expert systems technology [KOR92]. COMSOFT has developed a pilot of the delivery vehicle called the Management Support System (MSS), which includes levels of knowledge and was developed to support the AT&T Object Modeling Resource Base. Figure 13.9 describes the MSS framework for knowledge on development techniques. The staff at COMSOFT envisions a framework for technology transfer that includes some entity to synthesize and integrate research and make this knowledge available to organizations. The COMSOFT effort suggests a partnership between universities and private organizations to synthesize and address these gaps in knowledge.

Others in the industry [FOW92] have identified three views of technology transition: a research and development (R&D) life cycle view, an innovative organization view, and a technology-driven change view. Of these, the R&D view relates technology transition to a specific technical or organizational community and focuses on the technology as it matures. The innovative organization view concentrates on the development of a sound climate for change that enables technology to be immersed easily. This view often is

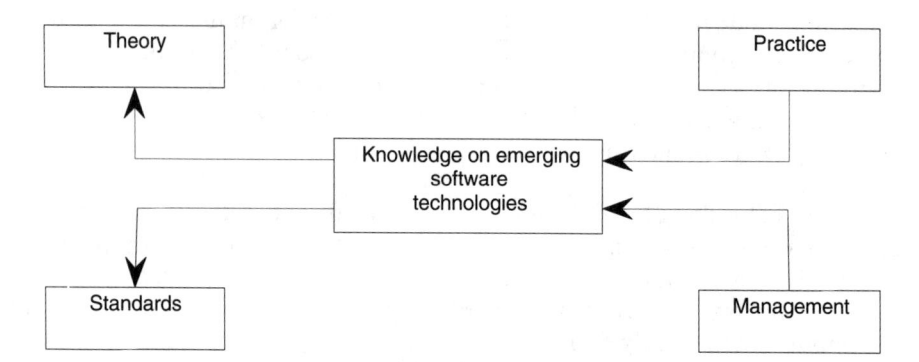

Figure 13.9
The Management Support System framework.

Diagram: Boxes labeled "Theory", "Practice", "Standards", "Management" all connected to a central box "Knowledge on emerging software technologies".

shared by TQM initiatives and a quality improvement perspective. The final view, where technology drives change, focuses on the change process itself and provides management and direction for this change.

However, as has been said so well in [FOW92], "Yet sets of transition mechanisms do not necessarily lead us to more effective transition planning or, even more important, to a strategic basis for that planning."

Others, including Dan Mosley, have expressed the process of technology transition in innovation life cycles. Mosley [MOS92] concludes that Bright's innovation chain equation [BRI69], shown in Figure 13.10, represents a model that can be adapted to fit the technology transition process. This life cycle includes stages for technological discovery and perception of a need for new technology, synthesis of existing knowledge as a basis for the new technology, verification of the conceptual basis for adoption, demonstration of the viability of the new technology, development of alternative versions and selection of prototypes to demonstrate the value of new technology, commercial introduction with limited use, widespread adoption of the technology, and proliferation of generic technology into new areas.

13.7 Experiences with Object-Oriented Development

One very helpful approach to consider when migrating to object technology is to study other organizations that have made the transition successfully. Because object technology is relatively new, there are not a large number of case studies in the adoption process, but those that have been published are valuable.

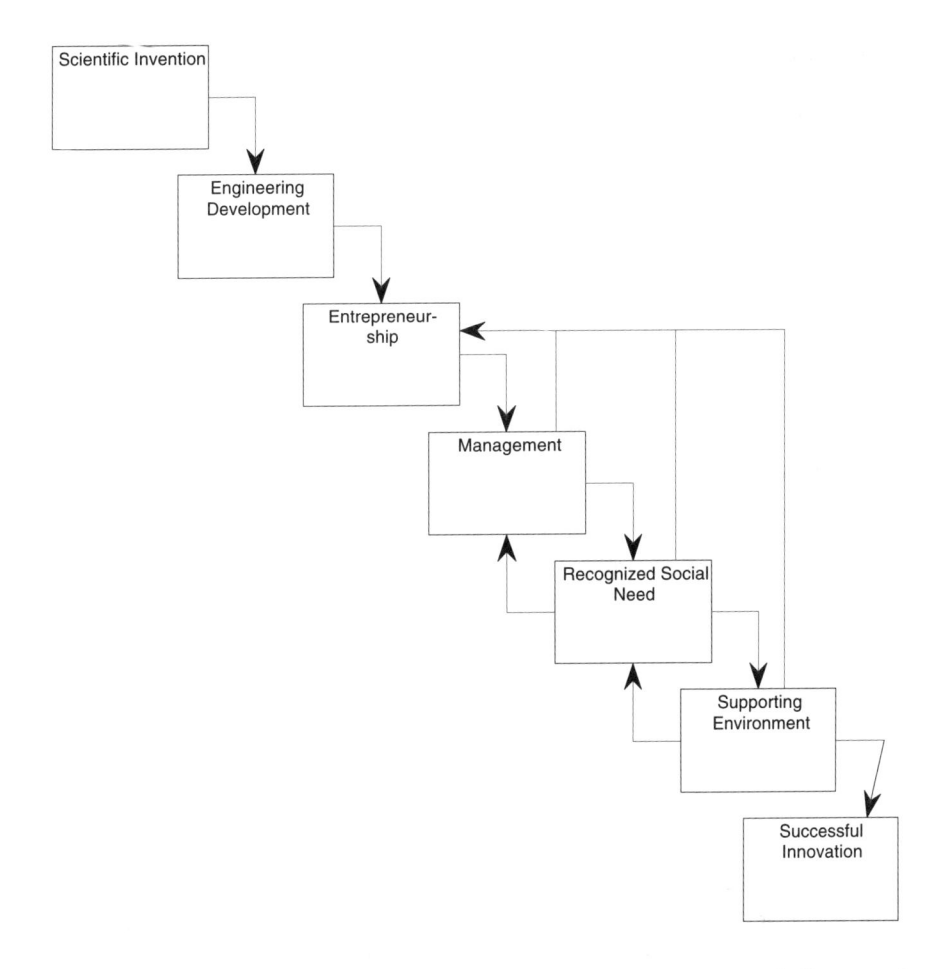

Figure 13.10 Bright's innovation chain.

In this section, I will review those experimental reports and discuss the observations and recommendations of those organizations that have begun migrating to object technology.

Taligent

In 1992, Taligent published a white paper on experiences of early adopters of object technology [TAL92]. The observations of these organizations, which included American Airlines, American Express, Anderson Consulting, British Airways, CIGNA, Eastman Kodak, EDS, Federal Express, Liberty Mutual, and Texas Instruments, are summarized as follows:

1. Educate management.
2. Recruit an executive sponsor.
3. Set appropriate expectations and goals.
4. Learn from experienced peers.
5. Recruit and manage outside consultants.
6. Look for staff with a motivation to learn OT.
7. Work in small, geographically close teams.
8. Plan for new staff roles (mentors, analysts, architects, etc.).
9. Look for specific applications that can benefit from OT.
10. Invest heavily in training.
11. OOA/Ds are difficult but must be done.
12. Build an enterprise model.
13. Choose an OOPL carefully.
14. Use an evolutionary prototype.
15. Conduct regular reviews.
16. Focus on system performance.
17. View reuse as a long-term benefit.
18. Develop organization structures to promote reuse.
19. Create incentives for reuse.
20. Develop and use metrics.

Cadre Technologies

Cadre began working with object technology in 1987 and rewrote part of their CASE tool product (Teamwork/Ada) in C++. Their experiences are described in [WYB90], and they report their code size went from 25K to 67K of C to 3K to 10K of C++, but their compile times almost doubled. They found that platform support for C++ varied causing numerous problems, that the class libraries that they used were not modular and took time to use efficiently, and that navigation was more difficult in C++ than C.

Cadre also found that configuration management was more complicated with C++ because of the "uses" and "inherits" relationships that must be maintained. Cadre reported that cohesion was sacrificed and functions tended to become scattered amongst parent/child classes, and this in turn created dependencies between class methods in the inheritance hierarchy. They also found that using C++ required more focus on analysis and design, that training staff was essential, that CASE tool selection was critical given the limited set of products, and that the OOD method that they used (Booch) tended to be oriented towards package-based OOPLs (i.e., Ada).

General Electric/Martin Marietta Advanced Concepts Center

General Electric (GE), another early user of object technology, developed their own OOA/D method (OOMT) and CASE tool, which they now sell [CON93]. The GE Advanced Concept Center (ACC) was recently purchased by Martin Marietta (MM). GE/MM ACC recommends selecting possible pilot projects for object technology as follows:

1. Pick a project that is relatively small (10 to 20 people).
2. Don't pick a project that is on the critical path for the organization
3. Use the best possible staff
4. Dedicate the team to the project
5. Provide introductory and intermediate training
6. Have mentors participating
7. Have a project manager and lead engineer
8. Provide adequate tools
9. Include users
10. Provide team members with current literature

GE's experiences with object technology resulted in an average of 10 lines of code (LOC) for each method and an average of 170 LOC for each class, 60% of the total effort was spent in analysis or design, and their productivity improved between 2 and 2.5 times over traditional structured development. GE suggests measuring object-oriented development for object dependencies (i.e., number of objects associated with each object, number of user interfaces, number of persistent classes, objects at stress points in application, and software defects).

GE also reported that their first object technology application took around 1.25 times as long as older methods to develop, and the following issues contributed to the increased costs:

- Inexperience of developers
- More emphasis on design
- Iterative process required

GE's experiences led them to recommend making a distinction between object-oriented and object-based languages. Object-based languages support data abstraction, while OOPLs support data abstraction and inheritance. Dynamic binding supports specific behavior for each class of object. Reuse for a framework is in the design domain, not the implementation. Dynamic binding allows a class to interact with other classes that need to know only the general appearance of the object, not the details.

The central design concept for dynamic binding is the concrete class (i.e., classes from which objects can be instantiated). An *abstract operation* is one that is declared but not implemented in a class. A *template operation* is one that includes an algorithm that is implemented in terms of one or more abstract operations. A base operation is one that is fully implemented in the abstract class.

Abstract operations define the calling interfaces, while template operations capture highly general patterns of control flow. Classes in a framework usually are tightly coupled. A contract is a specification of the capabilities and responsibilities of a class and its operations.

Colorado Technical University

Student programmers at Colorado Technical University were given a single problem and asked to program a solution in an OOPL and a traditional programming language [PLE93]. The resulting systems were measured for complexity (using McCabe's metrics) and productivity (using Halstead metrics) to determine if any significant differences existed. The results of the study indicated that:

- Hybrid OOPLs did not exhibit a statistically significant advantage in any of the measures used.
- Pure OOPLs did exhibit a statistically significant advantage in every measure used.
- Object technology can reduce complexity and increase productivity.

The results of this study suggest that, for an organization to realize the benefits of object technology, it must pursue pure object-orientation, not a hybrid approach. Also, any organization that is planning to transition to object technology should do so only if they are willing to make a commitment to gaining an understanding of object-orientation.

Digital Equipment Corporation (DEC)

To get started with object technology, DEC gave developers an intensive five-day OOA/D and OOP class [STA93]. The system that was developed, the BASEstar Integration Platform, was developed using four major areas: user interface objects (i.e., non-GUI), application-specific objects (file types, attributes, and behaviors specific to manufacturing), utility objects (abstract types referenced by many application-specific objects), and an object runtime environment (a layer between the application and utility objects and the operating system — persistent storage, garbage collection, inheritance, dispatching, etc.).

The BASEstar system was composed of 42 types or classes with 900 methods, of which 180 were public. The DEC developers were able to create 2.5 methods per day (three-times the number of methods in the previous version), and their productivity improved more than 25% over a previous version of the product.

During the first two months of the project, iteration occurred almost daily, while during the final two months, iterations occurred only twice. Domain analysis and peer reviews added expense and time to the project but helped focus on the issues of reuse and quality assurance for the classes and system.

DEC identified the following factors that influenced the decision to use object technology:

- Capabilities in the tools
- Assumptions made during prototyping regarding features, etc.
- Reliability of project estimates
- Need for full commitment to success of OT
- First project is as costly (if not more) as traditional
- Subsequent projects realize benefits
- Mentoring is best approach to limit impact of OT on team

NCR

NCR developed COOPERATION using object technology, and their effort took three years, involved over 100 developers, and resulted in over 12 major applications and services with over 350,000 lines of object-oriented code [GUT92]. COOPERATION was developed with 80% reusable objects, it was ported to three different operating environments (Windows, OS/2 and Unix), and NCR used the project to developed significant expertise in object technology.

NCR's observations in using object technology were that traditional hierarchical management structures might not be able to deal with object technology projects. Instead, a more flexible, matrix-style structure that can accommodate iteration and innovative thinking is required. Project management is directly tied to the object-oriented development process, and both formal and informal lines of communication should be used to facilitate the adoption.

NCR created task teams, with no formal reporting structure, to handle specific functional areas. Each team published minutes from their efforts that were distributed to other teams and had weekly meetings to discuss issues and status. Peer-to-peer communication thrived in this environment. NCR also used mentors, consultants with extensive experience in object technology, to help their staff adjust and get around some of the difficult design issues.

NCR setup three types of review teams — class, code, and architectural — that operated informally and didn't compete or interfere with traditional management processes. The goal of these review groups was to ensure that proper object-oriented techniques were used consistently in all phases of development.

NCR's observations on managing object technology include: use a different management structure; establish task teams for each work product and encourage peer-to-peer communications; use mentors to guide the process and provide design expertise; and setup review teams for classes, code and system architecture.

NCR found eight factors essential to success in transition:

- A strong software development process
- A strong mentoring program
- A high-level architecture development team
- A relatively flat development organization (peer-to-peer)
- Rewards for adding reusable classes
- Rewards for using existing classes
- Source control and configuration management
- Training management, along with developers

Bank of America

One early adopter of object technology is the Bank of America (BOA). BOA reported the following lessons that they learned from a migration to object technology [GAR93]:

- Education is expensive.
- Total development environment also is expensive.
- Paradigm shift is required but is hard to sell.
- Lack of formal deliverables.
- Hard to represent dynamics of object interactions.
- A mentor is a must.

- Use small teams with a true "believer."
- Requires a total management commitment.
- Users must play an integral role.
- Accommodate corporate bureaucracy.
- Reward reuse.

BOA also offered observations on the adoption process, including anticipating 30% to 40% effort for infrastructure development for the initial object technology project and at least a 6 month learning curve for development staff.

Anderson Consulting

Anderson Consulting, a big-six accounting firm, also reported on their experiences adopting object technology [POD93]. Anderson developed a product with two concurrent projects, a staff of 22, and a common technical architecture for both products, and they already were using a structured analysis when object technology was brought in.

The Anderson project consisted of a traditional requirements specification (via structured analysis), followed by the definition of a technical architecture, development of a prototype architecture, refinement of the architecture, and design/implementation of the applications using the Booch method. They report their training was ongoing for both OOD and C++ programming.

Anderson reported on the lessons that they learned, including team organization — smaller teams were required with deeper skills, no designer/programmer split was required, contractor relationships must be specified, a position should be defined for overall architect/OOD style critic, and they felt easy access to experienced personnel (i.e., mentors) was essential to success.

Other Experiences

Matthew Pittman [PIT93] suggests that object-oriented development differs from traditional development in the following ways:

- Object-oriented development requires different methods for management.
- Object-oriented development is iterative, incremental, and in some cases, both.
- OOA/D is an iterative process, where components are designed in detail, then implemented and tested, with a system acceptance test for the entire application.

- Object-oriented projects should be staffed differently from other projects — architects, class designers, class implementors, and programmers.
- As work packages are completed, tracking data should be fed back to management and the project plan adjusted as needed.
- Experience suggests that incremental development usually takes more time, and integration time is required; each increment of a component should provide some useful facility or proof of concept and should be rewarded.

In addition to these, still other experiences offer insight into the process of adopting object technology. Davis and Morgan report on their experiences migrating to object-oriented development at Brooklyn Union Gas [DAV93]. Their experience suggests reuse levels of 27% in the presentation layer, 5% in the process layer, and 65% in the business object layer of their object-oriented application.

Fayad *et al* report on the adoption of object-oriented analysis/design method (Shlaer/Mellor) at McDonnell Douglas. [FAY93]. Of the lessons that they report, several are repeated throughout other experiences, including that training and education plays a major role in the adoption process, the learning curve is a factor in adoption, a chief methodologist should be appointed to ensure that the methods and tools are used rigorously, and follow-up training should be provided as needed.

Summary of Experiences

When studying these experiences, there are several themes or observations that occur across many or even all the organizations. I summarize these observations in the following list:

- Training and education are keys to success with object technology.
- Expect at least a 6-month learning curve for developers to learn object technology.
- Reuse can occur but takes a lot of work and a long time.
- Object-oriented development requires new management techniques, tools and methods, life cycles, and roles and responsibilities for staff.
- Productivity can improve using object technology after the second or third project.
- Mentoring helps developers learn to use object-orientation in practice.
- Focus on software architecture and developing software in layers.

13.8 References

[ABD91]   Abdel-Hamid, T. and S. E. Madnick, *Software Project Dynamics: An Integrated Approach*, Prentice-Hall, 1991.

[AOY87]   Aoyama, "Concurrent Development of Software Systems: A New Development Paradigm," *ACM SIGSOFT (Soft. Eng. Notes)*, vol. 13, no. 3, July 1987, pp. 20-23.

[BAR92]   Barton, R., "Educating the Luddites: Technology Transfer is More than Training," *American Programmer*, vol. 5, no. 3, pp. 32-37.

[BOU89]   Bouldin, B., *Agents of Change: Managing the Introduction of Automated Tools*, Prentice-Hall, 1989.

[BOW93]   Bowman, C. F., "Achieving Object Nirvana: Practical Tips for Migrating to OT," *Object Magazine*, May-June 1993, pp. 47-49.

[BRI69]   Bright, J. R., "Some Management Lessons from Technical Innovation Research," *Harvard Business Review* (January/February 1969), pp. 36-41.

[CLA91]   Clay, A. W., G. Grzybowski, S. Webber, and E. Yourdon, "Quality Metrics at AG Communication Systems," *American Programmer*, vol. 4, no. 9, September 1991.

[CON93]   Conway, J., "Case Study: GE Facilitates the Transition to Object-Oriented Programming," *Education and Training*, SIGS Publications, 1993.

[COO94]   Cook, T. W., "Retraining Business Organizations for the Object-Oriented Era," *First Class*, vol. IV, issue 11, pp. 11-17.

[CST90]   Computer Science and Technology Board, "Scaling up: A Research Agenda for Software Engineering," *CACM*, 33, 3 (Mar. 1990), 281-293.

[CUT89]   Cutler, R. A., "A Comparison of Japanese and U.S. High-Technology Transfer Practices," *IEEE Trans. Eng. Manage.*, 36, 1 (Feb. 1989), 17-24.

[DSO93]   D'Souza, D., "An Educated Look at Education," *JOOP*, March-April, 1993, pp. 40-46.

[FAY93]   Fayad, M. E., L. J. Hawn, M. A. Roberts, and J. R. Klatt, "Using the Shlaer-Mellor Object-Oriented Analysis Method," *IEEE Software*, March 1993, pp. 43-52.

[FOW92]   Fowler, P. and L. Levine, "Toward a Defined Process of Software Technology Transfer," *American Programmer*, vol. 5, no. 3, pp. 2-10.

[GAR93]   Garewal, A., "Client/Server Computing Using Object Technology," *proceedings of the Excecutive Symposium on Object Technology*, September, 1993.

[GIB91]   Gibson, E., "Flattening the Learning Curve: Educating Object-Oriented Developers," *JOOP*, February 1991, pp. 24-28.

[GOL93]   Goldberg, A., "Wishful Thinking," *Object Magazine*, May-June 1993, pp. 87-88.

[GUT92]   Guttman, M. K. and J. R. Matthews, "Managing a Large Project: CASE Study of a long-term project at NCR," *Object Magazine*, November-December 1992, pp. 75-78.

[HUM91]   Humphrey, W., T. Snyder, and R. Willis, "Software Process Improvement and Hughes Aircraft," *IEEE Software*, July 1991, pp. 11-24.

[HUM90]   Humphrey, W., "Introducing Process Models into Software Organizations," *American Programmer*, September 1990, pp. 1-7.

[HUM89a]   Humphrey, W., *Managing the Software Process*, Addison-Wesley, 1989.

[HUM89b]   Humphrey, W., "CASE Planning and the Software Process," *Tech. Rept. CMU/SEI-89-TR-26*, SEI, Carnegie Mellon University, May 1989.

[HUN93]   Hunscher, D., "Stories from the Frontline: Managing Object-Oriented Development in an Engineering Evironment," *Object Magazine*, January-February 1993, pp. 75-78.

[KEL89]   Kellner, M. I., "Representation Formalisms for Software Process Modeling," *proceedings of the 4th Intl. Software Proces Workshop*; also in *Soft. Eng. Notes,* vol. 14, no. 4, June 1989.

[KER93]   Kerth, N. L. and E. Andreason, "Managing the Objects: Management's Role in a Successful Transition to Object-Orientation," *American Programmer*, vol. 5, no. 9, pp. 28-35.

[KOR92]   Korson, T. D. and V. K. Vaishnavi, "Managing Emerging Software Techhnologies: A Technology Transfer Framework," *CACM*, vol. 35, no. 9, pp. 101-111.

[LOV93]   Love, T., "Flying Over the Object Barrier," *Education & Training*, pp. 10-12.

[MCK93]   McKim, J., "Teaching Object-Oriented Programming and Design," *JOOP*, March-April 1993, pp. 32-39.

[MOS92]   Mosley, D. J., "A Framework for Technology Innovation," *American Programmer*, vol. 5, no. 3, pp. 20-26.

[OIV92]   Oivo, M. and V. R. Basili, "Representing Software Engineering Models: The TAME Goal Oriented Approach," *IEEE Trans. on Soft. Eng.*, vol. 18, no. 10, pp. 886-898.

[PIT93]   Pittman, M., "Lessons Learned in Managing Object-Oriented Development," *IEEE Software*, January 1993, pp. 43-53.

[POD93]   Podmolik, L., "Case Study: Engineering Data Management using the Booch Method," *Object World (Feb. 1993) proceedings*.

[PLE93]   Plews, M., "Programming Language Study: Evaluating the Claims Made for Object Orientation," *Object Magazine*, May-June 1993, pp. 54-55.

[PRE88]   Pressman, R. S., *Making Software Engineering Happen: A guide for instituting the technology*, Prentice Hall, 1988.

[PRE91]   Pressman, R. S., *Software Engineering: A Practitioner's Approach*, McGraw-Hill, 1991.

[REE92]   Reed, D. R., "Perspective: The Engineering Manager," *Moving from C to C++*, SIGS Publications, pp. 10-11.

[SEI92]   Huff, C. C., D. Smith, K. Stepien, E. Morris, and P. Zarrella, CASE Adoption Workshop, *Tech. Rep. CMU/SEI-91-TR-14*.

[STA93]   Startsman, T. and T. Zysk, "Case Study: Making the Transition at DEC," *Object Magazine*, May-June 1993, pp. 56-60.

[TAL92]   Taligent, "Leasons Learned from Early Adopters of Object Technology," 1992.

[TOP93]   Topper, A., D. Ouellette, and P. Jorgensen, *Structured Methods: Merging Models, Techniques, and CASE*, McGraw-Hill, 1993.

[WIE93]   Wiener, R. and L. Pinson, "OOP: An Academic Perspective," *Education & Training*, pp. 13-15.

[WU93]   Wu, C. T., "Teaching OOP to Beginners," *JOOP*, March-April 1993, pp. 47-50.

[WYB90]   Wybolt, N., "Experiences with C++ and Object-Oriented Software Development," *ACM SIGSOFT*, vol. 15, no. 2, April 1990, pp. 31-39.

[YEH91]   Yeh, R. R., D. A. Naumann, R. T. Mittermeir, R. A. Shlemmer, W. S. Gillmore, G. E. Sumrall, and J. T. Lebaron, "A Commonsense Management Model," *IEEE Software*, November 1991, pp. 23-33.

[ZEL90]   Zells, L., *Managing Software Projects*, QED Information Science, Inc., 1990.

The Future of COBOL

Chapter 14

The future of COBOL products looks bright, with the X3J4.1 task group delivering its recommendations for extending the language to support the concepts of object-orientation. Once the X3J4 committee accepts the recommendations, the COBOL community will begin to consider the standard and make comments on it. Hopefully, major COBOL vendors — including IBM, HP, Sun, Unisys, and DEC — will provide support for the COBOL 97 standard shortly after it is accepted.

Existing COBOL development tools must be modified by vendors to support the object-oriented standard, and additional products must be developed and delivered. For OOCOBOL to be effective, it must be incorporated with other object-oriented development tools. These include browsers, editors, incremental compilers and linkers, profilers, inspectors, debuggers, class libraries, and frameworks. As you already have seen, Micro Focus has led the way with development of these tools in its existing COBOL product line, and other COBOL vendors should follow this trend.

In this chapter, I will provide a glimpse of the future of software engineering in general, and where COBOL is going, with an eye towards the factors that will affect the next COBOL standard. I will review the most recent changes to the COBOL 97 standard and look at the evolving COBOL marketplace, distributed object management, and future software development trends.

14.1 COBOL 97 Standard Update

At the time that this book was completed, the Technical Committee X3J4 had received the OOCOBOL proposal from the X3J4.1 task group but had not yet accepted them or made them available for public comment and review. As of April 1994, the X3J4 committee had initiated a letter ballot on the proposal, and the X3J4.1 task group had disbanded.

The COBOL 97 standard, while still under review, currently calls for object-oriented extensions, enhancements to the CALL statement, file sharing, record locking, full support for the national character handling, portable results for decimal arithmetic, bit and boolean data types, exception handling, full-screen I/O, automatic validation based on data descriptions, support for recursion and user-defined functions, and a table SORT facility.

Some last minute issues under discussion by the committee related to the object-oriented features include standard class libraries, garbage collection, the CREATE command, string manipulation, and interfaces to non-COBOL systems. Micro Focus released its first production version (1.5) of the Object COBOL Option in June 1994, after over 18 months of beta testing.

Outstanding issues for OOCOBOL include technical aspects as well as acceptance from organizations that are heavily committed to older (i.e., pre-COBOL 85) applications. Technical issues include whether OOCOBOL should support multiple or single inheritance, static or dynamic binding, automatic garbage collection, persistent objects, and base class libraries.

Additional issues include how operating systems and graphical user interface APIs will be integrated with the OOCOBOL standard, how client/server standards efforts and the Object Management Group (OMG) will work with the OOCOBOL specification, and how other object-oriented products will be modified to work with OOCOBOL. Perhaps the most important issue to the success of OOCOBOL is how the language will be integrated with existing structured code and how, or even whether, existing systems will be modified to support object-oriented concepts.

14.2 Emerging COBOL Products

As the OOCOBOL standard is prepared for release and comment, many COBOL development products are available for a variety of development environments, mostly geared towards the personal computer (PC). PC-based COBOL development has been available for many years, but recently the prominent products have been modified to support development and deployment of PC-based applications. The major PC environments — including Microsoft Windows, IBM OS/2, DOS, and Apple Macintosh — now support COBOL development and deployment.

Micro Focus supports COBOL development on all these platforms, in addition to IBM mainframe (OS/MVS and VM), minicomputer (AS/400, HP 3000, etc.), and a variety of Unix platforms. Other COBOL vendors support all major operating environments and are beginning to include PC-based development and deployment options in their product sets.

Issues that remain to be resolved by these COBOL vendors for complete PC-based development and deployment include support for GUIs, PC-based DBMSs, network communication, remote procedure calls (RPCs), and interfaces with non-PC-based applications (i.e., mainframe-based legacy systems).

As COBOL becomes a more acceptable PC-based development tool, more utilities and operating environments will be supported. Currently, many of the PC-based COBOL products still have a mainframe-orientation regarding the user interface and file/database access. Most of these tools provide sufficient support for non-GUI development and RDBMS access, but few support full GUI applications development, event-driven behavior, Btrieve, or object-oriented DBMS access.

A new series of PC-based COBOL development tools is beginning to appear on the market. The Xinotech COBOL Composer is a good example of this type of product and includes an intelligent COBOL editor, a graphical display environment for COBOL, a code analyzer, and guidelines for COBOL development. All these components are integrated into the Composer under Microsoft Windows or Motif on Sun.

14.3 Distributed Object Management

As you saw in chapter 1, there are a variety of distributed computing standards that have been proposed to facilitate the development of applications in heterogenous environments [NIC93]. The one I will focus on most in this section is the OMG's CORBA. Each of the OMG members, with the exception of Microsoft, has indicated their plans to support the CORBA in the products. Many of these vendors already offer architectures that include support for CORBA or the DCE defined by the OSF (see Chapter 1). Figure 14.1 shows each of the major distributed architectures from the vendors and the standards they support. These architectures are described briefly in the following sections.

IBM — DSOM

System Object Model (SOM) was delivered with OS/2 2.x and included operating system extensions that support object-oriented concepts (i.e., inheritance, method dispatching and messages). SOM 2.0 includes support for multiple inheritance, C++ bindings, and an interface definition language (IDL) that works in combination with the CORBA standard. Delivered with the SOMobjects Developer Toolkit are frameworks for specific object management functions, including parsing support for binding other programming

Figure 14.1
Major distributed architectures.

Vendors	Architecture or Products	Standards Supported
DEC	Application Control Architecture (ACA)	CORBA
HP	Distributed Object Management Facility (DOMF)	CORBA and DCE
IBM	Distrubuted System Object Model (DSOM)	CORBA
Microsoft	OLE & Cairo	DCE
NCR	Cooperative Frameworks	OMG DOMF ?
Novell/HyperDesk	Distributed Object Management System (DOMS)	CORBA
Sun	Distributed Object Management Facility (DOMF)	CORBA

languages, persistent objects, and object replication. SOM 2.0 also supports distributed objects across a variety of platforms, including OS/2 and AIX, with future support for Windows and other Unix environments [RYM93b]. Under SOM, user objects and system objects can be defined and used. Within OS/2 2.x, the operating system components are available as SOM objects for manipulation and reuse.

IBM also has released Distributed SOM (DSOM) for workstation and workgroup distribution of objects and services following the SOM view. DSOM is planned for OS/2 and AIX and eventually will support TCP/IP, NetBIOS, and NetWare IPX. IBM also has announced plans to offer Distributed Application Environment (DAE) as a middleware product for a variety of operating environments, including AIX, OS/2, and VM. DAE will support messaging, system management, database access, and GUI interfaces based on Motif and OS/2 PM.

IBM and Hewlett-Packard (HP) are working together to incorporate portions of HP's Distributed Object Management Facility (DOMF) with IBM's SOM. IBM plans to ship developer tools for the DSOM with HP's DOMF services by the fall of 1993. IBM and Apple plan to incorporate DSOM into their Taligent products by 1995. Future IBM operating systems will be migrated to Taligent, and frameworks will be provided for DOS, OS/2, Unix, and the Macintosh (via the PowerOpen operating environment).

HP — DOMF

HP currently supports distributed computing via DOMF, the distributed computing environment (DCE), and the OpenODB standard. HP also has announced plans to provide a distributed version of Smalltalk in the near future. HP, IBM, and Sun agreed to provide cross platform services via the CORBA standard to help integrate applications. HP recently announced its plans to include ORB Plus with the HP/UX operating system. ORB Plus supports the CORBA standard and includes DOMF, object services, and development tools. ORB Plus also includes object notification, naming, and life cycle management.

DEC — ACA

DEC plans to extend its Application Control Architecture (ACA) services to support the OMG CORBA standard. DEC, in a strategic alliance with Microsoft, will allow PC-based Object Linking and Embedding (OLE) applications to use the CORBA as a transport mechanism for distributed communication.

Novell/HyperDesk — DOMS

Novell announced its plans to offer distributed object management services based on the CORBA standard using HyperDesk's Distributed Object Management System (DOMS) [RYM93a]. HyperDesk DOMS is available today and supports SunOS, Windows, and DG-UX. Novell plans to support DOMS in its Netware 3.*x* and 4.*x* products beginning in the fall of 1994. The major portions of DOMS are an object request broker (that supports the CORBA standard), an object repository, a remote execution environment (for RPCs), and programming tools and interfaces for developers.

Sun — DOMF

SunSoft is planning to deliver its own CORBA compliant Distributed Object Management Facility (DOMF) in 1994, which will be available for Solaris environments including SPARC, Intel, and PowerPC. Sun also is working on its own architecture, Distributed Objects Everywhere (DOE), which it hopes to begin shipping in 1994.

Microsoft — Cairo

Microsoft, a member of the OMG, has indicated that it will not directly support the CORBA standard in its future operating environment, code-named Cairo.

Microsoft already supports OLE as a pseudo-distributed mechanism (including directory, repository, and security services) but only on single PCs or workstations (see DEC plans). Microsoft also has reimplemented parts of the DCE in Windows NT so that there are questions about its plans for conformance with CORBA in the future.

Microsoft has indicated that Cairo will provide icon-based services for applications and operating facilities by extending the OLE to support access across an enterprise making resources accessible in a heterogenous environment. Cairo will be based on the DCE RPC architecture defined by the OSF.

NCR — Cooperative Frameworks

NCR has plans to offer distributed services for its platforms and other Unix environments via its Cooperative Frameworks. These frameworks will support directory services, security, and other communication services. NCR also plans to support the upcoming OMG's Distributed Object Management Framework standard.

NCR also developed a methodology that uses a distributed object manager with remote method invocation in its cooperative frameworks. Under this methodology, an object-oriented design can be created without explicitly considering distribution, and the objects can be distributed as desired without changing a single line of code in any object. Two types of objects are involved: *Active*, which support asynchronous, transaction-oriented tasks, and *passive*, which accept and issue only synchronous requests and participate in simple, atomic transactions.

14.4 Future Software Development

As organizations adopt and use OOCOBOL, they will find the software engineering community changing and evolving in the future. New tools and techniques for software development will be created, tested, and adopted, along with new deployment environments. In this section, I will provide a glimpse into the future of software engineering by looking at some interesting items under development or forthcoming so that organizations can begin to consider how these new methods and tools will affect their development environment.

14.4.1 Evolution of CASE and Formal Methods

The existing CASE marketplace has stagnated in the past few years, and CASE has received a bad reputation in the industry. This resulted from the hype attributed to CASE tools, wide-spread failure on the part of organizations adopting CASE, limited code generation and reverse engineering facilities, and failure on the part of CASE vendors to adopt and support integration mechanisms (i.e., repositories).

To be competitive, future CASE tools must evolve in a variety of ways, including support for object-oriented methods of analysis and design, support for GUI development, better support for maintenance tasks, and integration across the entire software development life cycle (SDLC). The promise of a standard for CASE repositories is yet unmet and might not be delivered before the year 2000. This lack of integration has been and will continue to be a major drawback to using CASE tools on large projects and across organizational lines.

CASE tools also will change to support both structured and object-oriented methods and OOA/D methods. Popular OOA/D methods will be merged or fused to form better methods, and CASE tools will have to support them. Multi-method support or support for metamethods (including structured, real-time, and object-oriented techniques) will be required of future CASE products. Some CASE vendors have recognized this and already offer support for many techniques and notations. Several CASE products (including ProtoGen, ObjectMaker, Ipsys, and the Visual Software Factory) already provide support for many popular notations. Future CASE products must move beyond simple notational support and provide technique and method support in the form of tailorable rule-checking for whichever method is used in an organization.

In addition, future CASE products will have to integrate all of the life cycle tasks and deliverables within a common repository. Likely these products also will include metrics and project and process management facilities. Sophisticated configuration management facilities will be required that can track requirements, can change requests, can test plans, goals and objectives, and can provide browsing for reusable components.

Underlying support for multiple methods will be a repository that can manage metadata about the development process. Examples of this data might include traditional deliverables (i.e., diagrams, textual specifications, etc.) but will include new media types.

14.4.2 CASE as a Method Advisor

Recent studies have shown that, for CASE tools to be more effective, they need to move from an impassive role in the development process to more of a guided or advisory role [VES92]. These and other findings suggest that CASE tools should enforce or guide developers in the selected method or technique to ensure that developers follow the proper intent of a technique. This leads to the concept of a CASE environment as an advisor to software developers. In the study cited, the authors identified three basic types of CASE tools.

Restrictive tools that are designed to encourage the developer to use them in a normative manner. For example, a restrictive tool that supports functional decomposition would require a developer to start a system at the top with a context diagram, then decompose the system down into lower-level detail.

Guided tools that are designed to encourage, but not to rigidly enforce, the developer to use them in a normative manner. Using the previous example, a guided tool would suggest, but not require, developers to use a top-down partitioning process.

Flexible tools that are designed to allow developers complete freedom in using them. Following collection of specifications, the developer could verify that the specifications are consistent and complete but would not be required to begin at the top when using the tool.

[T]his research suggests that tools providing support should not force the systems developer to follow a top-down process in designing a system. Rather, CASE tools should provide support primarily for the specifications produced... Hence, restrictive and guided CASE tools, which directly support the disciplined approach and indirectly the untrained personnel, might be the most likely to result in increases in software productivity, as well as quality. I. Vessey [VES92].

Already, some CASE tool vendors have incorporated expert systems into their products, but for verification checking only. There is much research underway on the role of CASE tools as software process advisors or guides for the development process [KAI88] [PUN88]. Some of these efforts include matching an expert system or knowledge-based support tool with a CASE repository.

The Knowledge-Based Requirements System (KBRS) under development at George Mason University provides computer support for collection and analysis of system- and software-level requirements and coordinates all aspects of requirements definition and tracking [PAL92]. Others incorporate knowledge-based systems with software process models. Softman is a process-driven CASE environment developed at the University of Southern California with a system for process guidance for developers that navigates through a software process model and integrates a CASE environment for forward and reverse engineering [MI92].

In the future, CASE tools will act more as advisors for the software development process and will include knowledge-bases of technique and tool expertise that will be drawn upon and applied to new development projects. There also will be a merging of development techniques (methodologies) and CASE environments, together with process and project management facilities, reuse, and measurements and estimation.

14.4.3 Hypertext and CASE

In the future, there will be a marriage of CASE tools, hypertext, groupware, and multimedia capabilities to create a complete team-oriented software development environment. Others have discussed the benefits of combining CASE and hypertext, most notably [AIK89] [BIG88]. You can expect to see these technologies combined in the future to help provide more of the advisor role in CASE discussed earlier. Many of the commercially available methodologies now are being offered in hypertext format with some plans for multimedia formats in the near future.

I can see a time when CASE environments eventually will include an expert advisor to software engineers and provide specific recommendations as well as suggestions for standards for software development. With the use of hypertext, the areas of training and supporting software development techniques can be greatly improved. Also, the verification and rule checking provided by a CASE tool can be based on the software process used and tailored to the software development process within the organization.

Existing research with CASE and hypertext has been undertaken at the Amdahl Australian Intelligent Tools Program and provides an architectural framework for integrating CASE tools [CYB92]. HyperCASE combines a hypertext-based interface with a knowledge-based document repository. Future work in this area will incorporate groupware, configuration management, planning and tracking, and multimedia document presentation.

Other research is underway on merging CASE with multimedia to produce interactive, flexible documentation to developers and users of software. Ed Yourdon, the father of structured development, argues that inexpensive CASE tools will become commonplace in the years to come, and will be extended to include multimedia capabilities and groupware functions and support pen-based development [YOU92].

Many in the industry have provided us creative insight into the possible future of software development environments. Interesting components of this future environment include groupware, multimedia, software factories with product and process integration, and hypertext.

The movement towards groupware support in software development tools will facilitate better communication between developers. Such a combination eventually might include electronic mail, calendars, facilities scheduling, document preparation, project and process planning, shared database access, and automatic message notification.

Ed Yourdon, an architect of many software development techniques, describes this possible combination as a "great leap forward" with CASE [YOU91]. Others, including [KAS91], see the eventual merging of CASE environments with distributed computing environments. The Xerox PARC and MIT Athena projects are examples of studies in these areas.

The incorporation of multimedia, including sound, video, animation and hypertext, inside a CASE tool should further enhance the development process. Recent papers have described the benefit of delivering documents and deliverables using multimedia [RAD92]. In addition, the concept of multimedia as a methodology training and support tool in combination with CASE capabilities can go along way toward reducing the costs of implementing and supporting software engineering.

14.4.4 Reverse Engineering

Future CASE tools also will provide facilities for extracting design information from existing legacy systems. This design recovery will allow organizations that have significant investments in 3GL systems without adequate documentation to capture the architecture, logic, and ultimately, the business rules and models that are buried within the older systems that are outdated and must be replaced.

Some existing CASE products, including Insight and Mark/V, can reverse engineer objects and methods from existing code. Some products can deliver portions of the design recovery, typically in the form of control flow or module hierarchy, but the difficult part will be to decipher the logic within the modules and to map this logic to design specifications.

Existing reverse engineering tools will have to be modified or new products created that can capture objects, classes, attributes, and methods from legacy systems as described in chapter 11. Some work has been done in this area in the laboratory, but much work remains before these products will be commercially available.

Undoubtedly, expert systems will be used in the future to analyze program code to infer about the underlying business rules, but people will always be required to make decisions regarding how the code should be represented and which code is redundant. The promise of reverse engineering is perceived as the silver bullet for the maintenance nightmare that most development organizations face, and this will be a difficult expectation to change in the future.

14.4.6 Integration of Object Technology and Other Products: Object Repository

As the CASE industry matured, it became obvious that standards for integration of products were essential to the continued growth and use of these products. Major CASE players (including HP, DEC, and IBM) have proposed CASE repository standards to facilitate the exchange of development information between different tools.

The object-oriented technology marketplace is very much like the CASE market was five or six years ago, with a wide variety of products covering a broad spectrum of capabilities, with little (if any) communication or exchange between products. What is required in the object technology marketplace is the same focus on standards for tool integration that the CASE market still is struggling with.

One positive step in this direction is the Object Management Group (OMG), which is beginning to establish standards for object services, methods, class libraries, and OODBMSs. As object technology matures, these standards will help to bring together the common aspects of object-oriented development and address early the issues of tool integration.

Future object-oriented development products will share a common object repository, probably in the form of an OODBMS, and use standard APIs and services that will be defined by the industry and its users. Object management, one critical aspect of object-oriented development, will be handled by an OODBMS, and class libraries will be available in standard formats and notations. When this future environment will come to pass, no one can say, but estimates range from three to five years.

14.4.6 Media Use in Software Applications

As more and more applications are developed and PCs are sold with multimedia support, the need will grow for developing systems that support alternative media types. The recent popularity of CD-ROMs, sound boards, and digital video in PCs that were sold through major retailers and distributed shows how the operating environment is changing rapidly.

The widespread use of alternative media types — sound, voice, handwriting, finger prints, photographs, graphic images, video, etc. — in future software applications must be supported by software engineering tools and methods. Multimedia development represents yet another paradigm shift for software engineering organizations, as well as for development tool vendors.

Pen-based computers now generally are available, along with personal digital assistant (PDA) equipment and wireless computers connected to LANs and WANs. Software developed in the future will support handwriting recognition, speech recognition, and perhaps even visual pattern matching. As more and more appliances and hardware components contain computers, the types of software that is required and the development tools will change dramatically.

In the short term, there will be an integration of RDBMS and OODBMS products to support older data storage and access together with newer media types. In the future, RDBMS data will contain references or pointers to objects and methods in an OODBMS, and the traditional numeric and textual information will be processed and delivered alongside audio, video, and graphic images.

14.5 Conclusion

As you saw in chapter 1, the nature of software development is changing, and for COBOL to continue to be a viable software engineering tool, it must change as well. The inclusion of object-oriented concepts in the COBOL 97 standard and support for these extensions in COBOL products help bring the language forward into the 1990s.

You as developers of COBOL applications have a unique opportunity to determine to a large extent what COBOL will look like and how it will change. Those of you who plan to take advantage of the features of OOCOBOL have an opportunity to determine which of the proposed facilities will be in the final COBOL 97 standard. As you review the OOCOBOL standard, you should recognize that you can use the object-oriented features in the standard or ignore them and continue using COBOL the way it has always been used. On the other hand, if you choose to, you can help define and shape the language and ensure that the features you need are in the eventual OOCOBOL products.

I encourage ereryone who currently is developing or maintaining COBOL applications to study the OOCOBOL standard, learn whatever they can about object-orientation, consider what features are available in other OOPLs, and submit their own comments on OOCOBOL to the X3J4 committee members. Micro Focus, by delivering an early version of an OOCOBOL compiler and tools, have provided everyone the opportunity to experiment with objects in COBOL today.

The experiences gained by experimenting with this early version of OOCOBOL might lead to modification of the resulting standard such that it better satisfies the needs of COBOL shops. This early use also might help organizations get a head-start in adopting object-orientation without the high learning curve for C++ or Smalltalk and help them focus on other object technology issues, including analysis and design, class libraries, configuration, and life cycle management.

With the help of COBOL developers around the world, the OOCOBOL standard can represent a powerful evolution of the COBOL that we all know and love to support the concepts of object-orientation. Those COBOL developers who ignore the OOCOBOL standard can continue to maintain existing applications and hope that future software development still requires their skills.

14.6 References

[AIK89]   Aiken, P. H., "A Hypermedia Workstation for Requirements Engineering," *doctoral dissertation*, George Mason University, Fairfax, VA., 1989.

[BIG88] Bigelow, J., "Hypertext and CASE," *IEEE Software*, March 1988, pp. 23-27.

[CYB92] Cybulski, J. and K. Reed, "A Hypertext-Based Software Engineering Environment," *IEEE Software*, March 1992, pp. 62-68.

[KAI88] Kaiser, G. E., "Intelligent Assistance for Software Development and Maintenance," *IEEE Software*, May 1988, pp. 40-49.

[KAS91] Kashdan, N., "CASE and Distributed Computing Environments," *American Programmer*, July 1991, pp. 30-35.

[MI92] Mi, P. and W. Scacchi, "Process Integration in CASE Environments," *IEEE Software*, March 1992, pp. 45-53.

[NIC93] Nicol, J. R., C. T. Wilkes, and F. A. Monola, "Object Orientation in Heterogeneous Distributed Computing Systems," *IEEE Computer*, June 1993, pp. 57-67.

[PAL92] Palmer, J. D. and N. A. Fields, "An Integrated Environment for Requirements Engineering," *IEEE Software*, May 1992, pp. 80-86.

[PUN88] Puncello, P., "ASPIS: A Knowledge-Based CASE Environment," *IEEE Software*, March 1988, pp. 53-65.

[RAD92] Radding, P. and M. Farrell, "Multimedia Documents," *American Programmer*, vol. 5, no. 5, pp. 44-49.

[RYM93a] Rymer, J., "Novell Drives into Distributed Object Computing," *Distributed Computing Monitor*, vol. 8, no. 2 (February 1993), pp. 3-7.

[RYM93b] Rymer, J., "IBM's System Object Model," *Distributed Computing Monitor*, vol. 8, no. 3 (March 1993), pp. 2-23.

[VES92] Vessey, I., S. Javenpaa, and N. Tractinsky, "Evaluation of Vendor Products: CASE Tools as Methodology Companions," *CACM*, vol. 35, no. 4, pp. 90-105.

[YOU92] Yourdon, E., "CASE: Whither or Wither?," *American Programmer*, November 1992, pp. 16-27.

[YOU91] Yourdon, E., "A CASE of the Blahs," *American Programmer*, July 1991, pp. 37-45.

Appendix

Appendix

Appendix **A**

Example Problems
OOA Results

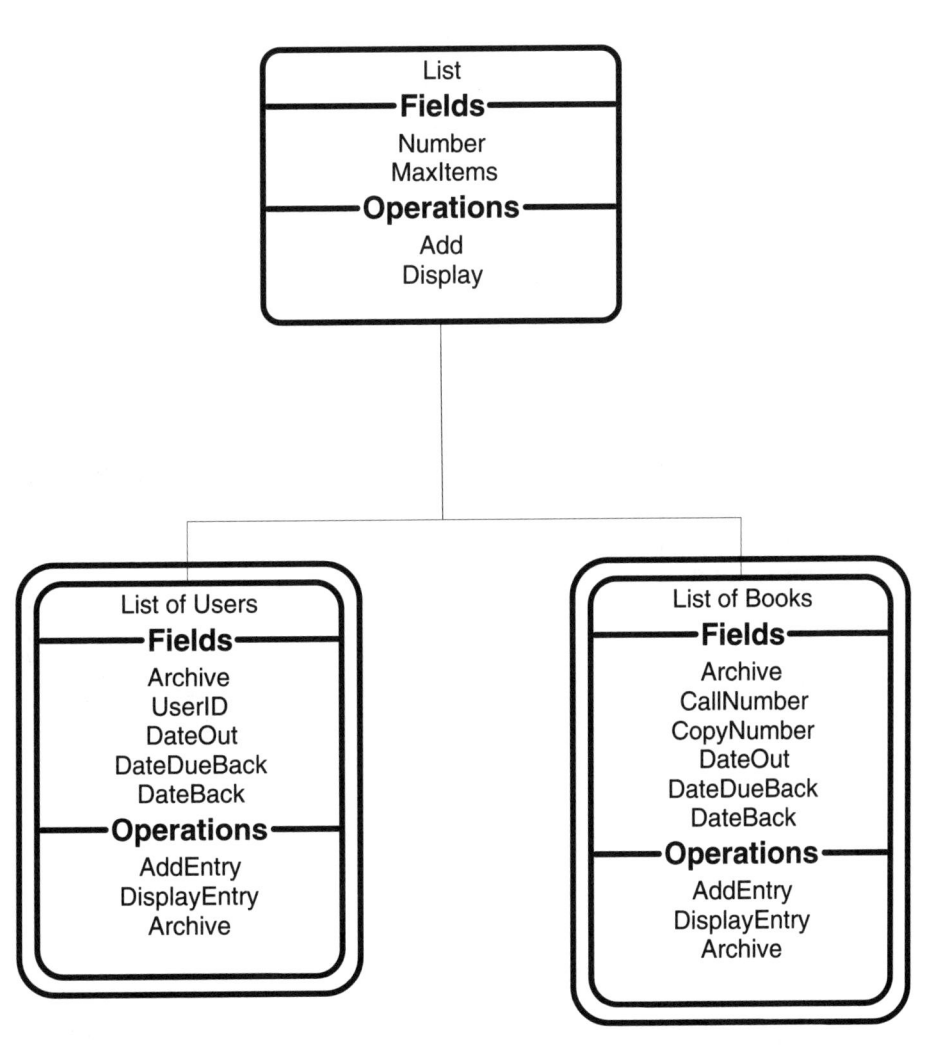

```
                    ┌─────────────────────┐
                    │        List         │
                    ├──── Fields ─────────┤
                    │      Number         │
                    │      MaxItems       │
                    ├──── Operations ─────┤
                    │       Add           │
                    │      Display        │
                    └─────────────────────┘
```

List
- Fields: Number, MaxItems
- Operations: Add, Display

List of Users
- Fields: Archive, UserID, DateOut, DateDueBack, DateBack
- Operations: AddEntry, DisplayEntry, Archive

List of Books
- Fields: Archive, CallNumber, CopyNumber, DateOut, DateDueBack, DateBack
- Operations: AddEntry, DisplayEntry, Archive

Figure A1.1 Library List class diagram.

Note: The examples in this appendix are incomplete, mostly because of space limitations, and are included to show the reader the format, syntax, and overall flow of possible OOCOBOL applications.

Book

Fields
- Title
- CallNumber
- Publisher
- DatePublished
- ISBN

Operations
- AddBook
- FindBook
- PrintBook
- RemoveBook

1,m   1,m

1

Author

Fields
- Name
- Birthdate
- Deathdate

Operations
- AddAuthor
- PrintAuthor

1

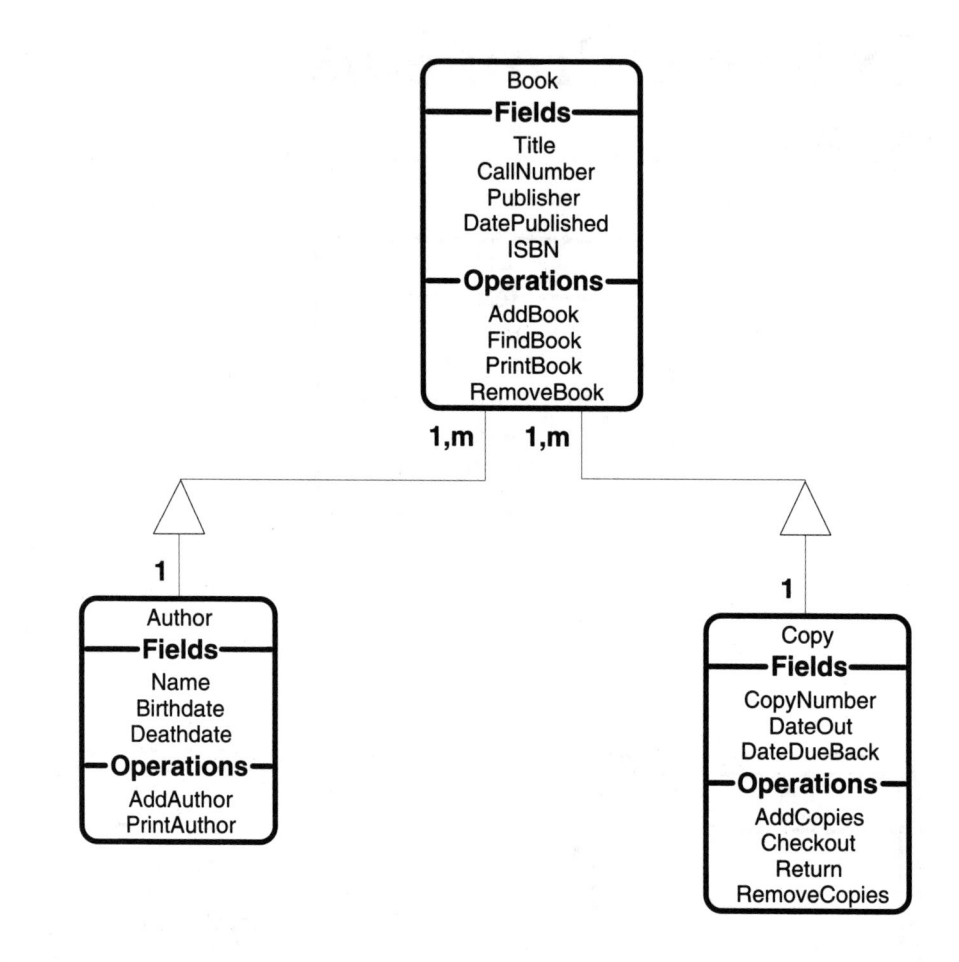

Copy

Fields
- CopyNumber
- DateOut
- DateDueBack

Operations
- AddCopies
- Checkout
- Return
- RemoveCopies

Figure A1.2 Library Book class diagram.

Library Menu	Books	User	Help
SignOn	Which books do I have?	Change Password	Contents
Exit Library...	Previous books I had		Search for Help on...
			How to Use Help
			Library Tutorial
			About LibraryManager...

Figure A1.3 Library user menu hierarchy.

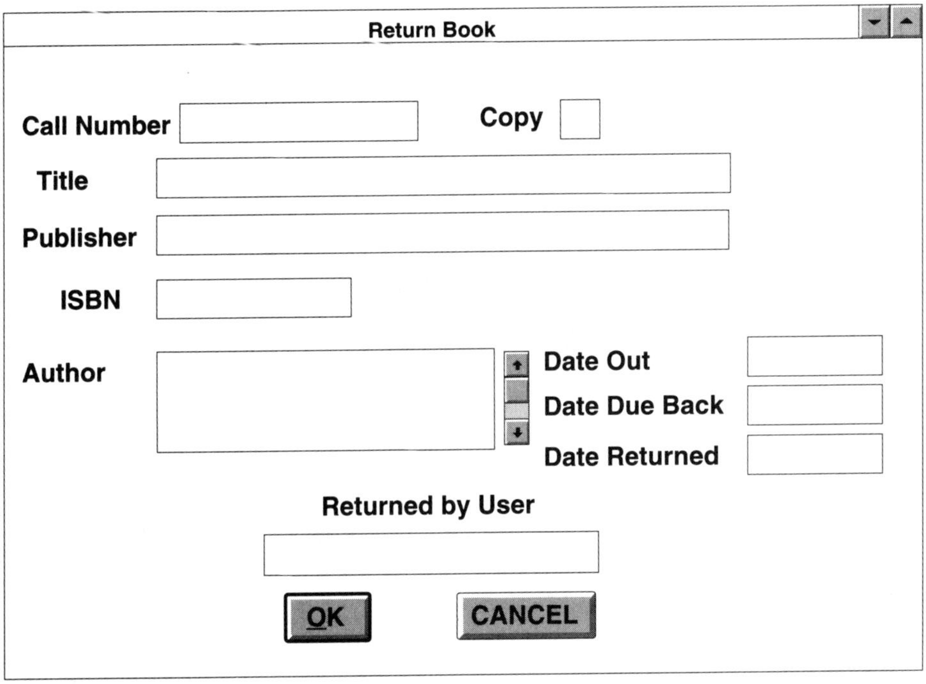

Figure A1.4
Library return book GUI screen.

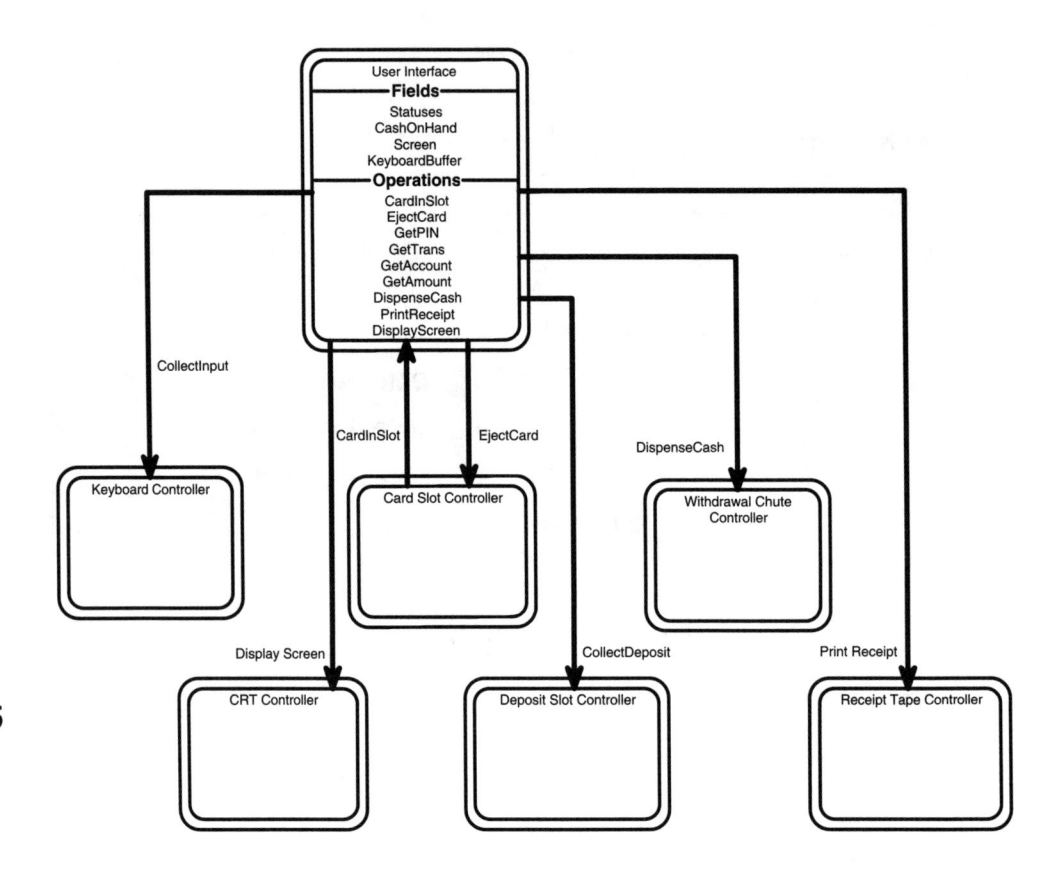

Figure A1.5
ATM user
interface
class diagram.

Class definition - all attributes   Page   1
Class : **ATM**
The ATM manages all sessions with bank customers. It interfaces directly with the Terminal Controller which manages all the hardware components, the Account Manager which manages all bank account information, and the ATM File Manager which manages all ATM transacitons.
Fields:
Date
Time
CashOnHand
Operations:
ATMSession
Cardinality:
Concurrency:
Generic Parameters:
Metaclass:
Interface:
Persistence: persistent
Space Complexity:
Superclasses:
Uses:
Visibility:
Class : **ATM File Manager**
The ATM File Manager logs all ATM transactions, and provides services to the ATM - find previous transactions.
Fields:
Date
Time
Type
PAN
AccountType
Balance
Amount
Operations:
LogATMTransaction
Cardinality:
Concurrency: active
Generic Parameters:
Metaclass:
Interface:
Persistence: persistent
Space Complexity:
Superclasses:
Uses:
Visibility:

Figure A1.6
Excerpts from Library and ATM class definition reports.

Class : **Account** (abstract)
Bank account.
Fields:
Number
Balance
Type
DateOpened
Name
Address
PIN
Operations:
Open
Close
Debit
Credit
Print
Cardinality:
Concurrency:
Generic Parameters:
Metaclass:
Interface:
Persistence:
Space Complexity:
Superclasses:
Uses:
Visibility:

Class : **Account Manager**
Manage access to all bank accounts.
Fields:
PAN
AccountType
PIN
Balance
Operations:
GetPAN
Debit
Metaclass:
Interface:
Persistence: persistent
Space Complexity:
Superclasses:
Uses:
Visibility:

Field Definitions   Page   1
Name   Update Date
Description
AccountType   11/06/93
The account type signifies the type of account each customer has. Valid types include 01=Saving, 02=Checking, 05=Money Market, 10=Loan, 11=Mortgage, 12=Line of Credit.
Address   11/02/93
The address of someone - where they live.
Answer   11/02/93
An option (or answer) selected by the user.
Archive   11/08/93
Defines whether a list has been archived to permanent storage.
AssociatedState   11/02/93
A table of states. The index is used to find the state and the element in the array maps to the state number.
Type: ATMState
AuthorName   11/02/93
The full name of an author.
Balance   11/06/93
The current balance in the account referenced by PAN and Account Type.
BirthDate   11/02/93
The date (MM/DD/YY) that the author was born.
BorrowLimit   11/02/93
The limit on the number of books a user may borrow at one time.
CRTStatus   11/06/93
The current status of the CRT. If working, 0, else -1.
CallNumber   11/02/93
The unique identifier for a book within the library.
CardStatus   11/06/93
The current status of the Card Reader. If working, status is 0, otherwise, -1.
CashOnHand   11/06/93
The available cash on hand for withdrawals. In $10 bills.
CompanyName   11/02/93
The name of the company where the system is running.
CopyNumber   11/02/93
Number of a copy of a book.
DateBack   11/02/93
The date a book was actually returned by this user.
DateDue   11/02/93
Date book copy is due back in the library.
DateDueBack   11/02/93
The date a book is due back.
DateHired   11/02/93
The date a library staff person was hired.
DateIn   11/02/93
Date book copy was returned to the library.

Figure A1.7
Excerpts from Library and ATM attribute/field defintion reports.

DateOut   11/02/93
The date that the copy was checked out by the user.
DateOute   11/02/93
The date a book was checked out by this user.
DatePublished   11/02/93
The date that the book was published.
DeathDate   11/02/93
The date (MM/DD/YY) that the author died.
DepositStatus   11/06/93
The current status of the deposit slot. If working, 0, else -1.
EmployeeType   11/02/93
The type of employee - S=Staff, F=Faculty, A=Administration, etc.
First   11/02/93
The first name of someone.
FirstScreen   11/02/93
The first screen in the ATM system.
ISBN   11/02/93
The unique identifier for the book in the Library of Congress.
KeyboardStatus   11/06/93
The current status of the keyboard. If working, 0, else -1.
Last   11/02/93
The last name of someone.
MaxItems   11/09/93
The maximum number of items in the list.
MenuOption   11/02/93
A menu option selected by a user.
Name   03/22/94
First + Last
NextScreen   11/02/93
The next screen to be displayed.
NextUserID   11/02/93
The next system-assigned userID.
Number   11/09/93
The number of items in the list.
NumberOut   11/02/93
Number of book copies currently checked out by the user.
PAN   11/06/93
The Person Account Number represents a logical account structure for all bank customers. Since a bank customer can have many accounts, the PAN represents a 9-digit number that is the master account. Each PAN is supplemented with a 2-digit account type.
Password   11/02/93
An access code associated with a UserID.
PrinterStatus   11/06/93
The current status of the receipt printer. If working, 0, else -1.
Publisher   11/02/93
The publisher of the book.

Appendix A OOCOBOL Examples   447

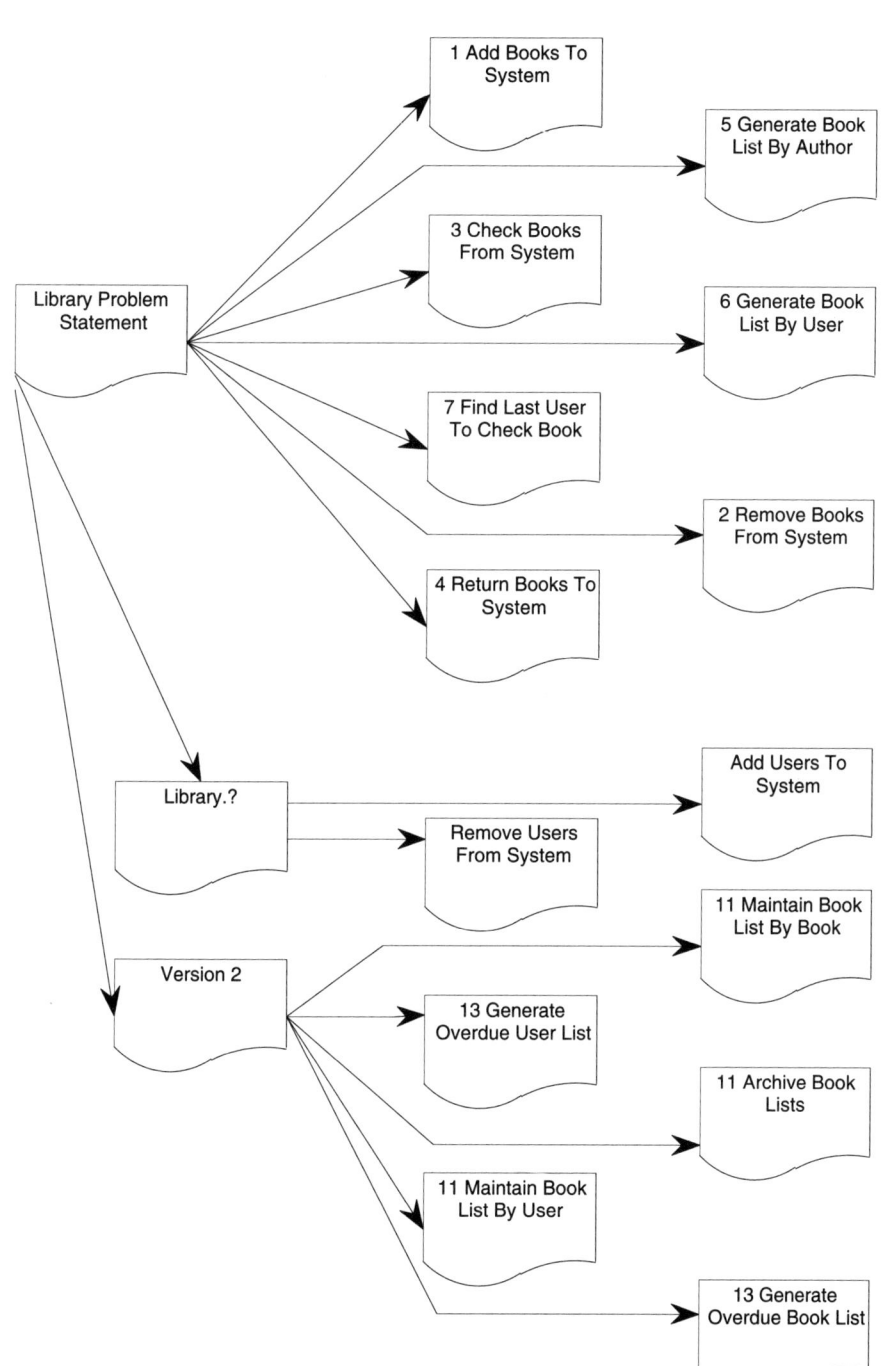

Figure A1.8
Library requirements document diagram.

448   Object-Oriented Development in COBOL

Figure A1.9
ATM requirements document diagram.

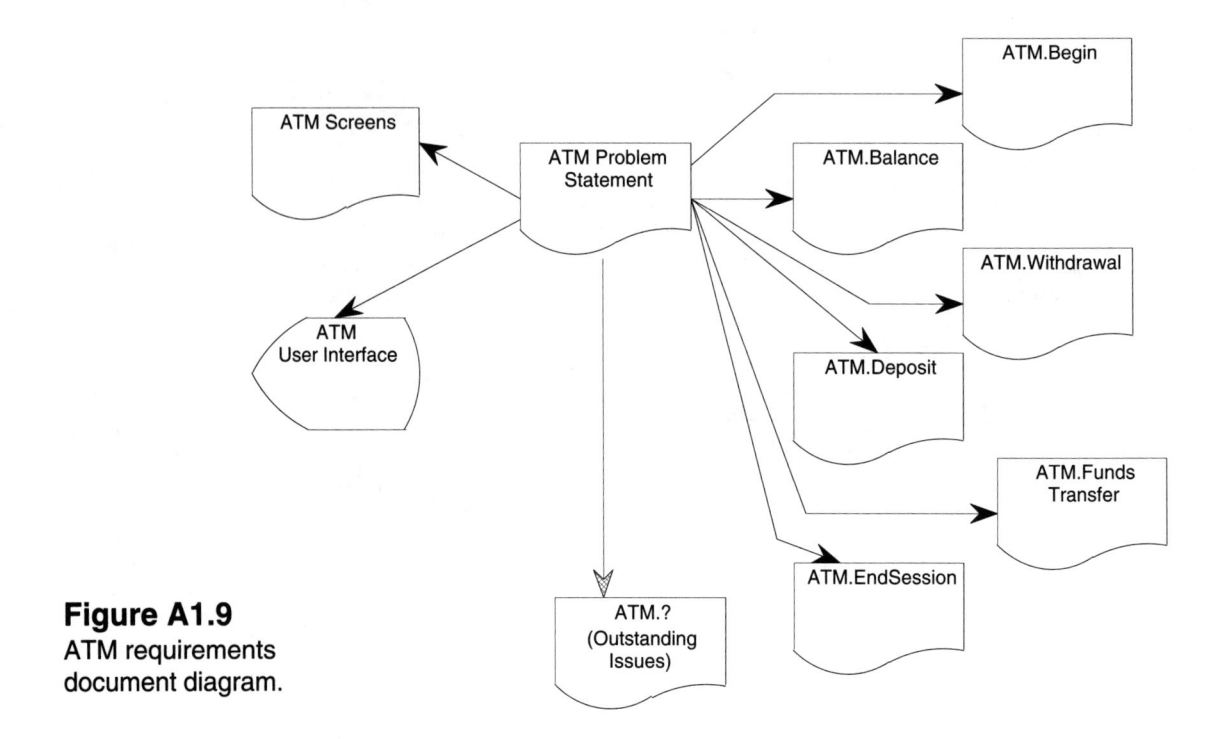

Requirements associated with diagram symbols   Page   1
Name - Description
    Name   Type

Add Books To System Get author, book, and copy information from the Publisher and User, and add it to the respective data stores.

Name	Type
Add Author	Process
Add Author	Module
Add Book	Module
Add Book Information	Module
Add Book Information	Process
Add Books To System	Document
Add Copy	Module
Add Copy	Process
Display Screen	Module
Find Book	Module
Find Book Information	Module
Get Book Information	Module
Get Call Number	Module
Library problem	Requirement
Verify Book Information	Process

Add Users To System Additional Issues - allow library users to be added to the system Get user information from the User and the next system-generated userID from the system, and add it to the Users data store.

Name	Type
Add User	Process
Add User	Module
Add Users To System	Document
Find User	Module
Library problem	Requirement
Verify User Information	Process

Archive Book Lists Version 2 Archive the CheckoutList and UserList data stores when they contain more than 100 entries.

Name	Type
Archive Book Lists	Document
Archive Lists	Process
Archive Lists	Module
Version 2	Requirement

Check Books From System Get user and book information from the User and assign a copy of the book to the user.

Name	Type
Assign Copy	Process
Assign Copy	Module
Check Book	Module
Check Books From System	Document
Display Screen	Module
Find Copy	Module
Find User	Module
Library problem	Requirement
Verify Book	Process
Verify Borrow	Process
Verify Limit	Process
Verify User	Process

Figure A1.10
Excerpts from the Library requirements traceability report.

Requirements associated with diagram symbols   Page   2
Name - Description
    Name   Type

Find Last User To Check Book Using the book's call number, display all copies of the book currently checked out.

Name	Type
Find Last User	Process
Find Last User	Module
Find Last User To Check Book	Document
Library problem	Requirement

Generate Book List By Author Get an author's name from the User and list all books written by the author.

Name	Type
Generate Book List By Author	Document
Generate List By Author	Process
Generate List By Author	Module
Library problem	Requirement

Generate Book List By User Get a list of all the books checked out by the user.

Name	Type
Generate Book List By User	Document
Generate List By User	Process
Generate List By User	Module
Library problem	Requirement

Generate Overdue Book List Version 3 List all users whose books are currently overdue.

Name	Type
Generate Overdue Book List	Process
Generate Overdue Book List	Document
Generate Overdue List By Book	Module

Generate Overdue User List Version 3 List all books currently overdue by a user.

Name	Type
Generate Overdue List By User	Module
Generate Overdue User List	Process
Generate Overdue User List	Document

Library problem The library problem is very popular in Software Engineering literature. It has been a conference problem at several major national and international conferences [WIN88], the Software Engineering Institute uses it in selected curriculum modules, has been extensively studied in the literature [HUR91], various CASE vendors use it as a demonstration problem. The Jackson design advocates claim it is the "best example" for their method [CAM86], and a very formal specification is given in [KEM85].

Problem Statement

Consider a small university library system with the following transactions or functions:

    1. Add a copy of a book to the library.
    2. Remove a copy of a book from the library.
    3. Check out a copy of a book from the library.
    4. Return a copy of a book to the library.
    5. Get the list of books in the library written by a particular author.
    6. Get the list of books currently checked out by a particular borrower.
    7. Find out which borrower most recently checked out a particular copy of a book.

Within the library system, there are two types of users: library staff and ordinary borrowers. Transactions 1, 2, 3, 4, 6, and 7 are restricted to library staff, while ordinary borrowers can use transaction 6 to find out which books they currently have checked out. Finally, there are three additional constraints on the library system:

8. All copies of books in the library must be either available for checkout or must be checked out. (i.e., no reserve books)

9. No copy of a book can be both available for checkout and be checked out at the same time.

10. An ordinary borrower may not have more than a predefined number of books checked out at one time. (i.e., there is a set borrow limit.)

In a software development project for the library problem, a first step would be to express the given requirements in written form. In the process of reexamining the stated requirements, it is likely that some flaws or unspecified issues in the original narrative description would be discovered. Some examples of outstanding issues for the library problem include:

A) How does the library system differentiate between staff users and ordinary borrowers? How are these users added and removed from the system?

B) What is the "predefined maximum borrowing limit" for a user? How is this information entered and stored?

C) Regarding transaction 5, what does "in the library" mean? The possibilities are: "available for checkout" (i.e., physically in the library) or "either available for checkout or checked out" (owned by the library).

D) Transactions 6 and 7 suggest data structures which, over prolonged system use, will grow very large. How will these structures be managed by the library system? (See item # 11 below.)

E) Where do library books come from? Where do they go when they are removed?

Library Problem Statement   Document
Library.?

A2 OOD Results

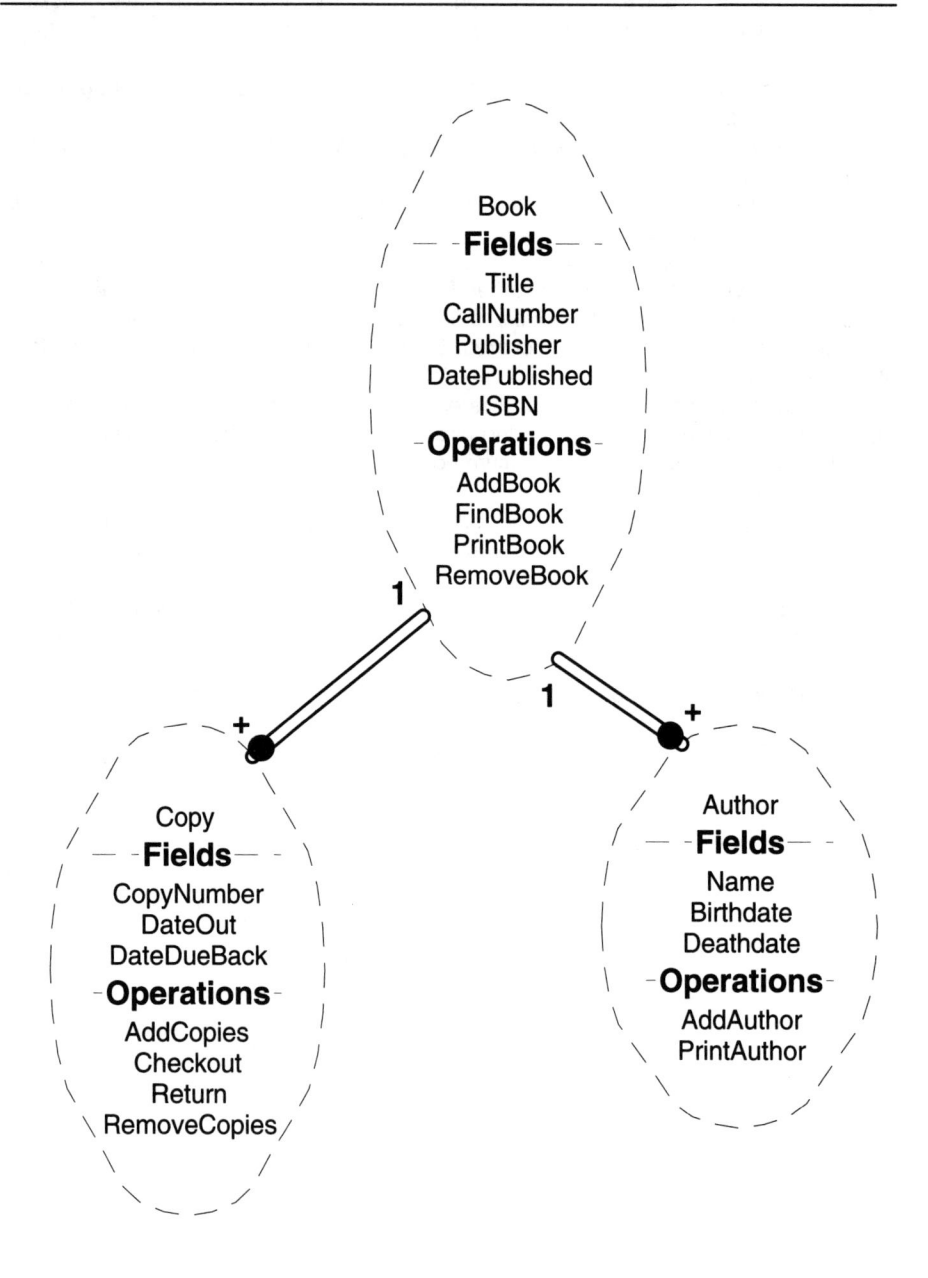

Book
Fields
Title
CallNumber
Publisher
DatePublished
ISBN
Operations
AddBook
FindBook
PrintBook
RemoveBook

Copy
Fields
CopyNumber
DateOut
DateDueBack
Operations
AddCopies
Checkout
Return
RemoveCopies

Author
Fields
Name
Birthdate
Deathdate
Operations
AddAuthor
PrintAuthor

Figure A2.1
Library book class diagram.

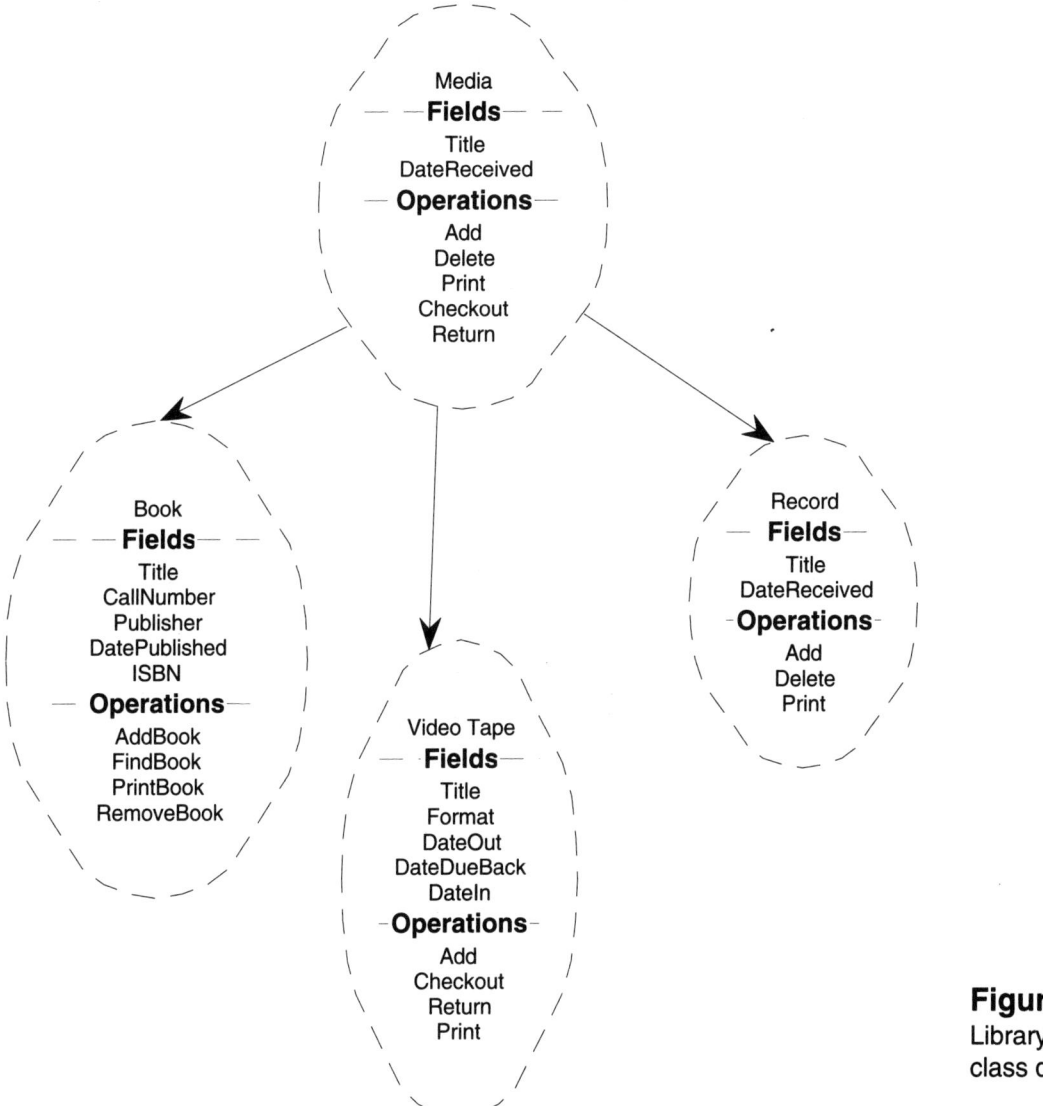

Media
— **Fields** —
Title
DateReceived
— **Operations** —
Add
Delete
Print
Checkout
Return

Book
— **Fields** —
Title
CallNumber
Publisher
DatePublished
ISBN
— **Operations** —
AddBook
FindBook
PrintBook
RemoveBook

Video Tape
— **Fields** —
Title
Format
DateOut
DateDueBack
DateIn
— **Operations** —
Add
Checkout
Return
Print

Record
— **Fields** —
Title
DateReceived
— **Operations** —
Add
Delete
Print

Figure A2.2
Library media class diagram.

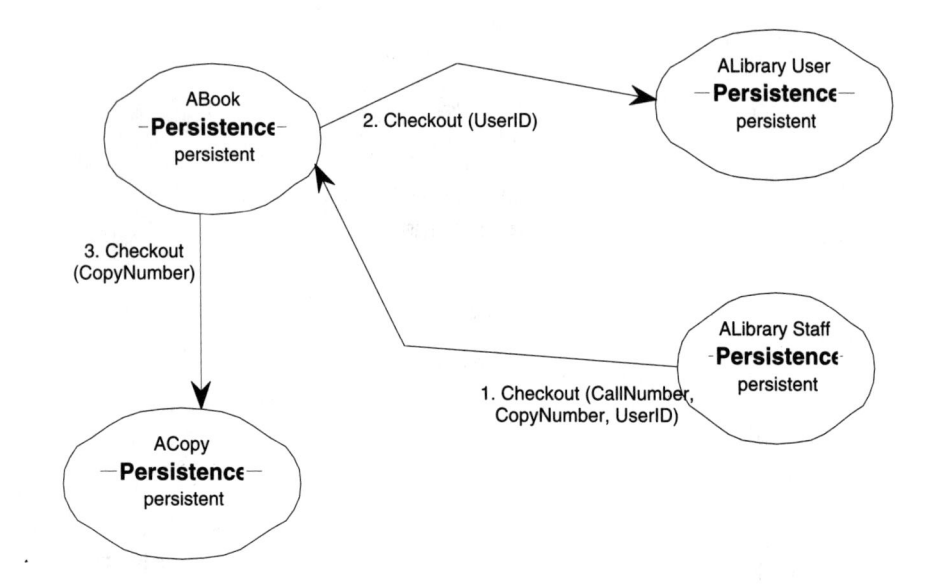

Figure A2.3
Library checkout book object scenario diagram.

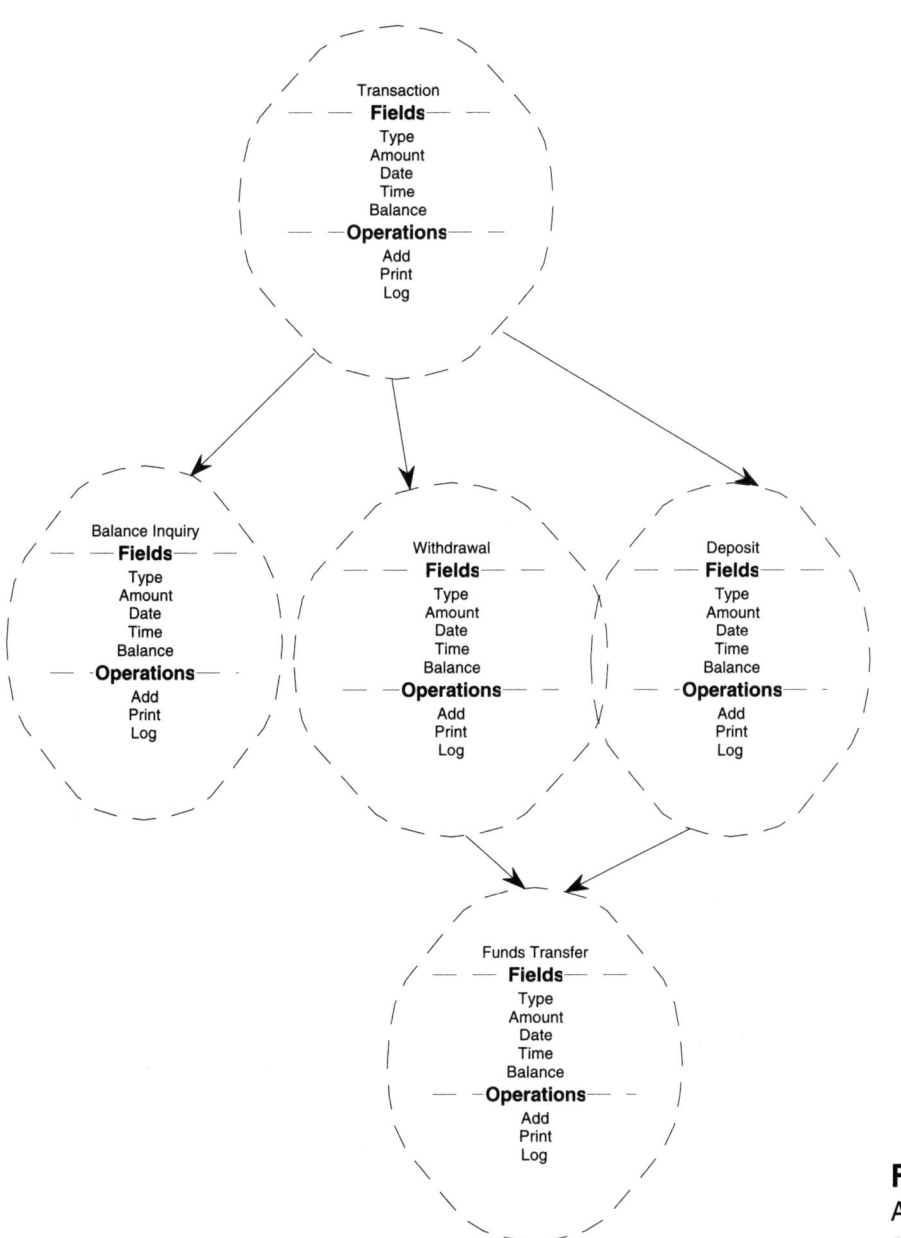

Figure A2.4
ATM transaction class diagram.

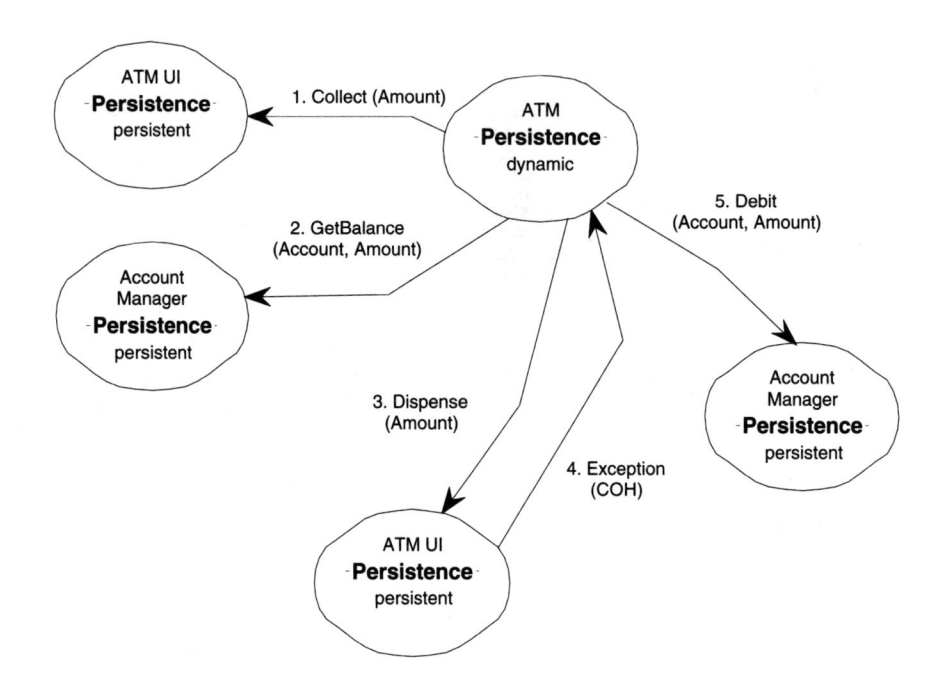

Figure A2.5
ATM withdrawal object scenario diagram.

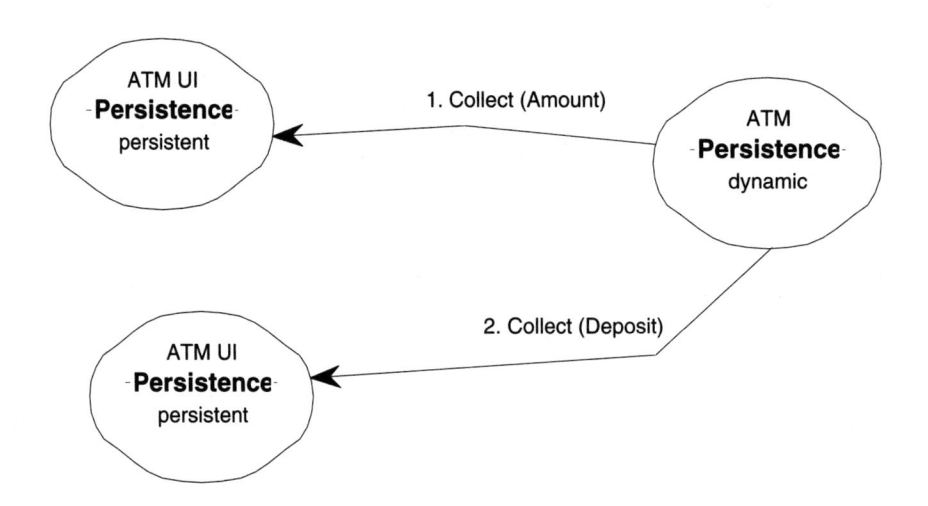

Figure A2.6
ATM deposit object scenario diagram.

Appendix A OOCOBOL Examples 457

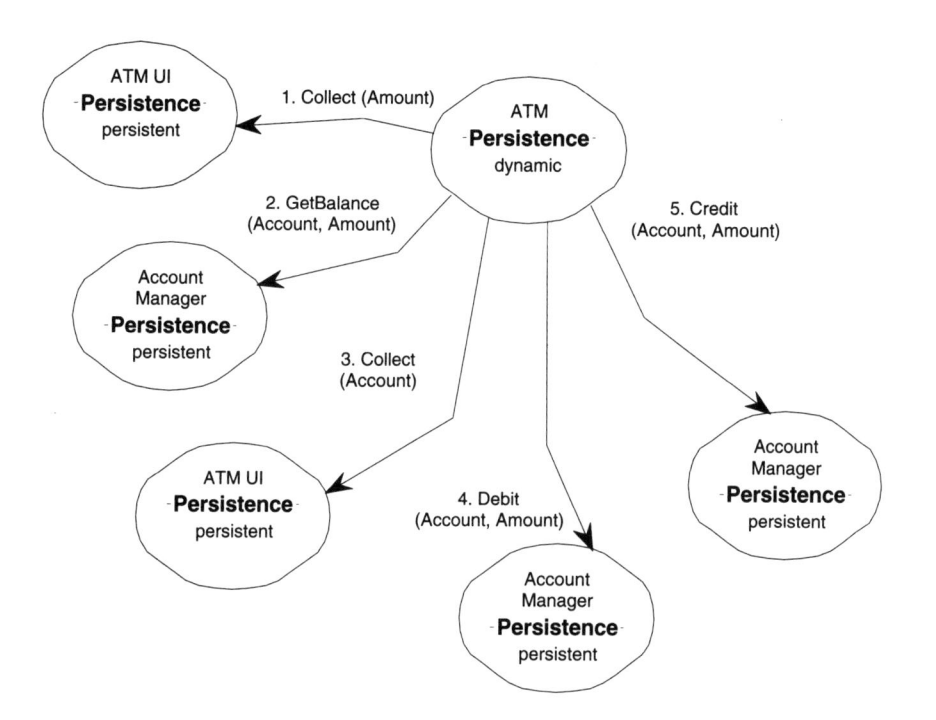

Figure A2.7
ATM funds transfer object scenario diagram.

ATMState - *Do* (state): executes actions of the current state
- *Display*(state): displays the screen associated with a state
- *GetAnswer*(Answer): gets the users answer/response
- *Process* (state, answer): processes the transition to the next state/screen

Process:
    NextState = StateTable (state, answer)

ATMSession logic
    Loop
        Perform ATMSession
        Until state/screen = 16.
        Perform SaveTransaction.
        State = 1.
    Forever
    or Until CashOnHand < 100.

ATMSession:
    Display (state)
    GetAnswer(answer)
    Do (state)
    state = *Process* (state, answer)

SaveTransaction:
    Save ATMTransaction data to file.
    Update ATM global variables.

Figure A2.8
ATM state and session module psuedocode.

A.3 OOCOBOL Code

Figure A3.1
Excerpts from deck of cards OOCOBOL source code.

*[CARDECK.CBL] Deck of Cards Example problem

Class-ID. CardDeck is factory
         data is protected
         inheriting base with data.

Special-Names.
         Factory CardDeck is "CARDECK"
         Factory base is "BASE"
         Factory sortedcollection is "CHARARRY".

Working-Storage Section.
77   NumberofCards   Value 52.
01   nil   object reference external.
01   SelectionMethodName   PIC X(30)   Value "SelectCards".

****
*   The New method is required of all classes and creates an instance of the object
*   CardDeck. This method also calls the initialize method to define the collection
*   and initialize the card suits, values and Dealt field.
*
****
Method-ID. "new".
Linkage Section.
01   thedeckofcards   object reference.
Procedure Division returning thedeckofcards.
         Invoke Super "new" Returning thedeckofcards
         Invoke thedeckofcards "initialize"
         Exit Program.
End Method "new".

Object.

Working-Storage Section.
01   DeckofCard-Storage.
         03   thecollection   object reference.
         03   othercollection   object reference.
         03   sortstyle PIC X.
               88   cmpordvalue   Value "O" "o".
         03   currentsuit   PIC X.
         03   currentsuitlen   PIC s9(9) comp-5.
         03   currentcard   PIC X.

```
            03       currentcardlen           PIC s9(9) comp-5.
            03       currentdealt             PIC 9(4) comp-5.
                     88      Dealt                       Value 1.
                     88      NotDealt                    Value 0.
            03       currentordvalen          PIC s9(9) comp-5.
```

Method-ID. "initialize".
`*****************************************************************************`
`*`   This method initializes the array of cards for their value, suit, and dealt fields.
`*`
`*****************************************************************************`

```
Working-Storage Section.
01      Work-Area.
            03       suit                     PIC X.
            03       value                    PIC X.
01      asize    pic x(4) comp-5.
Procedure Division.
        Move 52 to asize.
        Invoke characterarray "ofReferences"
                Using asize
                Returning thecollection.
        Perform Init-Suit
                Varying i from 1 by 1
                Until i = 4.
        EXIT PROGRAM.
Init-Suit.
        Perform Init-Value
                Varying j from 2 by 1
                Until j = 14.
Init-Value.
        Case i = 1: set suit to "H".
        Case i = 2: set suit to "C".
        Case i = 3: set suit to "D".
        Case i = 4: set suit to "S".
        Calc i + j to Index.
        Move suit to Suit[Index].
        Move j to TmpValue.
        Case j = 14: Move "A" to TmpValue.
        Case j = 11: Move "J" to TmpValue.
        Case j = 12: Move "Q" to TmpValue.
        Case j = 13: Move "K" to TmpValue.
        Move TmpValue to Value[Index].
        Move 0 to Dealt[Index].
```

End Method "initialize".

Method-ID. "AddCard".
```
*****************************************************************************************
*       This method adds a new card to the list of cards dealt.                          *
*****************************************************************************************
```
Working-Storage Section.
01   newcard   object reference.
01   returnobject   object reference.
Linkage Section.
01   p1   object reference.
01   p2   object reference.
01   p3   object reference.
01   p4   object reference.
Procedure Division Using p1 p2 p3 p4.
        Invoke DeckOfCards "NewCard" using p1 p2 p3 p4
             Returning newcard
        Invoke thecollection "add" using newcard
             returning returnobject
        Exit program.
End Method "AddCard".

Method-ID. "GetCard".
```
*****************************************************************************************
*       This method returns the value of a card as 2 of Hearts, etc.                     *
*****************************************************************************************
```
Linkage Section.
01   acard   object reference.
01   c1   object reference.
01   c2   object reference.
01   c3   object reference.
01   d4   object reference.
Procedure Division Using c1 c2 c3 c4.
        Invoke arecord "getCardValue"
             Returning c1
        Invoke arecord "getCardSuite"
             Returning c2
        Exit program.

End Method "GetCard".

Method-ID. "at".
```
*****************************************************************************************
*       This method locates the card at a specific point in the collection.              *
*****************************************************************************************
```
Linkage Section.
01   itemnum   PIC S9(9) comp-5.
01   aresult   object reference.
01   Index   PIC S99.

Procedure Division using itemnum returning aresult.
    Invoke thecollection "at" using itemnum returning aresult
    Exit Program.
End Method "at".

Method-ID. "shuffle".
```
*******************************************************************************
*    This method re-shuffles the deck of cards so that all cards are available.    *
*******************************************************************************
```
Working-Storage Section.
01   Work-Area.
        03   suit   PIC X.
01   asize   pic x(4) comp-5.
Linkage Section.
01   ACard   object reference.
01   Card   object reference.
01   c2   object reference.
Procedure Division Using Card Return ACard.
        Perform Init-Suit
            Varying i from 1 by 1
            Until i = 4.
        EXIT PROGRAM.
Init-Suit.
        Perform Init-Value
            Varying j from 2 by 1
            Until j = 14.
Init-Value.

        Calc i + j to Index.
        Move 0 to Dealt[Index].

End Progarm "shuffle".

Method-ID. "deal".
```
*******************************************************************************
*    This method deals or selects n cards from those available.    *
*******************************************************************************
```
Linkage Section.
01   numbercards   PIC S9(9) comp-5.
01   n   PIC 99   Value 0.
01   c1   object reference.
01   c2   object reference.
01   c3   object reference.
01   c4   object reference.
01   c5   object reference.
Procedure Division use n returning c1.
Begin:

Figure A3.2
Excerpts from Library OOCOBOL source code.

```
*[LIBRARY.CBL] Library Example problem

***************************************************************************************
*         Book Class
***************************************************************************************
IDENTIFICATION DIVISION.
CLASS-ID.      Book IS TRANSIANT COLLECTABLE
               INHERITS Base.
DATA DIVISION.
01     Book.
       03     Call_Number           PIC X(32).
       03     Title                 PIC X(60).
       03     Publisher             PIC X(60).
       03     Date_Published        PIC 9(8).
       03     ISBN                  PIC X(16).
       03     ListOfUsers                      USAGE OBJECT List_Of_Books.
01     Copy.
       03     Copy_ID.
              03     Call_Number    PIC X(32).
              03     Copy_Number    PIC 99.
       03     Date_Out              PIC 9(8).
       03     Date_Due_Back         PIC 9(8).
01     Author.
       03     Author_Name.
              05     Last_Name      PIC X(30).
              05     First_Name     PIC X(30).

METHOD-ID. "new".
WORKING-STORAGE SECTION.
01     TEMP                         USAGE OBJECT REFERENCE.
LINKAGE SECTION.
01     Book                         USAGE OBJECT REFERENCE.
01     Book_REF                     USAGE OBJECT REFERENCE.
PROCEDURE DIVISION USING Book_Ref RETURNING Book.
       INVOKE Super "new" RETURNING Book.
       INVOKE Book "Initialize".
       EXIT PROGRAM.
END METHOD "new".

METHOD-ID. "Initialize".          /* For Factory */
***************************************************************************************
*        Initialize Book class by creating the SQL table and indexes *
***************************************************************************************
WORKING-STORAGE SECTION.
01     SIZE                         PIC X(4) COMP-5.
```

```
        PROCEDURE DIVISION.
            CREATE TABLE BOOK
                PRIMARY KEY Call_Number.
            CREATE TABLE COPY
                PRIMARY KEY Copy_ID.
            CREATE TABLE AUTHOR
                PRIMARY KEY Author_Name.
            CREATE INDEX XBOOK
                ON BOOK (Call_Number).
            EXIT PROGRAM.
    END METHOD "Initialize".

        OBJECT.
        PROCEDURE DIVISION.
        METHOD-ID. Add.
       ********************************************************************************
       *     Add - creates the entry in the Book table with the proper values.
       ********************************************************************************
        PROCEDURE DIVISION USING Book RETURNING Book.
            INSERT INTO BOOK
                VALUES (Call_Number Title Publisher ISBN Author).
            INSERT INTO COPY
                VALUES (Call_Number Copy_Number Date_Out Date_Due_Back).
            INSERT INTO AUTHOR
                VALUES (Author_Name Call_Number).
            EXIT PROGRAM.
        END METHOD Add.

        METHOD-ID. BooksByAuthor.
       ********************************************************************************
       *     Print Books by Author table *
       ********************************************************************************
        PROCEDURE DIVISION USING Author RETURNING Report.
            SELECT * FROM BOOK WHERE Author_Name = Author.
            Perform PrintBook.
            INVOKE ListOfBooks Print
            EXIT PROGRAM.
        END METHOD BooksByAuthor.

        METHOD-ID. UsersByBook.
       ********************************************************************************
       *     Returns and prints a list of users that have checked out a book *
       ********************************************************************************
        PROCEDURE DIVISION USING CallNumber RETURNING Report.
            SELECT * FROM BOOK WHERE Call_Number = CallNumber.
            Perform PrintBook.
            INVOKE ListOfUsers Print
            EXIT PROGRAM.
        END METHOD UsersByBook.
```

METHOD-ID. FindBook.
```
***************************************************************************************
*        Returns specific book information                                             *
***************************************************************************************
```
PROCEDURE DIVISION USING CallNumber RETURNING Book.
    SELECT * FROM BOOK WHERE Call_Number = CallNumber.
    MOVE Title to Title.
    MOVE Author to Author.
    MOVE ISBN to ISBN.
    MOVE Publisher to Publisher.
    EXIT PROGRAM.
END METHOD FindBook.

METHOD-ID. FindCopy.
```
***************************************************************************************
*        Returns specific copy information                                             *
***************************************************************************************
```
PROCEDURE DIVISION USING CallNumber CopyNumber RETURNING Copy.
    SELECT * FROM BOOK WHERE Call_Number = CallNumber
        AND Copy_Number = CopyNumber.
    EXIT PROGRAM.
END METHOD FindCopy.

METHOD-ID. Remove.
```
***************************************************************************************
*        Remove all book information from the library                                  *
***************************************************************************************
```
PROCEDURE DIVISION USING CallNumber.
    DELETE FROM BOOK WHERE Call_Number = CallNumber.
    DELETE FROM AUTHOR WHERE Call_Number = CallNumber.
    DELETE FROM COPY WHERE Call_Number = CallNumber
        AND Copy_Number = CopyNumber.
    EXIT PROGRAM.
END METHOD Remove.

```
***************************************************************************************
*        User Class
***************************************************************************************
```
IDENTIFICATION DIVISION.
CLASS-ID.   User IS TRANSIANT COLLECTABLE
                 INHERITS Base.
DATA DIVISION.
01   User.
        03   User_ID   PIC 9(6).
        03   User_Name.
                05   Last_Name   PIC X(30).

```
                    05      First_Name              PIC X(30).
            03      Address.
                    05      Street                  PIC X(30).
                    05      Street_2                PIC X(30).
                    05      City                    PIC X(30).
                    05      State                   PIC XX.
                    05      Zip_Code.
                            07      Zip_5           PIC 9(5).
                            07      Zip_4           PIC 9(4).
                    05      Phone_Number.
                            07      Area_Code       PIC 999.
                            07      Phone_3         PIC 999.
                            07      Phone_4         PIC 9(4).
            03      Borrow_Limit                    PIC 99.
            03      ListOfBooks                     USAGE OBJECT List_Of_Books.

METHOD-ID. "new".
WORKING-STORAGE SECTION.
01      TEMP                                USAGE OBJECT REFERENCE.
01      NextUserID                          PIC 9(8).
LINKAGE SECTION.
01      User                                USAGE OBJECT REFERENCE.
01      User_REF                            USAGE OBJECT REFERENCE.
PROCEDURE DIVISION USING User_Ref RETURNING User.
        INVOKE Super "new" RETURNING User.
        INVOKE User "Initialize".
        EXIT PROGRAM.
END METHOD "new".

METHOD-ID. "Initialize".            /* For Factory */
*****************************************************************************
*       Initialize User class by creating the SQL table and indexes
*****************************************************************************
WORKING-STORAGE SECTION.
01      SIZE                                PIC X(4) COMP-5.
PROCEDURE DIVISION.
        CREATE TABLE USER
            PRIMARY KEY User_ID
            FOREIGN KEY User_Name.
        CREATE INDEX XUSER
            ON USER (User_ID).
            MOVE 0 to NextUserID.
        EXIT PROGRAM.
END METHOD "Initialize".
```

OBJECT.
WORKING-STORAGE SECTION.
01   Ref_List   USAGE OBJECT REFERENCE.
01   User   USAGE OBJECT REFERENCE.
PROCEDURE DIVISION.
METHOD-ID. Add.
****
*   Add - creates the entry in the User table with the proper values.
****
PROCEDURE DIVISION USING User RETURNING User.
        CREATE ListOfBooks RETURNING Ref_List.
        COMPUTE NextUserID + 1 to NextUserID
        INSERT INTO USER
                VALUES (NextUserID UserName Password BorrowLimit).
        EXIT PROGRAM.
END METHOD Add.

METHOD-ID. BooksByUser.
****
*   Returns and prints a list of books that have checked out to this user
****
PROCEDURE DIVISION USING UserID RETURNING Report.
        SELECT * FROM USER WHERE User_ID = UserID.
        Perform PrintUser.
        INVOKE ListOfBooks Print.
        EXIT PROGRAM.
END METHOD BooksByUser.

METHOD-ID. FindUser.
****
*   Returns specific user information by UserId, or if not found, by
*   UserName. If still not found, returns exception condition.
****
PROCEDURE DIVISION USING UserID RETURNING User.
        SELECT * FROM USER WHERE User_ID = UserID.
        If User_ID NE UserID
                SELECT * FROM USER WHERE User_Name = UserName.
        MOVE User_Name to User.UserName.
        MOVE Password to User.Password.
        MOVE Borrow_Limit to User.BorrowLimit.
        EXIT PROGRAM.
END METHOD FindUser.

METHOD-ID. UpdateBorrowLimit.
****
*   Update User Borrow Limit
****

```
PROCEDURE DIVISION USING UserID BorrowLimit.
    UPDATE USER SET BorrowLimit to BorrowLimit
        WHERE User_ID = UserID.
    EXIT PROGRAM.
END METHOD UpdateBorrowLimit.

METHOD-ID. UpdatePassword.
*****************************************************************************
*       Update User Password
*****************************************************************************
PROCEDURE DIVISION USING UserID Password.
    UPDATE USER SET Password to Password
        WHERE User_ID = UserID.
    EXIT PROGRAM.
END METHOD UpdatePassword.

METHOD-ID. Remove.
*****************************************************************************
*       Remove all user information from the library
*****************************************************************************
PROCEDURE DIVISION USING UserID.
    DELETE FROM BOOK WHERE User_ID = UserID.
    EXIT PROGRAM.
END METHOD Remove.


*****************************************************************************
*       Library Staff Class
*****************************************************************************

IDENTIFICATION DIVISION.
CLASS-ID.       Staff IS TRANSIANT COLLECTABLE
                INHERITS Base.
DATA DIVISION.
01      Staff.
        03      User_ID                         PIC 9(6).
        03      User_Name.
                05      Last_Name               PIC X(30).
                05      First_Name              PIC X(30).
        03      Address.
                05      Street                  PIC X(30).
                05      Street_2                PIC X(30).
                05      City                    PIC X(30).
                05      State                   PIC XX.
                05      Zip_Code.
                        07      Zip_5           PIC 9(5).
                        07      Zip_4           PIC 9(4).
```

```
            05    Phone_Number.
                  07    Area_Code       PIC 999.
                  07    Phone_3         PIC 999.
                  07    Phone_4         PIC 9(4).
      03    Borrow_Limit                PIC 99.
      03    Employee_Type               PIC XX.
      03    Date_Hired                  PIC 9(8).

METHOD-ID. "new".
WORKING-STORAGE SECTION.
01    TEMP                              USAGE OBJECT REFERENCE.
LINKAGE SECTION.
01    Staff                             USAGE OBJECT REFERENCE.
01    Staff_REF                         USAGE OBJECT REFERENCE.
01    NextStaffID                       PIC     9(8).
PROCEDURE DIVISION USING Staff_Ref RETURNING Staff.
      INVOKE Super "new" RETURNING Staff.
      INVOKE User "initialize".
      EXIT PROGRAM.
END METHOD "new".

METHOD-ID. "Initialize".          /* For Factory */
*******************************************************************************
*     Initialize Staff class by creating the SQL table and indexes
*******************************************************************************
WORKING-STORAGE SECTION.
01    SIZE                              PIC X(4) COMP-5.
PROCEDURE DIVISION.
      CREATE TABLE STAFF
            PRIMARY KEY User_ID
            FOREIGN KEY User_Name.
      CREATE INDEX XSTAFF
            ON USER (User_ID).
            MOVE 0 to NextStaffID.
            EXIT PROGRAM.
END METHOD "Initialize".

OBJECT.
WORKING-STORAGE SECTION.
01    Ref_List                          USAGE OBJECT REFERENCE.
01    Staff                             USAGE OBJECT REFERENCE.
PROCEDURE DIVISION.
METHOD-ID. Add IS PUBLIC.
*******************************************************************************
*     Add - creates the entry in the Staff table with the proper values.
*******************************************************************************
```

Object-Oriented Development in COBOL

```
        PROCEDURE DIVISION USING Staff RETURNING Staff.
            COMPUTE NextStaffID + 1 to NextStaffID
            INSERT INTO STAFF
                VALUES (User_ID Staff_Name Password Borrow_Limit Date_Hired).
            EXIT PROGRAM.
        END METHOD Add.

        METHOD-ID. Checkout.
       ******************************************************************************
       *       Checkout a book from the library
       ******************************************************************************
        PROCEDURE DIVISION USING UserID CallNumber CopyNumber DateOut
        DateDueBack.
            SELECT * FROM USER WHERE User_ID = UserID.
            SELECT * FROM BOOK WHERE Call_Number = CallNumber.
            SELECT * FROM COPY WHERE Call_Number = CallNumber
                    AND Copy_Number = CopyNumber.
            INSERT INTO CHECKOUT
                VALUES (User_ID Call_Number Copy_Number
                    Date_Out Date_Due_Back).
            EXIT PROGRAM.
        END METHOD Checkout.

        METHOD-ID. Return.
       ******************************************************************************
       *       Return a book checked out to a user
       ******************************************************************************
        PROCEDURE DIVISION USING UserID CallNumber CopyNumber DateCheckedOut.
            SELECT * FROM CHECKOUT WHERE User_ID = UserID
                    AND Call_Number = CallNumber
                    AND Copy_Number = CopyNumber.
            MOVE Date_Out to DateCheckedOut.
            MOVE Date_Due_Back to DateCheckedOut + 14.
            DELETE FROM CHECKOUT
                    WHERE UserID = User_ID
                    AND CallNumber = Call_Number
                    AND CopyNumber = Copy_Number.
            INVOKE Book FindBook.
            INVOKE Book FindCopy.
            INVOKE User Find.
            INVOKE ListOfBooks Add Using UserID CallNumber CopyNumber
                    DateCheckedOut.
            INVOKE ListOfUsers Add Using CallNumber CopyNumber UserID
                    DateCheckedOut.
            EXIT PROGRAM.
        END METHOD Return.
```

```
METHOD-ID. ModifyBorrowLimit.
*****************************************************************************
*       Modify the borrow limit for a user
*****************************************************************************
PROCEDURE DIVISION USING UserID BorrowLimit.
        SELECT * FROM USER WHERE User_ID = UserID.
        UPDATE USER Set Borrow_Limit to BorrowLimit
                WHERE User_ID = UserID.
        EXIT PROGRAM.
END METHOD ModifyBorrowLimit.

*****************************************************************************
*       List Class
*****************************************************************************
IDENTIFICATION DIVISION.
CLASS-ID.       LIST is factory
                INHERITS from SortedCollection.
ENVIRONMENT DIVISION.
CONFIGURATION SECTION.
SPECIAL-NAMES.
FACTORY SortedCollection is "srtdclln".
DATA DIVISION.
01      List_Of_Users.
        03      Number                  PIC 999.
        03      MaxItems                PIC 999.
        03      Archive                 PIC X(4) COMP-5.
                88      NotArchived                     VALUE 0.
                88      Archived                        VALUE 1.
        03      FILLER.
                05      User_ID         PIC 9(6).
                05      Date_Out        PIC 9(8).
                05      Date_Due_Back   PIC 9(8).
                05      Date_Back       PIC 9(8).
                05      Call_Number     PIX X(32).
                05      Copy_Number     PIX 99.
WORKING-STORAGE SECTION.
78  maxstringlen                                        value 18.
*****************************************************************************
*       Create a new list object.
*****************************************************************************
IDENTIFICATION DIVISION.
METHOD-ID       "new".
LINKAGE SECTION.
01  l1                                  usage object reference.
01  l2                                  usage object reference.
01  l3                                  usage object reference.
```

```
01  I4                                             usage object reference.
01  IsnewRecord                                    usage object reference.
PROCEDURE DIVISION using I1 I2 I3 I4 returning IsnewRecord.
      Invoke Super "New" Returning IsnewRecord.
      Invoke IsnewRecord "Initialize" Using I1 I2 I3 I4.
      Exit Program.
end method "new".

*******************************************************************************
*       Create a blank record.
*******************************************************************************
METHOD-ID.   "CreateDefault".
WORKING-STORAGE SECTION.
01  aCallNumber                                    usage object reference.
01  aUserID                                        usage object reference.
01  aDateOut                                       usage object reference.
01  aDateIn                                        usage object reference.
01  i                                   pic x(4) comp-5.
Linkage Section.
01  IsnewRecord                                    usage object reference.
Procedure Division returning IsnewRecord.
      Invoke Super "New" Returning IsnewRecord.
      Move 18 to i.
      Invoke CharacterArray "WithLength" Using i returning aCallNumber.
      Invoke aFName "copy" Returning aUserID.
      Invoke aFName "copy" Returning aDateOut.
      Invoke aFName "copy" Returning aDateIn.
      Invoke IsnewRecord "Initialize" Using aCallNumber aUserID
             aDateOut aDateIn.
      Exit Program.
End Method "CreateDefault".

OBJECT.
WORKING-storage section.
01  recordetails.
       03  CallNumber                              usage object reference.
       03  UserID                                  usage object reference.
       03  DateOut                                 usage object reference.
       03  DateIn                                  usage object reference.
*******************************************************************************
*       Initialize the new List entry.                                         *
*******************************************************************************
METHOD-ID. "Initialize".
Linkage Section.
01  aCallNumber                                    usage object reference.
01  aUserID                                        usage object reference.
```

```
01  aDateOut                                          usage object reference.
01  aDateIn                                           usage object reference.
procedure division using aCallNumber aUserID aDateOut aDateIn.
        Set Call_Number to aCallNumber.
        Set User_ID to aUserID.
        Set Date_Out to aDateOut.
        Set Date_In to aDateIn.
        Exit Program.
End Method "Initialize".

*****************************************************************************************
*       Set the Call Number                                                              *
*****************************************************************************************
METHOD-ID. "SetCallNumber".
Linkage Section.
01  aCallNumber                                       usage object reference.
Procedure Division Using aCallNumber.
        Set Call_Number to aCallNumber
        Invoke Self "changed"
        Exit Program.
End Method "SetCallNumber".

*****************************************************************************************
*       Set the DateIn                                                                   *
*****************************************************************************************
Method-id. "SetDateIn".
Linkage Section.
01  aDateIn                                           usage object reference.
Procedure Division Using aDateIn.
        Set DateIn to aDateIn
        Invoke Self "changed"
        Exit Program.
End Method "SetDateIn".

...

end object .
end class .
```

Figure A3.3
Excerpts from
ATM OOCOBOL
source code.

```
*[ATM.CBL] ATM Example problem
****************************************************************************
*           Account Class definition
****************************************************************************

        IDENTIFICATION DIVISION.
        CLASS-ID.       Account IS TRANSIANT COLLECTABLE
                        INHERITS Base.
        01      Account.
                03      Number                          PIC 9(8).
                03      Type                            PIC XX.
                        88      Checking                                VALUE "CK".
                        88      Saving                                  VALUE "SV".
                        88      Money_Market                            VALUE "MK".
                        88      Line_Of_Credit                          VALUE "LC".
                        88      Mortgage                                VALUE "MG".
                        88      Loan                                    VALUE "LN".
                03      First_Name                      PIC X(30).
                03      Last_Name                       PIC X(30).
                03      Address.
                        05      Street                  PIC X(30).
                        05      Street_2                PIC X(30).
                        05      City                    PIC X(30).
                        05      State                   PIC XX.
                        05      Zip_Code.
                                07      Zip_5           PIC 9(5).
                                07      Zip_4           PIC 9(4).
                        05      Phone_Number.
                                07      Area_Code       PIC 999.
                                07      Phone_3         PIC 999.
                                07      Phone_4         PIC 9(4).
                03      Balance                         PIC S9(6)V99.
                03      PIN                             PIX 9999.
                03      Date_Opened                     PIC 99/99/9999.
        WORKING-STORAGE SECTION.
        01      ACCT.
                03      ACCT_Number                     PIC 9(8).
                03      ACCT_Type                       PIC XX.
                        88      Checking                                VALUE "CK".
                        88      Saving                                  VALUE "SV".
                        88      MoneyMarket                             VALUE "MK".
                        88      LineOfCredit                            VALUE "LC".
                        88      Mortgage                                VALUE "MG".
                        88      Loan                                    VALUE "LN".
                03      ACCT_FirstName                  PIC X(30).
                03      ACCT_LastName                   PIC X(30).
```

```
            03      ACCT_Address.
                    05      Street              PIC X(30).
                    05      Street_2            PIC X(30).
                    05      City                PIC X(30).
                    05      State               PIC XX.
                    05      Zip_Code.
                            07      Zip_5       PIC 9(5).
                            07      Zip_4       PIC 9(4).
                    05      Phone_Number.
                            07      Area_Code   PIC 999.
                            07      Phone_3     PIC 999.
                            07      Phone_4     PIC 9(4).
            03      ACCT_Balance                PIC S9(10)V99.
            03      ACCT_PIN                    PIX 9999.
            03      ACCT_DateOpened             PIC 99/99/9999.
01      Next_ACCT_Number                        PIC 9(8).

METHOD-ID. "new".
WORKING-STORAGE SECTION.
01      TEMP                                    USAGE OBJECT REFERENCE.
LINKAGE SECTION.
01      Account                                 USAGE OBJECT REFERENCE.
01      Account_REF                             USAGE OBJECT REFERENCE.

PROCEDURE DIVISION USING Account_Ref  RETURNING Account.
        INVOKE Super "new" RETURNING Account.
        INVOKE Account "Initialize".
        EXIT PROGRAM.
END METHOD "new".

METHOD-ID. "Initialize".
******************************************************************************
*       Initialize a new Account entry.                                       *
******************************************************************************
PROCEDURE DIVISION.
        MOVE 10000000 TO Next_ACCT_Number.
        EXIT PROGRAM.
END METHOD "Initialize".

METHOD-ID. Open.
******************************************************************************
*       Open a new account.                                                   *
******************************************************************************
LINKAGE SECTION.
01      Acct_Name                   PIC X(60).
01      Acct_Number                 PIC 9(8).
```

```
01      Acct_Balance                    PIC S9(10)V99.
PROCEDURE DIVISION USING Acct_Name Acct_Balance
        RETURNING Acct_Number.
        ADD 1 to Next_Acct_Number.
        Move Next_Acct_Number to Acct_Number.
        EXIT PROGRAM.
END METHOD Open.

OBJECT.
PROCEDURE DIVISION.
METHOD-ID. GetPAN.
********************************************************************************
* Given an PAN, verify that it is a valid Account. If it is, return the PIN. If not, return 0. *
********************************************************************************
WORKING-STORAGE SECTION.
01      PAN                             PIC 9(8).
01      PIN                             PIC 9999.
PROCEDURE DIVISION USING PAN RETURNING PIN.
        FIND ACCOUNT USING PAN
        FOUND MOVE ACCT_PASSWORD TO PIN
        NOT FOUND MOVE 0 TO PIN.
        EXIT PROGRAM.
END METHOD GetPAN.

METHOD-ID. GetBalance.
********************************************************************************
*       Returns the current account balance. Assumes a previous GetPAN call was
*       successful.
********************************************************************************
WORKING-STORAGE SECTION.
01      PAN                             PIC 9(8).
01      Balance                         PIC S9(10)V99.
PROCEDURE DIVISION RETURNING Balance.
        MOVE ACCT_BALANCE TO Balance.
        EXIT PROGRAM.
END METHOD GetBalance.

METHOD-ID. Debit.
********************************************************************************
*       Debits (Decreases) an Account Balance based on the Amount passed.
********************************************************************************
WORKING-STORAGE SECTION.
01      PAN                             PIC 9(8).
01      Amount                          PIC S9(10)V99.
PROCEDURE DIVISION USING Amount.
        COMPUTER (ACCT_Balance - Amount) to ACCT_Balance.
```

```
          EXIT PROGRAM.
END METHOD Debit.

METHOD-ID. Credit.
********************************************************************************
*       Credits (Increases) an Account Balance based on the Amount passed.
********************************************************************************
WORKING-STORAGE SECTION.
01      PAN                     PIC 9(8).
01      Amount                  PIC S9(10)V99.
PROCEDURE DIVISION USING Amount.
        COMPUTER (ACCT_Balance + Amount) to ACCT_Balance.
        EXIT PROGRAM.
END METHOD Credit.

END OBJECT.
END CLASS Account.


********************************************************************************
*       ATMTransaction Class
********************************************************************************
IDENTIFICATION DIVISION.
CLASS-ID.       ATMTransaction IS PERSISTENT
                INHERITS OrderedCollection.
01      ATM_Transaction.
        03      Account_Number          PIC 9(8).
        03      Transaction_Type        PIC X.
                88      Withdrawal                      VALUE "W".
                88      Deposit                         VALUE "D".
                88      Balance_Inquiry                 VALUE "B".
                88      Funds_Transfer                  VALUE "F".
        03      Date                    PIC 99/99/9999.
        03      Time                    PIC 99:99.
        03      Amount                  PIC 9(4)V99.
        03      Balance                 PIC S9(6)V99.

METHOD-ID. "new".
WORKING-STORAGE SECTION.
01      TEMP            USAGE OBJECT REFERENCE.
01      NextUserID      PIC 9(8).
LINKAGE SECTION.
01      ATMTrans                USAGE OBJECT REFERENCE.
01      ATMTrans_REF    USAGE OBJECT REFERENCE.
PROCEDURE DIVISION USING ATMTrans_Ref RETURNING ATMTrans.
        INVOKE Super "new" RETURNING ATMTrans.
        INVOKE ATMTrans "Initialize".
        EXIT PROGRAM.
END METHOD "new".
```

```
OBJECT.
WORKING-STORAGE SECTION.
01      ATMTrans                        USAGE OBJECT REFERENCE.
01      ATMTransaction                  USAGE OBJECT REFERENCE.
PROCEDURE DIVISION.
METHOD-ID.  SaveTransaction.
*       Save Transaction to ATM File                                    *
        Exit Program.
END METHOD SaveTransaction.


***************************************************************************
*       ATM Class
***************************************************************************
IDENTIFICATION DIVISION.
CLASS-ID.       ATM IS PERSISTENT
                INHERITS Base.
01      ATM.
        03      Date                    PIC 99/99/9999.
        03      Time                    PIC 99:99.
        03      Cash_On_Hand            PIC S9(4).

METHOD-ID. "new".
WORKING-STORAGE SECTION.
01      TEMP                            USAGE OBJECT REFERENCE.
01      ATM.
        03      Date                    PIC 99/99/9999.
        03      Time                    PIC 99/99/99.
        03      CashOnHand              PIC S9(4).
        03      State                   PIC 99.
        03      NextState               PIC 99.
        03      Answer                  PIC 9.
01      ATMStates.
        03      Filler                  PIC X(5)        Value "20000".
        03      Filler                  PIC X(5)        Value "34500".
        03      Filler                  PIC X(5)        Value "45000".
        03      Filler                  PIC X(5)        Value "10000".
        03      Filler                  PIC X(5)        Value "60000".
        03      Filler                  PIC X(5)        Value "7E000".
        03      Filler                  PIC X(5)        Value "89ABD".
        03      Filler                  PIC X(5)        Value "AB000".
        03      Filler                  PIC X(5)        Value "5G000".
        03      Filler                  PIC X(5)        Value "CE000".
        03      Filler                  PIC X(5)        Value "E0000".
        03      Filler                  PIC X(5)        Value "E0000".
        03      Filler                  PIC X(5)        Value "E0000".
        03      Filler                  PIC X(5)        Value "F5000".
        03      Filler                  PIC X(5)        Value "10000".
        03      Filler                  PIC X(5)        Value "G0000".
```

```
01      ATMStateTable Redefines ATMStates.
        03      ATMStateScreen          Occurs 16 Times.
                05      ATMState        PIC X Occurs 6 Times.

LINKAGE SECTION.
01      ATM                             USAGE OBJECT REFERENCE.
01      ATM_Ref                         USAGE OBJECT REFERENCE.
PROCEDURE DIVISION USING ATN_Ref RETURNING ATM.
        INVOKE Super "new" RETURNING ATM.
        INVOKE ATM "initialize".
        EXIT PROGRAM.
END METHOD "new".

METHOD-ID. "Initialize".        /* For Factory */
****************************************************************************
*       Initialize the ATM for processing transactions
****************************************************************************
PROCEDURE DIVISION.
        MOVE COH TO CashOnHand.
        Call GETDATE Returning Date.
        Call GETTIME Returning Time.
        Move 1 to State.
        EXIT PROGRAM.

END METHOD "Initialize".

OBJECT.
WORKING-STORAGE SECTION.
01      Ref_ATM                         USAGE OBJECT REFERENCE.
01      ATM                             USAGE OBJECT REFERENCE.
PROCEDURE DIVISION.
METHOD-ID. ATMSession.
****************************************************************************
*       ATMSession processes all ATM Transactions using the ATM State Table.
****************************************************************************
PROCEDURE DIVISION USING State ATMStates CashOnHand Answer
                RETURNING NextState.
        Perform ProcessATM
        Until 1 = 0
        Or Until CashOnHand < 100.
        EXIT PROGRAM.

ProcessATM.
        Invoke ATM "Display" Using State.
        Invoke ATM "GetAnswer" Returning Answer.
        Invoke ATM "Do" Using State Answer.
        Invoke ATM "Process" Using State Returning NextState.
```

```
            Set State to NextState.
END METHOD .
END OBJECT.
END CLASS ATM.

*********************************************************************************
*       ATMUserInterface Class
*********************************************************************************
IDENTIFICATION DIVISION.
CLASS-ID.       ATMUserInterface is factory
                INHERITS from PanelsBase.
DATA DIVISION.
WORKING-STORAGE SECTION.
        78  maxstringlen   value 18.
WORKING-STORAGE SECTION.
PROCEDURE DIVISION.

END METHOD .
END OBJECT.
END CLASS  .


*********************************************************************************
*       ATMState Class
*********************************************************************************
IDENTIFICATION DIVISION.
CLASS-ID.       ATMState IS PERSISTENT
                INHERITS Base.

METHOD-ID. "new".
WORKING-STORAGE SECTION.
01      TEMP                        USAGE OBJECT REFERENCE.
01      ATM.
        03      Date                PIC 99/99/9999.
        03      Time                PIC 99/99/99.
        03      CashOnHand          PIC S9(4).
        03      NextScreen          PIC 99.
LINKAGE SECTION.
01      ATM                         USAGE OBJECT REFERENCE.
01      ATM_Ref                     USAGE OBJECT REFERENCE.
PROCEDURE DIVISION USING ATN_Ref RETURNING ATM.
        INVOKE Super "new" RETURNING ATM.
        INVOKE ATM "initialize".
        EXIT PROGRAM.
END METHOD "new".
```

* [ATMAIN.CBL] ATM Main Program.

****
*   ATM Main is the main program which initializes the main GUI application
*   the main phone application and sends events to the MF eventmanager.
****

Program-id. ATMMain.
Object Section.
Class-Control.

EventManager is class "p2emgr".

ATMApplication is class "ATMApp".
Working-Storage Section.
01 theEventManager   usage object reference.

Procedure Division.
        Invoke EventManager "new" Returning theEventManager.
        Invoke theEventManager "run".
        Stop Run.

End Program ATMMain.

* [ATMAPP.CBL] ATM Application Program
****
*   ATMApplication creates a new ATM object and manages the GUI
*   portion of the ATM system. and is responsible
****
Class-ID. ATMApplication inherits from dependent.

Object Section.
Class-Control.
        ATMApplication is class "ATMApp"
        Dependent is class "dependnt"
        Dictionary is class "dictinry"
        Association is class "associtn"
        MessageBox is class "msgbox"
        ATMSession is class "ATMSess"
        CharacterArray is class "chararry"
        Callback is class "callback"
        ATMWindow is class "pwindow"
        Window is class "window"
        Base is class "base"
        ATMRecord is class "record".

```cobol
Working-Storage Section.
01      i                                       pic x(4) comp-5.
01      astring                                 usage object reference.
01      OO-Desktop                              usage object reference external.
01      EventManager                            usage object reference.
01      ATMWindow                               usage object reference.
01      event                                   pic x(4) comp-5.
copy "pwindow.evt".
copy "p2cevent.cpy".

****************************************************************************
*       Create the callbacks for the ATM events such as button down, keyboard,  *
*       mose, etc. Then create a new ATM object and given over control the      *
*       MF envent manager                                                       *
****************************************************************************

Method-ID. "initialize".
Linkage Section.
01      atm-reference                           usage object reference.
Procedure Division Using atm-reference.

        Move zero to numberOfViews.
        Set ATM to atm-reference.
        Invoke EventManager "new" Returning anEventManager
        Invoke anEventManager "AutoCoordinates"
        Invoke anEventManager "initialize"
        Invoke Self "newNamedView" Returning ATMWindow.
        Exit Program.
end method "initialize".
end object.
end class ATMApplication.
```

Index

A

abstract data types
  (ADTs)   47, 52, 65, 120, 142, 384
AcuCOBOL   248
ANSI X3J4 committee   1, 19, 116, 139, 423, 435
Apple Macintosh   263
application frameworks   184

B

Booch, Grady   28, 32, 57, 192-196, 221, 373

C

CICS   272, 286, 329
  Application structure   288
class   57, 65
class browsers   131
class design   92
class library   58, 105, 131
  management   322
class relationships   142
class-based development   384
classification   57, 59, 329
client/server development   17, 326
  middleware   23
COBOL programming language   113-116
  data structures   121
  data types   118-120
  divisions   122
  history of   115
  software development   114
  subroutines   125
  use of   303
COBOL standards   15
  COBOL 68   15, 35, 115
  COBOL 74   15, 115
  COBOL 85   16, 35, 116
  COBOL 97   19, 116-140, 233-240, 423-424
common object requester broker access
  (CORBA)   23-24
computer-aided software engineering
  (CASE)   135, 175, 394, 429-433
  GUI support   283
  OOA/D tools   135, 183
  repositories   433-434
  reverse engineering   432-433

Conference on Data Systems Languages
  (CODASYL)   115
configuration management   133
controlling software complexity   38

D

database management system
  (DBMS)   121, 139, 199
decreasing maintenance   38
design recovery   335
distributed computing environment (DCE)   23-24
distributed object management systems   9, 24, 425-428
domain analysis   145, 338
downsizing   10

E

examples
  Automatic Teller Machines (ATM)   67, 254
    assumptions   163, 207
    maintenance   319
    OOA results   163-170
    OOD results   208-215
    OOP Results   254, 297
    prototype   207
    states and transitions   166
  Deck of cards   52, 120, 126, 185-187, 240
  Library problem   66, 250
    assumptions   156, 198
    maintenance   317
    object wrapper   346
    OOA results   155-156, 159-161
    OOD results   198-206
    OOP Results   251, 295
    SQL tables   252
  OOA issues   153

F

formal software development methods   12, 48, 429-432
fourth-generation languages (4GLs)
  GUI   278-284

G

Goldberg, Adelle   92, 146, 149, 418
Graham, Ian   327
Graphical User Interface (GUI)   11, 39, 138, 262-263
   asynchronous external events   265
   class library   270, 285
      Microsoft Foundation Library (MFL)   285
      NextStep   286
      ObjectWindows Library (OWL)   286
      Taligent   286
   components   268, 280, 293
   components hierarchy   267, 281
   development tools   283, 334
   dialog boxes   281
   event-driven behavior   264
   message-based   265
   messages   267
   modal processing   265
   user-centric   264, 274
graphical user interface (GUI) application
   architecture   265
   behavior   271
   design guidelines   280
   design process   276-278

H

Haythorn, Wayne   316
Henderson-Sellers, Brian   358
Humphrey, Watts   37, 386, 396, 406

I

improving productivity   38
improving software quality   37
inheritance   57
   multiple   57
   single   57

L

Liant Software
   RM/COBOL   247

M

MBP
   Visual COBOL   247
McCabe, Tom   314
messages   58, 61
methods   57

Meyer, Bertrand   214
Micro Focus
   dialog system   218, 291
   transaction manager   292
Micro Focus COBOL   21, 131, 246. *(See also* COBOL standards: COBOL 97)
   class library   243, 245, 292
      Base   239, 244
      CallBack   293
      Collection classes   244
      MenuItem   293
      PanelBase   292, 294
      Persistence Manager   244
   class library browser   250
   Object COBOL Option   116, 139
Microsoft Windows   264
   application logic   268
   architecture   268

N

Netron/CAP   22, 248-249
   frame hierarchy   249
   frames   248

O

object management group (OMG)   24, 39, 290
   Common Object Request Broker Architecture (CORBA)   290
object oriented COBOL task group (OOCTG)   19 (*See also* COBOL standards: COBOL 97)
object technology   433
object technology marketplace   7
object wrapper   326
   benefits of using   329
   capturing classes from existing systems   338-340
   case studies   347
   drawbacks   344
   methods   334
   strategies for using   332, 343
   tools   341
   types   330
      borrow   330-333
      handshake   330
      take-over   331-333
      translation   331-333
object-based development   384
object-orientation
   benefits of using   40
   concepts   13, 16, 59-65, 118

Index

abstraction 24, 52, 59-62, 327
  binding 58
  classification 54
  classification by inheritance 59
  encapsulation 24, 58, 122, 326
  garbage collection 59
  generalization 52, 65, 389
  information hiding 54, 58, 326
  inheritance 59
  message passing 59-62, 326
  persistence 58-59
  polymorphysm 24, 58
migration to 329, 383-384, 408
  experiences 410
  J curve 406
  scope of change 390
  select OOA/D method 386
  strategies for 385, 404
  training and education 402
problems with 41
roles and responsibilities 97, 108-109
object-oriented analysis
  (OOA) 45, 99, 134, 141-176
  Coad/Yourdon method 144, 150-153, 221
    notations 153, 160, 170
    technique 151
  data modeling 144
  domain analysis method 145
  finding classes 143
    data modeling 144
  informal analysis of textual requirements
    document 146
  object behavior analysis method 149
  object model 141-143, 181, 221
  OMT method 144, 148, 221
  popular methods 147
  Shlaer/Mellor method 144, 147, 154
object-oriented analysis and design methods
  comparing 222-231
object-oriented design
  (OOD) 45, 56, 99, 135, 174, 179-219
  Booch method 180, 192-196
    design guidelines 182
    notations 195-196, 202, 209
    technique 194
  object specification 179, 221
  OOSD method 190
  popular methods 187
  responsibility-driven design
    method 190, 223
  Shlaer/Mellor method 188, 221-223
  Synthesis method 189
  training 403

object-oriented development 384
  configuration management 321
  law of demeter 182
  manager training 404
  managing 351
    configuration management 374
    estimating 368
    evolution and iteration 354
    measuring 371
    milestones 370
    planning for 368
    prototyping 354
    staffing 370
  selecting OOA/D methods 385
object-oriented hype 6
object-oriented operating systems 9
  Cairo 10-12, 298, 428
  NextStep 29, 104
  Taligent 10-12, 264, 285, 298, 410, 425-428
object-oriented programming
  (OOP) 45, 100, 130, 233-259
object technology 1, 433-434
  learning curve 2
  types of products 7
  bendors 8
objects 57, 60
  attributes 60
  behavior 61
  interactions 61
  lifetimes 61
  relationships 65
  types 62
OOA/D methods
  CASE Tools 9, 429
OOCOBOL 22, 36, 124-130, 233-259, 423-424
  as an object-based OOPL 389
  class definitions 122, 126, 236-239
  class libraries 184, 201, 389
  development environment 131
  factories 235
  garbage collection 236
  intrinsic data types 138
  maintenance 304, 314, 320
  method definitions 122, 126, 237-243
  object definitions 122, 126, 237-243
  programmer training 403
  programming tasks 234
  standard 139, 423
  using objects 127, 238
OODBMS 9, 29
OOPL 46, 101, 233

Ada 28, 105
C++ 31, 103
CLOS 105
Eiffel 27, 103
Objective-C 104
OOCOBOL 32
SIMULA 27, 30
Smalltalk 28, 31, 101, 218-219
    Model/View/Controller (MVC) 270
vendors 8
visual tools 10
OOSDLC 81-109, 137, 180
    maintenance 108
    managing 107
    testing 106
OS/2 Presentation Manager 264
    application logic 269
    architecture 268
OSF/Motif 264

P

Pittmann, Matthew 368, 417
Pressman, Roger 37, 81, 386, 405
Prieto-Diaz, Ruben 357, 362
prototyping 137

Q

auality assurance 376

R

reusable software components 11, 37, 180, 183-184, 234, 330, 355
    classification schemes 362
    cost and benefits of 367
    experiences 360-361, 365-367
    managing 355
    organizational structure 358-360
    prohibitors to 361, 365
    reusability framework 364
    reuse group 359, 376
    two-library reuse model 358
    types 356
reuse-oriented programming 363
reverse engineering 117, 184, 331-333, 335-338, 432-433
Rumbaugh, James 144

S

software configuration management (SCM) 374
software development
    analysis 51
    history of 13
    management 352
        measurements 372
        planning 303
        tracking 303
    synthesis 51
software development life cycle (SDLC) 40, 81-83
    object-oriented 88, 93
    prototyping 88
    spiral 86
    waterfall 83
software engineering
    abstraction 52, 59
    cohesion 55
    coupling 55
    divide and conquer 50
    hierarchical ordering and partitioning 53
    incremental development 55, 91, 134, 330
    information hiding 54
    modularity 54
    notations 49, 393
    principles of 47, 133
    representations 49
    techniques 49, 393-394, 429-431
        data decomposition 50, 56
        functional decomposition 50, 56, 117, 129, 133
        generalization 65
        object decomposition 51, 56, 62
Software Engineering Institute (SEI) 392
    Software Process Maturity Model (SPMM) 396
software engineering triad 394
software layers 18, 326
software maintenance 303
    measuring 308
        complexity 310, 330
        cost 310
        structured programming 310
    strategies 312
        reverse engineering 312
    tasks 305
    types 307

software process   392-394
  improvement   401
  modeling   395
    common-sense management   400
    continuous quality improvement   399
    goal-oriented   400
    maturity   396
    models of interactions/communication   398
    roles and activities   398
    system dynamics   399
software production framework   391
System Object Model (SOM)   342, 425-427
system portions   4, 290, 327
  application processing   290
  data access   4, 10, 20, 37, 40-41
  user interface   263, 289

T

testing OOCOBOL programs   257

U

user interface (UI)   278
  color to highlight   277
  development   279
    types of software users   279
  future   298
  keyboard navigation   277
  performance support systems (PSS)   298

V

visual OOPLs   283, 342

W

WIMP (windows, icons, menus, and pointing device)   262
Wirfs-Brock, Rebecca   190

X

X3J4   1, 19, 32, 36, 116, 139, 245, 292, 423, 435